THE TRIAL PROCESS: LAW, TACTICS AND ETHICS

CONTEMPORARY LEGAL EDUCATION SERIES

LAW SCHOOL ADVISORY BOARD

CO-CHAIRS

Howard P. Fink
Isadore & Ida Topper Professor of Law
Ohio State University
College of Law

Stephen A. Saltzburg
Howrey Professor of Trial Advocacy
George Washington University
National Law Center

MEMBERS

Charles B. Craver
Merrifield Research Professor of Law
George Washington University
National Law Center

Jane C. Ginsburg
Professor of Law
Columbia University
School of Law

Edward J. Imwinkelried
Professor of Law
University of California at Davis
School of Law

Daniel R. Mandelker
Howard A. Stamper Professor of Law
Washington University
School of Law

Mark V. Tushnet
Professor of Law
Georgetown University
Law Center

The Trial Process: Law, Tactics and Ethics

Second Edition

J. ALEXANDER TANFORD
Professor of Law
Indiana University at Bloomington

THE MICHIE COMPANY
Law Publishers
CHARLOTTESVILLE, VIRGINIA

For Philippa

Preface

This second edition has been completely rewritten. My students have taught me a lot in the ten years since *The Trial Process* was first published. However, the spirit of the book remains the same: to provide an intellectually rigorous trial practice experience. Students should be taught to think critically about trial practice just as they are taught to think critically about constitutional law or corporations.

I owe special debts of gratitude to three people: Mike Saks, Sarah Tanford, and Philippa Guthrie. Mike Saks taught me social psychology. I was lucky enough to spend two semesters with him at Iowa, first on a sabbatical leave, and then on a CIC Fellowship. Along this path, I was helped and encouraged by my sister, Sarah Tanford, with whom I wrote an article on the interrelationship between psychology and trial practice. Philippa Guthrie provided the love and moral support that enabled me to complete this book — even when I spent Christmas Eve rewriting the cross-examination chapter instead of being with her family.

I am grateful to Indiana University and Dean Alfred Aman who provided support and the sabbatical leave that enabled me to write this book. Colleen Pauwels and the I.U. law library staff (especially Keith Buckley) have been indispensable and patient with me. Ken Dau-Schmidt has helped me on the sections raising economic issues. Mario Joven proofread the entire manuscript. Many of the people who influenced the first edition continue to influence this one: Linda Dague, Don Beskind, Maury Holland, Tom Read, Adrienne Fox, Jim Rowan, Brent Taylor, Joe Harbough, Ken Pye, and especially Tony Bocchino.

Throughout the book, I have taken considerable editorial liberties with passages quoted from statutes, cases, and other sources. I have omitted citations and footnotes, edited or abridged some of the material, and substituted gender-neutral language for old masculine forms. I generally have not indicated these editorial changes in the quotations themselves unless requested to do so by the original author. This is a book for teaching and learning, not a reference book.

J. Alexander Tanford

March 1, 1993
Bloomington, Indiana

Acknowledgments

The author acknowledges with thanks permission to reprint from the following materials:

American Bar Association for permission to reprint from the ABA Standards for Criminal Justice.

American Bar Association for permission to reprint from the ABA Model Rules of Professional Conduct.

Gary Bellow & Bea Moulton, The Lawyering Process (1978). Reprinted with permission of the Foundation Press.

Wayne Brazil, The Adversary Character of Civil Discovery: A Critique and Proposals for Change, 31 Vand. L. Rev. 1275 (1978). Reprinted with permission of the Vanderbilt Law Review.

James P. Brown, A Juryman's View, 2 Ga. St. B.J. (1965). Reprinted with permission of the Georgia State Bar Journal.

David Crump, Attorneys' Goals and Tactics in Voir Dire Examination, 43 Tex. B.J. 244 (March 1980). Reprinted with permission from Texas Bar Journal, Vol. 43, No. 3, pages 244-46.

David Edelstein, The Ethics of Dilatory Motion Practice: Time for Change, 44 Fordham L. Rev. 1069 (1976). Reprinted with permission of Fordham Law Review.

Monroe Freedman, Professional Responsibility of the Criminal Defense Lawyer: The Three Hardest Questions, 64 Mich. L. Rev. 1469 (1966). Reprinted with permission of the Michigan Law Review.

Lee Gaudineer, Ethics and Malpractice, 26 Drake L. Rev. 88 (1977). Reprinted with permission of Drake Law Review.

Ann Fagan Ginger, Jury Selection in Civil and Criminal Trials (2d ed., Lawpress 1984). Reprinted with permission of Lawpress.

Robert Keeton, Trial Tactics and Methods (2d ed. 1973). Reprinted with permission of Little, Brown & Company.

James McElhaney, Expert Witnesses and the Federal Rules of Evidence, 28 Mercer L. Rev. 463 (1977). Reprinted with permission from Mercer Law Review. Copyright © 1977 Walter F. George School of Law, Mercer University.

John Noonan, The Purposes of Advocacy and the Limits of Confidentiality, 64 Mich. L. Rev. 1485 (1966). Reprinted with permission of the Michigan Law Review.

A. Kenneth Pye, The Role of Counsel in the Suppression of Truth, 1978 Duke L.J. 921. Reprinted with permission of the Duke Law Journal.

Alvin Rubin, A Causerie on Lawyers' Ethics in Negotiation, 35 La. L. Rev. 577 (1975). Reprinted with permission of the Louisiana Law Review.

Jeffrey Rubin & Bert Brown, The Social Psychology of Bargaining and Negotiation (1975). Reprinted with permission of the Academic Press.

Arthur Train (pseud. Ephraim Tutt), Yankee Lawyer: The Autobiography of Ephraim Tutt. Copyright 1943 Ephraim Tutt; copyright renewed 1970 by Helen C. Train. Reprinted with the permission of Charles Scribner's Sons.

Robert Traver (John D. Voelker), Anatomy of a Murder (1958). Reprinted with permission of St. Martin's Press.

Hans Zeisel & Shari Diamond, The Effect of Peremptory Challenges on Jury and Verdict: An Experiment in a Federal District Court, 30 Stan. L. Rev. 491 (1978). Copyright 1978 by the Board of Trustees of the Leland Stanford Junior University.

Summary Table of Contents

Table of Contents

Chapter 1

INTRODUCTION

A. OVERVIEW

This book is about jury trials and the attorney's role in conducting them. It discusses law, ethics, tactics, psychology, and skills. If you expect to represent a client competently in a trial courtroom, you will have to master all these aspects of trial practice. The legal and ethical rules that regulate trials will define what you are permitted to do, the wealth of advice from experienced attorneys and psychologists on effective tactics will help you decide what you want to do, and the acquisition of basic trial courtroom skills will enable you to accomplish your goals.

Legal and ethical rules define how a trial is conducted and regulate the conduct of attorneys. Just as the rights and duties of citizens are generally defined by bodies of substantive law, so too will your conduct in court be regulated by the law of trials. This book will introduce you to this area of law and its major doctrines, so that you will understand the rules of the litigation game. The book also will raise common ethical issues that arise during trials, and will discuss the ethical considerations that further constrain your conduct.

A knowledge of the law and ethics of trial practice will tell you what you are required, forbidden, or permitted to do, but will not tell you whether doing something is a good idea. In order to make reasoned tactical choices, you must have an overall strategy, understand the psychology of juror behavior, and be familiar with the extensive literature concerning effective trial tactics. Although a growing body of empirical research on juror behavior exists, the field of trial practice is hardly a scientific one. Proper tactics are often a matter of hot debate among trial lawyers. Where there are differences of opinion, we will try to present a variety of viewpoints, discussing the pros and cons of each. That way, you will be encouraged to think critically about alternative solutions to problems rather than to accept and imitate one person's idea of good and bad tactics.

Finally, we will look at trial practice skills and techniques. You have to be able to put into effect what you have decided to do. These "how to's" are covered in the book, but you should not expect simple answers. Like tactics, skills and techniques are often subjects of dispute. Practitioners disagree vehemently about the right and wrong ways to do anything in a courtroom. The text will try to guide you away from the most serious pitfalls, and present a range of views on what constitutes effective trial techniques.

Every book carries with it the author's view of the world. This text is no exception. My own view of what constitutes good trial practice has dictated the contents and organization of this book. In the next few paragraphs, as I explain the structure of the book, those views should begin to become clear.

1

At the heart of every case is the preparation of a theory. A theory is your master strategy based on a thorough analysis of the strengths and weaknesses of your and your opponent's cases. That analysis looks at the facts and the law, and plots the most likely course through them that leads to a favorable verdict. Like any good battle plan, your case theory (if it is realistic) recognizes that you have some weaknesses, and will suffer some losses and setbacks. To formulate a good theory, you must gather as much information as possible, through interviewing, investigation, and legal research. Then, you must organize and analyze the information, assessing your strategic options, and discarding the weak ones. Your goal is to formulate a simple, workable theory of the case that will appeal to the jury and produce a favorable verdict. This process of trial preparation and theory formulation is presented in Chapter 2.

Chapters 3 through 9 consider the components of the trial in their natural order: Jury selection, opening statements, trial evidence, direct examination, cross-examination, expert witnesses, and closing argument. The final chapter in the book covers negotiation.

Perhaps more than any other course you will take in law school, a trial practice course is an integrative experience. While it will teach you a new body of law, new ethical rules, and how to use a specialized set of practical tools, it also should help you see how a lawyer must use all that is taught in law school. To effectively represent a client at trial, you will have to draw on your knowledge of substantive law, procedure, evidence, ethics, legal research and writing, trial law, and appellate procedure, as well as on your skills as a trial tactician. In a law school curriculum divided into discrete subjects taken a few at a time, it is often difficult to see how integrally each relates to the others. Beyond teaching you about the trial process, it is the goal of this book and any course in trial practice to help you see that the law is indeed a "seamless web," and that all you have learned fits together.

Although this book focuses on trial practice, you should not lose sight of the fact that the trial is only one part of the legal system. Many complaints never reach the courts. Most cases that do are settled and do not go to trial. Of those that are tried to a verdict, most continue afterwards through the appeal process. Nevertheless, the trial itself is the hub of the system. Everything that has gone before, such as the drafting and filing of pleadings, investigations, discovery, motions practice, settlement negotiations, and pretrial conferences, has been influenced by the looming specter of the trial. What comes after — motions for judgments n.o.v. or for new trials, appeals, briefs, habeas corpus petitions, suits to enforce judgments, certiorari petitions, more negotiation — looks back on what happened during the trial and focuses on the conduct of the judge and attorneys who performed it. Thus, no matter what stage of litigation you become involved in, you must understand the trial process.

B. HISTORY OF THE JURY TRIAL

Why does a trial have twelve jurors? Why not fifteen, or seven, or none? Why does the judge wear a black robe? Why do we require witnesses to testify in person? The answers to many such questions about the structure of the modern trial can be found in history.

Prior to the eleventh century, legal disputes in Britain were settled in two ways, both of which depended heavily on religious beliefs. One method was the "wager of law." A person accused of a crime or sued on a debt could clear himself or herself of the charge by taking an oath denying liability and producing a set number of compurgators (oath-helpers) who swore oaths supporting the accused. If the requisite number of compurgators — usually twelve — was produced, the defendant was discharged. Everyone assumed that fear of God would prevent a compurgator from swearing falsely. Wagers of law were used regularly in debt actions until about 1600.

The better known method of early dispute resolution was the ordeal. In an ordeal, a defendant's guilt was tested by his or her susceptibility to injury. A defendant was required to walk nine yards holding a pound of hot iron, retrieve a number of stones from a pot of boiling water, or walk barefoot across burning wood. If the defendant was burned and blistered from the ordeal, he or she was deemed guilty, because God would have intervened to protect the innocent from harm. A more lenient ordeal was the test of cold water, in which the defendant was bound and lowered into a pond that had been blessed with holy water. If the accused sank, the water had received the defendant with God's blessing (if they accidentally drowned, at least they went to heaven). However, if the accused floated, he or she was found guilty because pure water would not receive the body of an impure person. Ordeals by iron, hot water, and fire were abolished in 1215. Ordeals by cold water were used well into the seventeenth century for witchcraft trials.[1]

The seeds of the modern jury trial were brought to England by the Normans in the eleventh century. They introduced two concepts that have become the cornerstones of the trial process: adversarial dispute resolution and fact finding by a disinterested body of citizens.

The earliest form of the adversary system was trial by battle. Although still based on the assumption that God would make the truthful party victorious, trial by battle required that both parties to a dispute confront each other. Trials by battle were used most commonly to settle disputes over title to land. A party had a choice of fighting personally or appointing a champion to fight in the party's place. Some writers, with tongue firmly in cheek, have suggested that thus was born the trial lawyer. Although trial by battle died out by 1485, the idea that each litigant should have an equal chance to fight for his or her cause remained imbedded in the system.

The more important innovation of the Normans was the inquisition, a body of citizens summoned to give verdicts on legal issues. While the early compurgators had been summoned by the litigants themselves, inquisitors (or recognitors) were summoned by the government. Faith that God would prevent false swearing was replaced by the belief that disinterested citizens were better able to determine the truth and give a verdict accordingly. Accurate verdicts were further insured by replacing the fear of punishment in the

---

[1] Ordeals are described in colorful language in JOHN H. WIGMORE, A KALEIDOSCOPE OF JUSTICE 5-17 (1941).

hereafter with present criminal penalties for false swearing, by giving the parties the right to challenge biased recognitors, and by requiring that a verdict be agreed upon by twelve of the recognitors. The inquest could be summoned only by the monarch and originally was used solely when the crown was a party. By the end of the twelfth century, royal inquests were made available for settling important private controversies, and other private litigants began to agree to be bound by the verdict of unofficial recognitors modeled after the royal inquests.

These inquisitors performed the roles of witnesses, jurors, and judges at the same time. They were summoned from the neighborhood of the dispute because those persons were expected to know the facts already. If they did not know something, they were required to inform themselves by speaking to other witnesses. The inquisitors then had to determine the proper legal resolution of the controversy. They were assisted somewhat by the parties, who pleaded their causes, and by judges who clarified the precise issues of dispute and gave opinions on the law.

The modern form of the jury trial began to develop in the thirteenth and fourteenth centuries. A class of professional attorneys emerged who were permitted to represent and plead for litigants. They had the power to challenge jurors and recite their clients' versions of the facts to the jury. The number of jurors became fixed at twelve, and the requirement of a unanimous verdict was established. Reliance on outside witnesses became commonplace, and by the fifteenth century had become the rule rather than the exception. Most of the evidence was now presented in open court by witnesses questioned by the judge and the jurors. The role of attorneys was still minor, however. They gave opening statements about the facts and suggested witnesses who could prove them, although the jurors were free to ignore their advice. There are even scattered records from the fifteenth century of lawyers making objections to the relevancy of evidence.

By the sixteenth and seventeenth centuries, it had become uncommon for anyone, even the jurors, to give evidence except by sworn testimony in open court. Rules of evidence were created to regulate witness testimony, and jurors no longer were required to have independent knowledge of the controversy — although they still had to come from the neighborhood and not be wholly strangers to the facts. Since jurors were liable to serious penalties for returning false verdicts, the practice of asking a judge for instructions about the law had become common. The trial was still largely inquisitorial — the judge and jurors, not the attorneys, asked the questions. Many parties did not have lawyers at all. In a criminal case witnesses could be summoned only by the judge and the prisoner did not have counsel unless he or she assigned a point of law arising on the indictment. There were still few rules of evidence and procedure. Hearsay and conclusionary evidence were admissible, and the average trial lasted only a few minutes. Juries were still locked up without food and water, so lengthy deliberations were rare.

When the British colonized North America, they brought trial by jury with them. During the eighteenth century, the trial developed into its modern form. Judges became more passive and jurors became listeners. Advocates for the parties took over the presentation of evidence and made frequent arguments (often rhetorical) for the benefit of the members of the community who had come to watch. In criminal cases, the right of the defendant to call witnesses and have the assistance of counsel became established. Formal distinctions between direct and cross-examination emerged, and the first treatises on evidence rules were published. This was what a trial looked like when the Constitution was written, and supplies the basic meaning of the word "trial" that appears in the Constitution.[2]

Contemporary American trial practice is characterized by its diversity. At one time, the ninety-two federal district courts employed ninety-two different methods for selecting jurors, with even greater variations existing in state courts.[3] This diversity of practice is easy to understand: trial procedures are regulated by a crazy quilt of federal and state constitutions, statutes, and case law; state and local court rules and customs; and rules of professional ethics. When you add to this equation the preferences and personalities of trial lawyers and judges, and their differing views on the goals and purposes of trials, it becomes safe to say that probably no two trials today are conducted in exactly the same way.

NOTE

Trial by battle. Trials by battle were not abolished officially in England until 1819, in response to the case of *Ashford v. Thornton*, 1 B. & Ald. 405 (1818), in which one of the parties "threw a gauntlet into a startled court of the King's Bench." *See* JOHN H. BAKER, AN INTRODUCTION TO ENGLISH LEGAL HISTORY 11, 56, 64 (2d ed. 1979).

C. THE ADVERSARY SYSTEM AND THE SEARCH FOR TRUTH

What is a trial and what should it be? Many contemporary legal writers have turned their attention to these questions, but have been unable to articulate satisfactory answers. Is a trial a search for truth, a search for justice, a ritual played out for the good of society, or merely a game played by lawyers? Should the lawyer's goal be to win, to seek justice, or to further valuable social principles? Is an attorney the mouthpiece of the client or the client's conscience?

It is often said that trials should be a search for truth. The American adversary system has been criticized for rating truth too low among the goals of trials. This indifference to truth seeking probably is one of the chief reasons that the legal profession is held in dubious esteem. Lawyers often are criticized for being "hired guns" who advance their clients' interests without regard to right and wrong, and who try to sell their clients' stories to juries regardless of their merit, subordinating the truth to the struggle to win.

---

[2]*See* U.S. CONST. art. III, § 2 (The trial of all Crimes shall be by Jury); *id.*, amend. VI (In all criminal prosecutions, the accused shall enjoy the right to a trial by an impartial jury, to be confronted with the witnesses against him; to call witnesses in his favor, and to have the assistance of counsel); *id.*, amend. VII (In civil suits, the right of a trial by jury shall be preserved).

[3]Harold Hyman & Catherine Tarrant, *Aspects of American Trial Jury History, in* THE JURY SYSTEM IN AMERICA 23 (R. Simon ed. 1975).

Critics argue that this is unworthy of a learned profession — that we should pursue higher goals. But to expect trials to become effective vehicles for determining the "truth" is more idealistic than realistic. Truth is an elusive concept, perhaps totally meaningless in a courtroom where you are trying to reconstruct events long past through witnesses with faded and faulty memories.

The view at the opposite extreme is that a trial is only a contest played by rules, with the judge as the referee. This more correctly describes what trials have become, although it does not address what a trial ought to be. As in an athletic event, the trial is supposed to be fought out on a level playing field in which neither side is given an advantage apart from the strength of their witnesses. The judges act as referees, allowing the contestants to play out the game as they see fit, intervening only when a player violates a rule. The lawyers are left free to fight for their clients as long as they stay within the bounds of law.

This view of trials has the benefit of simplicity. The lawyer is not required to wrestle with difficult philosophical questions about the proper duty of attorneys to promote justice, nor to make moral judgments about the worthiness of the client's position. Rather, lawyers can embrace the heroic image of the champion battling for a cause, and can state with clear conscience: "My client: right or wrong." There is also an incidental financial benefit in holding this view — a client, especially one with a weak case, is more likely to pay enormous legal fees for a loyal, partisan fighter than for a neutral truth-seeker.

There also are drawbacks to this pure adversarial model of trials. Certainly it demeans the legal profession when lawyers participate in frivolous lawsuits, display arrogant disregard for truth, and assist greedy clients in grabbing whatever they can from others regardless of the justness of the result. The adversary ideal also has other more subtle weaknesses. It emphasizes the talent, cleverness, and experience of the lawyer. It rewards trickery and successful evasion of the rules. It increasingly places justice beyond the reach of the poor and middle classes who cannot afford to mount an expensive courtroom advertising campaign to sell their cases. All of these factors tend to derogate the process of arriving at a fair resolution of a controversy according to the facts.

The debate over adversariness may lead you to the mistaken belief that a trial lawyer actually has a substantial influence on the outcome of a case — that a clever lawyer somehow can turn a hopeless case into victory. While bad lawyering undoubtedly can ruin a good case, the reverse is rarely true. The role of the lawyer is limited by the facts, by rules of trial law, by professional ethics, and by rules of courtroom decorum. The most important thing to remember is that you are bound by the facts. To win, you will need facts that justify a verdict and facts that will persuade a jury. While you have a limited ability to manipulate facts — to choose the order of their presentation, to omit some and to emphasize others — you have no ability to change facts. You must overcome the law-school-induced perception that you can prevail on any position; that any case can be won by the right argument. Trials consist of the sworn testimony of witnesses who relate what they saw, and you must accept that these facts have more to do with who wins and loses than the lawyers. If a body is cold and blue and rigor mortis has set in, that body is dead, and no amount of clever argument can be expected to convince a jury otherwise.

NOTES

1. ***Verdict accuracy vs. adversary system.*** The major proponents of the theory that trials should serve society by being searches for accurate verdicts are JEROME FRANK, COURTS ON TRIAL (1949), and Marvin Frankel, *The Search for Truth: An Umpireal View*, 123 U. PA. L. REV. 1031 (1975). Critics of this idealistic view are many. *See* Richard Markus, *A Theory of Trial Advocacy*, 56 TUL. L. REV. 95, 96 (1981) (impossible to accurately reconstruct the past through witnesses with faded and faulty memories); L. RAY PATTERSON & ELLIOTT CHEATHAM, THE PROFESSION OF LAW 105-09 (1971) (trials are games played by rules; attorney owes no duty to opponent or society beyond promise to play by rules). The classic defense of the adversary system is Lon L. Fuller & John D. Randall, *Professional Responsibility: Report of the Joint Conference*, 44 A.B.A. J. 1159 (1958).

2. ***Can you win a weak case?*** Social psychologists who have studied the effects of argument and other factors on juror decision-making have demonstrated that the merits of a case have by far the greatest impact on how jurors vote; lawyers' tricks to enhance their persuasiveness have relatively little impact. *See* Martin Fishbein & Icek Ajzen, *Acceptance, Yielding and Impact: Cognitive Process in Persuasion*, in COGNITIVE RESPONSES IN PERSUASION (R. Petty et al. eds. 1981); Daniel Linz & Stephen Penrod, *Increasing Attorney Persuasiveness in the Courtroom*, 8 LAW & PSYCHOL. REV. 1, 45-46 (1984).

D. LEGAL AND ETHICAL FRAMEWORK

1. TRIAL LAW

You are not free to conduct a trial any way you see fit. Rules of law and ethics place limits upon your performance. Don't expect a trial judge to treat you like Perry Mason — peering over half-frame glasses and saying, "That's a bit irregular, counselor, but I'll allow it this once." Trials run according to set procedures, and legal ethics require you to follow them. A typical trial proceeds as follows:

- The case is called and both attorneys state their readiness to proceed. Any preliminary motions are discussed.
- A panel of prospective jurors is brought to the courtroom, sworn to truthfully answer questions, interrogated by the judge and attorneys, and a jury is chosen. In many jurisdictions, the judge will the read preliminary jury instructions.
- The plaintiff (or prosecutor) makes a brief opening statement describing plaintiff's case, and then the defendant makes an opening statement.
- The plaintiff calls and examines witnesses and introduces exhibits. The defendant cross-examines each witness. The plaintiff may conduct brief re-direct examination of some witnesses.
- The plaintiff rests and the defendant moves for a directed verdict.

- The defendant (having lost the motion) calls and examines witnesses and introduces exhibits, and the plaintiff cross-examines each witness. The defendant may conduct re-direct examination.
- After the defense rests, the plaintiff may produce rebuttal witnesses or exhibits.
- After both sides rest, they make motions for directed verdicts which are routinely denied.
- The plaintiff makes the first closing argument. The defendant makes the second argument. The plaintiff makes the final argument.
- The judge reads instructions on the law to the jury.
- The jurors retire, deliberate, and reach a verdict.

Trial procedure is not just a matter of local custom. It is controlled by statutes and rules of procedure. These codes can be very specific or quite general. Thus, the judge's discretion to deviate from the usual order of trial varies. A typical statute reads as follows:

> *Order of proceedings.* — The trial must proceed in the following order, unless the court, for special reasons, otherwise directs:
>
> 1. In the case of a jury trial, the jury is first selected and sworn;
> 2. After the jury is sworn, the plaintiff may state the issue and plaintiff's case;
> 3. The defendant may then state the defense, or may wait until after the close of plaintiff's evidence;
> 4. The plaintiff must then produce the evidence supporting plaintiff's claim;
> 5. The defendant may then produce evidence;
> 6. The parties may then respectively offer rebuttal evidence;
> 7. When the evidence is concluded, the plaintiff must commence the argument;
> 8. The defendant may then present argument;
> 9. The plaintiff may conclude the argument;
> 10. The court must then charge the jury.[4]

Rules of law also limit what you can do during trial in two different respects. First, you must expect to be hemmed in by the trial judge's conservative view of law. Sophisticated legal analysis, clever argument in favor of a minority view, thoughtful re-examination of established doctrine, exhaustive briefs, and arguments contrary to precedent are the province of the appeals courts. In the trial courts, you must expect the judge to rule quickly, to adhere to precedent, and to keep the trial safely within well established legal boundaries. You might still want to make a novel legal argument to preserve the issue for appeal, but you cannot expect the judge to allow you to rely on it for the trial.

Second, there is a law of trials comprising the familiar authorities: constitutional provisions, statutes, case law, and court rules. In the law of trials can be found everything from broad statements about your right to a jury trial, to

---

[4]This is a slightly modified version of CAL. CIV. PROC. CODE § 607.

narrow rules about whether you must sit or stand and whether time limits can be placed on your presentation.

Just below the surface of the law lie local customary practices concerning courtroom etiquette. These "rules" are usually unwritten, and may vary widely from courtroom to courtroom even in the same county. Local custom may govern where you sit, how free you are to move around the courtroom when questioning witnesses, how exhibits are handled and stored, the propriety of socializing with the trial judge, and a host of other factors. If we were to write them down, a typical set of rules of courtroom etiquette might read as follows:[5]

Model Rules of Courtroom Etiquette

General

Rule 1. Flag. — The flag of the United States and of this State shall at all times while court is in session be displayed on or in close proximity to the bench.

Rule 2. Food, beverages, and tobacco. — Neither food nor beverages shall be brought into the courtroom; tobacco in any form shall not be used.

Rule 3. Behavior of persons in the courtroom. — Dignity and solemnity should be maintained in the courtroom at all times by attorneys, court officers, witnesses and other persons; unseemly behavior shall be grounds for removal from the courtroom.

Rule 4. Disconcerting or distracting activities. — There shall be no unnecessary conversation, loud whispering, newspaper or magazine reading or other disconcerting or distracting activity by anyone in the courtroom during the progress of the trial.

Rule 5. Hats; headgear. — No one shall wear a hat or other headgear in a courtroom unless for religious purposes.

Rule 6. Formalities in opening court. — At the opening of each court day, the formalities to be observed shall consist of the following: the bailiff shall, by a rap of the gavel or other signal, direct all present to stand, and shall say clearly and distinctly:

> Everyone please rise! Hear Ye — Hear Ye — Hear Ye! The District Court of the County of _____, State of _____ is now open for the conducting of business. The Honorable Judge _____ presiding. Please be seated.

Rule 7. Duties of bailiff. — It shall be the duty of the bailiff to maintain order in and around the courtroom at all times; this includes the duty to admit persons to the courtroom and direct them to seats, and to refuse admittance to the courtroom in such trials where the courtroom is occupied to its full seating capacity.

---

[5] Many of these rules were borrowed from RULES FOR UNIFORM DECORUM IN THE DISTRICT COURTS OF MINNESOTA (1978) or suggested by Catherine T. Clarke, *Missed Manners in Courtroom Decorum*, 50 MD. L. REV. 945 (1991).

Rule 8. Swearing of witnesses. — No witness shall be required to take a religious oath. When the witness is sworn, the clerk shall have the witness give the reporter his or her full name, and after being sworn, courteously invite him or her to be seated on the witness stand.

Rule 9. Manner of administration of oath or affirmation. — The oath or affirmation shall be administered to jurors and witnesses in a slow, clear, and dignified manner. Witnesses when sworn should stand near the bench or witness stand, and the swearing of witnesses should be an impressive ceremony and not a mere formality.

Rule 10. Advising clients and witnesses of formalities. — The lawyers should advise their clients and witnesses of the formalities of court appearances, thereby avoiding embarrassment to all concerned.

Rule 11. Demonstrations in connection with verdict or testimony. — There shall be no demonstration in the courtroom in connection with the rendering of a verdict or other decision, nor any outburst, disruption or applause in connection with any testimony.

Lawyers

Rule 12. Officer of court. — The lawyer is an officer of the court and should at all times uphold the honor and maintain the dignity of the profession, maintaining at all times a respectful attitude toward the court, its personnel, and other lawyers.

Rule 13. Promptness. — Lawyers shall be on time for all court appearances; lawyers shall inform the clerk's office if unexpected circumstances will cause the lawyer to be late.

Rule 14. Addressing court or jury. — Lawyers should rise and remain standing while addressing the court or the jury. In addressing the court, the lawyer should refer to the judge as "Your Honor" or "The Court."

Rule 15. Approaching bench. — The lawyers should normally address the court from a position at the counsel table. If a lawyer finds it necessary to discuss some question out of the hearing of the jury at the bench, the lawyer may request permission to approach the bench, and, if invited, approach the bench for the purpose indicated. In such an instance, the lawyers should never lean upon the bench nor appear to engage the court in a familiar manner.

Rule 16. Examination of witnesses. — The lawyers may be seated or stand while examining witnesses, but shall not approach the witness except when identifying or examining exhibits, or when other circumstances so require.

Rule 17. Familiarity with witnesses, jurors or opposing counsel. — During trial, lawyers shall not exhibit undue familiarity with witnesses, jurors or opposing counsel, and the use of first names shall be avoided. In arguments to the jury, no juror should be singled out and addressed individually.

Rule 18. Clothing. — All lawyers and court officials shall refrain from wearing articles of clothing suited primarily for sports or leisure time activities during court appearances. Lawyers shall wear appropriate business attire.

Rule 19. Objections without argument. — Lawyers shall state their objections and the grounds therefor without argument; if there is to be an argument or offer of proof, it shall be made out of the hearing of the jury. When speaking to an objection or any other point of law, the lawyers shall address all remarks to the bench, and not address each other directly.

Rule 20. Exhibits. — At the beginning of trial, the lawyers shall give the court reporter a list of exhibits they intend to introduce, and the numbers by which they have been marked for identification; after an exhibit has been introduced, it shall be left in the custody of the court reporter when not being used by the lawyers.

Rule 21. Addressing jury. — When addressing the jury, the lawyers shall first address the court and ask leave to proceed.

Rule 22. Courtesy toward opposing counsel and witnesses. — The lawyer shall treat opposing counsel and witnesses with courtesy and respect.

Rule 23. Interruption of other lawyers; advice to witnesses as to manner of speaking. — The lawyers as far as possible shall refrain from interrupting each other or speaking at the same time in order to assist in making a proper record. Lawyers should instruct their witnesses to testify slowly and clearly so that the court and jury will hear their testimony, and should caution witnesses not to chew anything when testifying.

Judge

Rule 24. Dignity of judge. — The judge shall at all times be dignified, courteous, respectful and considerate of the lawyers, the jury and witnesses.

Rule 25. Punctuality. — The judge shall be punctual in convening court, and prompt in the performance of judicial duties, recognizing that the time of litigants, jurors and attorneys is of value and that habitual lack of punctuality produces dissatisfaction with the administration of the business of the court.

Rule 26. Impartiality. — During the presentation of the case, the judge shall maintain absolute impartiality, and shall neither by word or sign indicate favoritism toward any party.

Rule 27. Intervention. — The judge should refrain so far as possible from intervening in the examination of witnesses or argument of counsel; however, the judge may intervene to prevent a miscarriage of justice.

Rule 28. Addressing lawyers and officers of court. — The judge shall be impersonal in addressing the lawyers and other officers of the court.

Rule 29. Decorum in court. — The judge shall be responsible for order and decorum in the court and shall see to it at all times that parties and witnesses in the case are treated with proper courtesy and respect. Lecturing, browbeating, badgering or shouting at a witness shall not be allowed.

Rule 30. Accurate record. — The judge shall be in complete charge of the trial at all times and shall see to it that everything is done to obtain a clear and accurate record of the trial. Only the judge may give any directions to the court reporter concerning the record.

Rule 31. Critical statements regarding an attorney. — The judge shall exercise extreme care so as not to say anything before the jury or parties to an action that is critical of a lawyer or that may be embarrassing to the lawyer in front of a client or the jury. If the judge has a suggestion to make to the lawyer of a critical nature, the judge should call a recess or call the lawyer to the bench and speak in an undertone not audible to the jury.

Rule 32. Patience. — The judge shall at all times exercise the highest degree of patience.

2. TRIAL ETHICS

Finally, your conduct as a lawyer is limited at all times by the MODEL RULES OF PROFESSIONAL CONDUCT. The ethical standards that circumscribe the trial lawyer's bag of tricks are contained primarily in Rules 3.3 through 3.5.

Rule 3.3 Candor Toward the Tribunal

(a) A lawyer shall not knowingly:

(1) Make a false statement of material fact or law to a tribunal;

(2) Fail to disclose a material fact to a tribunal when disclosure is necessary to avoid assisting a criminal or fraudulent act by the client;

(3) Fail to disclose to the tribunal legal authority in the controlling jurisdiction known to the lawyer to be directly adverse to the position of the client and not disclosed by opposing counsel; or

(4) Offer evidence that the lawyer knows to be false. If a lawyer has offered material evidence and comes to know of its falsity, the lawyer shall take remedial measures.

(b) The duties stated in paragraph (a) continue to the conclusion of the proceeding, and apply even if compliance requires disclosure of information otherwise protected by Rule 1.6 [Lawyer-Client Confidentiality].

(c) A lawyer may refuse to offer evidence that the lawyer reasonably believes is false.

Rule 3.4 Fairness to Opposing Party and Counsel

A lawyer shall not:

(a) Unlawfully obstruct another party's access to evidence or unlawfully alter, destroy or conceal a document or other material having potential evidentiary value. A lawyer shall not counsel or assist another person to do any such act;

(b) Falsify evidence, counsel or assist a witness to testify falsely, or offer an inducement to a witness that is prohibited by law;

(c) Knowingly disobey an obligation under the rules of a tribunal except for an open refusal based on an assertion that no valid obligation exists;

* * *

(e) In trial, allude to any matter that the lawyer does not reasonably believe is relevant or that will not be supported by admissible evidence, assert personal knowledge of facts in issue except when testifying as a witness, or state a personal opinion as to the justness of a cause, the credibility of a witness, the culpability of a civil litigant or the guilt or innocence of an accused; or

(f) Request a person other than a client to refrain from voluntarily giving relevant information to another party unless:

(1) The person is a relative or an employee or other agent of a client; and

(2) The lawyer reasonably believes that the person's interests will not be adversely affected by refraining from giving such information.

Rule 3.5 Impartiality and Decorum of the Tribunal

A lawyer shall not:

(a) Seek to influence a judge, juror, prospective juror or other official by means prohibited by law;

(b) Communicate ex parte with such person except as permitted by law; or

(c) Engage in conduct intended to disrupt a tribunal.

The decision to conduct ethical trials, however, like the decision to obey the law, is a personal one. The sad fact is that many lawyers ignore professional ethics and few are ever disciplined for even the most outrageous trial conduct. Many trial lawyers attempt to justify abuse of the ethical guidelines with the argument that rules have to be "bent" in order to win cases. Other practitioners read the MODEL RULES OF PROFESSIONAL CONDUCT as if they were no more than adverse statutory authority to be distinguished away on some technicality, conducting trials with the attitude that the spirit of the rules may be freely violated if some intricate argument can be made that the conduct is not explicitly prohibited. Creating clever legalistic arguments that outrageous conduct does not technically violate any disciplinary rule, or following the principle that conduct is only unethical if you get caught, is not the same thing as being an ethical trial lawyer.

E. THE PSYCHOLOGY OF JURY TRIALS

In the 1950's, a pioneering team of lawyers and social scientists undertook the University of Chicago Jury Project to systematically study the jury decision process.[6] Since that time, social psychologists have studied the jury trial system in great depth. Using mock juries and simulated trials, they have investigated what constitutes effective communication, what influences ju-

---

[6]HARRY KALVEN & HANS ZEISEL, THE AMERICAN JURY (1966).

14

rors, and how jurors reach decisions. If you expect to be a good trial lawyer, you must understand the rudiments of the psychology of jury trials.

The consensus among social psychologists is that:

- Jurors base their decisions primarily on the evidence, and not on extraneous factors.
- Jurors are not easily tricked or persuaded by clever tactics or rhetoric.
- Jurors give more weight to vivid anecdotes, emotions and personal experiences, and less weight to statistics, science and abstract concepts.
- Jurors have difficulty understanding and following the instructions judges give on the law.
- Jurors reach decisions by the "story model" — arranging evidence in the form of a plausible story of human motives and actions, discarding evidence that does not fit, and picking the closest available verdict.

The most important of these points is that jurors reach decisions by constructing stories, not by engaging in orderly legal analysis. Based on their expectations about what makes a complete story, jurors construct narratives partly from the facts presented and partly from their knowledge of similar events. They arrange this information into a story of motives, actions, and consequences. A story usually comprises a series of discrete episodes. Each episode contains events connected by causal relationships: initiating events produce mental states in the characters which cause them to engage in actions which produce consequences. For example, in a criminal assault case, a juror might construct the following episode: the victim sees his girlfriend dancing with the defendant (initiating event) and becomes angry (mental state); he pulls a knife (action) and causes the defendant to back away (consequence), which leaves the defendant angry and wanting revenge (consequence).

If more than one story emerges, the jurors will tend to accept the one that provides the greatest coverage of the evidence and is the most coherent. Coverage refers to the extent to which the story accounts for the evidence offered at trial. Coherence refers to internal factors: whether the story is internally consistent, plausible, and complete. The greater the coverage and coherence, the more confidence a juror will have that it is the correct story. Only after they have agreed upon a story do jurors attempt to match it with the available verdict categories.[7]

Psychologists also have demonstrated that jurors are relatively good at understanding the facts of a case and basing their verdicts on them. Fears that jurors are swayed by emotions or racial prejudices are largely misplaced. Jurors pay attention to evidence, remember most of it, and correct each others' misunderstandings during deliberations.[8] However, not all "facts" are given equal weight. Jurors are disproportionately influenced by vivid anecdotes and concrete examples, tending to assume that these specific illustrations are

---

[7] See REID HASTIE, STEVEN PENROD & NANCY PENNINGTON, INSIDE THE JURY (1983); Nancy Pennington & Reid Hastie, A Cognitive Theory of Juror Decision-Making, 13 CARDOZO L. REV. 519, 521-33 (1991); Richard O. Lempert, Telling Tales in Court: Trial Procedure and the Story Model, 13 CARDOZO L. REV. 559 (1991).

[8] See, e.g., Valerie P. Hans, Jury Decision Making, in HANDBOOK OF PSYCHOLOGY AND LAW (D.K. Kagehiro & W.S. Laufer eds., 1993).

representative of the universe of similar events. They tend to undervalue abstract information, science, and statistical probabilities. The more important the decision, the stronger is this anti-scientific tendency.[9]

Not surprisingly, jurors make stereotypical judgments about the people and things in a trial. Based on their common sense knowledge about the way the world works, jurors make assumptions about the character and credibility of witnesses based on factors that might be thought to be legally irrelevant, such as race, class, attractiveness, status, and clothing.[10] They have preconceived notions (often called "schemas") about what is meant by terms like "supermarket." Any reference to a supermarket will automatically call up a specific mental image that includes a wealth of details, such as size, location, how crowded it is, and how brightly lit. These mental images are used as shorthand summaries in deciding the facts of a case.[11] If the facts of a case are unclear, because they are poorly presented or both sides have plausible stories, then these biases and attitudes can have a strong influence on a juror's decision.

Unfortunately, jurors have difficulty understanding and following the judge's legal instructions. Jury instructions are often written in complicated legal language, presented orally but not in writing, and given at the end of trial rather than the beginning. Jurors are generally prohibited from taking notes or asking any questions. Imagine taking an exam based only on lectures in which you were not permitted to take notes or ask questions! The difficulty is due in part to the fact that jurors tend to adhere to their preconceived notions of what a typical armed robbery or kidnapping is, and ignore technical legal instructions to the contrary. However, the news is not all bad. Jurors are more likely to follow the law if they hear it several times, see it in writing, and have it explained in plain English using analogies to common experience.[12]

Finally, it is probably reassuring to know that jurors are not swayed by extralegal tricks, techniques and rhetoric of lawyers. They base their decisions on the merits of the case as filtered through their common sense.[13]

F. WOMEN AND MINORITIES IN THE COURTROOM

In many jurisdictions, the trial courts remain a largely white male institution. Most trial judges and most trial lawyers are white males. They have been running the courts their way for years. If you are a woman, a person of

---

[9]See RICHARD E. NISBETT & LEE ROSS, HUMAN INFERENCE: STRATEGIES AND SHORTCOMINGS OF SOCIAL JUDGMENT 55-56 (1980); Michael J. Saks & Robert F. Kidd, *Human Information Processing and Adjudication: Trial By Heuristics*, 15 LAW & SOC. REV. 123 (1980).

[10]See J. Alexander Tanford & Sarah Tanford, *Better Trials Through Science: A Defense of Psychologist-Lawyer Collaboration*, 66 N.C. L. REV. 741, 748-50, 755-56 (1988); Christy Visher, *Juror Decision Making: The Importance of Evidence*, 11 LAW & HUM. BEHAV. 1 (1987).

[11]See Albert J. Moore, *Trial By Schema: Cognitive Filters in the Courtroom*, 37 UCLA L. REV. 273 (1989).

[12]The extensive literature on juror comprehension of instructions is summarized in Hans, *supra* note 8 and J. Alexander Tanford, *The Law and Psychology of Jury Instructions*, 69 NEB. L. REV. 71, 79-88 (1990).

[13]See Tanford & Tanford, *supra* note 10, at 752-59; Barbara F. Reskin, & Christy Visher, *The Impacts of Evidence and Extralegal Factors in Jurors' Decisions*, 20 LAW & SOC. REV. 423 (1986).

color, or a young beginner, you can expect to encounter a hostile, intimidating environment in some courtrooms. After all, you are an outsider trying to break into a small, exclusive club of litigators. Consider the following excerpts from the 1986 Report of the New York Task Force on Women in the Courts.[14] Similar comments could be made about the experiences of African-American, Latino and other minority lawyers.

> [In] recent years, there has been a significant improvement in the way women attorneys are treated in the courts, particularly by judges, and some judges are exemplary in their equal treatment of male and female counsel. Professional acceptance of women attorneys has not, however, been uniform. Irene A. Sullivan, President of the Women's Bar Association of the State of New York testified:
>
>> Too many women attorneys practicing law in our state describe their contact with our court system in negative terms. The comment of one lawyer that: "[W]e are too often either treated disrespectfully or simply ignored," was echoed by many others with whom I spoke.
>
> Elizabeth Holtzman, District Attorney of Kings County, reported that "discrimination against women exists in our courts and manifests itself in many forms: disrespectful and demeaning comments and behavior in the courtroom by male judges, court personnel and opposing counsel." [Holtzman] offered several examples:
>
>> (a) On a very hot summer day, after a male defense counsel was given permission to remove his jacket, an assistant district attorney in my office asked the male judge in open court if she too could remove her jacket. The judge replied: "Don't remove your jacket unless you intend to remove all your clothes."
>> (b) During a plea conference, another male judge told a buxom Brooklyn prosecutor, "My clerk and I have a bet on whether you have to wear weights on your ankles to keep you from tipping over."
>> (c) A woman prosecutor in my office who disagreed strongly with a male judge over a legal point was told, "I will put you over my knee and spank you."
>
> [Other attorneys shared their experiences]
>
>> (a) Women attorneys are frequently assumed to be litigants and told to wait outside of the courtroom or warned not to approach the bar. This attitude occurs with greater frequency towards minority women. For example, a black woman attorney in a business suit carrying a brief-case was told upon trying to enter a Family Court courtroom: "Only attorneys, please. Mothers wait outside."
>> (b) We have all endured the attitude by judges and/or our adversaries, of assumed incompetence. The general belief is that we cannot know what we are doing or talking about. We have also seen that our black

---

[14]The report is reprinted in 15 FORDHAM URB. L.J. 15 (1986-87).

and Latina sisters are presumed even more frequently to be incompetent.

(c) In Suffolk County ... [i]f a male attorney objects repeatedly during trial he is "going all out for his client" and is "a real fighter." If a female attorney objects similarly, she is a "bitch" or a "tough broad." Do you know one attorney actually came over and tried to kiss me to seal his victory after a hard fought trial?

G. A QUESTION OF STYLE

What makes a good public speaker, and how do you become one? Some are born, of course — but what about the rest of us? There are no clear answers. However, the following general suggestions may help you think about how to present yourself in a courtroom.

- *Be yourself.* Most of you are not professional actors, so don't try to be. If you try to act like someone else, you will probably appear insincere. Think about how you naturally argue when you are involved in a lunchroom debate — are you emotional or logical, loud or quiet? Do you gesture with your hands or draw diagrams on paper? Do you tend to suggest compromises or argue for a position? Do you support your arguments with statistics or stories about your family experiences? You will be most comfortable, coherent and persuasive if you work within your natural style, rather than trying to be someone else.
- *Be professional.* The second most important rule is probably "Thou shalt not try to be a country lawyer." Jurors will be quick to detect the insincerity. They expect you to be a lawyer, not Goober down at the gas station.
- *Be confident.* Know the case well enough that you are confident of your grasp of the facts and law. Convey that confidence to the jury.
- *Vary the volume, pitch and pace of your voice.* Nothing is more boring than a monotonous delivery. You can slow down or insert pauses for emphasis, speed up to convey excitement, raise your voice in indignation at an injustice, or drop to a whisper when disclosing a key fact.
- *Choreograph your presentations.* The courtroom is your stage, and you should think about where you want to stand and when you will move. You can move in or out of the jury's view, change positions during transitions, stand behind your client, stand at a chalkboard like a teacher, and employ a host of other stage techniques to complement your verbal presentation.
- *Use visual aids.* Even a dull speaker is more entertaining with well chosen visual aids.
- *Limit your use of notes.* The more tied you are to your notes, the less spontaneous and heartfelt will be your presentation. Most trial lawyers recommend that you use the minimum number of notes that still enable you to remember exactly what you wanted to do.
- *Watch good lawyers.* Watch the good lawyers and see what they do. How long are their presentations? How often do they use visual aids, gestures, or tell stories to illustrate their points? How do they move around the

courtroom? Do not try to copy anyone, but learn from what they are doing and see if you can incorporate any of it into your natural style. Check the law school library media department; it probably has dozens of videotapes of demonstrations by the country's best litigators.

• *Read.* The library is full of literature on trial techniques and tactics containing examples of how good lawyers phrase their questions and present their arguments. Many of these are listed in the bibliographies throughout this book.

NOTES

1. *Sample trial transcript.* For an excellent (and short) example of a full trial, see the trial transcript with comments in JAMES W. JEANS, LITIGATION, ch. 21 (1992).

2. *Becoming a good public speaker.* Speech problems can be overcome with effort. Many "great" public speakers worked hard to achieve that result. John F. Kennedy is a classic case. Most people remember the late president as a naturally great speaker. In fact, Kennedy's vocal afflictions were a laundry list of common speech problems: high pitch, rapid rate, and lack of pauses and emphasis. During the 1960 campaign, Kennedy was clocked at an astonishing 240 words per minute — almost 100 words per minute faster than normal speech. He employed several voice coaches and, by the time he delivered his inaugural address, he had earned a reputation as a great public speaker. For details of Kennedy's speech problems and improvement, see James Powell, *John F. Kennedy's Delivery Skills During the 1960 Campaign,* 32 WEST. SPEECH 59 (1968).

3. *Juror reaction.* How do jurors react to the various styles of courtroom behavior? James P. Brown, was senior vice president of a savings and loan association when called to serve jury duty. He later wrote an article called *A Juryman's View,* 2 GA. ST. B. J. 225, 227-29 (1965):

> The most important persons in the courtroom to the juror are the attorneys who participate in the trial.
>
> In all situations involving human beings, each person and each group of persons chooses a leader for guidance, and in a court of law the attorney is the leader. Invariably, the remarks in the jury room center on the impression made by the attorney. The verdict of the jury in every case reflects the skill of the attorney in presenting the case. The attorney is always on the spot and is the focus of attention; the attorney's appearance, manners, logic, and what the attorney puts value upon are the factors that bring jurors to conclusions.
>
> Case Situation in Point:
>
> A female witness is frightened and balky. The male attorney, with his obvious superior intellect, intimidates and finally traps the witness. He infuriates her as he calls her time and again by her first name and then by her nickname. He belittles her beyond reason. He struts and appears to enjoy confusing the witness. Later, in the jury room, the entire group expresses disapproval of the attorney's methods. Though

not on trial, the attorney was tried by the jury, a verdict reached, and his client suffered from his behavior.

No law, written or unwritten, infers or states that an attorney is to be on trial with the client; but to the juror, who must reach the verdict, the attorney is always on trial consciously or unconsciously.

The Juror evaluates attorneys by:

Their manners
Their sincerity
Their familiarity with all aspects of the case
Their attention to details
Their consideration of others
Their attire and general appearance
Their speech
Their method of communication
Their estimate of the jury's intellect

A juror reaches a verdict from the logical factors and from many intangible sources including the juror's background, and perhaps from the mysterious reason that caused the juror to be chosen for the particular case. However, what the attorneys did, said, or what they did not do or say overpowers other factors and influences the jurors' decision. In that dramatic moment when the verdict of the jury is read, the juror recalls the points won and lost by the attorneys.

H. SOME BASIC PRINCIPLES OF ADVOCACY

A substantial part of this book is concerned with the techniques of effective advocacy at the various stages of trial. However, there are some basic principles of advocacy that apply to all parts of your presentation, which you should begin thinking about.

- Prepare! Prepare! Prepare! Good advocacy is 90% preparation and only 10% talent.
- Develop a theory of your case and stick to it. Make sure that everything you do furthers that theory, and don't waste time on anything irrelevant to it.
- Keep it simple.
- Understand the law of the case as contained in the jury instructions. A good case fits squarely in the middle of it. Save your clever legal arguments about what the law should be and your interesting interpretations for the court of appeals.
- Know your adversary. Know your opponent's style, and also know what kind of case is going to be presented against you.
- Know the judge and the local rules of courtroom procedure.
- Be realistic. Never build a case around what a judge or jury might do, build it around what they will probably do. Sure, it's possible that jurors might believe that a drooling child molester with "Born to Lose" tattooed on his forehead is a credible witness, but it is not likely.

- Think carefully about the language that you use. Use words that personalize your witnesses and depersonalize your opponent's. Use colorful labels as mnemonic devices for the main facts.
- Corroborate rather than repeat. Exact repetition is boring, but corroboration from several angles is convincing.
- Use stories and anecdotes to illustrate your main points.
- Be positive rather than negative. Emphasize the strengths of your case, rather than the weaknesses of your opponent's.
- Ignore jurors who are going to vote against you. You lack the power to make them change their minds, and attempting to do so will probably only harden their adverse stand. Instead, present your case to the nice jurors who are already inclined to vote in your favor. Make sure they understand your position, will remember it in the jury room, and will be able to articulate reasons why it is a good explanation of the facts.

I. BIBLIOGRAPHY

1. COMPREHENSIVE

ANTHONY AMSTERDAM, TRIAL MANUAL 5 FOR THE DEFENSE OF CRIMINAL CASES (1988).
FRANCIS X. BUSCH, LAW AND TACTICS OF JURY TRIALS (1959).
BYRON K. ELLIOTT & WILLIAM F. ELLIOTT, THE WORK OF THE ADVOCATE (1888).
RALPH C. MCCULLOUGH & JAMES L. UNDERWOOD, CIVIL TRIAL MANUAL (2d ed. 1980).

2. LAW

RICHARDSON LYNN, JURY TRIAL LAW AND PRACTICE (1986).
J. Alexander Tanford, *An Introduction to Trial Law*, 51 Mo. L. REV. 623 (1986).

3. ETHICS

JEROME FRANK, COURTS ON TRIAL (1949).
Marvin Frankel, *The Search for Truth: An Umpireal View*, 123 U. PA. L. REV. 1031 (1975).
MONROE FREEDMAN, LAWYERS' ETHICS IN AN ADVERSARY SYSTEM (1975).
RICHARD H. UNDERWOOD & WILLIAM H. FORTUNE, TRIAL ETHICS (1988).

4. PSYCHOLOGY

JEFFREY T. FREDERICK, THE PSYCHOLOGY OF THE AMERICAN JURY (1987).
Valerie P. Hans, *Jury Decision Making, in* HANDBOOK OF PSYCHOLOGY AND LAW (D.K. Kagehiro & W.S. Laufer eds., 1993).
REID HASTIE, STEVEN PENROD & NANCY PENNINGTON, INSIDE THE JURY (1983).
HARRY KALVEN & HANS ZEISEL, THE AMERICAN JURY (1966).
SAUL M. KASSIN & LAWRENCE S. WRIGHTSMAN, THE AMERICAN JURY ON TRIAL: PSYCHOLOGICAL PERSPECTIVES (1988).
Lawrence J. Leigh, *A Theory of Jury Trial Advocacy*, 1984 UTAH L. REV. 763.

Richard O. Lempert, *Telling Tales in Court: Trial Procedure and the Story Model*, 13 Cardozo L. Rev. 559 (1991).

Daniel Linz & Steven Penrod, *Increasing Attorney Persuasiveness in the Courtroom*, 8 Law & Psychol. Rev. 1 (1984).

Albert J. Moore, *Trial By Schema: Cognitive Filters in the Courtroom*, 37 UCLA L. Rev. 273 (1989).

Nancy Pennington & Reid Hastie, *A Cognitive Theory of Juror Decision-Making: The Story Model*, 13 Cardozo L. Rev. 519 (1991).

Steven D. Penrod, Daniel Linz, Harry Heuer, Dan Coates, Michael Atkinson & Stephen Herzberg, *The Implications of Social Psychological Research for Trial Practice Attorneys, in* Psychology and Law (D. J. Muller et al. eds. 1984).

J. Alexander Tanford & Sarah Tanford, *Better Trials Through Science: A Defense of Psychologist-Lawyer Collaboration*, 66 N.C. L. Rev. 741 (1988).

J. Alexander Tanford, *The Law and Psychology of Jury Instructions*, 69 Neb. L. Rev. 71, 79-88 (1990).

Donald E. Vinson, Jury Trials: The Psychology of Winning Strategy (1986).

5. HISTORY

Morris S. Arnold, *Law and Fact in the Medieval Jury Trial: Out of Sight, Out of Mind*, 18 Am. J. Legal Hist. 267 (1974).

John M. Baker, An Introduction to English Legal History (2d ed. 1979).

Francis X. Busch, Law and Tactics in Jury Trials, vol. 1: 2-10, 481-84; vol. 2: 781; vol. 3: 473 (1959).

Adhemar Esmein, A History of Continental Criminal Procedure 322-50 (1913).

Stephen Landsman, *A Brief Survey of the Development of the Adversary System*, 44 Ohio St. L.J. 713 (1983).

Stephen Landsman, *The Rise of the Contentious Spirit: Adversary Procedure in 18th Century England*, 75 Cornell L. Rev. 497 (1990).

Frederick Pollock & Frederic W. Maitland, The History of English Law Before the Time of Edward I, vol. 1: 138-46 (2d ed. 1898).

John H. Wigmore, A Kaleidoscope of Justice (1941).

6. TACTICS

John Appleman, Preparation and Trial (1967).

F. Lee Bailey & Henry Rothblatt, Successful Techniques for Criminal Trials (2d ed. 1985).

Melvin Belli, Modern Trials (1954).

Paul Bergman, Trial Advocacy in a Nutshell (2d ed. 1989).

Joan M. Brovins, & Thomas Oehmke, The Trial Practice Guide (1992).

Asher Cornelius, Trial Tactics (1932).

Richard Crawford, The Persuasion Edge (1989).

Mark A. Dombroff, Dombroff on Unfair Tactics (2d ed. 1988).

Joseph Donovan, Tact in Court (1898).

Kenny Hegland, Trial and Practice Skills (1978).

JAMES W. JEANS, LITIGATION (2d ed. 1992).

JAMES W. JEANS, TRIAL ADVOCACY (1975).

ROBERT KEETON, TRIAL TACTICS AND METHODS (2d ed. 1973).

JOSEPH KELNER & FRANCIS MCGOVERN, SUCCESSFUL LITIGATION TECHNIQUES (1981).

JOHN G. KOELTL, THE LITIGATION MANUAL: A PRIMER FOR TRIAL LAWYERS (2d ed. 1989).

FRED LANE, LANE'S GOLDSTEIN TRIAL TECHNIQUE (3d ed. 1984).

Steve Lubet, *The Trial as a Persuasive Story*, 14 AM. J. TRIAL ADVOC. 77 (1990).

JAMES E. LYONS (ED.), WINNING STRATEGIES AND TECHNIQUES FOR CIVIL LITIGATORS (1992).

THOMAS A. MAUET, FUNDAMENTALS OF TRIAL TECHNIQUES (3d ed. 1992).

JAMES MCELHANEY, TRIAL NOTEBOOK (2d ed. 1989).

ALAN MORRILL, TRIAL DIPLOMACY (2d ed. 1972).

HENRY ROTHBLATT, SUCCESSFUL TECHNIQUES IN THE TRIAL OF CRIMINAL CASES (1961).

D. LAKE RUMSEY (ED.), MASTER ADVOCATE'S HANDBOOK (1986).

SYDNEY SCHWEITZER, CYCLOPEDIA OF TRIAL PRACTICE (2d ed. 1970).

HERBERT J. STERN, TRYING CASES TO WIN (1991).

LLOYD P. STRYKER, THE ART OF ADVOCACY (1954).

JANINE WARSAW, WOMEN TRIAL LAWYERS: HOW THEY SUCCEED IN PRACTICE AND IN THE COURTROOM (1987).

Chapter 2

TRIAL PREPARATION

A. INTRODUCTION

Preparation is the key to successful trial practice. Contrary to what you may see on television, no part of trying a case is extemporaneous. From opening statement, to cross-examination, to the objections you make, to your impassioned closing argument attacking the credibility of an adverse witness, everything you do and say in the courtroom is planned in advance. Any lawyer who tells you differently is simply justifying his or her own laziness.

Consider these introductory words from BYRON & WILLIAM ELLIOTT, THE WORK OF THE ADVOCATE 3-4 (1888):

> Preparation is the foundation of success in advocacy. Neither genius nor talent, neither tact nor cunning, can equip an advocate to try a cause as it is the duty of advocates to try causes, without a foundation well laid by thorough and complete preparation. The first step is to acquire a knowledge of the facts. It is not enough to obtain a knowledge of them in outline; they must be known in their breadth and depth and in their relation to each other and to the ruling principles of law. Knowledge less thorough will not enable an advocate to acquit himself with credit nor will it enable him to do his duty to his client. Cicero says: "What Socrates used to say, that all men are sufficiently eloquent in that which they understand, is very plausible but not true. It would have been nearer the truth to say that no man can be eloquent on a subject that he does not understand." No man can be strong where his knowledge of his subject is feeble. Preparation alone supplies the knowledge which makes trial lawyers strong. Biographers of advocates, like biographers of military heroes, sometimes take up the pen of the romancer, and, to magnify the man of whom they write, invent pleasant fictions. It is to this class of biographers that legal literature owes many stories of verdicts won, as they say, "by a flash of wit or a torrent of eloquence." There is more of rhetorical flourish than of sober truth in these stories. For the most part, legal controversies are not fields for display, but fields for hard work. The advocate cannot too strongly lay it to heart that preparation is absolutely essential to success. Speeches that are lauded as remarkable examples of extemporaneous speaking are almost always found, when the truth is known, to be the result of careful and laborious preparation.

This exhortation is just as true today as it was when it was written over 100 years ago.

The cornerstone of preparation is the development of a theory of the case. A case theory is your view of the best realistically possible interpretation of the facts and law. What do you think really happened, given the evidence and common sense? What is your best legal ground? In what areas is your case strong, and where is it weak? How would a verdict for your client advance the cause of justice? Not until after you develop a theory are you ready to plan any other part of your case. You will have to make decisions concerning which witnesses to call, what questions to ask, whether to introduce particular exhibits, and what arguments to make. You cannot expect to make sensible decisions about how best to try your case until after you have a clear overall theory.

In this chapter we will also discuss a range of other issues that fall into the general concept of trial preparation. We are not here concerned with specifically how to prepare a direct examination or a closing argument; that will be discussed in subsequent chapters. Rather, we will focus on aspects of general preliminary preparation:

- Case investigation: gathering the facts and learning the law (substantive, procedural and evidentiary) relevant to your case.
- Pretrial planning concerning such issues as the order of proof and the evaluation and selection of witnesses.
- Pretrial legal maneuvering: motions, jury instruction requests, pretrial conferences.
- Developing a case file.

One important thing to remember throughout this chapter and throughout your work in this course is that the best way to prepare is to write it down. Facts gathered will be forgotten if not recorded; ideas may dissipate if not written out; clever arguments may prove harder to articulate than you thought when you try to explain them in writing. A trial is like a book, consisting of characters, a conflict, a plot, and a dramatic trial scene. The true labor in preparation consists of writing and rewriting the book until all the pieces fit together in an intelligent and plausible whole. This is a time-consuming process, but it is the closest thing to a guarantee of a successful trial.

B. LEGAL FRAMEWORK

1. DUTY TO PREPARE

Is there a legal duty to adequately prepare for trial? Consider the following cases:

SHACK v. STATE

249 Ind. 67, 231 N.E.2d 36 (1967)

[The defendant appealed his conviction for murder on the ground of ineffective assistance of his trial counsel, James Nedeff.]

The gravamen of appellant's petition [is] that the attorney representing him before the Trial Court was incompetent and that such representation was inadequate. In order for us to make a determination as to whether or not Varderman Shack had adequate and competent counsel in the defense of this most serious indictment, we look first to what Mr. Nedeff, himself, said concerning his conduct of this case.

On the 7th day of January, 1963, Mr. Shack was unable to speak due to an injury that he had received. He was only able to talk two weeks prior to the time the trial was to commence; yet, Mr. Nedeff did not ask for any continuance in order to give him additional time to confer with the defendant or to prepare his case.

Mr. Shack furnished Mr. Nedeff with the names of witnesses to call on his behalf, but Mr. Nedeff was either unable to locate them, or felt they could be of no benefit to Mr. Shack and he did not request a continuance in order to locate any of the witnesses who were not found at that time. He did not call any witnesses for Mr. Shack, and the sole witness, for all practical purposes, was the appellant himself.

Mr. Nedeff devoted approximately eighteen (18) hours to the preparation of the defense of Mr. Shack.

Mr. Nedeff did not request any instructions on behalf of Mr. Shack from the Trial Court. During part of the eighteen (18) hours of preparation he did research work at the law library on homicides in various degrees. He did visit the scene of the crime. He does not know of any other preparation that he could have made for this case.

In many cases it would be impossible for this Court to fix guidelines as to the requisite number of hours that an attorney should spend in preparation of the defense of a case. This Court has written on the subject of adequate preparation and adequate time for preparation, but we must conclude that each case stands on its own facts. In *Wilson v. State* (1943), 222 Ind. 63, 51 N.E.2d 848, the following language is used:

> ... Nor need we now draw a line, if there is one, between competency and incompetency. The spirit of these constitutional provisions requires that an accused must have something more than a perfunctory presentation. It is true whether the attorney is appointed by the court or engaged by the accused.

Appellant has called our attention to the concurring opinion of Judge Emmert in *Hillman v. State* (1954), 234 Ind. 27, 123 N.E.2d 180, in which he stated:

> A careful lawyer would have double-checked the story of appellant. The transcript discloses that the prosecuting attorney, in compliance with the criminal code, endorsed the names of six witnesses on the back of the affidavit. None of these were ever called or interviewed by appellant's counsel, although as a matter of law he knew the state had listed them as witnesses against his client. Even a casual investigation of the evidence the police officers were prepared to give would have disclosed that a confession had been signed.

We believe it is unnecessary to labor this matter further. Varderman Shack did not have competent counsel in his trial nor did he have an adequate defense. We can decide as a matter of law that Mr. Nedeff did not make adequate preparation when he expended only eighteen (18) hours in factual investigation, legal research, inquiry concerning sanity, and all of the other facets of inquiry properly to be disposed of by an attorney in the preparation of a felony as serious as Murder in the First Degree. This is particularly true since Mr. Nedeff had never tried a homicide case. This would probably be true even with one of the legal giants of trial practice; but, a seasoned trial lawyer would deem it unthinkable to go to trial with only eighteen (18) hours of preparation. He would deem it malpractice not to seek a psychiatric examination of his client in order to determine whether or not a plea of insanity would be interposed. A mature practitioner who had tried many cases would spend several times eighteen (18) hours in legal research alone in order to properly prepare, for the Court's consideration, tendered instructions touching on the various elements of murder.

It is the concern of the bar of this State and this Court, which fixes the standard of competency, to have to set aside a conviction because of incompetency of a member of the bar representing a defendant in a criminal case. I therefore feel the competency of the attorney involved in this case should be referred to the Disciplinary Commission for investigation and report as to whether or not disbarment proceedings or other disciplinary action should be taken.

BEASLEY v. UNITED STATES

491 F.2d 687 (6th Cir. 1974)

[Defendant was convicted of attempted armed bank robbery and appealed, claiming ineffective assistance of his appointed counsel before and during trial.]

Turning to the claim of ineffective assistance of counsel before and during trial, the question we are faced with is how ineffective and incompetent an attorney's representation of a criminal defendant must be before an accused's Sixth Amendment right is violated. The District Court found that Petitioner's attorney had been incompetent and ineffective in several respects.

First, Counsel called as the sole defense witness (except for Petitioner) an FBI agent described by the District Court as:

> a man whom petitioner has advised counsel, prior to trial, is "out to get me;" a man who is not a *res gestae* witness; a man who is employed by the opposing party to the suit, and was not an agent on the case; a man whose only knowledge of petitioner's *modus operandi* came from information supplied by petitioner himself, a man whom the attorney, himself, has called a liar and perjurer on the witness stand only two months before trial; a man who is called as a witness without having been interviewed by counsel to discover what testimony he could give; a man who has interviewed petitioner and taken a statement, damaging to petitioner, which counsel has just read before calling this witness.

Calling this witness made sense only in the context of a bizarre defense strategy which the District Court characterized as "highly implausible." Defense counsel's only conceivable rationale for calling this antagonistic witness was to embarrass the Government by showing how zealous this FBI agent had been and to support the theory that a "pro" like Petitioner would not have pulled an amateurish operation like the attempted robbery in this case. The trial judge gave no credence to this strange defense reasoning. Calling the FBI agent, furthermore, allowed the prosecution to introduce damaging evidence of a past criminal record. The witness was called over Petitioner's protests to his attorney. His testimony did nothing but support Petitioner's guilt and criticize his character. The witness testified without advance questioning by defense counsel as to what he might say. The District Court found that it was "incompetency" to call this witness.

Third, although the trial judge ordered the Government to pay for an independent test of the fingerprint evidence, counsel never requested one. Evidence not disclosed until October 11, 1972, indicates that an independent test would have revealed a defect in the Government's crucial fingerprint evidence. At trial the Government introduced a corner of one of the two demand notes the attempted robber had handed to the bank teller, which contained six prints identified as Petitioner's. A Detroit Police expert testified on October 11, 1972, that tests run one day after the attempted robbery disclosed only two partial prints, neither of which was Petitioner's. Another print, not Petitioner's, was found on the fake "bomb" used in the attempted robbery. This evidence, never disclosed to Petitioner, would have tended to rebut the Government's fingerprint evidence. The man who could have disclosed this was called to the courtroom by defense counsel but was never called to the stand. Thus, although counsel had urged Petitioner to waive a jury trial because of complicated fingerprint testimony, he never used the favorable rebuttal evidence available and left the Government's identification of Petitioner unchallenged.

Fourth, there were several res gestae witnesses who were never called to testify, though they would have testified that they could not identify petitioner as the attempted robber. Because their testimony would not have aided the prosecution, the Government did not summon them. Defense counsel did not call them because he was under the mistaken belief that it was the Government's responsibility to subpoena all res gestae witnesses, the practice in Michigan state courts but not in federal courts.

Sixth, defense counsel failed to interview any res gestae witnesses before trial other than the one who gave mildly favorable testimony for the prosecution.

Seventh, counsel conducted "no more than a cursory investigation of the facts prior to trial." An alibi witness whom Petitioner had asked counsel to interview died before trial and without having been contacted by counsel, thus depriving Petitioner of his testimony in any form.

In this case the District Court found that Petitioner had been denied the competent and effective assistance of counsel in many respects. Whether this denial constituted a violation of Petitioner's Sixth Amendment right depends on the meaning of effective assistance of counsel.

In *McMann v. Richardson*, 397 U.S. 759 (1970), the Supreme Court stated that "It has long been recognized that the right to counsel is the right to the effective assistance of counsel." It held that the advice rendered by an attorney as to whether a confession would be admissible in evidence must be "within the range of competence demanded of attorneys in criminal cases." 397 U.S. at 771. "[I]f the right to counsel guaranteed by the Constitution is to serve its purpose, defendants cannot be left to the mercies of incompetent counsel, and ... judges should strive to maintain proper standards of performance by attorneys who are representing defendants in criminal cases in their courts." 397 U.S. at 771.

We hold that the assistance of counsel required under the Sixth Amendment is counsel reasonably likely to render and rendering reasonably effective assistance. It is a violation of this standard for defense counsel to deprive a criminal defendant of a substantial defense by his own ineffectiveness or incompetence. Defense counsel must perform at least as well as a lawyer with ordinary training and skill in the criminal law and must conscientiously protect his client's interest, undeflected by conflicting considerations. Defense counsel must investigate all apparently substantial defenses available to the defendant and must assert them in a proper and timely manner. It is a denial of the right to the effective assistance of counsel for an attorney to advise his client erroneously on a clear point of law if this advice leads to the deprivation of his client's right to a fair trial. Defense strategy and tactics which lawyers of ordinary training and skill in the criminal law would not consider competent deny a criminal defendant the effective assistance of counsel, if some other action would have better protected a defendant and was reasonably foreseeable as such before trial.

We hold that Petitioner did not receive the effective assistance of counsel before and during trial. Potentially exonerating defenses were not explored by counsel and were not developed at trial. Because Petitioner was represented by incompetent and ineffective counsel, his conviction cannot stand.

2. DUTY TO COMPLY WITH DISCOVERY REQUESTS

Should you try to evade discovery? Many lawyers seem to think that discovery is just a game, or that it is good "tactics" to try to evade all discovery requests. Consider *Chapman v. Pacific Telephone and Telegraph Co.*, 613 F.2d 193 (9th Cir. 1979):

> Deborah Halvonik was one of the attorneys for multiple plaintiffs in a Title VII action. During pretrial [discovery] she refused to comply with the order of the district court [and was held in criminal contempt].
>
> At a pre-trial conference on January 6, 1978, the district court orally ordered Mrs. Halvonik, lead counsel, to submit a written narrative statement of the direct testimony of each witness whom plaintiffs intended to call at the trial. The court observed that such statements would be helpful to the court in understanding the issues and would compel the parties to prepare adequately for trial. Appellant was given ten days to comply.
>
> She made no attempt to prepare the statements ... On January 26, she attended another pretrial conference. The court inquired what progress had been made in preparing the witness statements. Mrs. Halvonik informed the court that nothing had been done. The court held her in contempt but withheld fixing punishment until after the conclusion of her Title VII trial.
>
> When the court informed Mrs. Halvonik she was in contempt, she asked for and was granted a recess to consult with co-counsel. After the

recess, Mrs. Halvonik said she did not intend to comply with the order because she was confused. The court found her confusion "self-induced and self-perpetuated."

On that day, the court reduced its order to writing. Mrs. Halvonik still did not make even a good faith attempt to prepare witness statements.

Mrs. Halvonik argues that the order was not clear and definite. She portrays the court's infinite patience, its repeated explanations of the order and its attempts to mollify Mrs. Halvonik as vacillation. We are at a loss to see what more the court could have done to clarify and define its order.

Attorneys, as officers of the court, have a duty to cooperate with the court to preserve and promote the efficient operation of our system of justice.... The Rules of evidence and procedure are designed to lead to just decisions and are part of the framework of the law. Thus while a lawyer may take steps in good faith and within the framework of the law to test the validity of rules, [she] is not justified in consciously violating such rules and [she] should be diligent in [her] efforts to guard against [her] unintentional violation of them.

Mrs. Halvonik's conduct in this case far surpassed the bounds of a good faith testing of the district's court's order.

Mrs. Halvonik argues that she was privileged to disobey the court's order because it was invalid. An attorney who believes a court order is erroneous is not relieved of the duty to obey it. The proper course of action, unless and until the order is invalidated by an appellate court, is to comply and cite the order as reversible error should an adverse judgement result. *Maness v. Meyers*, 419 U.S. 449, 95 S. Ct. 584, 42 L. Ed. 2d 574 (1975).

The contempt order is affirmed.

NOTE

Sanctions for discovery abuse. Rules 11 and 37 of the Federal Rules of Civil Procedure provide a range of sanctions that may be imposed upon a party who abuses or delays the discovery process, from awarding expenses and attorney's fees to dismissal of the action. Sanctions usually are imposed against the client (who would then have to bring a separate malpractice action against the attorney), but the court has inherent power to hold the attorney in contempt. A few courts have local rules authorizing penalties to be imposed directly on attorneys, but they are rarely used. *See* ROBERT RODES, KENNETH RIPPLE & CAROL MONEY, SANCTIONS IMPOSABLE FOR VIOLATIONS OF THE FEDERAL RULES OF CIVIL PROCEDURE (Fed. Judicial Center, 1981). Rule 26 permits the court to limit discovery and requires attorneys to verify that discovery is not being undertaken for purposes of delay or economic warfare. *See* Edward Sherman & Stephen Kinnard, *Federal Court Discovery in the 80's — Making the Rules*, 95 FED. R. DEC. 245 (1982). Sanctions in general are discussed in MARK A. DOMBROFF, DOMBROFF ON UNFAIR TACTICS 153 (2d ed. 1988).

C. ETHICAL CONSIDERATIONS

1. AMERICAN BAR ASSOCIATION, STANDARDS RELATING TO THE ADMINISTRATION OF CRIMINAL JUSTICE (2d ed. 1980)

Standard 4-4.1. Duty to Investigate
(a) Defense counsel should conduct a prompt investigation of the circumstances of the case and to explore all avenues leading to facts relevant to the merits of the case and the penalty in the event of conviction. The investigation should include efforts to secure information in the possession of the prosecution and law enforcement authorities. The duty to investigate exists regardless of the accused's admissions or statements to defense counsel of facts constituting guilt or the accused's stated desire to plead guilty.

Standard 4-4.2. Illegal investigation
Defense counsel should not knowingly use illegal means to obtain evidence or information or to employ, instruct, or encourage others to do so.

The official commentary to these sections emphasizes that effective representation at trial requires thorough investigation and preparation before trial. In that commentary, the following steps are mentioned as ethically required in criminal cases:

- Search for and locate potential witnesses and try to secure their cooperation.
- Obtain independent laboratory analysis of fingerprints, handwriting, clothing, hair, blood, and weapons.
- Request formal and informal discovery from the prosecutor.
- Talk to the police who investigated the case and arrested your client.
- Investigate your client's background, education, employment record, mental and emotional stability, family relationships, and the like.
- Investigate the backgrounds and character of opposing witnesses to prepare for impeachment.
- Find out the conditions at the scene, especially those that may have affected eyewitnesses' opportunities for observation.

You are not relieved of your obligation to investigate by your client's admission of guilt or desire to plead guilty. The question before you is whether the prosecution can prove legal guilt, not whether your client "did it." However, you obviously cannot undertake illegal investigation through wiretaps or electronic surveillance devices, or by harassing or threatening witnesses.

2. ABA MODEL RULES OF PROFESSIONAL CONDUCT

The Model Rules address several aspects of trial preparation: the need to prepare thoroughly, the obligation to cooperate in discovery, and the development of a theory. Rule 1.1 makes adequate preparation the first rule of professional responsibility.

Rule 1.1 Competence

A lawyer shall provide competent representation to a client. Competent representation requires the legal knowledge, skill, thoroughness and preparation reasonably necessary for the representation.

Rule 3.4 addresses discovery. It imposes a general duty of fairness to opposing counsel. The discovery tricks everyone has heard about — evading legitimate discovery requests, stalling, hiding documents — are unethical.

Rule 3.4 Fairness to Opposing Party and Counsel

A lawyer shall not:

(a) Unlawfully obstruct another party's access to evidence or unlawfully alter, destroy or conceal a document or other material having potential evidentiary value. A lawyer shall not counsel or assist another person to do any such act;

(b) Falsify evidence, counsel or assist a witness to testify falsely, or offer an inducement to a witness that is prohibited by law;

(c) Knowingly disobey an obligation under the [discovery] rules of a tribunal except for an open refusal based on an assertion that no valid obligation exists;

(d) In pretrial procedure, make a frivolous discovery request or fail to make reasonably diligent effort to comply with a legally proper discovery request by an opposing party;

...

(f) Request a person other than a client to refrain from voluntarily giving relevant information to another party unless:

(1) The person is a relative or an employee or other agent of a client; and

(2) The lawyer reasonably believes that the person's interests will not be adversely affected by refraining from giving such information.

Rule 3.4 also addresses the preparation of a case theory. It cautions that a lawyer shall not:

(e) In trial, allude to any matter that the lawyer does not reasonably believe is relevant or that will not be supported by admissible evidence, assert personal knowledge of facts in issue except when testifying as a witness, or state a personal opinion as to the justness of a cause, the credibility of a witness, the culpability of a civil litigant or the guilt or innocence of an accused.

Thus, you must have a good faith *factual* basis for your theory. You must believe that evidence will be admissible and that witnesses will be available to testify to it, in order to include it in your theory.

Similarly, Rule 3.1 requires that you have a good faith *legal* basis for the case you present. You may not argue an unwarranted legal position because a jury just might buy it, or in order to set up a possible compromise in the jury room.

Rule 3.1 Meritorious Claims and Contentions

A lawyer shall not bring or defend a proceeding, or assert or controvert an issue therein, unless there is a basis for doing so that is not frivolous, which includes a good faith argument for an extension, modification or reversal of existing law. A lawyer for the defendant in a criminal proceeding ... may nevertheless so defend the proceeding as to require that every element of the case be established.

A special duty is placed on prosecutors that prohibits them from overcharging in a weak case in hopes that the jury will convict of something. Rule 3.8 states that the prosecutor shall "refrain from prosecuting a charge that the prosecutor knows is not supported by probable cause."

3. ENCOURAGING PERJURY

Perhaps the best known ethics hypothetical in all of trial practice occurs at the beginning of Robert Traver's novel, *Anatomy of a Murder* (1958):

I paused and lit a cigar. I took my time. I had reached a point where a few wrong answers to a few right questions would leave me with a client — if I took his case — whose cause was legally defenseless. Either I stopped now and begged off and let some other lawyer worry over it or I asked him the few fatal questions and let him hang himself. Or else, like any smart lawyer, I went into the Lecture. I studied my man, who sat as inscrutable as an Arab, delicately fingering his Ming holder, daintily fingering his dark mustache. He apparently did not realize how close I had him to admitting that he was guilty of first degree murder, that is, that he "feloniously, wilfully, and of his malice aforethought did kill and murder one Barney Quill." The man was a sitting duck.

And what is the Lecture?

The Lecture is an ancient device that lawyers use to coach their clients so that the client won't quite know he has been coached and his lawyer can still preserve the face-saving illusion that he hasn't done any coaching. For coaching clients, like robbing them, is not only frowned upon, it is downright unethical and bad, very bad. Hence the Lecture — an artful device as old as the law itself, and one used constantly by some of the nicest and most ethical lawyers in the land. "Who me? I didn't tell him what to say," the lawyer can later comfort himself. "I merely explained the law, see." It is a good practice to scowl and shrug here and add virtuously: "That's my duty, isn't it?"

"As I told you," I began, "I've been thinking about your case during the noon hour."

"Yes," he replied. "You mentioned that."

"So I did, so I did," I said. "Now I realize there are many questions still to be asked, facts to be discussed," I went on. "And I am not prejudging your case." I paused to discharge the opening salvo of the Lecture. "But as things presently stand I must advise you that in my opinion you have not yet disclosed to me a legal defense to this charge of murder. In fact, Lieutenant, for all the elaborate hemorrhage of words in the law books about the legal defenses to murder there are only about three basic defenses: one, that it didn't happen but was instead a suicide or accident or what not; two, that whether it happened or not you didn't do it, such as alibi, mistaken identity and so forth; and three, that even if it happened and you did it, your action was legally justified or excusable." I paused to see how my student was doing.

The Lieutenant grew thoughtful. "Where do I fit in that rosy picture?" he responded nicely.

"I can tell you better where you don't fit," I went on. "Since a whole barroom full of people saw you shoot down Barney Quill in apparent cold blood, you scarcely fit in the first two classes of defenses. I'm afraid we needn't waste time on those." I paused. "If you fit anywhere it's got to be in the third. So we'd better bear down on that."

"You mean," Lieutenant Manion said, "that my only possible defense in this case is to find some justification or excuse?"

My lecture was proceeding nicely according to schedule. "You're learning rapidly," I said, nodding approvingly. "Merely add legal justification or excuse and I'll mark you an A."

The Lieutenant's eyes narrowed and flickered ever so little. "Maybe," he began, and cleared his throat. "On second thought, maybe I did catch Quill in the act. I've never precisely told the police one way or the other." His eyes regarded me quietly, steadily. This man, I saw, was not only an apt student of the Lecture; like most people (including lawyers) he indubitably possessed a heart full of larceny. He was also, perhaps instinctively, trying to turn the Lecture on his lawyer. "I've never really told them," he concluded.

A lawyer in the midst of his Lecture is apt to cling to the slenderest reed to bolster his wavering virtue. "But you've told me," I said, pausing complacently, swollen with rectitude, grateful for the swift surge of virtue he'd afforded me. "And anyway," I went on, "you would have had to dispatch him then, not, as you've already admitted, an hour or so later. The catching and killing must combine. And that's true even if you'd actually caught him at it — which you didn't. I've just now told you that time is one of the factors in determining whether a homicide is a murder or not. Here it's a big one. Don't you see? — in your case time is the rub; it's the elapsed time between the rape and the killing that permits the People to bear down and argue that your shooting of Barney Quill was a deliberate, malicious and premeditated act. And that, my friend, is no more than they've charged you with."

Quietly: "You don't want to take my case, then?"

"Not quite so fast. I'm not ready to make that decision. Look, in a murder case the jury has only a few narrow choices. Among them, it might let you go. It might also up and convict you. A judge trying you without a jury would surely have to, as I have said. Now do you want to go into court with the dice loaded? With all the law and instructions stacked against you?" I paused to deliver my clincher. "Well, whether you're willing to do so, I'm not. I will either find a sound and plausible legal defense in your case or else advise you to cop out." I paused thoughtfully.

Lieutenant Manion produced the Ming holder and studied it carefully, as though for the first time. "What do you recommend then?" he said.

It was a good question. "I don't know yet. So far I've been trying to impress you with the importance, the naked necessity, of our finding a valid legal defense, if one exists, in addition to the 'unwritten law' you so dearly want to cling to. Put it this way: what Barney Quill might have done to your wife before you killed him may present a favorable condition, an equitable climate, to a possible jury acquittal. But alone it simply isn't enough." I paused. "Not enough for Paul Biegler, anyway."

"You mean you want to find a way to give the jurors some decently plausible legal peg to hang their verdict on so that they might let me go — and still save face?"

My man was responding beautifully to the Lecture. "Precisely," I said, adding hastily: "Whether you have such a defense of course remains to be seen. But I hope, Lieutenant, I have shown you how vital it is to find one if it exists."

"I think you have, Counselor," he said slowly. "I rather think now you really have." He paused. "Tell me, tell me more about this justification or excuse business. Excuse me," he added, smiling faintly, "I mean legal justification or excuse."

"Well, take self-defense," I began. "That's the classic example of justifiable homicide. On the basis of what I've so far heard and read about your case I do not think we need pause too long over that. Do you?"

"Perhaps not," Lieutenant Manion conceded. "We'll pass it for now."

"Let's," I said dryly. "Then there's the defense of habitation, defense of property, and the defense of relatives or friends. Now there are more ramifications to these defenses than a dog has fleas, but we won't explore them now. I've already told you at length why I don't think you can invoke the possible defense of your wife. When you shot Quill her need for defense had passed. It's as simple as that."

"Go on," Lieutenant Manion said, frowning.

"Then there's the defense of a homicide committed to prevent a felony — say you're being robbed —; to prevent the escape of the felon — suppose he's getting away with your wallet —; or to arrest a felon — you've caught up with him and he's either trying to get away or has actually escaped."

"Then there's the tricky and dubious defense of intoxication. Personally I've never seen it succeed. But since you were not drunk when you shot Quill we shall mercifully not dwell on that. Or were you?"

"I was cold sober. Please go on."

"Then finally there's the defense of insanity." I paused and spoke abruptly, airily: "Well, that just about winds it up." I arose as though making ready to leave.

"Tell me more."

"There is no more." I slowly paced up and down the room.

"I mean about this insanity."

"Oh, insanity," I said, elaborately surprised. It was like luring a trained seal with a herring. "Well, insanity, where proven, is a complete defense to murder. It does not legally justify the killing, like self-defense, say, but rather excuses it." The lecturer was hitting his stride. He was also on the home stretch. "Our law requires that a punishable killing — in fact, any crime — must be committed by a sapient human being, one capable, as the law insists, of distinguishing between right and wrong. If a man is insane, legally insane, the act of homicide may still be murder but the law excuses the perpetrator."

Lieutenant Manion was sitting erect now, very still and erect. "I see — and this — this perpetrator, what happens to him if he should — should be excused?"

"Under Michigan law — like that of many other states — if he is acquitted of murder on the grounds of insanity it is provided that he must be sent to a hospital for the criminally insane until he is pronounced sane." I drummed my fingers on the Sheriff's desk and glanced at my watch, the picture of a man eager to be gone.

My man was baying along the scent now. "How long does it take to get him out of there?"

"Out of where?" I asked innocently.

"Out of this insane hospital!"

"Oh, you mean where a man claims he was insane at the time of the offense but is sane at the time of the trial and his possible acquittal?"

"Exactly."

"I don't know," I said, stroking my chin. "Months, maybe a year. It really takes a bit of doing. Being D.A. so long I've never really had to study that phase of it. I got them in there; it was somebody else's problem to spring them. And I didn't dream this defense might come up in your case."

My naivete was somewhat excessive; it had been obvious to me from merely reading the newspaper the night before that insanity was the best, if not the only, legal defense the man had. And here I'd just slammed shut every other escape hatch and told him this was the last. Only a cretin could have missed it, and I was rapidly learning that Lieutenant Manion was no cretin.

"Tell me more," Lieutenant Manion said quietly.

"I may add that the law that requires persons acquitted on the grounds of insanity to be sent away is designed to discourage phony pleas of insanity in criminal cases." ... I paused and knocked out my pipe. The Lecture was about over. The rest was up to the student. The Lieutenant looked out the window. He studied his Ming holder. I sat very still. Then he looked at me. "Maybe," he said, "maybe I was insane."

Thoughtfully: "Hm.... Why do you say that?"

"Well, I can't really say," he went on slowly, "I — I guess I blacked out. I can't remember a thing after I saw him standing behind the bar that night until I got back to my trailer."

"You mean — you mean you don't remember shooting him?" I shook my head in wonderment.

"Yes, that's what I mean."

"You don't even remember driving home?"

"No."

"My, my," I said, blinking my eyes, contemplating the wonder of it all. "Maybe you've got something there." ... All right, I thought — maybe my man was insane when he shot Barney Quill. Maybe he was nuttier than a fruit cake and maybe he had blacked out and didn't remember a thing. So far so good. But there was one flaw, one small thorn in this insanity business, and one that had to be faced, and fast. And wasn't it far better to face it now, before I got committed in the case, than later on in the harsh glow of the courtroom? I turned back to my man.

"Look, Lieutenant. Hold your hat. I'm about to pitch you a fast ball .... Maybe you were insane. Maybe you didn't remember a thing. But you and the newspaper agree on one thing. Both of you tell me that right after you returned to the trailer park, after shooting Barney Quill, you woke up the deputized caretaker and told him: 'I just shot Barney Quill.' Now is that correct?" Again I held my breath.

I rather think he saw what was coming, but he replied steadily enough. "That is right," he answered because he had to, there was no other answer, no escape; he was already committed on that one far past the point of no return.

Slowly, easily: "All right, then, Lieutenant. Now tell me, how come you could tell the caretaker you had just shot Barney Quill if you had really blacked out and didn't remember a thing? Who told you?"

"Well," he began. Then he stopped cold and closed his eyes. He was stalled. It was the first time I'd seen him really grope. The silence continued. Was I, I wondered, developing into one of those incurable ex-D.A.'s, the unreconstructed kind who can always find more reasons for convicting their clients than acquitting them?

"Come, now, man," I pressed, "what could possibly have led you to tell the caretaker you'd just shot Barney if it is true that you didn't remember it?"

He spoke rapidly, jerkily. "All right.... It's coming back.... Barney Quill was the last man I saw before I blacked out.... In fact his was the only face I saw in the whole damned place.... My gun.... I knew when I entered the barroom the clip of my luger was loaded. When I got back to my trailer I saw it was empty. There's a thing that pops up...." He threw out his hands. "Don't you see? I figured I must have shot him, that's all. So I went and told the caretaker I had." He paused and looked up at me like a child who'd just recited his Christmas poem. Had he done all right?

It was the only plausible explanation he could have made.

Consider the following analysis of the defense lawyer's ethical role, from Monroe Freedman's classic article, *Professional Responsibility of the Criminal Defense Lawyer: The Three Hardest Questions*, 64 MICH. L. REV. 1469, 1478-82 (1966):[1]

> [Is it] proper to give your client legal advice when you have reason to believe that the knowledge you give him will tempt him to commit perjury[?] This may indeed be the most difficult problem of all, because

---

[1] Professor Freedman has amplified his views in MONROE FREEDMAN, LAWYERS' ETHICS IN AN ADVERSARY SYSTEM (1975).

giving such advice creates the appearance that the attorney is encouraging and condoning perjury.

Assume that your client, on trial for his life in a first-degree murder case, has killed another man with a penknife but insists that the killing was in self-defense. You ask him, "Do you customarily carry the penknife in your pocket, do you carry it frequently or infrequently, or did you take it with you only on this occasion?" He replies, "Why do you ask me a question like that?" It is entirely appropriate to inform him that his carrying the knife only on this occasion, or infrequently, supports an inference of premeditation, while if he carried the knife constantly, or frequently, the inference of premeditation would be negated. Thus, your client's life may depend upon his recollection as to whether he carried the knife frequently or infrequently. Despite the possibility that the client or a third party might infer that the lawyer was prompting the client to lie, the lawyer must apprise the defendant of the significance of his answer. There is no conceivable ethical requirement that the lawyer trap his client into a hasty and ill-considered answer before telling him the significance of the question.

A similar problem is created if the client has given the lawyer incriminating information before being fully aware of its significance. For example, assume that a man consults a tax lawyer and says, "I am fifty years old. Nobody in my immediate family has lived past fifty. Therefore, I would like to put my affairs in order. Specifically, I understand that I can avoid substantial estate taxes by setting up a trust. Can I do it?" The lawyer informs the client that he can successfully avoid the estate taxes only if he lives at least three years after establishing the trust or, should he die within three years, if the trust is found not to have been created in contemplation of death. The client then might ask who decides whether the trust is in contemplation of death. After learning that the determination is made by the court, the client might inquire about the factors on which such a decision would be based.

At this point, the lawyer can do one of two things. He can refuse to answer the question, or he can inform the client that the court will consider the wording of the trust instrument and will hear evidence about any conversations which he may have or any letters he may write expressing motives other than avoidance of estate taxes. It is likely that virtually every tax attorney in the country would answer the client's question, and that no one would consider the answer unethical. However, the lawyer might well appear to have prompted his client to deceive the Internal Revenue Service and the courts, and this appearance would remain regardless of the lawyer's explicit disclaimer to the client of any intent so to prompt him. Nevertheless, it should not be unethical for the lawyer to give the advice.

Essentially no different from the problem discussed above, but apparently more difficult, is the so-called Anatomy of a Murder situation. The lawyer, who has received from his client an incriminating story of murder in the first degree, says, "If the facts are as you have stated them so far, you have no defense, and you will probably be electrocuted. On the other hand, if you acted in a blind rage, there is a possibility of saving your life. Think it over, and we will talk about it tomorrow." As in the tax case ... the lawyer has given his client a legal opinion that might induce the client to lie. This is information which the lawyer himself would have, without advice, were he in the client's position. It is submitted that the client is entitled to have this information about the law and to make his own decision as to whether to act upon it. To decide otherwise would not only penalize the less well educated defendant, but would also prejudice the client because of his initial truthfulness in telling his story in confidence to the attorney.

Consider this thoughtful response by A. Kenneth Pye, in *The Role of Counsel in the Suppression of Truth*, 1978 DUKE L.J. 921, 926, 947-57:

A trial is not an athletic contest in which each side should have an equal chance to win. A defendant should win only when he is innocent or when the state cannot prove his guilt beyond a reasonable doubt by competent evidence. He has no inherent right to an acquittal. He may be acquitted because the prosecution errs, or for some other reason not related to his guilt, but not because of any sense of entitlement.

[In the *Anatomy of a Murder* situation, Biegler's conduct is indefensible — it amounts to suborning perjury. His] conduct in lecturing [Manion] concerning the legal consequences of different versions of what might have taken place was no more or less than a suggestion of the story that [Manion] should then relate. It was intended to produce the version of the facts related to [him] and was obviously so perceived by him.

The reason for [Biegler's] approach is likewise obvious. He might feel uncomfortable if he were required to call [Manion] to the stand to testify to a story that [he] had earlier denied. [Biegler] is in a much better position from the point of view of his conscience and of his ultimate success if he can start with a story that, if believed, will justify an acquittal. [Manion] also is happier if he can provide such testimony.

It clearly would make a better battle in many cases if the defendant had help in fabricating his story. The problem is that we are seeking not a good fight but an honest statement of the events as perceived by the witness. The ABA Standard is clearly correct when it states:

It is unprofessional conduct for the lawyer to instruct the client or to intimate to him in any way that he should not be candid in revealing facts ....[2]

Clearly, the confidential relationship is of immense significance to the operation of our system. But there is nothing in the history of the evidentiary privilege or of the professional obligation to suggest that it was designed to cloak active participation in the facilitation of perjury. A conclusion that a lawyer may immunize himself from professional responsibility for subornation by telling his client that his conduct is unlawful lacks a basis in authority or reason. Whether or not he has previously cautioned a client to tell the truth, when an attorney calls the client to

[2]1 ABA STANDARDS FOR CRIMINAL JUSTICE 4-3.2(b) (2d ed. 1980).

the stand knowing that he will lie, the attorney willfully procures perjury.

A broader justification for counsel calling any witness (including but not limited to the defendant) when he knows he will tell a falsehood is predicated upon the proposition that counsel is not required to be the judge of the credibility of any witness, including his client. It is argued that the trial is not a search for "truth" in the abstract, but is rather an effort to persuade the trier of fact that it should resolve the dispute by adoption of some version of the facts as testified to by witnesses.

Advocates of this approach would argue that counsel should advise witnesses and clients to testify only to what they believe in their own minds to be the truth and warn them of the pains of perjury and of the danger of effective cross-examination of a witness who is not truthful. After such warnings, the lawyer has arguably fulfilled his duty. He should not attempt to judge credibility but should permit the witness to relate any story the witness desires and then attempt to persuade the jury to believe the testimony elicited.

There is obvious appeal in such an analysis. Counsel is relieved of any ethical responsibility if a witness chooses to lie. Undoubtedly, defense counsel will sometimes be more successful than would have been the case if he could not have produced witnesses to testify about a defense that counsel knows did not exist.

The problem is that in some situations lawyers do "know" what in fact took place. When they do, the moral responsibility for producing testimony to the contrary is quite different from when counsel is ignorant of the true state of facts, or even when he believes (but does not know) that the facts are different from the version of the facts that the witness is prepared to relate. Knowledge simply brings with it moral consequences that are not present in its absence.

Furthermore, it is frankly impossible to explain to the public why a lawyer should be permitted to present with impunity evidence he knows to be false. It makes little difference whether the evidence is live testimony or a document. The public expects that the conduct of lawyers in a courtroom will be at least equal to the behavior expected of laymen in the ordinary affairs of life. To examine a witness who is telling a story under oath that the witness and the lawyer know to be false does not meet the minimum standard of conduct.

It is submitted that the lawyer should lay out the ground rules that will govern his representation at his first conference with the defendant: he will ask his client to relate his version of the facts. Counsel will not permit him to take the stand and testify to facts that the defendant has told counsel did not take place. After hearing the defendant's version, the lawyer will conduct his own investigation. If the lawyer's investigation of the case reveals evidence that tends to refute the defendant's story, and he concludes that the defendant's story will not be believed, he will so inform the defendant. If the defendant recants, the lawyer will then either attempt to negotiate a favorable plea agreement with the prosecutor or go to trial with the hope of preventing the government from meeting its burden of proof. If the defendant adheres to his story, counsel will proceed to trial, permit the defendant to testify if he so desires, and argue his version of the facts to the jury. Counsel will not, however, permit the defendant to change his version of the facts to meet the discovered unfavorable evidence. If the defendant either before or during trial changes his story and attempts to testify to a version of the facts earlier denied (unless this version of the facts is substantiated by counsel's independent investigation), counsel will seek to withdraw from the case. The client should be told that the lawyer's action in seeking to withdraw may or may not be permitted by the court and may have substantial impact upon the sentence imposed in the event of conviction.

Such caution at the beginning of representation might reduce the level of trust that the client has in counsel. It should. The client at the beginning should know that his lawyer is [not merely] a "hired gun," he is a professional who will zealously represent him, though only within certain limits. The client should be informed of the scope of these limits.

NOTES

1. **Duty of fairness toward opponent.** Rule 3.4, requiring fairness toward your opponent, was one of the most controversial of the Model Rules. In a public hearing when this rule was proposed, bar associations from New Jersey, Philadelphia, New York, and Wisconsin argued against it, urging that the provision requiring fair and diligent compliance with discovery laws be deleted. 51 U.S. LAW WEEK 2043, 2045 (July 20, 1982).

2. **Failure to prepare.** In *Ethics and Malpractice*, 26 DRAKE L. REV. 88, 94, 98-99, 108-09 (1977), Lee Gaudineer discusses the ethical duty to prepare:

Competency, as used in [Rule 1.1] embraces: (1) being qualified in an area of the law wherein representation has been undertaken, (2) adequate preparation under the circumstances, and (3) reasonable and proper attention to the client's case.

Closely related to being knowledgeable and properly applying one's knowledge is being prepared. One can be knowledgeable and skillful in applying that knowledge, but, unless the lawyer is prepared in a given case, the client will suffer. Proper preparation or attention to the details of the matter, both to the law and facts, is mandatory. Disciplinary cases under this rule have been few. Proper preparation, as competency in general, ordinarily was not a basis for disciplinary action prior to the adoption of the Code of Professional Responsibility. However, the changing view was well expressed by the Nebraska Supreme Court [in *State ex rel. Nebraska State Bar Ass'n v. Holscher*, 193 Neb. 729, 230 N.W.2d 75 (1975)]:

We have repeatedly recognized the ancient maxim that ignorance of the law is no excuse.... Of all classes and professions the lawyer is most sacredly bound to understand and uphold the law. Respondent was guilty of extreme negligence in his failure to familiarize himself with Section 77-1918, R.R.S. 1943, as amended. The fact that he was extremely busy with criminal prosecutions does not absolve him of his responsibility. It would have taken comparatively little time to have read the statute as amended. He admits that he did not know the law. He knew the statute had been amended and made no attempt to ascertain its provision. It is inexcusable for an attorney to attempt a legal procedure without endeavoring to ascertain the law governing that procedure.

It is clear that lack of preparation will be no longer condoned. It does not matter whether the preparation was needed in order to become qualified or in order for a qualified lawyer to update his knowledge.

Preparation, adequate in the circumstances, encompasses knowledge of the current law on the subject, ascertainment of the facts from the client, independent investigation, and employment of necessary discovery proceedings after a suit is started. A lawyer is expected to possess knowledge of those plain and elementary principles of law which are commonly known by well-informed attorneys and to discover those additional rules of law which, although not commonly known, may readily be found by standard research techniques. The lawyer must educate himself on the applicable principles of law so that he may exercise informed judgment and advise the client accordingly in regard to the client's rights. The court will take notice of those research tools available to and commonly used by the lawyer.

The attorney must also make an adequate investigation of the facts, both as they are favorable and unfavorable to the client. However, a lawyer may rely upon the facts related by the client. Investigation as to the truth or falsity of the facts related need not be made, but, if critical facts are not related, it is the duty of the lawyer to ascertain such facts. The lawyer may also have the duty to investigate and report to the client. If the client does not know what facts are material, it is the duty of the lawyer to inquire of the client in respect to such facts. If the client assumes the responsibility of ascertaining the facts, the lawyer need not. In all cases the lawyer's conduct is to be appraised in light of the surrounding circumstances existing prior to and during the course of such litigation and not solely according to the omniscience of hindsight gained after the litigation has been completed.

3. *Abuse of discovery rules.* The classic article on the abuse of discovery rules is Wayne Brazil, *The Adversary Character of Civil Discovery: A Critique and Proposal for Change*, 31 VAND. L. REV. 1295, 1303-4, 1311, 1313-15, 1320-26, 1329-31 (1978). Brazil argues that the inherent nature of trial practice as adversarial and competitive interferes with effective discovery:

The unarticulated assumption underlying the modern discovery reform movement was that the gathering and sharing of evidentiary information should (and would) take place in an essentially nonadversarial environment. That assumption was not well made. Instead of reducing the sway of adversary forces in litigation and confining them to the trial stage, discovery has greatly expanded the arenas in which those forces can operate. It also has provided attorneys with new weapons, devices, and incentives for the adversary gamesmanship that discovery was designed to curtail. Rather than discourage "the sporting or game theory of justice," discovery has expanded both the scope and the complexity of the sport....

Attorneys in litigation have five primary objectives: (1) to win; (2) to make money; (3) to avoid being sued for malpractice; (4) to earn the admiration of the professional community; and (5) to develop self-esteem for the quality of their performances....

The pursuit of victory psychologically dominates all other objectives of litigation. The means employed by litigators to achieve victory for their clients regularly involve manipulating people and the flow of information in order to present their clients' positions as persuasively and favorably as possible. This manipulation may involve any and all of the following general techniques: not disclosing evidence that could be damaging to the client or helpful to an opposing party; not disclosing persuasive legal precedents that could be damaging to the client; undermining or deflating persuasive evidence and precedents that are damaging to the client and are introduced by opposing counsel, by such means as upsetting or discrediting honest and reliable witnesses or by burying adverse evidence under mounds of obfuscating evidentiary debris; overemphasizing and presenting out of context evidence and precedents that appear favorable to the client; pressuring or cajoling witnesses, jurors, and judges into adopting views that support the client's position; deceiving opposing counsel and parties about the weaknesses of the client's case and the strengths of opposing cases; aggravating and exploiting to the fullest extent possible vulnerabilities of the opposing party and counsel that have nothing to do with the merits of a given dispute by such means as intimidating an anxious opponent, spending a poor opponent into submission, or "soaking" in settlement an opponent who has public image problems or who for other reasons cannot endure the risk and public exposure of a trial. None of these techniques is illegal or violates the letter of the ethical rules of the profession. Indeed, the refusal to resort to at least some of these devices may be construed as a breach of an attorney's obligation "to represent his client zealously within the bounds of the law."
...

Moreover, sophisticated obstructionist maneuvering during discovery, which is difficult to monitor and evaluate, can be very lucrative for lawyers. Since discovery constitutes such a significant percentage of most litigation activity, lawyers understand that they must make money during discovery. For the lawyer being paid by the hour, there is a great economic temptation to protract and complicate discovery. Most clients, furthermore, are completely incapable of determining which tactical ploys by attorneys are wise and justified and which are simply ways to increase the attorney's fees.... It is quite likely that attorneys will select those costly and obstructionist devices which simultaneously seem to promise them the most profit, the least risk of malpractice, and the greatest probability of victory.

Some attorneys serve lengthy sets of "canned" interrogatories for the purpose of psychologically or economically harassing an opposing party. *See, e.g.,*

Roadway Express, Inc. v. Piper, 447 U.S. 752, 757 n.4 (1980): "[L]awyers have long indulged in dilatory practices.... [M]any actions are extended unnecessarily by lawyers who exploit or abuse judicial procedures, especially the liberal rules for pretrial discovery." *See also In re U.S. Fin. Sec. Litig.*, 74 F.R.D. 497 (S.D. Cal. 1977) (defendants served 2,736 questions that would have cost the plaintiffs $24,000 to answer). Brazil goes on to say:

> Litigators also may use interrogatories to pressure or manipulate opposing counsel into doing such initial case preparation as factual investigation and legal research and analysis that properly should be undertaken by the propounding counsel and paid for by that counsel's client. One additional abuse of interrogatories about which lawyers frequently have complained is the "fishing expedition," which involves [requesting] information that might support new types of claims, uncover competitors' business secrets, or harass an opponent into a favorable settlement.

> The costs generated by interrogatories obviously will tend to increase as their purposes proliferate. Clients must pay for the time attorneys spend considering and carrying out various ways to use interrogatories for purposes other than obtaining relevant data. Moreover, canned interrogatories present tempting opportunities for litigators to increase their profit margins. An attorney may charge many different clients the full cost of drafting the original set of questions even though the use of the set in a given case requires only editing and copying, both of which often can be done by nonlegal personnel. Lengthy, multipurpose interrogatories also force opposing parties to commit extra resources in order to evaluate the objectives of the questions they receive and to tactfully answer or avoid improperly motivated inquiries.

> Like interrogatories, request for documents and for admissions suffer from obvious abuses. Demands for document production, for example, can be used to impose great economic burdens upon or to harass or intimidate opposing parties and lawyers, to disrupt normal business operations or professional schedules, to steal trade secrets, or to fish for evidence to support new claims. Moreover, the pressures generated by such abusive tactics can be exploited to coerce a settlement that bears no relation to the merits of the dispute.

> The dysfunctional effects that adversary pressures have on discovery are even more obvious in the ways litigators respond to interrogatories, demands for documents, and requests for admission. The principal goals of the responding attorney tend to be completely adversarial: to provide as little information as possible, and to make the process of acquiring that information as expensive and difficult as possible for the opposing party and lawyer. To do otherwise might be considered a breach of the ethical obligation owed to a client, thereby exposing counsel to the risk of a malpractice suit. Volunteering information rather than resisting its production may also deprive the litigator of opportunities to demonstrate his adversarial skills and to increase the size of his fee.

> There are many standard devices used by litigators to resist the disclosure of information and to mislead the opponent through their responses

to interrogatories, requests for admissions, and demands for documents. The responding adversary's first impulse is to construe all inquiries and requests as narrowly as possible, thereby limiting the amount of useful information that must be divulged.... An aggressive counsel also will refuse to respond to written requests that are not free of virtually all ambiguity, imprecision, overbreadth, irrelevance, or other technical deficiency.... Nor will litigators necessarily answer a request even after they have construed it as narrowly as possible, and have objected to every arguable technical deficiency. Responding counsel's next line of defense is built on the use of privileges and the work product doctrine. Conscientious litigators will scrutinize every probe from an adversary to determine whether it is directed at material that is arguably shielded from the disclosure.... At each stage in what can become a tortuous and very expensive process, resisting counsel can hope the opponent will abandon pursuit of the damaging material. It is worth emphasizing that these tactics of resistance fall short of such overtly unethical conduct as destroying or hiding incriminating documents.

Such "overtly unethical conduct" has been widely reported among the top law firms engaged in big cases. In one case, attorneys hid documents their opponents had requested and represented to the court that the materials had been discarded inadvertently. *See Berkey Photo, Inc. v. Eastman Kodak Co.*, 74 F.R.D. 613 (S.D.N.Y. 1977), discussed in Charles Renfrew, *Discovery Sanctions: A Judicial Perspective*, 67 CAL. L. REV. 264 (1979). In another, counsel refused to turn over requested documents, willfully misrepresenting that the documents did not contain relevant information. *Litton Sys. v. A.T.&T.*, 90 F.R.D. 410 (S.D.N.Y. 1981). MODEL RULES OF PROFESSIONAL CONDUCT Rule 3.4(a) prohibits destroying documents with evidentiary potential, whether or not it has yet been requested in discovery. The rule also prohibits "concealing" documents with evidentiary value, which probably prohibits the common obstructive device of burying significant documents in mounds of irrelevant or innocuous materials. Brazil continues:

> If the tactics discussed above fail to conceal damaging information, counsel may feel constrained to refuse to respond to interrogatories or document production requests until compelled to do so. The first ploy is to ignore the original discovery probe and its deadline. At least among seasoned litigators the fear of sanctions for missing one deadline is not great. If the opposing attorney then presses for a response, the next defensive maneuver is to make excuses, play on sympathies, and seek extensions. When the deadline for the first extension approaches, additional extensions are sought. Such self-conscious and systematic efforts at procrastination impose additional financial strains on opponents, may undermine their will to pursue the litigation, and give the defensive attorney time to negotiate a favorable settlement before the damaging evidence is disclosed.
>
> Depositions, like other discovery devices, are expensive and thus can be used to exert economic pressure on opposing parties and counsel. An aggressive litigator bent on straining the resources and testing the will of

an adversary can notice numerous depositions and can prolong each examination for extended periods. Because depositions can be used to require the presence of the deponent for lengthy periods of time, they also have great adversarial potential for harassing and embarrassing adverse parties or witnesses and for disrupting their lives and businesses.

Counsel may use many [stratagems] to regulate and restrict the evidence their client or witness provides during deposition. Counsel can assert privileges whenever they arguably apply and can direct the witness not to answer questions that might invade protected spheres. They also may attempt to pressure the examining attorney into abandoning sensitive areas of inquiry by aggressively interposing disruptive objections to the form or relevance of questions. Counsel even may try to delay indefinitely the taking of their witness' deposition or to manufacture excuses to limit the scope of permissible questions. Such tactics will communicate quickly to an opponent that he will have to work very hard, withstand unpleasant pressures, spend considerable money, and seek aid from the bench if he intends to pursue what may or may not be fruitful lines of inquiry.

4. *Unnecessary motions.* MODEL RULES OF PROFESSIONAL CONDUCT Rule 3.2 states that a "lawyer shall make reasonable efforts to expedite litigation." The commentary states that the rule prohibits dilatory practices that delay the trial without serving some other substantial interest. Consider the following excerpt from David Edelstein, *The Ethics of Dilatory Motion Practice: Time for Change*, 44 FORDHAM L. REV. 1069, 1069-73 (1976):

That motions can cause delay and can be employed for the purpose of causing delay is no secret to the legal community.

The advocate has at his disposal a broad spectrum of motions which may be employed for a "myriad of uses" during the course of litigation. Motion practice is available as a means of obtaining relief from the court before, during, and after trial. For the advocate practicing in the federal courts, the Federal Rules of Civil Procedure specify a great number of distinct motions. Additionally, there are established and recognized motions which are frequently made even though not explicitly authorized by the Federal Rules. The motion for reargument is one such motion.

Assuredly, motion practice is vital to our adversary system. It is the mechanism for bringing requests of counsel to the attention of the court, and it facilitates the disposition of meritless cases and cases in which there are no factual disputes. However, motion practice can produce the negative effect of retarding the judicial process. Every motion requires the attention of the court, and ... litigation cannot proceed until the motion is resolved....

Delay of disposition is detrimental to the adversary system. In criminal litigation, the Constitution demands speedy determinations of guilt or innocence. In civil litigation, there is no constitutional requirement of promptness; however, victimized plaintiffs and innocent defendants frequently have a strong interest in prompt relief or vindication. Moreover, it is in the public interest to expedite litigation of general concern and to maintain a system which stands ready and able to "secure the just, speedy, and inexpensive determination of every action."

Assuming that delay of any portion of the litigation process ... can be considered a form of harassment, counsel is required by the Code to insure that no motion is made merely to harass through delay. However, counsel apparently is not prohibited from submitting a motion which has multiple purposes; so long as at least one of those purposes is not to harass through delay, such a motion would not be designed "merely" to harass. Furthermore, the rule does not restrict motions which are not intentionally dilatory, or even motions that are intentionally dilatory but are not aimed at harassment.

See ABA Comm. on Professional Ethics, Informal Op. 557 (1963) (unethical to file change of venue motion solely to cause inconvenience and delay).

FED. R. CIV. P. 7(b)(3) states that "all motions shall be signed in accordance with Rule 11." This requires attorneys to certify that their motions are "well grounded in fact," "warranted by existing law," and "not interposed for any improper purpose, such as to harass or to cause unnecessary delay or needless increase in the cost of litigation." If an attorney files a dilatory motion anyway, the court shall impose a sanction on the attorney or party, which may include fees and expenses incurred in responding to such a motion. For a discussion of the justification for Rule 11, see James Underwood, *Curbing Litigation Abuses: Judicial Control of Adversary Ethics — Model Rules of Professional Amendments to the Rules of Civil Procedure*, 56 ST. JOHN'S L. REV. 625, 651-54 (1982).

D. TRIAL PREPARATION

1. PRELIMINARY INVESTIGATION

While there is no single correct procedure to follow in investigating every new case, the majority of attorneys in most cases take similar initial steps:

- Interview the client.
- Read any pleadings or other court papers connected with the case.
- No matter how intimately you are familiar with the legal theory of a claim or defense, do some legal research. Locate and re-read the controlling statute or a relevant section in a law encyclopedia.
- Conduct a factual investigation.
- File discovery requests.

It is important to conduct an immediate investigation into both the facts and the law. Judge Robert Keeton offers the following classic advice:

Your two investigations — on the law and on the facts — should proceed simultaneously, the scope of each being influenced by the results of the other. Should either receive priority?

If it were possible to anticipate all of the avenues of fact inquiry needed to support any legal theory you might later assert, or to meet any legal theory that your adversary might later assert, then clearly you should give priority to the fact investigation because of the advantages of completing this investigation while facts are fresh in the minds of witnesses, before the influences of time and discussion have affected their views of the facts, and before your adversary has interviewed them. Truth may be eternal, and facts may not change, but facts do not prove themselves, and fact-findings must be made by people with human failings. The ideas of the most conscientious witness will undergo some modification as [the witness] thinks about and discusses the facts of the case with others ....

There are disadvantages to giving priority to fact investigation. It is impossible to anticipate all the legal points that may affect the scope and importance of investigating certain aspects of the facts. You must also take account of limitations of time. Rarely is a trial lawyer able to devote enough time to preparation of a case [so that the lawyer feels] there is nothing more [to do] . Furthermore, thorough investigation often involves the use of services of others, and incurring expenses that must be borne eventually by the client; the feasibility of incurring expenses will depend on the amount involved in the case and the materiality and probable success of the investigative efforts. In view of these considerations, it becomes important to avoid wasteful investigation of facts that will not possibly be relevant under the theories of law applicable to the case.[3]

Gary Bellow and Bea Moulton provide useful advice on the kind of *legal* investigation that should be done at the early stages of a case:

As Robert Keeton points out, a case should not be presented in court, negotiated, or even investigated to any great extent until the lawyer has a clear idea of the applicable legal standards. The open texture of legal rules notwithstanding, most advocacy is conducted within a rule framework which sets clear limits on the theories and strategies counsel can pursue.

Our hunch is that many of you do not yet proceed in this fashion. Despite the amount of law training devoted to finding, reconciling, distinguishing and "Shepardizing" cases, very few students are comfortable with the sort of legal research and analysis that is essential to these preliminary efforts....

First, students are often trained in only one kind of legal research — the complete, painstaking analysis that is necessary in briefing an issue for an appellate court. This means that when a case comes in they either do very little research (because "there's not enough time"), or they retire to the library shortly after the client interview for days or weeks (we know of cases where research at this early stage went on for months), and return with comprehensive memos on issues that may never be pressed because the client has had to cope in other ways with his or her problem.

What are almost always needed in the early stages of a case are a series of frequent, short (20-60 minutes) visits to the library. Early in the case, for example, you should read carefully any immediately relevant statutory or regulatory material. If court-made law controls, a case note in a local law review or annual survey will tell you where your jurisdiction

---

[3] ROBERT KEETON, TRIAL TACTICS AND METHODS 308-09 (2d ed. 1973).

stands on the issue. You might even quickly read the leading or most recent cases. If your jurisdiction is unfavorable to the claim, checking the ALR or a digest will give you a sense both of how strong and how prevalent the contrary authority is.

Second, many students do not handle statutes or regulations well, even though such material is directly relevant and often controlling in many types of law practice. Because statutes and regulations control broad classes of transactions, guide administrative choices and practice, and are more apt to be deferred to by a judge than court-made law, they must be under control at a relatively early stage.

Third, many students have trouble organizing large bodies of law in their heads. In practice, the law will be most usable in black letter or outline form. Written guides, desk references, and annual surveys or updates can provide useful organizational schemes that you can change or elaborate as you learn the law in each case you handle, and as you follow advance sheets and reporting services. Such habits of organization and learning will serve you well in making judgments at any stage of a given case about "what the law is."

Fourth, students have considerable difficulty deciding when to stop researching. As a consequence, they don't develop usable research skills. In the long run, this makes them less willing and able to do relatively simple research jobs.[4]

Factual investigation consists of far more than filing discovery motions. You are all familiar with formal discovery from civil and criminal procedure courses. Formal discovery is one potential source of information, but rarely the primary source. Most information upon which you will rely at trial comes from an informal investigation process — a painstaking and methodical search for witnesses, documents and other useful evidence.

The scope of this informal investigation is as varied as the nature of your case and witnesses. It has three basic components: the search for and interviewing of witnesses, the search for documents and other tangible evidence, and an investigation of the scene and the actual instrumentalities involved in the litigated event. The following basic suggestions should help get you started:

- View the scene of the crime or event. Consider taking your client and key witnesses with you. Sketch or photograph the scene. Walk through a re-enactment of the event to get a sense for distances, times, and directions.
- Talk to witnesses as soon as possible. Memories fade with time; witnesses move out of town. Put your interviews in writing and ask the witnesses to read them over, make changes and sign them.
- Examine any instrumentalities involved, such as murder weapons, damaged automobiles, or defective table saws.
- Check local and state police records. In accident cases, the police will probably have investigated and collected names and statements of wit-

---

[4] GARY BELLOW & BEA MOULTON, THE LAWYERING PROCESS 356-59 (1978).

nesses and sketched the positions of the vehicles. In all cases, witnesses may have criminal records.

- Talk to emergency service personnel from ambulance crews, wrecker services, fire departments and public utilities. They often arrive before the police and talk to witnesses or participants.
- Check hospital records. This usually will require that you obtain a release from the patient.
- Read the local newspapers published around the time of the event. They may have photographs and names of witnesses.
- The county courthouse is full of public records concerning land, taxes, births, deaths, marriages, and so forth.
- City directories often list family and occupational data, and can help you identify who lives at a certain address or who has a particular telephone number.

The final stage of investigation is formal discovery. It is beyond the scope of this chapter to review the discovery rules of civil and criminal procedure. We assume that you already know them from other courses. However, it does seem beneficial to spend a few paragraphs discussing the tactical decisions you must make about which forms of discovery to use and the extent to which they are useful in trial preparation.

The best known discovery device is the deposition on oral examination. Deposing the opposing party is a universal practice. It provides information and enables you to see how that party performs as a witness. It also introduces you to opposing counsel. A deposition has the advantage of spontaneity, and is critical if you think a witness may be lying or exaggerating. Despite the universality of taking depositions, occasionally there may be tactical reasons to forgo the process. Disadvantages of depositions include: revealing your own theory of the case to your opponent, inadvertently strengthening the deponent's self-confidence and ability to withstand cross-examination, inviting reciprocal depositions of your client, and waiving a Dead Man's Statute objection to the opposing party's competency.

An alternative to the oral deposition is the deposition upon written questions provided for in FED. R. CIV. P. 31. This procedure has some disadvantages compared to oral depositions. Because questions have to be prepared in advance, it is difficult to anticipate follow-up questions. This is a disadvantage if the witness decides to become evasive, if the witness is an important one, or if the subject of the testimony is complex. Also, it is likely the deponent will be given a copy of your questions in advance and have time to think carefully about the answers. However, a Rule 31 deposition on written questions will probably be less expensive than the oral deposition, since no attorney need be present when the answers are given. It is especially useful for taking depositions of unimportant witnesses at distant locations.

A third discovery option is a set of interrogatories under FED. R. CIV. P. 33. Interrogatories are generally cheaper and more efficient than either kind of deposition. Interrogatories, however, are limited to parties, so are not an option for ordinary witnesses. When the respondent is a corporate party, a Rule 31 deposition permits you to name the exact employee to answer the questions, but the respondent gets to select who will answer interrogatories. The tactical disadvantages of interrogatories are obvious. Answers are written under the careful supervision of the opposing attorney. You do not get to view the witness's demeanor, nor can you expect candor. You are unable promptly to follow up interesting answers. However, interrogatories serve a valuable purpose when they are used *before* you take an oral deposition. You will usually be able to take a better deposition if you have basic information relevant to the incident in advance: names of witnesses, relevant documents, business statistics, dates of board of directors meetings, etc.

You can use FED. R. CIV. P. 34 to request the production of documents, permission to enter land, or the right to sample and test matter in the possession of your opponent. Under this rule, you may request "writings, drawings, graphs, charts, photographs, phono-records and other data compilations from which information can be obtained" such as computer printouts. This procedure is useful both before and after you take your opponent's deposition. Looking at documents or potential exhibits early in the case may be helpful when writing interrogatories or taking depositions. Also, the interrogatories and depositions will themselves reveal the existence of additional tangible objects you will want to personally examine or have your experts test.

The plaintiff, victim or other person whose state of health is a key issue may be ordered to undergo medical or psychiatric testing under FED. R. CIV. P. 35. The decision whether to request a physical or mental examination is normally not very difficult. If the person's condition is going to be a contested issue in the case, you must seek to have your own experts examine that person.

Requests for admission pursuant to FED. R. CIV. P. 36 are helpful at the end of the discovery process to define the issues for trial. Unlike other discovery devices, requests for admission do not seek new information. You already know the answers, but want to know if the other side will concede them to be true to expedite litigation. An admission under Rule 36 is conclusive, and your opponent may not thereafter introduce contrary evidence. In that sense, it is far stronger than an admission obtained in an interrogatory or deposition, which the party may later disavow. Requests for admission are commonly used to follow up a concession made in a deposition, and when proving an issue would be expensive, boring to the jury, or difficult. You do not want to request an admission on a fact that is easily and cheaply proved, makes your case look strong, or carries a favorable emotional impact.

2. DEVELOPING A THEORY OF THE CASE

Developing a theory of the case will be the single most important thing you do. This theory must be developed early, and will serve as your blueprint from which you will construct your case. As you prepare for trial, you will face a myriad of decisions, from which witnesses to call to which jury instructions to request. None of these decisions can be made intelligently unless you have a clear picture of the way you intend to prove your case. Thus, the development of a viable theory is the first order of business.

A theory is not a recitation of every fact or a pursuit of every remotely possible legal avenue. Presenting all the information you have gathered, or making every conceivable legal argument, will simply overwhelm the jurors and obfuscate the important matters. A theory is the simplest model that explains what happened and why you are entitled to a favorable verdict. To formulate a good theory, you must decide what evidence and arguments to ignore as well as which ones to emphasize. Your final product should be a cohesive, logical view of the merits of the case that is consistent with common everyday experience.

A case theory contains the following elements:

- *Law*. Your theory should clearly indicate the proper legal outcome of the case. You must understand the elements of your cause of action or defense, and whether and how you can prove them. If there are multiple legal issues, you must decide what is your strongest legal argument. Just because an issue could be argued does not mean you must do so. For instance, a defendant in a personal injury case could argue that the plaintiff cannot prove liability, or that the plaintiff suffered no damages, or both. If you represent a defendant who, at the time of an accident, was drunk, speeding, driving in the wrong lane, and did not have a license, could you sincerely argue that your client was not negligent? If the plaintiff suffered only whiplash injuries that cannot be medically verified, your theory of the case can more comfortably rest on an argument that the plaintiff cannot prove any injury.
- *Facts*. Your theory must be consistent with the weight of the evidence. It also should identify which are the most important items of evidence that support your version of the disputed events. Just because evidence is available does not mean it must be presented — even if you have spent time and effort to gather it. You must develop the ability to discern helpful from confusing information and the discipline to limit yourself to the presentation of facts supporting your theory.
- *Weaknesses*. You must recognize, acknowledge, and have an explanation for weaknesses, gaps, inconsistencies, and improbabilities in your case.
- *Emotions*. A good theory includes an emotional component. What injustice has been committed? Why is your client morally deserving of a verdict?
- *Opponent's case*. Recognize that there is another side to the story. Analyze your opponent's case to determine where the disputes will arise, identify the strengths and weaknesses of the adverse case, and develop an explanation for why your opponent's version is wrong.

3. DEVELOPING THE EVIDENCE

The major task of trial preparation is working with the facts — organizing the evidence you have, identifying and locating additional evidence you need, and planning effective ways of presenting it. Developing the evidence is an integral part of refining your case theory.

a. Is the Evidence Admissible?

If you have engaged in investigation and discovery, you already know about 90% of all the evidence that might be offered at trial. That means you can anticipate in advance evidence that should be objected to, and places where your opponent may object to your evidence. You need to decide whether the judge will sustain any of these objections and exclude the information. A good theory of the case must be based on a reasonably accurate prediction of what evidence will be admitted and what evidence will be excluded at trial. It is a waste of time to develop a theory premised on evidence that is inadmissible.

b. Diagramming the Case

One of the most common ways of organizing your presentation of evidence is to diagram the case. This technique involves making a chart in which the elements you need to prove are matched with a list of witnesses and exhibits available to you. You then can comb your interview notes, the prior statements, and the depositions for each witness, recording on your chart every important piece of admissible evidence that will help you prove your theory of the case. The chart can form an outline of your case and help assure that you call all witnesses and introduce all exhibits that help you. Figure 1 illustrates how a prosecutor might diagram a simple assault case.

Figure 1

State's Diagram of Simple Assault Case

Elements:	ASSAULT	INJURY	IDENTITY OF DEFENDANT	MOTIVE	NEGATE SELF-DEFENSE
Evidence: VICTIM'S TESTIMONY	defendant hit face with hand, felt something hit head	knocked out, woke up in hospital	knows defendant, can make in-court identification	defendant laid off after poor performance report prepared by victim	had beer in hand when hit, did not strike or threaten defendant, received prior threat
WITNESS TESTIMONY (BARTENDER)	heard shouting, saw defendant hit victim with fist, then with beer bottle	saw victim fall, saw blood, victim unconscious	can describe defendant		did not see victim hit defendant, saw victim's hands on table
ARRESTING OFFICER'S TESTIMONY	found victim on floor, table overturned	victim unconscious	when arrested, stated victim had it coming		no visible injury to defendant
DEFENDANT TESTIMONY	hit victim		knows victim, told police he had it coming	laid off, victim foreman, gave him poor performance report	
EXHIBITS	diagram to aid in description of attack	police photo of bruises, hospital record			

c. Searching for Corroboration

Assembling proof for trial is a process of both finding good witnesses and of bolstering their credibility. If you focus your attention solely on making sure you have minimally sufficient testimony on each element, you may survive a directed verdict motion but still be a long way from persuading the jury to believe your witnesses. One witness is legally adequate; two witnesses and a corroborating document are persuasive. Your goal is to make your case *persuasive*, not merely adequate.

Part of the preparation process is to do what you can to bolster the credibility of your witnesses. You have no control over some things — nuns are more credible than prostitutes. The background of those who happen to be witnesses already has been determined. However, you can make the testimony given by every important witness more credible by corroborating everything that witness says.

> It is vital to corroborate the [key witnesses] on every point on which corroboration is possible. Nothing should be left to rest on [their] unsupported testimony if there is any extrinsic proof of substance to support it. In particular, when the physical characteristics of sites or things are of any significance to the [witnesses'] testimony and can be proved by such relatively incontrovertible proof as photographs or demonstrative evidence, this should be done. The time when the [witness] left work should be corroborated by [his or her] timecard; the weather, by Weather Bureau records. Every matter on which [a witness] is supported by proof that the trier of fact is likely to believe has a capacity to spread and envelope his or her testimony with an atmosphere of veracity.[5]

In addition to corroboration through the use of exhibits and documents, witnesses can corroborate each other through their testimony. If you refer back to Figure 1, you can see that even though a witness may be called for one purpose, he or she may be able to corroborate witnesses who testify on another issue. For example, the arresting officer who arrives after the fight is over may know nothing about the fight; yet, the officer can describe the overturned table and chair, corroborating the witnesses who testify to the violence of the attack.

> The purpose here is to move from your conclusions and inferences to the "data" that would support them. For example, suppose you represent a client who claims she was defrauded in the door-to-door sale of a food freezer plan. She understood the salesman to say that she was leasing the freezer and could cancel at any time. She tried to cancel, but the company now insists that no such option was offered and is suing her for the balance. If the client's story were true, what else would be true? The

---

[5] Anthony Amsterdam, Trial Manual 5 for the Defense of Criminal Cases § 395 (1988).

following possibilities come immediately to mind: (i) the freezer, not the food plan, would be the money-maker for the company; (ii) the salesman might have been "working" the area and made similar representations to other purchasers; (iii) there may be company training manuals or written instructions to salesmen on the sales "pitch"; (iv) complaints about similar practices may be on file with better business or consumer protection agencies; (v) the salesman may have been under some particular pressure to make sales at the time he visited your client. Each of these suggests possible lines of inquiry and could lead to facts that corroborate your client's story.[6]

d. Filling in the Gaps in Your Case

Inevitably you will find weaknesses in your case — gaps in proof and places where you have only the uncorroborated testimony of a single witness. Often there will be nothing you can do but strengthen the other aspects of your case and hope that the logic of your argument will carry the jury safely over the weak spots. Sometimes, once these weaknesses are identified, a review of the witnesses and exhibits will disclose ways of shoring up your vulnerable points. You also should consider three ways of helping your case without additional evidence: legal presumptions, stipulations, and judicial notice.

Your legal research may uncover presumptions that shift the burden of proof to your opponent. Criminal defendants long have incorporated the presumption of innocence into their theories of the case. Prosecutors routinely use presumptions of possession based on close proximity, or of theft based on possession of recently stolen goods.[7] In civil cases, a wide range of statutory and common-law presumptions exist — from *res ipsa loquitur* to the presumption that a death is not suicide to a statutory presumption that acts of expatriation are voluntary.[8] In extreme cases, a presumption may eliminate completely the need to present any evidence; in others, the jury will be instructed to consider the presumption as evidence corroborating your theory.[9]

Stipulations are agreements between the parties that certain facts are true. This is another way of alleviating problems with your proof. If your adversary will agree to stipulate to a fact, then you will not be required to offer any proof on that issue. It must be remembered, however, that it is not your opponent's job to make it easier for you to prove your case. He or she may not agree to stipulate, or may demand an equivalent stipulation that helps your oppo-

---

[6]GARY BELLOW & BEA MOULTON, THE LAWYERING PROCESS 321 (1978).

[7]In criminal cases a presumption may shift the burden of going forward to the defendant, but cannot constitutionally shift the burden of persuasion to the defense to prove the presumption invalid. *Sandstrom v. Montana*, 442 U.S. 510 (1979); *County Ct. v. Allen*, 442 U.S. 140 (1979).

[8]*Vance v. Terrazas*, 444 U.S. 252 (1980).

[9]*See, e.g.*, ARKANSAS MODEL JURY INSTRUCTIONS, CIVIL No. 705 (3d ed. 1989): "One of the vehicles involved in this case was driven by _____ and was owned by _____ who was a passenger in it at the time of the occurrence. You may consider this fact in deciding whether the driver was acting as agent for the passenger."

nent's case. In addition, some attorneys are reluctant to ask for stipulations for fear of disclosing weaknesses to the other side. This fear is probably over-dramatized. If your adversary has adequately prepared, he or she already knows your weaknesses. Since you also know your adversary's weaknesses, an offer to exchange stipulations that results in a benefit to both sides may be gladly received. However, it generally is a bad idea to stipulate an issue where your proof is strong — you want the jury to see the strengths of your case, not its weaknesses.

Judicial notice is available to introduce many types of information not subject to reasonable dispute. Federal Rule of Evidence 201 provides for two categories: (1) facts "generally known" in the community, and (2) facts "capable of accurate and ready determination by resort to sources whose accuracy cannot reasonably be questioned," such as almanacs, encyclopedias, and newspaper television listings. If you seek to prove facts of the second type, you bear the responsibility for supplying a reference book to the judge. If the judge agrees to take notice of a fact, he or she will instruct the jury that it should accept the fact as true.[10] Judicial notice relieves you of the necessity to find and call witnesses, but has some of the same drawbacks as a stipulation, since it may not be as persuasive as the testimony of live witnesses.

4. DEVELOPING A STRATEGY

Once you have developed a theory, you need a strategy for selling your theory to the jury. A successful strategy should be solidly based in what social psychologists know about effective communication and persuasion. We suggest that you adopt some variation of the following general principles that are based on the empirical work of social psychologists:

- *Start strong*, to take advantage of the principle of "primacy." Primacy refers to the tendency of jurors to remember and be influenced by what they hear first. Psychologists have confirmed what our mothers always told us: first impressions are important.[11] This principle suggests that the first thirty seconds of each phase of your trial — your opening statement, each direct and cross-examination, and your closing argument — is a critical point in which you should focus on something you especially want the jury to remember.

- *End strong*, to take advantage of the principle of "recency." Recency refers to the tendency of jurors to remember what they hear last in a sequence. This principle suggests that the final thirty seconds of each phase of your trial — your opening statement, each direct and cross-examination, and your closing argument — is also a critical point in which you should focus on something you especially want the jury to remember.

---

[10] In civil cases, the judge will instruct the jury that the fact is conclusive. In criminal cases, if the fact helps the prosecution sustain its burden of proof, the judge will only instruct the jury that it *may* find the noticed fact to be true. *See* FED. R. EVID. 201(g).

[11] *See* SAUL M. KASSIN & LAWRENCE S. WRIGHTSMAN, THE AMERICAN JURY ON TRIAL: PSYCHOLOGICAL PERSPECTIVES 132-37 (1988).

- *Use themes and stories.* Familiar stories will be easier for jurors to remember than lots of small details. Try to package parts of your case in ways that take advantage of this. Jurors may not remember all the details of your argument that an opposing expert witness's opinions are purely subjective; but they will remember the story of Goldilocks and the three bears. They may have trouble envisioning what the scene of a crime was like until you tell them it looked like a scene from *Deliverance*.
- *Concentrate on a small number of points.* What are the five or ten most important facts in your case? Identify them in your case theory, and then emphasize them throughout your trial. If you can simplify your case, edit your presentations, and keep the jury focused on your main points, resisting the temptation to go off on less important tangents, you will present the jury with a case they can understand and remember.
- *Use repetition and corroboration.* Your main points should be repeated several times so that the jury is sure to remember them. Although too much repetition of the same message may cause boredom, you should plan to remind the jurors of your main points and facts several times, varying slightly the way you present it so that your presentation is corroborative rather than repetitive.
- *Admit your weaknesses.* Every case has weaknesses, e.g., witnesses with unsavory backgrounds or evidence that defies common sense. You cannot ignore these problems; weaknesses do not just go away. You cannot explain them away, but you can disclose them yourself in a way that makes them appear trivial. Psychologists have shown that you will usually be more persuasive if you bring out both sides of an issue yourself than if you adopt the "used-car-salesman" approach of trying to hide obvious points of vulnerability.[12] As a corollary to the principles of primacy and recency, however, weaknesses should usually be buried in the middle of each phase of your trial.

5. SELECTION AND ORDER OF WITNESSES

The following discussion on the strategy of witness selection assumes that you are in the happy situation of having more witnesses available than are necessary to establish your claim or defense. This often will not be the case. Frequently you will have to call every witness with relevant information in order to make out a minimally persuasive case. But whether you have available four or forty witnesses, you should make a positive choice of whether to call each individual, and not put every potential witness on the stand as a matter of course.

a. Whether to Call Any Witnesses

A decision to call no witnesses is rarely an option for any party except a criminal defendant. If you intend to prove your claim or defense, or to contest your adversary's proof, you must present evidence. Unless you stipulate to a

---

[12]*See* Daniel Linz & Steven Penrod, *Increasing Attorney Persuasiveness in the Courtroom*, 8 LAW & PSYCHOL. REV. 1, 13-14 (1984); Robert Lawson, *Relative Effectiveness of One-Sided and Two-Sided Communications in Courtroom Persuasion*, 82 J. GEN. PSYCHOL. 3 (1970).

set of facts or can introduce a deposition, this evidence will have to come from witnesses.

A criminal defendant is in a unique position. Because of the rigorous burden of proof placed on the prosecution, the accused may choose to present no evidence, relying instead on an argument that the state has failed to prove his or her guilt beyond a reasonable doubt. In some jurisdictions this gives the defendant a slight tactical advantage of going first and last in closing argument — reversing the normal order of summation.[13]

Criminal defense attorneys generally recommend planning your case under the assumption that you *will* call witnesses. Failure to call any witnesses usually is tantamount to admitting to the jury that you have no defense. Then at trial, if the state has put on a weak case, you can consider resting without presenting any evidence if your own defense is flimsy or if it might bolster a weakness in the state's case. For example, if an assault victim is unable to identify the defendant at trial, you might choose to rest without evidence if you had been planning a self-defense case. If you put on your evidence, you would be conceding the identity issue. If you had planned an alibi defense, however, you would obviously go ahead with it. Only in a most hopeless case, in which your client admits guilt and no defenses are applicable, should you plan ahead not to call witnesses.

b. Criteria for Selecting Witnesses

There are a number of criteria on which to make a decision whether to call a witness. They range from the obvious — whether the witness is available and has relevant testimony to give — to the not so obvious intricacies of personality. The goal, of course, is to call "good" witnesses and avoid calling "bad" witnesses. This is easier said than done.

Indications that you should call a witness:

- The witness is necessary to prove a prima facie case. If a witness is the only one who can supply testimony on an essential element of your case, that witness must be called.
- The witness will corroborate important points in your case. Social science research demonstrates that repetition will increase the likelihood that the important facts will be remembered.[14]
- Taken as a whole, the witness's testimony is more favorable to you than to your opponent.
- The person is someone (such as the client or victim) who was directly affected by the events.
- Your client's testimony will refer to the witness. The law allows an adverse inference from the failure to call an available witness with natural

---

[13] *See, e.g.,* N.C. SUPER. & DIST. CT. R. 10: "In all cases, civil or criminal, if no evidence is introduced by the defendant, the right to open and close the argument to the jury shall belong to him."

[14] *See* John T. Cacioppo & Richard E. Petty, *Effects of Message Repetition and Position on Cognitive Response, Recall, and Persuasion,* 37 J. PERSONALITY & SOC. PSYCHOL. 97 (1979), suggesting that three repetitions is the optimal number.

ties to your client. Thus, if your client claims three friends were in the car, you should call all three, even if they saw or remember little. Otherwise, the jury may infer that the missing witness was not called because he or she would have contradicted your client. Potential witnesses who are friends, family members, employees, or agents of your client should be called if the jury has any way of finding out their existence.

- The witness has a clear memory.
- The witness is attractive. Social scientists have shown that physically attractive witnesses are perceived as more intelligent and competent than unattractive witnesses.[15]
- The witness holds a professional job or is well-educated. Psychologists have shown that such persons are regarded as more trustworthy than either representatives of power groups or people in low status occupations.[16]
- The witness has a likeable personality or is an entertaining speaker. The more good-natured witnesses you can call, the more the jury will evaluate your case favorably.
- The witness possesses sympathetic characteristics, such as physical disability, youth, or old age.[17]
- Witnesses are likely to be of similar race, sex, and socioeconomic status to members of the jury.[18]

Indications that you should not call a witness:

- The witness will do damage to your case when facts favoring your opponent are brought out on cross-examination.
- The witness shares responsibility for the event and will be seen as trying to blame others.
- The witness was intoxicated, sleepy, or otherwise probably had difficulty accurately observing the events.
- The witness bears personal animosity toward the opponent or personal bias in favor of your client.
- The witness has a prior criminal record.
- The witness will contradict your client or important witnesses.
- You already have several witnesses on the same point. Some repetition is good, but too much may cause boredom.
- Character witnesses for the defense should be avoided. Most experienced lawyers think they are useless, and some empirical research suggests they actually may make your case worse.[19]

---

[15] *See* Ellen Berscheid & Elaine Walster, *Physical Attractiveness, in* 7 ADVANCES IN EXPERIMENTAL SOCIAL PSYCHOLOGY 158 (L. Berkowitz ed. 1974).

[16] *See* Rotter & Stein, *Public Attitudes Toward the Trustworthiness, Competence, and Altruism of Twenty Selected Occupations*, 1 J. APPLIED SOC. PSYCHOL. 334 (1971).

[17] *See generally* HARRY KALVEN & HAN ZEISEL, THE AMERICAN JURY 193-218 (1966) (empirical study of characteristics of criminal defendants as witnesses).

[18] *See* Ellen Berscheid, *Opinion Change and Communicator-Communicatee Similarity and Dissimilarity*, 4 J. PERSONALITY & SOC. PSYCHOL. 670 (1966), which suggests that the more similar two persons (witness and juror) are, the more they like each other, which increases the likelihood of persuasion.

[19] In two classroom experiments, students in evidence classes at Indiana University Law School were asked to decide the guilt or innocence of a defendant based on a summary of the evidence for

c. Whether the Accused Should Testify

Part of the witness selection process for the criminal defense attorney is the often difficult question whether to put the accused on the stand. Many factors are involved in the decision, and there are risks either way. Of course, if your client is a sympathetic witness with no prior record and you have a strong defense and many corroborating witnesses, the decision to call the defendant is easy. Conversely, if the state has presented a weak case, and your client has a long record, an evil appearance, and a patently incredible (and uncorroborated) story, the decision to keep the defendant off the stand is also easy. Most cases fall somewhere in between.

Most attorneys favor calling the defendant in the majority of cases. Despite the presumption of innocence, it is commonly believed that jurors do assume that the defendant is probably guilty if he or she fails to take the stand and offer a reasonable defense. A series of surveys by the National Jury Project revealed that 30-50% of prospective jurors expected a defendant to prove his or her innocence despite an instruction on the presumption of innocence.[20] Thus, the chances of conviction increase if the accused does not testify.[21]

Other factors may militate against calling the defendant as a witness. The most obvious is the existence of a criminal record. Studies have shown that a record of similar criminal activity increases the likelihood of conviction.[22] Other considerations include: whether the defendant's story is incredible or contradicts better defense witnesses; the weakness of the prosecution's case; and the unattractive dress, voice, speech patterns, physical characteristics, or body language of the defendant.[23] There is one final danger: the client's testimony may make admissible otherwise excludable evidence. Confessions suppressed because the defendant was denied counsel or not given adequate warnings can be used if the defendant testifies. Unconstitutionally seized evidence likewise may become admissible to impeach a testifying defendant.[24]

d. Order of Witnesses

After selecting your witnesses, you must decide the order in which you will present them. This determination obviously will be influenced by practical

and against him (before the students had studied character evidence). When given facts identical in all respects except for the presence of a character witness, the conviction rate was fifteen percent to thirty percent higher when the character evidence was introduced.

[20] NATIONAL JURY PROJECT, JURYWORK: SYSTEMATIC TECHNIQUES § 2.04 (2d ed. 1991) (Figure 2.2).

[21] See David R. Shaffer & Thomas Case, On the Decision Not to Testify in One's Own Behalf: Effects of Withheld Evidence, Defendant's Sexual Preference, and Juror Dogmatism on Juridic Decisions, 42 J. PERSONALITY & SOC. PSYCHOL. 335 (1982). In an experiment at Indiana University, hundreds of evidence students (who ought to know better) were given a trial transcript and asked whether they thought the defendant guilty. The conviction rate jumped thirty percent when the defendant did not testify (all other evidence being identical).

[22] See Anthony Doob & Herschi M. Kircschenbaum, Some Empirical Evidence on the Effect of § 12 of the Canada Evidence Act Upon the Accused, 15 CRIM. L. Q. 88, 89-95 (1972); Roselle Wissler & Michael Saks, On the Inefficacy of Limiting Instructions, 9 LAW & HUM. BEHAV. 37, 41-44 (1985).

[23] Henry Rothblatt, The Defendant — Should He Testify?, TRIAL DIPL. J. at 22-23 (Fall 1979).

[24] United States v. Havens, 446 U.S. 620 (1980); Harris v. New York, 401 U.S. 222 (1971). See also Craig Bradley, Havens, Jenkins, and Salvucci, and the Defendant's "Right" to Testify, 18 AM. CRIM. L. REV. 419 (1981).

factors beyond your control, such as the times when particular witnesses are available or the rules of evidentiary foundations that require calling some witnesses before others. However, within these practical restrictions, the effective ordering of witnesses will help you present a logical, understandable case that highlights your strengths and hides your weaknesses as much as possible. Consider the following suggestions:

- Start with a strong, important witness who can describe the event.
- Start with witnesses who can authenticate a diagram of the scene and identify important exhibits.
- In general, call witnesses in chronological order, e.g., the plaintiff and eyewitnesses first to describe the accident, then witnesses to prove damages.
- Call corroborating witnesses after a primary witness has testified.
- Call weak or minor witnesses in the middle of your case.
- If several witnesses are needed to lay a foundation, such as a chain of custody, call them seriatim.
- If you must read depositions or other documents, try to disperse them throughout your case so you do not bore the jury to tears.
- Call expert witnesses near the end, since they are generally drawing conclusions that will not make sense until the jury understands all the facts.
- Finish with a strong witness. This takes advantage of the principle of recency.
- Call all your witnesses in your case-in-chief. Never withhold evidence so you can "surprise" your opponent with it in rebuttal.

NOTES

1. *Pretrial court proceedings as sources of information.* The trial often will not be the first time that witnesses have testified about the facts of the case. One or more preliminary or related court proceedings may occur before the actual trial, at which proceedings potential trial witnesses will give testimony. You should attend all of them, and obtain transcripts if possible — you can learn useful information about the witnesses and the evidence. Criminal trials often are preceded by coroner's inquests, grand jury proceedings, preliminary hearings, and hearings on motions. A codefendant may be tried first and the same witnesses used. The police officers may testify in other cases. Civil cases may be preceded by a criminal trial, a traffic court appearance, or a hearing before a worker's compensation board or similar administrative agency.

2. *What do real lawyers actually do?* If you are interested in reading a survey of Arizona lawyers concerning how much investigation they actually conduct, see Note, *Adequacy of Fact Investigation in Criminal Defense Lawyers' Trial Preparation*, 1981 ARIZ. ST. L.J. 523, 534. The survey found, for example, that despite the advice given above, forty-five percent of lawyers did not visit the scene. However, in reading any such survey, be sure to remember that both competent and incompetent lawyers are included in it. Another survey was conducted by F. R. Lacy, *Discovery Costs in State Court Litigation*,

Table 1

	AVERAGE COST			AVERAGE NUMBER OF PROCEDURES		
	AMOUNT IN CONTROVERSY: $0-3,000 $3,000-10,000 $10,000+			AMOUNT IN CONTROVERSY: $0-3,000 $3,000-10,000 $10,000+		
All cases	$123	$313	$483	.85	1.54	2.27
Discovery cases	194	368	638	1.35	2.23	3.00
Tort cases	222	361	719	1.69	2.57	3.16
Other	149	379	489	1.10	1.63	2.67
Jury trials	207	354	626	1.40	2.31	3.00
Court trials	150	403	701	1.17	2.00	3.00
p/i auto	172	256	612	1.67	1.57	3.38
Other p/i	212	406	622	1.60	4.20	2.50

57 OR. L. REV. 289, 292, 297, 299-300 (1978). As indicated in Table 1, Lacy discovered that in small cases, lawyers rarely do anything except take the opposing party's deposition. Even in major cases, they rarely take more than two or three depositions.

3. Additional reading on the tactics of discovery. Two of the best discussions on the tactics of various discovery devices are RALPH McCULLOUGH & JAMES UNDERWOOD, CIVIL TRIAL MANUAL 283-374 (2d ed. 1980) and ROGER HAYDOCK & DAVID HERR, DISCOVERY PRACTICE (2d ed. 1988). *See also* DAVID BAUM, ART OF ADVOCACY — PREPARATION OF THE CASE §§ 8.30 TO 8.34 (1981); JAMES W. JEANS, LITIGATION §§ 4.01-4.24 (2d ed. 1992); JEFFREY KESTLER, QUESTIONING TECHNIQUES AND TACTICS ch. 7 (2d ed. 1992) (depositions).

4. Who are the most respected witnesses? The Gallup Poll conducts an annual survey of the relative prestige of various occupations. In GEORGE GALLUP, THE GALLUP POLL: PUBLIC OPINION 1990, at 23 (1991), the occupations are ranked for honesty and integrity as follows: (1) pharmacists, (2) clergy, (3) physicians, (4) dentists, (5) college professors, (6) engineers, (7) police officers, (8) funeral directors, (9) bankers, (10) reporters, (11) business executives, (12) senators, (13) lawyers, (14) local politicians, (15) building contractors, (16) real estate agents, (17) labor union leaders, (18) stockbrokers, (19) insurance agents, and (20) used car salespersons.

5. Selecting your first and last witnesses. Most good trial practitioners follow a strategy that you should start and finish with "strong" witnesses to take advantage of primacy and recency effects. If you have two strong witnesses, the usual advice is to call first the one who can give a more complete overall picture of the occurrence. BYRON K. ELLIOTT & WILLIAM ELLIOTT, THE WORK OF THE ADVOCATE 238-39 (1888); Mortimer Hays, *Tactics in Direct Examination, in* CIVIL LITIGATION AND TRIAL TECHNIQUES 366-67 (H. Bodin ed. 1976) (the plaintiff will often be the appropriate witness). There is some disagreement. Rothblatt advocates selecting the first witness solely on the basis of his or her ability to withstand cross-examination, since this will take the wind out of subsequent cross-examination attempts. HENRY ROTHBLATT, SUC-

wind out of subsequent cross-examination attempts. HENRY ROTHBLATT, SUC-
CESSFUL TECHNIQUES IN THE TRIAL OF CRIMINAL CASES 83 (1961). Psychologists suggest that the first witness should be one who can testify to the single
most important item of evidence in your case. For example, the prosecutor
could call either an eyewitness who can confidently identify the accused, or a
police detective who can introduce the defendant's confession. SAUL M. KASSIN
& LAWRENCE S. WRIGHTSMAN, THE AMERICAN JURY ON TRIAL: PSYCHOLOGICAL
PERSPECTIVES 135-36 (1988).

A number of trial practitioners recommend that your client be the final
witness, so that he or she has the opportunity to observe the whole proceeding
and explain any inconsistencies in the testimony. ANTHONY AMSTERDAM,
TRIAL MANUAL 5 FOR THE DEFENSE OF CRIMINAL CASES § 396 (1988). Others
suggest that an expert witness is a good one to call last, because doing so
enables you to summarize testimony through a hypothetical question. *See,
e.g.*, Robert Hanley, *Working the Witness Puzzle*, LITIG., Winter 1977, at 9.
Contra Philip Corboy, *Structuring the Presentation of Proof or Evidence*, TRIAL
DIPL. J., Summer 1978, at 26 (recommending calling the doctor first, even
though that is not the usual order).

What if you have only one strong witness? Should that witness be called
first or last? If the answer is not dictated by the nature of the testimony or
other practical considerations, some assistance can be found in the social
science studies on the relative effects of primacy and recency. Although the
results have been occasionally inconsistent and are affected by other factors
(such as the characteristics of the individual witness), experiments seem to
indicate that the plaintiff should call his or her strongest witness first and the
defendant should save the strongest witness until last. One study determined
that a juror's initial, tentative decision as to guilt or innocence had a disproportionate influence on final decisions, so the plaintiff or prosecution benefits
from calling the strongest witness first. Vernon Stone, *A Primacy Effect in
Decision-Making by Jurors*, 19 J. COMMUN. 239 (1969). Another study supports the defense tactic of calling the strong witness last. Norman Miller &
Donald Campbell, *Recency and Primacy in Persuasion as a Function of the
Timing of Speeches and Measurements*, 59 J. ABNORMAL & SOC. PSYCHOL. 1
(1959), found that a recency effect occurs when there is a long delay between
messages and assessment (deliberation) follows soon after the second message. Plaintiff cannot defeat this by calling a strong rebuttal witness, because
the same study showed that when the messages are close together there is a
primacy effect. The defendant's last witness benefits either way.

6. The defendant's relatives as witnesses. Don't bother. Empirical evidence suggests that relatives of a criminal defendant testifying on his behalf
have no impact on the jury's decision. Christy Visher, *Juror Decision Making:
The Importance of Evidence*, 11 LAW & HUM. BEHAV. 1 (1987).

7. Whether to use live witnesses or pre-recorded testimony. Occasionally, you will be faced with a choice between calling a witness in person or
presenting that witness's testimony through a stipulation or a transcribed or
videotaped deposition. It is generally assumed by lawyers that live witness
testimony is more persuasive than the other forms and is thus preferred for

important witnesses. Consider WELCOME D. PIERSON, THE DEFENSE ATTORNEY AND BASIC DEFENSE TACTICS 284 (1956):

> Regardless of the care employed in the taking of a deposition, or the presentation of the testimony in court, it is obvious that the testimony of a witness by deposition cannot possibly have the same probative effect on the jury as the same evidence would have if the witness were present in person. The witness is not before the jury. In civil cases the court instructs that in considering the credibility of a witness they may take into consideration his "demeanor while testifying and his apparent candor and fairness or lack of it." If the witness is not present in person, these privileges are denied to the jury. One lawyer states he "would rather have the testimony of one live witness than half a dozen depositions."

There is little objective support for the proposition that live testimony is preferable to stipulations and depositions. In one experiment comparing live with various kinds of recorded testimony, the results showed that there is no "best" format for presenting testimony. Some witnesses seemed to fare better when they did not appear in person. In that experiment, the jurors' perceptions of the plaintiff's competency and friendliness increased when his transcript was read, although their perceptions of his honesty and appearance went down. For the defense expert, reading a transcript improved juror perception of his honesty compared to live testimony, and showing a videotape improved perceptions of his friendliness and appearance. Gerald Williams, et al., *Juror Perceptions of Trial Testimony as a Function of the Method of Presentation: A Comparison of Live, Color Video, Black-and-White Video, Audio, and Transcript Presentations*, 1975 B.Y.U. L. REV. 375. *See also* Gordon Bermant, *Critique — Data in Search of Theory in Search of Policy: Behavioral Responses to Videotape in the Courtroom*, 1975 B.Y.U. L. REV. 467, 475-85, which cautions that there are many untested variables in the Brigham Young study, which makes evaluation of the results difficult.

In another experiment, researchers studied whether jurors remembered more facts from a live witness than a recorded one. They discovered that jurors actually remember more when testimony is presented on videotape than by a live witness. Gerald Miller, et al., *The Effect of Videotape Testimony in Jury Trials: Studies on Juror Decision Making, Information Retention, and Emotional Arousal*, 1975 B.Y.U. L. REV. 331, 357-64.

8. *Presenting deposition testimony.* When it is necessary to present a witness's testimony by deposition instead of in person, is there any reason to prefer playing a videotape to reading a transcript? Most lawyers would intuitively select the videotape, since it seems more like live testimony. There is some experimental evidence that bears this out, although the answer is far from clear-cut. In one experiment, mock jurors were asked to decide the value of condemned land, based on the conflicting testimony of two witnesses — one presented on color videotape and the other by transcript. The award they would have given favored the testimony of whichever witness was presented on videotape. Larry C. Farmer, et al., *The Effect of the Method of Presenting Trial Testimony on Juror Decisional Processes, in* PSYCHOLOGY IN THE LEGAL PROCESS 59-76 (B. Sales ed. 1977).

When lawyers must use transcripts, they employ various methods to avoid boring the jury with monotonous presentations. Consider WELCOME D. PIERSON, THE DEFENSE ATTORNEY AND BASIC DEFENSE TACTICS 284 (1956):

> Various methods are used to sustain the interest of the jury while a deposition is being read. Many lawyers adopt the practice of having an associate take the place of the absent person in the witness chair. The trial attorney then reads the questions and his associate reads the answers. The purpose is to create a visual impression of the witness testifying. If this method is followed it is important for the associate, who is acting as the witness, to be familiar with the deposition and to possess a fine speaking voice. The use of the practice is debatable.
>
> Some lawyers believe it is best for the trial attorney to take his place in the witness chair and read both questions and answers. The attorney is more familiar with the deposition and the points to be emphasized than his associate counsel. Care must be employed in the reading of the deposition. Of course the entire deposition should be read but it is not improper for an attorney to emphasize the portions favorable to his side of the controversy. Regardless of the care employed, juries frequently are inattentive to the dull reading of testimony by deposition. One juror, after listening to an entire day of the dull reading of depositions, remarked as he left the courtroom, "If I ever get to the place where I can't sleep at night, I want one of those attorneys to come out to my house and read a bunch of depositions."

9. *Planning rebuttal witnesses.* All too often, lawyers pay little attention to planning rebuttal witnesses. The plaintiff can (and should) give some thought to the evidence that probably will be introduced by the defendant, and can plan whether to call any witness to contradict or impeach that evidence. You must remember, however, that rebuttal is properly limited to responding to new matters raised by your opponent — either by contradiction or by impeaching the defense witnesses. It generally is not proper to introduce evidence in rebuttal that could have been introduced in your case-in-chief. If the defense merely contradicts your case, introducing no new issues, you cannot call rebuttal witnesses to strengthen your case-in-chief. *See generally* FRANCIS X. BUSCH, LAW AND TACTICS IN JURY TRIALS vol. 3: 960-97 (1960) (with extensive citations).

If you expect the defendant to raise an affirmative defense, and you have a witness who can negate it, should you call that witness in your case-in-chief or save the witness for rebuttal? Despite the temptation to "take the wind out of defendant's sails," most practitioners advise against trying to anticipate an affirmative defense or other new issue the defendant might raise. Not only may it be irrelevant to attempt it, but it may open up new lines of cross-examination favorable to your adversary. The defense evidence may never materialize, or may come out differently than expected, leaving the jurors confused as to why you introduced the testimony. In a few situations, however, anticipatory rebuttal may be advisable — when you are certain of the defense, and the rebuttal evidence fits together with your theory in your case-in-chief. This is especially true when the defense is a common one familiar to the jurors. For instance, in a self-defense assault case, the prosecution may prove the attack was unprovoked in its case-in-chief. *See* Starr, *Rebuttal & Surrebuttal, in* CIVIL LITIGATION AND TRIAL TECHNIQUES 608-11 (H. Bodin ed. 1976).

   10. ***Assuring attendance of your witnesses.*** Your planning and selection of witnesses will be for naught if they do not show up to testify. It is not enough to call them the day before trial and tell them to come down to the courthouse. Assuring that your witnesses will be there when you need them is a three-step process:

   1) Keep track of witnesses during the months or years it takes for the case to go to trial. People move, change jobs, change telephone numbers, and take vacations. You have to know how to contact a witness if you expect that person to show up. Witnesses also are curious about what is happening to a case in which they are involved. An occasional telephone call will keep you informed about the witness and the witness informed about the progress of the case.

   2) Issue subpoenas. Once the trial has been scheduled, all witnesses should be subpoenaed, not just "unfriendly" witnesses. Subpoenas to friendly witnesses will provide them with written reminders of the date and place of trial, give them the necessary documentation to be excused from their jobs, and eliminate the appearance that they are partial to and anxious to testify for your client. If you need a document or exhibit, especially if it is in the possession of a hostile witness, a subpoena duces tecum should be issued. If you expect to introduce a hearsay declaration or use the deposition of an unavailable declarant, you probably will have to show that you tried to subpoena that person as part of the foundation. Do not forget to subpoena your opponent's witnesses if you need them to be present for identification purposes.

   3) Keep witnesses available once the trial has started. If a witness is allowed to leave too early, the witness may not be available if you need unexpected rebuttal evidence.

E. FINAL PREPARATION

1. LEGAL MEMORANDA AND TRIAL BRIEFS

   The best lawyers prepare trial memoranda or trial briefs for the presiding judge. A trial brief sets out the legal issues, explains your theory, lists your witnesses and exhibits, and outlines the evidence you expect to prove to demonstrate a prima facie case. It can include a description of how you will lay the foundation for particularly important hearsay documents, or establish a chain of custody for narcotics. If a witness must be called out of order, the brief can show how the testimony will connect up to later evidence. Such a brief is likely to be of great help to the judge in following the evidence and understanding your argument on major evidentiary issues. It may even influence a judge who is uncertain how to rule on a particular point.

   You probably must serve a copy of the memorandum on your adversary. MODEL RULES OF PROFESSIONAL CONDUCT Rule 3.5(b) prohibits ex parte communication with the judge. This raises a potential dilemma if you serve a copy of your trial brief on your opponent but your opponent does not give one to you. If you cannot arrange mutual exchange of trial briefs, then you probably should wait until the day of the trial to hand in your copy. The judge is unlikely to look at it before then anyway. However, the fear that you will give something away by telling your opponent your theory of the case is overblown. With modern discovery, it is unlikely that there will be many surprises.

Some lawyers advise against including anything specifically about evidentiary issues in your brief. They argue that you should not cross a bridge before you come to it. What you anticipate as a question of evidence may not even be objected to. Mentioning it in a brief may tip off the opponent to grounds for objection he or she had not thought of. Therefore, they suggest that questions of evidence should be discussed on separate pages to be handed to the judge as needed.[25]

2. TRIAL MOTIONS

There are innumerable motions you can make in aid of your trial.

- *Suppression motions.* Motions to suppress illegally obtained evidence should be considered by the defense in all criminal cases. If the police have committed any constitutional errors in their investigation, you should consider filing a suppression motion. In some states, evidence obtained constitutionally but in violation of statutory guidelines also may be suppressible. These motions are usually made soon after the arrest.
- *Motions in limine.* A motion in limine is a pretrial motion asking for a ruling on a matter of evidence. Usually, the motion asks that the opposing attorney be prevented from referring to inadmissible evidence during voir dire, opening statement, or witness examination. Occasionally the motion may ask for a ruling that anticipated evidence will be *admissible*, so the moving party may be allowed to use it. Judges have inherent discretion to hear this kind of anticipatory motion, both in advance of and during trial, but are not required to rule on them.[26] Although you can move to exclude any kind of inadmissible evidence, the court is not likely to grant your motion unless the evidence is inadmissible as a matter of law.[27] Rarely will a court entertain such a motion just because the evidence is prejudicial,[28] or if its admissibility depends on the laying of a foundation.[29] For example, you can move successfully to exclude evidence of an offer of compromise, but you probably will not be successful in moving to exclude hearsay on the grounds that it falls within no exception. In some jurisdictions, you may be *required* to make certain kinds of objections pretrial or risk waiver. For example, an amendment to FED. R.

---

[25] See Harry S. Bodin, *Final Preparation for Trial, in* CIVIL LITIGATION AND TRIAL TECHNIQUES 199 (1976).

[26] *E.g., Logston v. State*, 535 N.E.2d 525 (Ind. 1989).

[27] *E.g., State v. Baker Bros. Nursery*, 366 S.W.2d 212 (Tex. 1963).

[28] See *United States v. Costa*, 425 F.2d 950 (2d Cir. 1969); *Lewis v. Buena Vista Mut. Ins. Ass'n*, 183 N.W.2d 198 (Iowa 1971).

[29] See *State v. Flett*, 234 Or. 124, 380 P.2d 634 (1963); *Bruckman v. Pena*, 29 Colo. App. 357, 457 P.2d 566 (1971); *Riley v. State*, 427 N.E.2d 1074 (Ind. 1981).

CIV. P. 23(a)(3)(c) proposed in 1992 would require that all objections to exhibits other than relevance be raised before trial, although it does not require the judge to rule on them until trial.

- *Motions to separate witnesses.* Motions to exclude all witnesses except the parties from the courtroom are made as a matter of routine by most lawyers at the start of trial in an effort to preserve minor inconsistencies among the opponent's witnesses. If witnesses are allowed to remain in the courtroom and hear what other witnesses say, they may consciously or unconsciously conform their testimony to what they have heard. These motions are granted as a matter of right in most jurisdictions.[30]
- *Motions for a directed verdict.* Under FED. R. CIV. P. 50, a motion for a directed verdict may be made at the close of evidence offered by an opponent. Most lawyers make such motions as a matter of routine. In criminal cases, a motion for judgment of acquittal may be made by the defense at the close of the prosecution's case if the evidence is insufficient to sustain a conviction.

You should prepare for these motions in advance. Put your own motions in writing, attaching a short legal brief in support. Prepare your arguments to be made in support of them. Try to anticipate obvious motions that might be made against you on the eve of trial or during it, and prepare arguments in opposition.

3. JURY INSTRUCTIONS

You have the right to submit requests for specific jury instructions. Most states have a rule to this effect:

(a) *Instructions.* At or before the close of the evidence, any party may file written requests that the Court instruct the jury on the law as set forth in the request. A copy of such requested instructions shall be served on the adverse parties. The court shall inform counsel of its proposed action on the requests prior to their arguments to the jury, and shall instruct the jury after the arguments are completed. No party may assign as error the giving or the failure to give an instruction unless the party objects thereto before the jury retires to consider the verdict, stating specifically the matter objected to and the grounds of the objection. Such objection shall be made out of the hearing of the jury.

(b) *Additional Instructions.* While the jury is deliberating the court may in its discretion further instruct the jury, in the presence of or after notice to counsel. Objections thereto shall be made in a motion for new trial.[31]

In general, you should do so. Although in theory the judge is responsible for preparing jury instructions and has a copy of the applicable pattern jury instruction manual, most judges expect you to undertake the task of actually deciding which of the hundreds of pattern instructions you want, and making

---

[30] *See, e.g.,* FED. R. EVID. 615.
[31] Based on MICHIGAN COURT RULE 2.516.

copies of them for the judge to read. Your requests should be prepared in advance as far as practicable, and in writing. However, it is obviously impossible to anticipate all the requests that may be needed. For example, a party is entitled to an instruction that the jury is to disregard evidence that has been stricken from the record,[32] or that a criminal conviction may be used only in evaluating credibility.[33] Whether these instructions are appropriate will depend on what happens during trial.

Bear in mind, however, that most jurisdictions now have pattern jury instructions that the court is required to use if they are applicable. It is rarely worth the trouble to ask a judge to give an instruction that differs in any way from the approved pattern instruction in the jurisdiction. For example, MICHIGAN COURT RULE 2.516(D)(2) states this rule:

> Pertinent portions of the Michigan Standard Jury Instructions (SJI) must be given in each [case if] (a) they are applicable, (b) they accurately state the applicable law, and (c) they are requested by a party.

If you want an instruction that is not in the pattern book, or if you want an instruction that deviates in any way from an approved instruction, you are engaging in an uphill fight. Each request should be followed by a legal memorandum that clearly explains why your proposed instruction more clearly states the law in your jurisdiction.

4. STIPULATIONS

A stipulation is an agreement between the parties to a lawsuit that certain facts are true. It is a contract between the parties, binding them to an agreement, and constituting a judicial admission, admissible against your client and uncontrovertible.[34] A stipulation of fact means that the fact is no longer contested and therefore not a material issue. Evidence concerning the stipulated matter becomes irrelevant.[35] However, many courts permit evidence consistent with a stipulation if it is helpful to the jury in understanding the complete context in which the litigated events took place.[36] Generally speaking, stipulations must be introduced into evidence in some way in order to have any practical effect. Because a stipulation is the admission of your opponent, you can offer it at almost any time. Most judges will permit you to read it, although some prefer to read all stipulations themselves. It probably is inappropriate to ask a witness to read a stipulation.

Stipulations are often used for mutual convenience, to save the expense of proving uncontested facts or laying evidentiary foundations. Should you stipulate? While stipulations certainly make for efficient judicial administration, there are some tactical considerations that may militate against entering into them:

---

[32] See D.C. BAR ASS'N, STANDARDIZED JURY INSTRUCTIONS FOR THE DISTRICT OF COLUMBIA 15 (rev. ed. 1968).

[33] See California Jury Instructions Civil 2.24 (7th ed. 1986).

[34] See *Ireland v. Stalbaum*, 162 Neb. 630, 77 N.W.2d 155 (1956); *Central Coat, Apron & Linen Serv. v. Indemnity Ins. Co.*, 136 Conn. 234, 70 A.2d 126 (1949).

[35] See *Martin v. Hunter*, 179 Kan. 578, 297 P.2d 153 (1956).

[36] See *United States v. Palmiotti*, 254 F.2d 491 (2d Cir. 1958).

- The party having the burden of proof usually gains more by a formal stipulation than the defendant.
- Items in a stipulation can be read and reread and emphasized in argument, often more effectively than ordinary testimony.
- Sometimes the language of a stipulation can become a subject of bitter controversy when an unscrupulous opponent tries to stretch it beyond its actual intent.

All of this suggests that a formal stipulation should be worded with meticulous care. Francis Busch suggests the following form:

"In order that the time of the Court and Jury may be conserved it is stipulated and agreed, for the purposes of this action, that the following facts are true:" here [you should] list each item by number, in the simplest language and in as short a sentence as possible; long and involved sentences are more susceptible of misconstruction than short and simple ones. This, if it is thought desirable, may be followed by a statement that: by the above stipulation it is not intended by either party that such and such specified facts are admitted, or, generally that the liability or damages (unless damages are admitted in the stipulation) are admitted.[37]

An offer to stipulate during trial also can be an effective weapon against relevant, but prejudicial, evidence. If you offer to stipulate to the contested fact, the prejudicial evidence is no longer needed, and the balance between probative value and prejudice may swing toward exclusion.

Stipulations that constitute important parts of your case should be read to the jury near the beginning of your case in chief. Stipulations that go only to formal matters, such as foundations, should be offered in connection with other testimony logically related to that matter. If you have stipulated to an evidentiary foundation, e.g., that a document is admissible, there is no necessity that the stipulation be read to the jury at all. When the document is offered, you can remind the judge that its admissibility has been stipulated.

5. PRETRIAL CONFERENCES

Pretrial conferences normally are associated with civil cases. Only rarely are they held in criminal actions.[38] The purpose of the pretrial conference is to save trial time by resolving as many problems as possible in advance. In most civil cases the parties will hold at least two such conferences: a preliminary attorneys' conference and the more formal pretrial conference with the court. The attorneys are expected first to meet informally to exchange exhibits and witness lists, enter into stipulations, obtain admissions, and explore the possibility of settlement. This is followed by a more formal conference with the trial judge, in which differences between the parties are ironed out, motions may be ruled on, and questions about procedure may be resolved. A formal

---

[37] FRANCIS X. BUSCH, LAW AND TACTICS OF JURY TRIALS vol. 2: 443 (1959).
[38] Cf. FED. R. CRIM. P. 17.1 (court may order pretrial conferences).

pretrial order (drafted by one of the parties) generally will be agreed on that embodies all of the agreements and rulings. The following rule[39] is typical:

> *Pretrial Conferences.* — (a) In any action the court may in its discretion and shall upon the motion of any party, direct the attorneys for the parties to appear before it for a pretrial conference to consider:
>
> (1) the simplification of the issues;
>
> (2) the necessity or desirability of amendments to the pleadings;
>
> (3) the possibility of obtaining admissions of fact and of documents which will avoid unnecessary proof;
>
> (4) a limitation of the number of expert witnesses;
>
> (5) an exchange of names of witnesses to be called during the trial and the general nature of their expected testimony;
>
> (6) the desirability of using one or more types of alternative dispute resolution; and
>
> (7) such other matters as may aid in the disposition of the action.
>
> (b) Unless otherwise ordered by the court the pre-trial conference shall not be called until after reasonable opportunity for the completion of discovery.
>
> (1) *Notice.* The clerk shall give at least thirty [30] days' notice of the pre-trial conference unless otherwise directed by the court.
>
> (2) *Participants.* At least one attorney planning to take part in the trial shall appear for each of the parties and participate in the pre-trial conference.
>
> (c) At least ten [10] days prior to the pre-trial conference, attorneys for each of the parties shall meet and confer for the following purposes:
>
> (1) *Exhibits.* Each attorney shall mark for identification and provide opposing counsel an opportunity to inspect and copy all exhibits which the attorney expects to introduce at the trial. Numbers or marks placed on such exhibits shall be prefixed with the symbol "P/T," denoting its pre-trial designation. When the exhibit is introduced at the trial of the case, the "P/T" designation will be stricken. The exhibits must also indicate the party identifying them. Exhibits of the character which prohibit or make impracticable their production at conference shall be identified and notice given of their intended use. Necessary arrangements must be made to afford opposing counsel an opportunity to examine such exhibits.
>
> (2) *Exhibit stipulations.* Written stipulations may be prepared with reference to all exhibits exchanged or identified. The stipulations shall contain all agreements of the parties with reference to the exchanged and identified exhibits, and shall include, but not be limited to, the agreement of the parties with reference to the authenticity of the exhibits, their admissibility in evidence, their use in opening statements, and the provisions made for the inspection of identified exhibits. The original of the exhibit stipulations shall be presented to the court at the pre-trial conference.

---

[39] The rule is a slightly modified version of INDIANA TRIAL RULE 16.

(3) *Fact stipulations.* The attorneys may stipulate in writing with reference to all facts and issues not in genuine dispute. The original of the stipulations shall be presented to the court at the time of the pre-trial conference.

(4) *Exchange list of witnesses.* Attorneys for each of the parties shall furnish opposing counsel with a written list of the names and addresses of all witnesses then known. The original of each witness list shall be presented to the court at the time of the pre-trial conference.

(5) *Discuss settlement.* The possibility of compromise settlement or of using alternative methods of dispute resolution shall be fully discussed and explored.

(d) It shall be the duty of counsel for both plaintiff and defendant to arrange for the conference of attorneys at least ten [10] days in advance of the pre-trial conference.

(e) If necessary or advisable, the court may adjourn the pre-trial conference from time to time or may order an additional pre-trial conference.

(f) The court may direct one of the parties to prepare a pretrial statement which recites the action taken at the conference, the amendments allowed to the pleadings, and the agreements made by the parties which limit the issues for trial. Such statement shall be filed with the court, and when entered shall control the subsequent course of action, unless modified thereafter to prevent manifest injustice.

(g) If without just excuse or because of failure to give reasonable attention to the matter, no appearance is made on behalf of a party at a pre-trial conference, or if an attorney is grossly unprepared to participate in the conference, the court may order either one or both of the following:

(1) the payment by the delinquent attorney or party of the reasonable expenses, including attorney's fees, to the aggrieved party; or

(2) take such other action as may be appropriate.

Judges differ in their attitudes toward pretrial conferences. Some are informal, others formal. Some judges take an active role, trying to encourage settlement and suggesting compromises on points of disagreement, while others are more passive, letting the attorneys control the issues raised and ruling only when requested to do so. Whatever the procedures, you should not forget that the pretrial is part of the formal proceedings in the litigation of your case. A pretrial conference should be taken as seriously as the other aspects of trial, and adequately prepared for in advance. The conference should not be scheduled at all until you are fully prepared and ready for trial.

NOTES

1. *Motions in limine and preserving the record.* A ruling on a motion in limine is not final. If the judge rules that the evidence is inadmissible, such ruling does not absolutely exclude the evidence; rather, it prevents your opponent from raising the matter in open court without first obtaining specific permission from the judge. *See Swearingen v. Swearingen,* 578 S.W.2d 829 (Tex. Civ. App. 1979). In the context of the evidence as it develops during trial, the judge has the discretion to reverse his or her ruling and permit the

evidence to be introduced. *E.g., France v. State,* 387 N.E.2d 66 (Ind. App. 1979). If excluded evidence is presented to the jury despite the order, you must make a new objection in order to preserve the issue for appeal. *E.g., Padgett v. State,* 364 S.W.2d 397 (Tex. Crim. App. 1963). Similarly, if the evidence is ruled admissible pretrial, and the evidence is later presented at trial, you cannot appeal the decision unless you preserve the issue by a timely objection during trial. *E.g., Riley v. State,* 427 N.E.2d 1074 (Ind. 1981). If your own evidence is excluded by a motion in limine, you must approach the bench during trial, make an offer of proof, and ask to be allowed to present the excluded evidence, in order to preserve the issue. *E.g., Alleyn v. State,* 427 N.E.2d 1095 (Ind. 1981).

2. *Pretrial motions.* For an extensive discussion of motions and written notices that should be considered, see FRED LANE, LANE'S GOLDSTEIN TRIAL TECHNIQUE §§ 7.01 TO 7.80 (3d ed. 1984). *See also* STEPHEN HRONES, HOW TO TRY A CRIMINAL CASE 57-113 (1982) (extensive list of possible pretrial motions with sample forms); MARK KADISH & RHONDA BROFMAN, CRIMINAL LAW ADVOCACY — TRIAL INVESTIGATION AND PREPARATION ¶14.02 (1992); ANTHONY AMSTERDAM, TRIAL MANUAL 5 FOR THE DEFENSE OF CRIMINAL CASES §§ 223-264 (1989).

F. THE TRIAL NOTEBOOK

The final stage of trial preparation is to gather all that you have prepared and organize it into some kind of convenient format for use during the trial. Practicing attorneys have developed a number of different solutions to this problem. By far the most popular is the trial notebook — a standard three-ring binder with tabbed dividers, into which all your notes can be placed and organized. An alternative format uses a large expanding file or briefcase filled with ordinary manila folders for individual topics. Many litigators are also experimenting with electronic notebooks stored in laptop computers. The goal is to provide a central, easily transportable storage place for everything you may need at trial, and to organize it so that you immediately can locate any part of that material. The general rule is that if you cannot find something within fifteen seconds at trial, it might as well not exist.

Although there are disagreements about the order, there is consensus among trial practitioners that the following sections should be included in your notebook:

- *Dramatis personae.* The names, addresses, and telephone numbers of everyone important to the case: judge, clerk, court reporter, opposing lawyer, client, and witnesses.
- *Case theory.* A section at the front containing your case theory and a diagram or outline of your proof. The outline of proof lists witnesses and exhibits that will establish all the elements of your and your opponent's cases. It makes an excellent quick reference in answer to directed verdict motions based on failure of proof, to support an offer to connect up evidence through later witnesses, or to answer any inquiries from the judge about your case. An outline of what your opponent needs to prove may

enable you to make an intelligent directed verdict motion if your adversary neglects to offer evidence on a necessary element.

- *Trial schedule.* A section for your trial schedule listing everything you intend to do at trial in the actual order you will do it. If you write down the scenario and refer to it as you go along, you will not forget to make a motion, ask for a recess so you can telephone a witness, submit a jury instruction, or call a witness. For example, the first part of a trial schedule might look something like this:

1. Approach bench, ask for preliminary instruction on cause of action.
2. Move to have voir dire recorded.
3. Move to separate witnesses.
4. Voir dire.
5. Telephone Jackson (ask for five-minute recess).
6. Move to have opening statements recorded if voir dire request not granted.
7. Opening statement.
8. Direct examination — Jackson.
9. Opponent's cross-examination.
10. Request that Jackson be allowed to leave courthouse and return to work.
11. Request judicial notice of traffic law § 9-142 (twenty-mile speed limit in school zone).
12. Read "school zone" stipulation.
13. Direct examination — Stevens.
14. Etc.

- *Last minute reminders.* A section containing checklists of things to do at the last minute, such as calling witnesses, getting a treatise from the library, arranging for a pitcher of water at your table, and so forth. It is better to have a place to write yourself notes than to rely on your memory when you are under the stress of an imminent trial.
- *Pretrial.* A section containing a list of queries for the judge at the start of trial, e.g., whether she will permit an exhibit to be used in opening statement and whether she prefers objections to be argued at the bench or in open court.
- *Court documents.* A section for the pleadings, rulings on motions, pretrial orders, and any other official court documents.
- *Jury selection.* Your notes for jury selection, a copy of the statute concerning grounds for challenge for cause, and a jury seating chart or other form on which to record information about the prospective jurors.
- *Opening statement.* Your notes for your opening statement.
- *Witnesses.* A separate section for each witness, both favorable and unfavorable, with copies of statements and documents relating to that witness and an outline of the direct or cross-examination. Prior statements and depositions should be carefully indexed so you immediately can locate passages needed to refresh recollection or impeach. You may find it beneficial to include an introductory paragraph about each witness's personality, intelligence, susceptibility to cross-examination, temper, and any-

thing else you learned during interviews that will help remind you about how you intended to handle the witness on the stand.

- *Trial motions.* Notes pertaining to your argument for or against a motion for a directed verdict.
- *Evidence research.* Copies of your evidence research and any briefs you have prepared to support your objections. If a convenient state evidence manual exists, you may be able to dispense with this section.
- *Closing argument.* Your notes for final argument, including sketches of any diagrams you plan to draw on the chalkboard.
- *Jury instructions.* A copy of the jury instructions approved by the court, and any requests for additional instructions.
- *Exhibits appendix.* Originals or copies of all documents you will use at any time during trial and a checklist for keeping track of which ones have been admitted into evidence. Keeping track of exhibits (your own and your adversary's) can be one of the most difficult tasks in the trial. Exhibits are marked, shown to witnesses, talked about, offered, withdrawn, admitted, and passed to the jury. Laying adequate foundations may require more than one witness. Few things are more frustrating than being told you cannot use an exhibit during closing argument because you neglected to move it into evidence. An exhibit checklist can help you keep a running record of the status of all exhibits.
- *Discovery appendix.* A section for answers to interrogatories and requests for admissions, and for transcribed depositions, if they are too bulky to include in the file set aside for the particular witness.
- *Index.*

NOTES

1. *Example of exhibit checklist.*

Figure 2

Sample Exhibit Chart

EXHIBIT CHART							
Exhibit number	Description	Marked for identification	Foundation laid	Offered	Admitted	Excluded	Shown to jury
1	Letter dated February 16	X	X	X	X		X
2	Return letter dated March 2	X	X	X	X		X
3	Bill of lading	X	X	X		X	
4	Cancelled check	X	X				
5	Receipt	X					

2. *Where to file exhibits.* A potential problem arises if you need to use a document or photograph in your opening statement, during witness examinations, and again when giving your closing argument. Where should you put it in your trial notebook? The usual advice is to put documents in a separate file at the end. *See* ANTHONY AMSTERDAM, TRIAL MANUAL 5 FOR THE DEFENSE OF CRIMINAL CASES § 297 (1989). However, if you use this approach, you may not be able to find it when you need it. Two solutions are possible. First, you might make enough copies so that one will be filed in each section where it will be needed. However, this system will not work if the best evidence rule limits you to using the original, or if witnesses will be making marks on a diagram which you will need in your closing argument. The second solution is to place the exhibit within the section in which it will be used first, accompanied by a written note reminding yourself where next to put it when you are done.

G. BIBLIOGRAPHY

1. GENERAL

DAVID BAUM, ART OF ADVOCACY — PREPARATION OF THE CASE (1981).

Harry S. Bodin, *Marshalling the Evidence, in* CIVIL LITIGATION AND TRIAL
   TECHNIQUES 18-27 (1976).
Harry S. Bodin, *Final Preparation for Trial, in* CIVIL LITIGATION AND TRIAL
   TECHNIQUES 199 (1976).
FRANCIS X. BUSCH, LAW AND TACTICS OF JURY TRIALS, vol. 2: 337-780 (1959).
Philip Corboy, *Structuring the Presentation of Proof or Evidence*, TRIAL DIPL.
   J., Summer 1978, at 26.
Robert Hanley, *Working the Witness Puzzle*, LITIGATION, Winter 1977, at 9.
HUBERT HICKAM & THOMAS SCANLON, PREPARATION FOR TRIAL (1963).
JAMES W. JEANS, LITIGATION, chs. 4-5 (2d ed. 1992).
JAMES W. JEANS, TRIAL ADVOCACY, ch. 6 (1975).
MARK KADISH & RHONDA BROFMAN, CRIMINAL LAW ADVOCACY — TRIAL INVES-
   TIGATION AND PREPARATION (1992).
ROBERT KEETON, TRIAL TACTICS AND METHODS 303-52 (2d ed. 1973).
FRED LANE, LANE'S GOLDSTEIN TRIAL TECHNIQUE, chs. 1-8 (3d ed. 1984).
THOMAS A. MAUET, FUNDAMENTALS OF TRIAL TECHNIQUES 369-414 (3d ed.
   1992).

2. CASE INVESTIGATION

James McElhaney, *Informal Investigation*, LITIGATION, Spring 1982, at 51.

3. DISCOVERY

Harry S. Bodin, *Depositions — Strategy and Tactics, in* CIVIL LITIGATION AND
   TRIAL TECHNIQUES 159 (1976).
ROGER HAYDOCK & DAVID HERR, DISCOVERY PRACTICE (2d ed. 1988).

4. MOTIONS IN LIMINE

Edna Epstein, *Motions in Limine — A Primer*, LITIGATION, Spring 1982, at 34.

5. ETHICS

Wayne Brazil, *The Adversary Character of Civil Discovery: A Critique and
   Proposal for Change*, 31 VAND. L. REV. 1295 (1978).
David N. Edelstein, *The Ethics of Dilatory Motion Practice: Time for Change*,
   44 FORDHAM L. REV. 1069 (1976).
Monroe Freedman, *Professional Responsibility of the Criminal Defense Law-
   yer: The Three Hardest Questions*, 64 MICH. L. REV. 1469 (1966).
Lee Gaudineer, *Ethics and Malpractice*, 26 DRAKE L. REV. 88 (1977).
A. Kenneth Pye, *The Role of Counsel in the Suppression of Truth*, 1978 DUKE
   L.J. 921.

6. TRIAL NOTEBOOKS

JAMES W. JEANS, LITIGATION § 5.05 (2d ed. 1992).
Charles Joiner, *The Trial Brief, in* ADVOCACY AND THE KING'S ENGLISH 47 (G.
   Rossman ed. 1960).
Paul Luvera, *The Trial Notebook*, PRAC. LAW., November 1973, at 37.

James McElhaney, *The Trial Notebook*, LITIGATION, Fall 1980, at 45.

7. THEORY OF THE CASE

James McElhaney, *The Sense of Injustice*, LITIGATION, Spring 1988, at 47.
HERBERT J. STERN, TRYING CASES TO WIN, vol. 1: 69-125 (1991).

8. PSYCHOLOGY

SAUL M. KASSIN & LAWRENCE S. WRIGHTSMAN, THE AMERICAN JURY ON
    TRIAL: PSYCHOLOGICAL PERSPECTIVES 132-37 (1988).
Daniel Linz & Steven Penrod, *Increasing Attorney Persuasiveness in the
    Courtroom*, 8 LAW & PSYCHOL. REV. 1, 13-14 (1984).

Chapter 3

SELECTING A JURY

A. INTRODUCTION

Before a jury trial can begin, it must have a jury. There must be a procedure for taking all the local citizens who were summoned for jury duty and reducing them to a specific six or twelve persons who will decide forever the fate of your client. The usual procedure goes something like this:

- Before the trial, citizens selected from voter lists, telephone books, and driver's license records are summoned for jury duty.
- Prospective jurors fill out questionnaires.
- At the start of a trial, a number of prospective jurors are brought to the courtroom. The judge administers an oath asking them to answer questions honestly.
- The clerk calls the names of a few jurors selected at random and asks them to take seats in the jury box. Copies of their questionnaires are distributed to the attorneys.
- The prospective jurors are then questioned — sometimes by the judge, sometimes by the attorneys, and sometimes by both. This questioning process is called a *voir dire*.
- If the questioning reveals that a prospective juror cannot be fair and impartial, one of the attorneys may challenge that juror.
- Unless the challenge is disallowed for some reason, the prospective juror is excused. The ones who are not challenged will serve on the jury.
- The clerk calls the names of more prospective jurors to take the places of those who were excused, and the process continues until the requisite number have survived and a jury has been created.
- The whole process takes an average of one to two hours.

Attorneys hold different views about what one should expect to accomplish during the voir dire. Most would agree that there are four main goals:

- Make a good first impression on the jury.
- Identify and remove jurors likely to vote for your opponent.
- Begin the process of persuasion.
- Do all this without putting the jury to sleep.

There is no consensus about how to achieve these goals. Attorneys employ many approaches and hold many different opinions, but have few real answers.

How important is the jury selection? Some attorneys believe it is the single most important part of the trial. Herald Fahringer, a prominent trial attorney, has written:

> Jury selection is the most important part of any criminal trial. If a lawyer has a difficult case, but succeeds in obtaining a jury sympathetic with [the] client's cause, the chances of winning improve substantially. On the other hand, a client may have an excellent defense, but if [there are] twelve antagonistic jurors, sometimes the skill of no lawyer can save him. In most cases, the defendant's fate is fixed after jury selection. Consequently, counsel's ability to select a favorable jury ... is of paramount importance.[1]

How realistic is it that an attorney can find out what a juror is really like in only a few minutes? Empirical studies of the effect of pretrial publicity showed that voir dire did not identify jurors who had been affected by the publicity, nor ameliorate its influence. Jurors simply do not admit they have been biased.[2] Fahringer pessimistically concludes:

> [I]t must be conceded that jury selection involves some guile on the part of lawyers. Lawyers announce to the panel that they want only jurors who will decide the case impartially, while, in fact, they want partisan jurors. Counsel is obliged to pick people who, by reason of their background, personality or attitudes, can be expected to find in [the] client's favor. This insincerity is quickly detected by the jurors. We lie to them and they in turn to us; this is a bad beginning for a project designed to discover the truth.[3]

NOTES

1. ***Attorney- vs. judge-conducted voir dire.*** There is a great debate in legal circles over whether it is better to have the judge ask questions, thereby preventing abuses by the attorney and saving time, or to have the attorney ask questions because he or she is in a better position to probe into potential biases. *See, e.g.*, S. Mac Gutman, *The Attorney-Conducted Voir Dire of Jurors: A Constitutional Right*, 39 BROOK. L. REV. 290 (1972). Empirical studies show that both premises are correct — judges are more efficient, but attorneys elicit more reliable information. Susan Jones, *Judge Versus Attorney-Conducted Voir Dire: An Empirical Investigation of Juror Candor*, 11 LAW & HUM. BEHAV. 131 (1987); David Suggs & Bruce D. Sales, *Juror Self-Disclosure in the Voir Dire: A Social Science Analysis*, 56 IND. L.J. 245, 251-52 (1981).

2. ***How long does it take?*** Everyone has heard stories about trials in which it took six weeks to pick a jury. However, judges estimate that the typical jury selection process averages less than one hour. GORDON BERMANT,

---

[1] Herald P. Fahringer, *In the Valley of the Blind: A Primer on Jury Selection in a Criminal Case*, 43 LAW & CONTEMP. PROBS. 116, 116-17 (1980).

[2] Norbert Kerr et al., *On the Effectiveness of Voir Dire in Criminal Cases with Prejudicial Pretrial Publicity: An Empirical Study*, 40 AM. U. L. REV. 665, 668-70 (1991); Gary Moran & Brian Cutler, *The Prejudicial Impact of Pretrial Publicity*, 21 J. APP. SOC. PSYCHOL. 345 (1991).

[3] Fahringer, *supra* note 1, at 117.

CONDUCT OF THE VOIR DIRE EXAMINATION: PRACTICES AND OPINIONS OF FEDERAL DISTRICT JUDGES 13 (1977); William Fortune, *Voir Dire in Kentucky: An Empirical Study of Voir Dire in Kentucky Circuit Courts*, 69 KY. L.J. 273, 299-300 (1981). Systematic observation indicates that voir dire rarely lasts more than a few hours. William H. Levitt et al., *Expediting Voir Dire: An Empirical Study*, 44 S. CAL. L. REV. 916, 958-60 (1971).

B. SAMPLE VOIR DIRE EXAMINATION

Because it often takes two hours or more to conduct a complete voir dire examination of prospective jurors, it is not possible to reprint an entire voir dire examination. The following abbreviated excerpt[4] should give you a feel for the process:

The Clerk: All rise, please. The superior court for Jackson County is now in session. All persons having business before this court draw nigh to be heard. The Honorable Janice McInney presiding.

The Court: Be seated. Call the case of Wilson versus Valley Electric Company. Are both sides ready?

Plaintiff's Attorney: Yes, your Honor.

Defendant's Attorney: We are ready, your Honor.

The Court: Is this our panel?

The Clerk: Yes, your Honor.

The Court: Ladies and gentlemen of the jury. In a few minutes we will begin the selection process for the case of Wilson v. Valley Electric Company. This is a civil case in which the plaintiff seeks to recover damages for injuries alleged to have been caused through the fault of the defendant. The basic allegation is that on February 1, 1992, the plaintiff, a twelve-year-old boy, climbed a utility pole owned and maintained by the Valley Electric Company, and came into contact with a high voltage line, resulting in serious injuries. The plaintiff claims that the defendant failed to take proper safety precautions. The defense claims contributory negligence — that the plaintiff's injuries were wholly or partly the plaintiff's own fault.

The plaintiff is still under age, so the suit is being brought on his behalf by his father, Peter Wilson. They are represented by John Bracey. The defendants, at the far table, are represented by Susan Oliver.

Under our procedures, we use a six-person jury in civil cases. We will call six of you up to the jury box where you will be questioned by the attorneys. Those of you who remain in the audience should listen closely to the questions also because you may be called up to take the place of one of the first six. It is very important that each of you keep your voices loud when answering questions so that we can all hear you.

Mr. Clerk, will you call the first six jurors?

---

[4]The example was drawn primarily by combining a hypothetical voir dire in PHILIP B. HEYMANN & WILLIAM H. KENETY, THE MURDER TRIAL OF WILBUR JACKSON 47-66 (1975) and a real one conducted by James Hullverson, in WARD WAGNER, ART OF ADVOCACY — JURY SELECTION §§ 4.00 TO 4.45 (1981).

The Clerk: Please answer when your name is called and take a seat in the jury box. Laura Jones. Levon Williams. Arnold Greenberg. Edwin Nussbaker. Mary Oswald. Irene Bell. [Whereupon all prospective jurors were duly sworn.]

The Court: Mr. Bracey, you may proceed.

By Mr. Bracey: Thank you. May it please the court and you, members of the panel. My name is John Bracey, and I represent the boy who was crippled and his family. That is his father, seated at our table. The child, John Wilson, is not here. He will not be here through much of the trial for two reasons. First, of course, he has to be in school. Also, we decided — his parents and I — that it would be better if he did not hear all the testimony about how serious, permanent, and hopeless his condition is. Can you understand that? Would any of you hold it against him in any way because he is not here?

A: (No response.)

Q: Seated over there is Ms. Oliver, an attorney with Harkins, Harrell, Boyd, and Long. They represent the defendant, the Electric Company. Do any of you know either myself or the defense lawyer? Do any of you know anything about or have you heard anything about the defense law firm? Mr. Greenberg, do you recognize the names of any of the lawyers?

Juror Greenberg: No.

By Mr. Bracey: How about you, Ms. Jones?

Juror Jones: Not that I know of.

Q: By the way, do you prefer being called Ms. or Mrs.?

A: I prefer Ms., thank you.

Q: Ms. Oswald, which do you prefer?

A: I know it's unfashionable, but I've been called Mrs. Oswald for thirty years, and I'd like to be called Mrs.

Q: And you, Ms. Bell?

A: I don't know, I guess Ms.

Q: The plaintiff — that is, the injured person who had to bring the suit — is John Wilson, a fourteen-year-old boy. When he was twelve, in February 1992, he climbed up an uninsulated utility pole and was electrocuted — excuse me, I don't mean he was killed; he was crippled from a potentially lethal seven thousand volts of electricity. His parents are Pete and Wanda Wilson, of 3614 Southbriar Road. John was attending Washington Middle School at the time. Do any of you know the Wilson family? Mr. Nussbaker, I noticed from your questionnaire that you have a fifteen-year-old daughter. Did she go to Washington Middle School?

A: No. She went to the Lakeview Christian Academy.

Q: Mr. Williams, you have a twelve-year-old. Does he go to Washington?

A: Yes, he does.

Q: Has your son said anything about this case or about a boy from the school who was crippled?

A: No.

Q: It would not prejudice you in any way because your son and John go to the same school, would it?

A: No, of course not.

Q: Does anyone else have any connections to Washington School or the Wilsons?

A: (No response.)

Q: The defendant is Valley Electric Company. Do any of you have friends or relatives who work for the Electric Company?

Juror Williams: I have a cousin who works for them in Center City.

Q: How often do you see your cousin, Mr. Williams?

A: I don't.

Q: What?

A: I don't see him.

Q: When was the last time you saw him?

A: About five years ago at a wedding.

Q: Would this influence you in any way, that your cousin works for the defendant?

A: No.

Q: Anyone else. Mrs. Oswald?

A: Well, I have a neighbor who works for them. I see a company truck parked in their driveway.

Q: Do you know these neighbors, or socialize with them?

A: No.

Q: Would the fact that you have a neighbor who works for the defendant cause you to favor the defendant?

A: No, of course not.

Q: Now, I know that we all have had some dealings with the defendant, because we have to pay our electric bills. And I am sure that we all worry about our electric bills because they keep going up. In this case, we are asking for five million, six hundred thousand dollars in compensation. Does anyone worry that a large verdict might cause your utility rates to go up? Ms. Jones?

A: I hadn't thought of it that way, but I guess they might.

Q: Mr. Williams?

A: No, I don't worry about it. They cover this whole part of the state and have millions of customers, so even if they did raise rates it wouldn't be by much.

Q: Ms. Bell?

A: I don't know. I think I agree with that other man that it wouldn't amount to much on my bill.

Q: Mr. Greenberg?

A: I do worry about it. They always pass on the costs to the customer. Like for Three Mile Island or these nuclear plants that cost billions, they just go to the state utility commission and get another twenty percent rate increase.

Q: Does that mean you would have reservations about voting for a large verdict?

A: I don't know. It wouldn't prove anything. It wouldn't punish the Electric Company because they would just pass on the cost.

Q: Well, do you understand that the purpose of this suit is not to punish the defendant, but to decide how much money will compensate John Wilson for a life in a wheelchair?

A: Yes.

Q: Do you have any problems with compensating John for his past and future medical costs?

A: No, of course not.

Q: So you could award large damages to cover real medical costs, even though your electric bill might go up a few cents?

A: Certainly.

Q: And if we proved that John will never be able to hold a job because of his injuries, could you compensate him for that?

A: Yes.

Q: Mrs. Oswald, do you also agree that an injured person should be compensated for being unable to work?

By Ms. Oliver: I object. He's asking for a legal opinion.

By Mr. Bracey: Let me rephrase. Mrs. Oswald, if the judge instructed you that you can consider lost earning capacity in awarding damages, could you do so?

A: Yes.

Q: You could follow the judge's instructions?

A: Yes.

Q: Mr. Nussbaker?

A: Yes, that only seems fair.

Q: If the judge instructed you that you can also compensate John for suffering and pain, would that present any problems?

A: No.

Q: Would anyone have any problems following the law and considering all three kinds of damages — medical expenses, lost earning capacity and pain and suffering — in arriving at a fair verdict?

Various jurors: No.

Q: Mr. Greenberg, if you decided that we had proved that these damages combined added up to five million, six hundred thousand dollars, would you reduce that amount out of concern about higher electric bills?

A: No, I guess that would be unfair.

Q: Ms. Jones, could you return a verdict of several million dollars if that is what it would take to compensate John?

A: That seems like a lot, but I could vote for it if you proved it.

Q: Ms. Bell?

A: Yeah.

Q: Mr. Williams?

A: Yes, if you proved it.

Q: Mrs. Oswald?

A: Could I vote for that much money?

Q: Yes.

A: I think so.

Q: You seemed hesitant.

A: That's a lot of money. I don't see how you could prove it.

Q: We are confident we can, but that will have to wait for the witnesses. I am only asking whether you could vote for a five million dollar verdict if you were persuaded by the evidence that that figure was fair, or whether you might return a lower one just because the defendant is the Electric Company.

A: Oh. No, I would vote for whatever I thought you had proved.

Q: Now, in connection with John's injuries, I need to ask some questions. John is, as you will see, confined to a wheelchair, and he has lost his arms. He now has mechanical arms. Does anyone know anyone or have any relatives in wheelchairs or who have to wear artificial limbs? Yes, Ms. Bell?

A: My father's in a wheelchair.

Q: Ms. Bell, I don't mean to pry, but sometimes we have to ask questions about personal matters. In this suit there is a lot at stake, and we have to be certain that the jurors who decide it can be completely impartial. Sometimes there are personal experiences that jurors have had that could cause them to react very emotionally or would make them uncomfortable sitting on a jury. Do you think that it would bother you or influence you in any way that your father is in a wheelchair like John?

A: No.

Q: Was he injured, is that why he's in a wheelchair?

A: No. He's very old and in a nursing home and has trouble with his legs.

Q: Could you put this out of your mind and decide this case solely on the facts presented?

A: I think so.

Q: Does anyone else have any experience with crippled people? Yes, Mrs. Oswald?

A: There's a family at our church that has a daughter in a wheelchair.

* * *

Q: I have a few follow-up questions based on those jury questionnaires you all filled out. Mrs. Oswald, I noticed that you do volunteer work at County Memorial Hospital, is that right?

A: Yes.

Q: In fact, you are president of the Women's Auxiliary, are you not?

A: Yes, I am.

Q: Do you work with the children's ward?

A: Yes, quite a bit.

Q: John Wilson was in that ward for more than two months, in February and March, 1992. Might you have seen him or worked with him?

A: No. When I said we worked with children, I meant the Women's Auxiliary did. We also run the gift shop, and I have worked only in the gift shop since about 1986. I did work on the wards before then.

Q: So you've been around hospitals and doctors for some time?

A: Yes, almost fifteen years.

Q: In that time I expect you've become pretty familiar with medicine and hospital care and so on?

A: Well, a little.

Q: Do you know Drs. Anthony Yeager, Mary Ann Stevenson, and Reynaldo Cortez?

A: Yes.

Q: They may be called as witnesses in this case. Without going into any details, is there anything you know about any of these doctors that would cause you to question their expert medical judgment in this case?

A: No, they're all good doctors.

Q: Does anyone else know these doctors or has anyone heard of them?

Various Jurors: No.

Q: So can I take it that you will all evaluate their testimony based solely on what you hear in the courtroom?

Various Jurors: Yes.

Q: Does anyone else have any knowledge of medicine or hospitals? Yes, Mr. Nussbaker?

A: I used to work at Crosstown Pharmacy.

Q: Did you have anything to do with prescription medicine?

A: No. I did some stock work.

Q: But you probably became familiar with some prescription drugs?

A: Sort of. I'm not sure I remember much.

Q: The doctors in this case may testify that they prescribed certain strong pain-killers for John, like Demerol and Percodan. Do you know much about them?

A: Not much.

Q: Is there anything in your experience that would cause you to question a doctor who said these were strong, dangerous drugs only prescribed in cases of extreme pain?

A: No. I think that's right.

* * *

Q: Mr. Greenberg, did you serve in the armed forces?

A: Yes.

Q: What branch?

A: Infantry.

Q: Where did you serve?

A: Vietnam.

Q: During the war?

A: Yes.

Q: Did you know people who were severely injured?

A: Yes, I did.

Q: Did you know anyone who lost both arms, like John did?

A: No, I don't think so. I knew people who lost arms or legs, but I can't remember anyone who lost both arms.

Q: Did this have an effect on you?

A: It's terrible. I mean, their lives are ruined.

Q: Would your experiences make it hard to be a fair and impartial juror in this case?

A: No, I don't think so.

* * *

Q: Mr. Nussbaker, you work at Westinghouse, is that right?

A: Yes.

Q: Are there any people working there who have lost both arms?

A: No.

Q: Ms. Bell, you work at Sears?

A: Uh huh.

Q: Do you know if there are any people who have lost both arms working there?

A: I don't think so.

Q: Mr. Williams, you work for the post office, do you not?

Juror Williams: Yes.

Q: Are there any people without arms there?

A: No.

Q: Ms. Jones, are there any people without arms working at your real estate agency?

A: No.

Q: Do any of you have anything to do with hiring or personnel?

Various Jurors: No.

Q: So none of you know whether anyone as handicapped as John has ever applied for a job or been hired where you work?

Various Jurors: No.

Q: Mr. Greenberg, you are retired, but did you ever work at the same job as a person without arms?

A: No.

Q: Mrs. Oswald, do you know anyone without arms who has a job?

A: Not exactly. There's a receptionist at the hospital who's disabled and is in a wheelchair, but she has some use of her arms or at least one arm is okay, because she can use the telephone.

Q: So she uses her arms, or at least one arm?

A: Yes.

Q: I asked these questions because there may be testimony from people at job agencies and who work in job placement about whether a person without arms can find a job. Is there anything that any of you have seen that would cause you to question a job counselor who said it was very unlikely that a person without arms could find and keep a job?

Various Jurors: No.

Q: Is there any reason why any one of you could not be fair and impartial?

Various Jurors: No.

By Mr. Bracey: I pass the jury for cause.

NOTE

Other examples. You can find other good examples of voir dire examinations in FRANCIS X. BUSCH, LAW AND TACTICS OF JURY TRIALS, vol. 1: 778-96, 849-62 (1959); JAMES W. JEANS, LITIGATION, at § 8.22 (2d ed. 1992); HERBERT J. STERN, TRYING CASES TO WIN, vol. 1: 523-620 (1991).

C. LEGAL FRAMEWORK

1. WHO ASKS THE QUESTIONS?

Courts follow three different procedures for conducting questioning. The traditional practice, still followed in some states, places responsibility for questioning prospective jurors on the attorneys. The federal practice requires the judge to conduct all or most of the questioning, and greatly restricts attorney participation. A compromise "cooperative" method is used in some jurisdictions, in which the judge asks general questions, followed by supplemental questions from the attorneys.

Attorney-conducted voir dire used to be ubiquitous. In New York, the judge was not even present during questioning unless requested by one of the parties.[5] Although concerns about efficiency have eroded the popularity of this procedure, it is still common. In a few states the task of questioning jurors is allocated to the attorneys by statute,[6] but more commonly it results from judicial discretion. In most states, the presiding judge has discretionary control over who asks the questions, and the practice may vary widely even within the same jurisdiction.[7] Often, the only way to find out if you are expected to conduct the entire voir dire is to ask.

In the federal courts, the voir dire is often conducted exclusively by the trial judge. The judge has discretion whether and to what extent to allow attorney participation.[8] Most judges severely limit it in the name of efficiency. This procedure obviously saves time — the judge is more likely to conduct a superficial job than the attorneys — and is spreading to some states. Under judge-conducted voir dire procedures, input by the attorneys is limited to the submission of written questions, which the judge may ask as written, may ask only after substantial editing, or may refuse to ask. In some courts, even this small degree of attorney participation may be denied.[9] The courts have generally upheld severe restrictions on active attorney participation in the voir dire. The judge may conduct the entire voir dire as long as he or she does so adequately to insure an impartial jury.[10]

Probably the most common modern method of voir dire is a cooperative procedure in which the trial judge conducts a general examination and then turns the questioning over to the attorneys. This is the method recommended by the American Bar Association's Standards for the Administration of Criminal Justice:

> *Standard 15-2.4:* Interrogation of jurors should be conducted initially and primarily by the judge, but counsel for each side should have the opportu-

---

[5] N.Y. CIV. PRAC. LAW § 4107 (McKinney 1992).

[6] *E.g.,* CONN. GEN. STAT. § 51-240 (1985): "In any civil action tried before a jury, either party shall have the right to examine, personally or by his counsel, each juror outside the presence of other prospective jurors as to his qualifications to sit as a juror in the action, or as to his interest, if any, in the subject matter of the action, or as to his relations with the parties thereto.... The right of examination shall not be abridged by requiring questions to be put to any juror in writing and submitted in advance of the commencement of the action."

[7] *See* William Fortune, *Voir Dire in Kentucky: An Empirical Study of Voir Dire in Kentucky Circuit Courts,* 69 KY. L.J. 273, 297-98 (1981), reporting that in Kentucky, where the trial judge has discretion, about twenty percent of judges give attorneys responsibility for the full examination.

[8] *See* FED. R. CIV. P. 47(a); FED. R. CRIM. P. 24(a).

[9] *E.g.,* ILL. ANN. STAT. ch. 110A, § 234 (1985) (the court *may* permit the parties to submit additional questions).

[10] *See, e.g., Fietzer v. Ford Motor Co.,* 622 F.2d 281 (7th Cir. 1980); *United States v. Dellinger,* 472 F.2d 340, 367-69 (7th Cir. 1972); *Labbee v. Roadway Express, Inc.,* 469 F.2d 169 (8th Cir. 1972).

nity, subject to reasonable time limits, to question jurors directly, both individually and as a panel.

2. THE MECHANICS OF QUESTIONING

The second procedural issue is how the jurors are to be questioned. The practices of courts vary widely. Questions may be posed in the courtroom, in the judge's chambers, in special jury rooms, or in written questionnaires before trial. The jurors may be questioned en masse, in groups of four to twelve, or individually. Individual questioning may be done privately or with the other jurors present.

Standardized written questionnaires that elicit general background information are commonly issued to prospective jurors prior to the start of trial. These questionnaires range from simple ones that merely track the statutory qualification requirements to more complex ones that include detailed demographic questions, questions about prior experiences with the legal system, and other questions normally asked during voir dire. In some individual cases, especially high-publicity cases, judges have departed from the standardized form and distributed detailed questionnaires to prospective jurors that have been tailored to fit the particular case.[11]

As an alternative to the questionnaire, general questions may be posed to all prospective jurors at one time. This kind of questioning usually is reserved for easily detectable disqualifications: nonresidency, recent jury service, physical disability, and so forth. It may be conducted in the common jury room or in the courtroom when a panel is first brought in.

Probably the most common practice is to question panels of four to twelve prospective jurors at a time.[12] Questions are posed to the panel as a whole, with follow-up questions to individuals when needed. In some cases, the jurors may be questioned one at a time. Obviously, individual questioning takes longer than group questioning, and it is usually reserved for special cases that have attracted considerable publicity.[13] Private questioning also may be used when it appears that further public questioning could taint the panel. For example, if in response to a general question, a prospective juror states that he or she has a reason for being biased against a party, it is within the discretion of the judge to remove that person from the hearing of the other jurors before inquiring further. The law seems to leave the question of group versus individual questions to the discretion of the trial judge.[14]

---

[11]See Robert S. Warren & Gail E. Lees, *Jury Selection, in* Winning Strategies and Techniques for Civil Litigators 41-42 (J. Lyons ed. 1992) (listing high-publicity trials that used customized questionnaires: *United States v. John DeLorean, Cippolone v. Liggett & Myers,* the *Central Park Jogger* case, *United States v. Imelda Marcos,* and the *MGM Grand Hotel* fire litigation).

[12]See Ill. Ann. Stat. ch. 78, § 21 (1985) (jurors to be examined in panels of four); Minn. R. Crim. P. 26.02(4) (jurors examined in groups of twelve).

[13]See *United States v. Hearst,* 466 F. Supp. 1068 (N.D. Cal. 1978). *But see Lackey v. State,* 578 S.W.2d 101 (Tenn. Crim. App. 1978) (not permitted).

[14]See *United States v. Bear Runner,* 502 F.2d 908 (8th Cir. 1979) (if individual prejudices are likely, individual questions should be asked).

3. REMOVING A PROSPECTIVE JUROR

At the heart of the voir dire system is the process of getting rid of unsatisfactory jurors. The lawyer's control over the composition of the jury is the
right to reject, not the right to select. Under the challenge system used in
most courts, a juror may be challenged for cause if legally unqualified, or
challenged peremptorily (without the need to state a reason) by one of the
parties. A few states substitute a system of "strikes" in place of peremptory
challenges.

In its most common form, this procedure works as follows:

1. Twelve potential jurors are seated in the jury box and questioned.
2. As soon as grounds for legal challenge arise, either lawyer may make a
   challenge for cause.
3. The court rules on the challenge for cause. The judge may ask additional questions or allow the other side to do so, or may hear legal
   argument. If the judge allows (sustains) the challenge, that juror is
   excused and another is called to take his or her place.
4. When the questioning is complete, six to twelve legally qualified jurors
   are seated in the jury box. The parties now have the opportunity to
   exercise peremptory challenges to remove jurors they dislike. Usually,
   peremptory challenges are exercised alternately, with plaintiff going
   first, until both sides either exhaust the number of allowable peremptory challenges or are satisfied with the remaining jurors.
5. The empty seats are filled with new prospective jurors, and the process
   starts over again for them. Those jurors agreed upon in the first round
   may not be reexamined.
6. Jury selection is completed when the jury box is full and both sides are
   satisfied with them all or unable to challenge any of them.

a. Challenges for Cause

A prospective juror may be challenged for cause for one of two reasons: (1)
legal disability, or (2) a likelihood of bias because of the peculiar facts of the
case. At common law, the former was known as a principal challenge for cause
and the latter a challenge for favor, distinctions no longer used. Challenges
for cause are now controlled primarily by statutes that set out the legal
grounds upon which they can be made. Such statutes commonly enumerate
minimal requirements for eligibility applicable to all trials, and also include a
general authorization for a challenge if it is determined that the juror cannot
be impartial in the particular case. Because challenges for cause go to the
legal disability (incompetence) of a prospective juror, they are unlimited in
number. A typical statute (the example happens to refer to criminal cases)[15] is
set out below:

> *Grounds for challenge for cause.* — A challenge for cause to an individ-
> ual juror may be made by any party on the ground that the juror:

---

[15] N.C. GEN. STAT. § 15A-1212 (1988).

(1) Does not have the qualifications required [to be a juror: resident of county, over eighteen, understands English, no felony convictions].

(2) Is incapable by reason of mental or physical infirmity of rendering jury service.

(3) Has been or is a party, a witness, a grand juror, a trial juror, or otherwise has participated in civil or criminal proceedings involving a transaction which relates to the charge against the defendant.

(4) Has been or is a party adverse to the defendant in a civil action, or has complained against or been accused by him in a criminal prosecution.

(5) Is related by blood or marriage within the sixth degree to the defendant or the victim of the crime.

(6) Has formed or expressed an opinion as to the guilt or innocence of the defendant. It is improper for a party to elicit whether the opinion formed is favorable or adverse to the defendant.

(7) Is presently charged with a felony.

(8) As a matter of conscience, regardless of the facts and circumstances, would be unable to render a verdict with respect to the charge in accordance with the law.

(9) For any other cause is unable to render a fair and impartial verdict.

b. Peremptory Challenges

Peremptory challenges (called "strikes" in some jurisdictions) are given to both sides by statute. The number varies widely — from two or three in misdemeanor and civil cases to twenty-six in capital murder trials. In general, the parties are free to exercise peremptory challenges in any manner they see fit. In *Swain v. Alabama*,[16] the Supreme Court stated:

> The essential nature of the peremptory challenge is that it is one exercised without a reason stated, without inquiry and without being subject to the court's control. While challenges for cause permit rejection of jurors on a narrowly specified, provable and legally cognizable basis of partiality, the peremptory permits rejection for a real or imagined partiality that is less easily designated or demonstrable. It is often exercised upon the sudden impressions and unaccountable prejudices we are apt to conceive upon the bare looks and gestures of another, upon a juror's habits and associations, or upon grounds normally thought to be irrelevant.

There is one important restriction on this freedom, however. No party — neither the prosecutor, a criminal defendant nor any civil party — may exercise peremptory challenges in a racially discriminatory manner. You may not challenge prospective jurors just because you do not like their racial or ethnic background. In *Batson v. Kentucky*,[17] the Supreme Court stated:

> Purposeful racial discrimination in selection of the venire violates a defendant's right to equal protection because it denies him the protection that a trial by jury is supposed to secure. "The very idea of a jury is a body

---

[16] 380 U.S. 202 (1965).
[17] 476 U.S. 79 (1986).

... composed of the peers and equals of the person whose rights it is selected or summoned to determine." Racial discrimination in selection of jurors harms not only the accused whose life or liberty they are summoned to try.... [B]y denying a person participation in jury service on account of his race, the State unconstitutionally discriminate[s] against the excluded juror.... Selection procedures that purposefully exclude black persons from juries undermine public confidence in the fairness of our system of justice.... Although a prosecutor ordinarily is entitled to exercise permitted peremptory challenges "for any reason at all," ... the Equal Protection Clause forbids the prosecutor to challenge potential jurors solely on account of their race or on the assumption that black jurors as a group will be unable impartially to consider the State's case against a black defendant.

Under the Supreme Court's guidelines, if the prosecutor challenges all or most minority prospective jurors, the prosecutor must have a race-neutral explanation for each one. The reason must be legitimately connected to the case and may not be pretextual. In *Edmonson v. Leesville Concrete*,[18] the Supreme Court extended the no-discrimination rule to all civil litigants, and in *Georgia v. McCollum*,[19] to criminal defendants. Lower courts are also extending the *Batson* principle to gender discrimination, prohibiting parties from using their peremptory challenges to remove women from the jury just because they are women.[20]

4. THE SCOPE OF VOIR DIRE

a. Questions About Statutory Qualifications

It always is proper to question prospective jurors about whether they meet statutory requirements for jury service. In many jurisdictions, however, the jurors will be prescreened by a clerk for compliance with residency, age, English-speaking, prior jury service, and criminal record requirements. It also is common for the presiding judge to question jurors on their competency to sit on the particular case. Either the court or attorneys may ask jurors whether they have already formed opinions, whether they have been involved in the case or have relationships with any of the parties, and whether they can follow the law that applies, or may ask about any other matter upon which competency depends.

b. Questions Concerning Impartiality

The law in most jurisdictions permits the attorneys to challenge for cause any juror who cannot be fair and impartial for any reason. Thus, any questions that are legitimately intended to probe for bias or sympathy that could affect the neutrality of a prospective juror should be permitted, subject to the rule that jurors usually need not answer questions calculated to humiliate or

---

[18] 111 S. Ct. 2077 (1991).

[19] 112 S. Ct. 2348 (1992).

[20] *E.g., United States v. DeGross*, 930 F.2d 695 (9th Cir. 1990). *See* Shirley Sagawa, *Batson v. Kentucky: Will it Keep Women on the Jury?*, 3 BERKELEY WOMEN'S L.J. 14 (1988).

embarrass them.[21] The extent of the questions the judge will permit is largely a matter of discretion.[22] However, the following subjects are usually legitimate topics of inquiry:[23]

- Whether any juror knows anything about the facts of the case.
  Personal knowledge
  Exposure to pretrial publicity
  Rumors
- Whether any juror has a social relationship with a party, witness or attorney.
  Friendships
  Neighbors
  Related by blood or marriage
  Business associates
  Employment
  Landlord/tenant
  Members of the same or competing organization
  Membership in social clubs and service organizations
  Stockholder in close corporation
- Whether any juror has had experiences similar to those involved in the present case.
  Crime victim
  Accused of crime
  Witnessed a crime or accident
  Accident victim
  Caused an accident
  Brought suit
  Was sued
  Served as juror in a similar case
- Whether any juror has had life experiences similar to the parties or main witnesses.
  Similar marital status to a party
  Has children of ages similar to a party
  Military service
  Members of same profession or trade
- Whether any juror has a feeling of sympathy or antipathy toward a party, witness, or attorney based on lifestyle.
  Homosexuality
  Single parenthood
  Prior criminal record
  Receiving welfare assistance
  Alcohol or other drug use
  Sexual activity
  Gun ownership

---

[21] See, e.g., Abron v. State, 523 S.W.2d 405 (Tex. Crim. App. 1975).
[22] See, e.g., Hamilton v. State, 487 So. 2d 407 (Fla. App. 1986).
[23] The list was compiled primarily from FRANCIS X. BUSCH, LAW AND TACTICS IN JURY TRIALS, vol. 1: 561-89, 662-778 (1959). That text is accompanied by citation to well over two thousand cases.

- Whether any juror has prejudices against a group to which a party, witness or attorney belongs, such as:
    Corporations
    Racial minorities
    National origin or ethnicity
    Gender
    Law enforcement
    Labor unions
- Whether any juror has biases concerning social issues involved in the case.
    The insanity defense
    Alcohol consumption, especially drunk driving
    Drug use
    Crimes against children
    Intrafamily torts
    Sexual harassment
    Medical malpractice and the "litigation crisis"
    Environmental damage
    Gun use or possession
    Obscenity/pornography possession
    Race relations
- Whether any juror has already formed an opinion on the proper outcome of the case.
- Whether any juror's family members or close friends fall into any of these categories.

Answers that place a juror within one of these categories of potential bias do not lead automatically to a challenge for cause. Unless a state statute provides for automatic removal of the juror, it must appear from the questioning that the juror cannot be fair because of one or more of these factors. If the juror says that he or she can lay aside emotional responses and decide the case impartially, or denies that he or she would be influenced at all, a challenge for cause ordinarily will be denied.[24]

c. Questions About the Law

Somewhat more controversial is the practice of asking jurors about their willingness to follow the law, especially unpopular laws. A few judges prohibit such questions, on the naive assumption that all jurors will follow the judge's instructions, and therefore such questions are unnecessary. Even a casual analysis of this view shows that it is unworkable. Does anyone really think that a member of "Operation Rescue" would be willing to follow a judge's instructions concerning the legality of abortion?

The better view, followed by most judges,[25] is to permit questioning about jurors' attitudes toward legal issues that will arise in the case. As long as the

---

[24] See, e.g., Commonwealth v. Smith, 540 A.2d 246 (Pa. 1988); Johnson v. New Britain Gen. Hosp., 525 A.2d 1319 (Ct. 1987). Cf. Whalen v. State, 492 A.2d 552 (Del. 1985) (it is the judge who must be satisfied that the juror can genuinely put aside biases and feelings).

[25] See, e.g., Fortune, supra note 7, at 313-15 (survey revealed that 70% of Kentucky trial judges routinely permitted attorneys to question jurors about the law).

attorneys do not *misstate* the law, they are usually allowed to ask jurors about whether the jurors can follow the law. The modern view recognizes that many laws are highly controversial in our society. People are polarized and have strong feelings on laws ranging from medical malpractice and punitive damages to the insanity defense and the death penalty. An impartial jury can be seated only if the lawyers are permitted to explore whether jurors harbor any such biases. The inquiry cannot, however, turn into a test on jurors' knowledge of the law.[26]

d. Questions to Acquire Information for Exercising Peremptory Challenges

To the extent that an attorney uses his or her peremptory challenges to excuse biased jurors who could not be challenged successfully for cause, no additional questions will be needed beyond those searching for evidence of partiality. Any question that might result in a juror admitting that he or she could not be fair will be allowed. The answers, of course, also can form the basis for choosing whom to challenge peremptorily.

A problem arises when an attorney seeks to ask questions on voir dire solely for the purpose of gathering information on which to base his or her peremptory challenges. Some judges will allow this kind of questioning even if the relevancy of the information sought is not readily apparent. Most courts at least pay lip service to the principle that a broad scope of voir dire questioning is required to provide a basis for the intelligent exercise of peremptory challenges; otherwise, the right to peremptory challenges would be meaningless.[27] In practice, however, many judges are likely to curtail questioning that does not appear relevant to identifying biases and prejudices associated with the particular case. Questions attempting to elicit personal information — what magazines a juror reads, the television programs watched, level of education, and so on — will not always be allowed.[28]

e. Questions Used to Begin Advocacy

Trial lawyers often have suggested that the voir dire is the best time to begin the process of persuasion, by indoctrinating jurors on a partisan view of the facts and by ingratiating themselves and their clients with the jury. This technique commonly involves a recitation of favorable facts and an explanation of how they lead to a particular verdict. The most frequent form is the hypothetical question:

> Q: Mr. Smith, suppose the evidence showed that my client is crippled for life and unable to work or even go to the bathroom by himself. Could you return a verdict for $500,000 if that's what you thought it would take to compensate him?

---

[26] See *People v. Williams*, 628 P.2d 869 (Cal. 1981). See James H. Gold, *Voir Dire: Questioning Prospective Jurors on Their Willingness to Follow the Law*, 60 IND. L.J. 163, 166-88 (1984).
[27] E.g., *Mu'Min v. Virginia*, 111 S. Ct. 1899 (1991).
[28] See *Abron v. State*, 523 S.W.2d 405 (Tex. Crim. App. 1975).

Courts are split on whether this form of questioning is proper. The extent to which it will be allowed is largely a matter of judicial discretion. It can be argued that if the juror should answer "no," then he or she could be challenged for cause; therefore the question should be allowed. Some courts have adopted this view, and give attorneys a relatively free hand.[29] The majority position, however, is that hypothetical questions are not proper when it is obvious that they are being asked in an effort to precommit a juror to a particular verdict. It generally is improper to ask a juror what verdict he or she would give if certain facts were proved or whether the juror could arrive at a specific verdict by applying the anticipated instructions to an assumed set of facts.[30]

The other common indoctrination question is one that combines an argument with a question. These questions are either rhetorical or merely ask about (and emphasize) some universal aspect of human experience. For example:

> Have you ever greeted a stranger because he or she looked like someone you knew, or has a stranger ever greeted you because of mistaken identity?

Because it is obvious that most people have had this kind of experience, the question is unlikely to elicit any new information about the jurors that would be relevant to the intelligent exercise of challenges, and is therefore argumentative.[31]

5. ERROR AND PROTECTING THE RECORD

Grounds for appeal, of course, must be based on the erroneous action of the trial judge. It is difficult, however, for the trial judge to commit clear error during jury selection because control of voir dire is almost completely a matter of judicial discretion. Unless the judge obviously has obstructed the seating of an impartial jury,[32] there is little chance that a ruling during voir dire will warrant reversal. For example, in *Ristaino v. Ross*,[33] the trial judge refused to permit the jurors to be questioned about racial prejudice in a trial with obvious racial overtones; the Supreme Court upheld the decision as being within the judge's discretion.

Even if an error is committed, it must be properly preserved for appeal. In many courts, preserving error in voir dire is nearly impossible because the procedure is not transcribed. The minimal requirement for preserving an allegation of error is to move that the court have a reporter present so that the objection and its basis will appear in the record.

If you challenge a juror for cause, and the judge overrules you, you can appeal only if you have complied with the following requirements:

---

[29] *E.g., Beaver v. State*, 736 S.W.2d 212 (Tex. App. 1987).

[30] *Renny v. State*, 543 So. 2d 420 (Fla. App. 1989); *Hopkins v. State*, 429 N.E.2d 631 (Ind. 1981).

[31] *See People v. Bowel*, 111 Ill. 2d 58 (1986).

[32] *See, e.g., Parkinson v. Hudson*, 265 Ala. 4, 88 So. 2d 793 (1956); *People v. Diedtman*, 58 Mont. 13, 190 P. 117 (1920).

[33] 424 U.S. 589 (1976) (black defendant charged with attempted murder of white security guard).

- *Specificity.* You must have clearly stated grounds for your challenge. A general challenge ("I challenge this juror for cause") is not sufficient. The court must be told the reasons.[34]
- *Timeliness.* Your challenge to the juror must have been timely. In many states, challenges for cause must be made as soon as the grounds become apparent, and before any peremptory challenges are exercised. In any event, you must exercise a challenge before the juror is seated and sworn.[35]

If your opponent challenges a juror for cause that should be denied, but the court erroneously grants it, you can appeal only if you make a timely objection (contemporaneous with the judge's ruling) and explain why you believe the challenge should not be allowed.[36]

Objections to particular lines of questioning are subject to similar specificity and timeliness requirements. If you want to prevent your opponent from asking prejudicial questions, e.g., raising the issue of insurance, you must make a timely objection stating specific grounds. If you are prevented from pursuing a legitimate line of inquiry, you must have made a motion to allow the questions, stating specific legal grounds.[37]

One final procedural trap may catch the unwary. If you fail to exhaust all your peremptory challenges, you cannot claim error on the wrongful denial of a challenge for cause, since you could have excused that juror. You must have no peremptory challenges left, so that you cannot remove the juror in question.[38] In some states, a claim of error also will be preserved if you use your last peremptory challenge to remove a juror who should have been removed for cause, if you are thereby unable to challenge another undesirable juror.

NOTES

1. ***Extent of questioning and judicial discretion.*** Although the topics discussed above are permissible areas of questioning, the judge does not have to allow them. Little other than the discretion of the presiding judge controls whether a particular topic may be raised or how extensively it may be pursued in a given case. *Compare Ham v. South Carolina,* 409 U.S. 524 (1973) (trial judge's refusal to question jurors extensively about racial prejudice was error in a case with overtones of racial conflict), *with Ristaino v. Ross,* 424 U.S. 589 (1976) (no error in judge's refusal to question about racial prejudice where victims were white and defendant black).

2. ***Judicial control of attorney-conducted voir dire.*** Just because attorneys are permitted to conduct voir dire does not mean they have unlimited freedom. Judges will often intervene and take control to cut off irrelevant or protracted questioning. William Fortune, *Voir Dire in Kentucky: An Empirical Study of Voir Dire in Kentucky Circuit Courts,* 69 Ky. L.J. 273, 297-98, 301

---

[34] *See Dukes v. State,* 578 S.W.2d 659 (Tenn. Crim. App. 1979).

[35] *E.g., Spencer v. Commonwealth,* 384 S.E.2d 785 (Va. 1989).

[36] *See Green v. State,* 771 S.W.2d 576 (Tex. App. 1989).

[37] *See Ramseyer v. Dennis,* 187 Ind. 420, 119 N.E. 716 (1917).

[38] *See, e.g., State v. Anaya,* 553 A.2d 297 (N.H. 1988); *Hopkins v. State,* 429 N.E.2d 631 (Ind. 1981).

(1981). In David U. Strawn, *Ending the Voir Dire Wars,* JUDGES J., Spring 1979, at 45, one judge suggests that judges should intervene and stop attorney questioning in the following situations:

(1) Questions about a juror's emotional response to legal concepts.

(2) Redundant voir dire, especially questions about legal principles already explained.

(3) Attempts to elicit commitments from jurors about facts, legal principles, or verdicts.

(4) Questions concerning the appropriateness or morality of the litigation.

(5) Hypothetical questions about the kind of verdict a juror might return if certain evidence were produced.

(6) Attempts to curry favor with the jurors.

(7) Questions likely to aggravate prejudice or racial bias.

3. What do judges really do? There are three empirical studies of what judges really do: GORDON BERMANT, CONDUCT OF THE VOIR DIRE EXAMINATION: PRACTICES AND OPINIONS OF FEDERAL DISTRICT JUDGES (1977); William Fortune, *Voir Dire in Kentucky: An Empirical Study of Voir Dire in Kentucky Circuit Courts,* 69 KY. L.J. 273, 297-98, 301 (1981); William H. Levitt et al., *Expediting Voir Dire: An Empirical Study,* 44 S. CAL. L. REV. 916 (1971). All showed a wide variety of practices regardless of the formal rule of procedure.

4. Is there a right to participate in voir dire? S. Mac Gutman argues in *The Attorney-Conducted Voir Dire of Jurors: A Constitutional Right,* 39 BROOK. L. REV. 290 (1972), that because the Sixth Amendment guarantees a defendant the right to an impartial jury, a criminal defendant has a right to participate directly in questioning jurors. *See People v. Williams,* 29 Cal. 3d 392, 628 P.2d 869 (1981) (reversing rule prohibiting criminal defense attorney from conducting voir dire). However, this view has not been adopted generally by the courts.

5. Use of visual aids. Case law is sparse on whether voir dire may be illustrated with exhibits, charts, or the use of a blackboard. In *Eichstadt v. Underwood,* 337 S.W.2d 684 (Ky. 1960), the court held that the plaintiff was permitted to use a blackboard during voir dire to write out the total damages requested. *But see Finley v. State,* 84 Okla. Cr. 309, 181 P.2d 849 (1947) (the use of mug shot photographs to identify probable witnesses was too prejudicial); *Palmer v. State,* 121 Tenn. 465, 118 S.W. 1022 (1908) (use of newspaper article was properly refused).

6. Sample juror questionnaires. The following is a typical juror questionnaire. It comes from MICHIGAN GENERAL COURT RULE 510 (1990):

JUROR PERSONAL HISTORY QUESTIONNAIRE

TO THE JUROR: You have already been found generally qualified to serve as a juror. However, you may or may not be suitable for service in a given case. In order to find out whether you are suitable for service in each case, you will be questioned by the judge or attorneys. Certain questions are asked in most cases, and to save time you are being required to fill out this questionnaire so that those questions do not have to be asked in court. You can appreciate the time and money this questionnaire will save. The questions asked in this questionnaire are questions which could be asked of you in open court. You are therefore given more privacy by having you answer them in this questionnaire. You are required by the rules of the Supreme Court to answer the questions truthfully. Refusal to answer, or the giving of a false answer, subjects you to fine or imprisonment, or both, for contempt of court. As you answer the questions it will become obvious to you why such questions must be asked.

ANSWERS MUST BE WRITTEN OR PRINTED BY THE JUROR HIMSELF.
1. Print name plainly: _____
              Last name   First name   Middle name
   (a) State any legal changes of name including maiden and previous married names. _____
2. Address: _____
         Street address   City or village   Telephone
   (a) How many miles will you travel from your home to the Court House? _____
3. When and where were you born? _____
             Give exact date
4. Sex: _____
5. Marital status (check one): Single ( ); Married ( ); Divorced ( ); Separated ( ); Widow or Widower ( ).
6. Name of spouse: _____
7. Occupation of spouse: _____
8. Spouse employed by: _____
9. Ages and number of children at home: _____

10. Have you any defects in your hearing? _____
11. Have you any defects in your vision? _____
12. Is your general health good? _____
13. Have you any physical infirmity? (Explain) _____

14. State briefly the extent of your business or professional experience or other employment: _____

15. What is your present occupation? _____
    If not employed give line of work. _____
16. Employed by: _____
17. If not employed, state your present means of livelihood (for example, housewife; pension; etc.) _____

18. What duties do you perform in your present job? _____

19. State what other occupations you have been in during the past 10 years and what duties you performed: _____

20. Are you, or have you ever been, an office-holder for any state, county, or municipality? (Specify) _____

21. Are you, or have you ever been, a law enforcement officer? (Specify) _____

22. Are you an employer, landlord, or tenant? (Specify) _____

23. Are you a freeholder (owner of real estate)? _____
    What county? _____

24. Have you ever studied law? (Explain): _____

25. Have you ever studied medicine? (Explain): _____

26. How far did you go in school? (Indicate highest grade completed or degrees received): _____

27. Have you ever served as a juror? _____

28. If so, when and in what courts? _____

29. Have you ever been discharged (not excused) from jury service? _____

30. If so, for what cause? _____

31. Do you drive a car? _____

32. Do you (or your spouse) own a car? _____

33. If so, is it insured? _____

34. With what company? _____

35. Have you ever been in an accident? (Explain): _____

36. Were you injured? _____

37. Was anyone else injured? (Explain): _____

38. Has any member of your family, or a close friend ever been in an accident? If so, explain: _____

39. Are you a director of, or do you own stock in, any insurance companies? ___

40. What companies? _____

41. Were you ever an inmate in a state or county institution? (Explain): _____

42. Have you ever been convicted of a crime or misdemeanor (other than for a non-moving traffic violation)? _____

43. If so, explain: _____

44. Have you ever been arrested and charged with any crime? (Explain): _____

45. If so, is that charge pending? _____

46. Have you ever been a party to any suit, either civil or criminal? _____

47. If so, state the nature and number of each suit and in what court:

_____

_____

_____

I certify that I have answered the above questions fully and truthfully. I
realize that a false answer subjects me to the penalties for contempt of court.

_____   _____
Date   Signature of Juror

See also William Fortune, *Voir Dire in Kentucky: An Empirical Study of Voir
Dire in Kentucky Circuit Courts*, 69 KY. L.J. 273, 323-26 (1981); ANN FAGAN
GINGER, JURY SELECTION IN CIVIL AND CRIMINAL TRIALS §§ 12.2 to 12.31 (2d
ed. 1984).

   7. *Opposition to the death penalty.* In *Witherspoon v. Illinois*, 391 U.S.
510 (1968), the Supreme Court held that prospective jurors may be challenged
for cause if they are so opposed to the death penalty that they would automatically vote against it, regardless of the facts of the case. This process has
become known as "death qualifying" a jury, and the removable jurors are
often called "Witherspoon excludables." The Supreme Court made it clear that
jurors may *not* be challenged for cause merely because they do not believe in
the death penalty or have conscientious or religious scruples against the in-
fliction of the death penalty. Only if they state that under no circumstances
would they vote to impose capital punishment are they excludable. The Court
held:

> A man who opposes the death penalty, no less than one who favors it can
> make the discretionary judgment entrusted to him by the State and can
> thus obey the oath he takes as a juror. But a jury from which all such men
> have been excluded cannot perform the task demanded of it. Guided by
> neither rule nor standard, "free to select or reject as it [sees] fit," a jury
> that must choose between life imprisonment and capital punishment can
> do little more — and must do nothing less — than express the conscience
> of the community on the ultimate question of life or death. Yet, in a
> nation less than half of whose people believe in the death penalty, a jury
> composed exclusively of such people cannot speak for the community.
> Culled of all who harbor doubts about the wisdom of capital punishment
> — of all who would be reluctant to pronounce the extreme penalty — such
> a jury can speak only for a distinct and dwindling minority.... In its quest
> for a jury capable of imposing the death penalty, the State produced a jury
> uncommonly willing to condemn a man to die.

   8. *The struck jury.* A few states use a struck jury as an alternative to the
peremptory challenge system. Under this procedure, an entire panel of jurors
is questioned, and then the attorneys alternately strike jurors until only the
requisite number remain. There is considerable variation among the states
that use a struck jury. It may be an available alternative to a common jury, or
the exclusive method of selection. A small panel may be called from which
only a few names can be struck, *e.g.*, VA. CODE § 8.01-359 (in routine civil

cases eleven jurors are called and six struck), or the list may include the names of all empaneled jurors. The Alabama statute reads as follows:

> § 12-16-100. *Drawing, selection and empaneling of juries in criminal cases.* In every criminal case the jury shall be drawn, selected and empaneled as follows: Upon the trial by jury in the circuit courts of any person indicted for a misdemeanor, or felonies not punished capitally or upon appeals to the circuit courts from lower courts, the court shall require two lists of all the regular jurors empaneled for the week who are competent to try the defendant to be made, and the district attorney shall be required first to strike from the list the name of one juror, and the defendant shall strike two, and they shall continue to strike off names alternately until only 12 jurors remain on the list and these 12 jurors thus selected shall be the jury charged with the trial of the case.

9. *Waiver problems.* You should make sure that all challenges for cause have been made before you exercise any peremptory challenges; otherwise the right to challenge for cause may be waived. *Bitting v. State*, 165 Ga. 55, 139 S.E. 877 (1927).

10. *The number of peremptory challenges.* The number of peremptory challenges allotted to each side varies considerably with the state, the size of the jury, and the type of case. Generally, both sides have the same number of challenges, but some jurisdictions give more challenges to a criminal defendant than a prosecutor. The total number can range from twenty-six in capital cases to two or three in misdemeanor and civil cases. If there are multiple parties on one side, that side may or may not be permitted extra challenges. *See, e.g.*, FED. R. CRIM. P. 24(b) (in capital cases, twenty for each side; in other felonies the prosecution has six and the defense ten; three each in misdemeanors); ARIZ. R. CIV. P. 47(e) (four each in civil cases); CAL. PENAL CODE § 1070 (twenty-six in capital cases); IOWA CODE § 813.2, Rule 17 (two each in misdemeanors).

11. *Challenges to the array.* Another form of challenge is the challenge to the array, or entire venire. Such a challenge must be based on errors in the method by which jurors have been summoned, that have resulted in a venire which is not representative of the demographics of the community. The Supreme Court has held that a criminal defendant has a right to a fair possibility for obtaining a representative cross section of the community on any jury. An impartial trial is denied by the systematic exclusion of African-Americans, *Peters v. Kiff*, 407 U.S. 493 (1972); women, *Taylor v. Louisiana*, 419 U.S. 522 (1975); or those with general objections to the death penalty, *Witherspoon v. Illinois*, 391 U.S. 510 (1968). Challenges to the array generally are made before trial upon written motion. *See* JAMES GOBERT & WALTER E. JORDAN, JURY SELECTION 145-91 (2d ed. 1990).

12. *Disqualifications and exemptions.* Disqualifications and exemptions from jury service often are confused with challenges for cause. In most juris-

dictions, statutes declare certain persons disqualified to serve as jurors at all. For example, 28 U.S.C. § 1865(b) provides:

> [A]ny person [is] qualified to serve on grand and petit juries in the district court unless [the person]:
>
> (1) is not a citizen of the United States eighteen years old who has resided for a period of one year within the judicial district;
>
> (2) is unable to read, write, and understand the English language with a degree of proficiency sufficient to fill out satisfactorily the juror qualification form;
>
> (3) is unable to speak the English language;
>
> (4) is incapable, by reason of mental or physical infirmity, to render satisfactory jury service; or
>
> (5) has a charge pending against him [or her] for the commission of, or has been convicted in a State or Federal court of record of, a crime punishable by imprisonment for more than one year and his [or her] civil rights have not been restored.

Other statutes specifically exempt persons who have certain occupations from jury duty. This is like a privilege, belonging only to the juror, who may waive the exemption and serve. A party may not challenge such a juror for cause on the ground that he or she is exempt. Most states exempt attorneys, physicians, dentists, pharmacists, military personnel, fire fighters, clergy, school teachers, government officials, and persons over a certain age. Francis X. Busch has collected more than ninety occupations exempt in at least one state, including everything from embalmers and fruit growers to librarians and school janitors. LAW AND TACTICS IN JURY TRIALS, vol 1: 457-60 (1959). Disqualified and exempt jurors are generally sent home by the judge or clerk long before they ever get called to a particular courtroom.

13. *Alternate Jurors.* Some jurisdictions select alternate jurors who serve if a regular juror becomes ill. If they are used, alternate jurors are selected through the same voir dire process, and the parties generally are given one or two extra peremptory challenges. Federal Rule of Civil Procedure 47(b) used to permit alternate jurors, but ended the practice in 1992. The advisory committee noted that this procedure was a major source of dissatisfaction with the jury system, because people had to sit through trials as alternate jurors and then were not allowed to participate in deliberations. Alternate jurors are not needed anyway, because the modern view is that juries do not have to consist of twelve people. If a juror becomes ill, the trial may proceed with eleven jurors and still reach a lawful verdict.

14. *Questions about exposure to pretrial publicity.* It is generally accepted that jurors can be questioned about their exposure to media coverage in a notorious case. *See, e.g., Fietzer v. Ford Motor Co.*, 622 F.2d 281 (7th Cir. 1980), involving a negligence claim against Ford for faulty design of a fuel tank that exploded on impact. The court held that if a party can show exten-

sive pretrial publicity, a presumption of prejudice arises that requires the trial judge to question the jurors on whether it has influenced them:

> [The judge] should have asked the jurors if any one of them had read or had heard about the article and, if so, whether anything read or heard stood out in his or her mind. After determining the jurors' degree of exposure to and interest in the article, the court would then have been able to have inquired whether he or she had formed an opinion about Ford's relative negligence in the case.

Id. at 286. *See also* Marjorie Schultz, *The Jury Redefined: A Review of Burger Court Decisions*, 43 LAW & CONTEMP. PROBS. 8, 21-22 (1980). The exercises may be futile, however, because jurors rarely admit they have been affected. Gary Moran & Brian Cutler, *The Prejudicial Impact of Pretrial Publicity*, 21 J. APP. SOC. PSYCHOL. 345 (1991).

15. *Questions that disclose the existence of insurance.* Because jurors can be questioned about their interest in or attitudes about the parties, they also should be subject to questions about their connections with or interest in the insurance companies that ultimately will pay the damages. *See, e.g., Carothers v. Montgomery Ward*, 745 S.W.2d 170 (Mo. App. 1987). Yet, some people fear that if disinterested jurors know the defendant is insured, they will award damages because "it's all going to be paid out of insurance anyway." The cases vary considerably on the extent to which insurance can be disclosed on voir dire. In general terms, good faith inquiry is permitted to determine if jurors will be influenced in their decisions by their interest in an insurance company. In many courts, the attorney must make a prima facie showing that such inquiry is justified (e.g., by a juror's answering a general question about occupation by stating the juror works for Allstate). Questions designed merely to inject the issue of insurance are not permitted and may constitute reversible error. *See* Alan Calnan, *The Admissibility of Insurance Questions During Voir Dire: a Critical Survey of Federal Approaches and Proposals for Change*, 44 RUTGERS L. REV. 241 (1992).

16. *Inquiring about religious beliefs.* Inquiring about a juror's religious beliefs usually is improper unless a religious issue is involved in the case. *United States v. Barnes*, 604 F.2d 121 (2d Cir. 1979); *Yarborough v. United States*, 230 F.2d 56 (4th Cir. 1956). *But see Wasy v. State*, 234 Ind. 52, 123 N.E.2d 462 (1955) (abortion case).

17. *Asking for jurors' home address.* *See United States v. Barnes*, 604 F.2d 121 (2d Cir. 1979), in which the judge refused to allow information on the background of jurors out of fear for their safety in the trial of a New York City drug kingpin.

D. ETHICAL CONSIDERATIONS

1. GENERAL STANDARDS

The MODEL RULES OF PROFESSIONAL CONDUCT contain no provision that explicitly applies to jury selection. Only the general prohibitions apply. A lawyer may not:

- Make "a false statement of material fact or law to a tribunal."[39]
- "Knowingly disobey an obligation under the rules of a tribunal."[40]
- Allude "to any matter that the lawyer does not reasonably believe is relevant or that will not be supported by admissible evidence."[41]
- "Assert personal knowledge of the facts in issue ... or state a personal opinion as to the justness of a cause, the credibility of a witness, the culpability of a civil litigant or the guilt or innocence of an accused."[42]

The American Bar Association, Standards for Criminal Justice, however, contain a specific provision addressing jury selection:

Standard 4-7.2. Selection of jurors

(a) The lawyer should prepare himself or herself prior to trial to discharge effectively his or her function in the selection of the jury, including the raising of any appropriate issues concerning the method by which the jury panel was selected and the exercise of both challenges for cause and peremptory challenges.

(b) In those cases where it appears necessary to conduct a pretrial investigation of the background of jurors, investigatory methods of the lawyer should neither harass nor unduly embarrass potential jurors or invade their privacy and, whenever possible, should be restricted to an investigation of records and sources of information already in existence.

(c) The opportunity to question jurors personally should be used solely to obtain information for the intelligent exercise of challenges. A lawyer should not intentionally use the voir dire to present factual matter which the lawyer knows will not be admissible at trial or to argue the lawyer's case to the jury.

Commentary

The process of voir dire examination of prospective jurors by the lawyer is often needlessly time consuming and is frequently used to influence the jury in its view of the case.... [Lawyers must] limit questions to those that are designed to lay a basis for the lawyer's challenges. The observation that the voir dire may be used to influence the jury in its views of the case is rejected as an improper use of the right of reasonable inquiry .... The use of the voir dire to inject inadmissible evidence into the case is a substantial abuse of the process. Treatment of legal points in the course of voir dire examination should be strictly confined to those inquiries bearing on possible bias in relation to issues in the case.

2. INTENTIONAL VIOLATION OF PROPER JURY SELECTION PROCEDURE

MODEL RULES OF PROFESSIONAL CONDUCT Rule 3.4(c) states that a lawyer shall not "knowingly disobey an obligation under the rules of a tribunal." It is

---

[39] Rule 3.3(a)(1).
[40] Rule 3.4(c).
[41] Rule 3.4(e).
[42] Rule 3.4(e).

therefore unethical to intentionally violate the rules of proper voir dire. You may not ask an improper question or engage in illegal conduct and then withdraw it or apologize if you get caught. That may satisfy the legal requirement by removing improper matter from the jury's consideration, but it is still unethical. Under this general rule, it is unethical to:

- Engage in racially motivated peremptory challenges and then come up with clever "non-racial" justifications for them.
- Ask fact-specific hypothetical questions, in jurisdictions that prohibit them.
- Elicit promises from jurors that they will return a specific verdict.
- Use questions about exposure to *favorable* pretrial publicity as an excuse to inform other jurors about the publicity.
- Ask questions that disclose inadmissible evidence (especially the defendant's large insurance policy) without a good faith basis for believing it will lead to the discovery of biased jurors.

3. REVEALING PERSONAL INFORMATION ABOUT YOURSELF

Russ Herman, past-president of the Association of Trial Lawyers of America, suggests that you should reveal private things about yourself during voir dire. It will make jurors more comfortable revealing personal information about themselves, and will help jurors identify with you. He suggests the following question:

> Jurors, this case invokes a claim by a seven-year-old boy against a toy manufacturer. *As the father of a boy and two girls, I am familiar with the brand name "X"*. Tell me, juror Edwards, do you have children? What are their ages? Can you tell what you know about brand "X"? How do you select toys for your eight-year-old son, Tony?[43]

In a similar vein, Gerry Spence, one of the best known trial lawyers in the country, suggests the following question:

> I want to introduce you to some of *my friends*. I'd like you to meet our clerk of the court, Mr. Jones. Another one of *my friends* is the reporter here. He's a very important person.[44]

Indeed, since a good voir dire is like a conversation between you and the jurors, it is almost impossible to conduct a good one without referring to yourself, revealing information about yourself, and forging personal ties between yourself and some of the jurors.

However, MODEL RULES OF PROFESSIONAL CONDUCT Rule 3.4 prohibits you from asserting your own personal knowledge of facts or stating your opinions about any aspect of the case. It may be effective advocacy for you to try to make friends with the jurors and ingratiate yourself with them, but there are

---

[43] Russ M. Herman, *Jury Selection in Civil Litigation*, TRIAL, Jan. 1989, at 71, 76 (emphasis added).

[44] Gerry Spence, *A Voir Dire Masterpiece*, TRIAL DIPL. J., Fall 1980, at 8, 9-10, 56 (emphasis added).

limits. You cannot accomplish this by violating the rule against injecting your own personal experiences into the trial.

NOTES

1. *The ethics of investigating jurors.* Lawyers often conduct some investigation of prospective jurors in advance of voir dire. The law and rules of ethics permit you to do this, as long as you do not violate the rule against improperly influencing them. The old MODEL CODE OF PROFESSIONAL RESPONSIBILITY DR 7-108(A) prohibited lawyers and investigators from communicating directly with any person known to be a prospective juror. This prohibition was subsumed by the new Model Rule 3.5, which prohibits both attempts to influence and any ex parte communication with prospective jurors. The prohibition against direct communication probably extends to jurors' families and close friends. *See* MODEL CODE OF PROFESSIONAL RESPONSIBILITY EC 7-31. Discreet investigations that do not invade the jurors' privacy are ethical.

2. *Using social science consultants.* Some lawyers have hired social science consultants to help them identify and remove biased jurors. A few writers have suggested that this is unethical, or at least somehow a subversion of the trial process. Some have made wild accusations that social scientists can somehow read prospective jurors' minds and may be able to stack the jury. Amitai Etzioni, a sociologist, has written ominous articles about the power of this new technique, arguing that it is so effective it should be banned as unfair, comparing the application of social science to jury selection with Adam's legendary bite of the apple. Amitai Etzioni, *Creating an Imbalance*, TRIAL at 28 (Nov.-Dec. 1974); *Threatening the Jury Trial*, WASH. POST, May 26, 1974, at C3, col. 1. If any of these assumptions about scientific jury selection were true, it would raise serious ethical issues. Responsible social scientists who have examined empirical data conclude that social scientists have no such power, that individual characteristics are relatively unimportant factors in most juror decisions, and that scientific jury selection is not significantly better at identifying biased jurors than the intuitions of experienced trial lawyers. *See* Reid Hastie, *Is Attorney-Conducted Voir Dire an Effective Procedure for the Selection of Impartial Juries*, 40 AMER. U.L. REV. 703, 718-19 (1991); Michael J. Saks, *Blaming the Jury*, 75 GEO. L.J. 693, 710-11 (1986); VALERIE HANS & NEIL VIDMAR, JUDGING THE JURY 90 (1986).

One moral issue remains. John McConahay, Courtney Mullin, & Jeffrey Frederick, *The Uses of Social Science in Trials with Political and Racial Overtones: the Trial of Joan Little*, 41 LAW AND CONTEMP. PROBS. 205 (1977) summarize their concern:

> We also are concerned, with Etzioni and others, that the use of these expensive techniques will magnify the already huge disparity between the quality of defense available to the rich and well-connected, and that available to the poor and marginal.... Moreover, routine use of these techniques by both prosecution and defense may simply cause each side to cancel the other out while raising the cost of a jury trial to both. Thus, we may raise the status quo ante in a system of justice that is already very expensive to both sides.

However, the problem of disparity of resources pervades society generally. It is hardly an issue of trial ethics. The whole issue is thoroughly discussed in Michael Saks, *The Limits of Scientific Jury Selection: Ethical and Empirical*, 17 JURIMETRICS 3 (1976).

E. PREPARATION AND PLANNING

Planning for jury selection does not occur in a vacuum, but as an integral part of your overall trial preparation. The choices you make concerning purpose, method, and questions should be based on your theory of the case. You will have to decide what you want to accomplish, what kind of jurors to look for, and what questions to pursue. Each of these concerns is discussed in more detail in the sections that follow.

1. PURPOSES OF VOIR DIRE

Before any detailed preparation can take place, you must decide exactly what you hope to accomplish in your voir dire. Most experienced trial lawyers suggest three main purposes:

- *Information.* Elicit information from prospective jurors upon which to base challenges.
- *Indoctrination.* Begin the process of presenting your case by focusing on the main points that make up the core of your theory.
- *Ingratiation.* Introduce yourself and your client to the jury in a favorable way; at least try not to alienate the panel.

The primary goal obviously is to obtain information that will help you identify and eliminate jurors likely to be hostile to your side of the case. However, there are a number of secondary goals lawyers often try to achieve during voir dire, as long as they do not interfere with the primary task of intelligent jury selection. These goals are summarized in David Crump, *Attorneys' Goals and Tactics in Voir Dire Examination*, 43 TEX. B.J. 244, 244-46 (1980):

> 1. *Emphasizing Favorable Law or Facts.* An attorney will usually simplify and explain [favorable] law ... in a way that makes it seem even more favorable. Thus a criminal defense lawyer will make an effort to define the prosecution's burden of proof so as to make it appear as heavy a burden as possible. A plaintiff's personal injury lawyer will explain that negligence means, simply, "carelessness."
>
> 2. *Limiting the Effect of Unfavorable Law.* In response to the defense lawyer's tactic of making the prosecution's burden of proof seem insurmountable, a prosecutor may ... talk about that burden — emphasizing the proper limits of it, saying, for example, that proof beyond a reasonable doubt does not mean proof beyond "all" doubt, or "a shadow of" a doubt, but a proof in the light of reasonableness." A personal injury defense lawyer will counter the plaintiff's gambit in equating negligence and carelessness by putting negligence in terms of the jury having to find "my client guilty of an unreasonable act" before finding negligence.

When done by skillful lawyers on both sides, this dialectic may lead to a better understanding by the jury of the concepts involved. When the skill of the lawyers is not balanced, however, the result can be lopsided.

3. *Inoculation Against Unfavorable Facts.* If the client has a felony conviction that is going to become known to the jury when he testifies, a lawyer often decides that it would be unwise to wait until that time to introduce the jury to it. The evidence may seem less catastrophic if the jurors have been expecting it all along. This technique is called "inoculation." Just as in medicine a vaccine inoculates against disease by introducing an element of the disease-causing agent into the body, so this use of voir dire examination inoculates against the unfavorable fact.[45] The lawyer may even succeed in persuading the jurors, before the trial even begins, that the conviction lacks relevance — "the mere fact of conviction — that wouldn't prejudice you? You wouldn't be unfair to him?"

4. *Obtaining Commitments.* "If I introduce evidence showing that my client has suffered substantially, could you award ... substantial damages — as the law requires? If you find that you're saying to yourself, it'd take more than a million dollars to compensate for that suffering, would you have any hesitation in awarding such an amount?" The lawyer presents the law to the jury as "the law," which the jurors must follow — and obtains their commitment to do so. The theory is that after having given such a commitment, the jurors are more likely to follow the law as the lawyer wishes them to.[46]

5. *Personalizing the Client.* A lawyer may introduce [the] client, tell a little about him [or her], or have [the client] stand and face the jury. Sometimes, this technique can be effectively used in conjunction with commitments from the jury: "Can you promise me that you'll require the prosecution to prove the case beyond a reasonable doubt? And — more importantly — can you promise John,[47] as he sits here on the hot seat, that you'll require the prosecution to prove the case beyond a reasonable doubt?" The client is John, not Mr. Smith — except that he is Mr. Smith, or John James Smith when referred to by the opposition. Incidentally, a corporation, to the lawyer representing it, becomes not "X Corporation" but (when an employee has sat through the trial in the view of the jury and they have gotten to know him) "John's company."

6. *Arguing the Case Itself.* Some lawyers use the voir dire examination as a kind of opening statement, highlighting the facts they want the jurors to anticipate. Some facts have to be given the jurors in order for them to answer questions intelligently. In the adversary system, it is inevitable that the facts become stated in an adversary light.

---

[45] Experiments by psychologists seem to verify this assertion. *See, e.g.*, William J. McGuire, *Inducing Resistance to Persuasion: Some Contemporary Approaches, in* ADVANCES IN EXPERIMENTAL SOCIAL PSYCHOLOGY 192 (L. Berkowitz ed. 1964).

[46] Classic social psychological research indicates that public commitments increase the likelihood that the promised behavior will be enacted. *See* JEFFREY T. FREDERICK, THE PSYCHOLOGY OF THE AMERICAN JURY 146-48 (1987).

[47] *But cf.* MINN. GEN. R. PRAC. 2: "During court proceedings, counsel shall not exhibit familiarity with the judge, jurors, witnesses, [or] parties ..., nor address them by first names."

7. *Conditioning the Jurors to Accept One's Proof.* This is a subtle tactic. It works in an indirect way. If, for example, one has a lot of evidence but expects the other side to nibble at it and seek to exclude as much as possible, one might depict oneself as just "trying to get all the facts out as expeditiously as possible" and might express the hope that one's adversary, Mr. Jones, "will be trying to do the same thing." If, on the other hand, one has very little evidence — only one's client, who is not enormously credible — one might point out that it is not the number of witnesses that counts, adding: "I always wonder about lawyers who drag a trial out with a string of witnesses. We probably could do that in this case. But I believe in getting right to the heart of the matter, and I've boiled the testimony I'm going to present right down to the essentials."[48] This statement might be followed with a request that the jury not hold it against one's client because one is going to try the case on the facts and without "a lot of irrelevant material thrown in." This tactic works because the jurors do not know that the lawyer who is using it tried another case last week in which he put on a complete dog-and-pony show.

Another way to get the jurors to accept one's proof is to get them committed to accepting proof that actually is weaker than one intends to introduce. One might, for example, explain that the law provides that the evidence of one witness is sufficient. That makes sense, one might add, because often persons who do wrong do it outside the view of large numbers of witnesses — sometimes with no witnesses at all — and if you have one witness who is credible, one is lucky. Can the jurors follow the law and find in one's favor, if there is only one witness but that witness is credible, the lawyer might ask? Of course, the case that the lawyer intends to present has not one witness but three, and the evidence is corroborated by physical evidence — and so the jurors will learn when the case is presented.

8. *Building Rapport.* Extreme diplomacy is called for. The jurors should be treated with as much politeness as is possible (but jurors will not respect a lawyer who doesn't protect his client adequately, so don't hold back from relevant questions unduly). The use of humor, homely analogies and folksy mannerisms, however corny they may appear, often pays off. "This case is sort of like what the old mountain man said about his pancakes: 'No matter how thin I slice 'em, there is always two sides.'" A silly thing to say, and not very highbrow humor — but if used properly, it can bring broad smiles from jurors who are tired of being herded around and a little leery of lawyers anyway.

Another technique is to orient the jurors in a way that shows concern for their function, comfort and duties — without appearing fawning. Explaining what is about to happen in the trial, for example, or what the questions will be like, can help, as can the statement, "I know those benches are getting hard to sit on; I think they must order special, extrahard benches for every courthouse."

---

[48]The ethics of this question are dubious. It makes personal references to the attorney and constitutes a false statement of fact to a tribunal.

9. *Stealing One's Adversary's Thunder.* "At the end of this case, no matter what the evidence shows, Mr. Jones is going to argue that his client ought to get a huge sum of money. He may even be extremely emotional. You ought to expect that, in fact. It's his job. But if the evidence shows otherwise, can you ignore all that emotional argument and decide this case on the evidence?"

10. *Increasing or Decreasing the Impact of Concerns That Are Outside the Evidence.* This tactic is often ethically dubious. Even though insurance may be outside the allowable evidence, for instance, the plaintiff's lawyer may imply the existence of insurance — indirectly. "Anyone work for an insurance company? Can you be fair, even though you work for a company that furnishes defense lawyers to individuals just like the defendant here on trial, Mr. Smith?" This sort of comment would not only raise ethical questions; it might be grounds for a mistrial. This kind of brinkmanship, however, is common in voir dire examination. It is the kind of effort that the adversary system calls forth from many lawyers, if not most.

There are a host of other concerns that can be relevant to mention in voir dire [even though] they are irrelevant to the case. Race of one's client (commitment to disregard it), the fact a corporation is a party — the list is endless. It comes down to this: one should think of all the factors — both within and without the evidence — that one would think might influence a juror and conduct the voir dire examination accordingly.

Sometimes the effort is to emphasize, rather than de-emphasize, matters outside the evidence. "Would anyone feel sympathy for the man on the other side, Mr. Jones, because two years ago his chauffeur had an accident that dented his Rolls-Royce?" Such a question would be dubious. But there may be legitimate uses even of this technique, in other circumstances.

11. *Guiding the Conduct of the Jurors in Deliberations.* Attorneys have been known to "nominate" the foreperson during voir dire examination." Mr. Smith, it may be necessary for you to serve as foreperson of the jury. Could you perform that function? Would you mind presiding over the jury's deliberations?" It may even be possible for a lawyer to influence the methodology of jury procedure. "And when you go into the jury room, after reading the charge, discuss the evidence before you vote. Take the witnesses one by one." This statement would be made by a lawyer wishing to engender uncertainty among the jurors. If the lawyer wanted to de-emphasize the jurors' consideration of defects in evidence and have them decide instead on an overall-picture basis, he might predict that "When you get back there in the jury room, and you first take your vote after the charge is read, I'm confident that you'll remember what's been said here."

12. *Disqualifying Unfavorable Jurors.* Lawyers in voir dire examination are not attempting to get a fair jury but a favorable one. This effort will be assisted by the disqualification of jurors who appear unfavorable. There are grounds for juror disqualification — such as bias, pecuniary interest, inability to read and write English, etc. A skillful lawyer does

not use these grounds in a vacuum, asking mechanically of the jurors whether they have bias, whether they can read or write, et cetera. Instead, skillful lawyers use these grounds to identify, disqualify and remove persons whom they consider unfavorable. That is the way the adversary system works. Indeed, it sometimes happens that the lawyer ... wishes to cause the juror's removal for reasons independent of the actual ground of disqualification. A highly skilled practitioner may first make the decision to remove an individual and pursue lines of questioning designed to disqualify that individual as a consequence.

2. PRETRIAL INVESTIGATION OF PROSPECTIVE JURORS

In most jurisdictions, it is possible to obtain a list of the names and addresses of all prospective jurors anywhere from a day to a month in advance of trial. This list gives you the opportunity to try to find out something about those jurors even before the voir dire begins. Should you take time to conduct such an investigation when much of the information could be obtained more easily (and cheaply) by asking the prospective jurors themselves during voir dire? The answer obviously is "Yes" if there is any credence to studies showing that an overwhelming number of jurors are not honest. Jurors tend to give socially correct answers to questions about their biases and prejudices, rarely admitting to such feelings in the public forum of the courtroom. Judge Robert Keeton suggests other reasons for conducting pretrial investigation: Certain areas of inquiry may not be permitted during voir dire, you can keep the discovery of favorable information from your adversary, and you have a check against the honesty of the juror's responses.[49]

If you decide to investigate jurors, where do you look?

- The official jury list will contain at least the name, address, and generic reference to occupation of each juror.
- If you drive by the jurors' homes, you may see bumper stickers on their cars or determine of it is an interracial neighborhood.
- Professional jury investigating services exist in larger cities which keep jury books to which any law firm can subscribe at a fairly reasonable rate.
- Private investigators.
- Public records may provide information on a juror's registered political affiliation, whether they have been involved in civil litigation, whether they have criminal records, etc. You may be able to check the signatures on petitions (many jurisdictions utilize petitions as a way of getting minority parties or referenda onto ballots or to initiate bond issues, and they are usually public records).
- City directories indicate whether a person owns a house and is married, divorced or widowed;
- In small towns, court clerks, sheriffs, ministers and local politicians may know many prospective jurors personally.

---

[49] ROBERT KEETON, TRIAL TACTICS AND METHODS 253 (2d ed. 1973).

- If you represent a business concern, a check of its records will disclose whether there have been any unsatisfactory dealings between a juror and your client.
- Local newspaper files (morgues or public library) may contain articles on jurors or letters to the editor they have written. This is particularly easy if the newspaper for your community is included in the NEXIS database.

3. PREPARATION OF VOIR DIRE QUESTIONS[50]

As with all aspects of the trial process, the key to a successful voir dire is preparation. The questions you ask should be planned in advance. If you trust to the luck of spontaneity, you may leave things out or state them poorly. This concept may appear counterintuitive — how can you plan your questions when you have no idea who you will be questioning or what prejudices they will have that need to be explored? Obviously, you will not be able to plan all of the follow-up questions you will ask a prospective juror whom you fear to be biased. Nevertheless, you can and should plan the areas of potential bias you want to explore as well as specific questions intended to indoctrinate the jurors or to ingratiate yourself with them. As a guide to that preparation, the following sections provide suggestions about the kinds of topics and questions that you may want to include in your voir dire.

a. Introductory Remarks to the Panel

When a jury panel is brought into the courtroom, its members have no idea what the case is about, and many will be totally unfamiliar with the customary rules and procedures of a trial. Thus, it has become standard practice in most courts to begin the voir dire with some kind of introduction to the case, the parties and attorneys, and the basic ground rules for conducting fair trials. In most jurisdictions, the judge will give this introduction. Some of the information may be contained in a juror handbook. In such cases it is unnecessary (and probably unwise) for you to go over the same ground again.

The first part of the preliminary statement usually consists of an introduction to the nature of the controversy. Whoever goes first — the judge or the plaintiff — should introduce the parties and attorneys and explain fairly what the case is about. For example:

> I'm Susan Fahr, the assistant district attorney, and this [pointing] is James Barnaby, the defense attorney. We are the lawyers who will be presenting the case to you. This is a criminal case in which David Jackson is accused of armed robbery. He is charged with stealing a woman's purse and car at gunpoint. He claims this is a case of mistaken identity.

Defense counsel will not need to repeat the introduction unless the plaintiff gave too partisan a summary or neglected to introduce the defendant, or if the nature of the defense still needs to be explained. Some attorneys also introduce important witnesses in their preliminary statements, while others prefer

---

[50] The discussion in this section assumes that you are allowed to question the jury panel directly under procedural rules permitting attorney-conducted voir dire. A note at the end of this section discusses how to make the most of judge-conducted voir dire.

to wait until they question jurors about their associations with those witnesses.

There is disagreement about whether your initial fact statement should be neutral or subtly slanted in your own favor. Some lawyers favor summarizing the controversy in such a way that it sounds like you are entitled to a favorable verdict, arguing this is a chance to start "selling" your case. Others caution against trying to slant the statement toward your own version. They point out that jurors must first understand the case before they can begin to take sides, and that they will be wary of "sharp" lawyers at the beginning. If you exaggerate the facts in the beginning, and your opponent points this out to the jury, your credibility may be so far compromised that you have done irreparable harm to your case. The latter view is supported by experiments which show that when an audience knows there are two sides, greater persuasion is accomplished by presenting both sides of the controversy than a partisan view.[51] Any shading of the case in your favor must therefore be subtle. For example, the prosecutor in our example could slightly modify her introduction as follows:

> I'm Susan Fahr, the assistant district attorney, and this [pointing] is the defense attorney. We are the lawyers who will be presenting the case to you. This is a criminal case in which David Jackson is accused of "carjacking" — stealing a woman's purse and car at gunpoint. The defendant may try to claim mistaken identity.

You might want to include two other preliminary matters to prevent the jurors from misunderstanding your apparent attitude toward them. Many experienced lawyers explain their reasons for asking questions that pry into the private lives of the jurors. They tell the panel that they need to search for the kinds of biases and personal feelings that interfere with complete impartiality. Otherwise, the jurors might resent the attorneys for forcing them to discuss private emotions and events in public. Second, it is probably a good idea for someone at the start to explain that socializing is not permitted; lawyers are not allowed to talk to the jurors outside the courtroom. You will see the jurors in the hallways and the elevator, and you do not want them to think you are ignoring them when you do not respond to their greeting, "Well, how's it going?"

b. Areas of Inquiry

The precise areas of inquiry you choose to cover in a particular case obviously will depend on the nature of that case. No cookbook recipe can be provided that lists questions that should be covered every time. It is generally agreed that you should elicit some basic demographic information on the jurors, such as:

- Occupation of juror and juror's family.
- Juror's residence.

---

[51] Robert Lawson, *Relative Effectiveness of One-Sided and Two-Sided Communications in Courtroom Persuasion*, 82 J. GEN. PSYCHOL. 3 (1970).

- Juror's marital and family status.
- Whether the juror belongs to or assists any local, state or national civic and special interest organizations, e.g., Boy Scouts, ACLU, National Rifle Association.

However, it is generally inadvisable to probe into jurors' private lives beyond these matters, e.g., religious, social and political affiliations, unless you have a specific reason for doing so.

In addition, there is general agreement that you should ask questions that probe for biases and subtle attitudes on the part of jurors toward specific aspects of your case that could cause them to favor one side or the other. These questions seek to link jurors' experiences to the issues that will arise in your case; e.g., what kinds of interactions jurors have had with the police, asked in criminal cases involving police officers as witnesses or participants. General consensus favors probing in four areas:

- The applicable rules of law governing claims, defenses, and burdens of proof.
- Weaknesses in your case.
- Who your client is and who the major witnesses are.
- Juror familiarity with the main facts of the event being litigated, from either personal knowledge or pretrial publicity.

(1) Questions about the Law

It is no secret that people may have strong emotional feelings for or against legal doctrine. Issues such as abortion, government-sponsored Christmas displays, sexual harassment, and the insanity defense are obvious examples. More subtle attitudes may affect jurors' views concerning whether driving in excess of the 55-miles-per-hour speed limit is negligence, whether damages should be awarded for pain and suffering, or whether possession of an illegal handgun is a crime or a necessity.

Therefore, all practitioners agree that you must probe the jurors for potential biases for and against the important legal issue in your case, at least those that have any chance of being controversial. Melvin Belli prefers the following question forms:

> Are you in sympathy with the rule of law that requires you to accord this defendant the benefit of reasonable doubt; you would not find him guilty of anything unless it were proved to you that he was guilty beyond a reasonable doubt and to a moral certainty, would you?

> Do you believe in the rule of law that the defendant is presumed to be innocent until the state has proved him guilty beyond a reasonable doubt and to a moral certainty?[52]

This form has two problems: some judges do not allow this kind of hypothetical questioning, and you risk insulting the jurors who have just taken an oath

---

[52] MELVIN BELLI, MODERN TRIALS 797 (1954).

to follow the laws of the state. It is more common to ask about legal principles as follows:

> Will you be able to follow an instruction that provides that the state must prove the defendant's guilt beyond a reasonable doubt?

But you should bear in mind that your primary mission in voir dire is to find out what the jurors think. Leading questions like these that tell the jurors the "correct" answer are argumentative, and will have the effect of making it *more* difficult to find out the jurors' true feelings. Jurors will tend to give "socially acceptable" answers in public.[53] If you expect to gain any useful information, consider a question along these lines:

> This is a criminal case, in which the defendant will assert an insanity defense. It's obvious that a lot of people have strong feelings about it — some people feel that a person should not be put in jail if they are mentally ill, but should be sent to a hospital; others feel that the insanity defense is a loophole that allows criminals to go free. Do you have any feelings one way or the other about the insanity defense?

Some attorneys go beyond this, and ask about uncontroversial laws. For example, a prosecutor may ask whether any of the jurors have any feelings about laws criminalizing child molesting, despite the fact that it is absurd to think that there are going to be several people on the jury who will be strongly opposed to making child molesting a crime. However, the better tactic is probably to skip this kind of indoctrination. It is not necessary to proselytize to the converted. The jury may become bored or even irritated at this pointless questioning. They know that the prosecutor is not *really* going to root out a nest of jurors who advocate lenient child molesting laws.

If you do intend to mention any rules of law during voir dire, you must be careful to state them briefly and accurately. Any misstatement of law will bring a quick rebuke from the judge — not a good way to make a first impression on the jury.

(2) Factual Weaknesses

Just as jurors may have strong feelings about certain controversial laws, they may have biases and negative attitudes about factual aspects of your case. If you represent a child molester or are seeking punitive damages against the local police department, you want to get the issue out in the open early and talk to the jury about it. It is far better to find out bad news (e.g., that everyone hates your client) early when you can still minimize its impact by removing the worst potential jurors, than to pretend that you have a strong case. The jury will find out the negative information eventually anyway. Consider a question such as this:

> My client will take the stand and admit to you that ten years ago he molested a 12-year girl. Since then he has had extensive counseling, and will testify that the sickness has been kept under control. Some people

---

[53] *See* J. FREDERICK, *supra* note 46, at 122-23.

think that this kind of problem can never be cured, while others think that it can be controlled with therapy and willpower. What do you think about this?

The following list of topics will give you some idea of the areas lawyers routinely inquire into:

Civil cases

- Large verdict requests, especially if they include pain and suffering damages.
- Punitive damages.
- Beliefs about the so-called litigation explosion and whether jurors think many claims are unfounded, especially in medical malpractice cases.
- Sympathetic plaintiffs (or, rarely, defendants), especially those who have been horribly injured.
- Prior accidents; either plaintiff's involvement in prior accidents, or the fact that other accidents happened that involved the defendant or its products.
- The presence of celebrities in the case — as parties, witnesses or attorneys (suppose you had to try a case against Alan Dershowitz?).

Criminal cases

- The need to rely on criminals as witnesses.
- Prior criminal record of the defendant.
- The defendant not testifying.
- Sympathetic impact of the victim, defendant, or their families.
- Exposure to extensive or lurid pretrial publicity.
- Attitudes favorable or unfavorable toward the police and other law enforcement personnel.
- The use of co-defendants as witnesses.

(3) The People Involved in the Case

Beyond the predictable areas where some aspect of your case is an obvious weakness likely to provoke hostile reactions by jurors, lie a range of issues where you *might* find such an emotional reaction. Suppose one of your major witnesses is a retired cook who worked for the last fifteen years at the local high school cafeteria. Okay, the food was always lousy, but this is the type of witness unlikely to provoke any particular emotional reaction. Nevertheless, there may be antagonism between a juror and this person that is uniquely related to an individual juror's experiences. One juror may know your witness — from school, from the neighborhood, from church — and dislike her for some personal reason. It could be an incident five years ago when the juror's son was wrongly accused of stealing food from the cafeteria, a simmering property line dispute, or resentment over your witness' changing the date of the church picnic.

To probe into these areas, you obviously must tell the jurors who your client and witnesses will be, and ask if they know any of them. However, you probably need to give the jurors some context. Attorneys suggest that you describe major demographic characteristics of your client and any particularly important witnesses, and then ask if any jurors have encountered them in the course of those activities. For example:

> My client, Sharon Deckard, is active in the First Methodist Church of Bayshore, and is an adult leader in the Girl Scouts. Do any of you know her in connection with either of these activities?

> Our primary medical witness will be Dr. Frank Grissom, who has practiced internal medicine here in town for twenty years. Have any of you, or any members of your families, ever been patients of his?

This technique has the advantage of allowing you to mention favorable traits of your client and witnesses that will enhance their credibility.

Do not forget that jurors may not only harbor dislike for your witnesses, they may be especially fond of the opposing party. It is a good idea to go through a similar set of questions concerning jurors' encounters with and knowledge of the adverse party and any of his or her major witnesses. This time, of course, you might mention a couple of the negative aspects of the opposition's witnesses. For example:

> The primary defense witness will be Lonnie Sagawa. Mr. Sagawa sold used cars at a place called "Honest Abe's Used Cars" a few years ago until he was fired. Did any of you ever buy a car from him, or know him in any other way?

(4) The Main Facts of the Case

The jurors may not know your primary medical witness, Dr. Grissom, but may have received treatment for an injury similar to your client's from the doctor down the street. Thus, you should probe for juror's knowledge and opinions on the very subjects that form the heart of your case. It is not important how realistic it is that a juror might have prejudices — you are seeking the *unlikely* prejudice (and pursuing your goal to indoctrinate jurors on the important facts of your case as well). Consider asking about the following topics:

- Do jurors have any personal knowledge of the facts? It is extremely rare that you will find a previously undiscovered eyewitness, but you might find jurors who are familiar with the scene of a crime.
- Have jurors heard or read anything about the facts? Even in cases that attracted no media publicity, there was probably a short article on the event in the paper, or jurors may have heard friends or family talk about the case. There is a danger in asking these questions, of course, that a prospective juror will have heard something horrible about your client, and will promptly inform the other jurors about it, so you must be circumspect.
- Have jurors formed any tentative opinions about the case? This is the standard follow-up question if jurors have any knowledge of the case or have heard anything about it.

- Do jurors have any similar experiences? Have they, or members of their families, been involved in a similar controversy? For example, in a personal injury case, jurors may previously have been involved in a similar accident, either as a party or an eyewitness.
- Do jurors have any relevant expertise? Jurors or members of their families may have experience in a special field of work or learning that may be involved in your case. For example, in a products liability case involving a drill press, you might want to ask if any juror works with a similar type of machinery.

Which facts are important enough to spend time on? You should ask about the facts that are important to your theory of the case, where the jurors' feelings would make a difference. If you have done a thorough job preparing a theory of the case, then you already have identified the key disputes and the major facts upon which your case will rest. The heart of your trial strategy is to keep the jury focused on these key points throughout the trial, not letting them become distracted by side issues. Your voir dire should reflect this strategy as well, sticking to the main points.

c. The Final Question

As with any other stage of the trial, the conclusion of voir dire should be planned carefully. As a general rule, you will want to take advantage of the recency effect, and use the end of your voir dire to emphasize one of the important aspects of your case. For example:

> All of you, of course, understand that the law places the burden of proof entirely on the prosecution to prove the defendant guilty beyond a reasonable doubt. Will any of you have any difficulty holding the State to this heavy burden?

Some attorneys, however, suggest that the end of your voir dire should leave the jury with good feelings about your integrity, and should communicate your confidence in the jurors, suggesting that it is too early to begin arguing. A standard final question along these lines is directed to the entire panel, and sounds something like this:

> Attorney: Finally, based on everything you have heard so far, can any of you think of any reason why you could not be fair and impartial to both sides?
> Various jurors: No.
> Attorney: Neither can I. I have no challenges for cause, Your Honor.

The final moments can also be used to soothe hurt feelings by asking if anything done or said has irritated the jury, and asking the jury not to hold it against your client.

> The other attorneys in my office tell me I can sometimes sound arrogant and make people mad. Has anything that I have done this past hour made you angry with me?

If I have said or done anything that irritated you, or if I inadvertently do something later in the trial, will you promise not to punish my client for it?

NOTES

1. *Additional purposes.* One other common purpose behind voir dire (especially lengthy voir dire) is rarely mentioned. Voir dire often is used as a stalling tactic by the plaintiff or prosecutor whose witnesses are not available. In urban areas where courts are backlogged, a case may be marked ready for trial days, weeks, or even months before it is assigned to a trial judge. Because witnesses cannot be kept always ready to appear while the case waits for an open courtroom, it takes time and effort to locate and summon them. Since a lawyer cannot conduct voir dire and telephone witnesses at the same time, he or she frequently will prolong voir dire until the end of the day, so that he or she will be free to contact witnesses after court has recessed. *See* ALAN MORRILL, TRIAL DIPLOMACY 1 (2d ed. 1972).

There are two further purposes, variations on the themes summarized by Prof. Crump: 1) In addition to trying to discover unfavorable jurors and get them to disqualify themselves, you should look for jurors biased in your favor and try to elicit their promise to be fair, inoculating them against being challenged for cause by your adversary. 2) In addition to personalizing your own client, you can begin the process of depersonalizing the opposing party.

2. *Assistance of social scientists.* The growth of social science jury consultants has been phenomenal in the last few years. Many lawyers now feel that, if you can afford the considerable expense, you should employ them in every case. These consultants can conduct surveys of community attitudes, correlate whether any attitudes might affect how jurors would vote in your specific case, and help design voir dire questions to reveal the key attitudes. *See* DONALD E. VINSON, JURY TRIALS: THE PSYCHOLOGY OF WINNING STRATEGY (1986). However, there is little evidence that this kind of social science assistance is of any significant help. The reason is that when people are highly involved in a cognitively demanding task and when they must reach group decisions, these personality and individual attitude factors become unimportant compared to the merits of a case. Both conditions would be present in most jury deliberations. Juror characteristics are mnore important in close cases. The leading social psychologists who study jury behavior conclude that scientific jury selection may be more reliable than using stereotypes based on sex, race and national origin, but is not ultimately very effective. Solomon M. Fulero & Steven Penrod, *The Myths and Realities of Attorney Jury Selection Folklore and Scientific Jury Selection: What Works?*, 17 OHIO N.U. L. REV. 229, 244-51 (1990); Reid Hastie, *Is Attorney-Conducted Voir Dire an Effective Procedure for the Selection of Impartial Juries*, 40 AM. U. L. REV. 703, 718-19 (1991); Michael J. Saks, *The Limits of Scientific Jury Selection: Ethical and Empirical*, 17 JURIMETRICS 3 (1976); VALERIE HANS & NEIL VIDMAR, JUDGING THE JURY 90 (1986).

3. *Is there any point in asking jurors whether they are biased?* Imagine you are a lawyer representing an African-American defendant charged

with looting following the 1992 riots in south central Los Angeles. Is there any point in asking prospective jurors whether they have any bias against black people? It seems highly unlikely that anyone will admit publicly to being a bigot. For that reason, most attorneys recommend an indirect approach to the subject of bias, suggesting questions along these lines:

> Did you have any contact with black people in the military?
> Do any African-Americans live on your block or go to your children's school?
> What do you think about affirmative action and the civil rights laws?
> Do you know any interracial married couples? What do you think of it? Do you think their children will face social problems?
> You previously stated you enjoyed playing bridge and participated in a duplicate bridge club. Are there any minorities who regularly play with that bridge club?

4. Making the most of judge-conducted voir dire. When voir dire is handled solely by the judge, lawyers often appear unwilling to move for additional attorney-conducted questioning. It may seem pointless and they may be afraid they will antagonize the judge. There seems to be a tendency to defer voir dire completely to the trial judge, even though a judge's questioning rarely is as probing as an attorney's would be. The attorneys on the National Jury Project, in JURYWORK: SYSTEMATIC TECHNIQUES § 2.12 (1992) criticize this deference, and offer some suggestions on how your input can maximize judge-conducted voir dire. There are three things you can do before trial:

- If you have reasons for believing judge-conducted voir dire will be inadequate, you should try to persuade the judge either to personally conduct an expanded voir dire or to allow you to do so. Even if your motion to participate in voir dire is denied, the judge may expand his or her questioning in the areas you requested.
- To facilitate this process, you should submit a list of twenty to thirty clearly relevant questions you would like asked. You must be prepared to defend each question, explaining why it is likely to reveal juror bias.
- Prepare possible follow-up questions in advance which can be submitted to the judge at the close of his or her voir dire. Essentially, this means preparing questions as if you were going to ask them yourself, noting follow-up questions you would have asked as the voir dire progresses, and submitting to the judge those questions that were not covered.

In addition, you can have an effect on the questioning itself by cautious interference in the judge's voir dire. If a juror appears hesitant in his or her response to a question, or otherwise indicates he or she might not have understood a question fully, you can ask for clarification. You might tell the court you found the question confusing and wonder if the juror did also, or that you did not understand the answer and wonder if the juror could explain it. If a juror acts like he or she would like to amplify an answer, or if the judge cuts off a juror's explanation, you can try interrupting and ask the judge to give the juror an opportunity to expand on his or her answer. Finally, you occasionally can request the court to ask a particular juror some follow-up question while looking at the juror — a tactic that sometimes will result in the juror's answering your question spontaneously.

5. *Questions about insurance.* If your jurisdiction permits questions that raise the insurance issue, should you ask them? It generally is assumed that juries are more generous in their verdicts when they think that damages will be paid out of a "deep pocket," such as an insurance company. Therefore, it is usually in plaintiff's interest to ask questions that remind the jury that the defendant is insured. This tactic is not without risk — a frank disclosure by the defense that there is insurance, coupled with questions about whether jurors will resist the temptation to give a higher verdict, may make the plaintiff appear to be deliberately appealing to prejudice rather than the merits of his or her case. *See* Harry S. Bodin, *Selecting a Jury, in* CIVIL LITIGATION AND TRIAL TECHNIQUES 236-39 (1976). For a discussion of this issue from an insured defendant's point of view, *see* WELCOME D. PIERSON, THE DEFENSE ATTORNEY AND BASIC DEFENSE TACTICS 305-13 (1956).

6. *Sources of sample questions.* Many books on trial practice include long lists of sample questions. Space limitations prevent reprinting them here; however, if you are interested in reading through them for ideas, *see* ANN FAGAN GINGER, JURY SELECTION IN CIVIL AND CRIMINAL TRIALS, vol. 1: 509-751 (2d ed. 1984); Herald P. Fahringer, *In the Valley of the Blind: A Primer on Jury Selection*, 43 LAW & CONTEMP. PROBS. 116 (1980); JAMES J. GOBERT & WALTER E. JORDAN, JURY SELECTION 352-443 (2d ed. 1990); FRED LANE, LANE'S GOLDSTEIN TRIAL TECHNIQUE §§ 9.92 TO 9.95 (3d ed. 1984); WARD WAGNER, ART OF ADVOCACY — JURY SELECTION §§ 1-A.01 to 5-A.02 (1981).

7. *Should you write out your questions?* Although you often will be unable to predict what follow-up questions will be necessary and therefore cannot write them out in advance, you will be able to plan most of your voir dire. Consider Herald Fahringer, *In the Valley of the Blind: A Primer on Jury Selection in a Criminal Case*, 43 LAW & CONTEMP. PROBS. 116, 126 (1980):

> Unless counsel is endowed with an infallible memory, the list of questions to be asked of prospective jurors must be outlined on a legal pad so that those topics can be reviewed periodically. Failure to ask one important question, such as, "Do you know any police officers?" can be ruinous.

See also FRED LANE, LANE'S GOLDSTEIN TRIAL TECHNIQUE § 9.11 (3d ed. 1984) (experienced lawyers require only one-word outlines, inexperienced attorneys should write questions out verbatim).

F. CONDUCTING THE VOIR DIRE

1. GATHERING INFORMATION FROM PROSPECTIVE JURORS

Gathering reliable information from prospective jurors about themselves is not as easy as it may appear. It is not simply a process of asking questions and listening to the answers. Jurors may be unaware that they hold biases. They may be reluctant to disclose personal or embarrassing information in public.[54]

---

[54] *See* Dwan V. Kerig, *Perceptions from a Jury Box*, 54 CAL. ST. B.J. 306, 307 (1979) (self-report of juror); J. FREDERICK, *supra* note 46, at 117-18.

Jurors have a tendency to conform — to give socially acceptable answers, even if their true opinions are different — when under the anxiety of public voir dire.[55] The major problem may be simply that prospective jurors lie. They hide their prejudices from the attorneys, deny that they have had similar experiences, and even may deliberately try to get on a jury in order to put their prejudices into effect.[56] This is not hard to understand. If a close friend of a criminal defendant, convinced of his innocence, were called for his jury duty, the friend undoubtedly would feel a strong desire to sit on that jury to insure that no miscarriage of justice occurred. If you are unable to reach any of this hidden information, you may not have enough data on which to make intelligent challenges. The suggestions in this section should help improve the reliability and detail of the information gathered.

a. Form of Questions

If you want to gather reliable information from prospective jurors about themselves, it is axiomatic that you must get them to talk as much as possible. The way you ask your questions plays a significant role. Questions addressed to the entire panel are least likely to elicit meaningful responses. Social psychologists point out that the pressure for group cohesiveness and conformity militate against honest self-disclosure to such questions as, "Do any of you have any preconceived opinions about the defendant's guilt?" The likelihood of reliable information is further reduced if the lawyer prefaces the question with some remark such as "You know that the defendant is presumed innocent." Therefore, most lawyers caution against asking group questions, at least on the topics on which you genuinely want information. Instead, questions should be directed to individuals. If you ask a question face to face, a juror is less likely to take refuge in group silence, but is obligated to give some kind of answer. The truth is usually easier to speak than a lie, so you will probably even get relatively reliable answers.

However, asking the same routine question of all jurors individually can be extremely boring. Two suggestions may help alleviate this problem. One is to prepare a variety of questions that seek the same kind of information. There is no reason why you must adhere to identical questions for all jurors. If you have alternatives, you can switch when one gets stale. The other tactic is to ask the question of one juror, and then to ask others if they agree or disagree. Such questioning might proceed like this:

> Q: Mr. Smith, did you read anything about this case in the papers?
> A: Yes, I think I remember reading that a little girl had been killed in an accident.
> Q: Do you remember any of the details?

---

[55] See, e.g., Robert Helmreich & Barry Collings, *Situational Determinants of Affiliative Preference Under Stress*, 6 J. PERSONALITY & SOC. PSYCHOL. 79 (1967); Paul McGhee & Richard Teevan, *Conformity Behavior and Need for Affiliation*, 72 J. SOC. PSYCHOL. 117 (1967); Irving Sarnoff & Philip Zimbardo, *Anxiety, Fear, and Social Affiliation*, 62 J. ABNORMAL & SOC. PSYCHOL. 356 (1961).

[56] Studies show that from seven percent to as many as fifty percent of all jurors fail to give honest responses during voir dire. *See* Dale Broeder, *Voir Dire Examinations: An Empirical Study*, 38 S. CAL. L. REV. 503, 510-14 (1965).

A: Yes, a truck hit a car.

Q: Have you tentatively decided whether anyone is at fault based on what you have read?

A: No, I don't think so.

Q: Do you remember your reaction on reading about it?

A: Yeah, I thought it was tragic that a little girl was killed.

Q: Did that make you think it was the truck driver's fault?

A: No.

Q: Who else might have read about this accident? Ms. Harris?

A: Yes, I remember something about it in the paper.

Q: What was your reaction?

A: It was terrible that a child was killed. I have children of my own.

Q: Did you think it might be the truck driver's fault?

A: Sure, but it was more like I wondered whose fault it was.

Q: It might have been the child's mother who was at fault?

A: Sure. That's terrible to think of, but she might have been distracted or something.

Q: Ms. Jones, do you agree?

A: Yes. You can't tell who was at fault by reading the paper.

Q: Mr. Wilson, do you agree? [And so forth.]

Getting a juror to divulge information is similar to interviewing a prospective witness, and similar tactics often are appropriate. Simple, open-ended questions that ask for explanations rather than a yes or no will elicit more accurate information. The interviewing technique of asking a broad, neutral question, and following it up with increasingly narrow probes often will prove effective.[57] Obviously, questions should be simple and straightforward, devoid of the convoluted, qualifying phrases popular with lawyers.

b. Keeping Track of Answers

The information you elicit from the jury will be for naught if you cannot remember which juror gave which answers when the time comes to exercise challenges. Unless you have a photographic memory, you will need some system of recording answers. Probably the most effective is to have an assistant take detailed notes at the counsel table. This frees you to engage in conversation with the jurors undistracted by the need to take your own notes. If you must take your own notes, consider using shorthand or working out a private code for recording information — it is faster than longhand, and has the added advantage of not being decipherable if accidentally seen by jurors or your opponent.[58]

It is commonly suggested that you use some kind of chart to record the information. The easiest approach is to draw a diagram of the jury box as illustrated in Figure 3. The name of each juror, and information about that person, can be placed in the box corresponding to the juror's seat.

---

[57] Interviewing techniques are discussed in Chapter 6, part E, *infra*.

[58] *E.g.*, S — single, D — divorced, W — widowed, M5 — married five years, B2 — two-year-old boy, † — particularly active in a religious organization, CrJ/V — served on criminal jury that reached a verdict, Ex — similar personal experience, Mil — military service.

Figure 3

Jury Diagram

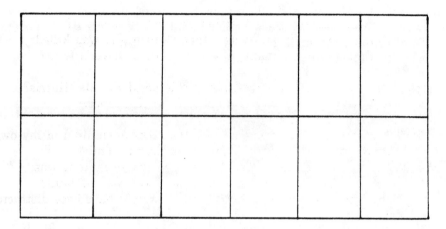

Some attorneys prefer to use a more detailed chart with spaces provided for answers to the questions they know they are going to ask in advance. A simple version of this kind of form is illustrated in Figure 4.

Figure 4

	JUROR 1	JUROR 2	JUROR 3	JUROR 4
Name				
Age				
Occupation				
Education				
Marital status				
Spouse's occupation				

c. Where to Stand

You must decide how to position yourself during voir dire: whether to stand, and if so, how far away from and at what angle to the jurors. Some lawyers prefer to remain at counsel table, believing that it is easier and less obtrusive to read questions and record answers from that position. Others prefer to stand and make use of the psychological advantage of being able to manipulate distance and angle. Experiments by social psychologists indicate that your distance from a prospective juror can influence how freely that person responds to questions. Distances between the attorney and juror of more than twelve feet are not conducive to self-disclosure. Closer distances facilitate communication and rapport. Studies show that jurors speak more and reveal more about themselves when the questioner stands between three and six feet away. A direct orientation of the interviewer's body toward the juror (face to face) may also elicit more verbalization.[59]

d. Style

Discussions of manner and style always must be preceded by a caveat. Style is a personal matter that depends on the personality of the lawyer. Too much effort to adopt someone else's manner of voir dire can make you appear affected and insincere. However, some general observations can be made about ways of encouraging jurors to talk.

David Suggs and Bruce Sales have summarized the social science literature and concluded that the style and demeanor of an attorney can have a significant effect on the amount of information disclosed by jurors.[60] Contrary to the beliefs of some attorneys, they advise against trying to appear just like the jurors (the "country lawyer" approach). Jurors tend to disclose more reliable information to a person of moderately higher social status than to an equal. Responses are also unreliable when the status difference is very large, so you should not be aloof. Not surprisingly, experimental data show that people prefer to talk to and reveal more of themselves to warm, friendly people. Experiments also have shown that nonverbal stimuli, such as head-nodding, can encourage the jurors to talk and produce longer responses. However, eye contact and body movement seem to work differently for men and women. Male attorneys appear to elicit greater self-disclosure from prospective jurors with limited eye contact and increased body motion (hand gestures, pacing), but the opposite appears to be true for female attorneys.

Suggs and Sales also report that there is a role for aggressive questioning. If you suspect that a juror may be lying about his or her biases, and friendly questioning does not seem to elicit honest responses, they suggest that you resort to aggressive questioning. This increases juror anxiety, a condition under which jurors are more likely to admit long-held prejudices. Obviously, such a tactic should be used sparingly because of its effect on the way other jurors will perceive you.

Other common stylistic suggestions include:

- Stay relaxed (easier said than done, however!).
- Ask your questions in a relatively rapid, unhesitating sequence, so you do not bore the jurors.
- Be courteous and treat the jurors with respect.
- Talk to all of the jurors and treat them all the same so you do not offend anyone by omitting them.

---

[59] See David Suggs & Bruce D. Sales, *Juror Self-Disclosure in the Voir Dire: A Social Science Analysis*, 56 IND. L.J. 245, 255, 262-64 (1981). *But see* EDWARD HALL, THE HIDDEN DIMENSION 108-09 (1966) (more effective if you stand at slight angle to prospective juror).

[60] Suggs & Sales, *supra* note 59, at 253-56.

- Remember and refer to jurors by their names to help build rapport. This is easy to do if you use the chart illustrated in Figure 3.
- Include your client by treating him or her warmly and referring to the client by name.
- Remain friendly but professional and avoid commenting on the jurors' personal lives. In a real trial several years ago, an attempt to be overly friendly resulted in the following dialogue:

> Q:Are you married, sir?
> A:Yes.
> Q:Do you have any children?
> A:Yes.
> Q:How many?
> A:Eight.
> Q:Eight? And what — I won't ask you each age. Approximately, what is the range?
> A:One through ten.
> Q:That's on a pretty regular basis.
> A:Thirty, forty times a month.[61]

2. INDOCTRINATING THE JURY

The detailed suggestions in the preceding section are based on the assumption that you want to make a serious attempt to gather information from the jurors in order to exercise challenges intelligently. What if your intentions are less than honorable? What if you wish to communicate information rather than collect it? Some techniques obviously will remain the same. Questions still should be simple and understandable, and asked in a friendly manner. However, many of the techniques will differ. You no longer want the jurors to do the talking; rather, you want to indoctrinate them.

It is important to remember that you cannot simply lecture the jury, telling them about your theory of the case. You must ask questions, and the questions must be justifiable as seeking information relevant to exercising a challenge. It usually is not proper to say:

> As you know, the prosecution bears a heavy burden of proving guilt beyond a reasonable doubt. The law requires you to acquit the defendant if this high standard is not met.

However, the same speech can be made in question form:

> When the judge instructs you that the prosecution bears the burden of proving guilt beyond a reasonable doubt, will you follow that law? Will each of you be able to vote for acquittal if the state fails to meet this high standard?

These questions obviously are proper because any juror who says he or she cannot follow the law could be challenged for cause.

---

[61] I am grateful to Terry Bethel for providing me with the transcript of the voir dire in which these questions appeared.

When seeking information, you want to ask open questions of individual jurors. When indoctrinating, most lawyers do the opposite. They ask closed, leading questions addressed to the whole panel. The idea is that they do not want a discussion, but merely want to start conditioning the jurors to accept their case theory. Through these "lecture questions," they begin to introduce the themes that will run throughout the case. Words are carefully chosen for their persuasive effect. Speaking distance can also be adjusted. Jurors may be discouraged from responding if you stand farther back, at least twelve feet from the jury.[62]

Another way of accomplishing this indoctrination is available that is more difficult, but perhaps more effective. It consists of provoking a discussion among the jurors and directing it toward the conclusion you want. In another context, you may know this as the Socratic method used in many law school classrooms. It has the advantage that if the jurors reach a conclusion themselves, they may be more likely to become committed to it.[63] If you simply tell them what the conclusion is, they may try to think up reasons why you could be wrong — a cognitive process called "reactance" by psychologists.[64] This method works especially well if you can identify a juror likely to give the answer you want. David Crump provides the following example:

> If an insurance company is trying to establish a defense of suicide, and if one of the panel members happens to know something about suicide — an ambulance driver, etc. — the defense lawyer might ask: "So you have seen lots of suicide cases, right? Have you seen [or heard about] many where the deceased drove his car into a concrete pier, like in this case ...?" A criminal defense lawyer claiming mistaken identification might ask a juror whether [the juror] has ever momentarily mistaken someone for someone he knew.[65]

This kind of voir dire is also more risky, because the jurors may draw conclusions that are different from those you want. The ambulance driver may say that in her experience people do not commit suicide by wrecking their cars; the juror may state that he has never mistaken a stranger for someone he knew if he had a reasonable chance to see the person.

3. WHOM TO CHALLENGE

What do you do with all this information? How do you decide whom to challenge? There is no consensus among lawyers. Many lawyers suggest that the only advice is to follow your intuition. Human behavior, and how people will react to your case, may simply be too complex to be reduced to sets of identifiable traits in prospective jurors that will make them more or less

---

[62] There is some evidence that distances over twelve feet are most conducive to one-way communication and persuasion. Stuart Albert & James M. Dabbs, *Physical Distance and Persuasion*, 15 J. PERSONALITY & SOC. PSYCHOL. 265 (1970).

[63] *Cf.* J. FREDERICK, *supra* note 46, at 187-88 (data on conclusion drawing are ambiguous).

[64] *See* SHARON S. BREHM & JACK W. BREHM, PSYCHOLOGICAL REACTANCE: A THEORY OF FREEDOM AND CONTROL (1981).

[65] David Crump, *Attorneys' Goals and Tactics in Voir Dire Examination*, 43 TEX ST. B.J. 244, 247 (1980).

likely to be receptive to your case. Studies by social psychologists confirm this. Attitudinal and demographic variables account for only ten to fifteen percent of the variability in verdict preference, causing social scientists to recommend that lawyers abandon the trait theories discussed below, and trust their intuition.[66]

However, assuming that you reject the tactic of simply taking the first twelve jurors called, and your intuition fails you, you probably would like some general advice. The following recommendations represent a sampling of the kinds of advice available in the books and articles on jury selection tactics. Their inclusion here is not meant as an endorsement of their efficacy; to the contrary, they should all be taken with a grain of salt — some with several grains.

- *Stereotyping.* The classic version of this approach suggests that the ideal juror for the civil plaintiff or criminal defendant is an overweight male between thirty and fifty-five years old, of Spanish, Irish, Jewish, French, or Italian origin, who works as an artist, laborer, salesman, or clerk, and who is serving jury duty for the first time. The ideal juror for a civil defendant or criminal prosecutor is an underweight, thin-lipped, young male or old female, neatly dressed, of German, English, or Scandinavian ancestry, who works in a white collar or managerial job, is a police or military officer, schoolteacher, clergyman's wife, insurance agent, accountant, or public utility employee, and who has prior jury experience.

- *Similarities.* This is probably the most common selection strategy. You look for jurors who share the characteristics of the adverse party and opposing witnesses, or who are likely to identify with them because they share similar backgrounds and experiences. This tactic assumes that women with children will identify with other women with children, college students with other college students, Latinos with other Latinos, accident victims with other accident victims, and so on. There is some empirical support for this idea that experiences produce behavior and behavior produces attitudes[67] influence juror decision making.[68]

- *Attitudes.* This method uses a social science consulting firm to help draw up a "scientific" profile of the typical juror likely to vote against you. The social scientists survey people in the judicial district in which the trial will be held and correlate demographic information to attitudes toward the kind of people and issues involved in the upcoming trial. The consultants run a statistical analysis and report back to the attorneys on any demographic or lifestyle characteristics that are statistically significant

---

[66] REID HASTIE, STEVEN PENROD & NANCY PENNINGTON, INSIDE THE JURY (1983); Solomon Fulero & Steven Penrod, *The Myths and Realities of Attorney Jury Selection Folklore and Scientific Jury Selection: What Works?*, 17 OHIO N.U. L. REV. 229, 247-48 (1990).

[67] SAUL M. KASSIN & LAWRENCE S. WRIGHTSMAN, THE AMERICAN JURY ON TRIAL: PSYCHOLOGICAL PERSPECTIVES 35-40 (1988).

[68] E.g., Harmon Hosch et al., *A Comparison of Anglo-American and Mexican-American Jurors' Judgments of Mothers Who Fail to Protect Their Children from Abuse*, 21 J. APP. SOC. PSYCHOL. 1681 (1991) (verdicts affected by gender but not ethnicity). *Compare* Marina Miller & Jay Hewitt, *Conviction of a Defendant as a Function of Juror-Victim Racial Similarity*, 105 J. SOC. PSYCHOL. 159 (1978) (white and black jurors twice as likely to convict if victim of same race) *with* Jeffrey Pfeifer & James Ogloff, *Ambiguity and Guilt Determinations: A Modern Racism Perspective*, 21 J. APP. SOC. PSYCHOL. 1713 (1991) (effect disappears with instruction on elements of offense).

in determining attitude about a case-related issue. In the voir dire, each juror is given a score for how many of the undesirable traits they have, and challenges are based on those scores.

- *Nonverbal behavior.* This tactic is based on the assumptions that a prospective juror will experience increased anxiety when being questioned by a party whom the juror dislikes, when discussing issues on which the juror has strong feelings (e.g., racial prejudice), and when lying. This anxiety will manifest itself in nonverbal communication cues, such as speech disturbances (self-interrupted sentences, repeating phrases, inappropriate laughter, etc.), use of an artificially formal speaking style, talking excessively long or fast, increase in the frequency of eye movements (shifty-eyed), facial expressions, hand movements, and body language.[69]

- *Authoritarianism.* Jurors with authoritarian personalities will tend to adhere to conventional middle-class values, submit to authority figures, punish violators of social norms, adhere to stereotypes, identify with power figures, be sexually repressed, and project their own feelings and attitudes onto others. Social science research on the authoritarian personality has been voluminous, and suggests that authoritarians are highly punitive, racist, politically conservative, rigid, and acquiescent to authority figures. They tend to render more severe verdicts than anti-authoritarians, except in rape cases. They also are more likely to change their opinions to conform to the opinions of experts.[70]

- *The "just world" hypothesis.* People differ in their tendencies to believe in a just world where one gets what one deserves (and deserves what one gets). To strong believers in a just world, good is rewarded and evil is punished. This is a defense mechanism enabling people to believe that bad things will not happen to them. Just-world believers tend to blame people for their own predicaments, and punish them for transgressions. Thus, they will tend to blame victims for provoking their own misfortunes, in order to perpetuate their own sense of safety. For example, women who believe in a just world will tend to blame a rape victim for dressing provocatively or accepting a ride home, because the belief enables them to feel safe from rape as long as they do nothing to provoke it.[71]

- *Prior jury service.* Some research suggests that a juror's prior jury experiences will affect how the juror will act in a later case. If the juror previously sat on a case involving a minor offense, he or she will expect a stronger case if the current charge is more serious, and will therefore be more likely to acquit than a new juror. On the other hand, if a prospective juror previously sat on a serious case, he or she will not demand that

---

[69] David Suggs & Bruce D. Sales, *Using Communication Cues to Evaluate Prospective Jurors During the Voir Dire*, 20 ARIZ. L. REV. 629, 632-38 (1978).

[70] *See* NATIONAL JURY PROJECT, JURYWORK: SYSTEMATIC TECHNIQUES § 18.07 (1992).

[71] *See* S. KASSIN & L. WRIGHTSMAN, *supra* note 67, at 33-34 (suggesting this tendency might not have much influence on jurors' final decisions).

the proof be as strong if the present case is less serious — thus, the juror will be more likely to convict.[72]

- *Leadership strategy.* Some lawyers believe that the final jury decision is most strongly influenced by one juror who emerges as the leader. If you identify someone you believe to be favorable to your side who is likely to become the jury leader because of the status and power the juror holds in the external world, this strategy suggests challenging other high-status jurors so your favorite remains as the natural leader.
- *The crackpot consultant.* Some lawyers have employed psychics, hypnotists, physiognomists, and handwriting analysts in an effort to predict juror behavior.[73]
- *The grandstand play.* Announce that you are so confident in the strength of your case, that you will take the first twelve jurors called.
- *Use more than one method.* Perhaps the one thing we can say for certain about juror selection strategies is that you should not challenge a juror on the basis of any one single factor. Most jurors will have some strengths and some weaknesses.

4. EXERCISING YOUR CHALLENGES

The exercising of challenges is a delicate act, necessary to get rid of bad jurors, but rife with dangers of irritating those who remain. As Melvin Belli points out:

> The prospective jury panel is a small community itself ... resenting encroachment on the right of privacy of one of its members. Thus, when exercising the peremptory challenge, while the lawyer might be most happy to be rid of that particular juror, [the lawyer] should not affront the remaining community of jurors or perhaps the remaining ... friend of that juror[.] I have seen trial counsel repeatedly, without even looking at a challenged juror, one who has lost a day's wages and a day's time, peremptorily dismiss such a juror without even a nod of his head or thanks.[74]

Although all lawyers agree that you should exercise challenges with courtesy, they do not agree how this is best accomplished. Belli suggests that you look at the juror and say, "We excuse Mrs. Jones. Thank you very much for your coming here today." Others favor making a request to the court and letting the judge excuse the juror. Mauet suggests saying, "Your Honor, at this time we would ask that Mr. Smith be excused," and then letting the court

---

[72] Dennis Nagao & James Davis, *The Effects of Prior Experience on Mock Juror Case Judgments*, 43 SOC. PSYCHOL. Q. 190 (1980).

[73] *See, e.g.*, Paul Luvera, *Plaintiff's Approach to Jury Selection in the Injured Child Case, in* NEW FRONTIERS IN LITIGATION 12-13 (G. Holmes ed. 1979) (handwriting analysts); John McConahay, Courtney Mullin & Jeffrey Frederick, *The Uses of Social Science in Trials with Political and Racial Overtones: The Trial of Joan Little,* 41 LAW & CONTEMP. PROBS. 205, 214 (1977) (psychic used to advise attorneys on jurors' aura, "karma," and psychic vibrations); S. KASSIN & L. WRIGHTSMAN, *supra* note 67, at 58 (expert advised picking jurors based on physiognomic cues (facial characteristics)).

[74] M. BELLI, *supra* note 52, at 795-96.

thank and excuse the juror.[75] There is consensus that, if possible, challenges should be made at the bench out of the hearing of the jury, especially challenges for cause in which you must state a reason why a particular juror is biased.

Every lawyer has his or her own secret strategy for exercising challenges. The trial advocacy literature is full of advice on how to trick your opponent into challenging a juror you also wanted removed, how to employ peremptory challenges in a way that leaves a particular juror as the most likely foreperson, how to confuse your opponent by challenging an obviously favorable juror, and so on. Most of this advice conflicts, and no two advocates seem to agree on what you should try to accomplish. In the typical case, you probably do not even have enough peremptory challenges to remove all the obviously hostile, unfriendly jurors, let alone to engage in that kind of delicate tactical maneuvering suggested. If you represent the intoxicated defendant in a personal injury case, and there are three of the plaintiff's friends and two members of M.A.D.D. on the jury and you only are allowed four peremptory challenges, most of the fine points of jury selection strategy can be safely ignored.

Nevertheless, a few general tactical suggestions can be made:

- Use challenges for cause before you use peremptory challenges.
- Be wary of using up your peremptory challenges too fast — someone worse will inevitably be called as the next juror.
- Try to identify jurors who are friendly with each other (by watching whom they sit with or talk to, or by asking them). If you challenge one, challenge them all to avoid making enemies.
- Use a pairing strategy which recognizes that, in jury deliberations, natural allies will tend to support each other, and isolated jurors will have little influence. For example, if you are down to your last peremptory challenge, it is better to use it to break up a pair of natural allies than to remove an unfavorable juror who is already isolated. Without an ally, psychologists have shown that most jurors are unable to resist pressure from the majority to conform.[76]

5. DOES IT MAKE ANY DIFFERENCE?

Does it make any difference? Does it matter who is on the jury and whom you challenge? Lawyers often claim that they win cases by the shrewd use of challenges, but they have no way of knowing what the outcome would have been with twelve jurors picked at random. Psychologists suggest that whom you challenge makes little difference in most cases. In the face of extensive relevant evidence, juror decisions are largely unaffected by their individual attitudes.[77]

Two empirical studies seem to bear this out. Norbert Kerr and his colleagues studied whether attorneys could identify and remove jurors adversely affected by pretrial publicity, and discovered no correlation between jurors

---

[75] THOMAS A. MAUET, FUNDAMENTALS OF TRIAL TECHNIQUES 22 (3d ed. 1992).

[76] S. KASSIN & L. WRIGHTSMAN, supra note 67, at 174.

[77] See S. KASSIN & L. WRIGHTSMAN, supra note 67, at 32; Fulero & Penrod, supra note 66, at 244-51.

challenged and their actual vote.[78] Hans Zeisel and Shari Diamond found similar results. In *The Effect of Peremptory Challenges on Jury and Verdict: An Experiment in a Federal District Court*, 30 STAN. L. REV. 491 (1978), they wrote:

> Normally, this question cannot be answered with precision. Because the excused jurors do not attend the trial, there is no way of knowing how they would have voted had they not been removed. Our experiment attempted to secure this missing information by asking the peremptorily excused jurors to remain as shadow jurors in the courtroom and to reveal at the end of the trial how they would have voted in the case. This allowed us to become retrospectively clairvoyant — to see how well the prosecutor and defense counsel performed in their attempts to eliminate hostile jurors. More important, by combining this knowledge with posttrial interviews of the real jurors, we reconstructed the vote of the jury that would have decided the case had there been no peremptory challenges — that is, if the first 12 jurors in the venire, not excused for cause, had formed the jury. By comparing what the reconstructed "jury without peremptory challenges" would have done with what the real jury did, we were able to gauge the effect, if any, of the peremptory challenges on the composition of the jury and its verdict.
>
> The experiment was conducted in 12 criminal trials before three judges of the United States District Court for the Northern District of Illinois.... After the real jury was impaneled and sent to the jury room, the court asked the peremptorily excused jurors and the remaining venire members to participate in the study. The judge emphasized the importance of the study and explained to the jurors that they would be paid for their participation as part of their regular jury service. Almost 90% of those invited agreed to serve in our experiment.
>
> In each case, the judge asked the peremptorily challenged jurors to form a shadow jury and seated them in the first row of spectator seats. The size of these shadow juries varied from case to case depending on the number of peremptorily excused jurors and their willingness to cooperate with the experiment. Although our study required only the pre-deliberation votes of the peremptorily excused jurors, we formed them into "juries" to ensure that they would take their task seriously.
>
> The court then formed a second shadow jury by random selection from the remainder of the venire. This jury was seated without the benefit of voir dire — that is, without questioning and challenges — and therefore was dubbed the "English jury," because challenges, although permitted in England, are almost never exercised.
>
> Thus, each case actually was tried to three "juries": the real jury, another composed of peremptorily challenged jurors, and still a third containing jurors randomly selected from the remainder of the venire.
>
> Table 4 summarizes the results of our experiment. The actual verdict of the real jury is recorded in column 5. Column 6 represents the shift in the probability of a guilty verdict as a result of the peremptory challenges. A

---

[78] Kerr et al., *supra* note 2.

TABLE 4

Comparison of the Reconstructed "Juries Without Challenges"
and the Real Juries After Challenges

	Percentage Guilty Votes On First Ballot		Corresponding Percentage Probability That the Verdict Will Be Guilty*			
	(1)	(2)	(3)	(4)	(5)	(4) (3)
Case No.	"Jury Without Challenges"	Real Jury	"Jury Without Challenges"	Real Jury	Actual Verdict	Percentage Shift in Probability of Guilty Verdict as a Result of Challenges
1**	49	42	41	23	NG	- 18
2	88	83	96	94	G	- 2
3***	41	42	22	23	NG	+ 1
4	50	33	42	11	NG	- 30
5	77	83	91	94	G	+ 3
6	53	50	55	42	NG	- 13
7	72	83	89	94	G	+ 5
8	100	100	100	100	G	0
9	50	50	42	42	Hung	0
10	72	92	89	97	G	+ 8
11	38	17	17	2	NG	- 15
12	67	33	84	12	NG	- 72

   * Percentages are interpolated from Graph 1. *See* note 23 *supra* and accompanying text.
  ** Assuming an initial vote of 5 to 7. *See* not 20 *supra*. If an initial vote of 6 to 6 is assumed, (1) becomes 54% and (2) becomes 50%; if 4 to 8 is assumed, (1) becomes 44% and (2) becomes 33%.
*** Assuming an initial vote of 5 to 7. If an initial vote of 6 to 6 is assumed, (1) becomes 46% and (2) becomes 50%; if an initial vote of 4 to 8 is assumed, (1) becomes 36% and (2) becomes 33%.

negative score indicates a decrease in the likelihood of a guilty verdict, a positive score indicates an increase, and a score of zero shows that the peremptory challenges did not affect the probability of a guilty verdict.

These data provide a preliminary answer to our question of whether peremptory challenges affect jury verdicts. In 7 of the 12 cases, the combined effect of the challenges was minimal and did not produce the expectation that the verdict of the "jury without challenges" would have differed from that of the real jury. In the remaining cases the probability of a guilty verdict shifted at least 13 points. The most striking shift in probability occurred in Case 12. The real jury in that case voted for acquittal, while the reconstructed jury almost certainly would have convicted the defendant.

Our data gave us some idea of how well the attorneys used their allotted challenges to excuse jurors who ... would have voted against their side. We designed a rough performance index that evaluated the extent to which counsel employed peremptory challenges to dismiss hostile or friendly jurors. [The performance index is calculated as follows: If peremptory challenges resulted in excluding hostile jurors and improving

TABLE 9

Attorney Performance Index

Case No.	Prosecutor	Defense
1	+ 23	+ 46
2	− 59	+ 6
3	+ 44	+ 30
4	− 20	+ 44
5	+ 31	+ 48
6	− 61	− 11
7	+ 9	− 10
8	− 32	− 62
9	0*	+ 12
10	+ 58	+ 46
11	+ 62	+ 36
12	− 61	+ 19
Average (Mean)	− 0.5	+ 17.0
Average Fluctuation Around the Mean	± 38	± 25

* The prosecutor exercised only one challenge, and the challenged juror did not participate in the study.

the proportion of favorable votes, the attorney received a positive score, representing a percentage of how well the attorney could have done. If the attorney excused friendly jurors and shifted the balance of guilty/not guilty votes in favor of the opponent, the attorney received a negative score.]

The collective performance of the attorneys is not impressive. The prosecutors' average score is close to zero (-0.5). Thus, in the aggregate, the prosecutors made about as many good challenges as bad ones. The defense counsel's average performance score (+17.0) is slightly better, which suggests that, on the average, defense attorneys shifted in their favor the proportion of not guilty votes in the venire. These averages are misleading, however, because the fluctuations around them are so large. The prosecutors' scores fluctuate between + 62 (Case 11) and -61 (Cases 6 and 12); the defense counsel's scores fluctuate between +48 (Case 5) and -62 (Case 8). The average fluctuations around the mean scores are ± 38 for the prosecutor and ± 25 for the defense, suggesting that in this limited sample of 12 cases, attorney performance was highly erratic. As a result even though attorneys' scores on the average were around zero, in some cases the attorneys performed very poorly, and in others very well. And if, in a case, one side performs poorly while the other side performs well, such disparity may have interesting results.

There is a correspondence between those cases that Table 4 indicates had the greatest shifts in the probability of a given jury verdict and those cases in which, as Table 9 shows, the difference between levels of attorney performance was greatest. In Cases 1, 4 and 12 — the cases in which the effects of voir dire on jury verdicts were most pronounced — the shifts in the likelihood of a guilty verdict are related to differential levels of attorney performance. Case 12, for example, showed the most dramatic shift in the probability of a guilty verdict (-72), it was also the case in which attorney performance differed the most. The prosecutor had a marked negative score (-61), while the defense attorney had a performance score that was noticeably positive (+19). In Cases 1 and 4, where the respective shifts in probability were -18 and -30, differences between the performance levels of opposing counsel similarly occur.

The present analysis does not take up the complex task of discovering why some attorneys performed better than others. We do not know how much of their performance was the result of superior skill or of luck or simply of easier choices. Nor do we know to what extent the ever-shrinking information that becomes available during voir dire contributes to that differential performance. But whatever the reasons, the generally poor and occasionally disparate performances of the prosecutor and defense counsel raise questions concerning the role of peremptory challenges in furthering the constitutionally prescribed goal of trial by an impartial jury.

The first conclusion emerging from this study is that there are cases in which the jury verdict is seriously affected, if not determined, by the voir dire. At times, one attorney will significantly outperform the opposing attorney in challenging hostile jurors. Lawyers apparently do win some of their cases, as they occasionally boast, during or at least with the help of, voir dire.

One way of averting the undesirable effects of disparate performance would be to increase the amount of information on which lawyers base their decisions. The more they learn in open court about the prejudice of potential jurors, the less opportunity there is for luck or private knowledge to determine which side benefits from the peremptory challenge process.

NOTES

1. *Group questions.* In reality, many lawyers (and almost all judges) use questions to the entire panel when seeking information, despite evidence that group questions rarely produce valuable information. Melvin Belli suggests that some questions are productive when asked of the entire panel, and should be used because they lower the chance of embarrassing a juror and save time. He includes those questions that cover prior acquaintance with participants and prior experience with lawsuits. MELVIN BELLI, MODERN TRIALS vol. 1: 809 (1954). *But see* Dale Broeder, *Voir Dire Examinations: An Empirical Study*, 38 S. CAL. L. REV. 503, 513 (1965), in which a juror who knew plaintiff's family well did not reveal it when the entire panel was asked about connections with the parties, and Neal Bush, *The Case for Expansive Voir Dire*, 1 LAW & PSYCHOL. REV. 9 (1976), in which jurors withheld that they had been crime victims or had relatives who were police officers after seeing other jurors challenged on that basis.

2. *Use of stereotypes.* Making assumptions about prospective jurors and exercising peremptory challenges based on broad stereotypes is no longer fashionable. Few lawyers today will admit to doing so, although undoubtedly many still do. ROBERT KEETON, TRIAL TACTICS AND METHODS 249 (2d ed. 1973), defends the practice: "The limited time available for your appraisal of individuals on the panel makes it necessary to rely to a great extent upon the assumption that attitudes of particular individuals on the panel conform to those usually held by persons of similar background." The problem is that broad generalizations relating individual juror characteristics and decision making simply have no validity. *See* Robert Plutchik and Alice Schwartz, *Jury Selection: Folklore or Science?*, CRIM. L. BULL. at 6-9 (May 1965), reporting the results of an experiment in which men were more emotional than women, wealthy jurors were less sympathetic to corporate defendants than the poor, and age had no noticeable effect. Most psychologists assert that selection of jurors based on stereotypes is unreliable. *See* SAUL M. KASSIN & LAWRENCE S. WRIGHTSMAN, THE AMERICAN JURY ON TRIAL: PSYCHOLOGICAL PERSPECTIVES 29 (1988); Steven Penrod et al., *The Implications of Social Psychological Research for Trial Practice Attorneys*, in PSYCHOLOGY AND LAW 439 (D. Muller et al., eds., 1984).

3. *Should the client participate in deciding whom to challenge?* It became popular during the political movement of the 1960s and 1970s to involve the client in the selection of jurors. *See, e.g.*, ANN FAGAN GINGER, JURY SELECTION IN CIVIL AND CRIMINAL TRIALS § 19.51 (2d ed. 1984), describing the jury selection for the defense in the Angela Davis case as a collective process involving lawyers, Ms. Davis, and the political team. *Compare* John Appleman, *Selection of the Jury*, 1968 TRIAL LAW. GUIDE 207, 220 (recommending that you give the appearance of consulting with your client because it looks good to the jury) with FRED LANE, LANE'S GOLDSTEIN TRIAL TECHNIQUE § 9.81 (3d ed. 1984) (suggesting that involving the client is good business practice for future relationships with the client). *But see* Philip Corboy, *Structuring the Presentation of Proof or Evidence*,TRIAL DIPL. J., Summer 1978, at 20, 22-23:

> During jury selection, I strongly recommend that your client never [even] be present .... I am fully aware of the practice of many lawyers ... who go through the charade of talking to their clients before excusing or accepting the juror. I think this is bunk. I don't believe that jurors think that a client has the first thing to say about who is going to be on the jury .... I don't think any lawyer worth his weight in salt is ever going to allow a client [to] help him select a jury.

4. *Attempts to ingratiate yourself with the jury.* A good (if somewhat exaggerated) example of an ingratiating voir dire can be found in Gerry Spence, *A Voir Dire Masterpiece*, TRIAL DIPL. J., Fall 1980, at 8, 9-10, 56:

> Juror: I'd like to say that I'm not used to sitting. There are a lot of things I'd like to be doing. And I just don't want to be here.
> Mr. Spence: And I can understand it too. I guess Jimmy (the defendant) can understand that. I guess Jimmy doesn't want to be here. I guess the

two of you have got that in common, don't you? I know how bad he wants
to go.

5. *Establishing juror bias.* A challenge for cause made on the ground
that the juror cannot be fair is a question of fact for the court. As a practical
matter, the judge is likely to try to avoid a challenge while the attorney
pushes for it. To result in exclusion, the voir dire of such a juror must elicit
evidence that clearly shows the partiality of the juror. This is not an easy
task, as the following excerpt shows. It is by Charles Garry in *People v. Huey
Newton*:

Q: As you sit there, Mr. Strauss, in your opinion, right now while you
are sitting there this minute, is Huey P. Newton guilty or not guilty?
A: Well, I don't know for sure whether he shot the officer or not, but the
officer is dead.
Q: And by that same standard, just because the officer is dead, you are
going to say that Huey Newton did it; is that right?
A: Well, that's got to be proven.
Q: Well, my question is: As you sit there right now, do you believe that
Huey Newton shot and killed, stabbed, whatever it was, Officer Frey?
A: I don't know whether he shot him or not. That I can't say.
The Court: Mr. Strauss, you see, under our law there is a presumption of
innocence to start with. When you start the case the defendant is pre-
sumed to be innocent, and it is up to the People, the prosecution, to prove
to you beyond a reasonable doubt that the defendant is guilty. Do you
understand that?
The Juror: Yes.
The Court: So, now, not having heard any evidence, you must start with a
presumption of innocence. Do you know what I mean by presumption?
You must say, "As far as I know the man is innocent." Do you understand
that?
The Juror: Yes.
The Court: "And it is up to the prosecution to prove to me that he is
guilty." Do you understand that?
The Juror: Yes.
The Court: So, therefore, as it stands right now, do you believe he is guilty
before you hear any evidence?
The Juror: No.
Mr. Garry: Well, do you really believe that as Huey Newton sits here
right now next to me, that he is innocent of any wrongdoing of any kind?
A: No. That I don't believe.
Mr. Garry: See? There you are, Judge. I challenge this juror for cause.
The Court: Well, you see, I will have to explain to you again and see if you
understand it, Mr. Strauss. The ... mere fact that he has been indicted by
the Grand Jury, you are not to infer or presume in any way that the
defendant is or must be guilty. Do you understand that?
The Juror: Yes.

The Court: Do you accept the rule of law? If you don't accept that rule of law, you don't understand it. Do you accept it? Do you understand what I am saying?

The Juror: (Juror nods head affirmatively.)

The Court: Now, under the rule of law, different places in the world have different rules of law, but it is the law of the United States and of the State of California that a defendant charged with a crime is presumed to be innocent until his guilt is established beyond and to the exclusion of every reasonable doubt. Do you understand what that means?

The Juror: (Juror nods head affirmatively.)

The Court: Now, if that is the case, you must — before you hear any evidence at all — you must start on the theory and believe that this man is innocent. But as soon as they produce proof which satisfies you beyond a reasonable doubt that he is guilty, then you can feel otherwise. Do you understand that?

The Juror: Yes.

The Court: Are you willing to start out with that theory? Are you willing to start out on that basis?

The Juror: Yes.

The Court: You may examine further.

Mr. Garry: But you are not willing, Mr. Strauss, as you have already stated, to accept the fact that Huey Newton is absolutely innocent as he sits right now, are you, sir?

A: Well, that's a question I can't answer before I hear the evidence.

Mr. Garry: I submit the challenge, Your Honor.

[The Court: You may examine, Mr. Prosecutor.]

Mr. Jensen: Let me ask you this, Mr. Strauss: If you walked out of this courtroom right now with this jury and you went upstairs and they gave you two verdicts to vote on, guilty or not guilty, and all you know about the case is what you know right now, would you find him guilty?

A: No, not alone on that, what I have heard here.

Q: So that there is no evidence at all for you to make a verdict; is that right?

A: That's correct.

Q: So there is no evidence that would justify you in finding the man guilty; is that correct?

A: (Juror nods head affirmatively.)

Q: In other words, as Mr. Newton sits there, you, as a juror, have no evidence about any of the charges in this case; is that correct?

A: Right.

Q: Now, the District Attorney, the prosecution has the burden of bringing some evidence in before anything can happen. Do you understand that?

A: Yes.

Q: Now, if the District Attorney does not produce any evidence at all, the man is not guilty. Isn't that correct?

A: That's right.

Q: So that if you are to deliberate right now you have no evidence; isn't that right?

A: That's right.

Q: So you would find him not guilty; isn't that right?

A: Yes.

Q: Is there any evidence as far as you are concerned right now that Mr. Newton is guilty of anything?

A: No.

Q: The fact that there has been a charge here, that is that he is charged with murder, assault, and kidnapping, is that, as far as you are concerned, evidence that he is guilty of anything?

A: No. That isn't evidence, no.

Q: As far as you are concerned, what is evidence?

A: What I am going to hear here in Court.

Q: Is that going to come from witnesses, as far as you are concerned?

A: From witnesses, yes.

Q: It is not going to be newspapers or anything like that?

A: No.

Q: Will you decide the case just on what the witnesses say?

A: Yes.

Mr. Jensen: As Your Honor said, I think this is a semantic problem.

The Court: You may examine further, Mr. Garry.

By Mr. Garry: Mr. Strauss, again I ask you that same question which you have answered three times to me now —

The Court: No. Please ask the question without preface.

Mr. Garry: As Huey Newton sits here next to me now, in your opinion is he absolutely innocent?

A: Yes.

Q: But you don't believe it, do you?

A: No.

The Court: Challenge is allowed.

ANN FAGAN GINGER, JURY SELECTION IN CIVIL AND CRIMINAL TRIALS § 17.4 (2d ed. 1984).

G. BIBLIOGRAPHY

1. GENERAL

GORDON BERMANT, CONDUCT OF THE VOIR DIRE EXAMINATION: PRACTICES AND
   OPINIONS OF FEDERAL DISTRICT JUDGES (1977).
FRANCIS X. BUSCH, LAW AND TACTICS OF JURY TRIALS vol. 1: 481-862 (1959).
William H. Fortune, *Voir Dire in Kentucky: An Empirical Study of Voir Dire
   in Kentucky Circuit Courts*, 69 KY. L.J. 273 (1981).
ANN F. GINGER, JURY SELECTION IN CIVIL AND CRIMINAL TRIALS (2d ed. 1984).
JAMES J. GOBERT & WALTER E. JORDAN, JURY SELECTION: THE LAW, ART, AND
   SCIENCE OF SELECTING A JURY (2d ed. 1990).
FRED LANE, LANE'S GOLDSTEIN TRIAL TECHNIQUE, chapter 9 (3d ed. 1984).

PATRICK McCLOSKEY & RONALD SCHOENBERG, CRIMINAL LAW ADVOCACY —
JURY SELECTION (1992).
NATIONAL JURY PROJECT, JURYWORK: SYSTEMATIC TECHNIQUES (2d ed. 1992).
David U. Strawn, *Ending the Voir Dire Wars*, JUDGES JOURNAL at 45 (Spring
1979).
WARD WAGNER, ART OF ADVOCACY — JURY SELECTION (1981).

2. LAW

S. Mac Gutman, *The Attorney-Conducted Voir Dire of Jurors: A Constitutional Right*, 39 BROOK. L. REV. 290 (1972).
J. Alexander Tanford, *Racism in the Adversary System: The Defendant's Use
of Peremptory Challenges*, 63 S. CAL. L.REV. 1015 (1990).

3. PSYCHOLOGY

Jeffrey T. Frederick, *Jury Behavior: a Psychologist Examines Jury Selection*, 5
OHIO N.U. L. REV. 571 (1978).
Solomon M. Fulero & Steven Penrod, *The Myths and Realities of Attorney
Jury Selection Folklore and Scientific Jury Selection: What Works?*, 17 OHIO
N.U. L. REV. 229, 244-51 (1990).
John McConahay, Courtney Mullin & Jeffrey Frederick, *The Uses of Social
Science in Trials With Political and Racial Overtones: The Trial of Joan
Little*, 41 LAW & CONTEMP. PROBS. 205 (1977).
Michael Saks, *The Limits of Scientific Jury Selection: Ethical and Empirical*,
17 JURIMETRICS 3 (1976).
David Suggs & Bruce D. Sales, *Using Communication Cues to Evaluate Pro-
spective Jurors During the Voir Dire*, 20 ARIZ. L. REV. 629 (1978).
David Suggs & Bruce D. Sales, *Juror Self-Disclosure in the Voir Dire: A
Social Science Analysis*, 56 IND. L.J. 245 (1981).
Hans Zeisel & Shari Diamond, *The Effect of Peremptory Challenges on Jury
and Verdict: an Experiment in a Federal District Court*, 30 STAN. L. REV.
491 (1978).

4. TACTICS

John Appleman, *Selection of the Jury*, 1968 TRIAL LAW. GUIDE 207.
Karen Blue, *How to Improve Your Chances For Selecting a Favorable Jury:
Proven Psychological Principles to Use During Voir Dire*, in WOMEN TRIAL
LAWYERS: HOW THEY SUCCEED IN PRACTICE AND IN THE COURTROOM 57 (J.
Warsaw ed. 1987).
Harry S. Bodin, *Selecting a Jury*, in CIVIL LITIGATION AND TRIAL TECHNIQUES
225 (1976).
RICHARD J. CRAWFORD, THE PERSUASION EDGE 49-100 (1989).
David Crump, *Attorneys' Goals and Tactics in Voir Dire Examination*, 43 TEX.
B.J. 244 (1980).
Bruce Davis & Richard Wiley, *49 Thoughts on Jury Selection*, 1965 TRIAL
LAW. GUIDE 351.

Herald P. Fahringer, *In the Valley of the Blind: A Primer on Jury Selection in a Criminal Case*, 43 LAW & CONTEMP. PROBS. 116 (1980).
JAMES W. JEANS, LITIGATION, chapter 8 (2d ed. 1992).
JAMES W. JEANS, TRIAL ADVOCACY, chapter 7 (1975).
ALAN MORRILL, TRIAL DIPLOMACY 1-21 (2d ed. 1972).
HERBERT J. STERN, TRYING CASES TO WIN, vol. 1: chapter 14 (1991).

Chapter 4

OPENING STATEMENT

A. INTRODUCTION

After the jury has been selected, the parties give their opening statements. The opening statements serve as the introduction to the trial. Most attorneys use this opportunity to give the jurors a summary of the facts in a logical outline so they can see how the evidence fits into a cohesive whole. Because evidence is presented in bits and pieces from numerous witnesses and exhibits, a clear opening statement of your case that the jurors can comprehend and remember is important. Opening statements help jurors understand the nature of the dispute, focus on the key evidence, and place witnesses and exhibits in their proper context.

Trial practitioners suggest that there are four main purposes to be accomplished in opening statements:

- Present a clear picture of the case to the jury: its major events, participants, instrumentalities, disputes and contentions.
- Arouse the interest of the jurors in your case and general theory so that they want to hear your evidence. If jurors become bored (or worse, if they become antagonistic), they may be inattentive while you present your witnesses.
- Build rapport with the jurors, speaking to them as intelligent people and communicating your sincere belief in your cause. This continues the process of establishing bonds with jurors that was begun in the voir dire.
- For the defense, the opening statement presents the opportunity to alert jurors that there will be two sides to the case so they do not make up their minds too soon.

Many trial practitioners assert that the opening statement is the most underrated and overlooked part of the case. As opportunities for extensive voir dire are reduced, the importance of a persuasive opening statement increases. While you cannot expect jurors to reach a decision in your favor based solely on your opening remarks, you can make effective use of the principle of primacy to begin this persuasion process. Too often, lawyers squander this opportunity to present their theory and highlight the pivotal evidence. Instead, they choose to read the pleadings, bury the important facts in a boring mass of trivial details, sacrifice coherence to plod through a witness-by-witness summary, ignore the facts in favor of broad generalizations, or waive opening altogether.

Proper opening statements are not arguments, although you occasionally will hear them referred to as such. Opening statements are supposed to be limited to the facts you intend to prove. The temptation to argue — to discuss legal standards, debate the respective credibility of witnesses, make inferences, and speak in broad terms about justice and truth — may be almost irresistible at times. Not only is succumbing to temptation objectionable; it may not be wise. After all, it was the evidence that convinced you to go to trial, and it will be evidence that carries the jury. This is your opportunity not to tell the jurors that you have the evidence on your side, but to show them. As Lloyd Stryker, one of the great trial lawyers put it, "Evidence itself is eloquence, and the facts, if properly arranged ... will shout louder than you possibly could."[1]

The most common problem seems to be that lawyers cannot resist overstating the evidence. Over 100 years ago, the first treatise on trial practice warned:

> A caution given by authors generally, is, never to overstate the evidence. Clearly right as this rule is, few are more often violated. Advocates very frequently exaggerate, and the result is generally disastrous, for jurors are quick to resent what they conceive to be an attempt to deceive them. Not only this, but they are very apt to think that all that is stated must be proved or else no case can be made out, and when the proof falls short of the statement they are quite likely to conclude that the advocate has no case. There is yet another reason supporting this rule, and that is this: where the evidence is stronger than the statement, the advocate secures credit for modesty and candor, and these are great virtues in the eyes of the jurors. It is never to be forgotten in stating the facts that keen and hostile eyes are watching, and that an unrelenting enemy is on the alert ready and eager to expose the least misstatement or mistake. It may be that the Roman priests were ... able to deceive Jupiter by chalking over the dark spots of the sacrificial bull; but, if they were, he was not so keen-eyed as an opposing counsel is likely to be, for chalking dark spots in a statement of facts will not deceive him. Fictions will not supply the place of facts.[2]

NOTE

How important is the opening statement? In Charles Becton & Terri Stein, *Opening Statement*, 20 TRIAL LAW. Q. 10, 10 (1990), appears the following statement: "Empirical studies conclude that after hearing opening statements, 65 to 80 percent of jurors not only make up their minds about the case, but in addition, in the course of the trial, they do not change their minds." This oft-repeated assertion is false. *See* William L. Burke, Ronald L. Poulson, & Michael J. Brondino, *Fact or Fiction: The Effect of the Opening Statement*, 18 J. CONTEMP. L. 195 (1992). Jurors do not make up their minds during opening statements (before they have heard any evidence). This piece of misinformation is usually attributed to the research of the University of Chicago Jury Project, but no actual source is ever cited, and all that the Chicago Jury Project found was that "the real decision is often made before the deliberation begins." Most jurors reach a tentative decision at the *end* of the trial, after

---

[1] LLOYD PAUL STRYKER, THE ART OF ADVOCACY 53 (1954).
[2] BYRON K. & WILLIAM F. ELLIOTT, THE WORK OF THE ADVOCATE 206-07 (1888).

closing arguments , and most verdicts reflect the majority's tentative decision. HARRY KALVEN & HANS ZEISEL, THE AMERICAN JURY 488-89 (1966). According to the late Hans Zeisel, no data was ever collected that could support a conclusion that jurors make a decision after opening statements.

The initial misinterpretation of the Chicago Jury Project's findings can be traced to JOHN APPLEMAN, PREPARATION AND TRIAL 189 (1967), who stated without citation: "Studies made by the University of Chicago indicate that approximately 65 percent of jury results are consistent with their beliefs arrived at immediately following opening statements. This does not mean, of necessity, that the opening statement alone has done the job." From there, like in the game of "telephone," this misinformation has been passed from lawyer to lawyer, and changed and exaggerated with each retelling. In all the articles citing these supposed findings, there is not one citation to a published study. *See* Orville Richardson, *Persuasion in the Opening Statement: The Plaintiff's Approach, in* OPENING STATEMENTS AND CLOSING ARGUMENTS 16 (G. Holmes ed. 1982) (reprinting a 1969 speech) (Chicago Jury Project study by Kalven showed that jurors make up minds "early" in case and never change); ALAN MORRILL, TRIAL DIPLOMACY 22 (2d ed. 1972) (study at Chicago established that sixty-five percent of jurors ultimately decide case consistent with first impressions formed after opening statements); Craig Spangenberg, *What I Try to Accomplish in an Opening Statement, in* EXCELLENCE IN ADVOCACY 17 (G. Holmes ed. 1971) (study of mock jurors showed that eighty percent made up their minds after opening statements and their opinions could not be changed); JAMES JEANS, TRIAL ADVOCACY 199 (1975) (study based on interviews of actual jurors showed that eighty percent made up their minds after opening statements); John Shepherd, *The Defendant's Approach in Opening Statement, in* PERSUASION: THE KEY TO SUCCESS IN TRIAL 21 (G. Holmes ed. 1977) (Professor Calvin's [sic] great work established that many cases are decided on the basis of opening statements alone); Tom Alexander, *The Opening Statement in the Product Case, in* OPENING STATEMENTS AND CLOSING ARGUMENTS 59 (G. Holmes ed. 1982) (attributing study to Case Western Reserve University); RICHARD J. CRAWFORD, THE PERSUASION EDGE 104 (1989) (may be even more than 80%).

B. EXAMPLE OF AN OPENING STATEMENT

It is difficult to provide you with a representative opening statement, because their length and detail vary widely with the complexity of the case and the freedom given to you in voir dire. The more complicated the case and the less participation you are allowed in voir dire, the longer and more detailed your opening will need to be. However, the following example, adapted from FRANCIS X. BUSCH, LAW AND TACTICS IN JURY TRIALS, vol. 2: 840-41 (1959), presents the issues discussed in this chapter, and should give you a feeling for the scope and organization of a typical opening statement.

May it please the Court, and you, Ladies and Gentlemen of the Jury: Our defense is that the witnesses for the State who have attempted to identify John Russo are mistaken. This man, John Russo, was nowhere near the scene of this hold-up when it occurred. As a matter of fact, he was more than 35 miles away. Like many a mystery, this one is a case of mistaken identity.

What will the evidence show? It will show that the crime was committed by two men who arrived and fled by automobile. John Russo owns no automobile and does not know how to drive one.

It will show that the hold-up men were armed. John Russo owns no gun, and no gun was ever found that can be connected to him.

It will show that the crime happened way out here [pointing to location on a map] south of the city on Western Avenue, about midnight. Yet John and his witnesses will testify that Russo lived with his widowed mother and sister at Orleans Street, on what is known as the near north side of Chicago [pointing to location on a map]. His house is about 11 miles north of where this hold-up occurred.

Russo works even farther away. For about six months before the hold-up, John was employed at a tavern and restaurant on Deerfield Road near the village of Niles [pointing to location on a map]. That is about 35 miles northwest of the scene of the crime. Russo's working hours at the tavern were from 4 p.m. to midnight. His job was that of a porter and handyman.

The testimony of the tavern owner and two other witnesses who were patrons of the place will be that on the night in question, March 13, Russo worked steadily at the tavern from 4 o'clock in the afternoon until midnight. At midnight, when the robbery was taking place, John was walking to catch the 12:20 suburban train which would take him to the Chicago Avenue station of the Elevated Railroad in Chicago. He caught the train, got off at Chicago Avenue, walked to his home and arrived there about 1:30. His mother was sitting up for him and will testify he arrived home at that time. His sister, who was 14 years old, was asleep. She is not allowed to stay up that late, so she did not see him until the next day at noon, when she got home from school.

The evidence will show that the train was the quickest and practically the only means of transportation which John could use. Neither Russo nor any of his family owns an automobile, and as I have stated, Russo had never driven an automobile, and did not know how to drive one.

John Russo will take the stand, and face you and the prosecutor, and tell his story. He knows nothing of this hold-up and will swear to you that he had nothing to do with it. He has been brought up and has always lived on the near north side. He had no business and no friends or acquaintances on the south side, and has never had occasion to be and never has been in the neighborhood of 115th Street and Western Avenue where this hold-up occurred. Based on this evidence I shall ask and expect you to return a verdict of not guilty.

NOTE

Other examples. Many other examples of opening statements can be found in LEONARD DECOF, ART OF ADVOCACY — OPENING STATEMENT (1982), ALFRED S. JULIEN, OPENING STATEMENTS (1980); RICHARD J. CRAWFORD, THE PERSUASION EDGE 118-37 (1989); JAMES W. JEANS, LITIGATION §§ 9.30-9.31 (2d ed.

1992); FRED LANE, LANE'S GOLDSTEIN TRIAL TECHNIQUE §§ 10.73-10.76 (3d ed. 1984); THOMAS A. MAUET, FUNDAMENTALS OF TRIAL TECHNIQUES 61-70 (3d ed. 1992).

C. LEGAL FRAMEWORK

1. RIGHT TO MAKE OPENING STATEMENTS

Opening statements by the attorneys are traditionally given at the start of the trial after the jury has been selected and sworn. The practice is so well established as part of the adversary system, that it probably rises to the level of a right. In *United States v. Stanfield*,[3] the court held:

> The practice of permitting attorneys to make opening statements is a practice long accepted as established and traditional in jury trials. It has the practical purpose of directing the attention of the jurors to the nuances of the proposed evidence in such a way as to make the usual piece-meal presentation of testimony more understandable as it is received.... We strongly believe that the well established and practical custom of permitting opening statements by counsel at jury trials in criminal cases should be continued in the district courts of this circuit.

The right to make an opening statement is not constitutionally required, however. It is not among the traditions of the adversary factfinding process that have been constitutionalized in the Sixth and Fourteenth Amendments. The court in *United States v. Salovitz*[4] traced the legal history of the opening statement:

> Some States provided by statute that the defendant might open after the prosecution had completed its case. Others provided that the defendant's opening might be made immediately following the prosecution's. Other States gave the defendant the option of opening either before or after the prosecution's proof. Some States permitted the defendant to exercise the option of reserving his opening statement until the close of the State's case only if the defendant was going to present evidence.
>
> Still other States, of which Connecticut is one, permit the trial court to decide in its discretion whether a defendant may open at all....
>
> We have held in a civil case that "opening is merely a privilege to be granted or withheld depending on the circumstances of the individual case."
>
> "The Constitution requires no more than that trials be fairly conducted and that guaranteed rights of defendants be scrupulously respected." *McGautha v. California*, 402 U.S. 183, 221, 91 S. Ct. 1454, 1474, 28 L. Ed. 2d 711 (1971); *see Cupp v. Naughten*, 414 U.S. 141, 146, 94 S. Ct. 396, 400, 38 L. Ed. 2d 368 (1973). We believe that an opening statement by the defendant is not such a guaranteed right, and that the making and timing of opening statements can be left constitutionally to the informed discretion of the trial judge.

---

[3] 521 F.2d 1122 (9th Cir. 1975).
[4] 701 F.2d 17 (2d Cir. 1982).

2. PROCEDURE

Opening statements customarily are given after the jury has been selected and sworn and before any evidence is produced. The party with the burden of proof — usually the plaintiff or prosecutor — gives the first opening statement, followed immediately by the defense. In most jurisdictions, the defense has the option of postponing (reserving) the opening statement until the beginning of its presentation of evidence. The trial judge generally has discretion to change the normal order of opening remarks in unusual circumstances.[5] In most jurisdictions, statutes or court rules determine the order and timing of opening statements. MICHIGAN COURT RULE 2.507(A) is typical:

> *Opening statements.* Before the introduction of evidence, the attorney for the party who is to commence the evidence must make a full and fair statement of that party's case and the facts the party intends to prove. Immediately thereafter, or immediately before the introduction of evidence by the adverse party, the attorney for the adverse party must make a like statement. Opening statements may be waived with the consent of the court and the opposing attorney.

Jurisdictions differ on whether a party may waive its opening statement altogether. Many, like Michigan, require the plaintiff to give an opening statement that presents a full and fair statement of its evidence, demonstrating that the plaintiff can establish a prima facie case.[6] Other jurisdictions allow the plaintiff to waive opening remarks.[7] Most jurisdictions permit the defendant to waive opening remarks,[8] although a few follow the Michigan rule and require opening statements from both sides.

3. THE CONTENT OF OPENING STATEMENT

The purpose of an opening statement is to inform the jurors in a general way of the nature of your case so that they will be better prepared to understand the evidence.[9] The farther you stray from this legitimate purpose, the more likely it is that an objection to "improper opening" will be sustained. Precisely how much latitude you will be given to discuss your case is left to the discretion of the trial judge. Not all trial judges will strictly enforce the law of opening statement discussed in this section. Only if impermissible remarks jeopardize the fairness of the trial will they warrant the granting of a mistrial.[10]

---

[5] *See, e.g.,* CAL. CIV. PROC. CODE § 607 (the trial must proceed in normal order "unless the court, for special reasons otherwise directs"); *State v. Guffey,* 205 Kan. 9, 468 P.2d 254 (1970) (court has inherent discretion to vary order seemingly required by statute).

[6] *See* MICH. CT. R. 2.507(A); *Fleetwood v. State,* 168 Ind. App. 545, 343 N.E.2d 812 (1976); *State v. Shaffer,* 260 La. 605, 257 So. 2d 121 (1971).

[7] *See* CAL. PENAL CODE § 1093; MINN. R. CIV. P. 39.04; *Mora v. People,* 472 P.2d 142 (Colo. 1970); *State v. Biggs,* 29 Utah 2d 183, 506 P.2d 1273 (1973).

[8] *E.g.,* CAL. CIV. P. CODE § 607.

[9] *Best v. District of Columbia,* 291 U.S. 411, 415 (1934).

[10] *E.g., Vosevich v. Doro, Ltd.,* 536 S.W.2d 752 (Mo. App. 1976).

a. The Prohibition Against Argument

The most basic rule of opening statements is that argument is prohibited.[11] The rule is easy to state, but hard to define precisely. Two common definitions are:

- If it is something you intend to prove, it is not argument. If you make a statement that is not susceptible of proof, it is argument.[12]
- Whenever you make a statement, if a witness could take the stand and make the same statement, it is not argument. However, if the rules of evidence would prevent such testimony, or if no such witness exists, the remarks are argumentative.[13]

However, these definitions are too limited. The cases permit something more than just a recital of evidence. Many judges will allow you to make fair inferences from the evidence, such as "We will prove that the defendant shot the victim for no good reason."[14] Judges also generally permit you to state your legal claim or defense in basic terms and to describe the nature of the case or the issues.[15]

The prohibition against argument must be understood in light of the reason for giving opening statements. As long as opening remarks will assist the jury in understanding the evidence, they are permissible. However, when they turn distinctly partisan, by asking the jury to resolve disputes, make inferences, or interpret facts favorably to the speaker, the remarks are argumentative.[16] Common examples of argumentation include:

- Asking the jury to resolve disputes in your favor. For example, you cannot refer to your witnesses as "disinterested," and therefore more worthy of belief that your opponent's witnesses.[17]
- Making negative judgments about your adversary or referring to the other party in scurrilous terms. You cannot, for example, call the defendant a "big cow."[18]
- Using colorful labels that characterize facts in a way distinctly favorably to your side. For example, the prosecutor cannot characterize a killing as a "slaughter."[19]

b. Discussing the Law

Jurisdictions vary widely on the extent to which you may talk about law in your opening remarks. Most jurisdictions do not permit the law to be discussed in any detail in opening statement.[20] However, most will permit you to

---

[11] See United States v. De Rosa, 548 F.2d 464 (3d Cir. 1977).

[12] LEONARD DECOF, ART OF ADVOCACY — OPENING STATEMENT § 1.06[1] (1982).

[13] JAMES JEANS, TRIAL ADVOCACY 206-07 (1975).

[14] Commonwealth v. Stevens, 419 A.2d 533 (Pa. 1980).

[15] State v. Freeman, 378 S.E.2d 545, 550-51 (1989). Cf. MINN. DIST. CT. R. 27(c)7 (attorney must confine himself or herself to stating facts).

[16] State v. Freeman, 378 S.E.2d 545, 551 (N.C. App. 1989).

[17] Lybarger v. Dep't of Roads, 128 N.W.2d 132 (Neb. 1964).

[18] Turner v. Commonwealth, 240 S.W.2d 80 (Ky. 1951).

[19] Hurst v. State, 356 So. 2d 1224 (Ala. App. 1978).

[20] United States v. Ziele, 734 F.2d 1447, 1455 (11th Cir. 1984); Lam v. Lam, 212 Va. 758, 188 S.E.2d 89 (1972).

state briefly the main legal issues on which the case depends. A Vermont court held:

> In an opening statement to the jury the plaintiff's counsel briefly out-lined his claim with regard to the law of negligence. The gist of the statement in this regard was that negligence is a shortage of duty; but some expressions were used which deviated from an accurate definition of negligence. Counsel expressly disclaimed that such statement was made in correct legal form, and at the outset reminded the jury that they were to take the law from the court. There was nothing of an inflammatory character in the statement, and what was said about the law was put forward in a way that suggested to the jury that the claim of the defen-dants would differ from that of the plaintiff. An exception was taken to the opening statement, but it avails nothing. In so holding there is no intention on the part of the court of giving countenance to the idea that counsel may argue the law to the jury, or read law to the jury, or treat as open questions of law upon which the court has ruled, or in any way seek to have the jury understand that they can do otherwise than to take the law from the court.[21]

When a cause of action is based on a statute, you usually will be permitted to read the statute or an approved jury instruction, but you will not be allowed to go further and argue how the law is supposed to be interpreted.[22]

c. Reference to Pleadings

Courts are split over whether it is permissible to read from or describe the pleadings during opening statement. The majority allow you to refer to the pleadings if doing so will explain the procedural posture of the case, clarify the factual contentions, or help identify which issues are contested and which have been admitted. This is a matter usually left to the discretion of the presiding judge.[23]

An exception to the general rule allowing you to refer to pleadings is the prohibition against telling the jury the specific dollar amount asked for in a complaint for damages. Most jurisdictions will not permit reference to the *ad damnum* clause, since the amount claimed — often in the millions of dollars — bears no necessary relationship to the damages actually sustained and provable.[24] However, damages may be mentioned if they are liquidated or capable of precise calculation and present no intangible issues such as pain and suffering or the value of property.

---

[21] *Lewes v. John Crane & Sons*, 78 Vt. 216, 219-20, 62 A. 60, 61 (1905). *Contra Williams v. Goodman*, 214 Cal. App. 2d 856, 29 Cal. Rptr. 877 (1963); *State v. Kendall*, 200 Iowa 483, 203 N.W. 806 (1925).

[22] *E.g.*, *Northern Trust Co. v. St. Francis Hosp.*, 522 N.E.2d 699 (Ill. App. 1988).

[23] *See, e.g.*, *Henderson v. Henderson*, 172 A.2d 956, 568 N.Y.S.2d 664 (1991).

[24] *E.g.*, *Botta v. Brunner*, 26 N.J, 82, 138 A.2d 713 (1958).

d. Discussion of Facts

Opening statements are supposed to be limited to summaries of the basic facts you intend to prove. Three rules follow from this: you may not refer to inadmissible evidence, you may not exaggerate or overstate your evidence, and you may not discuss evidence you expect your opponent to introduce that will not be part of your own case.

The basic rule is that you may not refer in opening statement to evidence that would be inadmissible at trial. If you do, your opponent may object, and the judge probably will instruct the jury to disregard your remark.[25] If the reference to inadmissible evidence is damaging enough, it may constitute grounds for a mistrial.[26] If the judge has excluded the evidence on a motion in limine,[27] then obviously it is error to mention it. Otherwise, however, judges will rarely sustain this objection unless the evidence is clearly inadmissible. If evidence is of borderline admissibility or depends for its admissibility on the laying of a proper foundation, the courts apply the "good-faith-basis" test. Under this standard, you may refer to any evidence that you have reasonable grounds to believe is admissible, and that you intend to offer.[28]

What does this mean in practical terms? The judge probably will sustain an objection that an attorney is discussing inadmissible evidence under the following circumstances:

- The evidence was excluded in a pretrial motion.
- The evidence could only come from a person who is not on the witness list.
- The evidence is privileged.
- The evidence violates one of the specific relevance exclusionary rules:

Rule 407:	Subsequent remedial measures.
Rule 408:	Offers to compromise.
Rule 409:	Payment of medical expenses.
Rule 410:	Plea discussions.
Rule 411:	Liability insurance.
Rule 412:	A rape victim's past behavior.

- The evidence violates the best evidence rule requiring production of the original document when its content are a material issue.

However, objections on the following grounds are difficult for the judge to sustain:

- Rule 402: General irrelevancy.
- Rule 403: The evidence is too prejudicial, confusing, or time-wasting.
- Objections based on the inability of your opponent to lay a foundation for:

Rule 404:	Character evidence.
Rule 406:	Habit.

---

[25] *Rutledge v. State*, 374 So. 2d 975 (Fla. 1979).

[26] *See Hall v. State*, 138 Ga. App. 20, 225 S.E.2d 705 (1976).

[27] Motions in limine are discussed in Chapter 2, part E, § 2.

[28] *E.g., Rutledge v. State*, 374 So.2d 975 (Fla. 1979); *Lybarger v. Dep't of Roads*, 128 N.W.2d 132 (Neb. 1964).

Rule 601: Competency to testify.
Rule 602: Personal knowledge.
Rules 607-610: Impeachment.
Rule 613: Prior statements of witnesses.
Rule 701: A lay opinion.
Rules 702-705: Expert testimony.
Rules 801-804: A hearsay exception.
Rules 901-902: Particular exhibits.

A closely related problem concerns exaggeration or overstatement of evidence. Overstatements can take two forms: promising evidence you know you cannot deliver, and making exaggerated inferences from the facts. The most obvious problem arises if an attorney discusses facts that cannot be proved. To do so is obviously error, but one that may not become known until the close of trial[29] — the trial judge obviously has not yet heard any evidence, so the judge cannot know what will be proved.

Making exaggerated inferences also is improper. For example, if you believe your witness will testify that the defendant's car was traveling 65 miles an hour, you may be tempted to tell the jury that you will prove the defendant was driving "much too fast." It is technically improper to state this kind of inference that involves subjective judgment, unless it reflects the *witness'* conclusion that the witness will draw on the stand. If the inference will have to be drawn by the *jury* based on the evidence, then it is improper to mention it in opening statement if it will be disputed. It is difficult for the courts to police this rule, however, because the judge cannot know in advance whether a witness will or will not testify to the particular conclusion stated by the attorney. Thus, the general standard of enforcement is to allow lawyers considerable latitude in stating what they expect to prove. The only remedy if your opponent abuses this license is to object at the time of the remark, and then move to strike it later after your opponent rests without proving it.

In general, you may not anticipate your opponent's defenses nor talk about the facts your opponent intends to prove. Unless you plan to offer the evidence yourself, you lack a good-faith basis that your statements will be supported by testimony, since you have no control over whether your opponent will call a particular witness or elicit testimony on a particular defense. However, once your opponents have committed themselves to a course of action in their pleadings, in voir dire, or in opening statements, then you may refer to it in a nonargumentative way.

Most jurisdictions permit you to go into as much detail as you want, as long as you do not overstate the actual evidence. Choice of the proper level of detail is a tactical one, subject to the judge imposing reasonable time limits. However, a few jurisdictions have rules prohibiting reciting the evidence in too much detail, although it is doubtful that a violation of this rule ever would be reversible error.[30]

---

[29] *E.g., Smith v. Covell*, 161 Cal. Rptr. 377 (1980).
[30] *See Stuthman v. United States*, 67 F.2d 521 (8th Cir. 1933). *Cf. United States v. De Rosa*, 548 F.2d 464 (3d Cir. 1977) (reversible if detailed description and evidence later excluded).

e. Exhibits

In most jurisdictions, you are permitted to use exhibits during opening statement. Exhibits that you reasonably believe will be introduced during the trial logically are evidence just like witness testimony, and you should be allowed to disclose them to the jury. Certainly the court should permit the use of accurate diagrams, charts and models that will help the jury understand the case, and most judges allow them.[31] Other kinds of exhibits that will be offered during trial, such as weapons, autopsy photographs, and bloody clothing, may be permitted at the court's discretion.[32] It is the custom in many courts to obtain the advance approval of the judge before using exhibits, especially potentially prejudicial ones.

f. Other Improper Matters

It is improper to include remarks in your opening statement that have nothing to do with the facts and issues of the case, especially if they tend to divert the jury's attention from the merits of the case. Thus, you should avoid the following:

- Making emotional appeals for sympathy for your own client, or antipathy toward the adverse party.[33]
- Appealing to racial, ethnic or other prejudices.[34]
- Personal remarks about the conduct, ethics, or character of the opposing party or attorney.[35]
- Referring to other similar cases or your own experience.[36]

g. Objections to Opening Remarks

If your opponent includes improper matter in his or her opening statement, you should object and move to strike the offending remarks. A prompt objection that states specific grounds is essential if you wish to preserve the matter for appeal.[37] Unless the remarks were extremely prejudicial, the court's granting of the motion and instructing the jury to disregard the objectionable statement will obviate the error.

---

[31] *E.g., Grimming v. Alton & So. Ry.*, 562 N.E.2d 1086 (Ill. App. 1990) (chart of damages). *Cf. People v. Reed*, 27 Cal. App. 2d 484, 81 P.2d 162 (1938) (prosecutor wrote name on blackboard several times to illustrate statement about handwriting identification).

[32] *E.g., Wapplehorst v. Kinmett*, 282 N.E.2d 53 (Ohio App. 1972). *Cf. State v. Posey*, 347 Mo. 1088, 152 S.W.2d 34 (1941) (even though alleged weapon not introduced at trial).

[33] *E.g., Nevels v. State*, 351 So. 2d 762 (Fla. App. 1977) (the suffering of a crime victim's family); *Horton v. Continental Volkswagen*, 382 So. 2d 551 (Ala. 1980).

[34] *See* Annot., 45 A.L.R.2d 303; Annot., 99 A.L.R.2d 1249.

[35] *See United States v. Stahl*, 616 F.2d 30 (2d Cir. 1980) (prejudice against defendant because of wealth); *Hartford Acc. & Indem. Co. v. List*, 424 S.W.2d 761 (Mo. 1968) (reference to plaintiff having a husband in prison).

[36] *E.g., State v. Stanley*, 123 Ariz. 95, 597 P.2d 998 (Ct. App. 1979) (telling jury that a co-defendant had pled guilty).

[37] *Haines v. State*, 170 Neb. 304, 102 N.W.2d 609 (1960).

4. LEGAL CONSEQUENCES OF OPENING STATEMENT

a. Directed Verdict After Inadequate Opening Statement

Some states require the party with the burden of proof to make a complete, legally sufficient opening statement. A legally sufficient opening is one that includes enough facts to make out a prima facie case on all essential elements of the cause of action. If you are unable to make out a prima facie case after a fair opportunity to do so, the court may grant a directed verdict against you before any evidence is introduced. The directed verdict will only be granted if it appears that you have stated all of your case and have been given the opportunity to amend your remarks to satisfy the requirement.[38] Courts exercise this power sparingly, and the law prefers that the case be tried on the merits. This is primarily a principle of civil procedure, although a few jurisdictions have extended the rule to criminal cases.[39] Not all jurisdictions approve such summary dispositions.[40]

b. Admissions

Factual admissions made during opening statement may constitute binding judicial admissions which preclude the party from contesting that fact. If it is a concession by the defense, it may relieve the plaintiff of the burden of proving it. If a factual concession is clear, unequivocal, and deliberate, it is likely to be held a binding admission.[41] Similarly, if you make a clear statement that you intend to rely on only one of several grounds asserted in your pleadings, or on only one of several defenses contained in your answer, you may be estopped from asserting the alternative grounds.[42] If there is any ambiguity in the statement, it is presumed that the attorney is not making an admission.

NOTES

1. *Denial of right to give opening statement.* In three situations, the parties may be refused the right to make opening statements. In some jurisdictions, the defendant may be denied the right if the plaintiff makes no opening. See *Stewart v. State*, 245 Ala. 511, 17 So. 2d 871 (1944). In some jurisdictions, the judge has discretion to dispense with opening statements if the issues are simple and have been clearly covered during the voir dire. See *United States v. 5 Cases, More or Less, Containing "Figlia Mia Brand,"* 179 F.2d 519 (2d Cir. 1950). In some jurisdictions, the defendant has a right to make an opening statement only if the defendant intends to call witnesses. See *Lewis v. United States*, 11 F.2d 745, 747 (6th Cir.1926); *Thompson v. People*, 139 Colo. 15, 336 P.2d 93 (1959).

---

[38]See *United States v. Donskey*, 825 F.2d 746 (3d Cir. 1987); *Best v. District of Columbia*, 291 U.S. 411, 415 (1934).

[39]See Annot., 75 A.L.R.3d 649.

[40]*E.g., White v. State*, 274 A.2d 671 (Md. 1971). Cf. *Uccello v. Laudenslayer*, 44 Cal. App. 3d 504, 118 Cal. Rptr. 741 (1975) (disfavored practice).

[41]See *Lystarczyk v. Smits*, 435 N.E.2d 1011 (Ind. App. 1982); *Miller v. Johnston*, 270 Cal. App. 2d 289, 75 Cal. Rptr. 699 (1969); *McLhinney v. Lansdell Corp.*, 254 Md. 7, 254 A.2d 177 (1969).

[42]Francis X. Busch, Law and Tactics in Jury Trials, vol. 2: 804 (1959).

2. *Inadequate opening statement as ineffective assistance of counsel.* *See* Annot., 6 A.L.R.4th 16 (circumstances under which a defense opening constitutes ineffective assistance of counsel).

3. *Order of opening in multi-party trials.* Where several attorneys represent multiple plaintiffs or defendants, the order of opening statements usually is resolved among counsel. If they are unable to decide, the court has the discretion to set the order. The party with the most to gain usually will go first for plaintiffs, and the party with the ultimate or primary liability or the largest financial interest usually will go first for the defendants. *See generally* Martin Littleton, *Opening to the Court or Jury, in* CIVIL LITIGATION AND TRIAL TECHNIQUES 309 (H. Bodin ed., 1976). With the consent of the court, attorneys representing multiple defendants may give their opening statements at different times, some immediately after the plaintiff, and others at the beginning of the defense case. Two openings generally are not permitted when multiple defendants are represented by the same attorney.

D. ETHICAL CONSIDERATIONS

Little specific attention has been paid to the ethical boundaries of opening statements. However, several general provisions of the MODEL RULES OF PROFESSIONAL CONDUCT are relevant:

- Rule 3.3: A lawyer "shall not knowingly make a false statement of material fact."
- Rule 3.4(e)(1): A lawyer may not "allude to any matter that the lawyer does not reasonably believe is relevant or that will not be supported by admissible evidence." It is not enough that the lawyer *hopes* evidence will be admitted, or believes there is a slim chance. The lawyer's belief must be objectively reasonable.
- Rule 3.4(e)(2): A lawyer shall not "assert personal knowledge of facts in issue."
- Rule 3.4(e)(3): A lawyer may not "state a personal opinion as to the justness of the cause, the credibility of a witness, the culpability of a civil litigant or the guilt or innocence of the accused."

Rule 3.4 also prohibits a lawyer from "knowingly disobey[ing] an obligation under the rules of a tribunal." Although the wording is vague, this provision probably makes it unethical to intentionally include in opening statement anything you know to violate the legal guidelines.[43] It is therefore unethical to try to get away with:

- Argument.
- Appeals to sympathy or prejudice.
- Discussions of the law.
- Exaggerated evidence or statements of facts and issues outside the scope of the pleadings.

---

[43] *See* RICHARD H. UNDERWOOD & WILLIAM H. FORTUNE, TRIAL ETHICS 309-16. The superseded MODEL CODE OF PROFESSIONAL RESPONSIBILITY was more explicit; DR 7-106(C)(7) provided that a lawyer was forbidden to "intentionally ... violate any established rule of procedure or of evidence."

- Attacks or negative comments on your opponent's case.

Consider the following case:

HAWK v. SUPERIOR COURT

42 Cal. App. 3d 108, 116 Cal. Rptr. 713 (1974)

In these proceedings by way of habeas corpus and certiorari, petitioner, an attorney, seeks to annul orders of the Solano County Superior Court adjudging him in direct contempt and imposing sentences totaling 54 days in jail and fines totaling $3,200.

The conduct found to be contemptuous occurred in the immediate view and presence of the court between August 14, 1972, and November 10, 1972, during the period petitioner was representing a defendant in a criminal case wherein the defendant was charged with 25 counts of murder.[44]

Contempt No. 5: Referring in his opening statement to two heart attacks suffered by the defendant "as the result of his arrest and incarceration." [The attorney] on numerous occasions, while examining prospective jurors, insinuated in certain questions asked by him that the defendant had been treated improperly and unfairly by the officers who arrested him[. T]he court had repeatedly admonished [him] that said statements and insinuations were improper[. N]evertheless, in his opening statement for defendant, contemnor did state "I would expect the county doctor to testify that Juan Corona suffered two heart attacks as the result of his arrest and incarceration."

The court found that contemnor's reference to the heart attacks was an effort to create sympathy in the minds of the jury for defendant and to create a prejudice against the prosecution, and that the reference constituted an improper and prejudicial attempt to influence the jurors at the trial of the action. In his opening statement a lawyer should confine his remarks to a brief statement of the issues in the case and evidence he intends to offer which he believes in good faith will be available and admissible. It is unprofessional conduct to allude to any evidence unless there is a good faith and reasonable basis for believing such evidence will be tendered and admitted in evidence.

Contempt No. 6: Referring to his client by his first name and making reference to his friendship for his client.... [W]hile examining prospective jurors, [the attorney] on numerous occasions referred to the defendant by his first name and on various occasions referred to his friendship for his client[. B]y such references contemnor intended to, and did, imply to the jury that he vouched for the character of his client[. T]he court repeatedly admonished contemnor that said appellation and references were improper; ... nevertheless, while making the defendant's opening statement to the jury, contemnor referred to his client as "Juan" and engaged in the following colloquy:

> MR. HAWK: Okay. Let me tell you about the man that I smuggled cupcakes into his cell up in Yuba City on his birthday in February of 1971 contrary to the Sheriff's office regulations about bringing in foodstuffs, which I did anyway.

---

[44] The defendant was Juan Corona, accused of murdering twenty-five migrant laborers. The case received nationwide publicity.

THE COURT: Mark the record for me, please, Mr. Reporter.

MR. HAWK: Let me tell you about Juan, the Christian.

MR. WILLIAMS: Objection ...

The court found that contemnor's continual references to his friendship and affection for the defendant constituted improper and prejudicial attempts to influence the jurors, a violation of the professional ethics of contemnor as an attorney-at-law, and an improper interference with the administration of justice in the trial of the case. As an officer of the court the lawyer should support the authority of the court and the dignity of the trial courtroom by strict adherence to the rules of decorum and by manifesting an attitude of professional respect toward the judge, opposing counsel, witnesses and jurors.

A court has authority to control courtroom conduct of an attorney that is in flagrant disregard of elementary standards of proper conduct and to temper his speech in order "to insure that courts of law accomplish that for which they were created — dispensing justice in a reasonable, efficient and fair manner." The record discloses that petitioner stubbornly defied the court's order to refrain from calling his client by his first name and from making reference to his friendship for his client. Petitioner's conduct, following numerous warnings, constituted a contempt of the authority of the court.

Contempt No. 7: Stating before the jury that the defendant "was stripped of his presumption of innocence by the press with the help of the Sheriff's Office." ... [C]ontemnor had been admonished on numerous occasions that certain of his statements and insinuations about the Sutter County Sheriff's Office were improper; ... nevertheless, in his opening statement on behalf of defendant, contemnor made the following statement:

> "Under oath it was alleged by one of the officers of the Sutter County Sheriff's Office, on which search warrants were had, and information which was passed out to the press, where Mr. Corona was stripped of his presumption of innocence by the press with the help of the Sheriff's Office."

The court found the references to be improper and prejudicial attempts to influence jurors, a violation of the professional ethics of contemnor as an attorney at law, and an improper interference with the administration of justice and the trial of the case. As we have noted, it is unprofessional conduct for a lawyer knowingly and for the purpose of bringing inadmissible matter to the attention of the judge or jury to make impermissible comments in the presence of the judge or jury.

NOTES

1. *"Bending" the rules.* In ALFRED JULIEN, OPENING STATEMENTS § 5.01 (1980) appears the following statement: "I am dissatisfied with any opening statement which does not at least draw from the district attorney the complaint that 'counsel is summing up.' There is no impropriety [in doing this]." What do you think of Mr. Julien's advice? At least two distinguished commentators on ethics agree with him. RICHARD UNDERWOOD & WILLIAM FORTUNE, TRIAL ETHICS 315 (1988) assert that "it is not unethical to [argue] unless

argument violates a standing order of the tribunal. Because it is rarely clear when a statement of the facts becomes argument, attorneys may legitimately press onward until halted by the court." The more common ethical advice is that if you intentionally argue to see if you can get away with it, you are acting unethically whether or not the opponent objects.

2. *Use of objections to interrupt your opponent's opening statement*. Using groundless objections to interrupt or harass your opponent is unethical. This problem is discussed more fully in Chapter 5, part B, § 4.

E. PREPARATION AND PLANNING

1. SELECTING A THEME

The first step in preparing an opening statement is to select a theme for your case that can be followed throughout the trial. Themes can be found in the elements of your case or in the characteristics of your client that arouse natural sympathy or coincide with universally admired principles. It is especially helpful if you can come up with a clever title for your theme. For example:

- *David and Goliath* — if you represent an individual against a large corporation.
- *Fighting city hall* — if you represent a person who has been the victim of inflexible policies of government bureaucracies or the unreasonable decisions of faceless officials.
- *Against all odds* — if you represent an heroic plaintiff who has fought back against the odds and refused to give up despite paralysis, blindness, or other serious, permanent injury.
- *Sold a bill of goods* — if you represent a products liability plaintiff who can be portrayed as the victim of relentless, high-powered sales tactics, convinced to use a product by the half-truths of modern advertising.
- *Caught in a sea of red tape* — if you represent a small business trying to comply with contradictory and arbitrary regulations and laws.
- *Law and order* — if your case is weak on sympathetic factors, but your client's actions were legally justified.

You should be cautious about overdoing it. Your presentation often can be structured so that the theme is invoked by inference rather than by hitting the jurors over the head with it. You do not have to explain to the jurors what it means to be an underdog or to be frustrated trying to correct an error in a computer-generated bill. As long as the subject is a familiar one, the jurors will recognize and respond to it.

In developing a theme, be sure it strikes a universal chord. It should be something within the experience and culture of every juror. In criminal cases, defense attorneys often use the theme that their clients are the "real victims" in the case — victims of false charges by angry ex-wives, police ineptitude, or perjury by co-conspirators. The problem with such a theme is that few of the jurors are likely to have ever been the victims of false charges or been framed. Most are likely to assume the police generally do a pretty good job. The theme therefore will not produce an empathetic reaction from the jurors, and may even weaken your case.

In general, you should probably stay away from "negative" themes which focus on a weakness in your adversary's case rather than a strength in your own. For example, imagine you represent the defendant in a criminal case where the victim's identification is shaky and the police did a poor investigation. It might sound clever to use the theme "the blind leading the blind." However, if you have a plausible alibi, you are probably better off with a less clever, but more positive theme, such as "you can't be in two places at once."

2. LENGTH

How long should your opening statement be? It is difficult to provide a definitive answer; obviously, the length will vary according to the complexity of the case and the amount of evidence. It is hard to state even general guidelines because trial practitioners hold widely varying opinions. Some advocate short openings: the minimal statement necessary to summarize the facts in a general way and pique the jurors' interest. This method has the advantages of minimizing the danger that you will promise to prove particular details to which witnesses later do not testify and maximizing the likelihood that you can hold the attention of the jury. This is probably the approach used by most trial lawyers today. However, some lawyers still prefer to give a long, detailed opening statement, organizing and presenting all of the witnesses and all of the anticipated testimony. They argue that longer openings give the jurors a better understanding of the favorable evidence, and the sheer quantity of supporting evidence can make a persuasive argument early in the trial.[45]

As a general rule, you probably should try to keep your opening statement short. Shorter statements are less boring and do not drown the important facts in a sea of details. Remember that the jurors know nothing about your case yet. The opening statement should give them the basic framework, not the entire case. A short opening statement that emphasizes your five or six main facts is more likely to be remembered by the jury and be helpful to them than a long, detailed one. Remember that the jurors will only *hear* your opening; they will not read it.

3. PLANNING CONTENTS OF STATEMENT

Opening statements can be divided into five stages: (1) introductory remarks; (2) the introduction of the witnesses, places, and instrumentalities involved in the case; (3) the identification of the major issues or contentions; (4) a summary of facts; and (5) the conclusion and request for a verdict. The following paragraphs provide suggestions on planning what to include in each segment of the opening statement.

a. Introductory Remarks

Probably most lawyers begin by introducing themselves, explaining the procedural order of the trial, and conveying the purpose of the opening state-

---

[45] *See, e.g.,* MELVIN BELLI, MODERN TRIALS, vol. 1: 862 (1954) (up to one and one-half hours).

ment. They frequently use an analogy to explain the role of opening remarks — e.g., opening statement is like the cover of a jigsaw puzzle box that previews what the finished puzzle will look like. They also commonly include the disclaimer that what is said in opening statement is not evidence. The typical introduction sounds like this:

> May it please the Court, and you, ladies and gentlemen of the jury: My name is John Smith, and I represent the plaintiff, Mary Wilson. Now that you have been accepted and sworn as jurors to try this case, it becomes the privilege of the lawyers on both sides to make opening statements of what they intend to prove. The plaintiff — that's me — makes such a statement first, and ordinarily the defendant's lawyer, Ms. Jones, follows with a statement in which she tells you what her defense is going to be. These statements are not evidence, but only a preview of the evidence — a road map, if you will, to help you find your way and understand where the trial is going. The evidence will come from the witnesses who take the stand and from exhibits. We will call witnesses first, and I will examine them and then the defendant will cross-examine. After I am done, Ms. Jones will call witnesses, she will ask them questions, and I will cross-examine. When we have called all the witnesses, both Ms. Jones and I will have the opportunity for closing arguments. When the lawyers are all finished, the judge will instruct you on the law and then the case will be in your hands to reach a verdict.[46]

This kind of opening has long been the standard for a number of reasons. The primary one is that making similar introductory remarks in all cases may help you overcome initial nervousness. Your familiarity with this generic introduction enables you to sound professional and confident, and the explanatory content may be helpful to the jurors, all of which helps you make a good first impression. The analogies and explanations about the trial process will make the trial less bewildering to the first-time jurors — always a good idea.

But what happened to our basic strategy of taking advantage of primacy by starting each phase of the trial by emphasizing some important aspect of the case? Obviously, it is an opportunity lost if you adopt this approach. Most of the better trial practitioners therefore recommend a more aggressive approach. They agree that the first few minutes of opening statement, when jurors are most likely to be paying attention, are crucial in making a good impression, but argue that you should give them a good impression of your *case*, not of *yourself*. It is probably better to avoid the traditional formalities and cliches about road maps. A juror does not want "to sit there and be told by some young pup what an opening statement is."[47] Instead, in the initial moments of opening statement, you should convince the jurors that justice is on your side. The modern trend is to begin directly with remarks that summarize

---

[46] Adapted from F. Busch, *supra* note 42, at 825.

[47] Mark R. McGarry, *McGarry's Illustrated Forms of Jury Trial for Beginners*, Litigation, Fall 1982, at 38, 39.

the nature of the case, state your theme, and arouse the interest of the jury. Consider the following two examples:

(a) On January 23, 1990, Mary Wilson walked into Riverside Hospital through the front door to have a minor operation to remove a growth on her arm. One week later, on January 30, she was carried out of the back door — dead. What happened in that short week to turn a routine operation into a life-and-death struggle, and why it never should have happened, is what this case is all about.[48]

(b) On November 8, 1991, a boy named Harvey Starr was killed at an amusement park through the carelessness of an untrained, substitute ferris wheel operator, who was filling in for the missing defendant. You and I will be examining the facts and asking, "Where was Waldo?" when this tragedy occurred.[49]

There are other reasons to eschew the standard opening. Analogizing your opening statement to a road map or the cover of a jigsaw puzzle box implies that your case is confusing. Your job is to make the case clear and simple. Stating that what you say is not evidence encourages the jurors to ignore your remarks as unimportant; you are not likely to fool the jurors into thinking you are nonpartisan by such a mock display of humility and fairness.

b. Introduction of Actors, Places and Instrumentalities

At the beginning of an opening statement, most trial practitioners introduce their clients and other important witnesses and set the scene, unless these matters were adequately covered during voir dire. By giving this background information first, they do not have to interrupt the summary of events to explain who certain people are or to describe a location or instrumentality.

The introduction of your client is most important. You should explain who he or she is in a way that personalizes the client. Imagine that you are trying to convince the jurors to go out on a blind date with your client. Jurors will be more receptive to testimony from a person if they have been introduced, are convinced the client is normal, and their interest has been piqued. Also, it is likely that jurors will be more receptive to people with characteristics that are similar to their own.[50] If your client shares the characteristics of particular jurors, you can consider mentioning it. For example, suppose your client is college-educated, divorced, has two teenaged children, and has worked as an administrator at the state university for twenty years. If the jury is predominantly blue-collar people with large families, you might introduce your client as "Jack Briggs, a man who has worked hard for twenty years to support his children."

You also should consider whether the jury should be introduced to any other important actors, and if so, what to say about them. This is not a recitation of your witness list. The purpose of opening statement is to describe *the incident*, not to describe the upcoming trial. Therefore, you should introduce the jury to

---

[48] *See* L. DECOF, *supra* note 12, at § A.01(e).
[49] *See* ALFRED S. JULIEN, OPENING STATEMENTS § 1.12 (1980).
[50] *See* JEFFREY T. FREDERICK, THE PSYCHOLOGY OF THE AMERICAN JURY 166-67 (1987).

the people who actually played out the crime or other event, not the witnesses who will later describe it. In doing so, bear in mind that the *role* they played is important to the jury's understanding who they are. Compare the following two examples:

> (a) Another important witness will be Randall Johnson. Mr. Johnson is married, lives here in Bayshore, and works at Lennie's Pizza. He will describe what happened at the scene of the accident.

> (b) Another important person is Randall Johnson. Mr. Johnson was driving the Lennie's pizza truck that smashed into Jennifer.

The first tells the jury nothing that is important about the case; the second introduces them to one of the critical people involved — the man who caused the wreck.

It has also been suggested that jurors will be better able to understand the events if they know the goals and motives of the participants,[51] and any obvious factors affecting credibility. You should add any of this additional information only if you can do so briefly. For example:

> Another important person is Randall Johnson. Mr. Johnson was driving the Lennie's pizza truck, trying to beat the 30-minute guarantee, when he smashed into Jennifer.

Finally, you should familiarize the jury with the important locations, times, and instrumentalities involved. The same kinds of considerations apply. Your goal should be not just to mention them, but to make them real to the jury. Locations can be pictured from the perspective of the client or eyewitness; instrumentalities and machines can be made to appear as complicated devices, difficult to control, or as simple extensions of the will of the operator; and times can be related in terms of rememberable events such as holidays or mealtimes. For example:

> Let me set the scene for you: It's 12:15 on Sunday afternoon. People are driving home from church services. Randy gets into this truck [holding up a photo] and drives to the Bond Street intersection [displaying diagram]. This is where the accident happened.

c. Identification of Disputes

Trial practitioners emphasize that it is helpful to describe the main *factual* disputes between the parties in opening statement. It usually is proper to mention the points of contention in order to help the jury focus on the real disputes, but not to start arguing about how they should be resolved. The usual advice is to tell the jury in plain, ordinary language what is claimed in the complaint and how the complaint was answered, stating the general na-

---

[51] *See* Daniel Linz & Steven Penrod, *Increasing Attorney Persuasiveness in the Courtroom*, 8 LAW & PSYCHOL. REV. 1, 3-7 (1984).

ture of the disputes they must resolve. You must be careful, however, not to begin attacking your opponent's case at this point. For example:

(a) The prosecution has charged Philip Green with murder. They say he intentionally killed the deceased, planned it in advance, and knew what he was doing. We have an honest defense. We do not deny that Phil Green caused the death of the deceased, but he was not responsible for this act. At the time the deceased was killed, Phil Green did not know what he was doing or that what he was doing was wrong. He had been driven crazy with fear of the deceased. Our evidence will therefore concentrate on the issue of Phil Green's mental condition.[52]

(b) We are claiming that David Wilson's injuries were caused by the negligence of the defendant. We will attempt to prove that the defendant was careless when he was driving, causing a wreck that seriously injured Dave and sent him to the hospital. In the papers filed before trial, the defendant asserts that he was driving safely and is not responsible for Dave's injuries. Thus, you will have to decide two issues: was the defendant driving carelessly, and if so, how much money will it take to compensate Dave Wilson for his injuries?

d. Summary of Facts

The main body of your opening statement tells the story of what happened. You should tell a narrative of the facts from your client's point of view, keeping it simple and using plain language. It is too soon in your case to join battle by stating your conclusions and contrasting your contentions with your opponent's.

A straightforward, chronological order is the safest, easiest, and most natural way to recount the important facts. It is used by most experienced trial attorneys. The jurors can follow it easily, and you can prepare and deliver it with only a minimal chance that you will leave out something important. A chronological organization is especially imperative in cases involving many separate incidents spread over a period of time.

Other organizational schemes also are possible. The most common alternative is a witness-by-witness method, in which you discuss the testimony of each witness independently. This is controversial, and some trial practitioners argue that it should never be used. Since witnesses inevitably will testify slightly differently than you anticipate, it is embarrassing (and potentially reversible error) to promise that a particular witness will testify to a fact and then discover that he or she testifies otherwise. Especially in cases involving numerous witnesses, jurors are more likely to remember a sequence of events, than a sequence of witness' names and narratives. On the other hand, there are rare occasions when a witness-by-witness method might be more effective — when your case hinges on the testimony of one or two principal witnesses, and you must build a case around their personal credibility. One other organizing method, called the flashback technique, is sometimes used in severe

---

[52] Adapted from F. LEE BAILEY & HENRY ROTHBLATT, SUCCESSFUL TECHNIQUES FOR CRIMINAL TRIALS 123-24 (1971).

personal injury cases in which the amount of damages is the primary issue. The plaintiff's current condition is described in categories — health, work, sports, personal life, family life, and so on — and each one is contrasted with the plaintiff's lifestyle before the accident. This method will work best if liability is conceded.

The main task in opening statement is to paint a vivid mental picture of what happened. The words you use and images you create should be chosen not only for their technical accuracy, but also for the effect they will have on the minds of the jurors. This is more than just avoiding the use of complex legal terms. The words you use should create images the jury will understand and remember; they should bring the story to life. This is especially important for conveying an accurate picture of emotions, pain, or a complex series of events difficult to describe in simple words. Certain words can trigger jurors' personal memories about the pain of a toe stubbed in the darkness or the anxiety of a dentist's waiting room. Different images are created by referring to an arm as hurt, injured, mangled, or shredded to the bone. Some words or phrases will spontaneously set off a whole string of images, emotions, and associations in the minds of the jurors — for example, Three Mile Island, Watergate and Thalidomide.

Another way to communicate a clear picture of places or events that are hard to describe is to use visual aids. Most attorneys favor the use of charts, diagrams, and exhibits to give the jury an accurate impression of the case. Exhibits used at this early point may have more impact than they would if introduced later. Visual aids should not be used indiscriminately, however, or they can detract from the clarity of your opening statement. They can interrupt the continuity of your narrative, divert the jurors' attention from your words, and may divert your attention as well, especially if you try to sketch out a diagram while talking. However, exhibits and diagrams that emphasize and clarify your main points will probably help the jury remember them. If the facts on a given point are especially complex, they may need to be visually reinforced for the jury even to understand them.[53]

Every case you take to trial will have some inherent weaknesses — gaps in your evidence, witnesses who lack credibility, the absence of corroboration on an important issue, unavailable witnesses, and so forth. Trial practitioners and psychologists agree that weakness in your case should be disclosed in the opening statement. By bringing them out yourself in as positive a manner as possible you take some of the sting out of them, appear honest, and lessen the negative impact when your opponent points them out.[54]

This does not mean you should tell the jury about every piece of conflicting evidence nor anticipate disputes your adversary may raise. These are not weaknesses in your own case. Rather, you must bring out and minimize those weaknesses that will emerge from your own presentation of evidence or that

---

[53] See Linz & Penrod, *supra* note 51, at 7-8 (complex facts need to be written on an exhibit to be remembered).

[54] See Linz & Penrod, *supra* note 51, at 13-14.

inhere in your theory of the case, regardless of what your opponent does. For example, suppose your client had consumed a couple of beers. You might say:

> Jack was sober when he got into his car. He had drunk only two beers over the course of the evening, and was still in full control of his faculties.

Or, if you anticipate that one of your witnesses cannot attend, you might say:

> Dr. Smith, who assisted at the operation, has moved to Chicago. If her busy surgical schedule permits her to travel here, she will testify in person. If she cannot get away — if her patients cannot wait — we still will have the benefit of her observations that were recorded in the official hospital record.[55]

One of the most difficult problems of opening statement in civil cases is how to deal with damages. Opinions differ greatly among trial lawyers. One school of thought is that damages, especially in catastrophic injury cases, should be treated only in very general terms, letting the facts speak for themselves. Those who favor this approach fear reaching a climax — the magnitude of the injuries and the enormous amount it will take to compensate the plaintiff — too early. Another school of thought opts for a detailed treatment of damages, because it helps the jury understand the case or because damages may be the stronger part of your case and may predispose the jury to want to find liability.

Intangible damages, such as pain and suffering, are the hardest to deal with. They are subjective and not susceptible to exact computation. Lawyers are split on the wisdom of naming a specific amount. Asking for a specific amount creates a frame of reference for the jurors, satisfies their curiosity, and communicates the seriousness of the case. On the other hand, it may appear too forceful too early. It may distract the jurors from focusing on the facts and reaching their own conclusions about the seriousness of the case. By committing yourself to a specific amount, you are gambling that the jurors eventually will accept your estimate of the value of pain and suffering and not decide you were overstating the case. Even among lawyers who do discuss damages, there are different approaches. Some list them in detail on the blackboard; others give only a general total figure at the end when asking for a verdict. For the novice, however, it is difficult to attach a dollar amount to intangible damages without being argumentative, so the best approach may be to discuss the facts underlying these damages, give the jury some idea of their dimensions, and leave the computation for closing argument.

e. Conclusion and Request for Verdict

Every good story must have an ending, and the opening statement is no exception. Your conclusion should summarize the theme of your case and ask the jury for a specific verdict, but it cannot be argumentative. This is a difficult line to draw. It usually is permissible to suggest that the evidence adds up

---

[55] *See* J. JEANS, *supra* note 13, at 201.

to a favorable verdict, as long as this is done simply and not at great length. For example:

> The bottom line is that the evidence will show that the defendant knew what he was doing when he killed Ralph Jones. He killed Ralph for revenge — an eye for an eye — because he blamed Ralph for the death of his daughter. The people of this state will therefore ask you at the close of the evidence to find him guilty of murder.

4. COMMON PROBLEMS IN OPENING STATEMENTS

The common problems that appear in opening statements can be summarized in one word: overstatement.

> An advocate can make no greater mistake in an opening statement than deliberately or carelessly to overstate his case. The deliberate inclusion of matters which cannot be established by admissible evidence may, as has been indicated, constitute reversible error. The more usual situation arises where an advocate, through overzealousness, makes an exaggerated statement of his proposed proof, or states as proposed proof matters [which he is later unable to prove because the evidence] is excluded as incompetent or irrelevant. In either event, the consequence may be fatal. An alert opponent will be quick to argue that [if] the opposing side had been able to prove what they solemnly told the jury they expected to prove, a different case might be presented; but as it has turned out, there has been a clear failure to prove the case. Such an argument is often persuasive, even though what has been proved is sufficient to make a case.[56]

There is empirical verification of this assumption. In controlled experiments with mock juries, when an attorney promised more than the evidence proved, and the overstatement was pointed out by the opponent, the overstatement had a negative effect on the verdict — the attorney was actually worse off than if he or she had given a more cautious opening statement.[57]

Overstatement takes several common forms.

- *Discussing your opponent's case.* In opening statement, you are supposed to discuss your own evidence. You lack a good faith basis for even *knowing* what your opponent is going to do; for all you know, the other side may rest without calling any witnesses! In any event, why would you want to emphasize the other side of the case? Other than a brief statement of the competing contentions of the two sides, you almost always are making a mistake to spend valuable time doing your adversary's work for her.

- *Discussing evidence of doubtful admissibility.* Obviously, you should include in your opening statement only evidence you think will be admit-

---

[56] F. BUSCH, *supra* note 42, at 796-97. *See also* Linz & Penrod, *supra* note 51, at 34-35 (psychological experiments show that overstatement lowers jurors' opinions of attorney's expertise and credibility).

[57] Tom Pyszczynski et al., *Opening Statements in a Jury Trial: The Effect of Promising More Than the Evidence Can Show*, 11 J. APPLIED SOC. PSYCHOL. 434, 440-41 (1981).

ted, and not mention clearly inadmissible evidence. But what about evidence of doubtful admissibility, which might either be allowed or excluded? There is a great temptation to discuss it, especially if it makes your case appear stronger. But of course, that is committing the sin of overstatement. You probably should not refer to dubious evidence, to avoid the risk of promising evidence you cannot deliver. One possible solution to this dilemma is to try to resolve the question of admissibility before trial, by stipulation or motion in limine.

• *Discussing the testimony of uncertain witnesses.* A closely related question is what to do about evidence from an uncertain witness. You may have doubts about exactly what a witness will say, or even if the witness will show up at all. Again, if you are uncertain what the witness will say, it is better not to mention the witness than to promise evidence you cannot deliver. Remember that a good opening statement describes what happened, not who will testify, so there will be nothing suspicious about your failure to mention the witness in opening statement if he or she eventually does testify. If a shaky witness is also a material actor, you will have to say something about the person, but should try to avoid specific details.[58]

5. SHOULD YOU WRITE OUT YOUR OPENING STATEMENT?

Most trial practitioners caution against writing out the opening statement word for word. Such a procedure encourages memorization or reading, neither of which is likely to produce a sincere, spontaneous opening. If your opening statement sounds like a prepared speech, it will result in less effective communication than if it sounds spontaneous. For these reasons, the usual advice is to prepare your opening in outline form, reducing it to a key word outline before trial. With practice, you will quickly learn that if you know the facts well, you can give an effective opening statement without notes.

A few trial lawyers disagree and urge that everything you plan to do during trial be written down exactly as you intend to present it — including the opening statement. This approach has two advantages. First, a written opening statement can be checked carefully in advance for overstatements, exaggerations, and objectionable arguments, and these weaknesses can be eliminated. Extemporaneous statements based only on outlines are more likely to contain overstatements. Second, you might know the points you want to make, but not realize how difficult they are to articulate until you try to turn a thought into a sentence. A persuasive presentation of your thoughts and concepts may require time and effort spent in preparation, in choosing the best words and phrases.

A good compromise is first to write out your opening statement word for word. That way you can check for length, complexity, word choice, and overstatement. You may want to leave your introductory and closing remarks written out fully, but the main body of your statement — the fact summary — should be reduced to an outline, and finally to a key word outline.

---

[58] ALAN MORRILL, TRIAL DIPLOMACY 24 (2d ed. 1972).

6. PRACTICE

The final stage of preparation is to practice your opening statement — in front of an audience if possible. This serves two functions. First, it will help you become more comfortable with your delivery, especially if you record your opening statement on video or audio tape. This gives you an opportunity to listen to yourself and correct delivery problems. Second, it may be useful in finding out whether your opening is adequate.

> Whether counsel has properly prepared her opening statement can be tested by "trying it out" on a spouse or lay friend. Most people have an interest in trials, so it will be a simple matter to induce one or more of them to listen to the opening statement.... If at the end of this test opening statement, the friend has too many questions about matters that he didn't quite understand, that opening statement should not be delivered. Such "testing" should become a matter of routine.[59]

A more sophisticated version of this "test run" is to use a genuine focus group. Social science consulting firms can supply attorneys with focus groups drawn from the community at large that will reflect the demographics of a real jury, so the attorneys can test-market their products.

NOTES

1. *Other common introductory remarks*. Trial practitioners sometimes use a number of other standard introductory remarks. Some explain that counsel is obligated to investigate the case, interview witnesses, and take depositions, and that the opening statement is based on that investigation, thereby giving credence to the factual summary. SYDNEY SCHWEITZER, CYCLOPEDIA OF TRIAL PRACTICE, vol. 1: 475 (2d ed. 1970). Some explain what is meant by plaintiff and defendant and give a short statement about how the parties got to court. RALPH McCULLOUGH & JAMES UNDERWOOD, CIVIL TRIAL MANUAL 579 (2d ed. 1980). In criminal cases, some prosecutors start by reading the indictment if that is permitted in the jurisdiction. A standard defense opening remark is that there are always two sides to every story. FRED LANE, LANE'S GOLDSTEIN TRIAL TECHNIQUE § 10.24 (3d ed. 1984).

2. *Allocation of time*. It is difficult to generalize concerning how much time you should devote to each of the various sections of your opening statement. In a case that turns on the credibility of the victim versus the defendant, such as a date rape in which the defendant claims consent, you may end up devoting most of your opening statement to the introduction of the two main actors. In a breach of contract case for shipping non-conforming goods, you may spend all your time explaining how a camshaft works. Nevertheless, in a typical case in which there are a variety of factual and legal disputes involving several witnesses, you might start from the following suggested range:

Introductory remarks: 1 minute
Introduction of actors, scene, instrumentalities: 2 minutes

---

[59] FRED LANE, LANE'S GOLDSTEIN TRIAL TECHNIQUE § 10.63 (3d ed. 1984).

Identification of disputes: 1 minute
Summary of facts: 5-10 minutes
Conclusion: 1 minute

3. *Two different models of a chronology*. There are two different ways to organize a chronology. The more common is to following your client chronologically through the event. For example:

> Ellen Gaston left her house at 3:15 to drive to the supermarket. She put on her seatbelt and drove east on Second Street. As she passed Rogers Elementary School on her right, she slowed down. She was watching the road in front and the schoolyard on her right, when she heard a sudden screeching of tires and was smashed into by the defendant coming out of a driveway on her left.

The other is to use a timeline, in which the movements of several people are charted minute by minute, but there is no protagonist. For example:

> It's 3:15. Ellen Gaston is leaving her house to go to the supermarket. The defendant is finishing his fourth beer in his apartment on Second Street. Kim Chua is sitting in his fifth grade classroom at Rogers Elementary School. At 3:16, Ms. Gaston gets in her car and fastens her seatbelt. The defendant goes to the refrigerator for another beer, but the cupboard is bare. Kim looks anxiously at the clock. From 3:16 to 3:20, Ms. Gaston drives east on Second Street. The defendant decides to go out for more beer, puts on his coat, and walks down to his car. Kim counts the minutes to the end of the school day. At 3:20, Ms. Gaston approaches Rogers School. The defendant guns his car down the driveway. The bell finally rings and Kim races out of the schoolhouse. At 3:21, these three people come together. Kim runs across the schoolyard. Ms. Gaston looks to her right to make sure he's not going to run into the street. The defendant flies into Second Street without stopping and smashes into Ms. Gaston's car.

See JAMES W. JEANS, LITIGATION, vol. 2: 595-99 (2d ed. 1992).

4. *Specially prepared charts*. For an example of charts specially prepared for use during opening statement, see John Elam, *My Approach to Opening Statements in Complicated Cases, in* OPENING STATEMENTS AND CLOSING ARGUMENTS 67-75 (G. Holmes ed. 1982).

5. *Saving surprises and otherwise gambling on your opponent's ignorance*. It was once popular to base decisions about what to disclose during opening statement on what you thought your opponent knew. For example, it has been suggested that you should disclose a weakness only if you think your opponent is likely to bring it out. *See* RALPH McCULLOUGH & JAMES UNDERWOOD, CIVIL TRIAL MANUAL 583 (2d ed. 1980). It also has been suggested that you hold back some surprise damaging evidence your opponent does not know about. *See* Martin Littleton, *Opening to the Court or Jury, in* CIVIL LITIGATION AND TRIAL TECHNIQUES 303-04 (H. Bodin ed. 1976). One experienced trial lawyer suggests that you should never disclose your rebuttal evidence. SYDNEY SCHWEITZER, CYCLOPEDIA OF TRIAL PRACTICE, vol. 1: 477 (2d ed. 1970).

Most practitioners now think this approach unwise. You may misjudge your opponent's knowledge and pass up the opportunity to present favorable evidence or to put a weakness in a favorable light. With modern discovery, it is unlikely you can surprise your opponent by keeping some evidence hidden. The only persons you are likely to surprise are the jurors — not a very good tactic. Thus, most lawyers recommend that you err on the side of safety, disclosing important weaknesses and giving the jury all the facts, and not concentrate on trying to outsmart your opponent. *See* LEONARD DECOF, ART OF ADVOCACY — OPENING STATEMENT § 1.18[3] (1982).

6. *Overuse of phrase "we expect to prove."* Many trial lawyers think that qualifying phrases such as "we expect to prove" or "the evidence will show" are overused. Many trial lawyers think that the repetitious use of these qualifiers before every sentence is unwise. Many trial lawyers think that this repetition breaks up the flow of the story and communicates that you are unsure of the evidence. Many trial lawyers think that it will be sufficient to state clearly at the beginning that the facts you will be summarizing are facts you expect the evidence to prove. *E.g.*, FRED LANE, LANE'S GOLDSTEIN TRIAL TECHNIQUE § 10.46 (3d ed. 1984). What do you think?

F. PRESENTING YOUR OPENING STATEMENT

1. WHETHER TO GIVE AN OPENING STATEMENT

Except in those jurisdictions that require the party with the burden of proof to make a prima facie opening, you have the option of giving or waiving your opening remarks. In many jurisdictions, the defense has the additional option of reserving opening statement until the start of the defendant's own case. However, the principle of primacy indicates that, in general, it is important to tell the jurors about your case early, because initial impressions may have a disproportionately large effect on their final decision. Trial practitioners unanimously agree that you should rarely, if ever, waive your opening remarks.

A defendant, however, should give some thought to whether it is better to present the opening statement immediately after plaintiff's or to reserve it. In the overwhelming majority of cases, it will be better to present your opening immediately. If jurors hear only one side of the case, they will have difficulty suspending their judgment. They will tend to form opinions based on the early evidence presented by the plaintiff. The only way that you can effectively combat the problem of early opinion formation is through "forewarning." Research by psychologists shows that if you forewarn jurors that the plaintiff will attempt to persuade them, and provide them with a summary of your facts, jurors will be able to resist their tendency to commit themselves prematurely to plaintiff's position.[60]

However, plausible grounds for deferring your opening statement have been suggested. If the plaintiff's or prosecutor's case could take a number of different paths and you have alternative defenses depending on the strength and

---

[60] *See* SAUL M. KASSIN & LAWRENCE S. WRIGHTSMAN, THE AMERICAN JURY ON TRIAL: PSYCHOLOGICAL PERSPECTIVES 104 (1988).

course of their case, you should consider reserving the opening. If you will have to concede or admit matters that your opponent might otherwise be unable to prove, you may choose to reserve opening until after you have made a directed verdict motion. Also, if plaintiff's case will take several weeks, you may want to reserve your opening; otherwise the jurors will have forgotten your side of the case by the time you get to present it.

2. BEGINNING YOUR OPENING STATEMENT

When the judge asks for opening statements, or looks at you expectantly, you have to begin. For some reason, these first few moments often seem to be the most awkward. The classic advice to the novice is this:

> Apparently two of the most difficult things for the trial lawyer to learn are how to get out of the chair, and [how to give] the salutation to the court and jury. When the court has told [you] to "proceed," [you should] stand up with the calves of [your] legs still touching the front part of the chair. [You] should address the court either, "May it please the Court" or "If the Court please." The salutation to the court is in a little higher pitched voice to create interest. [You] should remain standing until the judge recognizes [you] either by telling [you] to proceed, or calling [you] by name. Then [you] should walk to the front of the jury box [and] stand poised so that [you] can turn in any direction without moving [your] feet, put down [your] notes, make the jury look at [you], and address the jury in the same pitched tone of voice, the same respect, and the same dignity with which [you] addressed the court. [You] may acknowledge the presence of defense counsel, "If the Court please, Mr. Brown, Ladies and gentlemen of the jury" (or "Members of the jury").[61]

On television, lawyers always talk to the jury with one hand touching the railing on the edge of the jury box. Is getting right into the jurors' faces really a good idea? Where should you stand? In some jurisdictions, you may be required to stand behind a lectern. You also might use a lectern because you feel more comfortable with it. If you use one, do not become wedded to it. Use it as a place of sanctuary or a place for your notes, but get out from behind it to talk to the jury. Empirical research on communication shows that jurors are more likely to believe you if they can see you.[62] If your style tends to be informal and conversational, you should consider standing six to eight feet away from the jury at a slight angle.[63] If your style tends to be more formal or oratorical, empirical research suggests you should stand farther back — approximately twelve feet from the jury — for the most effective presentation.[64] Some lawyers scoff at social science research, and suggest you should stand

---

[61] F. LANE, *supra* note 59, at § 10.09.

[62] JURGEN RUESCH & WELDON KEES, NONVERBAL COMMUNICATION 128 (1972).

[63] Carol Lassen, *Effect of Proximity on Anxiety and Communication in the Initial Psychiatric Interview*, 81 J. ABNORMAL PSYCHOL. 226-29 (1973) (four to eight feet and oblique angle best distance for informal conversation).

[64] Stuart Albert & James M. Dabbs, *Physical Distance and Persuasion*, 15 J. PERSONALITY & SOC. PSYCHOL. 265 (1970) (twelve feet best distance for more formal, one-way persuasion).

wherever you feel most comfortable, as long as you are neither too close nor too far from the jury.

3. DELIVERY

Delivery is largely a matter of personal style. Trial practitioners agree that you should be sincere, friendly, conversational, and above all, natural. They do not, however, tell you how you can suddenly become all these things if you are not a naturally gifted public speaker. The answer is not to worry about it. Any one of us can sit down with a friend over a beer or cup of coffee and talk about the events of the day. If you can carry on a social conversation, you can make an opening statement. Talk to the jury as you would talk to a friend. If you naturally pace back and forth, gesture with your hands, and rant and rave when you talk, don't try to change your style and become a country lawyer because you happen to like "Matlock." If you tend to be shy, speak quietly, and feel uncomfortable raising your voice, you should stick to that style and not try to run around the courtroom pounding on tables just because you've seen lawyers do that on "L.A. Law."

Within the confines of your own style, there are a number of standard suggestions about how to deliver an opening statement:

- Use as few notes as possible. Whatever you do, don't read a prepared opening statement word for word.
- Maintain eye contact with the jurors, looking from one to another. If looking directly at an individual juror makes you nervous, look between two jurors.
- Use simple words and plain English. Avoid "legalese."
- Don't get too dramatic. Impassioned oratory, emotional outpourings, and bombastic ranting are rarely appropriate during the opening. This is the introduction to your case, not the climax. Too dramatic an opening can disconcert the jurors because it is out of place and it sets a fever pitch too early that cannot be maintained.
- Vary your pace, pitch and loudness. A monotonous, droning speaking voice will put jurors to sleep. You can vary the loudness of your voice as appropriate to the subject under discussion, starting softly, raising your voice when talking about car wrecks, or lowering it when discussing your client's intimate family relationships. Let your voice rise in pitch when talking about exciting events and lower when talking about nonexciting events.
- Keep up the pace of your speech, without letting it get so fast the jury cannot follow you. You may have heard the common advice that you should speak slowly and distinctly when you want to deliver a forceful message. That's usually bad advice — slow speech is boring, and jurors will start to daydream. Obviously if you talk too fast, you may sound nervous or be difficult to follow, but communication experts generally believe that fast speech is more effective than slow. Beware, too, of

uneven pace — halting sentences containing pauses or the repetitive use of sounds like "um," "er," and "y'know."[65]

- Use good posture. Despite what you see on television, the slouching country lawyer approach is not very effective. Most jurors see poor posture and leaning on courtroom furniture as inappropriate. They expect attorneys to be poised and confident professionals. Good posture (with your hands out of your pockets) can project an image of competence.[66]

An abstract understanding of common public speaking pitfalls is not likely to improve your delivery. In order to be useful, that knowledge must be coupled with an awareness of your personal style and deficiencies. The only ways to discover these is by videotaping a practice session and then watching the tape or by delivering your opening statement to friends and asking them to listen critically for problems. Once you identify them, any good speech textbook can provide simple exercises designed to correct difficulties with level, pitch, or pace.[67]

4. RESPONDING TO THE UNEXPECTED

a. Improper Opening by Opponent

If your opponent violates the legal or ethical guidelines in opening statement, you may object and move to strike the offending remarks. Such an objection would look like this:

> Defendant: ... and we will show that plaintiff's medical bills have already been paid by her own insurance company, so there were no actual damages ...
> Plaintiff [Stands up]: I object, Your Honor. Evidence about whether anyone has paid part of Ms. Butler's hospital bills is barred by the collateral source rule. I move to strike the remark, and request that the jury be instructed that plaintiff has an obligation to repay her insurance company.

Should you object? Most trial practitioners recommend that objections be made sparingly in opening statement, and only if you are sure of your ground and reasonably certain you will be sustained. The full tactical considerations of when to make objections will be discussed in the next chapter. However, as a starting point, consider the following suggestions:

When to object
- If your opponent talks about the credibility of witnesses, object as argumentative.
- If your opponent discusses how the jurors should resolve disputes, object as argumentative.

---

[65] *See* John Conley, William O'Barr, & E. Allen Lind, *The Power of Language: Presentational Style in the Courtroom*, 1978 DUKE L.J. 1375 (jurors find this kind of "powerless" speech less persuasive).

[66] *See* RALPH MCCULLOUGH & JAMES UNDERWOOD, CIVIL TRIAL MANUAL 583 (2d ed. 1980).

[67] *See, e.g.,* HORACE RAHSKOPF, BASIC SPEECH IMPROVEMENT (1965).

- If your opponent explains how the facts should be applied to the law, and whether elements of a cause of action have been satisfied, object as argumentative.
- If your opponent mentions prejudicial or privileged evidence that you are certain is inadmissible, you should object.
- If your opponent mentions his or her personal opinion, object that it is unethical do so.
- If your opponent disparages you or your client, object that it is unethical and argumentative.

When not to object
- If your opponent mentions evidence that you think is irrelevant or hearsay. The judge cannot rule in advance of trial on these objections.
- If your opponent is stating facts he or she will not be able to prove, you should forgo objection, because the judge cannot resolve this difference until the evidence is presented.
- If your opponent states the law correctly, an objection is pointless, even if it is a technical violation against discussing law.

Other tactics are available to respond to your opponent's overstatement. You can take careful notes (or obtain a transcript) of the remarks, and point out to the jury during closing argument how your opponent failed to fulfill his or her promises. If you represent the defendant, and speak second, you can immediately highlight the plaintiff's overstatements as factual issues, asking the jury to listen for the actual testimony. Many attorneys also suggest that you tie this into a statement to the jurors that what your opponent says is not evidence; that it is easy to say something is a fact, but the law requires it to be proved by evidence.

b. Responding to Objections

Objections also may be made by your opponent, of course. If there are objections, how should you respond? It probably is unwise to argue with the court or your opponent at this early stage. This is not the time to encourage the jurors to take sides. You are striving to give the jurors a comprehensive picture of your case, and lengthy interruptions detract from this purpose. If you must respond, a simple one is probably best. For example:

I am only stating what I expect the evidence to show.

If the objection is sustained, apologize and move on. If overruled, you should repeat what you were saying (if there is any chance the jurors may have been distracted by the interruption) and continue.

c. What If Your Opponent Already Said It?

As the defendant going second, you may find that much of what you wanted to say has been covered by the plaintiff in his or her opening. Should you repeat the material or omit it? The answer depends on the nature of the information. If the plaintiff has adequately covered the background information — the names of the attorneys, parties, and both sides' important witnesses, the scene, the instrumentalities, or the issues — and has done so in a neutral, informative way, there is no need to repeat it. Doing so is tedious and insults the intelligence of the jury. On the other hand, you want to give a smooth narrative of the facts as you see them, so it usually is not a good idea to omit part of the factual summary section of your opening just because the plaintiff already has discussed it. Besides, one of our strategies is to emphasize our main facts through repetition.

NOTES

1. ***Primacy effect.*** Social psychologists Daniel Linz and Steven Penrod argue that the data on the relative effect of primacy and recency effects are ambiguous. It may not be bad to defer opening — at least if you have had the opportunity to forewarn jurors in voir dire. There is evidence that the primacy effect favors the plaintiff when opening statements are delivered seriatim. If a second message is delayed, however, there are data suggesting a slight recency effect that would favor the defendant. Linz & Penrod, *Increasing Attorney Persuasiveness in the Courtroom*, 8 LAW & PSYCHOL. REV. 1, 15-16 (1984).

2. ***Objecting to your opponent discussing the law.*** Contrary to the advice given in the main text, Mark Dombroff advises you to object when your opponent presumes to "instruct the jury on the law." If you do not, your opponent gains the high ground and becomes the "expert," and your status is reduced. DOMBROFF ON UNFAIR TACTICS 345-46 (2d ed. 1988). This is not just a matter of ego. The jury in close cases may tend to defer to the attorney who appears to hold the higher status.

G. BIBLIOGRAPHY

1. GENERAL

FRANCIS X. BUSCH, LAW AND TACTICS OF JURY TRIALS, vol. 2: 781-840 (1959).
LEONARD DECOF, ART OF ADVOCACY — OPENING STATEMENT (1982).
ALFRED S. JULIEN, OPENING STATEMENTS (1980).
FRED LANE, LANE'S GOLDSTEIN TRIAL TECHNIQUE, ch. 10 (3d ed. 1984).
ABRAHAM P. ORDOVER, CRIMINAL LAW ADVOCACY — ARGUMENT TO THE JURY (1992).

2. LAW

James R. Lucas, *Opening Statement*, 13 U. HAW. L. REV. 349 (1991).
J. Alexander Tanford, *An Introduction to Trial Law*, 51 Mo. L. REV. 623, 644-56 (1986).

3. TACTICS

Tom Alexander, *The Opening Statement in the Product Case, in* OPENING STATEMENTS AND CLOSING ARGUMENTS 59 (G. Holmes ed. 1982).
Charles Becton & Terri Stein, *Opening Statement*, 20 TRIAL LAW. Q. 10 (1990).
Harry S. Bodin, *Opening the Trial, in* CIVIL LITIGATION AND TRIAL TECHNIQUES 283 (1976).

JOAN M. BROVINS & THOMAS OEHMKE, THE TRIAL PRACTICE GUIDE 111-25 (1992).

John Elam, *My Approach to Opening Statements in Complicated Cases, in* OPENING STATEMENTS AND CLOSING ARGUMENTS (G. Holmes ed. 1982).

JAMES W. JEANS, LITIGATION, ch. 9 (2d ed. 1992).

JAMES W. JEANS, TRIAL ADVOCACY, ch. 8 (1975).

Sharon Kleiman, *How to Deliver a Convincing and Winning Opening Statement in a Criminal Defense, in* WOMEN TRIAL LAWYERS: HOW THEY SUCCEED IN PRACTICE AND IN THE COURTROOM 275 (J. Warsaw ed. 1987).

George A. LaMarca, *Opening Statements — Effective Techniques*, 1977 TRIAL LAW. GUIDE 446.

Martin Littleton, *Opening to the Court or Jury, in* CIVIL LITIGATION AND TRIAL TECHNIQUES (H. Bodin ed. 1976).

James McElhaney, *Opening Statements*, LITIGATION, Summer 1976, at 45.

Orville Richardson, *Persuasion in the Opening Statement: The Plaintiff's Approach, in* OPENING STATEMENTS AND CLOSING ARGUMENTS 16 (G. Holmes ed. 1982).

John C. Shepherd, *The Defendant's Approach in Opening Statement, in* PERSUASION: THE KEY TO SUCCESS IN TRIAL 21 (G. Holmes ed. 1977).

Craig Spangenberg, *What I Try to Accomplish in an Opening Statement, in* EXCELLENCE IN ADVOCACY 17 (G. Holmes ed. 1971).

HERBERT J. STERN, TRYING CASES TO WIN, chs. 6-9 (1991).

Fred Wilkins, *The Art of the Opening Statement*, TRIAL, Nov. 1989, at 56.

Chapter 5

TRIAL EVIDENCE

A. INTRODUCTION

This chapter is not a comprehensive review of the rules of evidence. We assume that you have already taken a course in evidence and remember the basic doctrines of relevancy, hearsay, privilege, competency, and opinion testimony. This chapter concentrates instead on how to use evidence as part of your trial. We focus on:

- The tactical use of rules of evidence.
- How to make and respond to objections.
- How to make a record properly preserving evidentiary and procedural issues for appeal.
- The tactics of and procedures for using demonstrative evidence.

We also will introduce you to some evidentiary topics you may not have covered in your basic evidence course:

- Objections to the form of questions.
- Motions to strike.
- Offers of proof.
- In-court demonstrations.
- Jury views.

Throughout this chapter, we will focus on evidence as it is used in the course of a trial, not as it is argued on appeal. In the hectic atmosphere of the courtroom, precise in-depth legal analysis yields to advocacy, brevity, succinctness, and tactics. Your knowledge of evidence must be tempered with an understanding of discretion — both yours and the judge's. You have discretion whether to object and how to object. Your decisions concerning when to object, when to forgo objections, what to say when you object, and how to use exhibits, all will flow from your theory of the case. However, the most important thing to remember is the broad scope of the judge's discretion in ruling on objections. You must learn to accept the fact that, except in extraordinary circumstances, the trial judge's ruling is final, whether it is right or wrong. Few evidentiary errors warrant reversal on appeal.

NOTE

What happens if the judge rules incorrectly? You may have an erroneous impression that the court of appeals can somehow correct errors made by the trial judge. It cannot. All the court of appeals can do is reverse the judgment and send the whole case back for a very expensive new trial. How likely is it that the appellate courts will order a new trial for erroneous evidence rulings? An empirical study by Professor David Leonard suggests that the likelihood is small. He studied appeals based on FED. R. EVID. 608 and 611, and found that only 5 percent were reversed. David P. Leonard, *Appellate Review of Evidentiary Rulings*, 70 N.C. L. REV. 1155, 1214 (1992). This is far below the usual reversal rate of approximately 25 percent of cases. *See* J. Alexander Tanford, *Closing Argument Procedure*, 10 AM. J. TRIAL ADVOC. 47, 140 (1986) (Table 3).

B. OBJECTIONS

1. INTRODUCTION

If you go into any courtroom and watch a trial in progress, you probably will be struck by a disconcerting observation — most trial lawyers seem to make and handle objections poorly. Many lawyers make drawn out and poorly worded objections. Others just say, "Objection," without any explanation at all. Still others fail to make any objections. Knowing when and how to make and respond to objections is an integral part of being a successful trial lawyer. The materials in this section are designed to introduce you to the basic procedural, tactical, and ethical dimensions of the objection process.

2. OBJECTION PROCEDURE

The basic legal requirements for a proper objection are:

- Your objection must be timely — it must be made as soon as the grounds become apparent.
- Your objection must be specific — you must tell the judge which rule has been violated and how it was violated.

The timeliness requirement means you must object as soon as the grounds for objection become apparent. This usually means that you will have to object to your opponent's questions, because it usually will be clear from the question that the answer will violate the rules of evidence. You cannot wait until after you hear the testimony.[1] For example, if a witness is asked "What is your opinion of the plaintiff's character?" you must object at once. You cannot wait, hoping for a favorable answer, and object only if the answer goes against you. However, if the question is innocuous ("What happened next?"), but the answer violates the rules of evidence ("I wasn't there, but Harry told me that the car skidded"), an objection is timely if made to the answer.[2] As a general rule, you also must not object too soon, although the judge has discretion to permit a premature objection. Even if you think you know what the question will be, and that it is going to elicit objectionable testimony, you must wait until your opponent has finished asking it.[3]

---

[1] *See, e.g., State v. Matthews*, 748 S.W.2d 896 (Mo. App. 1988); *Wilkinson v. Duncan*, 294 Ala. 509, 319 So. 2d 253 (1975).

[2] *See, e.g., Terpstra v. Soiltest*, 63 Wis. 2d 585, 218 N.W.2d 129 (1974); MCCORMICK ON EVIDENCE § 52 (4th ed. 1992).

[3] *E.g., Flanagan v. DeLapp*, 533 S.W.2d 592 (Mo. 1976).

The specificity requirement means that you must direct the judge's attention to the precise reason why the evidence is inadmissible. You must state the exact ground for your objection, referring clearly to the rule being violated and explain how it is being violated.[4] Consider the following examples:

Insufficient objections

- "I object."
- "I object; irrelevant and incompetent."
- "Objection, the evidence is very prejudicial."
- "Objection. Counsel has not laid a proper foundation for the business record exception to the hearsay rule."

Proper objections

- "I object on the ground that this document violates the best evidence rule because it has not been shown to be the original."
- "I object under Rule 403. This photograph of the corpse has little probative value because the fact of death has been stipulated, and it will unfairly arouse the emotions of the jury."
- "I object to the document as hearsay. Counsel has not laid a proper foundation for a business record because she has not shown that the entrant had personal knowledge of the transaction."

Complying with these requirements will not necessarily preserve the issue for appeal. You must renew the objection if your opponent offers the same evidence a second time. You also must object to all similar evidence or you will waive the right to appeal the original erroneous ruling (it becomes harmless error).[5] To partially alleviate this burden, some jurisdictions allow a continuing objection to be made that preserves the error without requiring you to enter many useless objections to similar testimony when you know the judge will just overrule them.[6]

What if a judge has made a pretrial ruling on the admissibility of evidence? You still must enter an objection if the evidence is offered during trial. If the judge has *excluded* evidence, but your opponent tries to offer it anyway, you must renew your objection. Otherwise, the jurors will hear the evidence and you will have waived your right to appeal on the issue. If the judge has erroneously *allowed* inadmissible evidence to be used, you must object again when the evidence is offered at trial to preserve the issue for appeal.[7]

3. GROUNDS FOR OBJECTION

The grounds for objection are as numerous as the rules of evidence. A table of common objections and responses follows on the next two pages. You can object if offered evidence is irrelevant or is incompetent because it violates the

---

[4] *See, e.g., Brown v. State*, 417 N.E.2d 333 (Ind. 1981); FED. R. EVID. 103(a)(1).

[5] *See, e.g., State v. Wingo*, 403 S.E.2d 322 (S.C. App. 1991); *Jones v. State*, 425 N.E.2d 128 (Ind. 1981).

[6] *See, e.g., In re Powers*, 523 So.2d 1079 (Ala. App. 1988); N.C. R. CIV. P. 46(a)(1).

[7] *E.g., Riley v. State*, 427 N.E.2d 1074 (Ind. 1981); *Padgett v. State*, 364 S.W.2d 397 (Tex. Crim. App. 1963).

Table 3: Common Objections

Rule	Objection
PREJUDICIAL EVIDENCE	Unfairly prejudicial, confusing or misleading Cumulative
CHARACTER	Character evidence not admissible
OTHER CRIMES	Evidence of other crimes irrelevant No foundation that defendant definitely committed crime
SIMILAR EVENTS	No foundation of substantial similarity of conditions
HABIT	No foundation that person always acts this way
REMEDIAL MEASURES	Irrelevant to show liability or fault
INSURANCE	Evidence of insurance is inadmissible
CRIMINAL CONVICTIONS	No foundation: place, within 10 years, nature of crime
BIAS	Witness's attention not directed to specific event
PRIOR INCONSISTENT STATEMENTS	No foundation of circumstances of making statement Witness not asked to explain or deny
HEARSAY	Hearsay and no foundation laid for any exception
PERSONAL KNOWLEDGE	No foundation that witness has personal knowledge Speculation
OPINION RULE	Opinion not rationally based on witness's perceptions Details would be more helpful Legal conclusion
REAL EVIDENCE	No foundation connecting item to relevant event or person No foundation of unchanged condition
ILLUSTRATIVE EVIDENCE	No foundation that it is fair and accurate
WRITINGS	No authentication
DEMONSTRATIONS	No foundation of similar conditions
FORM OF QUESTION	Leading on direct examination Unintelligible, vague or compound Assumes facts not in evidence or misquotes a witness Argumentative comment
FORM OF TESTIMONY	Narrative, volunteered, or nonresponsive Beyond scope of previous examination

Common Responses to Objections

Rule	Response
PREJUDICIAL EVIDENCE	High probative value because issue is important Low prejudicial effect, jury already aware of it
CHARACTER	Defendant may prove own or victim's character Adverse party opened door Offered to impeach
OTHER CRIMES	Not offered to prove character, but to show motive, intent, knowledge, identity, inseparable part of events
SIMILAR EVENTS	Happened under similar conditions and shows notice or dangerousness, or how event happened
HABIT	Foundation shows invariable response to specific situation
REMEDIAL MEASURES	Proves contested issue: ownership/control/feasibility
INSURANCE	Offered to show agency, ownership, or bias of witness
CRIMINAL CONVICTIONS	Felony or crime of dishonesty within 10 years
BIAS	Act or statement by witness showing bias Act against witness raises likelihood of bias Extrinsic evidence always admissible
HEARSAY	Not hearsay because not for truth (specify purpose) Not assertion, but a question, command, or threat Admission of opposing party Present sense impression describing relevant event Excited utterance Present physical or mental condition Regularly kept business record Official record Witness unavailable and declaration against interest Witness unavailable and former testimony under oath
OPINION RULE	Opinion rationally based on personal observations Opinions on ultimate issues admissible under Rule 704
REAL EVIDENCE	Chain of custody only needs to eliminate reasonable possibilities of tampering
ILLUSTRATIVE EVIDENCE	Inaccuracies go only to weight
LEADING	Permitted on cross-examination or for hostile witnesses Preliminary matters and foundations Leading permitted to refresh recollection

rules against opinions and hearsay testimony. You also can object if a pretrial order is being violated, if your client's constitutional rights are being threatened, or if any rule of substantive law is being misapplied. There is not sufficient space here to review these matters in detail. However, Table 3 summarizes common evidence rules that arise during trial. It may be helpful in reminding you of how to make and respond to the most important evidence objections.

One group of objections appearing on the summary table may be new to you. They are called objections to the form of the examination. These are rules of evidentiary procedure, rather than substance, and are rarely covered in evidence courses. The following brief discussion will introduce you to any that are unfamiliar.

a. Leading Questions

A question is leading if it suggests that particular words, phrases, or ideas constitute the correct answer. Leading questions usurp the witness' power to choose his or her own words and explanations. They are usually answerable by a simple "yes" or "no," and often contain the phrase, "Isn't it true that ...." Leading questions generally are prohibited during direct examination but allowed during cross-examination. FED. R. EVID. 611(c) provides:

> Leading questions should not be used on the direct examination of a witness except as may be necessary to develop the witness's testimony. Ordinarily leading questions should be permitted on cross-examination. When a party calls a hostile witness, an adverse party, or a witness identified with an adverse party, interrogation may be by leading questions.

There is no precise definition of what constitutes a leading question. Like obscenity, exactly when a question is leading is in the eye of the beholder, and different judges will rule differently. The following examples may help:

(1) "Directing your attention to June 3rd at 4:00, can you tell us where you were?"	NOT LEADING.
(2) "Isn't it true that the light had just turned green?"	LEADING. Suggests an answer.
(3) "The light had just turned green, correct?"	LEADING. Suggests an answer.
(4) "Had the light just turned green?"	LEADING. Supplies information to the witness.
(5) "State whether or not the light had just turned green."	LEADING. Supplies information to the witness.
(6) "What color was the light?"	NOT LEADING.

Even if a question is leading, that does not mean a judge will sustain an objection. The judge has discretion to allow leading questions if he or she thinks they will be effective in developing complete testimony. In general, leading questions are permitted in the following situations:

- During cross-examination.
- When a witness displays hostility or evasiveness.
- During the direct examination of the adverse party or other witnesses closely aligned with the adverse party.
- When covering preliminary matters, such as a witness' background and the events leading up to the event in dispute.
- For laying evidentiary foundations.
- When asking about matters not in dispute.
- To direct a witness' attention to a time, place, or event.
- When examining difficult witnesses (e.g., young children).
- When inquiring into "delicate" (i.e., sexual) matters.
- In order to refresh a witness' memory.
- On redirect examination to save time.

b. Ambiguous, Unintelligible, and Vague Questions

Attorneys have an obligation to ask clear questions. If a question is incoherent, vague or ambiguous, and if it is likely to confuse the witness or jury, the judge can force counsel to rephrase the question in a clearer manner. For example, the following questions are unclear:

(1) "What happened in class today?" (if the witness had more than one class).
(2) "And you did, didn't you, when asked if you weren't hurt, reply in the affirmative?"

c. Compound Questions

Compound or multiple questions contain two or more separate factual inquiries. They usually are objectionable because of the possibility of confusion concerning which part of the question is being answered. For example:

(1) "Did you type this letter and send it to Mr. Pratter in the usual way?"
(2) "Didn't you kill your wife with this gun and then arrange with your accomplice to hide the body in the closet?"

d. Asked and Answered

Federal Rule of Evidence 611(a) gives the judge discretion to control the mode of interrogation so as to prevent needless consumption of time. When an attorney on direct examination goes over and over the same ground with a witness, the trial is delayed and there is a danger that the jury may become confused into thinking there were two or three similar events. Repetitious testimony may be objected to on the ground that it has already been asked and answered. The objection only applies to situations in which the same attorney repeats a question to the same witness who already clearly has answered it. Similar questions can, of course, be asked of different witnesses, by different attorneys, or on both direct and cross-examinations. On cross-examination, particularly of evasive witnesses, greater leeway is allowed to go over testimony several times to "sift" the witness. If a question is asked on direct and the matter is challenged on cross-examination, the same question can be repeated on redirect examination if it will help clarify the issue.

e. Narrative Testimony

Although a witness is supposed to testify in his or her own words, proper examination must be in a question and answer format. The attorney, not the witness, is supposed to select the topics and guide the testimony. If a witness testifies in a long narrative, in which the witness controls the choice of subjects to be testified about, the risk that inadmissible evidence will be injected into the interrogation is increased. If this happens, you may object that the testimony is taking the form of an unguided narrative. Judges have broad discretion to "exercise reasonable control over the mode ... of interrogating witnesses ... so as to make the interrogation and presentation effective for the ascertainment of the truth,"[8] so the judge may either permit the narrative or sustain your objection. Usually, the judge will not sustain this objection unless the witness demonstrates an inability to confine himself or herself to relevant information.

f. Argumentative Questions

Despite what you see on television, speeches and sarcastic comments by lawyers disguised as questions are objectionable as argumentative. The word "argumentative" refers not to arguing with a witness, but to making remarks that belong in closing argument. To be argumentative, a question must be more than just leading. A leading question seeks information — the lawyer who asks it wants the witness to agree to the lawyer's version of the facts. An argumentative question is one in which the lawyer wants to make a speech to the jury and does not care what the witness says. This objection is almost always directed at the attorney conducting cross-examination.

There are five common types of argumentative questions:

- *Speech-making*[9] (always recognizable, because lawyers turn toward the jury with smirks on their faces and raise their eyebrows just before asking the question).

  "So, Mr. Jones, since you testified you were looking the other way, you really have no idea what color the traffic light was, do you?"

- *Summarizing testimony.*

  Q: You were fifty feet away?
  A: Yes.
  Q: It was night?
  A: Yes.
  Q: There was no moonlight?

---

[8] FED. R. EVID. 611(a).
[9] *See, e.g., In re Kemp*, 236 N.C. 680, 73 S.E.2d 906 (1953).

A: No.

Q: And you saw the scar on his cheek?

A: Yes.

Q: So you are asking the jury to believe you could see a scar on a man's cheek from fifty feet away on a dark night?

Summarizing is not always objectionable. The judge may allow it when you are asking transitional questions, or refreshing the witness' and jurors' memories so that subsequent testimony will be in context. A summary question is also common when testimony is resumed after a recess.[10]

• *Pursuing a line of questions despite witness' denial of knowledge.*[11]

Q: Weren't you the one who robbed the store?

A: No, I wasn't even in town.

Q: You pulled the gun on the clerk, didn't you?

A: No.

Q: And you asked for money?

A: No.

Q: And you pulled the trigger, didn't you?

• *Comments to the jury* (usually attempts at sarcasm not in question form).[12]

Q: You claim to have seen the scar on his cheek from fifty feet at night?

A: Yes.

Q: You have remarkable vision, Mr. Witness. Did you see anything else?

• *"Would-it-surprise-you" questions,* in which the attorney states facts either not yet in the record or testified to by other witnesses.[13]

Q: Is it your testimony that the defendant was driving normally?

A: Yes.

Q: Would it surprise you to know that he had .08 percentage of alcohol in his blood that day?

g. Assuming Facts Not in Evidence

If a question assumes a fact that has not yet been testified to by the witness, it is objectionable until the witness has a chance to admit or deny the assumption upon which it is based.[14] To be objectionable, the question must be misleading; the mere fact that the question asks for a fact not in evidence does not make it objectionable — how else can the lawyer get the fact into evidence

---

[10] *See* Mark P. Denbeaux and D. Michael Risinger, *Questioning Questions: Objections to Form in the Interrogation of Witnesses*, 33 ARK. L. REV. 439, 485 (1980).

[11] *E.g., McDonald v. State*, 340 So. 2d 103 (Ala. 1976).

[12] *See, e.g., State v. Blount*, 4 N.C. App. 561, 167 S.E.2d 444 (1969).

[13] *Commonwealth v. Latimore*, 393 N.E.2d 370 (Mass. 1979).

[14] *See, e.g., Hopkinson v. Chicago Transit Auth.*, 570 N.E.2d 716 (Ill. App. 1991); *School City of Gary v. Claudio*, 413 N.E.2d 628 (Ind. App. 1980).

unless he or she asks? Attorneys are more likely to violate this rule during cross-examination when they are asking leading questions.

A classic example of this kind of question is, "Have you stopped using drugs?"[15] The question obviously assumes that the person ever used drugs in the first place. It is objectionable because the question does not ask the witness to affirm or deny this critical underlying premise. A proper question (at least as far as this rule is concerned) would be, "You used to be a heavy drug user, isn't that true?" If the witness confirms the premise, then you can follow up with the question, "Have you stopped using drugs?"

h. Misquoting the Witness

A question in which the attorney misquotes testimony (usually by exaggeration) is similar to an argumentative question or a question that assumes a fact not in evidence. It also commonly occurs during cross-examination. To be objectionable, the question must make it difficult for the witness to deny the premise of it, and the premise must misquote or exaggerate what the witness said.[16] For example:

> Q: Was the defendant drinking?
> A: Yes, he had two drinks.
> Q: What did this drunken man do next?

i. Nonresponsive Answers

If the witness' answer has nothing to do with the question, you may be able to strike it from the record. Answers that merely expand on or explain a narrow question, or that relate to the question in some way, are not objectionable. Some states require that a nonresponsive answer be otherwise inadmissible before it becomes objectionable.[17] Most jurisdictions allow only the examining lawyer to object on unresponsive grounds;[18] the opposing lawyer must object that the witness is giving narrative testimony or volunteering information without being asked a question, or make a motion to strike on substantive grounds. The matter rests entirely in the judge's discretion.

j. Questions Beyond the Scope of Preceding Examination

If questions or testimony on cross, redirect, or recross-examination relate to subjects that were not raised in the preceding phase of the examination of that witness, then it is within the judge's discretion to sustain a "beyond the scope" objection.[19] For example, suppose direct examination covers two issues: The witness claims to have seen the crime and also to have heard the defendant

---

[15]See 3 WIGMORE ON EVIDENCE § 780 n.1 (3d ed. 1940) ("May I ask if you have left off beating your wife?").

[16]See State v. Barcomb, 136 Vt. 141, 385 A.2d 1089 (1978); State v. Staten, 271 N.C. 600, 157 S.E.2d 225 (1967).

[17]E.g., State v. Ferguson, 280 N.C. 95, 185 S.E.2d 119 (1971).

[18]E.g., Bayshore Co. v. Pruitt, 334 S.E.2d 213 (Ga. App. 1985); Moschetti v. City of Tucson, 449 P.2d 945 (Ariz. App. 1969).

[19]E.g., FED. R. EVID. 611(b): "Cross-examination should be limited to the subject matter of the direct examination and matters affecting the credibility of the witness. The court may, in the exercise of discretion, permit inquiry into additional matters ...."

gloating about getting away with it. On cross-examination, the defense attorney asks only about the actual event, and nothing about the defendant's subsequent statements. It is now redirect examination. The prosecutor may ask further questions about what the witness saw, but it would be beyond the scope of the cross-examination to ask questions about the conversation. The rule applies universally to redirect and recross-examination, but not all states apply it to the primary cross-examination. Many allow the cross-examiner to raise any relevant issue, whether discussed on direct or not.

4. ETHICS OF OBJECTIONS

Objections often are used for reasons other than excluding inadmissible evidence. An attorney may make objections in order to disrupt the opponent's train of thought, tip off a witness to the answer, or distract the jury from damaging evidence. If a valid legal ground underlies the objection, there seems to be nothing wrong with using these secondary purposes as bases for making tactical decisions about the timing of an objection. However, making a *groundless* objection solely for these purposes would seem to be unethical because of the general prohibition in the MODEL RULES OF PROFESSIONAL CONDUCT Rule 3.1 against asserting an issue "unless there is a basis for doing so,"[20] and in Rule 3.3 against making "a false statement of law to a tribunal."

Probably the most common unethical objection is the "speaking objection" used as an excuse to present an argument to the jury. For example, you might be tempted to object to the opinion of a medical expert by saying, "This opinion is unreliable because it is based solely on the self-serving complaints of the plaintiff made after he knew he would need an expert to testify for him." If you have legal grounds for an objection, it is not unethical to phrase it in a manner designed to explain to the jury what is going on. However, if you do not have grounds, such an argumentative objection is unethical:

> Using a frivolous objection as a vehicle for expressing some argument to the jury is a practice condemned both by rules of procedure and by professional standards. On the other hand, expressing serious objections in a manner calculated to appeal to the jury as well as the court is generally regarded as a proper practice, and clearly it is proper to give attention to phrasing objections in such a way as to avoid causing an affirmatively adverse reaction by jurors. [However, if the argumentative part of the objection is overemphasized,] your statement is subject to the same criticism as a frivolous objection used for making an argument. The distinction is primarily one of degree, and great differences of opinion exist regarding such practices.... Some trial judges favor and practice limiting the lawyers strictly to [a minimal] statement of grounds of objection when objection is made; others favor and practice considerable leniency in this respect.[21]

---

[20] *See also* MODEL CODE OF PROFESSIONAL RESPONSIBILITY DR 7-106(C)(7) (a lawyer may not "intentionally ... violate any established rule of procedure or evidence"); *State v. Darnell*, 14 Wash. App. 432, 542 P.2d 117 (1975) (frequent objections without legal basis unethical).

[21] ROBERT KEETON, TRIAL TACTICS AND METHODS 196 (2d ed. 1973).

The second common unethical objection is the "warning" to a witness, in which an attorney tries to signal to the witness that the other lawyer is laying a trap. These objections often also suggest a good way to answer the question. For example, imagine the following cross-examination of a crucial eyewitness:

Q: You were 60 feet away?
A: Yes.
Q: This was 11:45 pm, correct?
A: Yes.
Q: There was no moon, correct?
A: Yes.
Q: And no streetlights?
Prosecutor: I object. Counsel is asking trick questions, trying to insinuate that the witness could not have seen the defendant's face clearly.
Court: Overruled.
Q: There were no streetlights, were there?
A: No, but I could see the defendant's face clearly.

Obviously, it is unethical to make such an objection. There are no legal grounds for it.

5. TACTICS OF MAKING OBJECTIONS

a. Whether to Object

Just because an objection *can* be made does not mean that it *should* be made. Before you object, you should have specific reasons for doing so. You should engage in a quick benefit-cost analysis, weighing the benefits against the risk that you will end up harming your own case. The decision will depend on the nature of the evidence offered, the grounds you can assert, the context of the particular controversy, and whether there is an alternative way of dealing with the evidence.

(1) Reasons to object

- *You are certain you will be sustained.* It is embarrassing to be overruled, and it gives the jury the impression you do not know what you are doing. If you make a number of objections that are sustained, however, then it may appear to the jury that your opponent is being unfair or is incompetent.
- *The evidence hurts your case.* This is often stated as the main reason to make an objection, but only if you are reasonably certain you will be sustained. To object to harmful evidence and lose will only highlight that testimony. If the evidence does not harm your theory of the case, there is usually no reason to object.
- *You need to protect your witness.* You must protect your witnesses from misleading questions asked during cross-examination. Your decision here will depend on how easily the witness can be trapped into giving a misleading answer. If the witness can take care of himself or herself, it is more effective if you allow the witness to do so. Questions that are argu-

mentative or assume facts not in evidence can confuse some witnesses, however, and you may need to object to them.

- *You wish to disrupt your opponent.* Although it is unethical to make groundless objections solely to interrupt your opponent's examination, there is nothing wrong with making valid objections for that purpose. A series of sustained objections may so fluster your adversary that he or she will lose track of the examination and forget to introduce important evidence.
- *You need to preserve a pretrial motion or previous objection.* If a pretrial motion to exclude or limit evidence has been denied, you must object again when such evidence is offered during trial if you wish to preserve the issue for appeal. If an earlier objection has been overruled, you must renew it if similar evidence is offered or the issue will not be preserved for appeal.
- *You wish to make a jury argument.* Using a frivolous objection as an excuse to make an argument to the jury is unethical. However, it is permissible to phrase a valid objection in a manner designed to inform the jury of the inherent danger in a misleading question, or point out the unfairness in (thereby lessening the effect of) prejudicial evidence.

(2) Reasons Not to Object

- *It would emphasize harmful evidence.* Your objection will call special attention to the harmful evidence. If you are overruled, the jurors are in effect told by the judge that it is proper that they consider the evidence; your unsuccessful objection having called it particularly to their attention, it is almost certain that they will consider it and give it more weight than if you had made no effort to exclude it.
- *The evidence will eventually be admitted anyway.* Questions in improper form, such as leading, can easily be rephrased and the evidence admitted. Some substantive objections, such as hearsay or lack of personal knowledge, also may be pointless if you are certain your opponent is going to call the original eyewitness.
- *Speculation is worse than hearing the truth.* If an objection is sustained so jurors do not hear evidence, they will undoubtedly become curious about what the witness might have said. In some situations, they may imagine the excluded evidence was far worse than the truth. For example:

> Prosecutor: Mr. Jones, were you ever convicted for any crimes such as child molesting and child pornography?
> Defense attorney: I object for lack of foundation under Rule 609.
> Court: Sustained.

How many jurors will speculate that your client has a prior record for child molesting and pornography? If the witness' answer would have been "I have been convicted of only one crime in my life, shoplifting when I was a teenager," you probably would have been better off if you had not objected at all.

- *Too many objections will cause an unfavorable reaction among jurors.*
  Many trial lawyers are concerned that the jurors will have an unfavorable reaction to objections because they view them as attempts to use technicalities to keep the jury from knowing the whole story. This is a persistent piece of courthouse folklore,[22] although it probably is not true. Two studies of actual juror reactions indicate that jurors have a high tolerance for objections, and in fact were often disappointed with attorneys who did not object. It is only picayune objections, or repeatedly overruled objections, that were viewed negatively.[23]
- *Evidence may open the door to otherwise inadmissible favorable evidence.*
  Sometimes, inadmissible evidence brought up by your opponent will open the door to otherwise inadmissible evidence that you wish to offer. By opening the subject matter, your adversary invites evidence in rebuttal and cannot successfully complain of its admission. For example, your opponent may offer evidence of the good character of a key actor, which opens the door for you to counter with proof of bad character otherwise inadmissible.
- *Alternative means of combating the objectionable evidence exist.* You may be able to counter the effects of the inadmissible evidence by following up the issue on cross or redirect examination. For example, if a witness testifies without personal knowledge, it may be more effective to expose the witness' lack of personal knowledge during cross-examination, and then move to strike the original conclusion. If you can at the same time prove a bias in favor of the adverse party, you have discredited the witness as well. Similarly, if your opponent has been asking misleading half-truth questions on cross-examination, a good redirect can both clarify the issue and expose the other attorney's unfair tactics.
- *The objection is petty.* Making petty objections irritates the judge and may cause your opponent to retaliate.

b. How to Make an Objection

Compliance with the timeliness and specificity rules is necessary in order to preserve an erroneous ruling as an issue for appeal. However, your goal at trial is not primarily to preserve issues for appeal — an appeal will be necessary only if you lose your case. Your principal trial objective is to win your objection at the trial court level. To make it easy for the judge to rule in your favor, consider using the following objection procedure:

- Stand up.
- Tell the judge that you object.
- State the exact grounds.
- Cite the legal rule.

---

[22] In 1888, Byron and William Elliott wrote that an attorney "who abounds in objections finds no favor with [the] jury.... What they want is full information, and they resent any effort to keep it from them." B. ELLIOTT & W. ELLIOTT, THE WORK OF THE ADVOCATE 245-46 (1888). Over 100 years later, lawyers are still giving the same advice. THOMAS A. MAUET, FUNDAMENTALS OF TRIAL TECHNIQUES 335 (3d ed. 1992).

[23] *See* Dale Broeder, *The Impact of the Lawyers: An Informal Appraisal*, 1 VAL. U.L. REV. 40 (1966); M. Michael Cramer, *A View from the Jury Box*, LITIGATION, Fall 1979, at 4.

- Give a one-sentence explanation.
- Allow your opponent to speak without interruption.
- Remain standing until the judge rules on the objection.
- Accept the judge's ruling gracefully.

Standing up and stating clearly that you object attract the judge's, jurors' and witness' attention. Obviously you need the judge's attention if you expect her to rule on your objection. Attracting the witness' attention tends to stop the testimony, thereby minimizing the damage that might be caused if the witness continued talking about inadmissible evidence. Attracting the jurors' attention away from the witness further minimizes the harm if the witness continues to talk about inadmissible evidence. Arguing from a standing position conveys a more positive attitude than sitting down.

Stating specific grounds is more than just complying with a rule of appellate procedure. No trial judge can be expected to recall all the intricacies of the rules of evidence in an instant. If you direct the judge's attention to the precise rule, you increase the likelihood of a favorable ruling. At least the judge will not overrule you because he or she has forgotten the rule of evidence on which you are relying.

A good objection cites the rule being violated and supports it with a "speaking brief" — a concise statement of *legal* reasons why your objection is sound. Your argument should rarely be more than a sentence or two. However, if you are making a novel or unusual objection, you probably should follow up with an offer to explain your legal grounds more completely outside the hearing of the jury. Be prepared to cite rules, cases, or treatises to support your position.

You also should give a one-sentence explanation of your objection in plain English so the jury understands its reasonableness. Although an objection is directed to the court, it is also attended to by the jury. For example, instead of making a purely legal objection, such as "Objection; leading question under Rule 611," explain the legal rule in a brief statement the jury can understand:

> "Objection; leading question under Rule 611. Defense counsel is telling the witness what to say."

There is a benefit in this practice, no matter what the ruling on the objection may be. If the objection is sustained, the jury understands why. If it is overruled, the jury understands it was not frivolous.

Allow your opponent to speak without interruption. The presentation should be professional and courteous. Remain standing until the judge rules on the objection. Remember that your remarks must be addressed to the judge, not the other attorney.

Accept the ruling gracefully. If you *win,* it is always good practice to be a gracious winner. If you gloat, smirk at your opponent, or comment upon your success, you might only succeed in angering the court or the jurors. If the judge overrules an objection to one of your questions, do not forget to elicit the answer. It is often a good idea either to repeat the question or to ask the court reporter to read it back to refresh the witness' and jurors' memories about the interrupted matter. If you *lose,* be a good loser. Remain professional and do not let yourself get upset or show anger, even if the ruling is the most stupid

one you have ever heard. Ordinarily, nothing is to be gained by arguing with
the judge after you have already lost the point. Rather, the effect of pointless
argument is to emphasize the very evidence you didn't want the jury to hear.

Obviously, the foregoing advice is directed to those situations in which you
can see an advantage (or, at least, no harm) in presenting and arguing an
objection within the hearing of the jury. There are other cases where the
ground for the objection or the explanation of it is something the jury should
not hear. For example, an innocuous first question, such as "Did you speak to
someone concerning the accident on November third," may be leading to a
settlement offer by an insurance adjuster. Neither the settlement offer nor
evidence of insurance is admissible. However, the defendant cannot very well
say in front of the jury, "I object that the question will elicit testimony that
the defendant offered to settle and is covered by insurance." In such situations, you will have to state that you object and ask to approach the bench to
state the grounds out of the jury's hearing.

6. TACTICS OF RESPONDING TO OBJECTIONS

a. Whether to Respond

When an objection is made by your adversary, you have three choices:

- Withdraw your question.
- Remain silent and let the judge rule.
- Make an argument against the validity of the objection.

Many attorneys automatically argue against every objection, while others
automatically withdraw or rephrase any question objected to. The first approach assumes your opponent is a complete idiot who can never be right on
an evidentiary issue; the second assumes you are the idiot. You should adopt
neither of these assumptions, but should make a conscious decision about how
to handle each separate objection.

(1) Reasons to Withdraw or Rephrase a Question

- *You agree that the objection is valid.* You lose credibility with the judge if
  you make silly arguments, and with the jury every time the judge rules
  against you.
- *The objection merely goes to the form of the question.* It is often best just to
  rephrase it, rather than get involved in a lengthy argument over
  whether it was a proper question.

(2) Reasons to Keep Silent and Let the Judge Rule

- *You are uncertain about the validity of an objection, but cannot think of a
  good argument.*
- *You have already withdrawn several questions.* If you continually ask
  questions and withdraw them if your opponent objects, it begins to look
  like bad faith. Let the court rule occasionally — the judge might even
  rule in your favor.

- *You don't want to interrupt the flow of your examination.* Every argument takes time and distracts the jury from the witness' testimony.
- *The judge is already taking your side.* If the judge questions the objector about the basis of the objection, or otherwise argues for your position in a colloquy with your adversary, it is probably best to keep quiet.
- *The judge does not appear to want to hear from you.* Some judges do not want to hear arguments, and tend to rule quickly on objections.
- *The objection is to testimony from a witness rather than to your question.* You can withdraw a question, but you cannot withdraw a witness' testimony.

(3) Reasons to Argue

- *You believe the evidence is admissible.*
- *The evidence is important to your case.* The more important the evidence, the greater the need to present an argument supporting its admissibility, even if your best argument is a weak one.
- *The judge expects it.* Obviously, if the judge asks you for a response, or looks at you expectantly, you should reply.

b. How to Respond

If you have a good argument against an objection and decide that you should respond, how should you go about it? In general, the same considerations apply to responses that applied to making objections:

- Stand up (if you are not already standing) and face the judge. Don't give in to the temptation to face the opposing attorney who is making the objection.
- State your responses succinctly, being as specific as possible about the legal grounds for admissibility. If you have support for your position — a case, treatise, or memorandum — offer to show it to the judge.
- Give a one-sentence nonlegal explanation for the benefit of the jury.
- Remain standing until the judge rules on the objection.
- Accept the judge's ruling gracefully.
- Make an offer of proof if you lose the objection. If the court sustains an objection against you and excludes evidence, do not forget to complete your record for appeal by making an offer of proof.

Sometimes a judge will sustain an objection against you quickly, before you have an opportunity to respond. It is not, as a general rule, a good idea to ask a judge to overturn his or her own ruling. The momentum is against you, and it puts you in the awkward position of arguing with the judge instead of opposing counsel. However, on rare occasions when important evidence has been wrongfully excluded, you may not be willing to acquiesce. You can ask the judge politely for a brief opportunity to be heard. Such a request probably will be granted if it is not made too often.

A similar problem is presented if the judge sustains a general objection. Your ability to appeal will be restricted unless the grounds for the ruling are in the record. It is proper to ask the judge to state the basis for his or her decision, but it is not wise to challenge the judge directly. The judge may respond by implying that you do not know your rules of evidence or may expound to the jury about why the evidence you offered was inadmissible. One alternative possibility is to shift the onus back onto opposing counsel by saying, "Excuse me, Your Honor, but I do not believe counsel stated the grounds for her objection. Could she specify her grounds for the record?"

NOTES

1. *Down at the courthouse.* In actual practice, few lawyers comply with the rule requiring specific objections. Trial attorneys, whether because of laziness or because they are unsure of their grounds, often object simply by saying, "Objection," and not stating grounds. Objections that are made in this general fashion *might* be sustained by the judge, but they also might be overruled. If you have neglected to follow the procedural requirements, you have no way to appeal incorrect rulings if you lose the case. In any event, it is generally a bad idea to learn trial practice by watching other lawyers until you know enough to recognize the good ones.

2. *Continuing objections.* ROBERT KEETON, TRIAL TACTICS AND METHODS 192-93 (1973), suggests that a continuing objection be phrased as follows:

> Your Honor, it is obvious that some additional questions raising this same point of law will be asked. In the absence of some special arrangement it might be asserted that I have forfeited my objection if I do not renew it by stating it fully each time a new question is asked. In order to avoid boring the court and jury with such repetition, may we have an understanding that I have the same objection I have stated to the last question, as a running objection to each question raising the same point and to the whole of this line of questioning, without the necessity of my objecting again to each question?

3. *What if the judge does not rule?* Your ability to appeal depends on the judge's issuing a ruling. Some judges, to avoid any chance of being reversed, may try to talk you into withdrawing a question or objection rather than ruling. Others may imprecisely ask you to move on to something else, or may instruct an attorney to proceed. Neither response is a definite ruling. Whether you are the objecting or offering party, you have the right to an explicit ruling and a statement of the grounds therefor. *State v. Staley*, 292 N.C. 160, 232 S.E.2d 680 (1977); *Kingston Pencil Corp. v. Jordan*, 115 Ga. App. 333, 154 S.E.2d 650 (1967). However, the judge may properly reserve his or her ruling until later and will frequently do so when the proponent offers to "connect up" seemingly irrelevant evidence. If the judge has reserved a ruling, the judge must make a decision eventually. You may have to remind the judge about this. Failure to request a ruling may be a waiver. *McElwain v. Schuckert*, 13 Ariz. App. 468, 477 P.2d 754 (1970).

4. *Requirement that objections to foundations be made pretrial.* An increasing number of jurisdictions are requiring in civil cases that foundation objections to exhibits and documents be raised pretrial. If no objection is raised before trial, the exhibit is admissible without the need for foundation

witnesses. Failure to raise the objection before trial is a waiver. *See* 1992 proposed amendment to FED. R. CIV. P. 26(a) (3)(c), 137 F.R.D. 90-91 (1991) (exhibit foundation objections must be made pretrial); TEX. R. CIV. EVID. 902(10) (business records self-authenticating unless objected to in advance).

5. *Objections to the conduct of non-witnesses*. You may object to the prejudicial actions, tactics, questions, or other conduct of people other than witnesses: attorneys, the judge, and members of the audience. You may object to improper remarks made by the opposing attorney, and you should move for a mistrial if they are seriously prejudicial. Objections also are appropriate when your opponent engages in unfair tactics, such as attempting to distract the jury during your examinations, or substituting a person of similar appearance in place of the client in an effort to defeat in-court identifications. *See* Alan D. Katz, *Meeting the Challenge (of Unfair Tactics)*, 1958 TRIAL LAW. GUIDE 249, 249-51. Making an objection to unfair or unethical tactics engaged in by your opponent can not only neutralize their effectiveness, but also reveal that unfairness to the jurors. For these reasons, some trial practitioners recommend that you object to all unfair tactics of your adversary. *See* FRED LANE, LANE'S GOLDSTEIN TRIAL TECHNIQUE § 13.122 (3d ed. 1984). Others suggest that if your adversary is mistreating one of your witnesses you should let it go unless that witness' testimony is being weakened or he or she is getting angry, because the jury will sympathize with the witness. *E.g.*, ROBERT KEETON, TRIAL TACTICS AND METHODS 175 (2d ed. 1973).

You may also object to gratuitous remarks made by the trial judge that reflect adversely on your client. *See Ginnis v. Mapes Hotel Corp.*, 470 P.2d 135 (Nev. 1970). Recognizing that it may be awkward to object to the actions of the judge in front of the jury, many jurisdictions permit you to wait and object when the jury is not present. *E.g.*, FED. R. EVID. 614(c). Objecting to the judge's prejudicial remarks or conduct, or to a question asked by the judge, is a delicate matter. It risks angering the judge (never a particularly good idea), and alienating the jurors who are likely to hold the judge in high regard. Nevertheless, such an objection may sometimes be necessary when the judge has seriously prejudiced your chances of winning. You probably should object to the judge's conduct in a quiet, respectful tone, out of the hearing of the jury. James W. Jeans suggests that you approach the bench and say:

> Your Honor, I want the record to reflect that when my client stated that he had never partaken of drugs before the night of this incident, that you leaned back in your chair and looked up at the ceiling, indicating to the jury your disbelief in the testimony.

JAMES W. JEANS, LITIGATION, vol. 2: 970 (2d ed. 1992). Your objection should be accompanied by a motion to strike if the judge made any prejudicial remarks within the hearing of the jurors, and a motion for a mistrial if seriously prejudicial. Jeans gives the following example:

> I request that you give an instruction to the jury now, that they are the sole judges of the credibility of the witnesses and that no action on the part of the judge is to influence them in this regard, and that you in no

manner intended to convey an impression to them regarding your appraisal of the witness' credibility.

Most practitioners suggest that objections to the conduct of the judge be made sparingly and only if you are sure of your grounds. *E.g.*, ANTHONY AMSTERDAM, TRIAL MANUAL 5 FOR THE DEFENSE OF CRIMINAL CASES § 418 (1988).

If members of the audience engage in disruptive or prejudicial behavior, that too is objectionable. *See* Annot., *Manifestations of Grief, Crying, and the Like by Victim or Family of Victim During Criminal Trial as Ground for Reversal, New Trial, or Mistrial*, 46 A.L.R.2d 949, 953-54.

6. *Should you make technical objections?* Objections on technical grounds, such as the form of the question, are the least likely to result in excluding harmful evidence (because they often can be rephrased easily) and the most likely to create a bad impression with the jury. For example:

> Q: Did you see the defendant enter the room?
> Attorney: Objection, leading the witness.
> Q: I'll rephrase. What happened next?
> A: I saw the defendant enter the room.

For these reasons, many trial practitioners do not make objections to the form of questions except for the purpose of exposing the unfairness of a pattern of misleading questioning or for the purpose of disconcerting an inexperienced opponent. The risks of making technical objections to relevant and helpful exhibits are even greater. There is a good discussion of these problems in FRANCIS X. BUSCH, LAW AND TACTICS IN JURY TRIALS, vol. 5: § 604 (1963). However, Keeton argues that if objections to form result in repeated rulings in your favor, the jury may being to wonder about the ethics and motives of the examiner. ROBERT KEETON, TRIAL TACTICS AND METHODS 171-72 (2d ed. 1973). It is also possible that a successful series of technical objections will result in your opponent's abandoning a line of questions or withdrawing the offer of an exhibit.

C. MOTIONS TO STRIKE

A motion to strike is closely related to an objection. If you can anticipate that inadmissible evidence is about to be disclosed to the jury, an objection is appropriate to prevent its disclosure. However, if a witness interjects inadmissible evidence unexpectedly, and the jury hears it, then you must use a motion to strike to remove it from consideration.

Of course, unlike an objection, a motion to strike will not prevent the jury from hearing the inadmissible evidence. For that reason, motions to strike are usually accompanied by additional requests for relief: that the jury be admonished to disregard the inadmissible evidence, and that a mistrial be declared if the jury has heard particularly prejudicial information. Admonitions to disregard prejudicial evidence are controversial — judges use them because they are deemed to "cure" the legal error, but social scientists have demonstrated that they are ineffective.[24]

1. PROCEDURE

If objectionable material has already been heard by the jury, trial procedure requires that you make a motion to strike it from the record. An objection by itself is not sufficient to preserve the issue for appeal, and it leaves the inadmissible evidence in the record and entitled to consideration by the jury.[25] Like an objection, a motion to strike must be accompanied by a specific statement of the legal basis for it.[26] If a motion to strike is granted, the judge is supposed to admonish the jury to disregard that evidence.[27]

Motions to strike are appropriate in five common situations:

- A witness gives an unresponsive answer to one of your questions.
- A witness volunteers inadmissible evidence in response to a proper question asked by your opponent. If the question itself clearly called for inadmissible evidence, you must have objected to the question. You cannot resort to a motion to strike unless the improper testimony could not have been anticipated from the question.
- A witness makes gratuitous or vindictive remarks.
- When subsequent testimony demonstrates that previous evidence was incompetent, or if your opponent fails to connect up testimony conditionally admitted.
- The opposing attorney makes gratuitous or improper remarks during witness examination or argument.

2. TACTICS

For the most part, the tactical considerations whether to move to strike improper testimony are the same as whether to object to an improper question. They will not be repeated. However, there are some important differences. A successful objection prevents the jury from ever hearing improper evidence. A motion to strike is made only *after* the jury has already heard the evidence. No matter how vehemently the judge admonishes the jury to disregard it, the evidence cannot be removed from the jurors' minds. The only effect of a motion to strike and admonition to disregard improper evidence is to emphasize the salience of that evidence.

The conventional wisdom among lawyers and judges is that striking out testimony after the jurors have heard it is not as effective as excluding it altogether by objection, but is better than doing nothing. Empirical data proves that the conventional wisdom is wrong. In the 1950's, investigators on the University of Chicago Jury Project conducted a series of mock civil trials,

---

[24] *See* J. Alexander Tanford, *Thinking About Elephants: Admonitions, Empirical Research, and Legal Policy*, 60 UMKC L. Rev. 645, 650-55 (1992).

[25] *E.g., Blinn v. State*, 487 N.E.2d 462 (Ind. 1986); *People v. Vetri*, 178 Cal. App. 2d 385, 2 Cal. Rptr. 795 (1960).

[26] *E.g., Cozine v. Hawaiian Catamaran Ltd.*, 412 P.2d 669 (Hawaii 1966); *Southern Elec. Gen. Co. v. Lance*, 269 Ala. 25, 110 So. 2d 627 (1959).

[27] *E.g., United States v. Nersesian*, 824 F.2d 1294 (2d Cir. 1987); *Isom v. River Island Sand & Gravel, Inc.*, 543 P.2d 1047 (Or. 1975).

varying whether the jurors heard evidence of the defendant's insurance cover-age. Evidence of insurance was used on the assumption that jurors would return a larger verdict if they knew it was being paid by an insurance com-pany. When the evidence was kept from the jury, verdicts averaged $34,000. When the existence of insurance was mentioned, average verdicts rose to $37,000. When insurance was mentioned, but the jury was admonished to disregard it, average verdicts climbed to $46,000.[28] Similar findings have been made in a dozen subsequent experiments.[29]

This leads to two important tactical differences between objections and motions to strike.

- Use motions to strike cautiously and infrequently.
- Base your decision on whether to move to strike testimony on its *legal* importance rather than the amount of factual harm it does to your case. If evidence is legally important but not titillating to the jury (e.g., testimony concerning venue or agency), you may use motions to strike freely. If evidence is legally important enough that you believe an erroneous ruling will be reversible error on appeal, you need to move to strike to preserve the issue. However, if evidence is factually prejudicial but has little legal importance (e.g., criminal record admitted to impeach), the damage has been done and there is little to be gained, so you rarely should move to strike.

D. OFFERS OF PROOF

Imagine in a products liability case that the judge erroneously sustains your opponent's objection to the testimony of your engineering expert. Your only evidence concerning a design defect is excluded. Without it, the jury decides against you and you appeal. You argue to the Court of Appeals that the expert should have been allowed to testify concerning a design defect, and that the trial judge's wrongful ruling was prejudicial error. The Court of Appeals turns to the record you submitted with your appeal, and lo and behold, the record does not reflect what the expert witness would have said. Obviously, if an objection was sustained, the evidence never got into the record, so the Court of Appeals cannot determine whether it was error to exclude it!

To solve this dilemma, the courts created a procedure known as an Offer of Proof. When an objection is made to a question and sustained by the court, the examining attorney may place into the record the evidence he or she expected to prove. Although the primary purpose is to perfect the record for appeal, the procedure also may help the trial judge rule correctly. Offers of proof are most commonly used when the issue is relevancy, and are unnecessary if the question itself indicates the nature of the evidence sought. For that reason, offers

[28] Harry Kalven, *A Report on the Jury Project of the University of Chicago Law School*, 24 INS. COUNSEL J. 368, 377-78 (1958).

[29] *E.g.*, Sharon Wolf and David Montgomery, *Effects of Inadmissible Evidence and Level of Judicial Admonishment to Disregard on the Judgments of Mock Jurors*, 7 J. APP. SOC. PSYCHOL. 205 (1977). This conclusion, the underlying experiments, and the courts' reactions to the problem are discussed in Tanford, *supra* note 24.

of proof are normally inapplicable to cross-examination, when the questions themselves are leading.

Offers of proof take three forms:

- The most formal offer of proof involves removing the jury from the courtroom, and then conducting the witness examination exactly as if the jury were present.
- An intermediate form comprises the attorney submitting a written or oral summary of the excluded evidence out of the hearing of the jury.
- The least formal offer of proof is the side bar conference, in which the attorney answers the judge's question, "Where are you going with this line of questioning?"

Remember that an offer of proof is *factual*. It is an opportunity to inform the judge what the evidence would be. It is not a *legal* argument explaining why you think the evidence is admissible.[30]

A formal offer of proof would proceed as follows:

PLAINTIFF'S ATTORNEY: Officer Novak, what happened next?
A: I asked whether there were any witnesses. One man stepped forth and identified himself as Franklin Stubbs. He appeared excited.
Q: What did you do next?
A: I asked him to tell me what he knew about the accident.
Q: What did Mr. Stubbs tell you?
DEFENSE ATTORNEY: I object. The testimony would be hearsay in violation of Rule 802. Mr. Stubbs can speak for himself.
PLAINTIFF'S ATTORNEY: It's an excited utterance, Your Honor. The witness testified Stubbs appeared excited.
DEFENSE ATTORNEY: No foundation, Your Honor. There is no proof the statement was made at or near the time of the event, and the officer's two questions mean Stubbs' answer is not spontaneous.
COURT: Sustained.
PLAINTIFF'S ATTORNEY: May I make an offer of proof, Your Honor?
COURT: Of course. Approach the bench.
PLAINTIFF'S ATTORNEY [Out of hearing of the jury]: We would like the jury excused and the witness allowed to testify to the content of Stubbs' statement.
COURT: Alright. Bailiff, please escort the jury to the jury room for a few minutes. [Jury leaves courtroom] Alright, counsel, you may proceed.
PLAINTIFF'S ATTORNEY: What did Stubbs tell you?
A: He told me that he had witnessed the accident. He said the driver of the blue Ford had gunned the engine and sped up when the light turned yellow, but the light was red by the time it got there. Stubbs said he was crossing the street ...
Q: By "he" you mean Stubbs?

---

[30] *See Moliere v. Wright*, 487 So. 2d 587 (La. App. 1986); *Wright v. Stokes*, 522 N.E.2d 308 (Ill. App. 1988).

A: Yeah. Stubbs said that he, Stubbs, had started to cross the street because the light had turned red for Walnut Street traffic, when the blue Ford came roaring through, almost hitting him. He said the driver of the Ford definitely ran the red light.

PLAINTIFF'S ATTORNEY: That's the end of the offer of proof, Your Honor.

COURT: Bring the jury back in. [Jury returns] You may continue.

PLAINTIFF'S ATTORNEY: After talking to witnesses, what did you do next?

A: I measured the skid marks and drew a diagram of the scene of the accident....

E. DEMONSTRATIVE EVIDENCE

An ancient proverb tells us that one picture is worth a thousand words. Melvin Belli, a pioneer in the effective use of exhibits and other kinds of demonstrative evidence, goes even further. Belli claims that, to a trial lawyer, "a picture can be worth much, much more. It could spell the difference between victory and defeat, or between a nominal award and an 'adequate' one."[31] This is probably an overstatement, but it serves a useful purpose. It often is easier and clearer to show something to the jury than to try to explain it in words alone. Also, an exhibit can be continual communication, remaining in front of the jury much longer than spoken words. Jurors may become distracted and miss important testimony, but it will be almost impossible for jurors not to see an exhibit passed to them. Some demonstrative evidence, such as photographs of injuries or a demonstration of what a witness means by "a threatening gesture," can convey information that may be impossible to communicate in words. Demonstrative evidence also tends to alleviate the boredom of hours of droning witnesses.

The preparation and use of demonstrative evidence is an essential part of the modern trial. Understanding demonstrative evidence requires that you learn four things:

- There is a body of procedural law that loosely regulates the method of offering demonstrative evidence.
- There also is a body of substantive law regulating what kinds of visual evidence are admissible. The substantive law divides demonstrative evidence into seven categories: real evidence, writings, illustrative evidence, silent witness exhibits, demonstrations, experiments, and views. Each type of evidence has its own unique foundation.
- One set of tactical considerations addresses whether to use demonstrative evidence and how best to inform the jury of its contents.
- Another set of tactical considerations concerns how to incorporate demonstrative evidence into the rest of your trial. What demonstrative evidence will help you make an effective opening statement, emphasize the main points in a direct examination, and provide punch to your closing argument?

---

[31] Melvin Belli, *Demonstrative Evidence: Seeing Is Believing*, TRIAL, July 1980, at 70.

1. LEGAL FRAMEWORK

a. Exhibits

Exhibits are divided into four distinct categories: real evidence, writings, illustrative exhibits, and silent witness evidence. Trial judges traditionally are given broad discretion to rule on the admissibility and use of exhibits.

(1) Real Evidence

McCormick defines real evidence as objects offered as having played "an actual and direct part in the incident or transaction giving rise to the trial,"[32] such as the actual murder weapon. When you offer real evidence, you must lay the following foundation:

- The exhibit is the same one involved in the incident.
- The exhibit is still in the same condition as it was at the time of the incident in all material ways.
- The exhibit can be connected to either the event or one of the main actors.

You may prove this foundation in either of two ways: direct evidence or circumstantial evidence. If the offered exhibit is unique, readily identifiable, and relatively impervious to change, the foundation may be laid by direct evidence. A witness who remembers seeing the item, either at the scene of the crime or in the possession of one of the main actors, testifies that the exhibit now offered is in fact the same one in the same condition.[33] For example, a gun with a serial number is unique and readily identifiable, so a police officer may lay the foundation by direct evidence as follows:

Q: What happened next?
A: I chased the defendant down an alley, caught him, placed him under arrest and handcuffed him.
Q: What did you do next?
A: I searched him and found a semi-automatic pistol in his jacket pocket.
Q: Do you recall the type of gun?
A: Yes, it was a Smith and Wesson forty-five caliber, serial number AP 45562 T.
Q: Handing you state's exhibit six, do you recognize this?
A: Yes. This is the handgun I recovered from the defendant. It is a Smith and Wesson, and here is the serial number, AP 45562 T.
Q: Has this exhibit changed in any way since you removed it from the defendant?
A: No, except that the clip has been removed.

If the offered evidence is not readily identifiable, because many similar such items exist, or because the item is susceptible to tampering or contamination, you must lay a circumstantial evidence foundation known as a "chain of

---

[32] McCORMICK ON EVIDENCE § 212 (4th ed. 1992, John W. Strong ed.).
[33] E.g., *Warriner v. State*, 435 N.E.2d 562 (Ind. 1982).

custody." The chain of custody traces what has happened to the item since it was originally recovered, so that it appears reasonably certain that the original item has not been contaminated or tampered with.[34] In a chain of custody, each person who had possession of the item testifies where it came from, that it was kept safely, and to whom it was eventually given. Drugs seized during an arrest are a good example of the kind of fungible item that requires a chain of custody.

Q: What happened next?

A: I chased the defendant down an alley, caught him, placed him under arrest and handcuffed him.

Q: What did you do next?

A: I searched him and found a plastic bag of white powder in his jacket pocket.

Q: What did you do with this powder?

A: I placed it inside a plastic evidence bag and sealed it to protect the powder from contamination. I took the defendant to the police station for booking, and then delivered the powder to the police laboratory at approximately 3:00 pm on September seventh.

Q: While it was in your possession, did you tamper with it or alter it in any way?

A: No.

Q: To whom did you deliver it?

A: To Susan Nelson, a police chemist.

Q: No further questions. We call Susan Nelson [Witness is sworn]. Ms. Nelson, were you on duty at 3:00 pm on September seventh?

A: Yes.

Q: Did you see Officer Johnson?

A: Yes. He gave me a sealed evidence envelope containing a white powder.

Q: What happened to it?

A: I locked it in the drug cabinet until I had time to test it the next day. On September eighth, I broke the seal, removed a small amount of the powder, and resealed the bag. I tested the powder and discovered that it contained cocaine.

Q: While the bag was in your possession, did you tamper with it or alter it in any way?

A: No.

Q: While the bag was open in your laboratory, could other substances have gotten mixed in with it?

A: No, I was very careful.

Q: To whom did you deliver the bag?

A: I delivered the bag to Detective Jennifer Boles on September fourteenth.

Q: No further questions. We call Jennifer Boles [Witness is sworn]. Detective Boles, were you on duty on September fourteenth?

A: Yes.

---

[34] See McCormick, *supra* note 32, at § 212.

Q: Did you see Susan Nelson that day?

A: Yes. She gave me a sealed evidence envelope containing a white powder.

Q: What happened to it?

A: I logged it into the evidence room at the police station. As far as I know, it just sat there for six months until today, when I retrieved it to bring it to the trial.

Q: Was it still sealed when you picked it up?

A: Yes.

Q: Did it appear to have been tampered with in any way?

A: No. It's unlikely, because the evidence room is always locked and there is always an officer on duty there, and only command officers have direct access to it.

Q: Handing you what has been marked as state's exhibit seven, do you recognize it?

A: Yes. This is the bag of powder I was referring to.

Real evidence also must be relevant, but no higher standard of probativeness is required for an exhibit than for testimony. If an item of real evidence tends to prove any issue, it is relevant. There is a common misapprehension that an exhibit must be connected to one of the parties to be admissible. The law is otherwise.[35] For example, a gun found at the scene of a robbery is admissible to help prove that the crime was *armed* robbery, whether or not it can be connected to the defendant.

(2) Writings

Written documents require the following foundation:

- The document must be authenticated by proving who wrote or created it.
- The document must satisfy the original document rule.
- The document must satisfy the hearsay rule.

The authentication requirement can be satisfied in two ways. Public and official documents are generally *self-authenticating*. Under rules such as FED. R. EVID. 902, a public document automatically satisfies the authentication requirement if an appropriate government official certifies in writing on the face of the document that it is true, accurate, and genuine. No additional evidence of who wrote or created the document is needed.

Rule 902. Self-Authentication. Extrinsic evidence of authenticity as a condition precedent to admissibility is not required with respect to the following:

(1) Domestic public documents under seal. A document bearing [an official] seal ... and a signature purporting to be an attestation or execution.

(2) Domestic public documents not under seal. A document purporting to bear the signature in the official capacity of an officer or employee of [a governmental] entity ... having no seal, if a public officer having a seal

---

[35] *See, e.g., State v. Moore,* 391 N.E.2d 665 (Ind. App. 1979).

[certifies] that the signer has the official capacity and that the signature is genuine.

(3) Foreign public documents. A document ... attested [by a foreign] official ... accompanied by a final certification as to the genuineness of the signature ... made by a ... consular agent of the United States....

(4) Certified copies of public records. A [certified] copy of an official record ....

(5) Official publications. Books, pamphlets, or other publications purporting to be issued by public authority.

(6) Newspapers and periodicals. Printed materials purporting to be newspapers or periodicals.

To authenticate private writings, you usually must call a witness to establish the genuineness of the document. FED. R. EVID. 901(b) contains four commonly accepted ways of accomplishing this.

Rule 901. Requirement of Authentication or Identification. (a) *General provision.* The requirement of authentication ... is satisfied by evidence sufficient to support a finding that the matter in question is what its proponent claims.

(b) *Illustrations.* By way of illustration only, and not by way of limitation, the following are examples of authentication or identification conforming with the requirements of this rule:

(1) Testimony of witness with knowledge. Testimony that a matter is what it is claimed to be.

(2) Nonexpert opinion on handwriting. Nonexpert opinion as to the genuineness of handwriting, based upon familiarity not acquired for purposes of the litigation.

(3) Comparison by trier or expert witness. Comparison by the trier of fact or by expert witnesses with specimens which have been authenticated.

(4) Distinctive characteristics and the like. Appearance, contents, substance, internal patterns, or other distinctive characteristics, taken in conjunction with circumstances.

If the exhibit is signed, you can prove its authenticity by calling the witness who actually signed it or another witness who recognizes the signature. Handwriting experts are sometimes used to compare a questioned document to a handwriting sample (called an "exemplar") known to come from a particular person, or the jury can do this comparison itself. If the document is unsigned, its authenticity must be proved by circumstantial evidence based on its contents or other distinctive characteristics. The most common example is a reply letter that contains references to an original letter or telephone call, indicating that the author of the reply letter was the person to whom the first communication was directed.[36]

A writing also must satisfy the original document rule. This does *not* mean it must be the original. The original document rule (sometimes called the "best evidence rule") only requires the original writing to be produced when

---

[36]*See* CAL. EVID. CODE § 1420.

its terms are material; even then, you do not have to produce the original if it is unavailable. The Federal Rules of Evidence are typical:

Rule 1002. Requirement of Original. To prove the content of a writing ... the original writing ... is required, except as otherwise provided in these rules or by Act of Congress.

Rule 1003. Admissibility of Duplicate. A duplicate is admissible to the same extent as an original unless (1) a genuine question is raised as to the authenticity of the original or (2) in the circumstances it would be unfair to admit the duplicate in lieu of the original.

Rule 1004. Admissibility of Other Evidence of Contents. The original is not required ... if —

(1) Originals lost or destroyed. All originals are lost or have been destroyed, unless the proponent lost or destroyed them in bad faith; or

(2) Original not obtainable. No original can be obtained by any available judicial process or procedure; or

(3) Original in possession of opponent. At a time when an original was under the control of the party against whom offered, that party was put on notice, by the pleadings or otherwise, that the contents would be a subject of proof at the hearing, and that party does not produce the original at the hearing; or

(4) Collateral matters. The writing, recording, or photograph is not closely related to a controlling issue.

Rule 1005. Public Records. The contents of an official record ... if otherwise admissible, may be proved by copy, certified as correct in accordance with Rule 902 or testified to be correct by a witness who has compared it with the original. If a copy which complies with the foregoing cannot be obtained by the exercise of reasonable diligence, then other evidence of the contents may be given.

Rule 1006. Summaries. The contents of voluminous writings ... which cannot conveniently be examined in court may be presented in the form of a chart, summary, or calculation. The originals, or duplicates, shall be made available for examination or copying, or both, by other parties at reasonable time and place. The court may order that they be produced in court.

Writings, like real evidence, must also be shown to be free from tampering. They must be the same in all material ways as when they were involved in the transaction. To satisfy this rule, the document must be free from alterations on its face, but otherwise carries a presumption that it has not been altered unless the opponent raises legitimate questions of its accuracy.

A typical foundation for a document sounds like this:

Q: What happened next?
A: I got a call to pick up a fare at the Hillcrest Nursing Home. I started the cab and entered the time into my trip log.

Q: Handing you state's exhibit five for identification, do you recognize it?
A: Yes. That's my trip log from March 12th of this year.
Q: Whose handwriting is this?
A: My own.
Q: Whose initials are at the bottom of the page?
A: Mine — "P.M.G."
Q: Is this the original page from your logbook?
A: Yes.
Q: Have any changes or alterations been made on it?
A: No.
Q: Is keeping this logbook a regular part of your job as a taxicab driver?
A: Yes. The Yellow Cab Company provides the forms and all drivers must fill them out every time we get a call to pick up a passenger.
Q: Do you make these entries at or near the time of the event from your own personal knowledge?
A: Yes.
Q: Your Honor, we move state's exhibit five into evidence as a business record.

(3) Illustrative Evidence

Exhibits that played no direct role in the transaction, but are offered to illustrate a witness' testimony and make the evidence more comprehensible to the jury, are commonly known as illustrative exhibits. These are the visual aids of the trial: maps, charts, diagrams, scale models, photographs, movies, and similar items used to help illustrate how events occurred and what things looked like. The specific identity or source of an illustrative exhibit is irrelevant. For example, it makes no difference whether you use a diagram drawn by the witness or one prepared by a surveyor. The only foundation required is:

- The exhibit is a fair and accurate depiction of something a witness observed. The true accuracy of the exhibit is seldom pertinent; what is important is that it depicts things the way the particular witness remembers them.[37]
- The judge believes that the use of the exhibit will be helpful to the jury in understanding that witness' testimony.[38]

The foundation for an illustrative exhibit requires that you prove it is an accurate depiction *from the witness' perspective*, not that it is objectively accurate. Because two witnesses may have perceived an event differently, a diagram that appears accurate to one witness may appear inaccurate to another. Therefore, if you use a diagram or scale model of the accident scene, you should lay the foundation separately for each witness who wishes to use it.

[37] See *Smith v. Ohio Oil Co.*, 10 Ill. App. 2d 67, 134 N.E.2d 526 (1956) (the inaccuracy of an exhibit is not grounds for objection unless it is so inaccurate that it is misleading and therefore not helpful).
[38] See, e.g., *Masters v. Dewey*, 709 P.2d 149 (Id. App. 1985); *Jackson v. State*, 426 N.E.2d 685 (Ind. 1981).

Each witness must verify that the exhibit accurately depicts his or her recollection before using it. For example:

Q: What happened next?
A: I arrived at the intersection of Fifth and Walnut Streets.
Q: Are you familiar with that intersection?
A: Sure. I drive that way to and from work almost every day.
Q: Do you remember what it looked like on April 3rd?
A: Yes.
Q: I am going to ask you to describe what happened at that intersection, including the locations and movements of the plaintiff and defendant. Would it help you if we could refer to a diagram of that intersection?
A: Yes.
Q: Handing you plaintiff's exhibit three for identification, is this a fair and accurate diagram of that intersection as it appeared to you on April 3rd?
A: Yes it is.
Q: Your Honor, we move into evidence plaintiff's exhibit three as an illustrative exhibit.

Photographs present some unique problems and must be distinguished from other kinds of illustrative evidence. Jurors are likely to assume that a photograph is correct, even to the minute details recorded. They may forget that it is offered only as a general representation — a mistake they are not likely to make with a diagram. A photograph, because of its ability to record detail, also carries a higher potential for being dramatic and emotional than other kinds of exhibits. Two considerations follow from these differences: gruesome or dramatic photographs are more likely to be excluded because of their prejudicial effect,[39] and the judge may require a stricter foundation on the accuracy of a photograph before admitting it.[40]

(4) Silent Witness Exhibits

A fourth kind of exhibit is now recognized in many jurisdictions: the silent witness. If a witness with personal knowledge is available to describe the events depicted in a photograph, the photograph is admissible as an illustrative exhibit. But what happens if no witness can verify that the photograph is an accurate representation of events? For example, a bank robbery, recorded by automatic cameras, can take place in the absence of eyewitnesses. Since no witness saw the robbery and can verify the accuracy of the events depicted, the foundation for illustrative evidence cannot be laid and the photographs must be excluded under that rule even if they clearly show the faces of the robbers. This peculiar result has led many courts to develop a new category of

---

[39] *See Commonwealth v. Chacko*, 480 Pa. 504, 391 A.2d 999 (1978). However, the court has broad discretion to admit gruesome photographs that are relevant. *See People v. Jackson*, 28 Cal. 3d 264, 618 P.2d 149, 168 Cal. Rptr. 603 (1980); *Brandon v. State*, 268 Ind. 150, 374 N.E.2d 504 (1978); *State v. Morales*, 120 Ariz. 517, 587 P.2d 236 (1978).

[40] *See Hopper v. Reed*, 320 F.2d 433 (6th Cir. 1963); *Lee v. Crittenden Co.*, 216 Ark. 480, 226 S.W.2d 79 (1950); *Virginian Ry. v. Hillsman*, 162 Va. 359, 173 S.E. 503 (1934).

exhibits. Photographs or other Media that accurately recorded events at the time they occurred, are admissible as silent witnesses.[41]

Since no human witness is available to verify the accuracy of a silent witness exhibit, you must find some other means for establishing a likelihood that the contents of the photographs are accurate. The most common procedure is to call an expert witness who can establish that the process involved in recording and reproducing an image is likely to produce undistorted results. Some courts require testimony that the camera was in good working order and properly loaded with film, and that the film was properly handled and developed.[42] Some require the opinion of experts that the photograph appears untampered with and accurate.[43] A single set of foundation requirements for all silent witness exhibits does not yet exist.[44] Instead, you must convince the court of the probable accuracy and relevancy of your photographs by some reasonable method.

FED. R. EVID. 901(b)(9) states somewhat vaguely that a silent witness exhibit is available based on "evidence describing a process or system used to produce a result and showing that the process or system produces an accurate result." Such a foundation might proceed as follows:

Q: What happened next, Detective?

A: After planting the microphone in the defendant's apartment, I returned to the vacant apartment down the hall to run a sound test. My partner walked around the defendant's apartment speaking out loud, and I turned on the tape recorder. We made a sample tape and then listened to it. Everything was working fine; I could hear my partner's voice loud and clear.

Q: Have you used this equipment before?

A: Oh sure. It's our standard recording equipment we use on all our electronic surveillance.

Q: Have you ever had any trouble with it?

A: No.

Q: What did you do next?

A: Turned on the machine and left the premises. Next day, we returned and picked up the tape.

Q: Did it appear that anyone had tampered with the recording equipment overnight?

A: No.

Q: What did you do with the tape?

A: Took it back to the station and listened to it. I found a two-minute conversation between two males recorded at approximately 2:15 a.m.

Q: Did you recognize either voice?

---

[41] See United States v. Clayton, 643 F.2d 1071 (5th Cir. Unit B 1981); Bergner v. State, 397 N.E.2d 1012 (Ind. App. 1980); Ferguson v. Commonwealth, 212 Va. 745, 187 S.E.2d 189 (1972); People v. Doggett, 83 Cal. App. 2d 405, 188 P.2d 792 (1948).

[42] E.g., United States v. Clayton, 643 F.2d 1071 (5th Cir. Unit B 1981); Bergner v. State, 397 N.E.2d 1012 (Ind. App. 1980).

[43] E.g., Bergner v. State, 397 N.E.2d 1012 (Ind. App. 1980); People v. Doggett, 83 Cal. App. 2d 405, 188 P.2d 792 (1948).

[44] A variety of approaches are summarized in State v. Pulphus, 465 A.2d 153 (R.I. 1983), and 41 A.L.R.4th 812.

A: Yes, one was the defendant's voice. The other voice was unknown to me.

Q: During that conversation, did either person say anything about drugs?

A: Yes.

Q: Officer, have you brought that tape with you?

A: Yes.

Q: Handing you state's exhibit two for identification, is this the tape you have been referring to?

A: Yes.

Q: Is it still in the same condition as the night it was made?

A: Yes.

Q: No alterations, erasures, or changes of any kind?

A: None.

Q: I move state's exhibit two into evidence.

(5) General Procedure for Introducing Exhibits

The procedure for introducing exhibits varies from jurisdiction to jurisdiction. However, it is safe to say that most courts require something approximating the following steps:

- Mark the exhibit with a letter or number for identification. This is often done by the attorneys before trial, but you also may request the clerk or court reporter to mark exhibits just before you use them.
- Lay the appropriate foundation through your witness, referring to the exhibit only by its identification mark.
- Show the exhibit to opposing counsel or ask the court if opposing counsel would like to examine it.[45]
- Formally offer the exhibit into evidence, referring to it only by number or letter. For example, "Your Honor, we offer defendant's exhibit C into evidence."
- If appropriate, hand the exhibit to the bailiff (or directly to the judge) for the court to examine. You probably should in all cases ask the judge if he or she wishes to view the exhibit.
- The opposing lawyer may conduct a *voir dire* examination of the witness concerning foundation matters, and/or may make objections to the admission of the exhibit.
- The court rules on whether to admit or exclude the exhibit.
- If the exhibit is received into evidence, publish it to the jury. With simple documents and photographs, you can distribute copies to individual jurors.[46] Real evidence can be passed among them. In either case, you should request the court's permission to approach the jury. Large diagrams or charts can be placed where all jurors can see them. If anything about the exhibit needs to be explained, you must do so through witness

---

[45] See *Hazdra Homes, Inc. v. DuPage Cty.*, 27 Ill. App. 3d 685, 326 N.E.2d 561 (1975) (exhibit not admissible unless opponent has prior opportunity to examine it).

[46] See *Wilkins v. Cash Register Serv. Co.*, 518 S.W.2d 736 (Mo. App. 1975) (broad discretion to permit distribution of copies).

testimony — you are not allowed to talk about the exhibit yourself at this time without explicit permission from the court.

b. Demonstrations and Experiments

Whether to allow a witness to demonstrate something to a jury is a matter left almost entirely to the discretion of the trial judge.[47] No precise set of foundation requirements exist, but the following is probably sufficient in most jurisdictions:

- The demonstration is relevant and would neither create undue sympathy nor place anyone in danger.
- The demonstration can be conducted under "similar conditions and circumstances" to those existing at the time of the original event. Variations in conditions generally affect weight, not admissibility.[48]

Persons other than witnesses, such as attorneys and jurors, generally are not allowed to participate in demonstrations.[49]

With respect to the demonstration of injuries, courts have reached a variety of results. *Exhibiting* injuries, scars and wounds is almost always permitted to illustrate the nature and extent of an injury, regardless of the gruesomeness of it.[50] However, *manipulating* an injury in an attempt to produce a cry of pain or to demonstrate limitations on natural movement is more easily feigned and more emotional, so is more often prohibited.[51]

c. Views

A jury view of the scene at which a disputed event took place is closely related to a demonstration. Although courts have inherent authority to permit the jury to leave the courtroom to view the scene, statutory authorization also exists in most jurisdictions.[52] Under most procedures, the jury is transported by a bailiff to the scene and permitted to view it, but nothing else. It is improper for the lawyers or the bailiff to explain the significance of certain details or to direct the jurors' attention to particular features.[53] Despite what you see on television, it is extremely rare for a judge to reconvene court at the scene to enable witnesses to testify about it, and rarer still for the judge to authorize a reenactment of the events.

It is more common for a view to be granted when land is involved than in cases not involving real property. Nevertheless, Wigmore argues that views

---

[47] *See Patterson v. F.W. Woolworth Co.*, 786 F.2d 874 (8th Cir. 1986); *Way v. Hayes*, 513 P.2d 1222 (Nev. 1973).

[48] *E.g., Shorten v. State*, 751 S.W.2d 262 (Tex. App. 1988); *Ivey v. State*, 369 So.2d 1276 (Ala. 1979).

[49] *But see Gesel v. Haintl*, 427 S.W.2d 525 (Mo. 1968) (jurors permitted to pull on hand scale to help them correlate force with the foot-pound scale).

[50] *See LeMaster v. Chicago, Rock Island & P. R.R.*, 35 Ill. App. 3d 1001, 343 N.E.2d 65 (1976) (amputated stump could be shown).

[51] *See Peters v. Hockley*, 152 Or. 434, 53 P.2d 1059 (1936).

[52] *See, e.g.*, IND. CODE § 35-37-2-5 (in criminal cases), § 34-1-21-3 (in civil cases); MINN. STAT. § 546.12 (civil; real property only); PA. R. CIV. PROC. 219.

[53] *E.g., State v. Musgrove*, 582 P.2d 1246 (Mont. 1978). *Cf. Rodrigues v. Ripley Indus.*, 507 F.2d 782 (1st Cir. 1974) (improper to conduct experiments, but proper to direct jurors' attention to relevant features).

are appropriate for any kind of object that must be seen in order to be properly understood and which cannot be brought into the courtroom. He cites cases in which jurors have been allowed to view automobiles, machinery, manufacturing plants, cattle, horses, trucks, and trains.[54] Whether and under what circumstances to permit a view is a decision left to the trial court's discretion.[55] Views are becoming increasingly uncommon as the need for trial efficiency increases and videotaping technology becomes more sophisticated.

2. ETHICS OF DEMONSTRATIVE EVIDENCE

The major ethical considerations concerning demonstrative evidence can be divided into two categories: the attempted introduction of exhibits despite the absence of foundation, and non-evidentiary displays or "sideshows."

MODEL RULES OF PROFESSIONAL CONDUCT Rule 3.4 prohibits a lawyer to "allude to any matter that the lawyer does not reasonably believe is relevant or that will not be supported by admissible evidence." Thus, it is unethical to attempt to let the jury see an exhibit that you expect the judge to ultimately rule inadmissible. For example, a prosecutor may not hand a witness a shotgun in plain view of the jury unless the prosecutor reasonably believes that this witness will be able to properly authenticate it and lay the foundation for its admissibility.

The second problem concerns sideshows. These are non-evidentiary visual displays staged for the jurors' benefit, that the lawyer will not offer into evidence but wants the jury to see. In their book, TRIAL ETHICS, Richard Underwood and William Fortune give the following examples:

- In a personal injury case in which plaintiff lost a leg, plaintiff's lawyer left an L-shaped package wrapped in butcher paper on the counsel table throughout trial.
- In a case brought by a widower for the wrongful death of his wife, the defendant's lawyer arranged for an attractive young woman to pretend to be the plaintiff's new girlfriend, sit near him during trial, and occasionally lean over and ask him innocuous questions, and touch him gently.
- In a criminal case, the defense attorney arranged to have the defendant's infant son crawl up to the attorney during closing argument by smearing Gerber's peaches on his cuffs. The attorney apologized to the court and handed the child to the defendant, who then held the child throughout closing argument.
- Defense counsel arranged for a look-alike to don the defendant's clothes and sit in the defendant's place, while the real defendant sat in the back of the courtroom. This caused several eyewitnesses to misidentify the accused.

Such tactics are unethical. They constitute attempts to get before the jury information that the lawyers have no reasonable basis to believe is admissible, and thus violates Rule 3.4. If you do not tell the court what you are doing,

---

[54] 4 WIGMORE ON EVIDENCE 364-65 (Chadbourn rev. 1972).
[55] *See, e.g., People v. Favors*, 556 P.2d 72 (Colo. 1976).

these tactics amount to a fraud on the tribunal, and contravene the general principle of Rule 3.3 that you owe a duty of candor toward the court.

3. TACTICS OF DEMONSTRATIVE EVIDENCE

Demonstrative evidence should not be used indiscriminately. Just because you have an exhibit available, or can conduct a demonstration, does not mean that you necessarily should use it. It is possible to overuse visual aids. The primary value of demonstrative evidence is its potential to stand out from oral testimony, attract the jurors' attention, and emphasize the particular facts it portrays. This effect can be weakened if you use visual aids too often. Therefore, most attorneys favor only using demonstrative evidence if it is necessary to prove your case, will provide ammunition for your closing argument, or emphasizes important witness testimony on a central issue. Thus, if a matter such as medical expenses is essentially uncontested, you reasonably may forgo introducing lots of bills for small amounts in favor of a one-page summary that shows the total cost.

a. Exhibits

Exhibits should cause as little disruption as possible in most situations. To accomplish this, you should have the exhibit readily accessible and premarked with its number or letter so that you can move smoothly from testimony to the exhibit. Some practitioners recommend that it is in the best interests of both sides to stipulate to the admissibility of exhibits so that the flow of testimony is not interrupted even for laying a foundation. Of course, you should stipulate to your opponent's exhibits only if you know that a proper foundation can be laid and that your opponent is capable of doing it.

The method you use to lay the foundation for an exhibit can affect the jurors' view of its importance. The less important exhibits, and those being used only to illustrate a witness's testimony, should be introduced as simply as possible — preferably by stipulation. However, if you want to focus the jurors' attention on an important exhibit, you can emphasize the foundation. Some attorneys suggest calling an expert witness — the photographer who took a photograph, or the draftsman who prepared a scale drawing — who can testify to the accuracy of it. You can raise or lower your voice and prolong or emphasize the foundation testimony to build up the jurors' interest. Keeping the exhibit hidden under a sheet or in a box while the foundation is being laid also can arouse the jurors' curiosity.

An exhibit can be useful for reasons completely apart from its ability to communicate; reasons related to the witness who uses it. For example, a plaintiff with crippling injuries can make a dramatic impression on the jury as he or she struggles out of the witness chair in order to mark locations on a chart. An expert who stands up and uses the blackboard may appear more knowledgeable than one who testifies sitting down. Similarly, using an exhibit may be inappropriate for a particular witness. For example, if you represent a defendant who claims to have killed someone in the heat of passion, you probably should not ask your client to calmly reconstruct minute details of the event on a diagram.

b. Using a Diagram

Diagrams and other illustrative exhibits are used with the expectation that they will make a witness' testimony more easily understood. To accomplish this, you should:

- Make sure the exhibit is large enough to be seen.
- Make sure neither you nor the witness blocks the jurors' view of the diagram.
- If possible, go to the courtroom in which your case will be tried with the witness, and practice. Have someone sit in the jury box and make sure the use of the diagram is visible and understandable.

You also have another audience: the court of appeals. The use of illustrative exhibits can have a deleterious effect on the appellate judges' ability to understand the evidence. All too often, the record will read like this:

Q: Using this diagram, tell the jury what happened next.
A: I parked my car here and walked over here. Just then I saw a person get out of a small truck.
Q: Who was this person?
A: That man, sitting over there.
Q: What happened next?
A: He walked over to a car parked here and then to a car parked here. I heard gunshots and ducked behind a car over here. I looked out and saw him fall to the ground, and another man run off in this direction.

Obviously, the court of appeals has no way of figuring out what actually happened, which will make their review of the factual record difficult. Yet you obviously cannot conduct a direct examination that sounds like this:

Q: Using this diagram, tell the jury what happened next.
A: I parked my car here.
Attorney: Let the record reflect that the witness has pointed out a location on the upper left corner of exhibit six, between what is marked as Sixth Street and what is marked as Kirkwood Avenue, on the left side of what is marked as Walnut Street. Continue, please.
Witness: Well, then I walked over here.
Attorney: Let the record reflect that the witness has indicated a path in a southwesterly direction representing approximately three inches on exhibit six, beginning at a point on the upper left corner of exhibit six, between what is marked as Sixth Street and what is marked as Kirkwood Avenue, on the left side of what is marked as Walnut Street, and ending at a point on the right side of Walnut Street in front of a location marked as The Book Corner. What happened next?
Witness: I saw a person get out of a small truck parked here.
Attorney: Let the record reflect the witness has indicated a point in the approximate center of exhibit six, on the south side of what is marked as Kirkwood Avenue ....

You need to use a diagram in a way that is understandable both to the jury and to the court of appeals. Two methods are available for these combined purposes: having the witness make marks on the diagram to indicate locations, and having the witness give adequate descriptions in words other than "here" and "there." Both are illustrated in the following example.

Q: Using this diagram, tell the jury what happened next.
A: I parked my car here.
Q: Will you mark that spot with a "W-1"?
A: Sure.
Q: What happened next?
A: I walked over here.
Q: Across Walnut Street to the Book Corner?
A: Yes.
Q: What did you see?
A: I saw a person get out of a small truck parked here.
Q: Will you mark that place with a "P-1"?
A: Sure.
Q: Who was this person?
A: That man, sitting over there.
Q: The plaintiff, Harry Purcell?
A: Yes.
Q: What happened next?
A: He walked over to a car parked here and then to a car parked here.
Q: Will you mark those places as "P-2" and P-3"?
A: Sure.
Q: What happened next?
A: I heard gunshots, and ducked behind a car over here.
Q: Will you mark that "W-2"?
A: Sure.
Q: What happened next?
A: I looked out and saw the plaintiff ....

Another technique is to let the witness tell a block of testimony, and then go back over it using a diagram. This has two advantages: you get to repeat important testimony two or three times, and you get to choose which parts of the narrative to emphasize and which to omit. It is not necessary to clarify every use of a "here" or "there" by a witness. This technique also has a potential disadvantage of jumbling chronological order. It works like this:

Q: Using this diagram, tell the jury what happened next.
A: I parked my car here and walked over here. Just then I saw a person get out of a small truck. He walked over to a car parked here. I heard gunshots and ducked behind a car here. When I looked up, the man was slumping to the ground.
Q: Please mark a "W" to show where you were when you heard the gunshots.
A: Okay.

Q: Please place a "P" on the diagram to show where the plaintiff was when he fell to the ground.
A: Okay.

Note that the attorney did not bother to have the record reflect where the witness initially parked her car. The matter is unimportant, either to the jury or to the court of appeals.

c. Communicating Contents of Exhibits to the Jury

For many kinds of exhibits, it is easy to make sure the contents and details are communicated to the jury. Large diagrams can be seen at a distance; most real evidence can be passed around the jury box. For other exhibits, such as multi-page documents, small photographs, and dangerous weapons, it is more difficult to devise an adequate way to make sure all jurors get a good look at them. Any document or small exhibit could be just passed around the jury, of course, but this is a time-consuming process. For example, if a four-page document is introduced that takes five minutes to read, it will take an hour for one copy to circulate among twelve jurors. If you resume testimony during this hour, then the jurors become distracted — each juror must decide whether to read the document or listen to the witness. You obviously would like them to do both, but the judge is not likely to let you suspend direct examination for an hour, nor would this be a good tactic, since each juror would have to sit there doing nothing for fifty-five minutes while other jurors read the document.

Trial practitioners suggest a number of methods for effectively communicating the contents of an exhibit to the jury. Every photo-finishing store can turn photographs into slides that can be projected large enough for all to see, or into 20" x 30" poster-size enlargements. You can make a dozen copies of photographs or simple documents so that each juror (and the judge) has one. Documents and diagrams can be made into transparencies and shown on an overhead projector. For short documents, one alternative is to ask a witness to read it to the jury. For this to be effective, it must be appropriate for the witness to read it, as in the case of a witness who wrote or received a document, and the witness should have a good speaking voice.

The need for an effective method of communicating the contents of an exhibit is especially strong in the case of complicated documents. You could use any of the techniques just discussed, but this can still be an unsatisfactory solution when you only want to emphasize one paragraph of a twenty-page commercial lease agreement. One solution is to introduce the whole document into evidence, but read only the portions you need. This procedure usually is permitted, although your opponent may have the right to compel you to read other relevant excerpts at the same time to prevent you from taking sections out of context.[56] You also may be able to enlarge just the one paragraph you consider important and display it on an easel. If you have any doubts about the propriety of a method you want to use to communicate an exhibit to the

---

[56] See FED. R. EVID. 106.

jury, check with the trial judge before trial. If the judge will not let you do it your way, you still will have time to prepare to do it the judge's way.

d. Demonstrations, Experiments, and Jury Views

Closely related to exhibits are demonstrations, experiments and jury views. Like an exhibit, these procedures create visual evidence for the jury. Unlike an exhibit, however, these procedures are done "live" in the jury's presence. You can rehearse, but you cannot prepare them in advance. They may not come out the way you planned!

The tactical considerations governing demonstrations, experiments and views are essentially similar to those governing the use of exhibits, except that the risks are magnified because you lack control over precisely what will happen. The procedure and foundation are similar to but less formal than those controlling illustrative exhibits. Broad discretion is given to the trial judge to decide whether and under what conditions to permit these live exercises.

You should use demonstrative or experimental evidence cautiously. It is conducted live in front of the jury, and if it comes out differently than you expected, your case may be in trouble. With modern technology, there rarely is a need for live demonstrations. Most jurisdictions permit the use of videotaped demonstrations offered for illustrative purposes. The advantage of videotaping your demonstration is obvious — if it doesn't come out right, you can do it again.

Nevertheless, many attorneys continue to use live demonstrations even for important testimony. If you do, bear the following in mind:

- Make sure the demonstration faces the jury, so they can see the event unfold. If you want the jury to see what the advancing gunman looked like, the witness must demonstrate it in a way that the gunman advances toward the jury.
- It is very difficult for one witness to demonstrate what two people were doing simultaneously. Demonstrations are more effective if the witness is demonstrating what one person did.
- You should not participate in the demonstration. You are not a witness and cannot place evidence into the record. If you cannot plan a demonstration that the witness can conduct with you out of the way, then don't do it at all.
- If you need a second person in a demonstration, use the jury. If you want the witness to demonstrate that she was close enough to the robber to see his face clearly, ask the witness to demonstrate that distance in relation to the front row of jurors, not in relation to you, to your co-counsel, or to some inanimate object in the courtroom.
- Do not conduct a demonstration without rehearsing. This means you probably should never ask a witness on cross-examination to demonstrate anything.
- Save them for important facts. Demonstrations, like exhibits, will emphasize the facts being demonstrated.

e. Making a Record of a Demonstration

Some kinds of demonstrations are unavoidable. Witnesses will use gestures to help explain their testimony. They point to the accused, indicate size with their hands, and shake their heads in answer to questions. While this evidence is clear to the jurors, at least to those who are looking at the witness, it will rarely be reflected in the record, because the court reporter can take down only what he or she hears. You must make sure that this nonverbal conduct is translated into words. We are all, of course, familiar with one common way of doing this — the attorney announces, "May the record reflect that the witness has pointed out the defendant."

Tactically, it usually is better for witnesses to provide the verbal descriptions in their own words. For example, if a witness indicates a distance with his or her hands, you can ask the witness to estimate that distance verbally. If the witness does so, no further statement need be made for the record. Indeed, no further statement should be made. You should avoid needless repetition. If the witness answers a question about size by spreading his or her hands two feet apart and saying "About two feet," it is unnecessary for you to add, "May the record reflect that the witness has indicated a distance of about two feet." Sometimes, of course, you may want to make a formal request for the record to reflect a gesture such as pointing out the accused, because it creates a moment of drama that emphasizes important evidence.

The following transcript indicates how demonstrations might be included in the record:

> Q: What happened next?
> A: We were standing in front of the trailer when the defendant turned to his wife and said he was going to beat the stuffing out of her if she didn't get back inside.
> Q: Are you sure those were his words?
> A: Yes.
> Q: How close were you standing to him?
> A: Real close.
> Q: With the court's permission, will you step down and demonstrate that distance? Will you approach the jury and stop when you are the same distance from the front row as you were from the defendant when he said he was going to beat the stuffing out of his wife?
> A: Sure [witness takes a position].
> Q: So you were about four feet apart?
> A: Yes.
> Q: Did you observe the position of the defendant's arms at that time?
> A: Yes, I did.
> Q: Will you demonstrate to the jury what the defendant did with his arms as he made the threat?
> A: Sure. He made fists like this [demonstrates] and took a step toward her like this [demonstrates].
> Q: We have to put this into words for the court reporter. Describe exactly how the defendant was holding his fists.

A: Both fists were doubled [demonstrating again], down at his side. He took a step toward her and held the left fist up at shoulder level and the right fist about at his waist, like a boxer's stance.

NOTES

1. *Suggestions on types of demonstrative evidence*. An excellent discussion of a variety of kinds of exhibits, with illustrations, can be found in JOAN M. BROVINS & THOMAS OEHMKE, THE TRIAL PRACTICE GUIDE 165-94 (1992). For innovative suggestions concerning demonstrative evidence, see Roger J. Dodd, *Innovative Techniques: Parlor Tricks for the Courtroom*, TRIAL at 38 (April 1990).

2. *Using leading questions to lay foundations*. It is proper in most jurisdictions to use leading questions to lay foundations. Nevertheless, some lawyers suggest that you use open-ended questions such as "Do you recognize this exhibit? What is it?" Even if well-prepped, a witness is unlikely to use the proper words of art to lay a foundation without some prompting from you. If the judge permits it, it is more efficient (and will result in less confusion) for you to guide the witness through the foundation with leading questions.

3. *Examples of demonstrative evidence foundations*. For sample transcripts showing how to lay foundations for demonstrative evidence, *see* Jersey M. Green, *Demonstrative Trial Technique: The Introduction of Illustrative Exhibits*, TRIAL DIPL. J., Summer 1991, at 65; EDWARD J. IMWINKELRIED, EVIDENTIARY FOUNDATIONS 37-81 (2d ed. 1989).

4. *Inaccuracies and dissimilarities*. Illustrative exhibits such as drawings or photographs of the scene of an accident can never be 100% accurate. No demonstration or experiment will exactly duplicate the conditions that existed at the time of an event. Does this matter? The contemporary view is that inaccuracies and dissimilarities affect weight, not admissibility. As long as the problems are clearly pointed out to the jury, the demonstrative evidence will be admissible. *See Moyer v. United States*, 312 F.2d 302 (9th Cir. 1963); *Botz v. Krips*, 267 Minn. 362, 126 N.W.2d 446 (1964). Courts have broad discretion in this regard. *See Tumey v. Richardson*, 437 S.W.2d 201 (Ky. 1969). Mark Dombroff suggests that you may be able to object to photographs as misleading if they appear accurate but: a) the distances are exaggerated or foreshortened by the use of telephoto or wide-angle lenses; b) important landmarks have been omitted because of the way the photograph was framed or cropped; c) it has been printed reversing left and right; or d) it has been over- or underexposed, distorting the light or color. DOMBROFF ON UNFAIR TACTICS 486-88 (2d ed. 1988).

5. *Showing exhibit to opponent*. This is a tricky procedure. You must remember that you are in open court and on the record. While court is in session, you are not supposed to make any remarks directly to your adversary. It is at least technically improper to turn to your opponent and ask, "Marva, do you want to examine this?" It is both improper and may irritate the jurors or the judge for you to walk over to the other counsel table and engage in a whispered conversation about the exhibit. We recommend that, in general, you say nothing. The record does *not* need to reflect that you have handed an

exhibit to your adversary. If you feel the overwhelming need to make some remark, consider something along these lines: "Your Honor, may I show this exhibit to Ms. Leonard?"

6. *Disclosing contents of exhibit before it has been admitted*. It is improper during the evidentiary phase of trial for you to show the jurors an exhibit or mention its contents before it is formally admitted. To do so would be to communicate evidence to the jurors that has not been properly introduced. James McElhaney, *Steps in Introducing Exhibits*, LITIGATION, Winter 1975, at 55. Therefore, you must refer to exhibits by their numbers or letters and not by a description of them. For example, you should say "Handing you plaintiff's exhibit three, do you recognize it?" rather than "Handing you a copy of the lease, do you recognize it?" When exhibits are large and obvious, you probably cannot introduce it without prematurely displaying it to the jurors. If you successfully move it into evidence, of course, any error in disclosing it prematurely will be cured. If your exhibit is excluded, however, a mistrial may be required if the jury has seen it. Belli suggests that such an exhibit should not be brought into the courtroom at all without first obtaining the court's permission, and if brought in, should be covered or kept in a container. MELVIN BELLI, MODERN TRIALS, vol. 2: 941-42 (1954). Assuming you are confident it will be received, this tactic also heightens the jurors' interest.

7. *Exhibits in the jury room*. Despite popular myths about jurors examining exhibits during deliberations, not all jurisdictions permit exhibits to go to the jury. Most exclude depositions and other testimonial substitutes. *E.g.*, MINN. R. CRIM. P. 26.03 (19). Some allow real evidence and writings but exclude purely illustrative exhibits. *See United States v. Soulard*, 730 F.2d 1292 (9th Cir. 1984). Some leave to the court's discretion which exhibits are sent to the jury. *See* ABA STANDARDS FOR CRIMINAL JUSTICE 15-4.1 (2d ed. 1980). In some courts, no exhibits go to the jury unless requested by counsel, N.Y. CRIM. PROC. LAW § 310.20; demanded by the jury, CAL. PENAL CODE § 1137; or requested by the jury and consented to by all parties, N.C. GEN. STAT. 15A-1233(b).

8. *Objections to exhibits*. Apart from the usual substantive objections (e.g., relevance, hearsay) and objections that the full foundation has not been laid, some special objections can be made to exhibits. These are discussed in Elwyn Cady, *Objections to Demonstrative Evidence*, 32 Mo. L. REV. 333 (1967). If an illustrative exhibit is an incorrect representation, it can be objected to on grounds that it distorts facts, exaggerates an injury, or is otherwise misleading or confusing. The mere fact that an exhibit is not absolutely correct (not to scale, containing identifying marks, retouched or posed photographs) does not make it objectionable unless it is also misleading. Gruesome or indecent exhibits (bloody clothing, photographs of corpses, obscene movies) can be objected to on the grounds that they will unduly arouse or inflame the emotions of the jury or have some other articulable prejudicial effect. *See* FED. R. EVID. 403. An objection on the sole ground that an exhibit is inflammatory, cumulative, gruesome, or indecent is rarely successful, however. An increasing number of jurisdictions require objections to exhibits to be raised before trial in civil cases or risk waiver. *See* 1992 proposed amendment to FED. R. CIV. P. 26(a)(3)(c), 137 F.R.D. 90-91 (1991).

9. *Dramatic use of exhibits*. Usually an exhibit is an aid to a witness's testimony, so you want to introduce it with little disruption so you do not distract the jury from that witness. Occasionally, however, you may want to introduce an exhibit in a disruptive or dramatic flourish. This technique should be used rarely and only for especially persuasive evidence. For example, prosecutors often introduce gruesome photographs of a murder victim with as much drama as possible. Melvin Belli was famous for the dramatic exhibit technique. He once represented a 685-pound plaintiff, supposedly "too heavy" for an ambulance or the courthouse elevator. His client was delivered to the courthouse in a moving van and lifted through a courtroom window by a crane. *See* MELVIN BELLI, MODERN TRIALS, vol. 1: 26-33 (1954).

F. BIBLIOGRAPHY

1. OBJECTIONS

E. Maurice Braswell, *Objections — Howls of a Dog-Pound Quarrel*, 4 CAMP. L. REV. 339 (1982).

Mark Denbeaux & Michael Risinger, *Questioning Questions: Objections to Form in the Interrogation of Witnesses*, 33 ARK. L. REV. 439 (1980).

JAMES W. JEANS, LITIGATION, ch. 14 (2d ed. 1992).

JAMES W. JEANS, TRIAL ADVOCACY, ch. 13 (1975).

ROBERT KEETON, TRIAL TACTICS AND METHODS 166-214 (2d ed. 1973).

FRED LANE, LANE'S GOLDSTEIN TRIAL TECHNIQUE, ch. 13 (3d ed. 1984).

Steven Lubet, *Objecting*, 16 AM. J. TRIAL ADVOC. 213 (1992).

David P. Leonard, *Appellate Review of Evidentiary Rulings*, 70 N.C. L. REV. 1155 (1992).

James McElhaney, *Making and Meeting Objections*, LITIGATION, Fall 1975, at 43.

James McElhaney, *I Object!*, LITIGATION, Nov. 1992, at 90.

2. OFFER OF PROOF

JAMES W. JEANS, LITIGATION, ch. 15 (2d ed. 1992).

JAMES W. JEANS, TRIAL ADVOCACY, ch. 14 (1975).

FRED LANE, LANE'S GOLDSTEIN TRIAL TECHNIQUE, §§ 13.28-13.33 (3d ed. 1984).

Jon Waltz, *The Offer of Proof*, 1972 TRIAL LAW. GUIDE 385.

3. DEMONSTRATIVE EVIDENCE

Melvin Belli, *Demonstrative Evidence: Seeing Is Believing*, TRIAL, July 1980, at 70.

Kenneth Broun, *Laying the Foundation for the Admission of Real and Demonstrative Evidence, in* MASTER ADVOCATE'S HANDBOOK 159 (D.L. Rumsey ed., 1986).

JOAN BROVINS & THOMAS OEHMKE, THE TRIAL PRACTICE GUIDE, ch. 10 (1992).

Elwyn Cady, *Objections to Demonstrative Evidence*, 32 Mo. L. REV. 333 (1967).

Roger Dodd, *Innovative Techniques: Parlor Tricks for the Courtroom*, TRIAL, Apr. 1990, at 38.

EDWARD J. IMWINKELRIED, EVIDENTIARY FOUNDATIONS 37-81 (2d ed. 1989).

JAMES W. JEANS, LITIGATION, ch. 12 (2d ed. 1992).

JAMES W. JEANS, TRIAL ADVOCACY, ch. 11 (1975).

Janeen Kerper, *Documents: Keeping Judge and Jury Awake*, LITIGATION, Spring 1981, at 18.

George A. LaMarca, *Courtroom Use of Demonstrative Evidence*, TRIAL DIPL. J., Winter 1980-81, at 28.

FRED LANE, LANE'S GOLDSTEIN TRIAL TECHNIQUE, ch. 12 (3d ed. 1984).

ASHLEY LIPSON, ART OF ADVOCACY — DEMONSTRATIVE EVIDENCE (1988).

James R. Lucas, *Props: An Overview of Demonstrative Evidence*, 13 AM. J. TRIAL AD. 1097 (1990).

James McElhaney, *Steps in Introducing Exhibits*, LITIGATION, Winter 1975, at 55.

James McNeal, *Silent Witness Evidence in Relation to the Illustrative Evidence Foundation*, 37 OKLA. L. REV. 219 (1984).

Bruce T. Wallace, *Demonstrative Evidence: Some Practical Pointers*, TRIAL, Oct. 1976, at 50.

Chapter 6

DIRECT EXAMINATION

A. INTRODUCTION

Direct examination is the most important part of the trial. Cross-examination may be more exciting and closing argument more eloquent, but it is the direct examination of witnesses that supplies most of the facts from which jurors draw their conclusions. Effective direct examinations that present the facts on which your case is based in a clear, logical, and persuasive manner are essential if you expect the jury to understand and accept your position.

Unfortunately, direct examination often is done poorly. Witnesses are not presented effectively, and attorneys fail to elicit coherent evidence from them. You cannot just put a witness on the stand and ask, "What happened?" Your direct examination must elicit what the witness knows in a manner that helps the jury understand, remember, and believe it. Several obstacles stand in your way that must be overcome:

- Your witness is only human. A witness may know only a portion of the entire story, may have a poor memory, and even may contradict other witnesses.
- Witnesses testify only in response to the questions you ask, which places a burden on you to be comprehensive and articulate.
- The rules of evidence limit the form of questions and the content of testimony. Many rules, such as the hearsay rule, defy common sense, make telling the complete story difficult, and make testimony different from normal conversation.
- Your opponent can object and interrupt testimony, diverting the attention of the jurors.
- The separation between direct and cross-examination may result in one topic being discussed at two different times, separated by an hour or more of unrelated information.

The goal of direct examination is to overcome these obstacles and present the testimony of witnesses in an understandable and persuasive manner. This requires a clear, logically organized presentation in which each witness describes the activities he or she observed or participated in. It requires that you concentrate not only on presenting enough evidence to make out a prima facie case, but also on making that evidence persuasive and rememberable. A legally sufficient case is not enough — you must persuade a jury that your client deserves a favorable verdict. Direct examination can help accomplish this goal only if it is carefully prepared and conducted.

What makes direct examination effective? Most trial practitioners agree on two fundamental principles.

- Let the witness dominate the direct examination. You should make a conscious effort to be as unobtrusive as possible — by standing out of the way, keeping your questions short and simple, and trusting your witnesses.
- Prepare your witnesses in advance to give complete and descriptive testimony. The better prepared your witnesses are, the easier it will be for you to fade into the background and let them tell their own stories.

B. EXAMPLE OF DIRECT EXAMINATION

The following abbreviated example[1] of the direct examination of the plaintiff in a personal injury case is designed to illustrate the basic principles discussed in this chapter.

Plaintiff's attorney: We call the plaintiff, George Woods.
[Plaintiff walks to the witness stand with the aid of a cane.]
Bailiff: Raise your right hand. [Plaintiff raises right hand; cane falls to floor]. Do you swear or affirm to tell the truth, the whole truth and nothing but the truth?
Witness: I do.
Q: What is your name?
A: George Woods.
Q: Where do you live?
A: 1130 South Paulina Avenue, here in Chicago.
Q: How long have you lived here?
A: All my life, forty-eight years. I moved into the house on Paulina Avenue eighteen years ago when I got married.
Q: Any family?
A: Yes, my wife Charlotte, and two children, Vicky and Sally. Vicky is sixteen and Sally is thirteen.
Q: Where do you work?
A: The Beverly Engineering Company.
Q: How long have you worked there?
A: Twenty-three years. I started as a draftsman, and rose to chief field engineer. Then I was in the bus wreck and my knees got all smashed up, and now I'm back working as a draftsman again.
Q: Let's start at the beginning. Where did you go to school?
A: In 1962, I graduated from Englewood High School and entered Illinois Institute of Technology to study design engineering. I did some graduate work at M.I.T., and then got a job with the Beverly Engineering Company in 1969.
Q: Doing what?
A: I started as a draftsman. That's the usual entry level position. You do final drawings of other people's construction plans.

---

[1] Adapted from FRANCIS X. BUSCH, LAW AND TACTICS IN JURY TRIALS, vol. 3, 397-418 (1960).

Q: How was your health back then?

A: It was fine. Except for the flu, I had never really been sick. I had no problems as far as I know.

Q: How about your legs?

A: They were fine. I broke my right leg once sliding into third base in a freak accident. I was playing on the company softball team.

Q: When was that?

A: In 1971.

Q: What happened to your leg?

A: I guess it healed. I was able to play softball the next year, and it never gave me any problems again.

Q: Will you describe your jobs over the next few years?

A: Sure. In 1974, I was promoted to the position of estimator. In 1976, I was made an assistant design engineer and later that same year I was promoted to field engineer. In 1981, I was made chief field engineer.

Q: What were your responsibilities?

A: I supervised all on-site architectural engineering projects for Beverly Engineering Company. That meant I had to travel all over the midwest. We might have as many as six construction projects going at once. This was what I had always wanted to do. I usually delegated most of the preconstruction planning, but I loved to direct the actual construction. That is when most of the crucial decisions had to be made. For instance, we might be working on the steel frame for a twenty-story building, and a steelworker would notice that the girders were not lining up properly. Then it was a challenge to find and correct the problem. Sometimes it was a risky job. I had to be able to climb around the steel framework like the steelworkers, testing for alignment and tension and so on.

Q: Did this job require a good memory?

A: Yes, of course. You have to be able to remember lots of details about different projects. You can't carry sixty sheets of blueprints with you when you're climbing steel girders twenty stories aboveground.

Q: Directing your attention to April 1992, were you still working as chief field engineer?

A: Yes.

Q: At what salary?

A: My base salary was $65,000 a year. I also averaged about five hundred a month in bonuses.

Q: Do you remember the events of April 20, 1992?

A: God, yes. That was the day of the bus wreck.

Q: What happened? Start at the beginning of the day.

A: Well, my car was in the shop, so I went to catch the bus to get to work. I walked to the corner of Paulina and Halstead Street and got on a downtown bus.

Q: About what time?

A: About 8:20 a.m.

Q: Did you pay your fare?

A: Yes.

Q: What kind of bus was it?

A: A regular city bus that said Chicago Transit Authority on the side.

Q: What did you do next?

A: I sat down in the second seat, next to the window, and started reading over some preliminary estimates prepared by my staff.

Q: Can you describe the seating in more detail?

A: Sure. I was in a two-person seat, next to the window. There was no one beside me. I was facing the front, on the right side. There was one seat in front of me.

Q: Did anyone sit there?

A: Yes, one person, but she got off before the wreck.

Q: Did you know anyone else on the bus?

A: No, I rarely ride the bus.

Q: How much space was there for your legs?

A: Well, of course I never measured it, but it was pretty close, sort of narrow for your legs. I would say six to eight inches or so. My knees brushed against the seat back.

Q: What did that seat back look like?

A: It was a flat sheet of metal of some kind, probably aluminum.

Q: Do you have any familiarity with scale models?

A: Of course, we work with scale models all the time in construction engineering.

Q: With the court's permission will you step over to this table and examine plaintiff's exhibit one?

A: Of course.

Q: Can you tell what it is?

A: Yes, it's a good scale model of the inside of the bus I was riding in.

Q: Is it fair and accurate, especially with reference to the front seats?

A: Yes.

Q: What about the view out the front window?

A: Yes, that looks correct.

Q: Will this exhibit help you in explaining what happened next?

A: Yes.

Plaintiff's attorney: We offer this into evidence as plaintiff's exhibit one, and ask that we be allowed to move it where the jury can see it.

Court: It will be received.

Q: Will you indicate where you were sitting?

A: Right here, in the right-hand seat, second from the front.

Q: What happened next?

A: I was reading my reports and not paying much attention, when there was a terrible crash.

Q: What was the first thing you noticed?

A: Well, it all happened very fast. I remember hearing the squeal of tires and I felt myself floating out of the seat. It was very quiet and I remember trying to reach out to grab this metal bar on the seat in front of me but my arms wouldn't move. For a moment I felt sort of suspended in mid-air, and then my face smashed into the top of the seat in front of me. I hit the metal bar, here, and I blacked out.

Q: Do you remember anything else?

A: I remember looking out the front window while this all was going on, and seeing nothing — no street, no sky, or anything. Then in a fleeting second I realized that the reason I couldn't see anything was because I was looking at the back end of another bus right in front of us, only a few inches away.

Q: You may sit down. What happened next?

A: Everything was black. My eyes felt like they were open but I couldn't see. I could hear voices way off in the distance. I thought I was dead and started to cry.

Q: Do you remember anything else from the scene of the accident?

A: No.

Q: What is the next thing you remember?

A: Waking up in a hospital bed. My glasses were gone and there were bandages all over my head. I tried to move, but couldn't. At first I was just numb, then my head and legs began to ache. Sometimes there were shooting pains in my legs. I don't remember much from those first few days; they — the nurses — kept giving me shots, and I would fall into a sort of half-sleeping stupor.

Q: Do you remember hearing anything?

A: No. Sometimes there would be voices, sort of indistinct and far away.

Q: What happened next?

A: I became increasingly aware of myself, and slowly recovered my consciousness. As I did, the pain in my legs became worse. It is hard to be precise, because I had no sense of time.

Q: Can you describe the pain?

A: I have never felt anything quite like it. By comparison, the pain I felt when I broke my leg back in 1971 was nothing. This was like a constant itch, and I wanted to hit my legs or cut them off to make it go away. At times there would be sudden pains like when you crack your shin against a table — sometimes a series of ten spurts of pain in a second or two. Sometimes the nurses would come in and hold me down by my shoulders and I would realize that I was crying and screaming. I don't remember much else. The pain shut out everything else around me.

Q: Do you remember your wife being there?

A: No. All I was conscious of was the pain. I do remember the first time I saw Charlotte there. The pain had subsided, and I saw her looking at me. I said hi and asked what time it was. She started crying and said I'd been in the hospital for ten days.

Q: What else did you notice?

A: That my legs were both in casts from the foot to mid-thigh.

Q: Showing you plaintiff's exhibit two, do you recognize it?

A: Yes. That's a photograph of me in the hospital bed with my legs elevated and the casts on.

Q: Is it accurate?

A: Yes.

Plaintiff's attorney: We offer this into evidence as plaintiff's exhibit two.
Court: Received.

Plaintiff's attorney: We have copies for the jury, the court, and opposing counsel. May I distribute them?

Court: Yes, go ahead.

Q: How long did you wear these casts?

A: Six weeks.

Q: Any problems?

A: Other than the pain from what used to be my knees, the only other problem I had was itching under the cast. It felt like little bugs were crawling on my legs, and I couldn't scratch it because it was under the casts.

Q: What kind of treatment did you receive?

A: Twice a day, they would come in and put me in a metal contraption that fitted under my arms. It was like a cage on wheels and moved when you pushed with your foot. They would tell me to try to walk.

Q: With casts on both legs?

A: Yes.

Q: Showing you plaintiff's exhibit three, do you recognize it?

A: Yes. That's a photograph of me in the metal cage during a therapy session, taken by my wife.

Q: Is it accurate?

A: Yes, it is.

Plaintiff's attorney: Your Honor, we offer this into evidence as plaintiff's exhibit three, and ask to be allowed to distribute copies as before.

Court: Of course; it will be allowed.

Q: What happened during these sessions?

A: I couldn't move much. I could push a little with my left foot, but every leg movement was very painful.

Q: How long did this continue?

A: Until the casts came off, and then a little beyond then. I don't remember the exact day, but it went on for about seven weeks from the time I woke up.

Q: Did your treatment change after that?

A: Yeah. The nurses started coming in four or five times a day to massage my legs. That felt good. But I dreaded it, because the doctors would come in afterwards to try to bend them.

Q: How did that feel?

A: Excruciating, like when your finger is bent backwards the wrong way. It made me scream. After a few times, I would beg the doctors not to bend them whenever they came in.

Q: How long did this go on?

A: Another four weeks, until I left the hospital.

Q: Did you try to bend your legs yourself?

A: Not at first, the pain was just too great. About the time I left the hospital, I could bend my knees if I moved them very slowly. It still hurt, but not as much.

Q: Did you try to walk?

A: Yes. They gave me crutches, and I learned to hobble around a little. On the day I was released, they got me up and helped me walk without the crutches. I could take a few steps, but the pain got so bad after three or four steps that I fell. I was told to practice walking every day.

Q: When were you released?

A: July 15th, my sister's birthday.

Q: Did you practice walking after that?

A: No, not every day. Sometimes I just couldn't bear to go through the agony, knowing that walking would bring the pain back.

Q: Did it get better?

A: Yes. I gradually improved for another six weeks or so, until I got to the point where I could walk across a room without much pain. It felt awkward. My left knee would bend okay, but my right one would only move a little, and it hurt whenever I tried to walk. I could get around better with the crutches, but still not far.

Q: During this time did you go to a doctor?

A: Yes. I went to Dr. Tinsley three times a week. He had been the doctor who operated on me and treated me in the hospital.

Q: Is that Dr. Walter Tinsley?

A: Yes.

Q: What happened next?

A: Around the end of August, I got to where I could get around pretty well using only a cane. I worked up to where I could walk about three blocks if I was careful not to stumble or put any strain on my legs. After three blocks, my knees would give out. Any farther and the pain would come back.

Q: What happened then?

A: I stopped improving. Dr. Tinsley said there was no reason to continue to see him regularly. I should go in only if there was some change.

Q: When was this?

A: Early in September.

Q: Did you see him again?

A: No.

Q: Did you go back to work?

A: Yes, on October first.

Q: Five months after the crash?

A: Yes.

Q: Did you get any paychecks during this time?

A: Yes. I had accumulated a month's sick leave, so I was paid for May.

Q: And after that?

A: Nothing. Why should they pay me? I wasn't working.

Q: When you went back to work, did you return to your old position as chief field engineer?

A: No.

Q: Why not?

A: I couldn't do it — physically, I mean. The position of chief engineer involved traveling every day to the firm's job sites, and walking through buildings under construction — some of which covered a large area. It involved walking up and down stairs and climbing over temporary and incomplete constructions, and sometimes scrambling around on steel beams and girders. Altogether, it was a strenuous job and required a person in excellent physical condition.

Q: What did you do?

A: The firm was very good to me. They let me go back to being a draftsman, a job that can be done in the office, sitting down.

Q: At what salary?

A: The same as the other draftsmen, thirty-four thousand a year.

Q: About half what you had been making?

A: Right.

Q: What about bonuses?

A: Draftsmen do not share in the bonus program because they are involved before construction begins, and have no part in bringing in a job ahead of schedule or under budget.

Q: So that cost you how much?

A: About five hundred a month.

Q: Why didn't you go back to one of the other jobs — estimator, design engineer, or field engineer?

A: They all involve travel, on-site design, and lot of walking around job sites and partially completed constructions. I can't do that because of my damn knees.

Q: Is your job satisfying?

A: No, it's frustrating. I had always wanted to be a chief engineer — that is an important and respected position. Now I'm back where I started, as a draftsman. All the other draftsmen are young men and women on their way up, twenty years younger than me. They work hard and enthusiastically, looking to the future. We have nothing in common — they look at me with pity, like I was some token cripple hired by the company for public relations purposes.

Q: Do you look to the future?

A: Yes, but only with dread. Upper level management in the firm is changing, and I'm afraid that one day they will forget that I used to be chief engineer, and fire me because I have no potential for advancement. Every time some young person gets promoted I'm reminded of the career I lost.

Q: Can you get away from it all on weekends at least?

A: Not really. I used to swim and play golf and now I can't anymore. My legs just won't work. I tried and tried, but the pain was too great and my knees too weak, so I had to give up. So my weekends are a constant reminder of the fact that I'll never get any better.

Plaintiff's attorney: No further questions.

NOTE

Other examples. Examples of direct examinations can be found in SCOTT BALDWIN, ART OF ADVOCACY — DIRECT EXAMINATION §§ 4.01 to 4.45 (1981); THOMAS A. MAUET, FUNDAMENTALS OF TRIAL TECHNIQUES 86-104 (3d ed. 1992).

C. LEGAL FRAMEWORK

In criminal cases, the defendant has a right to call witnesses and elicit their testimony under the Compulsory Process Clause of the Sixth Amendment. The Supreme Court has held that the defendant is entitled to present the direct examination of any witness who possesses "material and favorable" testimony.[2] Beyond this basic constitutional rule, direct examination is controlled primarily by the discretion of the trial judge and the rules of evidence. FED. R. EVID. 611(a) provides:

> The court shall exercise reasonable control over the mode and order of interrogating witnesses and presenting evidence so as to (1) make the interrogation and presentation effective for the ascertainment of the truth, (2) avoid needless consumption of time, and (3) protect witnesses from harassment or undue embarrassment.

The advisory committee noted that spelling out detailed rules to govern every aspect of direct examination was neither desirable nor feasible. However, a number of legal and procedural issues are well settled, and we will review them in the paragraphs that follow.

1. DIRECT EXAMINATION PROCEDURE

Direct examination procedures are generally uniform from jurisdiction to jurisdiction. The examining attorney requests that a witness be called, and either the judge or bailiff asks the named witness to come forward. If witnesses have been excluded from the courtroom, usually a bailiff or court officer will summon that person from the witness room. The witness walks over to the witness stand, is sworn by the bailiff, and sits down.

It now becomes your responsibility to question the witness. In some courts you must do so from counsel table or a lectern; in others you are free to move around the courtroom and stand wherever you want. In most jurisdictions no formal rule exists, and local practice and the preference of the judge will determine your freedom of movement. In many courts, you must obtain permission from the judge to approach the witness or the bench for any reason. Even if not strictly required, asking leave to approach the witness or the bench is always good courtroom etiquette.

The judge also controls the manner of eliciting testimony. Whether to allow a narrative form or require specific questions and answers is in the judge's discretion. Many judges prefer the specific question and response format because it affords the opposing counsel greater opportunity to object, and tends to keep the testimony of witnesses within the limits of the rules of evidence more than a narrative format. Such judges often will sustain objections to long, narrative testimony, especially if the objecting attorney articulates a fear that specific inadmissible evidence may be testified to by the witness. Of course, the trial court has discretion to permit narrative testimony if it is a reasonable way of eliciting testimony from a particular witness. At the other extreme, you are generally prohibited from asking leading questions. Narra-

---

[2]*United States v. Valenzuela-Bernal*, 458 U.S. 858 (1982).

tive testimony and other matters of the proper form of questions and answers were discussed in detail in Chapter 5, part B, § 3.

Beyond these few procedural requirements, however, you are free to conduct direct examination as you see fit, as long as you remain within the rules of evidence.

2. THE RULE AGAINST "BOLSTERING"

It is generally accepted that you may not bolster the credibility of a witness before that witness has been impeached. The usual rationale for the rule is that it would be a waste of time to open up side issues of a witness' good character and credibility until we know whether the other side intends to impeach.[3]

However, a distinction must be drawn between improper bolstering and bringing out relevant background information from a witness that will have the effect of making the witness more credible. The bolstering rule prohibits two kinds of evidence: testimony that the witness has not done an act falling under any of the impeachment rules, and evidence of acts of good character. Thus, you may not begin a direct examination by eliciting testimony that the witness has no criminal record, has no bias against the other party, has made consistent statements in the past, or once saved a child from drowning.[4] However, the rule does not prohibit general background information from the witness, such as address, family, occupation, education and so on. Nor does the rule prohibit enhancing a witness' credibility in ways that are directly relevant to the witness' testimony, such as proving that an eyewitness has good vision.

3. REFRESHING RECOLLECTION

During direct examination, it is proper to refresh the recollection of a witness whose memory of specific events proves to be insufficient. Most jurisdictions require a foundation that the witness cannot recall all the facts of an event or that the witness' memory is exhausted. You then can attempt to jog the witness' memory by any means. The two most common are asking leading questions, and letting the witness examine the witness' prior statement.

The most common method of refreshing recollection is to use a writing. Proper procedure consists of the following steps:

- Establish that the witness' memory is exhausted.
- Mark a document for identification.
- Show the document to opposing counsel, or refer to it by page and line if it is a deposition.
- Hand the document to the witness.
- Ask the witness to read silently the specific portion of the document that covers the forgotten material.

---

[3]*E.g., Lawrence v. State*, 464 N.E.2d 923 (Ind. 1984). *See also* FED. R. EVID. 608(a) (evidence of truthful character is admissible only after the character of the witness for truthfulness has been attacked).

[4]*See Anderson v. State*, 471 N.E.2d 291 (Ind. 1984).

- Retrieve the document.
- Ask the witness if his or her memory has been refreshed.
- Continue the examination if the witness now remembers the information.

A few jurisdictions permit you to refresh recollection only with writings prepared by the witness at or near the time of the event, but most follow the common-law rule permitting you to use any kind of writing: tax returns, police reports, summaries prepared for trial, depositions, and so forth.[5] However, it is generally improper to elicit any details about the document itself on direct examination unless it is independently admissible.[6]

4. REDIRECT EXAMINATION

Redirect examination after a witness has been cross-examined is not an absolute right. The scope and extent of redirect examination rests largely in the discretion of the trial judge.[7] However, courts routinely allow redirect on any new matters brought out during the cross-examination. This principle is so well established that it may be an abuse of discretion if the judge does not permit at least this limited scope of redirect examination.[8] Redirect examination has two proper purposes: the clarification of matters brought out on cross-examination, and rehabilitation if the witness has been impeached.

The main purpose of redirect examination is to clarify any confusion and correct any misunderstandings that may have arisen during the cross-examination, so that the entire examination of a witness will represent fairly his or her complete knowledge. You do not have the right to use redirect examination for the introduction of new matters that should have been presented in the examination in chief, although the judge has the discretion to permit you to ask questions inadvertently omitted from the direct examination. Courts generally have held that it is permissible to use redirect examination for the following purposes: to correct a mistake or misstatement made during cross-examination;[9] to explain or qualify an apparent contradiction between testimony given on direct and cross-examination;[10] to explain ambiguous or incomplete testimony, or to place a misleading answer in proper context;[11] to explain a prior inconsistent statement;[12] to explain or qualify apparent interest or bias (but not to justify a bias by giving the reasons for it);[13] to elicit testimony about a whole transaction or conversation when the cross-examiner

---

[5]*E.g., Baker v. State*, 371 A.2d 699 (Md. 1977). *See* MARK A. DOMBROFF, DOMBROFF ON DIRECT AND CROSS-EXAMINATION 80-81 (1985).

[6]*See* Joseph Kalo, *Refreshing Recollection: Problems with Laying a Foundation*, 10 RUT.-CAM. L.J. 233, 233-38 (1979).

[7]*E.g., United States v. Eniola*, 893 F.2d 383 (D.C. Cir. 1990); *United States v. Mackey*, 571 F.2d 376 (7th Cir. 1978).

[8]*E.g., United States v. Ruggiero*, 934 F.2d 440 (2d Cir. 1991). *See* ARK. STAT. § 28-710; CAL. EVID. CODE § 774 (providing right to conduct redirect on new matters).

[9]*See, e.g., Gurliacci v. Mayer*, 590 A.2d 914 (Ct. 1991).

[10]*See, e.g., Watkins v. Holmes*, 93 N.H. 53, 35 A.2d 395 (1943).

[11]*See, e.g., United States v. Walker*, 421 F.2d 1298 (3d Cir. 1970); *People v. Tucker*, 142 Cal. App. 2d 549, 298 P.2d 558 (1956).

[12]*See, e.g., United States v. Panebianco*, 543 F.2d 447 (2d Cir. 1976) (received death threat); *People v. Nakis*, 184 Cal. 105, 193 P. 92 (1920) (bribed by defendant's brother).

[13]*See Clark v. State*, 264 Ind. 524, 348 N.E.2d 27 (1976); *Hovey v. State*, 29 Ala. App. 149, 195 So. 282 (1940).

only referred to a part taken out of context;[14] to refresh a witness' recollection after he or she testified to a lack of memory on cross-examination;[15] and to show mitigating circumstances surrounding a criminal conviction.[16] In many jurisdictions, you are also permitted to elicit prior consistent statements on redirect examination if the witness has been impeached by prior inconsistent statements.[17]

The second purpose of redirect examination is to rehabilitate the credibility of a witness who has been impeached. The rule against bolstering prevents you from proving the absence of bias or interest, the absence of a criminal record, prior consistent statements, or acts of good character until after the witness has been impeached. If your opponent does not impeach the witness, these issues may not be brought up. But if your witness is impeached, then you may respond to it in redirect examination. You may introduce prior consistent statements to rebut an express or implied charge of recent fabrication, improper influence, or motive to fabricate.[18] Evidence of truthful character is admissible to rebut evidence of untruthful character.[19] Evidence suggesting bias may be rebutted with proof that the witness had no social or business relationships with either party, was compelled to come to court by a subpoena, is not receiving any compensation for the testimony, was available to both sides, and, in general, has no bias, motive, interest, or prejudice one way or the other.[20]

Whether a leading question may be asked during redirect examination is primarily a matter for the court's discretion. As in direct examination, leading questions that directly suggest the desired answers generally are improper; however, those used to bring a particular matter to the witness' attention or to make the need for explanation obvious often are allowed. Some judges use their discretion to permit leading questions during redirect examination to save time or to help a witness who has become genuinely confused.

NOTES

1. *Direct examination of the adverse party.* In most civil suits, you may call the adverse party to give direct testimony in your own case. An adverse party may be interrogated by leading questions and may be impeached. The direct examination thus resembles cross-examination. If the adverse party is a corporation or other artificial entity, you usually will be allowed to call its officers, directors, and managing agents as adverse witnesses, *e.g., Stauffer Chem. Co. v. Buckalew*, 456 So. 2d 778 (Ala. 1984). Under FED. R. EVID. 611(c), you also may use cross-examination techniques when questioning witnesses identified with the adverse party, such as lower level employees or the insured in a direct action against the insurance company.

---

[14]*See, e.g., Nitzel v. Austin Co.*, 249 F.2d 710 (10th Cir. 1957).

[15]*E.g., Duncan v. State*, 20 Ala. App. 209, 101 So. 472 (1924).

[16]*See Castillo v. State*, 490 So. 2d 1066 (Fla. App. 1986).

[17]*E.g., Thompson v. State*, 223 Ind. 39, 58 N.E.2d 112 (1944). *Cf. State v. Paige*, 272 N.C. 417, 158 S.E.2d 522 (1968) (prior consistent statement admissible if there has been any attack on credibility).

[18]FED. R. EVID. 801(d)(1)(b).

[19]FED. R. EVID. 608(a).

[20]*See* McCORMICK ON EVIDENCE § 47 (4th ed., J.W. Strong ed., 1992).

2. Hostile witnesses. A witness who is unfriendly or hostile may be asked leading questions. A witness is never presumed to be hostile, but must demonstrate actual hostility or unwillingness to testify before you can resort to cross-examination techniques such as leading questions. *See* McCORMICK ON EVIDENCE § 35 (4th ed., John W. Strong ed., 1992).

3. Consultation between lawyer and client during direct examination. Usually, there is no opportunity for a lawyer to consult with the client in the middle of direct examination. However, what happens if there is a recess in the middle of a direct examination? Can the trial judge prohibit the lawyer and client from consulting during that recess, out of fear of perjury? The answer is probably "yes" in civil cases, but "no" in criminal cases. In *Gedders v. United States*, 425 U.S. 80 (1976), the Supreme Court found that such an order interfered with the client's right to counsel, because it prevented legitimate consultation over trial strategy along with "coaching." *See also Mudd v. United States*, 798 F.2d 1509 (D.C. Cir. 1986).

D. ETHICAL CONSIDERATIONS

1. PREPARING WITNESSES TO TESTIFY

There is no bright line between legitimate witness preparation and unethical coaching. The classic distinction is that it is unethical to tell a witness what to say (coaching), but permissible to refresh a witness' recollection and suggest better ways in which a witness could frame his or her answers. The following scenario is unethical:

> Lawyer: How did it feel?
> Client: It hurt real bad.
> Lawyer: When I ask you that question at trial, I want you to say that it felt like your hand was stuck on a hot stove and you couldn't get it off, okay?
> Client: Sure.

On the other hand, most lawyers probably would see nothing unethical in the following example, although whether there is really any difference between the two is dubious:

> Lawyer: How did it feel?
> Client: It hurt real bad.
> Lawyer: When I ask you that question at trial, I want you to give a more vivid description but still be truthful. Would it be accurate to say that it felt like your hand was stuck on a hot stove and you couldn't get it off?
> Client: Yes, that's sort of what it felt like.

Where do you draw the line? No competent attorney would dream of calling a witness, especially a client, without adequate preparation. Consider the following excerpt from Monroe Freedman, *Counselling the Client: Refreshing*

Recollection or Prompting Perjury?, in Lawyers' Ethics in an Adversary
System 62-64, 68-69, 72-76 (1975):

The lawyer must try to elicit all relevant facts and to help the client —
who, typically, is not skilled at articulation — to marshal and to express
his or her case as persuasively as possible. For example, the poorly educated day laborer who has suffered an injury, and who can only say, "It
hurts bad," must be helped to articulate what the pain is like, when it is
present, and how it interferes with work, sleep, family life, and recre-
ation. In addition, the statement "I hurt myself while I was working," will
not be enough. The relevant details must be elicited through skilled questioning, and the witness must then be sufficiently rehearsed to assure
that no important evidence will be overlooked in testimony at trial, where
leading questions will not be permitted.

That is done by asking questions and by explaining to the client how
important the additional information may be to the case. If the client can
be made to understand your thoughts, he may tell you facts which otherwise would have been inadvertently overlooked or consciously and erroneously discarded by him as immaterial [through] subconscious suppression, psychologically induced by the wish to put one's best foot forward or
by nature's trick of inducing forgetfulness of what one does not like to
remember. That is, people will, in perfectly good faith, relate past events
in a way that they believe (rightly or wrongly) to be consistent with their
own interests. Necessarily, therefore, in pressing the client for additional
information, and in explaining the relevance and importance of that information, the lawyer will be affecting the ultimate testimony.
[A]lthough it is improper to prompt or suggest an answer to one's witness
during the actual testimony, the interview affords full play to suggestion
and evokes in advance of trial a complete verbalization, the importance of
which cannot be overlooked.

The process of preparing or coaching the witness, of course, goes far
beyond the initial eliciting of facts. In the course of polishing the client's
testimony, [some lawyers recommend] as many as fifty full rehearsals of
direct and cross-examination. During those rehearsals, the testimony is
developed in a variety of ways. The witness is vigorously cross-examined,
and then the attorney points out where the witness has been "tripped"
and how the testimony can be restructured to avoid that result. The
attorney may also take the role of witness and be cross-examined by an
associate. The attorney's "failures" in simulated testimony are then discussed, and the attorney then may conduct a mock cross-examination of
the associate. In that way, new ideas are developed while all the time the
client is looking on and listening. He probably is saying, "Let me try
again." And you will then go through the whole process once more. By
that time, as one might expect, the client "does far better." In fact, after
many weeks of preparation, perhaps on the very eve of trial, the client
may come up with a new fact that may perhaps make a difference between victory and defeat.

Nowhere in [the writing on trial advocacy] relating to the preparation of witnesses is there any analysis of the ethical implications of the model practices that are set forth.... If people do respond to suggestion, and if the lawyer helps the client to "fill in the gaps" and to avoid being "tripped," by developing "new ideas" in the course of repeated rehearsals, it is reasonably clear that the testimony that ultimately is presented in court will have been significantly affected by the lawyer's prompting and by the client's self-interest. Whether the end product is well within the truth, the whole truth and nothing but the truth, is therefore subject to considerable doubt.

Obviously, therefore, we are faced with another dilemma. On the one hand, we know that by telling the client that a particular fact is important, and why it is important, we may induce the client to "remember" the fact even if it did not occur. On the other hand, important facts can truly be lost if we fail to provide the client with every possible aid to memory. Furthermore, since the client's memory is inevitably going to be affected by reconstruction consistent with self-interest, a client who has a misunderstanding of his or her own legal interest could be psychologically inclined to remember in a way that is not only inconsistent with the client's case, but also inaccurate.... There does come a point, however, where nothing less than "brute rationalization" can purport to justify a conclusion that the lawyer is seeking in good faith to elicit truth rather than actively participating in the creation of perjury.

2. INTENTIONALLY VIOLATING RULES OF EVIDENCE

MODEL RULES OF PROFESSIONAL CONDUCT Rule 3.4(c) states that a lawyer shall not "knowingly disobey an obligation under the rules of a tribunal" (including its evidence rules), nor allude to any matter that is probably inadmissible.[21] Yet, it is common for lawyers to ask leading questions in direct examination, to pace examination quickly to limit their opponents' abilities to object, and to offer evidence of doubtful admissibility. These practices often are justified on the grounds that they are not per se violations of the rules of evidence — the judge might permit leading questions or might admit evidence even though the weight of authority is against it. Perhaps something in legal education makes lawyers think it is proper to violate the spirit of a rule of ethics if they can concoct an argument that they are not violating the letter of the rule.

It is unethical to intentionally conduct improper direct examination. You may not ask an improper question and then withdraw it if your opponent objects. That may satisfy the legal requirement by removing improper matter from the jury's consideration, but it is still unethical. Similarly, you may not

---

[21] The superseded MODEL CODE OF PROFESSIONAL RESPONSIBILITY was clearer. DR 7-106(C) provided: "In appearing in his professional capacity before a tribunal, a lawyer shall not: (1) state or allude to any matter that he has no reasonable basis to believe is relevant to the case or that will not be supported by admissible evidence .... (7) Intentionally or habitually violate any established rule of procedure or of evidence." *See also id.*, EC 7-25 (a lawyer should not by subterfuge put improper matters before a jury).

try to elicit inadmissible hearsay just because it would be entitled to consideration if your opponent fails to object. Under Rule 3.4, it is unethical to:

- Assume facts not in evidence.
- Misquote witnesses.
- Use leading questions except when one of the exceptions[22] applies.
- Ask a witness to repeat testimony by pretending you did not hear the answer.
- Use narrative testimony when you anticipate inadmissible evidence may arise, in order to make it more difficult for your opponent to object.

However, the line between the ethical and the unethical eliciting of testimony is not always clear. For example, leading questions often are permitted during direct examination and may be allowed by the judge to help refresh recollection. It is common, therefore, for attorneys to use leading questions to help a witness in trouble:

Q: What happened next?
A: Uh, let's see, I saw the red car turn left, and, let's see, it hit the truck
...
Q: Wasn't it the truck that hit the car?
A: Oh, yes, I mean the truck hit the car.

One way of looking at this is that the witness is having trouble remembering (probably because of anxiety), the attorney knows from previous interviews what the witness means, leading is permitted to refresh recollection anyway, and the attorney's intervention is necessary to make sure the truth emerges instead of a misstatement. However, there is another, equally likely scenario: the attorney is afraid the witness is about to say something that will hurt the case, so the attorney deliberately uses a leading question to tell the witness the "correct" answer, even though no foundation has yet been laid for refreshing memory. Isn't the attorney intentionally violating a rule of evidence?

3. DISCLOSING PERJURY

If any of your witnesses (other than your client) change their testimony on the stand and testify falsely, you have the unequivocal obligation to disclose this immediately to the court. MODEL RULES OF PROFESSIONAL CONDUCT Rule 3.3 states: "If a lawyer has offered material evidence and comes to know of its falsity, the lawyer shall take reasonable remedial measures." The comments make it clear that "the lawyer must refuse to offer" false evidence provided by a person other than the client.

If your client commits perjury, the ethical duty is less clear. If you learn of your client's intent to commit perjury before trial, you have a duty either to "remonstrate with the client confidentially [or] seek to withdraw."[23] The dilemma comes when your client changes his or her testimony on the stand. In

---

[22] *See* Chapter 5, part B, § 3.
[23] MODEL CODE OF PROFESSIONAL CONDUCT Rule 3.3 cmt. 11.

the case of a civil litigant or prosecutor, the question is resolved by Comment 6 following Model Rule 3.3:

> Except in the defense of a criminal accused, the rule generally recognized is that, if necessary to rectify the situation, an advocate must disclose the existence of the client's deception to the court or to the other party. Such a disclosure can result in grave consequences to the client, including not only a sense of betrayal but also loss of the case and perhaps a prosecution for perjury. But the alternative is that the lawyer cooperate in deceiving the court, thereby subverting the truth-finding process which the adversary system is designed to implement.

In criminal cases, however, there is disagreement. Some practitioners suggest that a defendant has a right to tell his or her story; it is too much to expect a person faced with the horrors of imprisonment not to lie or exaggerate to avoid that penalty. Therefore, the attorney is not obligated to do anything if the client commits perjury. Others argue that any use of testimony known to be perjurious is unethical. If you make it clear to the client that you will not tolerate false testimony (either before trial or during a short recess after surprise perjury), but the client persists in perjury, then you are relieved of your obligation to the client. If you cannot withdraw, that leaves only your obligation to the judicial system in operation, and you must disclose the perjury.[24] This is the view endorsed by the Supreme Court in *Nix v. Whiteside*.[25] In other words, the lawyer's role is that of a professional who agrees only to fight for the client within the bounds of the law; the lawyer is not simply a mouthpiece for the client. A compromise position has been suggested: allow the defendant to commit perjury if he or she cannot be dissuaded, but do not assist the direct examination, nor refer to it in closing argument.[26]

NOTE

Perjury and the criminal defendant. What happens when a criminal defense lawyer figures out that a client is going to commit perjury? Under the old MODEL CODE OF PROFESSIONAL CONDUCT DR 7-102(A)(4), you could not present perjured testimony if you found out in advance, and would have to withdraw from the case under DR 2-110(B)(2) if your client insisted on going forward with perjured testimony. See also ABA Comm. on Professional Ethics and Grievances, Formal Op. 87-353 (1987). *But see* MONROE FREEDMAN, LAWYER'S ETHICS IN AN ADVERSARY SYSTEM 31-32 (1975), arguing that it would be a betrayal of confidence to refuse to represent a client who insisted on going forward with perjured testimony. The problem with the withdrawal solution is that most defendants are represented by public defenders or assigned counsel

---

[24] *See* William R. Meagher, *A Critique of Lawyers' Ethics in an Adversary System*, 4 FORDHAM URB. L.J. 289, 290-95 (1976). *Cf.* William D. Popkin, *Client-Lawyer Confidentiality*, 59 TEX. L. REV. 755, 763 (1981) (withdrawal not satisfactory under MODEL RULES OF PROFESSIONAL CONDUCT).

[25] 475 U.S. 157 (1986).

[26] Warren Burger, *Standards of Conduct for Prosecution and Defense Personnel*, 5 AM. CRIM. L.Q. 11, 12-14 (1966). *But see State v. Robinson*, 290 N.C. 56, 224 S.E.2d 174 (1976) (holding that this approach violates a defendant's right to effective assistance of counsel because it creates inherent prejudice by conveying the impression that the lawyer does not believe the defendant).

who will not be permitted to withdraw. THE ABA STANDARDS FOR CRIMINAL JUSTICE 4-7.7 (2d ed. 1980) suggest that if you are not permitted to withdraw, you should place on the record that your client is testifying against your advice, and you should not actively aid in eliciting direct examination, but you should not reveal the perjury. The new MODEL RULES OF PROFESSIONAL CONDUCT seem to require more. Rule 3.3 requires that you disclose material facts necessary to prevent frauds and crimes by your client. It is discussed in William D. Popkin, *Client-Lawyer Confidentiality*, 59 TEX. L. REV. 755, 762-63 (1981). *But see* MODEL CODE OF PROFESSIONAL RESPONSIBILITY DR 7-102(B)(1) ("A lawyer who receives information clearly establishing that his client has ... perpetrated a fraud upon [the] tribunal shall ... reveal the fraud ..., *except when the information is protected as a privileged communication") (emphasis added)*.

E. PREPARING DIRECT EXAMINATION

Preparing direct examination is unique because it involves a joint effort between attorney and witness. For every other phase of the trial you can prepare alone. When you prepare for direct examination, however, you must do so in cooperation with the witness. Not only must you think about the topics you will raise, the exhibits you will use, and evidentiary issues that may arise, but you must also work with your witnesses on what they will say and how they will say it. In every other phase of the trial, you address the jury using your own words. In direct examination, the witness must address the jury, while you remain mostly silent.

This dual preparation is an interactive process. Based on your interviews with a witness, you sketch out a direct examination. Then you go over that direct examination with the witness and work on particular sections. During this "prep" session, you will undoubtedly learn more about the witness' testimony, which will require that you revise your direct examination, which you will then have to go over with the witness. It is not uncommon for a lawyer and key witness to go back and forth on direct examination a half dozen times before trial.

This section of the chapter is organized into three subsections that approximate this sequence of events: interviewing witnesses, preparing an outline of the direct examination, and preparing your witness to testify.

1. INTERVIEWING

It is beyond the scope of this book to present an in-depth analysis of the interviewing process. Interviewing may be the single most important part of the litigation process, because you cannot present a case to a jury effectively unless you know what the facts are. The trial process is one of gathering, sorting, analyzing, culling and then effectively presenting facts. Those facts are acquired largely through interviews. Thus, the primary goal of interviewing is to maximize the flow of accurate[27] information from the witness to you.

---

[27] Obviously, when we speak of "facts" and "accurate information" we do not mean objectively verifiable data. We mean pieces of information that a witness believes to be real. A trial is not a

The interviewing process is not as simple as asking witnesses to tell you everything they know about an event. Many factors influence the information flow, distorting and limiting it. The witnesses themselves will be of all personality types and come from all levels of society. Your own personality, attitude, and manner of asking questions will have a profound impact on the information you receive. Interviewing is a dynamic process that depends upon interaction between two persons.

Interviewing is useful not only for discovering facts, but also for learning something about the people involved in the case. Knowing how witnesses appear and how they react to questioning is essential for preparing their direct examination.

a. Barriers to Gathering Accurate Information

You must accept the fact that the information you gather from your witnesses, no matter how thoroughly you interview them, is not "accurate." Witnesses remember things incorrectly, forget other things, and neglect to tell you other information they think is irrelevant or embarrassing. Your own biases will cause you to misunderstand some things your witnesses tell you.

- Witnesses get the facts wrong. In one classic psychology experiment, a professor staged a simple assault in front of his class and then asked his students to describe what had happened. The student who was most accurate nevertheless gave twenty-six percent erroneous statements; the least accurate witness was wrong eighty percent of the time. The student-witnesses put words into the mouths of people who had been silent, attributed actions to participants that had not been done, and completely forgot essential parts of the event.[28]
- Witnesses may "see" what their preconceived ideas tell them they will see.
- Witnesses have great difficulty making accurate identifications of strangers, especially across racial lines. The most widely cited study on this point compared the ability of students at a predominantly white university with students at a historically black university to identify photographs of black and white males. The students were able to recognize faces of their own race two to three times as often as faces of another race, whether those students were black or white.[29]

A witness' memory can be distorted at three different stages. At the acquisition stage, information simply may not have been perceived because the witness was not looking, the lighting was bad, the event did not seem important, or many events took place in a very short time. During the retention stage, memory can become distorted through forgetting or through superimposition of new information over the old. A witness may "remember" details learned from newspaper accounts or conversations with other witnesses. Finally, even

---

scientific process. Matters that come to us as facts do so only after being filtered and distorted by the imperfect perception and memory of witnesses.

[28] Described in HUGO MUNSTERBERG, ON THE WITNESS STAND 49-51 (1908).

[29] Roy Malpass & Jerome Kravits, *Recognition for Faces of Own and Other Race*, 13 J. PERSONALITY & SOC. PSYCHOL. 330 (1969).

the way in which information is retrieved from memory can alter it. Asking specific questions to probe for details causes witness to remember as many false details as true ones.[30] In a famous experiment,[31] subjects were shown a film of a car accident and then asked how fast the cars were going when they "smashed," "hit," or "contacted." When the word "smashed" was used, answers averaged 41 miles per hour; when "hit" was used they averaged 34 miles per hour, and when "contacted" was used, answers averaged 31 miles per hour.[32]

Your own biases and stereotypes will also interfere with accurate information gathering. As the witness tells the story, you will probably think of similar situations in your own experience, or similar cases you have seen. Then the story becomes adulterated with what you have read into it.

Robert Gorden, in his book INTERVIEWING: STRATEGY, TECHNIQUES AND TACTICS (2d ed. 1975), lists the following additional factors that can inhibit the free flow of accurate information during an interview:

- *Competing demands for time.* The witness may have other things the witness wants or needs to do.
- *Ego threat.* The witness may withhold information which threatens the witness' self-esteem. In extreme cases, embarrassing information may have been repressed; more commonly, it is just embarrassing and the witness will be reluctant to talk about it.
- *Etiquette barriers.* Witnesses may feel that it is inappropriate to tell you something that involves sex, immorality, or bad taste, or that would create an inappropriate intimacy. Especially if you are a young attorney, witnesses may be afraid the things they have seen will embarrass or shock you.
- *Trauma.* It may simply be too painful for the witness to talk about some things.
- *Chronological confusion.* The witness may confuse the chronological order of events, either by being unsure of the sequence in which two distinct events happened, or by incorrectly assuming that a condition existing at one time probably existed at other times.
- *Inferential confusion.* A witness may make mistakes because of faulty induction when converting details into a general conclusion, or by faulty deduction when asked to give details in support of a conclusion.
- *Unconscious behavior.* A witness may have difficulty answering questions about things done out of habit, reasons for an emotional response, or actions taken in times of severe stress and shock.

---

[30] *See* Jack Lipton, *On the Psychology of Eyewitness Testimony,* 62 J. APPLIED PSYCHOL. 90 (1977); Keith Marquis, James Marshall & Stuart Oskamp, *Testimony Validity as a Function of Question Form, Atmosphere, and Item Difficulty,* 2 J. APPLIED SOC. PSYCHOL. 167 (1972).

[31] Elizabeth Loftus, *Reconstruction of Automobile Destruction: An Example of the Interaction Between Language and Memory,* 13 J. VERBAL LEARNING & VERBAL BEHAV. 585 (1974).

[32] *See* ELIZABETH LOFTUS & JAMES M. DOYLE, EYEWITNESS TESTIMONY 10-83 (2d ed. 1992); LAWRENCE TAYLOR, EYEWITNESS IDENTIFICATION 1-97 (1982).

DAVID BINDER & SUSAN PRICE, LEGAL INTERVIEWING AND COUNSELING 10-14 (1977), suggest a number of other potential inhibitors:

- *Case threat.* Some witnesses may have a specific interest in the outcome of the litigation. If such a witness believes that revealing information will be harmful to the case, he or she may withhold it. In this manner, a defendant may deny that he or she had a motive for or was in the vicinity of a crime.
- *Role expectations.* Clients and witnesses have certain preconceived ideas of what attorneys look like, how they talk and dress, what their offices will look like, and so on. These role expectations may be barriers in themselves, e.g., a client who expects the lawyer to define what is important and therefore waits to be asked specific questions. Also, if a witness expects a lawyer to be a well-dressed, middle-aged, white male, and meets someone of different appearance, this failure to fulfill expectations can cause distrust and reluctance to communicate.
- *Perceived irrelevancy.* If the witness does not think information is relevant, he or she is not likely to offer it, and the witness may not give serious consideration to the answer even if asked.
- *Greater need.* A witness may have a more immediate need to discuss one issue than another, and may be unable to concentrate on topics the lawyer wishes to explore. A first offender in jail awaiting trial, having heard stories about sexual attacks, may be so desperate to get out on reduced bail he simply is unable to talk about the facts of the offense. Similarly, a witness to a crime may believe her life is in danger if she testifies, and this greater need will cause her to deny that she knows anything relevant.

b. Techniques for Facilitating Interviewing

The news is not all bad. Psychologists suggest a number of techniques that can facilitate the flow of reliable information in an interview. Gorden suggest the following factors:

- *Fulfilling expectations.* Making your expectations clear will help. The witness will tend to try to fulfill the reasonable expectation of the interviewer, especially when the interviewer is the "expert" in the legal system. Most witnesses will tend unconsciously to conform to the norms of legal interviewing process.
- *Recognition.* Giving the witness sincere praise and recognition will encourage responsive communication. Witnesses, especially if they are new to the legal system, want to feel appreciated and recognized for playing the game well.
- *Altruistic appeals.* Some witnesses, but not all, may respond well to altruistic appeals to provide information helpful to other innocent people (e.g., other potential rape victims).
- *Sympathetic understanding.* Human beings need the sympathetic understanding of others with whom they are intimate. Some witnesses develop close relationships with attorneys, others (e.g., police detectives) do not.

This desire to have someone offer a sympathetic ear will help elicit information from many types of witnesses: teenagers who need to complain about their parents, older people who have problems which no one takes time to hear, and so on.

- *New experience.* An interview can provide a new experience for a witness who welcomes the adventure of becoming involved in a lawsuit. As long as the risks are not too high, the witness may respond favorably to the prospect of being at the center of a case.
- *Catharsis.* A witness who has pent-up feelings and frustrations, especially of guilt, concerning events related to your case may respond well to an opportunity for catharsis. The release of tension, especially if not judged harshly, may facilitate communication.
- *The need for meaning.* Witnesses caught up in a tragic case may need to understand why they or their friends were victims. The question "Why do events happen as they do?" often is a strong motivation for the witness to talk things out if you communicate that you, too, are interested in a search for meaning.
- *Extrinsic rewards.* A witness may be motivated to participate by extrinsic rewards — the prospect of a few days away from work with pay, being treated to a fancy lunch, or the prospect of being in the spotlight (maybe even appearing on television).

c. Facts Versus Conclusions

Effective communication requires that the witness provide details, not conclusions. Conclusions communicate meaning only if the speaker and listener share a frame of reference. Is Des Moines a big city? People from New York City and Podunk Center, Iowa, probably would answer differently.

When probing for information, you must listen carefully for the kind of conclusory statement that means different things to different people. Suppose, for example, you have a custody hearing coming up, and are interviewing the child about his new stepmother. He tells you "She's really cool. I like her a lot." You must recognize that your definition of "really cool" and the child's may be quite different, and ask a follow-up question:

Q: That's good. Why do you like her?
A: She lets me stay up late and doesn't make me do my homework. Mom always made me do my homework, but she lets me play Nintendo all day.
   or
A: She plays with me and takes me to neat museums and stuff. We saw dinosaurs last week.

Your strategy at the custody hearing may be quite different depending on which answer he gives.

d. Types of Questions

Questions can be divided into four types depending on how broadly or narrowly they define the information sought:

- *Open-ended questions* provide no guidance to the witness, but allow the witness to select both the subject matter and which details are relevant. For example, "What happened on November sixth?"
- *Directed questions* limit the witness to a particular subject, but allow the witness to select which details to talk about. For example, "Will you describe the fight between the bartender and the defendant?"
- *Narrow questions* define both the subject matter and the particular detail sought. For example, "At the start of the fight, who actually threw the first punch?"
- *Leading questions* define the subject matter and the particular detail sought, and also suggest a particular answer. For example, "At the start of the fight, the defendant threw the first actual punch, didn't he?"

Standard interviewing technique moves from open to narrow questions. Starting with open-ended questions permits the witness to tell the story in his or her own words. This is necessary at the beginning because the lawyer does not yet know enough about the facts to direct the witness. Social psychologists also point out that the facts reported by witnesses in a free narrative will be those the witness is most confident about, and therefore the most accurate information you will get. Once you start probing with more specific questions, your interference will affect the witness' memory and the kind of information the witness gives you, reducing its accuracy.

However, open-ended questions alone do not usually provide enough details. People tend to speak in conclusions and to withhold information about which they are uncertain. After the witness has told the story once, most lawyers go back over it with directed questions to fill in logical gaps and elicit details where the witness gave only conclusions. Finally, specific narrow questions can be asked to flesh out the details. Leading questions do not gather information, they provide it from the lawyer to the witness. Therefore, leading questions are not generally used in interviewing.

e. A Five-Stage Interview Model

To conduct an effective interview, it may help to conceptualize the interview in five stages:

- *Mutual evaluation.* An introductory stage where you break the ice, explain your purpose, and begin the process of building trust and rapport. This stage can be quite short, especially if you previously have met the witness.
- *Witness' overview.* Obtain the witness' recollection of the events in narrative form, without interrupting to ask for details. Your job during this stage is to listen, not to talk or take notes. This phase provides you with the outline of the important events from the witness' perspective. If you need to probe for information during this stage, do not resort to narrow

questions. Try using silence, non-committal remarks like "I see," or neutral questions that do not contain a suggested topic, like "what happened
next?"

- *Find the starting point.* Before you begin to probe for details, you must
  identify the point at which the witness' story begins. A probable starting
  point will have emerged from the witness' summary version of the events.
  You need only to probe briefly to see if anything relevant might have
  happened earlier. Common sense is your only guide. Ask the witness
  about the specific people, things, and events in the story — whether the
  witness had any previous contact with them or knew anything about
  them before the main event.

- *Detailed chronology.* In this stage, you fill in the details with directed and
  narrow questions. In most cases, a straight step-by-step chronological
  order will maximize the completeness of the information. Some system of
  note taking usually is recommended during this phase, since particular
  important details, such as the names and addresses of other witnesses,
  are difficult to remember accurately. During this stage, you must take
  control of the tempo and the scope of detail of the interview, preventing
  the witness from jumping ahead, and probing for explanations, details,
  and clarifications.

- *Conclusion.* It is recommended that in conclusion, you summarize the
  main facts for the witness and make sure the witness agrees with them.
  You need also to set an agenda for any future meetings, including
  whether the interview will be reduced to a witness statement you will
  want the witness to read over and sign.

NOTE

Using leading questions in interviewing. DAVID BINDER & SUSAN PRICE,
LEGAL INTERVIEWING AND COUNSELING 92-96 (1977), suggest one instance in
which leading questions are used in interviewing: you are seeking sensitive or
embarrassing information from a client.

> There are many instances when a lawyer must talk with a client about a
> situation involving socially aberrant behavior. In these instances, the
> lawyer may well wish to use leading questions as a means of obtaining
> reliable information. Thus, to the extent it is pertinent to get into the
> subject of a past criminal record with a client whom the lawyer strongly
> suspects has such a record, the lawyer might try a phrase such as: "I
> guess you've had trouble with the police before?" Stated with an accepting
> tone of voice, this question may make the client more willing to talk
> about the record than a question such as: "Have you ever been arrested
> before?"

2. PLANNING THE DIRECT EXAMINATION

Planning is the key to a successful direct examination. Although a good
direct examination may appear spontaneous, it cannot be improvised at trial.
You must know in advance what testimony you will elicit and what exhibits

to introduce, the order in which you will proceed, the evidentiary issues that are likely to arise, and how you will emphasize and make persuasive the most important points.

a. What Topics to Cover

Direct examination is not simply putting a witness on the stand and asking the witness to tell the jury everything the witness knows. Your most important job is to *select* which topics to cover and which to omit. This selection is based on your theory of the case, which tells you which issues you will pursue, what important themes and facts you will emphasize, and which items of evidence will help the jury resolve disputes. You should include:

- Sufficient facts to make out a prima facie case on every issue on which you bear the burden of proof.
- Any testimony from the witness on one of your main points of emphasis.
- Testimony that corroborates your other witnesses, especially your client.
- Information about the witness's background that makes his or her particular evidence more credible.
- Testimony that is necessary to lay a foundation for other evidence.
- Testimony that provides continuity and makes the story understandable.

b. Organization

It has long been the collective opinion of trial lawyers that most direct examinations should be organized chronologically. This keeps the witnesses from becoming confused, makes their testimony easy for the jury to follow, and allows you to use simple, nonleading questions such as "what happened next?" knowing that all events will be covered.

Chronological order is safe, but strict adherence to it is not the most effective. Part of our overall strategy is to take advantage of the principles of primacy and recency by placing special emphasis on what we do first and last. A direct examination structured to take advantage of these effects will probably be more effective. Instead of a strict chronological order that might bury the important facts in the middle, consider starting with the most important point you want the jury to remember and ending with particularly important details.

A typical order for direct examination is summarized in the following sections.

(1) The Beginning

To take advantage of the primacy principle, you should put one of your most important broad facts first. Using such an organization, the direct examination of a criminal defendant might start as follows:

Q: You are Mr. Harvey Wilson?
A: Yes.
Q: You know, don't you, that you are charged with an armed robbery of the Eastwood Quick-Pick store on July 4?

A: Yes.

Q: Mr. Wilson, please tell the jury whether you committed that crime.

A: I did not. I did not go into that store on July 4th. I was not even in town. I was visiting my wife's family all day in Chicago, celebrating the Fourth of July.

(2) Background Information

The first major topic in most direct examinations is the witness' background — age, address, occupation, family, and so forth. The most commonly stated reason for putting neutral biographical questions at the beginning is that they present familiar topics that are easy for witnesses to talk about, thereby helping them over their initial nervousness. This also is consistent with a chronological presentation, and it helps the jurors get to know something about a witness before they are asked to accept that person's testimony. In a case in which the credibility of a witness is an important issue, you often can kill two birds with one stone by beginning with background information that will enhance credibility as your initial point of emphasis.

Eliciting background information may be counterproductive if you dawdle too long or fail to draw a distinction between relevant and irrelevant background. If this stage of examination lasts a long time, the jurors may lose interest. In general, people pay close attention at the beginning, but the ability to pay attention falls off as time passes. You also run the risk of losing the attention of the jurors if you ask a lot of seemingly irrelevant background questions. Many attorneys ask the same pro forma questions of every witness: age, residence, employment history, marital status, and children. There is nothing magical about these particular questions — any background questions will help the witness feel at ease.

You can select instead particularly relevant background items that tie into and credit the testimony the witness will give. If the witness is a police officer who is going to talk about an investigation, experience on the police force is more relevant than the names of the officer's children. In a will contest case, the strong family ties between the testator and claimant can be emphasized. You also may choose to emphasize civic and social similarities between your witness and members of the jury. If you discover during voir dire that three jurors served in the Navy, it probably would make sense to bring out the military service records of your witnesses.

(3) Setting the Scene

As a transition from background matters to the facts of the case, you should consider having your witnesses describe their familiarity with the people, equipment, and locations involved in the occurrence. That way, a witness will not have to interrupt his or her description of the action to explain this background information. Such a transition might proceed like this:

Q: (After the witness testifies about his employment) Do you know Bill Barry?

A: Yes. He works with me at the factory.

Q: Do you ever do things together?

A: We usually go out for a beer a couple of nights a week after the shift ends.

Q: Where do you usually go?

A: We always go to the same place, Fast Company on Main Street.

Q: What is it like?

A: It's sort of a dive, usually pretty crowded between five and seven when we go there. There's a bar along one wall, a pool table in the back, and a row of tables on the other wall.

Q: Is it well lit?

A: Between five and seven it is, because the sunlight comes in the front window.

Q: Would you recognize a drawing of the floor plan of Fast Company if you saw one?

A: I think so.

Q: Handing you state's exhibit five, is this a fair and accurate drawing of the floor plan of Fast Company?

A: Yes it is.

[State's exhibit five moved into evidence]

Q: Directing your attention to August tenth, at about 5:30 p.m., where were you?

A: I was at Fast Company with Bill Barry. We were seated at this table closest to the window, when all of a sudden ....

This technique probably is more effective if the scene is simple than if the testimony will involve many people and more than one location. In complicated cases, there is a danger that the jurors may forget background information if it is explained out of context in this manner.

(4) Telling the Story

The body of the direct examination consists of a narrative that tells the witness' story. In general, you should direct the witness' attention to a specific time and place and ask the witness to tell the jury what happened. You then guide the witness through his or her narrative in chronological order. If you have done your job and gotten the preliminaries out of the way, you will not have to interrupt your story to explain who people are, or how they got to know each other, nor to describe the scene or instrumentalities involved in the crime or event.

The more your direct examination sounds like a story, the better. Stories are easier to follow, understand, and remember. Compare the following two possible direct examinations of a witness to a crime:

Q: Directing your attention to October 12, the kitchen of your home at about 10:00 a.m., please tell the jury what happened.

A: My mother gave me a basket of goodies and asked me to take them to my grandmother's house in the woods. I put on my red riding cape with the hood, and set out for grandma's house.

Q: What happened next?

A: I walked through the woods, taking a shortcut. Along the way I met Mr. Wolf. He asked me some questions about what was in the basket, and I showed him. He looked very hungry.

Q: What happened next?

A: Mr. Wolf went on his way. I walked another fifteen minutes, and then got to grandma's house. I knocked and a voice said, "Come in."

Q: What did the voice sound like?

A: Very scratchy. It didn't sound like grandma at all, but I figured maybe she had a bad cold.

Q: What happened next?

A: I entered the house. It was very dark. I tried turning on a light switch, but the lights didn't work. I went over to grandma's bed. She looked real bad — she had big eyes, big dog-like ears, and lots of sharp teeth. Or at least that's the way it looked in the dark.

Q: Did you question her about this?

A: Yes. I said, "What big eyes you have." She answered, "The better to see you with, my dear." Then I said, "What big ears you have." She answered, "The better to hear you with, my dear." I was getting nervous, because she didn't sound at all like herself. Then I said, "What big teeth you have. New dentures?"

Q: What happened then?

A: The person in the bed jumped up and grabbed me. It was Mr. Wolf wearing grandma's nightgown. He sneered and said, "The better to eat you with, my dear." I screamed for help.

Obviously, this version makes an effective story. Too often, however, a direct examination sounds like this:

Q: Directing your attention to October 12, the kitchen of your home at about 10:00 a.m., please tell the jury what happened.

A: My mother gave me a basket of goodies and asked me ...

Q: Handing you state's exhibit one, do you recognize it?

A: Yes, that's the basket.

Q: Is it still in the same condition as when your mother handed it to you?

A: The basket, yes. Of course, the contents have since been eaten or thrown out.

Q: What had the basket contained at the time?

A: Cookies, a fruitcake, fresh baked bread, cheese, and a bottle of wine.

Q: A bottle of wine? Does your grandmother drink?

A: Only occasionally. I've never seen her drunk.

Q: So to the best of your knowledge, she was not drunk on October 12 when she was eaten by Mr. Wolf?

A: No.

Q: What did you do with this basket?

A: I took it to my grandmother's house in the woods.

Q: Would that be 2501 Lonely Lane, Bayshore?

A: Yes.

Q: What were you wearing?

A: I put on my red riding cape with the hood.

Q: Showing you state's exhibit two, is this the cape?

A: Yes it is.

Q: And is it still in substantially the same condition as it was on October 12?

A: Yes.

Attorney: Move state's exhibit two into evidence.

Court: Received.

Q: What happened next?

A: I set out for grandma's house, through the woods, taking a shortcut. Along the way I met Mr. Wolf.

Q: Had you ever seen Mr. Wolf before?

A: No.

Q: Had you done anything to attract Mr. Wolf's attention?

A: No.

Q: Looking around the courtroom today, do you see the person who accosted you on the path?

A: Yes, he's over there.

Attorney: May the record reflect that she has identified the defendant?

Court: Fine.

Q: What happened next?

A: Mr. Wolf asked me some questions about what was in the basket, and I showed him.

Q: That's the same basket we referred to earlier? State's exhibit one?

A: Yes.

And so on.

(5) What to Do With Weaknesses

When should you elicit testimony disclosing inherent weaknesses? Since jurors will best remember what comes at the beginning and end, the middle would seem an obvious choice. Yet, unless damaging evidence fits logically into the middle of direct examination, a sudden break to insert damaging evidence out of its natural order will only emphasize it. Trial practitioners have reached no consensus. If it does not fit naturally into the sequence of events, some recommend that damaging information be disclosed at the beginning, and others that it be saved until the end. The research of social psychologists tends to support the latter view — in most cases, especially when no mitigating explanation is available, weaknesses should be included near the end, but not last.[33]

---

[33]See Brian Sternthal, Lynn W. Phillips, & Ruby Dholakia, *The Persuasive Effect of Source Credibility*, 42 PUB. OPINION Q. 285 (1978) (unexplained unfavorable information reflecting adversely on a witness' credibility appears to taint everything that comes afterward).

(6) Conclusion

The examination should end with an important detail to take advantage of the principle of recency. You can use this opportunity to emphasize one of the main points you want the jury to remember. For example:

Q: Can you prove you were not in town on July 4?
A: Yes, I can. I filled my car up with gas at a Shell station in Chicago about 2:00 that afternoon, just before we left to drive home. I paid by credit card, and I got a receipt with the date on it.
Q: Handing you defense exhibit F, is this that receipt?
A: Yes, here's my signature.
Defense Attorney: We move defense exhibit F into evidence. No further questions.

(7) Redirect

You should give some advance thought to planning your redirect examination. You may be able to anticipate that your opponent will impeach your witness by proving acts that suggest bias, bringing up a criminal conviction, or eliciting a prior inconsistent statement. If so, you can plan what questions you will ask to rehabilitate your witness, so that you and your witness are ready with an explanation for apparent bias or a prior consistent statement.

In most cases, you can anticipate that your opponent will use some means to try to cast doubt on the veracity of your witness, even if you are unsure exactly how the attack will take shape. You should therefore have several questions planned in advance that permit the witness to restate the witness' most important testimony. You can always decide not to ask a question if that part of the direct examination has gone unchallenged.

c. Making the Testimony Persuasive

The body of the direct examination consists mainly of eliciting from a witness what he or she remembers perceiving and doing. It is not enough, however, just to elicit the basic factual details and rest. Your job is to make the testimony *persuasive*. For testimony to be persuasive, four things must happen:

- The jury must hear it.
- The jury must understand it.
- The jury must remember it.
- The jury must trust the witness who says it.

You must accomplish two things to insure that the jury hears your important evidence:

- *Attract and keep the jurors' attention.* Most direct examination is boring. Much of it is not very important. Therefore, you want to assure that the jurors' attention is focused on the witness before you cover the most important parts of the direct examination. You can attract jurors' attention to the witness by having the witness do something unusual. For example, you can hand the witness an exhibit, have the witness get up and demonstrate something, or have the witness walk to a diagram. You can keep the jurors' attention by being brief and using visual aids.

- *Get your evidence admitted.* The jurors cannot hear your evidence if it is ruled inadmissible by the judge. This means you must anticipate objections your adversary might make, and prepare to circumvent them. With advance preparation, you can come equipped with research that supports admissibility. You can make sure that your direct examination contains sufficient evidence to satisfy foundations. You can prepare alternative theories of admissibility, such as offering evidence for a limited purpose. And, you can be prepared to look for other alternative methods of proof, perhaps through other witnesses, in case your evidence is excluded.

Obviously, once you have the jury's attention, you must present evidence the jury can understand. To a large extent, this is accomplished by working with the witness to make sure the witness can communicate in simple, clear language to the best of the witness' ability. This process is discussed at length in the next section on Witness Preparation. There are five additional techniques you can employ over which you have somewhat more control.

- *Maintain chronological order.* A story is easier to follow if it is in chronological order. Rarely is there any reason why you should deviate from it.
- *Subdivide direct examination into smaller units.* If you break up a long story into "episodes" it will be easier for the jurors to understand and remember it. Thus, you might divide up the plaintiff's story of a traffic accident into six segments: the plaintiff's happy and active life before the accident; the events of the day leading up to the accident; a detailed account of the accident itself; the minutes immediately following the accident; the next few days in the hospital; and what plaintiff's life has been like since the accident.
- *Plan transitions between segments.* It will be easier for the jury to follow your story if they understand when one "episode" stops and another starts. You should therefore plan verbal and visual transitions between segments. A transition is made up of three parts: a clear closure on one segment, an interruption of the flow of the direct examination, and then a clear beginning to the next segment. You can close a segment with a question such as, "Do you recall anything else about the accident?" For an interruption, you may remain silent for a few seconds, move to a different location, have the witness sit down if the witness was standing, and/or insert a phrase such as, "Let's move on to the events following the accident." You can open the next segment with the same kind of topic question you use to start the chronology: "Directing your attention to immediately after the accident, tell us what happened."
- *Elicit facts and details, not conclusions.* Conclusory testimony depends for its success on the witness and jurors sharing a common frame of reference. It is unlikely that all jurors will share the witness' view on what constitutes "large," "fast," or "a good look at the suspect." The more you are able to provide the jurors with the details of important points, the more certain you can be that the jury will understand it. Thus, you want

your witness to say "six feet tall and two hundred pounds" rather than "large," "going over eighty miles an hour" rather than "fast," and "close enough to read the words 'born to lose' tattooed on his upper arm" rather than "got a good look at the suspect."

- *Use appropriate visual aids.* Miscommunication is least likely if you can show the jury the actual objects and places involved in a litigated event. Photographs, diagrams and other illustrations also reduce the likelihood of misunderstanding.

If you expect the jury to remember the important parts of the direct examination, you must emphasize them. A large number of emphasis techniques are available. Basically anything you do that is different and makes evidence stand out will emphasize it. It is the contrast that makes this technique work, so you must remember that you cannot emphasize everything. Rather, you want your basic direct examination to consist of a verbal witness narrative with little interference from you. Then, when a particularly important item of evidence is coming up, you interfere in the direct, cause a little commotion, and focus the jury's attention on the important item. The following are common emphasis techniques:

- *Going into specific detail.* The more details you elicit, the more you emphasize the event being described. If the witness testifies, "I was walking down the street when the defendant pulled a gun on me and said, "Give me a hundred dollars," the jurors might miss the gun reference. If you wanted to emphasize it, you could break in at that point and elicit details:

  A: I was walking down the street when the defendant pulled a gun on me and said ...
  Q: Did you get a good look at the gun?
  A: Yes.
  Q: What color was it?
  A: Black.
  Q: About how big was it?
  A: It was pretty compact, about the size of an open hand.
  Q: Short barrel or long barrel?
  A: Short. I would call it a snub-nosed gun.
  Q: Automatic or revolver?
  A: Revolver.

- *Changing your questioning pace or pattern.* If you have been conducting a normal direct examination, you have been asking simple neutral questions such as "What happened next?" and "What did you see?" If you suddenly vary the type of question you ask, it emphasizes the testimony to follow. You can use a signal question, such as "Now think about your answer carefully, and tell the jury ...." Or, you can change from narrative questions to slow, narrow, detailed questions. For example:

  Q: What happened next?

A: I went down to the street to see if I could be of any help. It looked like a bad accident. I got down there and found the defendant sitting in his car. I went up to see if he was okay.

Q: How close did you get to his face?

A: About a foot.

Q: Could you hear his voice?

A: Yes.

Q: Clearly?

A: Yes.

Q: Could you understand any of what he said?

A: Yes I could.

Q: What did the defendant say?

A: He said, "I wish I hadn't had that last drink."

- *Changing your position or the witness' position.* For example, if you have been standing near the corner of the jury box, you could walk over to your table before asking an important question. Or, you can ask the witness to step to a diagram just before eliciting some crucial fact.

- *Using visual aids.* Perhaps the most effective tactic is to use visual aids or demonstrations. If an exhibit can be introduced at any one of a number of places during the direct examination, why not offer it at a time when it will help emphasize something important? If a witness picks up an exhibit or walks to a blackboard, it attracts the jury's attention. Whatever the witness says immediately after this will receive particular emphasis because of that attentiveness. The introduction of an exhibit often can be effectively combined with a series of preliminary questions going into considerable detail describing the exhibit.

- *Repeating the evidence.* Psychologists have demonstrated that repetition of a message several times increases the likelihood that it will be remembered and believed, as long as it is not repeated to the point where it becomes boring.[34] Repetition can take three forms: similar testimony from different witnesses, similar testimony elicited more than once from a single witness, and repetition of testimony by the attorney. Clearly, if you use all three methods, the message will be repeated too many times and become boring. The calling of multiple witnesses is easiest, if they are available. Repetition within a single witness' direct examination is more difficult, because of the "asked and answered" objection. However, it is permissible to ask a similar question, or have the witness explain an event once in words and then show the location on a diagram. It is often the case that there will be an opportunity to repeat some of the evidence in one of your questions during this process. For example:

Q: What happened next?

---

[34] One experiment found that the optimal number of repetitions was three; after that, the effects become negative. John T. Cacioppo & Richard E. Petty, *Effects of Message Repetition and Position on Cognitive Response, Recall, and Persuasion*, 37 J. PERSONALITY & SOC. PSYCHOL. 97 (1979). *See* Daniel Linz & Steven Penrod, *Increasing Attorney Persuasiveness in the Courtroom*, 8 LAW & PSYCHOL. REV. 1, 28-29 (1984) (more than 3 or 4 repetitions produces psychological reactance).

A: I saw the defendant pick up a beer bottle and hit poor Charlie over the head with it.

Q: Will you step to the diagram, state's exhibit one, and point out exactly where the defendant was when he hit Charlie with the beer bottle?

A: Sure. The defendant was standing here next to the bar. He grabbed a bottle off the bar and smacked Charlie with it as Charlie walked by.

The jury will probably hear conflicting testimony. Your opponent may tell a story quite different from yours. Therefore, you should do what you can to enhance the credibility of your witnesses. Several techniques are available:

- *Enhancing the witness' personal credibility.* Subject to the rule prohibiting bolstering, it is helpful to show that a witness is likely to be credible in this particular case. You can show the witness is unbiased by eliciting that he or she has never met your client before. You can prove that the witness is trustworthy by showing the witness holds a responsible job. You can forge links to the jury by eliciting background concerning the witness' family, social status, occupation, and residence. For example:

    Q: Where do you live?
    A: 2333 East Third Street, Bayshore.
    Q: Is that a house or apartment?
    A: Well neither, actually. It's a rectory.
    Q: A rectory — are you a priest?
    A: Yes, for St. Charles Catholic Church.
    Q: But you're not wearing one of those black and white special collars.
    A: They are optional.
    Q: Should I address you as Father Brown?
    A: We're generally called by our first names. My parishioners call me Father Paul.
    Q: Father Paul, do you know the plaintiff?
    A: No.
    Q: Are any of the parties in this case members of your parish?
    A: No.
    Q: Where were you on January 16th?
    A: Well, I had just finished Mass and was on my way to the hospital to visit the sick, when ...

- *Enhancing the credibility of the witness' story.* Regardless of the witness' inherent credibility, techniques are available to enhance the likelihood that the witness' story is accurate. You may prove that the witness has a good memory by having the witness so testify, eliciting things the witness did to preserve recollection such as taking notes, and eliciting detailed testimony about the event itself. If the event was an ordinary one, you can elicit any reason the witness has for remembering this one transaction out of many similar ones, such as the event being particularly pleasant, painful or embarrassing. Specific dates and times can be fixed by reference to some contemporaneous event or activity. The reliability of the witness' observations may be enhanced by proving good eyesight and hearing, good health, lack of fatigue, a particular reason for paying attention, or favorable conditions for observing (distance, obstructions, lighting). For example:

Q: How do you know it was 6:25?
A: I looked at my watch. I was waiting for my brother to pick me up, and he said to be there by 6:30 or he'd leave without me, so I double-checked the time.

- *Proving the witness' expertise and familiarity with the subject matter.* A witness' opinions and observations of other events and people are more credible if the witness is familiar with that type of event or the people involved. If a witness is going to describe a traffic accident, bring out that the witness used to be a cab driver. If a witness is going to testify about the condition of the testator at the time a will was executed, bring out the witness' knowledge of the details of the testator's general life, family, habits, mannerisms, and so forth. For example:

Q: Did you recognize the intruder's voice?
A: Yes.
Q: How did you recognize it?
A: I had heard it before. It belongs to a friend of my son's named Joey. Joey calls on the phone often, and also has been to our house.

- *Proving motives that are consistent with conduct.* People do things for reasons. If the reasons and motives are explained, the conduct makes more sense. If a witness acted out of habit, jealousy, love, shame, curiosity, or any other common emotion, proving the emotional state will make the conduct seem more logical. For example:

Q: What drew your attention to the corner booth?
A: It's my table. One of my jobs as a waitress is to keep an eye on my tables, and try to sell another round every time someone's glass is empty.

- *Admitting your weaknesses.* Every witness has weaknesses in their backgrounds, demeanor, or testimony. There is nothing you can do about this — your case is always bound by its facts. Many lawyers simply avoid these unfavorable matters, apparently hoping they will go away. If the harmful matter is something that your opponent does not know about, that is unconnected to the main issues, or that your opponent probably will not bring up, then it may make sense to avoid bringing it up in direct examination. However, if harmful evidence is likely to come out, it can have a serious impact on the perceived credibility of the witness if you appear to be trying to hide it. It does less harm if you disclose weaknesses yourself in a way that minimizes them. Once the jurors have decided that the weakness is not particularly important, they will be inoculated against your opponent's attempt to make it seem important during cross-examination.[35] For example, suppose your witness had been drinking:

Q: What kind of place is Mulligan's?
A: Like a pub, you know. They sell food and beer.
Q: Did you have anything to eat or drink while you were waiting?
A: Yes, a cheeseburger and a couple of beers. I didn't want to have too
     much, because Al and I were going to a party later where the beer
     would be free.

3. WITNESS PREPARATION

Witness preparation has two aspects: preparing the content of a witness' testimony and preparing the witness to give that testimony in the courtroom. The first task involves working with the witness on how to communicate persuasively what he or she knows. The second involves preparing the witness to present that knowledge as effectively in the courtroom setting as the witness does in the informal atmosphere of your office.

The importance of witness preparation cannot be overemphasized. Witnesses who are confident in their ability to give effective testimony and who know what to expect in the courtroom can only give more persuasive testimony than they would otherwise. However, most trial practitioners warn against over-preparation. If testimony appears too rehearsed, the jury may become suspicious of it. If too much emphasis is placed on using specific words or descriptions, the witness may become panicky because of a fear he or she will not remember the exact words learned in your office.

a. Preparing the Content of Testimony

The first task in preparation is to work with the witness on the content of the direct examination. This does not mean that you should tell the witness what to say, or try to change the testimony. Such conduct is unethical and may amount to suborning perjury. Rather, your task is to help the witness remember and articulate details, reduce conclusions to their underlying facts, and choose words and descriptions that are vivid and accurately convey the witness' perceptions in his or her own words.

The need for preparation is obvious:

> Many witnesses have a woefully inadequate conception of lapsed time. Others have no judgment of distance. Others will glibly describe an automobile as traveling at 75 miles an hour, and have no idea of the distance a car traveling that speed would traverse in a matter of seconds. It is better to spend some extra time with these witnesses in the office than to be embarrassed by their ill-considered answers on the witness stand. When a witness is asked how long he had an approaching automobile within his vision before a collision and answers "four or five minutes,"

---

[35] Arthur Lumsdaine & Irving Janis, *Resistance to Counterpropaganda Produced by One-Sided and Two-Sided Propaganda Presentations*, 17 Pub. Opinion Q. 311 (1953); William McGuire, *Persistence of the Resistance to Persuasion Induced by Various Types of Prior Belief Defenses*, 64 J. Abnormal & Soc. Psychol. 241 (1962).

pull a watch on him and show him what four or five minutes mean. After the demonstration he will probably say he meant "seconds." If he estimates a distance at 50 feet, test his judgment by asking him the distance between two fixed points within his view, and when he has given his estimate measure that distance with a tape or rule. If it develops he has no judgment of distance, tell him to say so on the witness stand. If he is overestimating the speed of an automobile, figure out for him on a piece of paper how far a car going at, say, 75 miles an hour, would travel in five seconds.[36] All of these measures, it is submitted, are justified in order to aid the witness in giving accurate testimony, and protecting him from the consequence of ill-considered answers.[37]

A second task of preparation is to help your witnesses break conclusions down into the underlying facts so that they are prepared to communicate the kinds of details that will make their testimony credible. For example, a witness to an accident might tell you that she was looking out her window and saw a car strike an obviously drunk pedestrian who had stumbled into its path. If you want the jury to see a vivid picture of the intoxicated pedestrian, the witness is going to have to do better than that. This is the time to make sure your witness will be able to give such a description. Preparation might proceed along these lines:

Lawyer: Ms. Gonzalez, how could you tell the pedestrian was drunk?
Witness: Well, he looked drunk, you know, weaving and stuff.
L: Tell me everything you remember about him.
W: He sort of stumbled and wasn't walking straight.
L: When did you first see him?
W: When he stepped off the curb.
L: Describe his clothes.
W: Rumpled, an old shirt — I think it was untucked.
L: Okay, describe that first step he took.
W: Oh, I remember, he stumbled then, and almost lost his balance, swaying from side to side.
L: Was he carrying anything?
W: Not that I remember.
L: Did you see a liquor bottle?
W: No.
L: Okay, how was his posture?
W: His head hung over, like this.
L: The chin almost on the chest, eyes looking down?
W: Yeah.
L: Did he walk into the street next?
W: No, he sort of looked around. Then he walked, sort of shuffling.
L: How straight a line did he follow?
W: Not at all straight, he weaved from side to side.
L: How far — a foot, two feet to one side or the other?

---

[36] Approximately 550 feet.
[37] FRANCIS X. BUSCH, LAW AND TACTICS IN JURY TRIALS, vol. 2: 529-30 (1959).

W: Probably about a foot to the left, then a few steps, then to the right a foot or two.

L: Did he keep his balance?

W: No, he almost fell again, and then lurched forward into the path of the car.

L: What did he do with his arms when he stumbled?

W: Reached out like he was trying to grab something.

L: All right, now when you testify in court, it is important to be as detailed as possible. So when you describe this man, can you go into details like these?

W: Sure.

L: As I understand it, then, you saw him on the curb in rumpled clothes with his shirt untucked. He almost fell stepping into the street, swayed from side to side, then he shuffled into the street, weaving a foot to the left, taking a few steps, then weaving to the right. He almost fell down again, reached out his arms, and then lurched into the path of the car.

W: That's right.

L: And you figured he had to be drunk?

W: Yes.

The final stage of preparation is to help the witness improve his or her choice of words for their maximum vividness and persuasive effect. The words used to describe an event can have an impact on how the jurors picture it. An incident or accident may sound like a minor matter to the jury, while a collision, wreck, or smash-up may sound more serious. However, if you are dissatisfied with a witness' word choice, it is dangerous to suggest a particular word you like better. If a witness tries to use words that do not come naturally, the witness may end up sounding like Archie Bunker and lose credibility with the jurors.[38] A better tactic is simply to ask the witness to use a more descriptive word or to let the witness pick a better one from a list of alternatives.

The most difficult task may be helping a witness find words to describe intense sensations or emotions. Pain is especially hard to convey through words. Many injured people will describe pain as "bad," but this general conclusory description will not be sufficiently meaningful to the jurors. Your witness will need to conjure up a mental picture of the intensity of the pain. Help your witness analogize his or her pain to a type of pain some of the jurors are likely to have experienced. The range is limitless: stubbing toes, cracking shins, hitting heads underneath kitchen cupboards, burning fingers on hot dishes, stepping on a tack, hitting fingers with a hammer, childbirth, and so forth.

Many trial practitioners encourage their witnesses to use descriptive phrases such as the following:

(1) "My head felt like the top had been blown off by a shotgun."

---

[38] In one experiment, it was found that witnesses who used "hypercorrect" speech (e.g., an assistant ambulance attendant who described an unconscious person as "comatose") were viewed as less convincing, less competent, and less intelligent than witnesses who used normal speech. John Conley, William O'Barr, & E. Allan Lind, *The Power of Language: Presentational Style in the Courtroom*, 1978 DUKE L.J. 1375, 1389-90.

(2) "It felt like someone was sticking a knife in my eye and twisting it."

Are these really any better than general descriptions? None of the jurors has had his or her head blown off or been stabbed in the eye.

b. Preparing Witnesses for the Courtroom

Part of the preparation process is preparing your witnesses for the court-room so they will be able to communicate effectively with the jurors.

As a first step, witnesses should be familiarized with courtroom procedures. Tell them (or show them) where the courthouse and courtroom are, where to park, where you will be, where they will wait, where the restrooms are, who will summon them to the courtroom, which seat is the witness chair, whether they should remain standing until sworn, and so on. Explain the order of questioning, including the possibility of redirect examination. Witnesses should be warned that the judge may ask questions, too. You also should describe the process of objections and the need to wait for a ruling before answering. It is a good idea to visit the courtroom with your witnesses so they can see how a trial really looks. If they have not testified before, witnesses probably have a seriously distorted view of trials acquired from television. A visit to a real courtroom will help relieve any anxiety they have about an alien system, and will give you the opportunity to discuss how they should act on the stand.

Witnesses also must be prepared to be good witnesses. Lawyers frequently give their witnesses the following general advice:

- Do not attempt to answer a question unless you have heard and under-stood it clearly.
- If you want a question repeated, say so. It is your right.
- Always answer courteously.
- Keep your voice up so the jury can hear you.
- Look at the jury when you speak.
- Do not try to be funny or sarcastic.
- Correct any mistakes you might make, interrupting if necessary.
- Answer with words rather than gestures.

In addition, trial practitioners stress the need to work with your witnesses to correct bad habits and distracting mannerisms — nail biting, mumbling, constantly saying "y'know," looking at the floor, and so on. The best vehicle for this process is a practice examination in which you ask a witness the kind of questions you will ask at trial. This will help alleviate a witness' fear of the unknown, and will increase his or her self-confidence. It also will provide a context in which to discuss proper procedures and point out bad testifying habits. A practice examination provides an opportunity for the witness to become familiar with handling and referring to exhibits, drawing diagrams, and so forth, so that these parts of the direct will run smoothly at trial. If the witness will have to mark exhibits during trial or conduct a demonstration, the witness can practice this in advance to reduce the possibilities of confusion or error. If the facilities are available to enable you to videotape the practice examination, you can show the witness exactly how he or she appears, which will make your constructive criticism more readily understood.

Finally, your witnesses should be given advice (tactfully, of course) about how to dress for the courtroom. Witnesses who dress conservatively but appropriately for their occupation and social status seem to be more effective than witnesses who overdress. Obviously, witnesses should avoid heavy make-up, ostentatious jewelry, extreme hairstyles, or inappropriate clothing — soiled overalls, short skirts, bermuda shorts, evening dresses, tuxedos, and so on. However, this does not mean all witnesses should dress alike. In general, both lawyers and psychologists advise that witnesses are most effective if they dress the way they would for work unless local court rules require more formal attire.[39]

NOTES

1. *Integrating foundations into your direct examination.* For other examples of how foundational questions are incorporated into direct examination, *see* HERBERT J. STERN, TRYING CASES TO WIN, vol. 2: 156-89 (1991); Emile Z. Berman, *Foundations for Evidence, in* CIVIL LITIGATION AND TRIAL TECHNIQUES 344-63 (H. Bodin ed. 1976); THOMAS A. MAUET, FUNDAMENTALS OF TRIAL TECHNIQUES 106-17, 138, 162-98 (3d ed. 1992); EDWARD IMWINKELRIED, EVIDENTIARY FOUNDATIONS (1980).

2. *Should you try to create sympathy for a witness?* You may be tempted to emphasize emotional testimony by the victim of a crime or accident in order to produce jury sympathy. Lawyers do this frequently, apparently believing that jury sympathy for a plaintiff or crime victim will increase the likelihood of a verdict against the defendant. Interestingly, such tear-jerking testimony may have the exact opposite effect. Social psychologists have discovered that jurors react negatively to the misfortunes of a victim, and an attempt to arouse sympathy for him or her merely undermines the victim's credibility and reduces the jurors' liking for that person. People are reluctant to face the fact that tragedy can strike them, so they tend to convince themselves that victims are different — more stupid, more careless, or more responsible for their own misfortunes.

While people react positively to a victim who is emotionally distressed immediately after a traumatic event, *see* Calhoun et al., *Victim Emotional Response: Effects on Social Reactions to Victims of Rape*, 20 BRIT. J. SOC. PSYCHOL. 17 (1981), they seem to expect victims to have recovered and regained a positive attitude toward life by the time the case goes to trial. In one experiment, subjects were more favorably impressed with a crime victim who minimized the trauma of the event and maximized her positive attitude about

---

[39] Albert Mehrabian & Martin Williams, *Nonverbal Concomitants of Perceived and Intended Persuasiveness*, 13 J. PERSONALITY & SOC. PSYCHOL. 37 (1969) showed that witnesses who overdressed for their social status were less persuasive than those who underdressed. Ellen Berscheid & Elaine Walster, *Physical Attractiveness, in* 7 ADVANCES IN EXPERIMENTAL SOC. PSYCHOL. 158 (L. Berkowitz ed. 1974), showed that attractive witnesses are more persuasive than unattractive ones. For those reasons, you should probably discuss clothing with all witnesses, and ignore advice that most witnesses will dress appropriately even if you say nothing. Why take the chance?

the future than with a victim who was still suffering and unable to forget the crime. Dan Coates, Camille Wortman & Antonia Abbey, *Reactions to Victims, in* NEW APPROACHES TO SOCIAL PROBLEMS (I. Freize et al. eds., 1979). The research is summarized in Steven Penrod et al., *The Implications of Social Psychological Research for Trial Practice Attorneys, in* PSYCHOLOGY AND LAW 443-44 (D. Muller et al., eds., 1984).

3. *Additional techniques of witness preparation.* Many trial practitioners recommend that you take your witnesses to visit the scene of the occurrence to help assure the accuracy of their recollections of details about angles, obstructions, times, and distances. *See, e.g.,* HENRY ROTHBLATT, SUCCESSFUL TECHNIQUES IN THE TRIAL OF CRIMINAL CASES 82 (1961).

4. *Remedying witnesses' bad habits.* One of the most common habits that reduces the credibility of a witness is speaking in an unconvincing style dubbed "powerless speech." Powerless speech is characterized by hedging ("I think," "sort of," "you know"), hesitation ("well," "um"), polite forms ("please," "sir"), and frequent use of intensifiers ("very," "definitely," "surely"). In one study, witnesses who spoke in this style were viewed as less convincing, less truthful, less competent, less intelligent, and less trustworthy than those whose speech was free from these habits. John Conley et al., *The Power of Language: Presentational Style in the Courtroom,* 1978 DUKE L.J. 1375, 1379-86. Although this kind of speech habit may be hard to remedy, if you make a witness aware he or she is doing it (preferably through videotape playback), that person may be able to change. *See also* WELCOME D. PIERSON, THE DEFENSE ATTORNEY AND BASIC DEFENSE TACTICS 213-14 (1956).

A number of other common problem characteristics of witnesses are summarized in ALAN MORRILL, TRIAL DIPLOMACY 34-36 (2d ed. 1972). Judge Morrill suggests that the remedy for most bad habits is repeated rehearsals and practice examinations in which the bad habits are pointed out. Long-winded witnesses should be told that their answers are unnecessary or unresponsive, short-winded witnesses should be forced to give more complete answers, opinionated witnesses should be made to stick to the facts, antagonistic witnesses should be warned not to attack the other side, egotistical witnesses must be convinced to be more humble, slow talkers should be speeded up, and fast talkers should be slowed down. Witnesses who try to be dramatic or emotional may be cured by videotaping their practice testimony and playing it back, so they can see how phony it looks. Witnesses with stage fright might be helped by a practice run in an empty courtroom, preferably with other persons (members of your firm, other witnesses, members of the witness' family) present. There is no guarantee that practice will change a witness' style of speaking, but it is probably worth a try.

5. *Eye contact with the jury.* The usual advice given by trial practitioners is that you should coach your witnesses to look at the jurors when giving important testimony. This advice is based on the commonly held belief that a person who does not look you in the eye, or who averts his or her gaze, has something to hide. *See, e.g.,* ALAN MORRILL, TRIAL DIPLOMACY 35 (2d ed. 1972) (people who do not look you in the eye are liars); Henry Rothblatt, *The Defendant — Should He Testify?,* TRIAL DIPL. J., Fall 1979, at 21, 23-24 (if your client does not establish eye contact, jurors will believe the client is hiding

something). Is this good advice? Despite what our mothers taught us, eye contact is not necessarily synonymous with persuasiveness or perceived credibility. Experiments have been inconclusive. Gordon Hemsley & Anthony Doob, *The Effect of Looking Behavior on Perceptions of a Communicator's Credibility*, 8 J. APPLIED SOC. PSYCHOL. 136 (1978), concluded that a male defendant's credibility was reduced if he averted his gaze from the jury. However, Albert Mehrabian & Martin Williams, *Nonverbal Concomitants of Perceived and Intended Persuasiveness*, 13 J. PERSONALITY & SOC. PSYCHOL. 37 (1969), found that more eye contact increased the persuasiveness of female communicators, but less eye contact increased the persuasiveness of male communicators.

6. *Preparing for the unexpected.* During trial, your witnesses are likely to do two things: omit certain facts to which you wanted them to testify, and forget or misstate other facts. While you can be sure this will happen, you cannot know when it will occur. Trial practitioners have suggested some techniques for handling these unexpected annoyances that require pretrial preparation. One suggestion is to work out a signal — a particular question you will ask when the witness has made a mistake. In ALAN MORRILL, TRIAL DIPLOMACY 37 (2d ed. 1972), the author suggests that you tell your witness you will use the question, "Is there anything else you can recall?" as a signal he or she has omitted something, and that you warn the witness always to answer that his or her memory is exhausted if the witness cannot figure out what was omitted. *Accord* LOUIS SCHWARTZ, PROOF, PERSUASION, AND CROSS-EXAMINATION, vol. 1: 310-11 (1973). *But see* GARY BELLOW & BEA MOULTON, THE LAWYERING PROCESS 692 n.39 (1978): "It has been suggested that counsel should arrange ways of signalling to the witness that [something] has been omitted ... [T]his strategy often only increases the anxiety that produced the ... omission in the first place." To reduce anxiety, you should consider telling your witness that you will help him or her out by asking leading questions if the witness becomes confused or forgets things. *Id.* at 690-92.

Some practitioners also suggest that you have your witnesses prepare special written statements containing everything you want them to testify about, in the order in which you will proceed. These statements can be used conveniently to refresh recollection and will make it easy for the witnesses to find their places. *Id.* at 692. Such a statement may be more effective than refreshing memory from a deposition because it is more compact, organized in the same order as direct examination, and contains little that can benefit your opponent if your adversary exercises the right to introduce it (unless the statement has been made too one-sided). *See* FED. R. EVID. 612. *But cf.* ROBERT KEETON, TRIAL TACTICS AND METHODS 29-30 (2d ed. 1973) (providing witness with outline of direct examination has the disadvantage of interfering with spontaneity).

7. *Enhancing the credibility of witnesses.* For an excellent discussion of techniques for enhancing the credibility of witnesses, *see* LOUIS SCHWARTZ, PROOF, PERSUASION AND CROSS-EXAMINATION: A WINNING NEW APPROACH IN THE COURTROOM, vol. 1: 207-08, 305-08, 516-17, 706-08, 717-18, 1005-08, 1216, 1411, 1416 (1973).

F. CONDUCTING DIRECT EXAMINATION

1. PREPARATION OF A GOOD OUTLINE

Conducting direct examination is like conducting an orchestra. You are in charge, but others must produce the sounds. Despite careful preparation, many trial lawyers have difficulty accomplishing their goals when they conduct direct examination. Part of the explanation may be that they are unfamiliar with the techniques of conducting effective examinations discussed in the next section. In many cases, however, the problem lies elsewhere. No conductor would think of trying to lead an orchestra without a detailed score, yet many trial practitioners advise that you should not use notes when conducting direct examination. They argue that notes are inevitably inflexible and interfere with spontaneity.

The reason that some lawyers have found notes less than useful may be that they were outlining the wrong thing. Since you are most familiar with preparing and outlining what *you* will say, your instinct will be to write out or outline the questions you will ask. The first time the witness gives a longer, shorter, or otherwise different answer than expected, you have nothing prepared. Either you will ask your next prepared question, thereby either skipping over or repeating facts, or you will flounder around trying to phrase a question when you cannot remember precisely what the witness should say next.

Direct examination is different from closing argument, opening statement, and even cross-examination in one major respect. In all other phases of the trial, you do most or all of the talking; therefore, it makes sense to outline what you intend to say. During direct examination, the witness will do most of the talking. Does it not make sense to outline what *the witness* will say? Recall the orchestra conductor's score — on it are the notes the musicians will play.

An outline of questions is useless. An outline that focuses primarily on what the witness will say is helpful. One such model outline is presented here. This outline uses a piece of paper or note card that has been divided into three columns. In the right-hand column is a detailed outline of the witness' testimony as you have worked it out in preparation. Essential testimony on your most important parts is written out in detail; unimportant testimony is summarized. In this way you will know when testimony is important enough for you to interrupt a witness to elicit more detail. In the middle column are your notes on what you will do — when you will move, when you will pick up an exhibit, and so forth. For some testimony, such as evidentiary foundations, it may be important for you to phrase a question in a particular way. Such questions also can go in the middle column. In the left-hand column you can summarize your evidentiary research, writing out the responses you will give if there is an objection. An excerpt from the outline for a witness to an automobile accident is presented on the following two pages:

Leading permitted to direct attention. Rule 611(c), Starks v. State	DIRECTING YOUR ATTENTION TO JUNE 24 1991, AT ABOUT 11:15 PM, WHERE WERE YOU?
	Corner 5th & Main On Main Street Headed south Stopped Light was red No other cars on Main Streetlights on corners Nothing blocking view Radio off Heard roar Car without muffler
Helpful opinion based on perception, Rule 701	Getting louder Saw car to left On 5th Street 75-100 feet away Coming west Toward me Car was blue Ford Watched 1-2 seconds
	(2 steps up) BASED ON YOUR OBSERVATIONS, HOW FAST WAS THE CAR GOING?
Opinion of speed based on perception, AMC v. Robbins	About 45 mph
	(pause, step back)
	Light turned green Waited anyway Didn't think car would stop
Relevant state of mind to explain why he didn't go on a green light	(walk to table, pick up photo)
	Car sped through Estimate speed 50 mph Car swerved left Hit pick-up truck On 5th Street Headed east Stopped Completely in own lane Had not seen truck before Attention focused on car Big crash Ran to scene

Photo admissible as illustrative evidence Garcia v. State	WOULD PHOTOGRAPH OF TWO VEHICLES ASSIST YOU IN DESCRIBING SCENE? MAY I APPROACH WITNESS? HANDING YOU PL EXHIBIT 1, DO YOU RECOGNIZE IT? IS IT FAIR & ACCURATE DEPICTION OF ACCIDENT SCENE AT ABOUT 11:15 PM (show to opponent) OFFER PL EX 1 INTO EVIDENCE AS ILLUSTRATIVE EV
	(Put photo on easel) WILL YOU DESCRIBE EXACTLY WHAT YOU SAW? (Walk back to table) 'Cars smashed up Glass all over Gasoline on road Ran to truck Driver looked dead Blood on face Blood on chest Ran to car 2 people in it Woman passenger Dazed but conscious Eyes open Looked at me 2 feet away 30 seconds since crash (Move to end of jury box)
Excited utterance Rule 803(2)	Asked if she was OK She said "He didn't stop for light" "Fool was speeding" DID SHE SAY ANYTHING ELSE? DID YOU HEAR IT CLEARLY? WHAT WERE HER EXACT WORDS? "We had been drinking" (Remove photo, give to bailiff)

As the witness testifies, you can follow along on the outline. As long as the witness is covering the desired facts, you can let the witness talk. If the witness omits a fact, you will know it immediately and can interrupt to ask for it. If the witness stops, you need only ask "what happened next?" or direct the witness to the next subject. If an objection is made, you can respond crisply and professionally, giving your reason and citing the rule or case supporting admissibility. When it is important that questions be phrased precisely, they are written out. Yet for most of the testimony, you can preserve spontaneity by focusing your attention on the testimony the witness is giving and not on yourself.

2. DOMINATION BY WITNESS

Most trial practitioners agree that the single most important principle of direct examination is to keep the jurors' attention focused on the witness. The attorney should fade into the background, doing as little as possible to distract the jury and letting the witness be the dominating presence during testimony.

> After all, a witness will be believed and remembered because of the manner and content of [the] testimony, not because the questions asked were so brilliant. Witness credibility is determined by who the witness is (background), what [the witness] says (content), and how [the witness] says it (demeanor). If the jurors remember one of your witnesses as being particularly convincing, but are not sure who conducted the direct examination, you have done your job.[40]

Since your primary role consists of asking questions, the extent to which you insert yourself into the direct examination will depend on what kinds of questions you use.

a. Narrative vs. Fragmented Testimony

If the witness is going to dominate direct examination, it would seem that the witness must do most of the talking. To accomplish this, you should ask broad questions that allow the witness to tell the story in his or her own way, at least to the extent that long, narrative answers are allowed by the judge. Although there are tactical risks inherent in giving free rein to your witnesses — unresponsive answers, the inclusion of irrelevant matters, the omission of essential details, chronological confusion — the collective wisdom of trial practitioners is that spontaneous statements of the witness will carry more weight with the jury than answers that appear tailored to fit a lawyer's questions. The narrative of a witness is also likely to be more interesting and less boring than a monotonous repetition of narrow questions and short answers, the endless cadence of which has been described as dull torture, "not unlike being nibbled to death by ducks."[41]

While the preference for a narrative might seem intuitively obvious, it may be that there is little actual difference between the two styles. When social scientists tested the effects of narrative and fragmented testimony in direct examination, they found only weak support for this principle. Occasionally, narrative testimony was more effective than fragmented testimony, but often it appeared to make no difference. However, fragmented testimony was never

---

[40] THOMAS A. MAUET, FUNDAMENTALS OF TRIAL TECHNIQUES 71-71 (3d ed. 1992).
[41] JAMES JEANS, TRIAL ADVOCACY 213 (1975).

significantly more effective than narrative.[42] It probably depends more on who your witness is — if a witness is comfortable doing most of the talking, you should let the witness do so. But if the witness is reluctant and responds better to specific questions (or if the judge requires them), don't panic! Using fragmented testimony appears to have little negative impact.

b. Phrasing Questions

The way in which questions are asked can greatly affect whether the witness dominates direct examination. If you ask long, complicated, leading questions, you will end up doing most of the talking, and the jurors will have to pay more attention to you than to your witness. For this reason, trial practitioners long have recommended that you ask short, simple, positive questions:

- *Ask only one question at a time*, and not a question with several parts. Compound questions are sometimes hard to understand. Answers to compound questions are worse; they are likely to be incomplete, ambiguous, or both.
- *Avoid negatives in the question*, if possible. Consider this exchange:

    Q: You do not know whether Jones was there?
    A: Yes.

    Did the witness mean "Yes, I know," or "Yes, it is true that I do not know," or "Yes, Jones was there"?
- *Make the question brief.* Both the witness and the jurors must remember all of the question in order to understand it.
- *Use simple words.* Use words that are used in everyday conversation. You want all of the jurors to understand both the questions and the answers, and this requires words that the least educated among them will understand. This is not a recommendation for using slang or bad grammar, however; that practice, unless it comes naturally, probably will be recognized and resented as talking down to the jury.
- *Avoid leading questions.* Not only might they be objected to, which interrupts the flow of testimony and distracts the jurors from the witness, but also they severely limit the witness' answers. You end up testifying instead of the witness.

    Facts should come from the witness. It is, therefore, clumsy work to frame questions, even if allowed, so that the answers shall be a mere affirmative or negative. If, for instance, the advocate asks, "Did the accused kill the deceased by a pistol shot?" and the witness answers, "Yes," the testimony is not so effective as if the killing is described in detail.[43]

---

[42] Conley, O'Barr, & Lind, *supra* note 38, at 1386-89.
[43] Byron K. Elliott & William Elliott, The Work of the Advocate 273 (1888).

3. CONTROL OF WITNESS

Maintaining control over a direct examination may appear at first glance to be inconsistent with the goal of letting your witness dominate. Yet failure to keep the direct examination on its planned course can be disastrous. Witnesses given complete freedom may omit essential details, make inadvertent errors, wander off into irrelevant matters, or leave the jurors confused by ambiguous testimony. You must either reach a delicate balance, keeping witnesses on track without appearing to control them, or give up and resort to the less effective technique of using narrow questions.

a. Controlling the Content of Testimony

To make sure that your witnesses cover all important matters in sufficient detail, you must maintain control over the substance of their testimony. If your witnesses have been well prepared, most of their narrative answers will be adequate, so that you will not have to do anything. Inevitably, however, witnesses will give some answers that are incomplete, confusing, or wrong. In these situations, you must either let the answer stand or find some way to elicit better testimony.

It is axiomatic that you must hear a bad answer in order to do anything about it. Therefore, the first step in controlling the content of testimony is to be aware of exactly what your witnesses say. As surprising as it may seem, many trial lawyers simply do not listen to what their witnesses are saying. This may be caused by thinking about how to phrase the next question or by making the risky assumption that witnesses will say in court what they said in the office.

If a witness gives a bad answer, you must decide whether it is worth interrupting his or her testimony to remedy the situation. You pay a price for interrupting a witness in the middle of a narrative. One experiment indicated that jurors' opinions of the fairness and intelligence of the lawyer went down significantly if he or she interrupted a witness.[44] Interruption also may be interpreted as a lack of trust in your witness.

Nevertheless, interruption may sometimes be preferable to letting the testimony continue. If the witness begins crying and cannot continue, or begins to panic on the stand, you may have to stop the direct examination altogether and ask for a recess. If the witness gives incomplete or inadequate testimony, some trial practitioners argue that you must interrupt in order to amplify or clarify it. This is certainly sound advice if the witness is testifying about something important. However, if the witness omits an unimportant detail or testifies incorrectly on a tangential issue, the better course would seem to be to let it stand and move on to the important matters.

If you decide that it is necessary to amplify an incomplete answer, a number of techniques are available. You could go through the process of refreshing the witness' recollection with a document, but this is a cumbersome and distracting practice, better suited to major lapses of memory than to the forgetting of small details. It may be better to try asking narrow questions that direct the

---

[44] Conley, O'Barr, & Lind, *supra* note 38, at 1390-92.

witness' attention to the omitted detail and, if this fails, to use a leading question. For example:

Q: What happened next?

A: The red Camaro went through the red light at about thirty miles per hour and smashed into the Cadillac. I heard the sound of brakes only after the Camaro was in the intersection.

Q: Do you remember any pedestrians?

A: Oh yes, there was a person in the crosswalk who the Camaro missed by inches.

Q: Do you recall anything the driver of the Camaro had in his hands?

A: I'm not sure I remember.

Q: Did he have a beer can in his hand?

A: Oh, yes, now I remember. His arm was out the window, facing me, and he had a beer can in his hand.

Occasionally, witnesses will get confused and inadvertently give incorrect testimony. This presents a particularly delicate problem. Any attempt to correct the misstatement may sound like coaching, yet correction may be essential.[45] One suggestion is to drop the matter and return to it later with a different, more leading approach, hoping the witness will give the right answer. The problem with this method is that the witness may repeat the same incorrect information. The same problem arises if you immediately ask the witness, "Are you sure about that answer?" hoping he or she will admit uncertainty so that you can refresh recollection. The witness is more likely to say that he or she is certain of the answer, making it even more difficult to extricate yourself from your predicament.

The solution may be simply to confront the witness with the misstatement and suggest the correct answer:

Q: What happened next?

A: I saw the defendant run away from the store. He ran south to Kirkwood Street, turned west, and disappeared from sight.

Q: Wait a minute. West is toward the downtown area. Don't you mean that he turned east, away from the downtown area?

A: Let's see. Yes, that would be east, not west. He ran to the east.

b. Controlling the Witness' Delivery

You can do little during trial to improve the manner in which your witnesses deliver their testimony. You must work with your witnesses during the preparation stage on their appearance, demeanor, and speaking style. However, you may be able to correct two common problems that occur during the presentation of testimony. If a witness is speaking too quietly, you can ask the witness to speak louder, or you can move farther away so that the witness will naturally speak louder. If you want a witness to look at the jury, you can employ similar tactics. You can phrase a question so that it asks the witness

---

[45] MODEL RULES OF PROFESSIONAL CONDUCT Rule 3.3 (a)(4) states: "If a lawyer has offered material evidence and comes to know of its falsity, the lawyer shall take reasonable remedial measures."

to "tell the jury" what happened, or you can position yourself at the far end of the jury box so that the witness will be looking at the jurors when he or she looks in your direction.[46]

4. MANNER AND STYLE OF ATTORNEY

Manner and style are largely matters of personal taste and personality. The general advice is to be yourself, and not to try to be an actor. However, regardless of the style you choose, there are some general ideas about effective presentation that will probably help your performance.[47]

- *Convey honesty and sincerity.* Your personal integrity is vital. Be honest and avoid "cheap shots."
- *Manifest confidence and belief in the witness.* Show the jury that you believe in the case you are presenting. Act like you care.
- *Be professional.* It is always better to err on the side of being too formal than to let your performance slide into sloppiness, slouching, or the dreaded "country lawyer" approach.
- *Respect the judge.* You should be respectful of the judge, without becoming subservient. The trial judge is the most powerful person in the courtroom. But remember that you are the second-most powerful. It is unseemly to brown-nose a judge.
- *Address all remarks to the bench.* Questions are directed to the witness; every other remark is directed to the judge. Do not speak directly to the opposing lawyer, and do not make comments to the jury.
- *Ask permission to approach* the bench, the witness or the jury, or to have the witness step out of the witness chair.
- *Dress in normal business attire.* Don't worry about anything you may have read about power clothing or dressing for success. If you wear something you think you look good in, and in which you are comfortable, your overall confidence will improve.
- *Use a conversational tone of voice.* Speak clearly and distinctly, using ordinary language. It probably is better to be too loud than too soft. The judge, witness, jurors, and court reporter have to be able to hear what you say.
- *Let your voice reflect the emotional level of the examination.* You probably should question a physician in a formal, professional manner, but when you examine an injured child, let your voice reflect your compassion and understanding.
- *Don't let negative feelings show* in your face and voice. If disaster happens, don't reveal that you are angry, irritated, or frustrated.
- *Do not try to suppress all human emotion.* Laugh if something funny happens. If you win a difficult battle over an objection, allow yourself a quick smirk of triumph.

[46] This position has been recommended by social psychologists. *See* Steven Penrod, et al., *The Implications of Social Psychological Research for Trial Practice Attorneys, in* PSYCHOLOGY AND LAW 442 (D. Muller et al., eds., 1984).

[47] *See* SCOTT BALDWIN, ART OF ADVOCACY — DIRECT EXAMINATION § 1.05 (1981); M. DOMBROFF, *supra* note 5, at 41-49.

- *Watch the witness*, so you see what the jury is seeing. Watch for signs of nervousness or confusion. Be careful not to get distracted staring at your notes.
- *Watch the judge.* Look for signs of irritation or a raised eyebrow. You also need to watch for visibly negative reactions that could affect the jury, such as the judge shaking her head in disbelief.
- *Watch the jury* for their reactions. Are they attentive, bored, falling asleep? Have they begun to look at your witness like the witness has some loathsome disease?
- *Keep an eye on opposing counsel.* Some unethical attorneys may try to distract the jurors' attention away from the direct examination.

5. REDIRECT EXAMINATION

Redirect examination is available to rehabilitate an impeached witness or to correct mistakes, clarify uncertainties, and refute misleading inferences from cross-examination. Before you undertake a redirect examination however, you should appraise carefully whether any further questions will improve the situation. If cross-examination has not weakened the direct, then you would be wise to forgo redirect examination. If the cross-examination has seriously discredited the witness or testimony, redirect is indicated, subject to these provisos:

- You should usually limit redirect to important items and skip over minor points.
- You must be reasonably certain that you can effectively rehabilitate the witness or counteract the cross-examination, and will not simply dig yourself deeper into a hole. Redirect examination is always risky — you may do more harm than good by focusing the jurors' attention on damaging evidence. An attempt to clear up a misstatement may fail, reinforcing the error, or you may signal to the jury that you are dissatisfied with your own witness.

If you decide to conduct a redirect examination, how should you proceed? Some lawyers believe a redirect examination should be as short as possible and be limited to issues fundamental to your case or that bear heavily on the witness' credibility. They argue that jurors have a sense of proportion and are not too concerned with minutiae. Busch suggests that there might occasionally be a justification for asking about unimportant issues. If the cross-examination has left the witness confused and upset, you can begin redirect on unimportant matters to restore the confidence of the witness before going into more vital issues.[48]

Trial lawyers have a tendency to ask complicated, leading questions on redirect examination that summarize the direct testimony and the cross-examination and suggest an explanation all in one sentence. For example:

Q: Mr. Smith, in your cross-examination, when you were talking about the second fistfight, you said that it was five to ten minutes from the

---

[48] F. BUSCH, *supra* note 37, at 952-53.

time you first saw the plaintiff to the time the defendant arrived, yet on direct you said the whole incident took less than two minutes; didn't you mean five to ten seconds?

There is no reason to vary from the principle of direct examination that short, simple questions that encourage the witnesses to talk are most effective. Redirect examination can follow the same format as direct examination: direct the witness' attention to the controversy and ask the witness to explain it. For example:

Q: Mr. Smith, could you clear something up for me. Do you recall the second fistfight?
A: Yes, I do.
Q: How long did it last altogether?
A: Maybe two or three minutes.
Q: When did the defendant arrive?
A: After the plaintiff, maybe five or ten seconds later.

NOTES

1. *Dealing with unexpected hostility.* Occasionally, a witness you thought would be helpful turns on you and gives unexpected, damaging testimony. This presents a special problem. Consider FRANCIS X. BUSCH, LAW AND TACTICS IN JURY TRIALS, vol. 3: 395-96 (1960):

A few general observations, based upon observed practice, may be made. First, the advocate must maintain control of the situation at all times; by this is meant that he must keep his wits about him, and avoid any conduct likely to create the impression that his confidence in his case has been weakened by the untoward occurrence. When the examiner first senses a feeling of hostility, he should proceed warily, by well-worded, direct (but not leading) questions to show unmistakably that hostility exists. Having done this, an appeal should be made to the court to permit the further examination of the witness by leading questions.

If the witness has made a previous written statement, contradictory of the direct testimony which he has given on the stand, he should be first presented with such statement and asked to refresh his recollection. If he is disturbed by the statement and shows a disposition to adjust his present testimony to it, he should, with the court's permission, be pressed relentlessly by sharp, short leading questions, directed to each contradiction in the statement, as to whether, when he made the particular statement, it was true or false. If, on the other hand, the witness shows a disposition to repudiate the statement, and the law of the particular forum permits it, the foundation for his later impeachment should be carefully laid, as on the cross-examination of an adverse witness. In the course of the examination of such a witness, amazement and contempt at his duplicity may be as effectively registered by the manner of the examiner as by the content of his questions. It should, however, be borne in mind that "whom the gods destroy, they first make mad." Whatever the outward show, the advocate must at all times and under all conditions have his emotions under complete control. Finally, such a witness should be "dropped" at that psychological moment when the advocate feels he has reached the peak of his examination; and that is when an answer has been elicited which clearly reveals the treachery of the witness.

2. *Conducting the examination: standing or sitting?* In some courts you may be required to conduct examinations while seated, while standing, or at a lectern. In other courts you have a choice. Many lawyers think that they are supposed to stand while examining witnesses, but there is no general rule requiring it. There are advantages to standing, of course — you can place yourself in a favorable position from which you can see the judge, jury, witness and opponent; you can handle exhibits smoothly; and you can easily change positions for emphasis or to make a witness speak louder. Conducting direct examination while seated also may have advantages. If you need extensive notes or will use many exhibits, and it would be awkward to carry them with you around the courtroom, you may want to remain seated where you can refer to notes less obtrusively. *See* LEONARD PACKEL, TRIAL PRACTICE FOR THE GENERAL PRACTITIONER 9-10 (1980).

One group of social psychologists, after reviewing the social science literature, cautiously suggests that you conduct direct examination from behind the corner of the jury box farthest from the witness. This helps reduce the possibility that your witness will be seen as lacking credibility because he or she is "shifty-eyed" (witness' gaze shifts between the jurors and the attorney asking questions). If you stand behind the jurors (or at least as close to behind the jury as the walls of the courtroom permit), a witness can gaze at both the jurors and you with only minimal shifting of eye contact. Steven Penrod et al., *The Implications of Social Psychological Research for Trial Practice Attorneys,* in PSYCHOLOGY AND LAW 442 (D. Muller et al., eds., 1984).

No matter where you stand, be sure of at least one thing: do not stand between the jury and a witness or exhibit where you might block the jurors' view. *See* THOMAS A. MAUET, FUNDAMENTALS OF TRIAL TECHNIQUES 84 (3d ed. 1992).

3. *Advice about expressing emotions.* Contrary to the advice given in the main text, many lawyers say that you should not allow feelings of joy or triumph to show on your face, just like you would not display dismay. *See* MARK A. DOMBROFF, DOMBROFF ON DIRECT AND CROSS-EXAMINATION 42 (1985). Certainly this advice to keep a "poker face" is a good goal. You should not jump up and down or shout out "All right!" when you win a battle over an objection to a crucial piece of evidence. However, it is doubtful that you can suppress a fleeting grin at a victory, nor is there any real point in trying.

G. FINAL CONSIDERATION: PREPARING YOUR WITNESS FOR CROSS-EXAMINATION

You also should prepare your witnesses for cross-examination. Most trial lawyers recommend some combination of lectures or written instructions to the witnesses, and subjecting them to practice cross-examinations. The following is typical of the advice given to prospective witnesses.[49]

- *Tell the truth.* Tell the truth, the whole truth, and nothing but the truth. Do not exaggerate. Do not leave anything out.
- *Admit weaknesses.* Be honest about any weaknesses, failings, or criminal activity you are asked about on cross-examination. Don't act embarrassed or be evasive. Nobody expects you to have led a perfect life. Remember that the lawyer who asks these questions is just doing a job.
- *Give yes/no answers.* If you can answer a question "yes" or "no", do it.
- *Don't volunteer information you were not asked.* The lawyers are in charge of deciding which topics to bring up. Limit your answers to the subject matter of the question. Information you volunteer may be inadmissible under rules of evidence, which could cause the judge to rebuke you in front of the jury. That would only hurt our case. If you think something important has been left out, speak to me before you leave. You can always be re-called for more testimony.
- *Don't give explanations.* If any explanation is called for, one of the lawyers will ask for it during redirect examination.
- *You can refer to documents if you need to.* If you need to see a document in order to refresh your memory, ask for it.
- *Don't speculate or guess.* If you are not sure of the answer to a question, just say so. The lawyer may be trying to trick you into giving testimony that you are not competent to give. If you know most of the answer, but not all, say what you remember and tell the lawyer what parts you are uncertain about.
- *Keep calm.* The cross-examining lawyer may try to get you angry. When you are angry, you are likely to say things that are not true. The best thing to do is remain calm, even if questions are insulting or the lawyer is being sarcastic. Remember that if the lawyer is picking on you, the jury will be on your side.
- *Don't argue with the lawyer.* If the lawyer seems to want to pull you into an argument, don't fall for it.
- *Make sure you understand the question.* First, you must listen carefully to the whole question before answering. Then, if you don't understand it, tell the lawyer you don't understand the question.
- *Ask for clarification if you need it.* If you do not understand a question, or if the question is ambiguous, you may ask the lawyer for clarification. For example, if the lawyer asks what you were doing on a certain day, you may ask the lawyer to clarify what time of day the lawyer is asking about.
- *Beware of leading questions containing lies and half-truths.* The other lawyer will try to put words in your mouth, and will ask you to agree with his or her view of the events. Such leading questions often contain false

---

[49] Based on suggestions by Richard Givens, Advocacy: the Art of Pleading a Cause 151-55 (1980); Jeffrey Kestler, Questioning Techniques and Tactics 581-606 (2d ed. 1992); D. Lake Rumsey, *Selecting, Preparing, and Presenting the Direct Testimony of Lay Witnesses, in* Master Advocate's Handbook 88-90 (1986).

statements and half-truths. If any part of a question is false, say so. If you think your answer is misleading, say so.

- *Listen for objections and stop.* If I make an objection, stop talking immediately. Wait until the judge decides whether you should continue.
- *Beware of agreeing to exact measurements.* The cross-examining lawyer may ask you to agree to exact distances and times of events when you are uncertain. His or her suggestion may sound plausible. However, do not agree to a specific measurement unless you are personally sure the measurement is accurate.
- *Have you talked to a lawyer?* Of course you have. You have talked to me, and may have talked to the other lawyers in this case. Some cross-examiners may try to trick you by asking questions such as whether you discussed, planned, or rehearsed your testimony. If asked, tell them you talked to me. That is the truth.
- *You may be asked about prior statements.* The other lawyer may ask you to recall exactly what you said in a prior statement or deposition. If you do not remember, say so. If you wish to look at the prior statement before answering, say so. Don't be upset if there are some inconsistencies. Think about it, and make sure that your testimony reflects the truth.
- *Don't look at me.* Look at the attorney who is asking the questions, and look at the jury when giving your answers. Don't look over at me for reassurance, because the jury may think I am giving you signals.

H. BIBLIOGRAPHY

1. GENERAL

SCOTT BALDWIN, ART OF ADVOCACY — DIRECT EXAMINATION (1981).
FRANCIS X. BUSCH, LAW AND TACTICS OF JURY TRIALS, vol. 3: 1-472 (1960).
RICHARD GONZALEZ, EXAMINATION OF WITNESSES (1989).
ROBERT KEETON, TRIAL TACTICS AND METHODS 10-92 (2d ed. 1973).
FRED LANE, LANE'S GOLDSTEIN TRIAL TECHNIQUE, ch. 11 (3d ed. 1984).
PATRICK MCCLOSKEY & RONALD SCHOENBERG, CRIMINAL LAW ADVOCACY — WITNESS EXAMINATION (1992).

2. LAW

EDWARD J. IMWINKELRIED, EVIDENTIARY FOUNDATIONS (2d ed. 1989).
Joseph J. Kalo, *Refreshing Recollection: Problems with Laying a Foundation*, 10 RUT.-CAM. L.J. 233 (1979).
J. Alexander Tanford, *An Introduction to Trial Law*, 51 Mo. L. REV. 623, 656-67 (1986).

3. ETHICS

Warren E. Burger, *Standards of Conduct for Prosecution and Defense Personnel*, 5 AM. CRIM. L.Q. 11 (1966).

4. INTERVIEWING

David Binder & Susan Price, Legal Interviewing and Counseling (1977).
Robert Gorden, Interviewing: Strategy, Techniques, and Tactics (rev. ed. 1975).
Robert L. Kahn & Charles C. Cannell, The Dynamics of Interviewing (1957).

5. WITNESS PREPARATION

John Applegate, *Witness Preparation*, 68 Tex. L. Rev. 277 (1989).

6. PSYCHOLOGY

John Conley, William O'Barr & E. Allan Lind, *The Power of Language: Presentational Style in the Courtroom*, 1978 Duke L.J. 1375.
Jack Lipton, *On the Psychology of Eyewitness Testimony*, 62 J. Applied Psychol. 90 (1977).

7. TACTICS

Mark A. Dombroff, Dombroff on Direct and Cross-Examination (1985).
James W. Jeans, Litigation, ch. 10 (2d ed. 1992).
James W. Jeans, Trial Advocacy, ch. 9 (1975).
Jeffrey T. Kestler, Questioning Techniques and Tactics (2d ed 1992).
James McElhaney, *An Introduction to Direct Examination*, Litigation, Winter 1976, at 37.
James McElhaney, *More on Direct Examination*, Litigation, Fall 1981, at 43.
Louis E. Schwartz, Proof, Persuasion and Cross-Examination: A Winning New Approach in the Courtroom (1973).

Chapter 7

CROSS-EXAMINATION

A. INTRODUCTION

An aura of mystery and excitement seems to surround cross-examination. Television dramas portray cross-examinations as exercises in pyrotechnics, in which the lawyer asks hostile and sarcastic questions, mixed with clever asides to the jury. Cross-examination causes Captain Queeg to reveal his mental instability in *The Caine Mutiny*; it wrings a confession from the defendant's wife in *Witness for the Prosecution* that she has been lying to frame her husband. This may make good theater — the dramatic confrontation between good and evil — but it hardly paints an accurate portrait of cross-examination. The reality is less exciting. Rarely in your career will you ever have to face a scheming, dishonest witness, knowing that you must break that witness' testimony in order to save an innocent client.

If cross-examination is not usually a battle of wits between a scheming witness and a clever attorney, how should it be understood? Like direct examination, it is primarily a method of eliciting testimony from a witness. Its success depends not on your ability to ask clever questions, but on the answers actually given. Cross-examination can best be understood by describing how it differs from other phases of the trial.

- Cross-examination is often difficult or impossible to rehearse. Witnesses called by your opponent sometimes will refuse to talk to you at all, and they frequently will refuse to participate in the kind of rehearsals you engage in with your own witnesses.
- Cross-examination follows direct examination, so the witness will have told his or her story once before you can ask any questions. All the answers you were seeking may already be in evidence, or the testimony you expected to be elicited on direct examination may have been omitted.
- Cross-examination occurs in the midst of your opponent's case. Its timing allows you to raise issues of your own during the presentation of the adverse evidence, but may separate the issues from related testimony in your case-in-chief by a large time gap.
- Because of its popular image, jurors usually expect cross-examination to be antagonistic. This preconception means that you occasionally can mount a ruthless attack on a witness' credibility without necessarily arousing the anger of the jurors.
- The witness on the stand also may expect the cross-examination to be antagonistic. Normal courtesy might come as a surprise and disarm a hostile witness more effectively than aggression. You also should expect the witness to be defensive, and perhaps unfriendly toward or uncooperative with you, if he or she expects you to attack.

You will notice that the list of differences does not include that cross-examination is spontaneous or unplanned. Indeed, the characteristics that distinguish cross-examination from other phases of the trial make thorough preparation essential. Your inability to rehearse a cross-examination, coupled with the potential hostility of the witness, means that you must work especially hard in advance to assure that witnesses will testify in helpful ways. Trial practitioners basically agree on several fundamental techniques for accomplishing this:

- If you cannot rehearse your examination with a witness, you must find another source for determining what that person is likely to say on the stand — usually depositions, written statements, or interviews.
- You cannot expect to be able to prep an opposing witness to improve the quality of his or her testimony, so you must build suggestions carefully into your questions.
- Since your opponent usually will conduct a thorough direct examination, you can limit the scope of your cross-examination to a few favorable points. You need not worry about cluttering up your examination with inconsequential details to fill in the background. If you focus on only a few important topics, you can take maximum advantage of the opportunity to remind the jury of your side of the case and increase the likelihood that the points will be remembered until you can tie them into your case-in-chief.
- Because the witness, especially a partisan witness, may expect you to attack and is likely to be hostile, your cross-examination must be planned carefully to control the examination and limit the witness' opportunity to repeat testimony that favors the other side.

Despite thorough preparation, cross-examination is still an uncertain phase of the trial process during which disconcerting things are likely to happen. It is the paradigm of the gladiatorial aspect of litigation, and you can anticipate occasional unexpected thrusts and parries from witnesses. Many lawyers believe that it is often the witness who comes out ahead if you get into unplanned skirmishes. One of the great nineteenth-century lawyers, Joseph Donovan, observed that "more good cases are ruined by [unwise] cross-examination than by any other cause."[1] My own experience in 15 years of watching law students conduct their first trials is that his observation is still valid 100 years later.

The goal of this chapter is to provide you with a solid theoretical base upon which you can build effective cross-examinations, thereby helping you avoid ruining your own cases through unwise cross-examination. At a minimum, you must remember that cross-examination is only one small part of the trial, and you cannot win the entire case with one devastating interrogation.

---

[1] JOSEPH DONOVAN, TACT IN COURT 102 (1898).

B. EXAMPLE OF A CROSS-EXAMINATION

The next few pages contain an illustrative example of cross-examination in a personal injury case, *Blake v. Dillon*. The plaintiff has alleged that, as he was crossing a street, he was struck and injured because of the defendant's negligent driving. The defendant claims that the plaintiff stepped out suddenly from between two parked cars. An eyewitness, Ms. Rogers, is called by the plaintiff. She says on direct examination that she saw the accident; the defendant was traveling seventy miles per hour; the victim was knocked fifty feet; the defendant's car traveled 150 feet before it stopped, and when the defendant got out of his car, he appeared to be drunk. The defendant's cross-examination follows:[2]

Q: Ms. Rogers, I'll try not to take too long, as I know you have other things to do. On the day of the accident, were you looking out your window at about 7:15 p.m.?

A: Yes, when the accident happened.

Q: And you kept watching immediately after the accident?

A: Yes.

Q: Did you see the driver get out of his car?

A: Yes.

Q: Did you get a good look at him?

A: Yes.

Q: You're sure it was my client, Mr. Dillon?

A: Oh, yes.

Q: Did you watch him for several seconds, then?

A: Yes. He got out of his car and walked quickly up to the front of it and knelt down by Mr. Blake's body.

Q: Did Mr. Dillon go straight to where Mr. Blake was lying?

A: Yes.

Q: He didn't fall down, did he?

A: What?

Q: Mr. Dillon didn't fall down, did he?

A: No.

Q: And he didn't stagger around?

A: No.

Q: And he appeared to be walking quickly but normally, is that right?

A: Yes.

Q: Just before the accident, what were you looking at?

A: I don't know. I was just looking at the street.

Q: There were cars parked on Woodlawn, weren't there?

A: Yes.

Q: There were cars parked on the far side of the street?

A: Yes.

Q: That would be the south side, wouldn't it?

A: Yes.

---

[2] Adapted from FRANCIS X. BUSCH, LAW AND TACTICS IN JURY TRIALS vol. 3: 847-53 (1960). Much of Mr. Busch's original cross-examination has been quoted directly.

Q: Between your house and the corner?

A: Yes.

Q: Weren't they parked close together?

A: Yes.

Q: Woodlawn runs west to east, doesn't it?

A: I think so, I'm not very good at directions.

Q: Ms. Rogers, how long have you known the plaintiff?

A: Well, I didn't know him very well before the accident.

Q: But you do know him?

A: Slightly, yes.

Q: Do you know where he lives?

A: Yes, sir.

Q: Do you know any members of his family?

A: I know he has a wife and daughter.

Q: You knew his wife, didn't you?

A: I had met her.

Q: Where?

A: At a PTA meeting a few years ago.

Q: Did you know the daughter?

A: Yes.

Q: How old is she?

A: Sixteen.

Q: You have a fifteen-year-old daughter, don't you?

A: She will be sixteen in June.

Q: Your daughter and the plaintiff's daughter are friends, aren't they?

A: Yes, I think you could call them friends.

Q: The Blake girl visited in your home before the accident, correct?

A: Yes.

Q: Many times?

A: Oh, I don't know how many times.

Q: Give us some idea — a dozen times, maybe?

A: Well, possibly that many; maybe more.

Q: Ms. Rogers, do you consider yourself a good judge of distance?

A: I think I'm average.

Q: Well, let's see about that for a moment. How far would you say it is from where you are sitting to the rear of the courtroom — the far wall over there?

A: Oh, I would say about 100 feet.

Defendant's Attorney: Your Honor, I have a tape measure here. I wonder if Your Honor would allow your bailiff to hold one end of it while we measure that distance?

Court: That will not be necessary. It has been measured before. The distance is 44 feet.

Q: Now about the collision. The window in your house that you were looking out of is an ordinary two-sash window, isn't it; not one of those wide picture windows?

A: Yes, it's an ordinary window you can raise or let down from the top.

Q: Would you say about this wide (indicating with hands)?

A: Yes.

Defendant's Attorney: Can we agree that that distance is between 2½ and 3 feet?

Court: A little less than 3 feet, I would say.

Plaintiff's Attorney: That's fine.

Q: That window faced south, didn't it?

A: Yes.

Q: And the window is west of the entrance to your house. Is that right?

A: Yes.

Q: Showing you defense exhibit A (photograph of front of house), this accurately shows your house and that window, doesn't it?

A: It shows the house and two windows.

Q: As you count from east to west, or right to left on exhibit A, your window is the second window?

A: Yes.

Q: And you were standing right in front of that window?

A: Yes.

Q: Standing in the front of that window, you could not see all the way down to the crosswalk. Is that correct?

A: I don't know. You have probably tried that out, and I don't want you to mix me up.

Q: I am not trying to mix you up, Ms. Rogers. I am just asking you if from where you were standing at that window you could see all the way to the end of the block, to the west crosswalk?

A: Maybe not. I don't know.

Q: This whole thing — the accident, I mean — happened very quickly, didn't it?

A: Yes, it did.

Q: The defendant's car was in your view for only a second or two, correct?

A: Yes. Not very long.

Q: Now, you said you thought Mr. Dillon might have appeared drunk. Did you go out of your house after this accident occurred?

A: No.

Q: Of course, from where you were with the window between you and the man out in the street, you could not smell his breath?

A: Of course not.

Q: And you could not hear the driver say anything, could you?

A: No.

Q: Nor see whether his eyes were bloodshot?

A: No.

Q: Your statement then that he might have been drunk is simply your conclusion, not based on anything specific that you saw, heard, or smelled?

A: Yes.

Q: Sometime after the accident you learned that it was Mr. Blake that was hurt?

A: Yes.

Q: From whom did you hear it?
A: My daughter told me, and then I went to see Mrs. Blake and she told me.
Q: And then you told her that you had seen the accident?
A: Yes.
Q: And that you would be a witness for Mr. Blake?
A: Not then, but later Mrs. Blake and their lawyer came to see me, and told me I would be a witness for them.
Q: And you said you would be glad to be a witness for Mr. Blake, isn't that right?
A: Well, not until after the lawyer talked to me and told me I could help Mr. Blake.
Defendant's Attorney: That is all, Ms. Rogers.

NOTE

Sample cross-examinations. Several sample cross-examinations can be found in THOMAS A. MAUET, FUNDAMENTALS OF TRIAL TECHNIQUES 226-34 (3d ed. 1992); and JAMES JEANS, LITIGATION §§ 15.33-15.34 (2d ed. 1992).

C. LEGAL FRAMEWORK

1. THE RIGHT TO CROSS-EXAMINE

It is safe to say that all litigants have the right to cross-examine witnesses who give adverse testimony. For defendants facing criminal charges, this right is found in the Sixth Amendment guarantee that the accused has the right "to be confronted with the witnesses against him." In civil cases, the right to cross-examine is part of the fundamental due process to which all parties are entitled. However, this does not mean that cross-examination is completely unbridled in scope and duration. A party is entitled to a full and fair opportunity to cross-examine, but not to raise irrelevant issues or to mislead the jury.

In *Mattox v. United States*,[3] the Supreme Court held that under no circumstances shall the accused be deprived of the right to subject prosecution witnesses to the ordeal of a cross-examination. In *Pointer v. Texas*, the Court stated: "[I]t cannot seriously be doubted at this late date that the right of cross-examination is included in the right of an accused in a criminal case to confront the witnesses against him."[4] This right includes the opportunity to test the recollection and sift the conscience of the witness, and to give the jury the chance to view the witness' demeanor.

Other parties also have the fundamental right to cross-examine witnesses called by their opponents. The prosecutor is entitled to cross-examine defense witnesses, including the defendant, if he or she has waived the privilege against self-incrimination by giving direct testimony.[5] In civil cases, refusal to allow cross-examination on relevant matters covered during direct testimony

---

[3] 156 U.S. 237, 244 (1895).
[4] 380 U.S. 400, 404 (1965).
[5] *See Trawick v. State*, 431 So. 2d 574 (Ala. App. 1983); *Viener v. State*, 257 S.E.2d 22 (Ga. 1979).

is a denial of a fundamental right and is usually a sufficient ground for reversal on appeal. While a judge has more discretion to limit cross-examination in civil cases, the judge may do so only after a party has had a fair and substantial opportunity to exercise the right.[6]

This fundamental guarantee is accompanied by a few secondary rules of law designed to assure its enforcement. The right of cross-examination encompasses not merely the right to ask questions, but also the right to elicit testimony. A witness can and should be compelled by the judge to answer proper questions. Continued refusal to answer may subject the witness to punishment for contempt. In extreme cases, where cross-examination is effectively denied, the court may strike out all or part of the direct examination[7] or grant a mistrial — even if the denial of an opportunity for full cross-examination is no one's fault.[8]

2. CROSS-EXAMINATION PROCEDURE

As a general rule, cross-examination follows the completion of the direct examination, although it is within the discretion of the trial judge to allow the cross-examination to take place at another time. The most common deviation from the usual order is the "voir dire" examination. Judges generally will allow brief cross-examination concerning the admissibility of evidence — the qualifications of a proposed expert, the authenticity or chain of custody of an exhibit, or the foundation for a hearsay exception — at the time it is offered during direct examination.[9] A judge also may allow a party to re-call a witness for further cross-examination later in the trial, either because a subsequent witness' testimony opens up new matters, or the cross-examiner realizes he or she simply forgot to ask an important question the first time.[10] The timing of cross-examination rests completely in the discretion of the trial judge.

Leading questions are generally permitted throughout cross-examination, although the judge has discretion to stop an interrogation that appears to be eliciting unreliable or distorted evidence. Contrary to what you see on television, however, you may not ask misleading or trick questions, nor frame your questions in such a way as to elicit half-truths and distortions. Questions that misquote a witness, assume facts not in evidence, are compound, or are argumentative, are impermissible. The rules concerning proper question form are discussed in detail in Chapter 5, part B, § 3.

The right to ask leading questions carries with it the right to insist that the witness give direct, responsive and limited answers. If your question was fair and simple, you usually may have all unresponsive and evasive portions of an answer stricken from the record. However, the witness generally will be al-

---

[6]*See, e.g., Kekua v. Kaiser Hosp.*, 601 P.2d 364 (Haw. 1979).

[7]*E.g., Lawson v. Murray*, 837 F.2d 653 (4th Cir. 1988).

[8]*See Henderson v. Twin Falls Co.*, 80 P.2d 801 (Idaho 1938) (witness died before cross-examination could be completed). *Cf. United States v. Siefert*, 648 F.2d 557 (9th Cir. 1980) (witness asserted Fifth Amendment privilege to only a few questions, answered the rest, no mistrial).

[9]*See, e.g., Martin v. State*, 251 Ind. 587, 244 N.E.2d 100 (1969) (preliminary cross-examination on competence allowed before direct examination).

[10]*See People v. Lewis*, 180 Colo. 423, 506 P.2d 125 (1973); *Parham v. State*, 53 Wis. 2d 458, 192 N.W.2d 838 (1972).

lowed to give a relevant explanation if neither a "yes" or "no" would be accurate.

3. SCOPE OF CROSS-EXAMINATION

There are two different rules on the permissible scope of cross-examination. A majority of jurisdictions limit cross-examination to the issues raised on direct. However, a sizeable minority follows the English practice of allowing cross-examination on any issue relevant to the trial.

FED. R. EVID. 611(b) states the majority rule: "Cross-examination should be limited to the subject matter of the direct examination and matters affecting the credibility of the witness." There are innumerable variations on this rule, and its interpretation and enforcement are matters of judicial discretion. The strict view, which originated in *Philadelphia & T.R. Co. v. Stimpson*,[11] is that your right to cross-examine a witness only extends to facts and circumstances connected to matters brought up on direct and to the general credibility of the witness. If you wish to inquire into other relevant matters, you must call the witness on direct examination in your own case. Rule 611(b) has modified the federal practice somewhat, by giving the judge discretion to permit cross-examination into new matters "as if on direct examination," i.e., without the benefit of leading questions. Another common variation is the so-called "Michigan rule."[12] This version permits inquiry into matters raised on direct and anything that will modify, explain, or rebut what was said or implied. Under this rule, it is the tendency of the direct examination that determines the scope of cross, not the particular facts and circumstances to which the witness testified.

The English rule, followed in a number of states, permits wide open cross-examination on any relevant issue, whether or not it was inquired about during direct examination. Under this variation, you not only may pursue issues brought out on direct, but also may use the full power of leading questions to elicit facts on new topics that form part of your own affirmative case.

Regardless of which rule is followed, all jurisdictions permit cross-examination that tests the credibility of the witness and the weight to be given his or her testimony. Although not every jurisdiction permits all of them, courts recognize at least nine categories of permissible impeachment:[13]

- Lack of opportunity or physical inability to reliably perceive the events about which the witness testified.
- Memory problems, either inherent in an event long past or particular to the witness.
- Distortions caused by a witness's poor communication skills.
- Bias, interest, prejudice, or other emotional traits that could cause a witness to testify falsely.
- Prior criminal convictions.
- Prior acts of misconduct reflecting adversely on veracity.

[11] 39 U.S. (14 Pet.) 448 (1840).
[12] So called because it was announced in *Campau v. Dewey*, 9 Mich. 381 (1861).
[13] *See* Irving Younger, *The Art of Cross-Examination 2-16* (ABA LITIGATION SECTION MONOGRAPH No. 1, 1976).

- Prior inconsistent statements.
- A bad reputation in the community for truth and veracity.
- Lack of the moral or religious belief necessary to feel obligated by the oath.

4. USING DIAGRAMS AND EXHIBITS

Although exhibits normally are associated with direct examination, in some situations they may be used on cross-examination as well. Any document, photograph, chart, map, model, or other exhibit introduced during the direct may be referred to on cross-examination. Such an exhibit may be shown again to the witness and further questions may be asked about it. If the direct examiner used a blackboard or other illustrative exhibit without formally introducing it, that exhibit similarly may be used. Objects and documents referred to during direct, but not introduced, usually can be produced and offered into evidence on cross-examination.

The more difficult question is whether new exhibits may be offered into evidence during cross-examination. Certain types of collateral exhibits usually are permitted: documents may be used to refresh memory, and prior inconsistent statements and certified records of criminal convictions may be offered to impeach.[14] However, there may be restrictions on your ability to introduce new substantive exhibits. The matter lies in the discretion of the trial judge and is related to the rules governing the scope of cross-examination. In states that have wide-open cross-examination, new exhibits probably will be allowed. In jurisdictions that have rules restricting the scope of cross, there are different interpretations. Some judges think that a new exhibit is per se beyond the scope of the direct, and therefore must wait until the cross-examiner's case-in-chief or rebuttal. Other courts have held that if the general subject matter is relevant to issues brought out during direct testimony or if they are used to impeach, then new exhibits properly may be introduced during cross-examination.[15] The introduction of new exhibits, whether substantive or merely impeaching, may constitute opening your case, thereby waiving the right to make a directed verdict motion.[16] The practice with regard to new exhibits is likely to vary considerably from jurisdiction to jurisdiction.

5. RECROSS EXAMINATION

If your adversary conducts a redirect examination, then you may ask the court for permission to conduct recross examination. The court has discretion to permit or refuse it. Unlike the primary cross-examination, recross is not a matter of right unless new matters have been raised by the redirect.[17] When permitted, recross usually is limited strictly to issues raised on redirect. How-

---

[14] *See, e.g.*, FED. R. EVID. 609 (impeachment by evidence of conviction of crime); FED. R. EVID. 613(b) (extrinsic evidence of prior inconsistent statement of witness).

[15] *See, e.g., Kellerher v. Porter*, 20 Wash. 2d 650, 189 P.2d 223 (1948).

[16] *See Grimsley v. State*, 304 So. 2d 493 (Fla. App. 1974) (defendant lost right to open and close argument by introducing an exhibit during cross-examination).

[17] *See Kinser v. Cooper*, 413 F.2d 730 (6th Cir. 1969).

ever, it is within the discretion of the judge to allow recross on matters inadvertently omitted from the primary cross-examination; it is also within the judge's discretion not to permit it.

NOTES

1. *When a witness does not answer questions.* Whether the direct examination must be stricken from the record because of the witness' failure to submit to cross-examination is largely a discretionary decision for the trial judge. It depends not on whether the witness was justified in not answering, but on whether it is fair to permit the direct to stand unchallenged. *Compare Villegas v. State,* 791 S.W.2d 226 (Tex. App. 1990), (claiming Fifth Amendment privilege requires striking direct *with People v. Chin,* 67 N.Y.2d 22, 490 N.E.2d 505 (1986) (a Fifth Amendment claim does not require striking of direct). *Compare Stephan v. United States,* 133 F.2d 87 (6th Cir. 1943) (refusal to answer questions for no reason, direct not stricken) *with Commonwealth v. Kirouac,* 542 N.E.2d 270 (Mass. 1989) (unjustified refusal to answer questions required direct to be stricken).

2. *When a witness gives unresponsive answers.* At the other extreme is the witness who answers more than he or she was asked or who gives unresponsive answers to cross-examination questions. While the rules against misleading questions allow a witness to explain some answers, the witness must remain responsive to the question asked. In many jurisdictions, the cross-examiner may move to strike the unresponsive part of a witness' answer. *See City of Indianapolis v. Heeter,* 355 N.E.2d 429 (Ind. App. 1976).

3. *Scope of cross-examination of criminal defendant.* The majority rule limiting the scope of cross-examination to matters raised during direct is premised in part on the ability of the cross-examiner to call the witness for direct examination. What happens under limited-scope rules if a criminal defendant takes the stand, but limits his or her testimony to only one of the material issues? The prosecution would seem to be prohibited by the Fifth Amendment from calling the defendant as a witness against himself or herself for direct examination (although one can argue that the defendant waived this protection by testifying), and by the rules of scope from pursuing the other issues during cross. There is a split of opinion. Most judges probably would allow broader cross-examination of a defendant than of other witnesses because a defendant cannot be re-called. However, appellate courts tend to state that the rule is the same for defendants as for other witnesses: a defendant subjects himself to cross-examination to the same extent as any other witness, "but he does not subject himself to cross-examination and impeachment to any greater extent." *Tucker v. United States,* 5 F.2d 818, 822 (8th Cir. 1925). *See also United States v. Palmer,* 536 F.2d 1278 (9th Cir. 1976) (claim of alibi opened door to cross-examination about motive); *People v. Zerillo,* 36 Cal. 2d 222, 223 P.2d 223 (1950) (general denial of guilt permits wide scope of cross). For a discussion of cross-examination of defendants under a wide-open scope rule, *see Neely v. State,* 272 N.W.2d 381 (Wis. App. 1978).

4. *Interpretation of limited scope rules.* The degree to which the limited scope rule is enforced varies considerably from jurisdiction to jurisdiction and

from case to case. In *McNeely v. Conlon*, 216 Iowa 796, 248 N.W. 17 (1933), the court took a very narrow view. A witness testified on direct about the facts of an accident and about going up to the victim, who was lying in the street. The court held that the victim's spontaneous statement overheard by the witness at that time was beyond the scope of the issues raised by the direct. However, in another Iowa case, *Eno v. Adair Cty. Mut. Ins. Ass'n*, 229 Iowa 249, 294 N.W. 323 (1940), the court adopted a broad view. A witness testified on direct about the existence of an insurance contract and about having seen plaintiff's severely damaged barn. Questions about the origin of the fire that caused the damage were held to be within the scope of that limited direct examination.

5. *Inadmissible evidence received during direct examination.* Inadmissible evidence may be admitted during direct examination if you do not object. The fact that it is admitted does not automatically create a right to cross-examine on that subject — cross-examination is limited to matters both within the scope of direct and which are relevant to the controversy. The rationale behind this restriction is that pursuing irrelevant matters would only multiply the inadmissible evidence. *See People v. McDaniel*, 59 Cal. App. 2d 672, 140 P.2d 88 (1943).

6. *Using your opponent's exhibits.* It frequently is suggested in books on tactics that you should use diagrams introduced by your adversary so that any inconsistencies are clearly marked on the adversary's own exhibit. Is it proper to mark up an exhibit introduced by the other side? There is very little case law on the subject. The matter is probably within the judge's discretion, and permission often will be granted provided that the purpose is legitimate. *See* ROBERT KEETON, TRIAL TACTICS AND METHODS § 3.16 (2d ed. 1973).

D. ETHICAL CONSIDERATIONS

1. INTENTIONAL VIOLATION OF PROPER CROSS-EXAMINATION PROCEDURE

MODEL RULES OF PROFESSIONAL CONDUCT Rule 3.4(c) states that a lawyer shall not "knowingly disobey an obligation under the rules of a tribunal." It is therefore unethical to intentionally conduct improper cross-examination. Contrary to what you see on television, you may not ask an improper question or make an insinuation, and then withdraw it if your opponent objects. Your withdrawal may satisfy the law by removing improper matter from the jury's consideration, but it is still unethical. Under this general concept, it is unethical to:

- Make gratuitous sarcastic remarks. For example:
    Q: You say the suspect ran east?
    A: Yes.
    Q: Toward the river?
    A: Yes.
    Q: So the river has moved to the east side of town?
    A: Excuse me?
    Q: Don't you mean he ran west?
    A: I guess so.

Q: Have you flown your own airplane?

A: What? No.

Q: I recommend that you don't.

• Ask an argumentative question. For example:

Q: You seem to be having difficulty remembering the details. Who told you to have a faulty memory?

• Ask a witness to comment on some other witness' testimony.[18] For example:

Q: Mary Jones says it was 3:30 when you left the bookstore, not 4:00. Is she lying?

• Assume facts not in evidence or misquote direct testimony.

2. REQUIREMENT OF A "GOOD FAITH" BASIS FOR QUESTIONS

The MODEL CODE OF PROFESSIONAL CONDUCT requires a good faith basis for any question asked on cross-examination. Rule 3.4(e) provides:

A lawyer shall not in trial, allude to any matter that the lawyer does not reasonably believe is relevant or that will not be supported by admissible evidence.

The good-faith basis test has two parts. First, you must have a *factual* basis for the question. You must be in possession of reliable information that the underlying fact is true. Even an innocuous question, such as: "Have you ever been convicted of a crime?" ethically may not be asked unless you have some indication that the witness has been convicted. The very act of asking such a question may cause jurors to assume there is some truth to it. If the witness denies it, the potential danger is compounded. The jurors may think that the witness not only committed a crime, but also lied by denying it.

Second, you must have a *legal* basis for the question. You must have a reasonable belief that the matter is admissible under the rules of evidence. Thus, it is unethical to ask a witness if he or she has been convicted of drunk driving (even if true) if the rules of evidence limit impeachment to felonies and crimes of dishonesty.[19] You may not ask a question alluding to inadmissible or imaginary evidence, and then "withdraw" it if the other side objects. As one court put it, it is improper for an attorney to ask a question "which he knows and every judge and lawyer knows to be wholly inadmissible and wrong."[20]

The good-faith-basis rule is backed up by two other ethics rules. Rule 4.4 prohibits using cross-examination to harass, embarrass, or degrade a witness.

---

[18] *Cf.* RICHARD UNDERWOOD & WILLIAM FORTUNE, TRIAL ETHICS 350-51 (1988) (may be proper in some jurisdictions).

[19] *See, e.g.,* FED. R. EVID. 609. *See also Hawk v. Superior Ct.,* 42 Cal. App. 3d 108, 116 Cal. Rptr. 713 (1974) (lawyer held in contempt for deliberately asking a question about an inadmissible misdemeanor conviction).

[20] *People v. Wells,* 100 Cal. 459, 462, 34 P. 1078, 1079 (1893). Of course, lawyers and judges will frequently have legitimate disagreements on whether evidence is admissible. It is not unethical to have asked a question just because an objection was sustained.

It requires that lawyers respect the rights of third persons, including witnesses being cross-examined. It prohibits using any means "that have no
substantial purpose other than to embarrass" a witness. Rule 3.3(a) states
that a lawyer shall not "make a false statement of material fact" nor "offer
evidence that the lawyer knows to be false."

Consider the ethics of the following cross-examination, from ARTHUR TRAIN,
YANKEE LAWYER: THE AUTOBIOGRAPHY OF EPHRAIM TUTT 364-69 (1943):

I had been assigned to the defense of a man named Mooney who had
served a short prison term and was now charged with carrying a con-
cealed weapon — a convenient method sometimes availed of by the police
to get rid of undesirable citizens. It is enough for present purposes for me
to say simply that the case against my client was of the flimsiest character, but Delaney the policeman, who had made the arrest, had urged the
prosecutor to convict him if he could. Now while the only testimony
against Mooney was that of the officer who claimed that he had taken a
loaded pistol from his pocket — which he may well have done after first
placing it there — it was legally enough; and unless Mooney took the
stand and denied that the weapon was his, the jury would have practically no choice. So I put him on the stand.

The prosecutor was my ancient enemy Francis Patrick O'Brien, and the
fact that I was for the defense made him more than ever zealous for a
conviction. Having proved that Mooney was an ex-convict, he asked:

"You come from the Gas House district, don't you?"

"No," replied Mooney.

"Ever hear of the Gas House gang?"

"Yes, but I'm not one of them."

"Oh, you're not, eh? I didn't ask you that. Why were you in such a hurry
to slip that in?"

"Because," retorted Mooney, "you were trying to make the jury think I
was."

"Maybe you're right!" replied O'Brien with a grin. "Now, how many
times have you been convicted of crimes in other states?"

"Never!" cried Mooney indignantly, "and you can't prove it, either!"

"Well, maybe I can't prove it," admitted O'Brien, "but," he added
insinuatingly, "I can inquire how many times you have committed burglaries — say in New Jersey."

"I never committed any burglary."

"No burglaries? What kind of crimes, then, have you committed?"

"None!" declared Mooney defiantly.

And then O'Brien pulled the dirtiest trick in court that has ever come
to my attention. He took a copy of Inspector Byrnes' Professional Criminals of America and, holding it so that the jury could plainly see the title,
opened it and ran his finger down a page as if reading what he had found
there.

"Did you not, on September 6, 1927," he demanded, "in company with
Red Birch, alias the Roach, Toni Sevelli, otherwise known as Toni the
Greaser, and Dynamite Tom Meeghan, crack the safe of the American

Railway Express at Rahway, New Jersey, and get away with six thousand dollars?"

Mooney leaped to his feet.

"It's a lie!" he shouted. "I never knew any such people. I never was in Rahway in my life!"

"So you say!" taunted O'Brien. "But don't you know that both the Roach and the Greaser swore you were there?"

Bang! went Babcock's gavel....

"That's all," said O'Brien, ostentatiously tossing Professional Criminals of America on the table in front of the jury box.

"If the Court please," I said, "for some reason the district attorney has not seen fit to offer in evidence the loaded pistol which Officer Delaney has produced here and swears he found in the defendant's pocket. Unless this is done I shall move to dismiss."

O'Brien arose languidly.

"The merest oversight, Your Honor! I offer the pistol in evidence."

"I object unless it is made to appear upon the record from whose custody it is produced, how it got here and that it is in the same condition as when received," I said.

"Mr. Tutt is technically correct," ruled Judge Babcock. "If he insists you will have to be sworn."

"I do insist," I said.

So O'Brien with the pistol in his hand ascended the stand, took the oath, and testified that it was in precisely the same condition as when delivered to him a few days before by Delaney.

"Have you any cross-examination?" inquired His Honor.

"I have," I replied. "Are you one of the public prosecutors of this county, Mr. O'Brien?"

"I am," he snapped. "As you very well know."

"And you are sworn to prosecute those of whose guilt you are satisfied, through the introduction of legal evidence in a legal manner?"

"Correct."

"Where were you born?" I asked.

"New York City."

"Do you come from the Gas House section?"

One of the jury sniggered and the judge raised a finger in admonition.

"Your question seems rather unnecessary, Mr. Tutt."

"This is cross-examination," I answered. "But I will withdraw it. How much did you pay for your appointment as assistant district attorney?"

Judge Babcock brought down his gavel.

"That will do. The jury will disregard the question."

"I have as much right to attack this witness' credibility as he has to attack that of my client," I asserted stoutly. "Did you not pay five thousand dollars to Michael McGurk to be delivered to Joseph Morrison in consideration of your appointment?"

"I did not!" shouted O'Brien. "Is Your Honor going to permit me to be insulted in this way?"

But a bewildered look had settled upon the learned justice's counte-
nance. Wasn't what was sauce for the goose sauce for the gander?

"Haven't you regularly contributed ten per cent of your salary each
month to the treasury of Tammany Hall?" I persisted.

His Honor flushed. That was getting near home.

"Kindly answer the question," I said.

"I object," roared O'Brien.

"Only a few more trifling questions, Mr. O'Brien," I went on.

"Have you ever been convicted of a crime?"

"No!" he replied, but he had turned unexpectedly gray.

"Have you ever committed one?" O'Brien choked.

"I won't force you to answer that," I continued.

But Babcock thought he saw his chance.

"Have you any basis for that question?" he demanded sharply.

I smiled at the jury and then at the bench.

"Your Honor," I said, "you and I belong to a generation which has old-
fashioned ideas of honor. Honor demands that I admit having no basis for
most of the questions which I have just asked this witness; yet, in a sense,
honor demanded that I should ask them, although I might later have to
disown their sincerity. But, sir, I do not abandon my attack upon this
witness' credibility. I have but one more question to ask him and upon his
answer I stake my client's liberty. Let him answer any way he sees fit —
yes, or no, I care not which — let him make any reply at all which may be
officially recorded here and not hereafter be disputed or denied by him —
and this jury may return a verdict against my client. — It is this: Mr.
O'Brien, when you took that book in your hand" — and I lifted Byrne's
Professional Criminals from where it lay upon the table — "and pretended to read from its pages, were you reading something that was
printed there or not? YES — or NO!"

In the silence that followed all those in the courtroom could distinctly
hear the ticking of the clock upon the rear wall.

"Tick-tock! Tick-tock! Tick-tock!" — "Yes-no! Yes-no! Yes-no!"

O'Brien squirmed and gazed at the floor.

"Tick-tock! Tick-tock!" went the clock.

"Yes — or no! Yes — or no!" I echoed.

O'Brien hung on dead center. If he answered "Yes" — insisted that he
had been reading from the book — I would have put it in evidence and
sent him up for perjury. Yet if he answered "No" — admitted that he had
made the whole thing up — that there was not a word about Mooney in
the book at all — it would be almost as bad....

O'Brien moistened his lips and swallowed twice. He coughed and fum-
bled for his handkerchief. After all, I could see him thinking, he had done
nothing that was not strictly legal. He had not charged that Mooney was
a professional crook; he had only asked him the question. You could ask
anything you chose so long as you were bound by the witness' answer.
Wouldn't that save him? Then that hope faded. While I might be bound by
his answer in the case at bar he would be forever bound by the written

record. He could never get rid of the millstone his yes or no would hang about his neck. I could have him disbarred.

"No," he muttered in a woolly voice, so low as hardly to be audible. "I — was — not — reading from the book."

A more difficult question arises if the cross-examiner asks a question out of ignorance. Advocates of the "fishing expedition" type of cross-examination say that sometimes you may have to probe, searching for a ground to impeach the witness. Can you ask the witness, for instance, whether he or she has biases against your client if you are sincerely searching for relevant information? If your question is neutral ("How do you feel about my client?"), it probably is ethical because you are not suggesting the existence of specific facts. However, if your question suggests an answer ("You hate my client, don't you?"), you must have a good-faith basis for it. If you have no idea what the witness' answer will be, that basis is absent.

3. DISCREDITING A TRUTHFUL WITNESS

Is it proper to try to discredit a witness whom you know to be telling the truth? This is one of the most troubling ethical questions, especially for criminal defense attorneys. If you try to convince the jury that a truthful witness is mistaken, are you not violating MODEL CODE OF PROFESSIONAL CONDUCT Rule 3.3's prohibition against offering false evidence, Rule 3.4's good-faith-basis test, and Rule 4.4's requirement of fairness toward the witness?

Professor Monroe Freedman thinks there is nothing unethical about discrediting such a witness. In *Professional Responsibility of the Criminal Defense Lawyer: the Three Hardest Questions*,[21] Freedman poses the following hypothetical:

> Your client has been falsely accused of a robbery committed at 16th and P Streets at 11:00 p.m. He tells you [he was in the vicinity] at 10:55 that evening, but that he was walking east, away from the scene of the crime, and that, by 11:00 p.m., he was six blocks away. At the trial, there are two prosecution witnesses. The first mistakenly, but with some degree of persuasion, identifies your client as the criminal.... The second prosecution witness is an elderly woman who is somewhat nervous and who wears glasses. She testifies truthfully and accurately that she saw your client at 15th and P Streets at 10:55 p.m. She has corroborated the erroneous testimony of the first witness and made conviction virtually certain.

Can you attempt to destroy the witness' credibility through cross-examination designed to show that she is easily confused and has poor eyesight, so she probably is mistaken in her identification? Freedman concludes that you should:

> [I]f you should refuse to cross-examine her because she is telling the truth, your client may well feel betrayed, since you knew of the witness'

――――――――――
[21] 64 MICH. L. REV. 1469, 1474-75 (1966). Professor Freedman has amplified his views in MONROE FREEDMAN, LAWYERS' ETHICS IN AN ADVERSARY SYSTEM (1975).

veracity only because your client confided in you, under your assurance
that his truthfulness would not prejudice him. [T]he same policy that
supports the obligation of confidentiality precludes the attorney from
prejudicing his client's interest in any other way because of knowledge
gained in his professional capacity. [If] a lawyer fails to cross-examine
only because his client ... has been candid with him, [the lawyer is using
those confidences against his client.] The client's confidences must "upon
all occasions be inviolable," to avoid the "greater mischiefs" that would
probably result if a client could not feel free "to repose [confidence] in the
attorney to whom he resorts for legal advice and assistance."[22] Destroy
that confidence, and "a man would not venture to consult any skillful
person, or would only dare to tell his counsellor half his case."[23]

Therefore, Freedman concludes, the attorney is obligated to attack the reliability or credibility of the witness.

Professor John Noonan disagrees. He asserts that the only way to justify Freedman's view is to hold the view that a trial is only a modern form of trial by battle. He argues that a trial should be something more dignified.

Professor Freedman ... has merely expressed as a norm what is, in fact,
current practice for some practitioners.... [However, a] more appropriate
view of a trial and of the adversary system is the view endorsed in 1958
by the Joint Conference on Professional Responsibility of the Association
of American Law Schools and the American Bar Association.... A trial is
seen as a process "within which man's capacity for impartial judgment
can attain its fullest realization,"[24] and the function of the advocate is to
assist the trier of fact in making this impartial judgment.... In this view
of the system, "the advocate plays his role well when zeal for his client's
cause promotes a wise and informed decision of the case."... In the process
of assisting the trier in attaining this final result, [may counsel] may
properly obscure or impugn testimony which, while true, would not be
relevant to the determination of guilt [?] By destroying the true but irrelevant testimony, it is argued, the advocate would, in fact, contribute to a
wise ultimate result. This reasoning, however, does not seem persuasive.
Rather, it resembles the paternalism which is so often invoked as an
excuse for not trusting others with the truth. Instead of attempting to
destroy the testimony it would be better to refrain from impeaching the
truthful witness and to trust the trier of fact to draw the right conclusions. The law itself provides mechanisms for excluding irrelevant and
prejudicial evidence; where evidence is not clearly irrelevant, a lawyer
should not attempt to exclude it at the cost of attacking a truthful witness. Repeated acts of confidence in the rationality of the trial system are
necessary if the decision-making process is to approach rationality.[25]

[22] ABA Comm. on Professional Ethics and Grievances, Formal Op. 150.
[23] *Greenough v. Gaskell*, 1 Myl. & K. 98, 103, 39 Eng. Rep. 618, 621 (Ch. 1833).
[24] Lon Fuller and John Randall, *Professional Responsibility: Report of the Joint Conference*, 44 A.B.A. J. 1160-61 (1958).
[25] John Noonan, *The Purposes of Advocacy and the Limits of Confidentiality*, 64 MICH. L. REV. 1485, 1486-88 (1966).

NOTE

What constitutes a good faith factual basis? Opinions differ on what
constitutes a sufficient factual basis for asking a question. In *State v. Williams*, 297 Minn. 76, 210 N.W.2d 21 (1973), the Minnesota Supreme Court
stated that an FBI "rap sheet" indicating that a witness had been convicted
was not a sufficient factual basis for asking the witness about those convictions. The court held that a properly certified record from the court in which
the conviction occurred was necessary. The District of Columbia Court of
Appeals took the opposite view in *Hazel v. United States*, 319 A.2d 136 (1974),
requiring only that a question not be totally groundless. Under this more
lenient view, you may cross-examine as long as you can point to any source
that is not inherently incredible. This latter view is probably the more common interpretation.

E. PLANNING CROSS-EXAMINATION

Despite the apparent spontaneity of cross-examinations, the best ones are
as meticulously planned as any other aspect of a trial. Brilliant cross-examination is the result of thorough investigation, research, and preparation done
well in advance, not of some sixth sense for detecting human weaknesses.
Good cross-examination derives from your theory of the case, not from anything that happens for the first time when the witness is on the stand.

1. SHOULD YOU CROSS-EXAMINE?

No rule of trial practice requires you to cross-examine a witness. If there is
nothing to be gained, then a cross-examination either will amount to nothing
or actually will help your opponent.

Reasons to forgo cross-examination

- The witness has no helpful or corroborating testimony to offer.
- The witness has testified on an uncontested issue or otherwise has not
  hurt your theory of the case.
- Even if the witness has hurt you, you have no ammunition for an attack.

Reasons to conduct cross-examination

- The witness can help your case by supplying favorable evidence on a
  contested issue.
- The witness can help your case by corroborating your important witnesses.
- The witness hurts your theory of the case, but you can prove the witness'
  perception of the events was unreliable.
- The witness hurts your theory of the case, but you can prove the witness'
  memory of the events is faulty.
- The witness hurts your theory of the case, but you can prove the witness
  is an unreliable person.

Occasionally a witness' testimony will hurt your case, but you will lack the
ammunition to attack it. In that situation, some attorneys recommend against

cross-examination, favoring a casual "No questions," hoping that the jury will have been asleep. Others favor an approach called "apparent" cross-examination, a phrase coined by the Elliotts in 1888:

> An apparent cross-examination keeps off on the edges and fringes of the case. It is employed where there is danger in attacking the strongholds yet it is felt that there must be something like an examination, lest it be concluded by the jury that the testimony is confessedly too strong to be met. Such an examination should keep away from the points of danger as much as possible, and yet it must not appear to be an idle or unmeaning procedure. The prudent course is to ask many questions upon matters where answers do no harm when it is evident that his testimony cannot be shaken either by showing a mistake or falsehood.[26]

Mauet suggests that in an apparent cross-examination, you can ask such tangential questions as whether your adversary asked the witness to testify, whether the witness volunteered or was subpoenaed, whether the witness discussed the testimony with the adverse lawyer or party, and what kinds of prior statements the witness made or used to prepare for testifying.[27]

2. SELECTING A PURPOSE

The first step in preparing a cross-examination is to decide what you hope to gain from it. How will cross-examination further your theory of the case? What evidence can you elicit that will help you in closing argument?

There are two very different goals you may try to accomplish: eliciting testimony which will help you build your own case, and attempting to weaken your opponent's case. Testimony that will help build your own case may take the form of important information that you need to prove your case, or facts that will corroborate the testimony of your witnesses. Cross-examination that will weaken your opponent's case also has different forms. You may decide to attack the personal credibility of a lying witness or expose the shakiness of a mistaken witness' testimony. You may choose to emphasize inconsistencies between this witness and other witnesses called by your opponent. You also may decide that there is more than one purpose for cross-examining a witness.

a. Constructive Cross-Examination

Despite the popular conception of cross-examination as an attack on a witness, the primary purpose of cross-examination, like any other aspect of the trial, is to help build your own theory of the case. Few witnesses possess information useful solely to one side. A search of the statements and depositions of opposing witnesses probably will yield potential testimony that will aid your own cause. It may even be that a jury is likely to remember and give special credence to evidence favorable to your case that comes from a witness called by the other side. You should look for:

---

[26] BYRON ELLIOTT & WILLIAM ELLIOTT, WORK OF THE ADVOCATE 288-89 (1888).
[27] THOMAS A. MAUET, FUNDAMENTALS OF TRIAL TECHNIQUES 263-64 (3d ed. 1992).

- *Favorable testimony on a contested issue.* Occasionally, a witness called by your opponent to testify against you on one issue will possess significant information you need to help prove a contested issue. If the favorable testimony was mentioned on direct, you can reemphasize it on cross. If the matter was avoided, then you should bring it up on cross-examination unless the topic cannot be raised because of limited scope rules.

- *Testimony corroborating your main witnesses.* It often will be possible to elicit testimony on cross-examination that enhances the credibility of your witnesses by corroborating parts of their testimony. The possibilities are endless. It can be as simple as eliciting testimony that your witness was present at the scene, or as complex as bringing out evidence of the truthful character of one of your witnesses. The most fruitful line of inquiry is likely to concern the opportunity for your own witnesses to observe the events. An adverse witness, especially one who uses a diagram of the scene to aid his or her direct examination, always should be able to corroborate that there would have been a good line of sight from another location. Using opposing witnesses to corroborate the actions of your client also is important. For example, if opposing witnesses saw your client trying to avoid an accident, rendering assistance to the victim, or driving safely just before it occurred, or if they overheard your client's explanation of the events, you should bring out these facts.

- *Testimony consistent with your theory of the case.* Rarely are more than a few issues really contested in a trial. The controversy usually boils down to a few disputed facts. Even if nothing else is possible on cross-examination, you always can elicit testimony about those uncontroverted facts that form part of your theory of the event. Professor Bergman uses the example of a petty theft charge for shoplifting a calculator. On direct, the defendant admits putting the calculator in his pocket, but denies intent, claiming he stepped out of the store only to get his checkbook from his wife. The cross-examination of the defendant could consist of the following questions on uncontested facts:

  "So you did pick up the calculator?"
  "And you put it in your pocket?"
  "Then you walked to the nearest exit?"
  "And left the store?"
  "And all the time you never took the calculator out of your pocket?"[28]

b. Destructive Cross-Examination

Cross-examination is used most commonly as a destructive technique through which the cross-examiner attempts to weaken his or her opponent's case. This form of cross-examination probably is overused. Lawyers have a tendency to attack every witness called by their opponents, just because it is cross-examination. However, some witnesses may be called who are neutral or even helpful to you. To attack them is unnecessary and may be counterproductive. For other witnesses, you may not have the ammunition for a successful

---

[28] Paul Bergman, *A Practical Approach to Cross-Examination: Safety First*, 25 UCLA L. REV. 547, 550-51 (1978).

attack. You therefore should choose to attack cautiously and infrequently, saving it for those witnesses who really hurt your case and using it only when you are sure of success. Since jurors tend to identify with witnesses more than lawyers, they are likely to resent an unsuccessful attack. Also, if you attack every witness, the jurors can tell that you are only playing a game. Like the little boy who cried "Wolf!" you may find that no one pays any attention when it comes time to attack a witness who is a real threat to your case.

Convincing a jury that a witness is not believable requires two things: facts showing a *likelihood* that they are wrong, plus some *actual evidence* that they are wrong. You may be able to convince a jury that a witness is likely to be wrong for any of three reasons: 1) the witness is an evil, lying perjurer; 2) the witness has forgotten the truth; or 3) for some understandable reason, the witness did not perceive events correctly in the first place.

(1) Attacking the Witness Personally

One form of cross-examination is to attack the personal veracity of a witness by proving the witness is lying. Even if the witness is a liar, the witness is not likely to admit it, so this is rarely a productive line of inquiry. Nevertheless, lawyers persist in personal attacks, hoping to convince the jury that a witness is not to be trusted. Some common forms of impeachment fall into this category:

- The witness has a personal motive to testify falsely based on bias, prejudice, or interest.
- The witness has previously been convicted of a crime, which shows the witness to be the type of person who would lie.
- Prior inconsistent statements may indicate that the witness has lied on one occasion.

For this type of attack to be successful, you must have an appropriate situation where an obvious motive and partisanship will readily allow the jury to believe it possible for the witness to commit perjury.

(2) Attacking the Witness' Memory

It is somewhat easier to convince a jury that the witness' testimony is unreliable because of faulty memory. This is still a personal attack on the witness, but no longer requires that you convince a jury the witness is evil, so it is easier to sell it to the jury. You can attack memory in several ways:

- Prior inconsistent statements cast doubt on how well the witness is able to remember the events.
- Inability to recall collateral details *of similar importance* may cast doubt on the reliability of a witness' memory. The most famous example of this kind of cross-examination is from the early nineteenth-century British trial of Queen Caroline for adultery. The star witness testified that on a certain voyage the queen slept every night in a tent occupied by another man. The cross-examination was as follows:

  Q: Where did Hieronimus (another passenger) sleep?

A: I do not recollect.

Q: Where did Countess Oldi sleep?

A: I do not recollect.

Q: Where did the maids sleep?

A: I do not know.

Q: Where did Captain Flynn sleep?

A: I do not know.

Q: Where did the livery servants sleep?

A: I do not remember.

Q: Were not you yourself a livery servant?

A: Yes.

Q: When Her Royal Highness was going to sea on her voyage from Sicily to Tunis, where did she sleep?

A: This I cannot remember.

Q: When she was afterwards going from Tunis to Constantinople on board the ship, where did Her Royal Highness sleep?

A: This I do not remember.

For this kind of cross-examination to be successful, the facts forgotten must be of equal importance to the facts remembered. If a witness claims to remember a startling event ("I saw the defendant pull a shotgun and shoot two people"), it probably will be a waste of time to ask if the witness remembers what other people were doing.

(3) Attacking the Witness's Initial Perception

Instead of (or in addition to) attacking the witness personally, you may decide to attack the accuracy of the particular testimony given. This involves implying to the jury that, for some excusable reason, the witness perceived matters inaccurately from the beginning. This is the easiest case to make to the jury of the three approaches. You can establish likelihood of error in several ways:

- Prove the witness was at an unfavorable vantage point from which to view the events.
- Demonstrate that the witness has physiological limitations, such as poor eyesight or hearing.
- Show that the witness was in poor condition to observe at the time of the event due to intoxication or fatigue.
- Show physical conditions limiting the witness' opportunity to observe the events, such as objects obstructing the witness' view, inadequate lighting, a great distance separating the witness from the event, distractions, or a very short time in which to make observations.

Once you have established a likelihood that the witness could make mistakes, you must prove that the witness has in fact testified incorrectly at least once. You may establish that a witness is mistaken either by showing that the witness' testimony is inconsistent with common sense, or that it is inconsistent with the testimony of more credible witnesses.

(4) Proving that Testimony is Inconsistent with Common Sense

You can convince a juror that a witness is wrong by bringing out facts that make the testimony inconsistent with ordinary human experience or with physical evidence. If the witness' version of the events is improbable, you can set up an effective closing argument by making sure that all of the unlikely details have been brought out. This is particularly effective for pointing out exaggerations in a witness' estimates of speed and distance. For example:

> Q: You estimated that the car was going about sixty miles per hour?
> Q: You watched it for a distance of two hundred feet?
> Q: You watched the car for at least ten seconds?

You can then do the math during closing argument to show that the testimony is impossible.[29] Note that there is no suggestion that you should ask the *witness* to do the math during cross-examination and then confess to being a bald-faced liar.

(5) Establishing Inconsistencies with Other Witnesses

If your opponent's witnesses are in disagreement among themselves on specific facts, then someone must be wrong. This is an extension of the principle underlying impeachment by prior inconsistent statements: two different versions of the events cannot both be correct. This tactic is especially effective when the other side has the burden of proof. If the inconsistency already has been testified to on direct, there is a risk in reemphasizing it on cross-examination: the witness may change it or explain it away. The tactic is dangerous, however, when *both* versions hurt you. The net result of your attack may be that the jury picks one of the two versions and decides against you anyway.

The other reason to establish inconsistencies, however, is to convince the jury that a particular witness is wrong because the witness is contradicted by more credible witnesses. This tactic should not be attempted unless you can also successfully impeach the witness by proving one of the three reasons the witness is likely to make mistakes. Otherwise, establishing inconsistencies is a two-edged sword. The jury may choose to believe your opponent's version of the inconsistent events rather than yours, especially if the witness being cross-examined offers satisfactory support for his or her version.

3. WHAT TOPICS TO INCLUDE

At the early stages of preparation, you must distinguish between "topics" and "questions." A topic is a discrete issue you want to raise on cross-examination because you expect to be able to establish something helpful to your theory of the case. A question is a means of trying to achieve that end. For example, you may want to prove that the witness and the defendant got into a fight last year, to support an argument that the witness is biased against the

---

[29] A car travelling sixty miles per hour would cover about ninety feet per second (lawyers use a standard formula: mph × 1.5 = feet per second). A car taking ten seconds to drive 200 feet is going twenty feet per second, or approximately fourteen miles per hour.

defendant. That is a topic you will pursue on cross-examination. However, several questions will be needed to accomplish this goal; e.g.:

Q: Directing your attention to August 14, 1990, you attended a party at Mary Royce's house, correct?

Q: You saw Conrad Stevens at that party, didn't you?

Q: About 10:00 p.m., you and Mr. Stevens began arguing, didn't you?

Q: Isn't it true you punched Mr. Stevens?

Q: And then you told him you hated him, correct?

At the beginning stages of preparation, you should decide what topics you want to go into on cross-examination, and not worry about individual questions. Choice of topics is a two-step process of first generating a list of potential topics, and then winnowing it down to the most important ones. Generating a list of potential topics is the easy part. Go back through the list of purposes, and then look through your evidence for both helpful testimony and possible lines of attack.

Once you have generated a list of potential cross-examination topics, you need to winnow it down and decide which ones you will actually pursue. The following suggestions may help this process.

a. Does It Advance Your Theory of the Case?

You should not pursue a topic on cross-examination just because it is available. You may possess a certified copy of a witness' prior conviction for perjury, but unless your theory calls for a personal attack on the witness, there is no reason to bring it up.

b. How Important Is It in Relation to Other Topics?

In some cases, there may be only one or two potentially productive topics that advance your theory, so you can pursue them all. However, if you have a large number of potentially productive topics that could be raised, you will have to choose which ones to include in your cross-examination. The general advice of experienced advocates is that you should limit cross-examination to a few important issues rather than take the "shotgun" approach. After all, jurors have finite capacities to retain information, so they may forget your main points if you bury them among less significant issues.

c. Is it Inconsistent with Other Topics You Want to Raise?

The most common dilemma arises when you have an opportunity both to elicit helpful testimony and to impeach the witness. If you do both, then your impeachment weakens the effect of the favorable testimony. If you choose not to impeach, then the adverse testimony goes unchallenged. If you leave out the helpful testimony, you might not have enough evidence to prove your case. The best approach often will be to do both, but to develop the affirmative evidence first. There are two reasons for this approach: 1) The witness undoubtedly will become less cooperative once the witness realizes he or she is under attack; and 2) experiments have shown that jurors pay less attention to testimony after the source of it has been shown to be unreliable.[30] If the favorable testimony elicited is particularly important, then some consideration should be given to forgoing impeachment.

d. How "Safe" Is the Topic?

Trial lawyers stress the need to maintain control during a cross-examination. The witnesses you will cross-examine possess information favorable to your opponent. Many will be hostile, and most will react defensively to any attempts to impeach them. If you fail to control the topics raised on cross-examination, the chances are that the witness will end up repeating the direct examination and avoiding or explaining away the weaknesses in it and the impeachment of it.

It is a common piece of trial lawyer folklore that one way of making sure the testimony stays on favorable grounds is never to ask a question to which you do not already know the answer. However, this advice cannot be taken too literally. You never will know for certain what answer a witness will give. No matter how many times the witness has said something before trial, no matter how many sworn statements have been made, the witness still may say something completely unexpected when asked about it at trial. What this aphorism means, therefore, is something slightly different: *you have the greatest control over a witness when you are asking for evidence that the witness has previously given in an interview, statement, deposition, or prior trial.* If a witness said it once, the witness is likely (but not certain) to say it again, and may at least be impeached if the witness says something different.

The principle behind this approach to controlling cross-examination is that if a witness said something before, you have the ability to impeach or refute testimony if it is unexpectedly different. If a witness made a prior statement that the traffic light was green, she cannot now say it was red, she did not see it, or she cannot remember, without being impeached. Professor Paul Bergman calls this a "high-safety" topic, and proposes a model for cross-examination in which you select your topics based on the relative safety with which you can pursue them.[31]

High-safety topics are those where you have a reason to believe that the witness will give certain testimony, and have the ability to refute a bad answer:

- You are asking for information the witness has previously given in a statement or deposition that would be admissible as a prior inconsistent statement if the witness testifies differently.
- You are asking about information the witness should know which is also contained in admissible exhibits, such as photographs or records of criminal convictions.
- You are asking about information the witness should know that other more credible witnesses will testify to.

---

[30]*See* Brian Sternthal, Lynn W. Phillips, & Ruby Dholakia, *The Persuasive Effect of Source Credibility*, 42 PUB. OPINION Q. 285, 289 (1978).
[31]Bergman, *supra* note 28, at 555-56.

Medium-safety topics are those where the nature of the case raises a likelihood that the witness will testify a certain way, but you have no direct way to refute a bad answer:

- You are asking for facts consistent with human experience where an unfavorable answer would contradict common sense.
- You are asking the witness about facts in situations in which the witness assumes that an independent refutation witness is available.
- You want the witness to confirm something implied in or inferred from a prior statement, but the witness has not previously been asked directly to confirm or deny it.
- You are seeking to prove that something did *not* happen because the witness says nothing about it in an otherwise detailed prior statement. For example, if a police officer's accident investigation report is silent on whether your client had been drinking, there is a likelihood that the officer will admit that there was no evidence of intoxication. Common sense tells us that a police officer would have reported intoxication.

Low-safety topics are those where you engage in wishful thinking. Circumstances suggest that a witness might know something relevant, but the witness has never said anything one way or the other. Thus, you have no reasonable basis to believe the witness' testimony will actually help you, but the witness also has never explicitly said anything to the contrary, so (you think) *maybe* the witness will unexpectedly provide favorable evidence. These are the kinds of topics lawyers caution against pursuing when they warn you not to ask questions if you do not know the answer. The risk is especially high under the following circumstances:

- The witness acted inconsistently with the fact sought. For example, you may be trying to corroborate your client's testimony that the victim pulled a knife on him. A written statement by the victim's roommate indicates that he was "eating pizza and watching TV" just before the shooting. Asking the roommate whether he saw the victim pull a knife is a low-safety topic. It is unlikely that the roommate would have continued calmly eating pizza while a knife was being waved about.
- The weight of the testimony of other witnesses is to the contrary. For example, if four witnesses claim the victim had no knife, it is risky to ask the fifth if she had seen a knife, even if her statement is silent on the point.
- The evidence would contradict common sense. For example, if you are cross-examining an eyewitness to a crime that occurred at night but in a well-lighted parking lot, it would be risky to ask whether it was too dark to see clearly.

Unsafe topics are those where you ask a witness to change his or her testimony. You want the witness to agree to elements of your version of the story, despite the fact that the witness has given prior statements or testimony to the contrary. It is almost impossible to pursue such a topic without being argumentative, and it is just plain silly to try it. Bergman writes:

> The "your story" mode of cross-examination is often used in dramatic works [and] would result in asking these kinds of questions of the defendant [claiming self-defense]:
> "Mr. Jones, you actually struck the first blow, didn't you?"
> "And then you picked up a stick?"
> "And you chased Mr. Smith with this stick?"
> In drama, the witness breaks down and admits that the cross-examiner is correct. In actual trials, however, the witness usually just keeps saying "No." After all, the implicit question, "Aren't you an abject liar?" is rarely answered in the affirmative.[32]

4. ORDER OF CROSS-EXAMINATION TOPICS

a. Where to Begin

The most common advice on organizing a cross-examination is to "begin strong." This view is consistent with our overall strategy to take advantage of the primacy effect. For example, Francis X. Busch writes that "[e]xperienced advocates stress the importance of commencing a cross-examination with a sharply-worded, surprise question, calculated to embarrass the witness and throw him off balance; the idea being that he may not only be immediately disconcerted but may lose his assurance and fumble his subsequent answers."[33] The advice is not universal, however. Some advocates favor a more cautious beginning. Asher Cornelius argues that "it is frequently advisable to ask as one's first question something competent and admissible but entirely foreign or apart from the controversial elements of the case ... and from thence gradually and easily gain [the witness's] confidence."[34]

Most lawyers advise against beginning cross-examination on the point where the direct ended, especially if you are attacking. Witnesses do not readily admit to errors in their testimony. If you start in on a subject still fresh in the witness' mind, the witness will be likely to figure out where it leads, and may be able to weaken the point you want to make. However, Bergman suggests that if you have the ammunition to refute the last point made in the direct examination, you might want to "[b]egin cross on whatever point direct finishes. Like the bull who makes a dramatic entrance by charging directly at the matador, you leap into the fray by taking up right where the direct left off."[35]

b. Order of Topics

Most lawyers agree that cross-examination should not follow the chronological order of direct examination, especially if you intend to impeach the witness. The witness, through pretrial preparation, is likely to have learned this

---

[32] Bergman, *supra* note 28, at 572-73.
[33] F. BUSCH, *supra* note 2, at 770-72 (with examples).
[34] ASHER CORNELIUS, CROSS-EXAMINATION OF WITNESSES 261-62 (1929).
[35] PAUL BERGMAN, TRIAL ADVOCACY IN A NUTSHELL 164 (2d ed. 1989).

sequence well and be ready with damaging testimony before you have even asked your questions. If the order is changed so that it jumps around in the chronology, then the witness will not have time to anticipate the direction of the examination. However, Judge Robert Keeton criticizes this "hop, skip, and jump" organization as having the same effect on the jurors as it does on the witness: they will have so much difficulty following the sequence that they will not think about the answers.[36]

Keeton's criticism assumes that the jury will have difficulty following a non-chronological cross-examination because it will be in no particular order. This need not be the case. You can deviate from chronological order and yet still allow the jury to follow the cross-examination. Most cross-examinations will contain only a few topics, which can easily be arranged according to the purpose for which they are offered. You might consider the following order:

- High-safety favorable evidence on contested issues.
- High-safety evidence that corroborates your main witnesses.
- Medium-safety favorable evidence.
- Medium-safety impeachment evidence.
- High-safety impeachment attacking the witness' testimony.
- High-safety impeachment attacking the witness personally.

Within each topic, related issues can be grouped together. Inconsistencies with other witnesses can be linked to proof of bias or prejudice that motivated the witness to see things differently. Cross-examination demonstrating the witness' lack of memory about details can be linked to proof that the witness had a poor opportunity to observe the events.

c. Final Topic

Most trial lawyers agree that the final topic should be one of the most important points you wish to raise in your cross-examination, to take advantage of the recency effect. Many trial lawyers believe that the end is even more important than the beginning, so that the most important topic should come last. However, experimental evidence is inconclusive on the relative importance of primacy and recency. Since the general order of cross-examination is to start with helpful information and end with impeachment, the final topic will often be your strongest impeachment evidence.

Two other tactics sometimes are recommended in planning the final topic. Some lawyers recommend that the cross-examination end with one or more summary, or wrap-up questions. They argue that the jury needs to be told, in conclusory form, the point of your cross-examination. The danger with such a tactic is twofold: 1) summary questions are usually objectionable as argumentative, and 2) the witness has a chance to answer your "question," and will often dispute your conclusion. Either way, the impact of your final point may be lost.

A second tactic sometimes recommended is to start to sit down, and then ask an "afterthought" question. This approach is based on the assumption that an antagonistic witness will relax when the witness thinks the examina-

---

[36] ROBERT KEETON, TRIAL TACTICS AND METHODS 139 (2d ed. 1973).

tion is over, and will therefore be more likely to give a favorable answer if caught off-guard. This tactic has two dangers: 1) the jurors also may have thought the cross had ended and miss the final point, and 2) the maneuver may appear too staged, especially if you try it more than once during a trial.

NOTES

1. *When to use prior convictions.* Many lawyers automatically bring up prior convictions on cross-examination. Is this a good practice? *See* Louis Schwartz, Proof, Persuasion, and Cross-Examination, vol. 2: 1611 (1973), suggesting that prior convictions should not be used unless they are genuinely probative of dishonesty. Research by social psychologists seems to confirm Schwartz's advice: convictions not directly related to credibility, at least minor ones, have no effect on jurors' assessments of witnesses' credibility. *See* Roselle Wissler & Michael Saks, *On the Inefficacy of Limiting Instructions*, 9 Law & Hum. Behav. 37, 43-44 (1985). Of course, many prosecutors use impeachment as an excuse to prove the prior criminal record of a defendant when they really want it as substantive proof that the defendant is a "criminal type" (once a criminal, always a criminal), an ethically questionable practice.

2. *Attacking witness vs. attacking testimony of witness.* Choosing a cross-examination that attacks a witness personally, instead of one that attacks the probability that his or her testimony is accurate, is dangerous. In Byron Elliott & William Elliott, The Work of the Advocate 316-17 (1888), the authors point out that cold-blooded liars are rare:

> Witnesses are often mistaken, but they are seldom guilty of perjury. It is unintended error rather than deliberate falsehood that makes human testimony unreliable. There are, it is true, many false witnesses, but there are many more whose deviation from the truth is attributable to mistake rather than intentional wrong. If, therefore, there is nothing known of the character of a witness that subjects him to suspicion, and nothing in his demeanor or the substance of his testimony that justly excites a belief that he is testifying falsely, the better course is to assume that he is mistaken, and cross-examine on that assumption.

A personal attack also may not go over well with the jury. Consider Sydney Schweitzer, Cyclopedia of Trial Practice, vol. 2: 634 (2d ed. 1970):

> The type of witness being cross-examined will also govern to a large extent your cross-examination as to possible motive to distort or exaggerate. Where the witness is of the superior type, as a clean-cut young executive who is able to impress the jury with his ability and inherent honesty, it would be folly to over-stress his friendship or relation with the other side in your cross-examination.

3. *Questionable purposes of cross-examination.* A few other purposes for cross-examination are recommended by some lawyers and rejected by others. The most common of these is to use cross-examination to insinuate a set of facts that does not exist. This kind of cross-examination by innuendo

has become infamous because of the "Isn't it true you really enjoyed it?" kind of question asked of rape victims. One attorney proudly claims that he won an acquittal for the renowned blues singer Billie Holiday because the jury believed her to have been framed based on his own questions that were objected to or stricken from the record. JOHN ERLICH, THE LOST ART OF CROSS-EXAMINATION 142-47 (1970). The empirical evidence suggests that this kind of cross-examination is rarely successful. Saul Kassin, Lorri N. Williams & Courtney Saunders, *Dirty Tricks of Cross-Examination: The Influence of Conjectural Evidence on the Jury*, 14 LAW & HUM. BEHAV. 373, 381 (1990). It also is obviously unethical.

Another closely related purpose is to use cross-examination for argument; that is, to ask the witness to agree to a statement summarizing your own theory of the case. For example: "Isn't it true that what really happened was that my client acted in self-defense after you pulled a knife on him?" Those who support this as a legitimate purpose point out that it gives you the opportunity to preview your closing argument. *See* F. LEE BAILEY & HENRY ROTHBLATT, SUCCESSFUL TECHNIQUES FOR CRIMINAL TRIALS § 193 (1971). *But see* ROBERT KEETON, TRIAL TACTICS AND METHODS 141 (2d ed. 1973): "[I]t is a crude way of doing what generally can be done more effectively through other means. Long before cross-examination you have ample opportunity to present your theory of the case ... when you are examining the jury panel, reading your pleadings, or making an opening statement." By asking such a question, you give a witness the chance to refute your theory, which is likely to be more detrimental than beneficial.

Although most attorneys reject the idea, William Gallagher suggests that there are times when one should plan a "fishing trip," or exploratory cross-examination. This consists of having the witness repeat the direct testimony, as damaging as it may be, probing for a weak spot. He suggests using this as a last resort for a witness who tips the scales in favor of the opponent. Gallagher, *Technique of Cross-Examination, in* CIVIL LITIG. AND TRIAL TECHNIQUES 552-72 (H. Bodin ed. 1976). Before attempting this path, you should ask yourself what your chances are of discovering anything new that did not appear during pretrial investigation, interviews, and depositions of the witness. *See* SYDNEY SCHWEITZER, CYCLOPEDIA OF TRIAL PRACTICE, vol. 1: 614 (2d ed. 1970):

> Where the witness has left no loophole in his direct examination, and you know of no weak points that could profitably be exploited on cross-examination, do not attempt to cross-examine. Dismiss the witness with a curt gesture that says: "too unimportant to bother about." [Do not] trust to providence that your interrogation will develop one or more weak points. [Unfavorable testimony] carries more weight than it would have had it been elicited on direct examination.

Finally, Harry S. Bodin suggests that it may be possible to compel an adverse witness to change his or her testimony by the inexorable logic of facts from which he or she cannot escape. Bodin, *Principles of Cross-Examination, in* CIVIL LITIGATION AND TRIAL TECHNIQUES 444 (1976). Is this a realistic possibility? Consider FRANCIS L. WELLMAN, THE ART OF CROSS-EXAMINATION 10 (1923):

> It is absurd to suppose that any witness who has sworn positively to a certain set of facts, even if he has inadvertently stretched the truth, is going to be readily induced by a lawyer to alter them and acknowledge his mistake. People as a rule do not reflect upon their meager opportunities for observing facts, and rarely suspect the frailty of their own powers of observation. They come to court, when summoned as witnesses, prepared to tell what they think they know; and ... they resent an attack upon their story as they would one upon their integrity.

4. *Should you cross-examine a witness who testifies on an uncontested issue?* If a witness testifies against you on an uncontested issue, and has no favorable evidence you need to elicit, there is no reason to cross-examine even if you have the ammunition. If you plead payment as a defense to a debt, why attack a witness who merely testifies to the origin of the debt? Your cross-examination must be consistent with your theory of the case. *See* Paul Bergman, *A Practical Approach to Cross-Examination: Safety First*, 25 UCLA L. REV. 547, 549-50 (1978).

5. *Cross-examination on unimportant details.* There is some dispute over whether it is ever advisable to raise trivial matters on cross-examination. Advocates of the "apparent" cross-examination strategy support the occasional raising of collateral matters when there are no other issues to pursue. Other trial lawyers recommend avoiding "petty triumphs "on cross-examination. Consider ASHER CORNELIUS, THE CROSS-EXAMINATION OF WITNESSES 20 (1929):

> No greater mistake can be made by any lawyer than to attempt to make capital out of trifling discrepancies in testimony. The jurors know very well that human beings cannot always be accurate regarding dates and figures and that each witness to a transaction will observe the thing from a slightly different angle and will honestly vary in his testimony thereto. Therefore, when the cross-examiner pounces upon a witness because of an error in dates, or as to the number of people present, or because he on one occasion testified that he arrived home shortly after nine and on another occasion he arrived home about nine-thirty, he is not only wasting his energy, but is actually aiding his adversaries.

6. *Use of exhibits during cross-examination.* On appropriate occasions, you may want to use diagrams or other exhibits during cross-examination, assuming the rules of evidence in your jurisdiction permit it. This tactic should be employed cautiously. Before introducing a *new* exhibit, remember that you must lay a foundation, and the witness may not be cooperative. If you try to introduce a diagram, the witness may find fault with it, claiming it to be a distortion. FRANCIS X. BUSCH, LAW AND TACTICS IN JURY TRIALS, vol. 3: 560 (1960). Not only could you not use it then, but future use by your own witnesses would be tainted. For this reason, some lawyers recommend against using your own exhibits, *e.g.*, LOUIS SCHWARTZ, PROOF, PERSUASION, AND CROSS-EXAMINATION, vol. 2: 1612 (1973). There would seem to be little risk in using exhibits introduced or referred to on direct, although a court may limit your ability to put marks on your adversary's exhibits. *See* ROBERT KEETON, TRIAL TACTICS AND METHODS 131-33 (2d ed. 1973).

7. *When to raise low-safety topics.* If you absolutely must pursue a low-safety topic, where should you put it? Occasionally there will be a question you would like to ask, but you are afraid of getting a bad answer. Little attention has been paid to this problem beyond the common advice not to pursue it at all. If you decide to raise the topic anyway, it must be put someplace. The logical point would seem to be in the middle, where weaknesses are traditionally placed. Since you should cover helpful testimony first and impeachment last, beginning and ending with strong points, the only place left is somewhere in the middle. Then, if your fears prove justified, you can still finish with safe topics.

F. PREPARING CROSS-EXAMINATION QUESTIONS

The key to successful cross-examination is control. The witnesses you will cross-examine possess information favorable to your opponent and harmful to you. That is why your adversary called them in the first place. Some witnesses will be hostile, some suspicious, and some defensive. None will react with gratitude when you attack their character. If you fail to control the cross-examination, you invite disaster. If you allow a witness to choose the subject matter of the testimony, the chances are that the witness will end up repeating the direct examination and avoiding or explaining away the weaknesses in it and the impeachment of it.

The single most important step in controlling the cross-examination is the preparation of good questions. Good questions are leading, simple, brief, nonargumentative, and use the witness's own words whenever possible. Accomplishing this may require that you write out your questions word for word.

1. WRITING OUT YOUR QUESTIONS

Trial lawyers disagree about whether you should write out cross-examination questions before trial. Some lawyers recommend that you write out every question exactly as you intend to ask it, especially at the beginning of your career. They argue that if you use no notes, or only sketchy and inadequate ones, the cross-examination can become disorganized or a topic omitted. Worse, a question that is not phrased precisely can disrupt your entire examination if it is objected to by your opponent or if it is broad enough to provide the witness with an opportunity to repeat damaging testimony.

With experience, many lawyers prefer to use outlines rather than writing their questions out verbatim. Melvin Belli argues that written questions are too confining and too inflexible in responding to unexpected answers. He recommends using only a simple outline of topics.[37] Irving Goldstein recommends a compromise position consisting of an outline of topics to be inquired into, with all vital questions written out in full.[38] However, before you decide

---

[37] MELVIN BELLI, MODERN TRIALS, vol. 2: 1560 (1954).

[38] Irving Goldstein, *The Cardinal Principles of Cross-Examination*, 1959 TRIAL LAW. GUIDE 331, 355.

to forgo writing out your questions verbatim, ask yourself whether you are certain you can remember the exact foundation questions necessary to impeach with a criminal conviction, or exactly how many feet away from an accident scene each of several witnesses was. If not, then you might be well advised to write out your questions.

2. HOW TO PHRASE A CROSS-EXAMINATION QUESTION

Many books and articles contain how-to-do-it instructions for conducting the perfect cross-examination.[39] In sum, they consist of suggestions about how to phrase your questions to keep you in control and limit the answers of the witness.

a. Break Your Topics Down Into the Smallest Possible Units

This is the most important concept of successful cross-examination: a topic and a question are different things. Your must divide a topic up into its smallest practical "fact units," and ask about each one separately. For example, suppose you represent the defendant in a personal injury action. Your expert will testify that most of plaintiff's medical problems were the result of pre-existing injury. To corroborate your expert, you intend to elicit from the plaintiff on cross-examination the fact that she had the pre-existing injury. You could just ask:

> Q: Ms. Roslyn, isn't it true that your back had previously been injured in an automobile accident in 1988?

Your goal, however, is to break this topic down into small fact units which can be strung together in a fast-paced, effective cross-examination, such as:

> Q: Ms. Roslyn, after the February 15th accident, you experienced back pain?
> A: Yes.
> Q: Stiffness?
> A: Yes.
> Q: Difficulty sleeping?
> A: Yes.
> Q: Difficulty walking?
> A: Yes.
> Q: You were also in an accident in March, 1988, is that right?
> A: Yes.
> Q: That's two years before the collision with David Simpson, right?
> A: Yes.
> Q: In 1988, you were hit by a city bus, weren't you?
> A: Yes.
> Q: And you went to the hospital?

---

[39] *See, e.g.,* FRED LANE, LANE'S GOLDSTEIN TRIAL TECHNIQUES §§ 19.20-19.92 (3d ed. 1984) (The "Do's" and "Don'ts" of Cross-Examination); LOUIS E. SCHWARTZ, PROOF, PERSUASION, AND CROSS-EXAMINATION, vol. 2: 1610-11 (1973) (How to Conduct Cross-Examination); *id.* at 1611-12 (What Not to Do on Cross-Examination); Busch, *Direct and Cross-Examination*, 23 MISS. L.J. 321 (1952); Garry, *Cross-Examination and Trial Tactics*, 11 LINCOLN L. REV. 77 (1979).

A: Yes.

Q: In fact, you spent two weeks in the hospital, isn't that right?

A: Yes.

Q: Following that first accident, you experienced back pain, didn't you?

A: Yes.

Q: Stiffness?

A: Yes.

Q: Difficulty sleeping?

A: Yes.

Q: Difficulty walking?

A: Yes.

Q: And you were treated by Dr. Sidney Greenstreet?

A: Yes.

Q: Is he a back specialist?

A: Yes.

Q: Isn't it true that he told you in early 1989 that these symptoms might never go away?

A: Yes.

b. Ask Only One Fact Per Question

Questions should be narrowly tailored, each one containing a single fact. For example, suppose you ask, "At 11:00 p.m., you went downstairs to the kitchen to get a drink of water, but you forgot your glasses, is that right?" The witness could answer the entire question "no" if the witness went to get an apple, despite the fact that the witness in fact forgot her glasses when she went down to the kitchen at 11:00 o'clock. You will be especially prone to asking compound questions in situations like this, in which most of the facts are uncontested or unimportant. However, good cross-examination breaks this topic down into single fact questions:

Q: Were you home at 11:00 p.m.?

Q: You went downstairs, didn't you?

Q: You went to the kitchen?

Q: You got a drink of water, right?

Q: You were not wearing your glasses, were you?

c. Always Ask Leading Questions

Each question should suggest the desired answer. The usual form is to state a fact and ask the witness to agree with it:

Q: You went downstairs, is that correct?

Using a positive question such as "is that correct?" or "Is that right?" is preferable to the negative "Is that not correct?" Compare the following two examples:

(a) Q: You did not lock the door, is that not correct?

(b) Q: Is it true that you did not lock the door?

However, a whole series of questions ending in "is that right?" will drive the jury crazy.

> Q: You went downstairs, is that right?
> Q: You went to the kitchen, is that right?
> Q: You opened the knife drawer, is that right?
> Q: You took out a butcher knife, is that right?
> Q: You cut an apple with it, is that right?

If you break your questions down into small units and ask them one after another, you can omit the suggestion part of the question while remaining in control. Your voice inflection can make the statement of fact sound like a question. For example:

> Q: You went downstairs, is that right?
> Q: You went to the kitchen?
> Q: You opened the knife drawer?
> Q: You took out a butcher knife?
> Q: You cut an apple with it?

d. Keep Your Questions Simple

Your question must be understandable to both the witness and jurors. Keep the language simple and universal, especially when cross-examining a witness used to speaking in jargon. Compare the following:

> (a) Q: Did you then proceed to exit your patrol vehicle?
> (b) Q: Did you get out of your car?

e. Do Not Repeat Damaging Direct Examination

If a message is repeated several times, it is more likely to be remembered and believed.[40] Thus, you help your adversary persuade the jury if you permit a witness to repeat direct examination. Yet, this is one of the most common mistakes of cross-examination. It occurs most frequently when a lawyer repeats harmful testimony in order to impeach it.

> Q: Mr. Barrolli, you stated on direct that you clearly saw my client point the gun at the victim and shoot him, is that right?
> A: Yes, I sure did.
> Q: Are you sure you could see the events clearly?
> A: Oh, yes.
> Q: But isn't it true that you were about 100 feet away at the time?
> A: Yes.

The repetition of the damaging direct was completely unnecessary. All you needed to ask was whether the witness was 100 feet away.

---

[40] *See* John T. Cacioppo and Richard E. Petty, *Effects of Message Repetition and Position on Cognitive Response, Recall, and Persuasion*, 37 J. PERSONALITY & SOC. PSYCHOL. 97 (1979).

f. Use the Witness' Own Words Whenever Possible

A corollary of the principle that a topic is of highest safety if you can impeach a bad answer with a prior statement is that you should stick to the exact words used in that prior statement whenever possible. Save the inferences, explanations and exaggerations for closing argument. For example, suppose a witness said in a deposition that he had consumed five beers before the accident. Suppose you ask:

Q: You were drunk the night of the accident, weren't you?
A: No.

What has happened to your high-safety question? Nowhere in the witness' statement did he say he was intoxicated. You may eventually be able to convince a judge that "five beers" is inconsistent with "not drunk," but you have lost control of the examination. Suppose you had asked:

Q: You had five beers the night of the accident, is that right?

What would the witness have said?

g. Ask About Facts, Not Conclusions

The time for drawing conclusions is closing argument, not cross-examination. Asking conclusory questions is often argumentative, and always a bad idea. It is not the *witness* who must agree to your conclusions, but the jury. One common type of conclusory question asks the witness to agree to your characterization of the facts. It invites the witness to disagree with you.

Q: It was 2:00 a.m.?
Q: It was raining?
Q: There are no streetlights, are there?
Q: *So it was very dark that night, wasn't it?*

The other common type of conclusory question is the summary of testimony.

Q: It was 2:00 a.m.?
Q: It was raining?
Q: There are no streetlights, are there?
Q: You were in your car?
Q: You were a block away from the scene?
Q: *So it's your testimony that on a dark rainy night you could clearly identify the defendant from a block away when there were no streetlights?*

h. Don't Ask the Witness to Explain an Answer

As soon as you ask a witness "Why?" you have given the witness free rein to say anything the witness wants. The classic illustration of this problem is the story about a case in which the defendant was charged with battery for biting off the complaining witness' ear. On cross-examination, the eyewitness admitted that he did not actually see the defendant bite off the victim's ear, but was nevertheless certain the accused had done so. The defense attorney asked the fatal question:

> Q: If you didn't see the defendant bite the victim's ear, how can you say you are certain he did so?
>
> A: Because I saw him spit it out.[41]

NOTES

1. ***Asking non-leading questions.*** Is there ever a justification for asking a non-leading question during cross-examination? The answer depends on whom you turn to for advice. Some writers take the position that you never should ask anything but a leading question, whether you are impeaching or eliciting helpful testimony. *See, e.g.*, Irving Younger, *The Art of Cross-Examination* 22-23 (ABA Litigation Section Monograph No. 1, 1976). Others suggest that open questions sometimes may be appropriate, either to break up the monotony of leading questions, to avoid the appearance of putting words in the witness' mouth, or when on a fishing expedition necessitated by a desperate situation. *Paul Bergman, A Practical Approach to Cross-Examination: Safety First*, 25 UCLA L. REV. 547, 553 n.12, 573-74 (1978).

The advantage of leading questions is that you can choose the most persuasive words available. Word choice can affect how the jurors conceive the events. In one famous experiment, subjects were shown a film of a car accident. Some then were asked how fast the cars were going when they "hit," and gave estimates averaging thirty miles per hour. When another group was asked how fast the cars were going when they "smashed," answers averaged over forty miles per hour. Elizabeth Loftus, *Reconstruction of Automobile Destruction: An Example of the Interaction Between Language and Memory*, 13 J. VERBAL LEARNING & BEHAV. 585 (1974).

2. ***Indexing prior statements and depositions.*** The main reason for preparing specific safe questions based on the witness' own prior statements is for control. If the witness deviates from his or her prior version of the events, at least as to material issues, you have the ability to impeach that inconsistent statement. However, this ability is lost if you cannot *find* the specific prior statement. Looking through a hundred pages of a deposition to find the place where the witness said there were two people present, not three, can be an impossible task. For that reason, most experienced trial lawyers develop some kind of indexing method. The simplest way is to note beside each question you prepare exactly where it came from. If it is a high-safety question that comes directly from lines 11-13 on page forty-six of the witness' deposition, you might make some notation like "D46/11-13" in the margin beside your question. That way, if you need to impeach, you can pick up the deposition and go right to the appropriate sentence. If you are asking a medium safety question that cannot be refuted, you could put an "X" in the margin. That tells you just to move on if the witness gives a bad answer. In major litigation, it is becoming common to also enter all depositions into a laptop computer, so an asso-

---

[41] I first heard the story from the late Irving Younger. It also appears in F. LANE, *supra* note 39, at § 19.30.

ciate can conduct word searches for prior inconsistent statements that arise unexpectedly.

3. *Disguising the purpose of your questions*. A more sophisticated technique for cross-examination, especially of a hostile witness, is to learn to disguise the true purpose of a line of questions. The following example illustrates how this is done. In a criminal case, suppose that an alibi witness has testified that he and the defendant went to a particular movie between 9:00 p.m. and 11:00 p.m. and you are convinced he is lying. You have a rebuttal witness (the theatre manager) who will say that the particular movie was not playing on that date. If you confront the witness directly about the name of the movie, he may answer, "We go to movies all the time, so I might have the title confused." Consider instead, asking questions that suggest that the witness is wrong as to the day of the week they went to the movie. In order to strengthen the alibi, is it not reasonable to expect that the witness will become increasingly positive about his memory, more and more certain that he and the defendant went to that movie on the day of the crime?

4. *Being subtle*. You can sometimes catch more flies with honey than with vinegar. In the following example, suggested by FRANCIS X. BUSCH, LAW AND TACTICS IN JURY TRIALS, vol. 3: 563-64 (1960), the plaintiff brought suit for damages for his unlawful discharge from employment. The defense called a witness who testified that the plaintiff was incompetent and therefore deserved to be discharged. Cross-examination was designed to reveal that this witness was biased against the plaintiff because of a broken romantic relationship. One possibility would have been to have asked the witness bluntly:

> Q: Isn't it true that you are making all this up just to get even with the plaintiff, who left you for another woman?

It is not likely that the witness would have admitted this. Instead, the plaintiff's attorney asked the following questions in a friendly and non-threatening way:

> Q: Prior to your complaining about the competence of the plaintiff, had you ever gone out with him?
> A: What do you mean by that?
> Q: Have you ever gone out socially with him, to the theatre or to dinner?
> A: Yes, a few times.
> Q: How many?
> A: I don't remember.
> Q: I am not suggesting anything improper, because you were divorced and the plaintiff was single, isn't that so?
> A: Yes.
> Q: When was the last time you went out with him?
> A: In the spring.
> Q: How often during the week did you go out?
> A: I'm not sure.
> Q: Now, the first time that you complained to the manager about his competence was in the summer, was it not?
> A: Yes, that's true.

Q: And that was after he had stopped going out with you?
A: The two had no relationship.
Q: I am sure of that. One last question, was not the plaintiff married in late spring of that same year?
A: I don't know. I think so.

G. CONDUCTING THE CROSS-EXAMINATION

1. PRELIMINARY STEPS

In order to conduct an effective cross-examination, there are several last minute matters you should attend to.

- *Assemble the file before trial.* You should have with you in court, in one file, all the necessary documents for cross-examining the witness: 1) your written cross-examination questions; 2) all prior statements, depositions, or other writings of the witness that could be used to impeach inconsistent trial testimony; and 3) any exhibits or certified copies of convictions you may want to introduce.
- *Listen to the direct examination.* Never assume a witness will testify in exactly the same way at trial as the witness did in a deposition. If you already have your cross-examination prepared, you can devote direct examination to listening carefully to the testimony rather than thinking up questions. Witnesses occasionally will say extraordinary things or may open the door to previously inadmissible evidence that you may miss if your attention is focused elsewhere.
- *Decide whether to abandon any planned questions.* Based on the direct examination, you may face a decision whether to forgo questions because they were covered on the direct examination. Generally, of course, you should proceed with your planned cross-examination. Repetition of favorable evidence is a good idea. However, in three situations you may choose to forgo a line of questions: 1) you may have to drop some topics because your opponent limits the scope of the direct examination; 2) you may decide to forgo impeachment if the impeaching effect of some prior act is explained away; or 3) the witness may unexpectedly put evidence in a *more* favorable light than you expected, and might retract it or dilute it if you repeat the question on cross-examination.
- *Decide whether to impeach by prior inconsistent statement.* Obviously, you cannot know in advance whether a witness will give direct testimony inconsistent with prior statements. Listen during direct examination, and decide whether it is worth impeaching any inconsistencies. In general, the only statements you are concerned about are those where the witness changes from favorable to unfavorable testimony. In such a case, you should drop the matter from the beginning of your cross where you had planned it, to the middle. If you have done your preparation, you already have noted in the margin where the matter was covered in the deposition, so you will be able to impeach effectively. If the witness gives inconsistent statements on unimportant issues, you probably should forgo impeachment, unless you can string together a lot of small inconsistencies. The

problem will be finding the original versions of these small details among dozens of pages of deposition. The task may be impossible unless the depositions are on a computer.

2. MAINTAINING CONTROL

Preparing good questions was the first step in controlling cross-examination. Now you have to deliver those questions effectively so as to maintain control and limit the answers of the witness. Recommendations cover a range of issues, such as whether to demand short, responsive answers, what kind of style and manner to adopt, and knowing when to beat a strategic retreat. These suggestions will be discussed in detail in the sections that follow. First, it is important to bear in mind one caveat:

> The technique of cross-examination is not one for which it is possible to lay down principles that can be rigidly observed. In fact, it is difficult to determine at times what is the basic rule and what is the permissible exception. That which may be classed as the exception by one may well be considered the rule by another. For instance, some experienced practitioners follow the rule that the examiner should never permit the witness to stray from the point in issue. Undoubtedly that is, at times, a sound doctrine. On the other hand, it is equally sound, and very frequently extremely effective, to encourage or even to lead the witness away from the main issue. In other words, when a witness, under cross-examination, attempts to leave the main highway and seek refuge in a side street, it is often good practice not to pull him back upon the highway. Chase him down the side street. It will often prove a dead-end street for him.... Thus, the advocate should not set a rigid course for himself but should be flexible in his offensive and adapt himself to developments.[42]

a. Should You Try to Limit the Witness' Answers?

Handling a witness who is evasive, keeps volunteering information, or insists on explaining or justifying "yes/no" answers can be a precarious problem. You can harm yourself in many ways if you try to stop these explanations; the witness can harm your case if you do not.

Many lawyers believe that controlling the cross-examination is paramount. They recommend several techniques for trying to limit a witness' answers and preventing the witness from volunteering testimony:

- Ask the witness to limit his or her answers to "Yes" or "No."
- Move to strike volunteered portions of the testimony.
- Ask the judge to instruct the witness to limit his or her answers to "Yes" or "No."

---

[42] William H. Gallagher, *The Technique of Cross-Examination, in* CIVIL LITIGATION AND TRIAL TECHNIQUES 541-42 (H. Bodin ed. 1976).

Other techniques may be used if the witness is evasive or offers self-serving justifications.

- Repeat the question or have it read back.
- Move to strike the evasive answer as not being responsive to your question.

However, other lawyers argue that the better approach is to tolerate the explanations and evasions, for several reasons: 1) Many judges feel that witnesses should be allowed to give explanations. You do not want to be rebuked by the judge. 2) You run the risk of giving the jurors the impression you are trying to keep something from them. There is some psychological data that an attorney who appears too one-sided is less persuasive than one who appears to consider both sides.[43] 3) Your opponent is likely to elicit the explanation on redirect examination anyway. 4) You may not realize that you have phrased the question in a way that it is not answerable by "Yes" or "No," in which case you will look like an idiot.

If you decide that you have to do *something* to try to control a hostile, loquacious witness, what should you do? Lawyers disagree on what is the best tactic.

- *The preventive approach.* Some lawyers recommend that you begin your cross-examination with a question such as, "I am going to ask you some specific questions, so please answer them with a simple 'Yes' or 'No' if possible; can you do that?"
- *The formal-objection approach.* Other lawyers recommend that you do not try to deal with a difficult witness yourself, but that you enlist the help of the judge by objecting to anything beyond a "yes" or "no" answer, such as "If the Court please, I object to the volunteered portion of the witness' answer and ask that the portion of it following the answer 'yes' be stricken."[44]
- *The self-help approach.* Some lawyers suggest that you appear weak and inexperienced if you have to go crying to the judge for help. They recommend that you handle the matter yourself. You may simply cut off volunteered testimony by stating, "Thank you, you have answered the question," or "Your lawyer can ask for explanations on redirect." Alternatively, you can be more sarcastic, saying something like, "Perhaps you did not hear my question. All I asked you was [repeat the question]. Do you think you can try to answer it?"

b. Knowing When to Abandon a Line of Questions

There are two reasons for deciding to stop pursuing a line of questions, one good and one bad. It will occasionally happen that the witness will give you an unexpectedly favorable answer partway through a planned line of questions. If you continue to press, the witness may retreat from that position and the point is lost. For example, suppose a defense attorney had prepared the follow-

---

[43] *See* JEFFREY T. FREDERICK, THE PSYCHOLOGY OF THE AMERICAN JURY 188 (1987).
[44] F. LANE, *supra* note 39, at § 19.78.

ing cross-examination of an eyewitness to a car-pedestrian accident, pointing out the witness' poor opportunity to observe:

Q: You did not see the defendant's car before the collision, did you?
Q: You were talking to a friend, correct?
Q: You were looking at your friend, is that right?
Q: Then you heard brakes squeal?
Q: You did not look toward the car until after the sound of the brakes, right?
Q: So you did not see whatever it was that caused the driver to slam on the brakes, did you?

Suppose the actual cross-examination went like this:

Q: Did you see the defendant's car before the collision?
A: No.
Q: You were talking to a friend, correct?
A: Yes.
Q: You were looking at your friend, is that right?
A: Yes — well, except for when my friend pointed out the plaintiff, who was walking down the middle of the street with a bottle of vodka in his hand.

You probably should not continue the line of questions!

The second reason to stop cross-examining is because you were pursuing a medium-safety topic, and the witness starts giving bad answers. Continuing the example above, suppose the cross-examination went like this:

Q: Did you see the defendant's car before the collision?
A: Yes.
Q: But weren't you talking to a friend just before the accident?
A: No, that was several minutes before the accident.

It is probably time to abandon this line of questions.

c. Choreography: Control Through Movement

In conducting a cross-examination, you should give some thought to where you will sit, stand or move during stages of the examination. Although some courts have local rules that restrict a lawyer's ability to move around the courtroom, most permit you to do pretty much what you want, except that *you may not approach too close to the witness*. Despite what you see on television, most judges will not permit you to lean on the edge of the witness box or get right up in the witness' face.

Standing and using fully the available space in the courtroom enables you to emphasize and focus the jurors' attention on certain questions by moving to the blackboard, picking up an exhibit, or changing your position. During the first part of your cross-examination, when you are eliciting helpful information, you can stand at the side of the jury, where you would for direct examination. This way the witness looks in the direction of the jury. During the impeachment phase, you can move closer to the witness and away from the jury. This may increase the tension on the witness and cause the witness to look away from the jurors. Either move may lessen the perceived credibility of that witness.[45]

d. Handling Interruptions by Opposing Counsel

Some lawyers will unethically try to interrupt cross-examination and tip off their witnesses to "correct" answers. They may make a vague objection that your question is misleading:

> I object. Counsel's question might mislead the witness. Counsel is obviously trying to insinuate that if the witness is talking to a friend, she cannot also be watching traffic. This witness was doing both at the same time.

You should object to this tactic. You might say:

> I object to the interruption by opposing counsel. He appears to be telling the witness what to say.

e. Handling Interruptions by the Judge

The trial judge has a right to interrupt a cross-examination to clarify testimony and bring out points overlooked by the attorney. The judge is not required to sit by and permit a miscarriage of justice. Therefore, the judge has discretion to interrupt and ask questions of the witness, but generally is not permitted to completely take over the cross-examination of a witness.[46]

Objecting to the judge's intervention is difficult, especially if you must do so in the presence of the jury. Goldstein suggests you phrase your objection as follows:

> If the Court please, I don't believe Your Honor intended to prejudice our case but I am afraid that the jury might take your questions to this witness in the wrong way. I feel that the record should show that we object to Your Honor's questions and the witness' answers.[47]

3. IMPEACHING WITH A PRIOR INCONSISTENT STATEMENT

The reason that high-safety questions are recommended is because you can impeach a witness who changes testimony. This obviously helps you control the cross-examination. However, this whole process of preparing safe questions containing single facts, using the witness' own words, and limiting yourself to leading questions, will control the cross-examination only if you know

---

[45]Psychologists have found that some witnesses appear less credible when tense, Albert Mehrabian & Martin Williams, *Nonverbal Concomitants of Perceived and Intended Persuasiveness*, 13 J. PERSONALITY & SOC. PSYCHOL. 37 (1969), or when they look away from the jury. Gordon Hemsley & Anthony Doob, THE EFFECT OF LOOKING BEHAVIOR ON PERCEPTIONS OF A COMMUNICATOR'S CREDIBILITY, 8 J. APPLIED SOC. PSYCHOL. 136 (1978).

[46]*See* Annot., Manner or Extent of Trial Judge's Examination of Witnesses in Civil Cases, 6 A.L.R. 4th 951.

[47]F. LANE, *supra* note 39, at § 19.89.

how to effectively carry out the impeachment. To do this, you must understand six things:

- *Impeachment is not the same as refreshing recollection.* If, in answer to a
  safe question taken directly from a prior statement, a witness testifies he
  or she does not remember, then you may choose to refresh recollection.
  However, if a witness gives an answer unexpectedly different from one
  contained in a prior statement, it does not mean the witness has forgotten
  the facts. You cannot refresh memory when the witness claims to be able
  to remember (nor has a proper foundation been laid to allow it); you must
  impeach and show the current memory to be unreliable.
- *You are not trying to talk a witness into recanting testimony, but to prove
  the witness is unreliable.* You are supposed to be impeaching, not trying to
  talk the witness into changing his or her testimony. You must accept the
  fact that the witness' memory has changed. No matter how sure you are
  that it was just an inadvertent misstatement, you will not convince the
  witness to testify differently, no matter how many times you ask the
  witness to re-read a prior statement. The only thing that will happen if
  you try is that the witness will just repeat and emphasize the unfavorable
  testimony, you will have completely lost control of the examination, and
  you will have wasted the opportunity to impeach. If it turns out the
  witness actually had made only an inadvertent misstatement, the witness probably will make the correction anyway when confronted with a
  prior inconsistent statement, so you lose nothing by assuming the worst
  and impeaching accordingly.
- *Inconsistent testimony does not mean the witness is evil.* When a witness
  testifies to facts different from those contained in a prior statement, it
  may be an inadvertent misstatement, a result of the natural process of
  erosion of memory. It might be an intentional change due to deliberate
  perjury, but is not necessarily so.
- *You impeach direct examination testimony, not cross-examination.* The
  general rule governing impeachment by prior inconsistent statements is
  that you may impeach facts testified to on direct examination only. If you
  bring up an issue for the first time on cross-examination and get bad
  answers, your only recourse is to abandon the line of testimony.
- *You may impeach specific factual assertions, not inferences.* You can impeach a witness who disagrees with a specific fact or opinion written
  down in a previous statement. However, if the witness disagrees with
  your *interpretation* of those facts, that cannot be impeached. For example,
  suppose a witness stated in a deposition that the defendant's car was
  traveling 60 miles an hour. If she testifies the car was going 30 miles per
  hour, you can impeach. If you ask for an interpretation, such as "Was the
  car going very fast?" and the witness says "No," you cannot impeach her
  by proving that she once said the car was going 60 miles per hour.
- *Impeachment always entails risk.* Witnesses will often be able to explain
  away an apparent inconsistency, and you will often be unable to successfully complete the impeachment. Therefore, conduct this kind of impeachment at the same time as other risky cross-examination — in the middle.

The technique for impeachment is as follows:

- Lock the witness into a definite answer.
- Prove that a prior statement on the subject was made.
- Reveal to the jury that the prior statement on this specific subject was materially different.

The first requirement is that the witness must have given actual testimony on the subject. Assume you represent the defendant in a personal injury case who is accused of running a red light and striking a pedestrian. The plaintiff calls a witness who said in a prior statement that the light was still green when your client drove through. On direct examination, suppose the witness cannot remember the color of the traffic signal. Can you impeach? No; the witness has not given any testimony on the matter.

Step one: Lock the witness into a definite answer.

Suppose the witness testifies on direct examination that the light was red — an obvious inconsistency. Your first step in the impeachment process is to lock the witness into a definite answer to a specific question. Try to do this without unnecessarily repeating the unfavorable testimony. It is probably a bad idea to ask the witness, "Are you certain of your testimony?" For example:

Q: You said the light was red?
A: That's right.
Q: Are you sure?
A: Oh yes, I looked at it very carefully.
Q: Could you be mistaken?
A: No.

Instead, remember you are laying a foundation for impeachment, in which you will suggest that the witness has recently changed his or her testimony. Emphasize the *old* version (the one that was changed), not the trial version. For example:

Q: The light was green, wasn't it?
A: No, it was red.
Q: Not green?
A: No.

Sometimes a witness who is aware of the inconsistency will refuse to be pinned down. For example:

Q: The light was green, wasn't it?
A: No, I think it was red.
Q: Are you saying definitely it was not green?
A: No, I'm not saying that, only that it might have been red. I wasn't paying close attention.

If the witness testifies to an inability to recall accurately, *you have accomplished your purpose* of proving that the witness' memory is unreliable, and it is pointless to continue. Recall that you are *not trying to get the witness to change his or her testimony.* If you press the matter, the witness will probably only explain away the prior statement by repeating that he or she is uncertain.

Step two: Prove that a prior statement on the subject was made.

Once you have the witness locked into a specific answer, you must prove that the witness made a prior statement covering this issue. You can do this by asking the witness about it, being specific about the time, place, and circumstances. For example:

> Q: Do you remember talking to an investigator named Sarah Frandsen at your house?
> A: Yes.
> Q: That was on September 16?
> A: Yes.
> Q: She asked you about the facts of this case, right?
> A: Right.
> Q: Do you remember answering questions about the scene of the accident?
> A: Yes.

In most jurisdictions, you are required to inform the witness of the time, place, and circumstances of the prior statement before you can refer to it. Even if not strictly required, it is good tactics to do so. It shows the witness and jury that you have a specific prior statement to which you are referring, and are not just fishing.

At this point in the process, some trial attorneys ask additional questions to build up the reliability of the prior statement. While most prior statements are hearsay unless they were made under oath,[48] and you cannot argue that the jurors should believe a prior statement for its truth, you may demonstrate that the prior statement is just as trustworthy as the trial testimony. This strengthens your impeachment, because it eliminates any logical explanation for the inconsistency other than bad memory or dishonesty. For example:

> Q: Two days later, Ms. Frandsen returned to your house, is that right?
> A: Yes.
> Q: She showed you a typed summary of your earlier conversation, is that right?
> A: Yes.
> Q: She asked you to read it over and sign it if it was accurate, correct?
> A: Yes.
> Q: Handing you defense Exhibit G for identification, is that your signature at the bottom?
> A: Yes.
> Q: You read the statement over before signing it, correct?

---

[48] FED. R. EVID. 801(d)(1)(A).

A: Yes.

Two other questions commonly are asked, but their legitimacy is dubious:

(a) Q: Wasn't your memory better one week after the accident than it is today, two years later?

(b) Q: Were you telling the truth when you made this statement or were you lying? (or worse) Were you telling the truth then or now?

The first question is irrelevant because the prior statement is being admitted to impeach, not for its truth. You can only argue that the earlier statement was the correct one if it meets a hearsay exception. Both types of questions are argumentative and tactically unnecessary.

Step three: Reveal to the jury that the prior statement on this specific subject was materially different.

The final phase of this impeachment is to prove the contents of the prior statement and expose the inconsistency. Remember that you are proving this to the *jury*, not the witness. You must reveal the contents of the prior statement to the jury; it is irrelevant whether you reveal it to the witness. The easiest way to do this is to read aloud the precise inconsistent passage and ask the witness to confirm that he or she made it. For example:

Q: Directing your attention to the second line in the second paragraph of that statement, did you say: "When the car drove through the intersection, it had a green light?"

If you are impeaching based on a deposition, the process is slightly more cumbersome:

Q: Directing your attention to page twenty-six, lines four through seven, is it true that you were asked these questions and gave these answers: Question: "What color was the light?"; answer: "Green"; question: "Are you certain?"; answer: "Yes"?

As a courtesy, you might lean over and show the witness the page and line you are referring to, but *do not hand the document over to the witness and ask the witness to peruse it.* You are not trying to convince the witness the testimony is inconsistent, but the jury.

If the witness admits the inconsistency, then the impeachment is complete, and you usually are not permitted also to introduce the statement into evidence unless you can lay the foundation for a hearsay exception. However, if the witness denies or does not remember making the statement, you may introduce it and read the inconsistent portion to the jury. Under FED. R. EVID. 613, the statement is admissible without further foundation, but in some jurisdictions, the statement must first be shown (not merely read) to the witness.

4. IMPEACHING WITH A PRIOR INCONSISTENT OMISSION

The most difficult kind of impeachment is to demonstrate that trial testimony is inconsistent with what was not said in a prior statement. Often, a witness will testify to something that was not mentioned in a prior statement at all or that seems to go so far beyond the statement that the witness must be making it up.

For example, a police accident report may contain no mention of any evidence of the defendant's intoxication, a notation that the plaintiff appeared "shaken" but that no ambulance was called, and a calculation that the defendant had been traveling at an (unspecified) excessive speed based on skid marks. Suppose that the officer testifies at trial that the defendant appeared intoxicated, the plaintiff appeared seriously hurt, and the defendant was driving approximately eighty miles per hour. Given the prior statement, the officer's testimony seems exaggerated, but there is no direct inconsistency.

To successfully impeach the officer's testimony, it is not sufficient merely to prove the prior statement. It is not necessarily inconsistent with the trial testimony. Rather, you first must establish that the failure to mention a fact in the prior statement is the equivalent of an explicit statement that the fact did not exist. This may be a difficult task, especially if the witness is aware of the problem and has a logical explanation for why some observations were omitted from an otherwise detailed statement.

Your first step is to use some common sense, and ask yourself whether the prior omission really amounts to an inconsistency. Two factors affect the likelihood of this: how detailed the prior statement is and how important the omitted fact is in relation to facts included. Thus, if the police report consisted only of a general one-paragraph summary, then it would not mean much that facts were omitted. But if the accident report were detailed, failure to include any reference to a driver's intoxication (surely an important fact to the police) logically suggests that the officer saw no evidence of it.

The second step is to decide whether there is a significant inconsistency, even assuming the prior statement represents all of the witness' knowledge. In our example, there is certainly an inconsistency between testifying to intoxication and the report's implication that there was no evidence of intoxication. There is also an inconsistency between the testimony that the plaintiff appeared seriously hurt and the report's implication that the apparent injuries were minor. But is there an inconsistency between "approximately eighty miles per hour" and "excessive speed"? Even assuming that the officer's failure to be specific in the statement meant he was unsure of the exact speed, that is not inconsistent with — in fact it corroborates — the trial testimony. The giving of further consistent details at trial that make prior damaging statements even more damaging is not making inconsistent statements, nor is it wise to emphasize such damaging testimony by going over it.

If you decide to attempt to impeach based on a prior omission, you must add one preliminary step to the impeachment technique discussed for prior inconsistent statements: you must eliminate (as far as possible) the possibility that the fact testified to was inadvertently omitted because the witness thought it unnecessary to include it. For example:

Q: Officer Jones, you investigate many similar cases, don't you?
A: Yes.
Q: You testify often about accidents?
A: Yes.
Q: Do you prepare an accident investigation report for each one?
A: Yes.
Q: You use the reports to refresh your recollection about a particular case before trial, correct?
A: Yes.
Q: They help you keep the facts straight?
A: Yes.
Q: So it is important that you be accurate in these reports?
A: Yes.
Q: You include all important facts you observe, don't you?
A: Yes.
Q: You include all facts that might have some bearing on who was at fault?
A: Of course.
Q: And you would include any facts that showed one driver might have violated a traffic law, isn't that correct?
A: Yes.
Q: Do you also write down if anyone was seriously injured?
A: Yes.
Q: Handing you defense exhibit B for identification, is this the report you prepared in this case?
A: Yes.
Q: On direct, you testified that the defendant was intoxicated, didn't you?
A: Yes.
Q: Please look over your report and answer this question: Did you make any mention whatsoever of any evidence of intoxication?
A: No.
Q: The plaintiff did *not* appear to be seriously injured, correct?
A: No, he looked seriously hurt.
Q: Again, I direct you to your report. Is there any mention in your report of anyone being seriously hurt?
A: No.
Q: In fact, you wrote that the plaintiff only appeared "shaken," isn't that right?
A: Yes.

5. MANNER AND STYLE

a. Fairness Toward the Witness

You should remember to maintain an attitude of fairness toward the witness. Most people seem innately to distrust lawyers (probably with good reason) and feel that they deliberately use tricks and loopholes to create misimpressions. Thus, jurors may penalize a lawyer who attempts to trick or confuse a witness. They will usually side with the witness against a lawyer who takes advantage of his or her training to trick the witness into distorting the testimony by a cleverly phrased question.

Unfairness can take many forms, all of which probably should be avoided. It once was popular to ask witnesses whether they have discussed their testimony with the opposing lawyer. If the witness answered "yes," it sounded like the testimony was coached. If the witness answered "no," the attorney would argue that the witness obviously was lying. A few lawyers still recommend the use of such questions, but most caution against it — it is improbable that jurors will hold it against a witness that the witness was outsmarted by a clever lawyer.

A more common form of unfair question is one that attempts to distort the true meaning of a witness's testimony. Lawyers are especially adept at taking matters out of context, putting unrelated facts together, and trying to stretch the testimony of a witness beyond the truth. Facts are not so easily manipulated. Misstating or distorting facts to try to create an incorrect impression is a bad tactic. It may cause the witness to argue with you, it will be resented by the judge and jury, and it is improper both legally and ethically. Whenever you are tempted to try it, remember that your adversary has an opportunity for redirect. Not only can he or she put things back into their proper context, but your opponent also can show the jury how unfair you were.

b. Style

Style is largely a personal matter. You may be naturally aggressive and stubborn or you may be quiet. Your strengths may lie in your ability to reason logically, to argue emotionally, or to persuade cleverly. So, too, the manner in which you conduct cross-examination should suit your personality. Just because lawyers are aggressive, hostile, arrogant and sarcastic on television does not mean you should try to adopt such a style. Consider the following discussion by FRANCIS X. BUSCH, LAW AND TACTICS IN JURY TRIALS, vol. 3: 526-33 (1960):

> Politely, but firmly, the cross-examiner should insist that the witness answer his questions in sufficiently loud voice and distinctly, so that the jury may hear and understand each response. The examination should, at all times, be conducted with dignity and reserve; slang should never be resorted to, and sarcasm employed sparingly. The examiner should not appear over-smart. If he does so appear, and succeeds in eliciting a favorable answer on cross-examination, it is apt to be attributed by the jury not so much to the unreliability of the witness as to the sharpness of the lawyer. Cross-interrogation should ordinarily be put in even, rapid se-

quence; and closely directed to one subject at a time. The purpose of putting questions rapidly is threefold: the attention of the jury is better maintained; the witness has less time to consider the effect of his answers; and rapid questioning is calculated to produce rapid answers. A witness answering rapidly is more likely to contradict himself than one who answers after having been given plenty of time to deliberate.

A hesitant, rambling cross-examination cannot be effective. Some lawyers, usually the inexperienced ones, are given to repeating all, or the last part, of every answer made by a witness.[49] The habit is pernicious and minimizes the chances of success in an examination. This automatic repetition emphasizes the witness's answers, slows up the examination, and gives the witness an added opportunity, between an answer and the next question, to weigh the effect of his last answer and prepare for the next question.

At all times must it be kept in mind that the witness is entitled to courteous treatment. The most direct, searching and damning cross-examination, even of one who is hostile and deemed to be dishonest, can be conducted with an observance of proper courtesy.

In this connection, it is pertinent to observe that the trained advocate never loses his temper, whatever the provocation may be. Simulated anger, like pretended surprise, may sometimes be resorted to with telling effect; but this is far different than an actual loss of temper. Loss of temper means loss of mental control; and unless he has complete mental control of himself at all times, the advocate is risking a wrecking of his cause.

The style of an advocate's cross-examination will necessarily depend to a greater or lesser extent upon the natural disposition of the examiner. The trained advocate, however, will cultivate and employ the style which he thinks is best calculated to produce effective results. Speaking generally, there are two prevailing styles: the savage, slashing, "hammer-and-tongs" method of "going after a witness to make him tell the truth"; and the smiling, soft-spoken, ingratiating method directed to lulling the witness into a sense of security and gaining his confidence. Neither style can be adopted to the exclusion of the other for every situation that may be presented. There are many situations where a vigorous, rapid-fire examination is likely to produce the best results, just as there are many situations where a quiet, easy, friendly examination will elicit more that is favorable to the examiner. The experienced advocate, like the seasoned baseball pitcher, relies upon his ability to change the pace to suit the varying conditions in the game. It is submitted that in most cases the gentler approach is better calculated to elicit the concessions which the

---

[49] For example:

Q: You were walking home, correct?
A: Yes, I was.
Q: You were. This was about 8:00 p.m.?
A: Yes. Maybe 8:05.
Q: Okay, 8:05. Then you arrived at Wilson's drug store?
A: No, I stopped first at the post office to mail a letter.
Q: After you mailed your letter at the post office, did you go to the drug store?

examiner desires. The savage, vehement style of cross-examination ordinarily makes the hostile witness more hostile. In some cases, such an examination angers the witness to the point of impelling him to make vicious answers. While this may weaken the effect of his direct testimony by emphasizing his partisanship and hostility, the content of the answer may be such as to lead the jury to believe that the witness is beating the examiner at his own game. Only the complete success of such an examination will keep the advocate in the jury's good graces. The repeated failure of such examinations is incalculably prejudicial. The witness is the "underdog" and the jury's sympathies are ordinarily with him.

NOTES

1. *Should you decline to cross-examine after a confusing direct examination?* Charles Garry, a prominent trial attorney, suggests that you should "not cross-examine an honest witness who tells his story in a rambling, illogical way and so buries it in insignificant details, that the jury cannot make it out. If you do, every question you ask him may awaken some forgotten fact." Garry, *Cross-Examination and Trial Tactics*, 11 LINCOLN L. REV. 77, 90 (1979). This is a risky decision. To opt for this approach, your evaluation must be accurate, because you will be passing up the opportunity to weaken the testimony. If it later turns out that the jury did understand the direct examination, the testimony will be unchallenged.

2. *Using sarcasm.* The temptation to use a sarcastic tone or make sarcastic remarks when cross-examining a witness who has testified to absurd or ridiculous facts often is irresistible. It is one of the most dangerous tactics to adopt, since it depends entirely for its success on the jurors' agreeing with you that the testimony was as ridiculous as you thought. If the jurors disagree, you have accomplished "negative persuasion." *See generally* Robert Abelson and James Miller, *Negative Persuasion Via Personal Insult*, 3 J. EXPERIMENTAL SOC. PSYCHOL. 321 (1967). Sarcastic remarks also violate the rule against being argumentative during cross-examination, and any persistent use of sarcasm is ground for being held in contempt. *Hawk v. Superior Ct.*, 42 Cal. App. 3d 127, 116 Cal. Rptr. 713 (1974). In most cases, it is better to wait until closing argument to point out the improbability in the testimony. Still, there are successful trial lawyers who believe that occasional sarcasm, when you are certain the jurors will agree with you, can be effective. Consider the following suggested cross-examination from DAVID COHEN, HOW TO WIN CRIMINAL CASES BY ESTABLISHING A REASONABLE DOUBT 631 (1977):

> Q: Mr. Johnson, isn't it a fact that you are approximately six feet tall?
> Q: And offhand, I would say that you weigh about 200 pounds, is that correct?
> Q: You have testified that you are a construction worker, isn't that so?
> Q: So then you do heavy manual work in your occupation?
> Q: You are not a weak man, are you?
> Q: Mr. Johnson, do you know that my client is only five feet seven inches in height?
> Q: And do you know that he weighs 160 pounds?

Q: And did you know that he is a music teacher at Monroe High School?
Q: And it is your testimony, is it, that this puny five-foot-seven-inch,
160-pound music teacher savagely beat a six-foot 200-pound construction
worker?

3. *Maintaining composure.* It is important that you maintain your composure during cross-examination. Not all cross-examinations will be successful. Situations frequently will arise in which you will get hit with an unexpected and damaging answer. The impact of the answer is not lost on the jury.
Since most jurors are convinced that the lawyers know the real truth about
the case, they may look at you to observe your reaction. If you seem unper-
turbed, the jurors may think that the answer was not as damaging as it first
appeared. *See, e.g.,* F. LEE BAILEY & HENRY ROTHBLATT, SUCCESSFUL TECH-
NIQUES FOR CRIMINAL TRIALS § 182 (1971). Also, remember that if you get
angry, you lose control. MARK A. DOMBROFF, DOMBROFF ON DIRECT AND CROSS-
EXAMINATION 210 (1985).

H. BIBLIOGRAPHY

1. COMPREHENSIVE

FRANCIS X. BUSCH, LAW AND TACTICS OF JURY TRIALS, vol. 3: 473-978 (1960).
JOHN E. DURST & FRED QUELLER, ART OF ADVOCACY — CROSS-EXAMINATION OF
     LAY WITNESSES (1988).
FRED LANE, LANE'S GOLDSTEIN TRIAL TECHNIQUE, chs. 19-20 (3d ed. 1984).
PATRICK McCLOSKEY & RONALD SCHOENBERG, CRIMINAL LAW ADVOCACY —
     WITNESS EXAMINATION (1992).

2. LAW

J. Alexander Tanford, *An Introduction to Trial Law*, 51 Mo. L. REV. 623,
     667-74 (1986).

3. ETHICS

RICHARD H. UNDERWOOD & WILLIAM H. FORTUNE, TRIAL ETHICS 341-54 (1988).

4. TACTICS

ROBERTO ARON ET AL., IMPEACHMENT OF WITNESSES: THE CROSS-EXAMINER'S
     ART (1990).
Paul Bergman, *A Practical Approach to Cross-Examination: Safety First*, 25
     UCLA L. REV. 547 (1978).
Harry S. Bodin, *Principles of Cross-Examination, in* CIVIL LITIGATION AND
     TRIAL TECHNIQUES (1976).
ASHER CORNELIUS, THE CROSS-EXAMINATION OF WITNESSES (1929).
William Gallagher, *Technique of Cross-Examination, in* CIVIL LITIGATION AND
     TRIAL TECHNIQUES (H. Bodin ed. 1976).
JOHN IANNUZZI, CROSS-EXAMINATION: THE MOSAIC ART (1982).
JAMES W. JEANS, TRIAL ADVOCACY, ch. 13 (1975).
ROBERT KEETON, TRIAL TACTICS AND METHODS 94-164 (2d ed. 1973).

Jeffrey T. Kestler, Questioning Techniques and Tactics (2d ed. 1992).
Steven Lubet, *Understanding Impeachment*, 15 Am. J. Trial Advoc. 483 (1992).
James McElhaney, *Constructive Cross-Examination*, Litigation, Winter 1988, at 49.
James McElhaney, *The Story Line in Cross-Examination*, Litigation, Fall 1982, at 45.
James McElhaney, *Impeachment By Omission*, Litigation, Fall 1987, at 45.
Louis E. Schwartz, Proof, Persuasion, and Cross-Examination (1973).
Francis Wellman, The Art of Cross-Examination (1923).
Irving Younger, *The Art of Cross-Examination* (ABA Litigation Section Monograph No. 1, 1976).

Chapter 8

EXPERT WITNESSES

A. INTRODUCTION

For trial lawyers, this is the era of the expert witness. The trial of cases is becoming dominated by the opinions of experts to an extent never before seen in the judicial system. Virtually all cases that go to trial today involve the testimony of expert witnesses. One study of civil jury trials revealed that expert witnesses were called in 86% of cases, at an average rate of four experts per case.[1] This is hardly a surprising development in our modern technological society. The types of cases being brought to court increasingly involve questions of science, engineering, psychology and economics. The routine personal injury case now involves every kind of expert from the family doctor to technicians who operate complicated diagnostic equipment to professional job counselors and economists to predict the future. Product liability and routine tort cases require engineers, architects, physicists, and designers. Criminal cases need psychiatrists and chemists. Whole new fields of expertise have been invented to serve the trial system, such as forensic medicine and accident reconstruction.

It is therefore of the utmost importance that you know how to use expert witnesses effectively and how to cross-examine your opponent's experts. In many ways, the techniques and tactics of examining expert witnesses are the same as those for other witnesses. However, there are also some issues unique to experts. This chapter discusses the law and tactics specially related to expert witnesses, assuming that you already know how to examine ordinary witnesses. You should not attempt to conduct either a direct or cross-examination of an expert without first reading Chapters 5 through 7, covering trial evidence, direct examination and cross-examination.

NOTE

Sample witness examinations. Several good examples of the direct and cross-examinations of expert witnesses can be found in JAMES W. JEANS, LITIGATION, §§ 11.29, 16.15 (2d ed. 1992); FRED LANE, LANE'S GOLDSTEIN TRIAL TECHNIQUE, ch. 16 (3d ed. 1984); and THOMAS A. MAUET, FUNDAMENTALS OF TRIAL TECHNIQUES 124-37 (3d ed. 1992).

B. LEGAL FRAMEWORK

The legal rules concerning expert testimony fall into five categories:

- *Qualifications.* The witness must be properly qualified to be an expert.

---

[1] Samuel Gross, *Expert Evidence*, 1991 WISC. L. REV. 1113, 1119.

- *Necessity.* The subject matter must be sufficiently complicated that expert testimony will be helpful to the jurors.
- *Scientific reliability.* Techniques and theories used or relied on by an expert must be scientifically reliable.
- *Opinion rule.* Experts may testify to a wide range of opinions based on personal knowledge, reliable hearsay, or facts presented in a hypothetical question.
- *Learned treatises.* Experts may be cross-examined concerning inconsistent statements in learned treatises.

1. QUALIFICATIONS NEEDED TO BE AN EXPERT

In order for a witness to testify as an expert, he or she must be qualified by reason of knowledge, skill, experience, training, or education in a field of specialized knowledge.[2] The question of the witness' competency is left to the sound discretion of the trial judge,[3] although in the modern era it is rare for a judge to refuse to qualify a witness. In order to lay the foundation, you must call your witness to the stand and elicit testimony about that person's credentials, unless your opponent stipulates to the witness' expertise.[4] Since the possession of sufficient qualifications concerns the competency of the witness to testify, your opponent has the right to conduct a voir dire — to cross-examine the witness on his or her qualifications *before* the witness gives further testimony.[5]

After you have elicited the witness' qualifications, you should formally tender the witness to the court as an expert in a particular field of specialty. Forgetting to make this formal offer is not fatal, however; a qualified witness may give opinions whether or not previously tendered to the court as an expert.[6] If your opponent has any objections to the witness being accepted as an expert, or to the areas in which he or she is qualified, these objections probably should be made at the time the witness is tendered as an expert.

2. ISSUES ON WHICH EXPERT ASSISTANCE IS PERMITTED

Before a qualified expert will be permitted to testify, the judge must determine that the issues are complex enough to warrant expert testimony. This is a relevance determination: Will the assistance of an expert provide probative information that the jury would otherwise be without? The modern trend

---

[2]See FED. R. EVID. 702. See also Balfour v. State, 427 N.E.2d 1091 (Ind. 1981) (police officer held to be an expert after only four hours of training); Central Ill. Light Co. v. Porter, 96 Ill. App. 2d 338, 239 N.E.2d 298 (1968) (wildlife biologist, conservation officer, and duck hunter all qualified to give opinions on effect of power lines on duck hunting).

[3]See United States v. Lopez, 543 F.2d 1156 (5th Cir. 1977); McCORMICK ON EVIDENCE § 13 (4th ed., J. Strong ed., 1992).

[4]Since the jury must evaluate testimony based on the credibility of witnesses, you may refuse a stipulation and prove your expert's qualifications. See Murphy v. National R.R. Passenger Corp., 547 F.2d 816 (4th Cir. 1977).

[5]See State Highway Comm. v. Barnes, 151 Mont. 300, 443 P.2d 16 (1968). See also EDWARD J. IMWINKELRIED, EVIDENTIARY FOUNDATIONS 16-17 (2d ed. 1989).

[6]See Dickens v. Everhart, 284 N.C. 95, 199 S.E.2d 440 (1973).

favors the use of experts whenever they will be of any assistance to the jury. FED. R. EVID. 702 provides:

> If scientific, technical, or other specialized knowledge will assist the [jury] to understand the evidence or to determine a fact in issue, a witness qualified as an expert ... may testify.

Under older common law, the test was stricter. Expert testimony was not admissible unless an issue was completely beyond the understanding and common experience of the average juror.[7] The modern trend seems more consistent with other rules of relevancy that admit any nonprejudicial testimony with probative value, even if the probative value is small. Expert testimony with a high potential for confusing the issues or arousing prejudice can be ruled inadmissible despite having some probative value, just like any otherwise relevant evidence.[8]

3. SCIENTIFIC RELIABILITY

In conducting their investigations and arriving at opinions, experts rely on scientific theories, principles, techniques and equipment. For example, in diagnosing a patient, an expert neurologist may rely on X-rays, spinal taps, brain scans, and electroencephalograms performed by the technical staff of the hospital. Thus, the reliability of the neurologist's diagnosis depends on the competence of the staff, the proper functioning of the equipment, and the correctness of the underlying scientific principles. Before the expert can testify about the results of such tests, a three-part foundation must be laid: (1) the person conducting the test must have been qualified to do so; (2) the equipment used must have been in good working order and been operated properly; and (3) the underlying theories, principles and techniques must be scientifically reliable.

The first two issues are questions of competence — whether the person conducting the test was properly qualified and whether the test was properly performed. The strictness with which courts require proof of the competency of staff and technicians varies.[9] It is likely that the more important or conclusive an individual test is, the greater the showing of reliability required; the less important an individual test is, the less strict the foundation required. For example, when a neurologist runs a battery of tests designed to overlap each other, repeated at two-day intervals, and then forms conclusions based collectively on all the information gathered, the importance of any one test is low. As with other competency issues, the decision whether a sufficient foundation has been laid that the results are reliable is left to the court's discretion.

The courts are not in agreement concerning how to prove scientific reliability. The traditional foundation requirement is known as the *Frye* test: the scientific theories, principles and techniques used must be generally accepted

---

[7] *E.g., State v. Maudlin*, 416 N.E.2d 477 (Ind. App. 1981).

[8] *See* James McElhaney, *Expert Witnesses and the Federal Rules of Evidence*, 28 MERCER L. REV. 463, 475 (1977).

[9] *E.g., State v. Magoon*, 264 A.2d 779 (Vt. 1970); *State v. Baker*, 56 Wash. 2d 846, 355 P.2d 806 (1960).

within the scientific community.[10] If there is controversy in the scientific community about the validity of the principles involved, the court should not permit testimony about them. It is under this doctrine that courts for the last fifty years have excluded testimony about polygraph tests.[11] However, recent cases have tended to repudiate the *Frye* doctrine and permit evidence of controversial testing procedures if there is some evidence of reliability, leaving to the party who opposes it the task of producing his or her own experts who can point out the controversial nature of the procedures.[12]

4. EXPERT OPINIONS

The purpose for calling an expert is to elicit the expert's opinion concerning an issue in the case that may not be obvious to the untrained juror. If that opinion is based on facts and data personally known to the expert through observation and experimentation,[13] it presents no unusual evidentiary issues. Any witness who has personal knowledge of relevant facts is competent to testify to those facts and can give opinions logically based on them. Thus, the physician who personally examined an injured person can testify to his or her diagnosis based on that first-hand knowledge.

It goes almost without saying, however, that experts also take into account what they read or are told. Yet, the hearsay rule would seem to prevent them from disclosing this information to the jury. For example, an emergency room physician may make a diagnosis of a concussion in part because the nurse said that the ambulance attendant said the patient seemed to slip in and out of consciousness. The dilemma is obvious — if we follow the hearsay rule and exclude this information, the conclusion drawn by the doctor may appear to the jurors to be unsupported by the evidence or may even be excluded altogether.

Modern evidence law resolves this problem with a compromise. An expert opinion may be based facts or data "made known to the expert at or before the hearing." If of a type reasonably relied upon by experts in the particular field in forming opinions or inferences upon the subject, the facts or data need not be admissible in evidence."[14] The expert may, however, discuss the hearsay basis for an opinion — not for its truth, but to help the jury evaluate the credibility of that opinion.[15]

Under modern practice, there are few formalities of expert testimony. The expert may give his or her opinion in any manner the expert chooses, as long

---

[10]*Frye v. United States*, 293 F. 103 (D.C. Cir. 1923). *See also Reed v. State*, 283 Md. 374, 391 A.2d 364 (Ct. App. 1978) (applying *Frye* test to exclude voiceprint analysis).

[11]*See* Note, *Courtroom Status of the Polygraph*, 14 AKRON L. REV. 133 (1980).

[12]*See United States v. Williams*, 583 F.2d 1194 (2d Cir. 1978); *United States v. Baller*, 519 F.2d 463 (4th Cir. 1975); *State v. Williams*, 388 A.2d 500 (Me. 1978); *Coppolino v. State*, 223 So. 2d 68 (Fla. App. 1968). *See generally* Paul Giannelli, *The Admissibility of Novel Scientific Evidence: Frye v. United States a Half a Century Later*, 80 CALIF. L. REV. 1197 (1980); J. Alexander Tanford, David Pisoni & Keith Johnson, *Novel Scientific Evidence of Intoxication: Acoustic Analysis of Voice Recordings from the Exxon Valdez*, 82 J. CRIM. L. & CRIMINOLOGY 579, 591-602 (1991).

[13]Pretrial experiments must be conducted under "substantially similar conditions" to those existing at the time of the actual event. *See Barnes v. General Motors Corp.*, 547 F.2d 275 (5th Cir. 1977).

[14]FED. R. EVID. 703.

[15]*See* Gross, *supra* note 1, at 1157.

as it is confined to the expert's own field of specialty.[16] Older common-law procedure dictated strict rules of form and procedure that often excluded expert testimony because one or two magic words were omitted — either the expert failed to testify "to a reasonable certainty,"[17] or the expert used the wrong causation standard.[18]

It used to be that the facts upon which an opinion was based had to be in evidence before the opinion could be given. If an expert had personal knowledge of these underlying facts, the expert first recited the facts and then gave an opinion.[19] If an expert was relying on second-hand information, however, the process was more complicated. Information told to the expert or contained in written records had to be proved first in court by witnesses with personal knowledge. After all the facts were in evidence, the examining attorney had to restate all the important facts in a hypothetical question.[20] This process is cumbersome and tedious, and the hypothetical question is prone to objection that important facts have been omitted or misstated, or that it contains facts not in evidence. In one famous case, the hypothetical question covered eighty-three pages of the transcript and the objection pointing out important facts omitted or misstated covered fourteen additional pages.[21]

Many jurisdictions have followed the lead of the Federal Rules of Evidence and modernized these archaic rules. The Federal Rules have abrogated the old rule which limited opinions to those based on admissible evidence and presented in hypothetical questions:

> *Rule 703. Bases of Opinion Testimony by Experts.* The facts or data in the particular case upon which an expert bases an opinion or inference may be those perceived by or made known to the expert at or before the hearing. If of a type reasonably relied upon by experts in the particular field in forming opinions or inferences upon the subject, the facts or data need not be admissible in evidence.

> *Rule 705. Disclosure of Facts or Data Underlying Expert Opinion.* The expert may testify in terms of opinion or inference and give reasons therefor without prior disclosure of the underlying facts or data, unless the court requires otherwise. The expert may in any event be required to disclose the underlying facts or data on cross-examination.

Even in jurisdictions that have retained the requirement of a hypothetical question, the trend is to relax the foundation. As long as the question is not so distorted that it would mislead the jurors, it will be permitted. If the opponent

---

[16] *See* FED. R. EVID. 705; *Gibson v. Healy Bros.*, 109 Ill. App. 2d 342, 248 N.E.2d 771 (1969).

[17] *E.g., Strohn v. N.Y.L.E. & W.R.R.*, 96 N.Y. 305 (1884) (expert testified a result was "very likely" instead of "reasonably certain"; case reversed).

[18] *Compare Keith v. United Cities Gas Co.*, 266 N.C. 119, 146 S.E.2d 7 (1966) (expert must testify to what "could have" been the cause and not to what "did" cause a result) *with Stone v. Thomas*, 84 N.Y.S.2d 257 (Sup. Ct. 1948) (expert must testify to what "did" cause result, not to what "could have" caused it).

[19] *E.g., State Hwy. Comm. v. Barnes*, 151 Mont. 300, 443 P.2d 16 (1968); *Mutual Life Ins. Co. v. Jay*, 112 Ind. App. 383, 44 N.E.2d 1020 (1942).

[20] *See Dahlberg v. Ogle*, 268 Ind. 30, 373 N.E.2d 159 (1978); *Dean v. Carolina Coach Co.*, 287 N.C. 515, 215 S.E.2d 89 (1978).

[21] *Treadwell v. Nickel*, 194 Cal. 243, 228 P. 25 (1924).

thinks it assumes facts not in evidence, omits essential facts, or does not contain sufficient facts to be reliable, he or she may explore such issues on cross-examination and may ask additional hypothetical questions. The question itself is not objectionable.[22]

5. CROSS-EXAMINATION AND IMPEACHMENT

Experts may be cross-examined and impeached like other witnesses. You can inquire into their abilities and opportunities to observe the events to which they have testified, test their memories about those events, and bring out facts tending to impeach their credibility, such as biases, interest in the outcome, motives to testify falsely, prior inconsistent statements, bad character for truthfulness, and prior criminal convictions.[23] You can explore the factual bases underlying their opinions and elicit further details about matters brought out in direct examination.

In addition, three special rules concerning the cross-examination of experts deserve your attention and are discussed below: inconsistent statements in learned treatises, fees and financial interest, and bad reputation as an expert. Only the first two are permitted.

Expert witnesses may be impeached by showing that the basic texts and treatises in their fields come to different conclusions or state different views than those they testified to. At common law, these are treated like prior inconsistent statements — because they are hearsay, they are admissible only to impeach the expert and not for their truth. FED. R. EVID. 803(18) created an exception to the hearsay rule for this use of learned treatises, which permits you not only to introduce them, but also to argue that the treatise is more reliable than the expert who contradicts it:

> *Rule 803(18).*   To the extent called to the attention of an expert witness upon cross-examination or relied upon by the expert in direct examination, statements contained in published treatises, periodicals, or pamphlets on a subject of history, medicine, or other science or art, established as a reliable authority by the testimony or admission of the witness or by other expert testimony or by judicial notice [are admissible]. If admitted, the statements may be read into evidence but may not be received as exhibits.

You may use a learned treatise to impeach if two requirements are met: the treatise is established as a reliable authority, and the expert is confronted with it before it is read into evidence. Under the federal rule, this is easy. You can prove reliability by inducing the expert to admit to it, by calling your own expert to authenticate it, or if well known enough, by judicial notice. The confrontation requirement is satisfied either if the expert refers to the book in direct examination or if you call it to his or her attention during cross-examination. At common law, depending on the jurisdiction, you might be restricted

---

[22]*See Ramsey v. Complete Auto Transit*, 393 F.2d 41 (7th Cir. 1968); *City of Indianapolis v. Robinson*, 427 N.E.2d 902 (Ind. App. 1981).

[23]*See* Gross, *supra* note 1, at 1166-68. *See also Scott v. Spanjer Bros.*, 298 F.2d 928 (2d Cir. 1962) (bias); *Young v. Group Health Co-op*, 85 Wash. 2d 332, 534 P.2d 1349 (1978) (prior inconsiste.it statement).

to treatises specifically referred to by the expert, treatises actually relied on by the expert in forming his or her opinion, or treatises the expert admitted were reliable.[24]

Experts also can be impeached by inquiring into their financial interests and the fees they receive for testifying. The courts generally agree that you can show that the expert is being paid for his or her time, the amount of compensation, and that this amount exceeds the statutory witness fee. If the expert has not yet been paid, you can cross-examine about the amount he or she expects to be paid. In addition, you usually are permitted to prove that the expert is on retainer to, has testified previously for, or has an ongoing financial relationship with an attorney, a party, or an insurance company.[25]

What if the other side calls a real crackpot witness, whom all your experts agree is a fraud — can you impeach that witness by showing his or her bad reputation as an expert? The answer seems to be no, although the issue comes up rarely.[26] Presumably, if the witness really is so bad, you will be able to impeach that person successfully by showing a lack of qualifications and education, and by using learned treatises and your own experts to contradict the pseudo-expert's testimony.

NOTES

1. *Judicial discretion to determine qualifications.* Whether a witness is qualified to be an expert is a matter for judicial discretion. This is well-illustrated by *Thornton v. Galliard*, 111 Ga. App. 371, 141 S.E.2d 771 (1965), in which the judge found a witness to be an expert despite the witness' testimony that he did not consider himself an expert. The appellate court said that "the mere fact that the witness in his testimony may disclaim to be an expert is no reason for refusing to allow him to testify as one."

2. *Opinions on the "ultimate" issues.* Under older common law, experts were not permitted to state opinions on the ultimate issues the jurors were supposed to decide. Thus, in a negligence case, experts could not "invade the province of the jury" by giving an opinion on whether injuries were caused by an accident. Although some jurisdictions still pay lip service to this doctrine, it has largely disappeared. Initially, courts created semantic ways of circumventing the rule: experts could testify that injuries were "consistent with" an accident of the type being litigated, or they were permitted to testify that the accident "could" or "might" have caused the result. *Keith v. United Cities Gas Co.*, 266 N.C. 119, 146 S.E.2d 7 (1966). More recently, jurisdictions have eliminated the rule altogether. FED. R. EVID. 704 explicitly states that an opinion "is not objectionable because it embraces an ultimate issue to be decided by the trier of fact." *Accord DeVaney v. State*, 259 Ind. 483, 288 N.E.2d 732 (1972); *Metropolitan Life Ins. Co. v. Saul*, 189 Ga. 1, 5 S.E.2d 214 (1939). *But see Mitchell v. State*, 154 Ga. App. 399, 268 S.E.2d 360 (1980) (expert cannot give opinion on exact ultimate issue before the jury). However, experts

---

[24] *See Miller v. Griesel*, 297 N.E.2d 463 (Ind. App. 1973) (relied on); CAL. EVID. CODE § 721(b) (referred to, relied on, or admitted).

[25] *See* Michael Graham, *Impeaching the Professional Expert Witness by a Showing of Financial Interest*, 53 IND. L.J. 35, 41-50 (1977).

[26] *See, e.g., Adams v. Sullivan*, 100 Ind. 8 (1884).

still may be prevented from giving purely legal opinions. *See, e.g., Marx & Co. v. Diners' Club, Inc.*, 550 F.2d 505 (2d Cir. 1977) (opinion on legal obligations of parties under a contract inadmissible).

3. *Court-appointed experts.* Because of the venality of some professional expert witnesses, it is rarely difficult to find someone to testify on any side of almost any issue. The professional "consultant" who makes a living selling his or her opinions to attorneys is a fact of life in litigation. No matter what the issue, no matter how extreme the facts, it seems that every lawsuit ends up with experts on both sides. It is no wonder that courts are suspicious about the academic neutrality of expert witnesses. This is not a new phenomenon. *See, e.g., Schlagenhauf v. Holden*, 379 U.S. 104, 125 (1964) (Douglas, J., dissenting) ("a doctor for a fee can easily discover something wrong"); *Opp v. Pryor*, 294 Ill. 538, 128 N.E. 580 (1920) (expert testimony is "generally discredited and regarded as the most unsatisfactory part of judicial administration ... because the expert is often the hired partisan, and his opinion is a response to a pecuniary stimulus"). In order to make more reliable experts available, modern evidence codes usually provide for court-appointed experts. Judges always have had, but rarely have used, an inherent power to appoint their own experts. *See* John M. Sink, *The Unused Power of a Federal Judge to Call His Own Expert Witnesses*, 29 S. Cal. L. Rev. 195 (1956). With the adoption of Fed. R. Evid. 706, this practice has become more common, but is still underused.

4. *Can you subpoena a reluctant expert?* Some jurisdictions greatly restrict your ability to subpoena an expert witness, even prohibiting it altogether. The majority permit you to subpoena an expert with personal knowledge of controverted facts or one who already has formed an opinion, such as a neurologist called in by the treating physician as a consultant. However, most jurisdictions do not permit you to compel an expert to perform tests or review a file for the purpose of reaching an opinion. There is great variation. *See* Note, *Compelling Experts to Testify*, 44 U. Chi. L. Rev. 851 (1977). *See also United States v. International Bus. Mach. Corp.*, 406 F. Supp. 178 (S.D.N.Y. 1976) (enforcing a subpoena).

C. ETHICAL CONSIDERATIONS

Little attention has been paid to the abuses of the expert witness rules. The Model Rules of Professional Conduct contain no mention of expert witnesses, failing even to acknowledge the problems of plaintiffs' whiplash doctors and defendants' in-house experts. Considering the pervasiveness of the use of experts, the importance of their testimony and its influence on jurors, and the growing problems of partisan expert witnesses, the lack of attention to these issues seems a strange oversight at best.

1. SELECTION AND PRESENTATION OF EXPERT TESTIMONY

The most serious ethical issues arise in the selection and presentation of expert testimony. Perhaps caught up in adversarial zeal, many lawyers see nothing wrong with shopping for expert witnesses who will testify in their favor, rejecting all those who come to different conclusions, regardless of the merits of the case. The sad fact is that, even if all respectable experts hold a contrary view, if you look long enough you can find someone who will pass as an expert to testify on your side.

The classic example of this practice is the case of a psychiatrist in Texas who became known as "Dr. Death" after he was called by the prosecution in more than fifty death sentence hearings. According to one account, in every case, whether he had examined the defendant or not, he testified that in his medical opinion the defendant had no regard for human life and was a remorseless sociopath who would continue his violent behavior if released. In all but one case, the jury then imposed a death sentence. The psychiatrist was well-known to favor the death penalty, and he could be counted on to give devastating testimony supporting capital punishment. Prosecutors continually used him to give such testimony despite the fact that the American Psychiatric Association has said that no psychiatrist can accurately predict long-term behavior under these circumstances.[27]

Is calling an expert known to be biased, who can be counted on to give favorable testimony regardless of the facts, unethical? It does not amount to subornation of perjury in the same sense as hiring a witness willing to testify to anything for a fee. It does not run afoul of the prohibition in Rule 3.3 against offering evidence *known* to be false. If frequency of occurrence were the measure of ethical conduct, there would be nothing wrong with this practice.

Professional ethical standards, however, appear to require something more. To say simply that it is proper to present experts such as "Dr. Death" because you can comply with the minimal legal requirements of expert testimony is to beg the ethical question. Ethics require that you refrain from using false or fraudulent evidence, and that you may (and probably should) "refuse to offer evidence that the lawyer reasonably believes is false."[28] Ethical Considerations promulgated under the superseded MODEL CODE OF PROFESSIONAL CONDUCT reminded lawyers they were supposed to avoid bringing about unjust results[29] or inflicting needless harm on others.[30] Lawyers owe a duty to the system of justice to utilize procedures that command public confidence and respect,[31] and are under a general obligation not to engage in conduct involving dishonesty or misrepresentation.[32] Selecting a person to testify as an expert who can be counted on to give a favorable opinion, even if the evidence is insufficient to support it, is difficult to rationalize as anything other than deceiving the court.[33]

---

[27] Tybor, *Dallas' Doctor of Doom*, NAT'L L.J. at 1 (Nov. 24, 1980). One of his cases has been the subject of a Supreme Court opinion, although not on the ethical issues. *See Estelle v. Smith*, 451 U.S. 454 (1981).

[28] MODEL RULES OF PROFESSIONAL CONDUCT Rule 3.3(c).

[29] MODEL CODE OF PROFESSIONAL RESPONSIBILITY EC 7-14.

[30] *Id.* EC 7-10.

[31] *Id.* EC 7-20.

[32] MODEL RULES OF PROFESSIONAL CONDUCT Rule 8.4(c).

[33] *See* Martin L. Norton, *Ethics in Medicine and Law: Standards and Conflicts, in* LAWYERS' ETHICS 269-70 (A. Gerson ed. 1980). The comments following Rule 3.3 prohibit the lawyer from cooperating in deceiving the court and thereby subverting the truth-finding process. Rule 8.4 prohibits the lawyer from engaging in conduct involving fraud or deceit.

2. PAYMENTS TO EXPERT WITNESSES

If you paid five thousand dollars to an ordinary witness to encourage him or her to testify for you, you would be subject to disciplinary action and possible prosecution for bribery. Yet, legal ethics permit you to pay large sums of money to experts to induce them to testify for your client, as long as the inducement is not "illegal."[34] This distinction seems strange. Are experts any less susceptible to financial inducements? Not all experts are wealthy neurosurgeons. Consider the pressure on a young scientist or professor who is told that if he or she reaches a favorable conclusion, then the attorney will employ that person for five thousand dollars as an expert witness. The practice often is defended on the ground that experts must be compensated for their time or to make up for income lost because the person could not be seeing paying clients. Again, this rationale is weak and seems based on the assumption that all experts are physicians in private practice. Many experts from industrial or university jobs receive a yearly salary and suffer no income loss by taking time off to testify. If a self-employed expert happened to witness a traffic accident, he or she might lose as much time through interviews, depositions, hearings, preparation and testimony without being compensated. Jurors and nonexperts take as much time away from their jobs as expert witnesses, but are compensated only by statutory fees (usually very small).

The official ethic of our profession, however, prohibits only contingent fees. An expert who is to be paid only upon a favorable verdict may be induced to give stronger or more positive testimony than he or she otherwise would give. For that reason, ethical rules have always prohibited such arrangements,[35] although the explicit prohibition has been dropped from the latest version of the ABA Model Rules.

3. PREPARING EXPERT WITNESSES

Experts who are hired as consultants to evaluate a file and render an opinion lack personal knowledge of the facts. So where do they get their information? From the lawyer, of course. It should be obvious that you must provide your expert with *complete* information. You may not withhold test reports or notes from investigators that are unfavorable, nor may you screen out information you think is irrelevant. You lack the expertise to decide what is relevant. Deliberate manipulation of the information your expert may rely on is nothing more nor less than participating in the creation of false evidence.[36]

Despite the obviousness of this ethical rule, experienced litigators give tactical advice to the contrary. One writes that you should provide only "enough

---

[34] MODEL RULES OF PROFESSIONAL CONDUCT Rule 3.4(b). *See also* MODEL CODE OF PROFESSIONAL RESPONSIBILITY DR 7-109(C)(3); EC 7-28.

[35] *See* Note, *The Contingent Compensation of Expert Witnesses in Civil Litigation*, 52 IND. L.J. 671 (1977); Note, *Contingent Fees for Expert Witnesses in Civil Litigation*, 86 YALE L.J. 1680 (1977). For an interesting opinion holding the prohibition against contingent fees unconstitutional because it discriminates against the less affluent who cannot afford to hire experts, *see Person v. Association of the Bar*, 414 F. Supp. 144 (E.D.N.Y. 1976), *rev'd*, 554 F.2d 534 (2d Cir. 1977).

[36] *See* MODEL RULES OF PROFESSIONAL CONDUCT Rule 3.4(b) (a lawyer shall not assist a witness to testify falsely).

information so that the expert will be well prepared," but withhold "materials that would open the door to ... cross-examination." In that way you will assure that only "helpful opinions are reached."[37] Another urges that you should not give your expert facts or documents unless "you do not mind if the opposition does learn or see them."[38] Such advice flies in the face of the ethical rules and amounts to nothing less than a recommendation that you deliberately manufacture false evidence.

4. CROSS-EXAMINATION OF EXPERT WITNESSES

The law of evidence permits you to test the knowledge of an expert witness by asking hypothetical questions that assume facts about which no evidence has been introduced. To do so ethically, you must make it clear that you are only speaking hypothetically. You may not stretch this rule to justify the creation or presentation of false evidence, nor to insinuate the existence of facts you know you cannot support with admissible evidence.

The limits on cross-examination to test expertise were explored in *In Re Metzger*,[39] in which an attorney was charged with misconduct for the following cross-examination of a handwriting expert. The expert had testified that a letter (exhibit "G") and an envelope (exhibit "F") were written by the defendant.

> [T]he respondent, giving to the clerk a receipt for the three papers, withdrew the letter, the envelope and the [exemplar] and retained them in his possession until the Monday morning shortly before the opening of the trial. [Respondent] fabricated ... a facsimile of [the exemplar], duplicating the typewritten matter and the handwritten matter as closely as he could. [When trial resumed,] the respondent, retaining the genuine [exemplar] in his custody, handed to the clerk of the court the letter and the envelope which he had received from the clerk and the spurious [exemplar]. When [the expert] took the stand ... the respondent said to the clerk of the court: "You got that exhibit there, so that Mr. Bailey may see it?" [T]he clerk handed to the respondent and the respondent handed to the witness the letter (exhibit "G") and the spurious [exemplar.] Upon handing these two papers to the witness the respondent immediately resumed his cross-examination as to the peculiarities of the handwritings, saying to the witness: "Then on the card the 'g' seems to have a characteristic something like this (drawing on blackboard); had you not noticed that?" Lengthy and detailed cross-examination followed, relating to the peculiarities, similarities and dissimilarities of the writings on the letter and on the spurious [exemplar.]

The trick worked. The expert never noticed that the exemplar was a fake, and testified at some length as to how similar it was to the letter and envelope. When it was revealed that the expert had been unable to identify forged

---

[37] James E. Daniels, *Managing Litigation Experts*, A.B.A. J., Dec. 1984, at 64-66.
[38] Peter I. Ostroff, *Experts: A Few Fundamentals*, LITIGATION, Winter 1982, at 9.
[39] 31 Haw. 929 (1931).

handwriting, the impeachment was complete. The court, however, was not amused:

> There can be no doubt that it was the right and the duty of the respondent, who was entrusted with the defense of two men who were on trial for their lives, to expose if he could what he believed to be a lack of ability and a lack of credibility or accuracy on the part of the witness who had testified as an expert on handwriting; but there was a limitation upon that right and that duty and the limitation was that the test and the exposure must be accomplished by fair and lawful means, free from falsehood and misrepresentation. The so-called "necessities of the case," the keenness of the desire of the attorney to defend the accused to the best of his ability, cannot in our judgment justify falsehood or misrepresentation by the attorney to a witness or to the clerk of the court, whether that falsehood or misrepresentation be expressed in direct language or be conveyed by artful subterfuge. We are unwilling to certify to the younger attorneys who are beginning their experience at the bar of this court, or to any of the attorneys of this Territory, that it is lawful and proper for them to defend men, even though on trial for their lives, by the use of falsehood and misrepresentation, direct or indirect. The conduct of the respondent was unethical and unprofessional.

One judge dissented:

> Metzger's right to impeach ... Bailey's opinion that the letter, envelope and card were written by the same hand it seems to me must be conceded. Indeed it was not only his right to do this but his duty to do so — his duty to his clients, to the jury and to the court. Of course if he had known that the letter and the envelope were in the handwriting of one of his clients, as he knew that the writing on the card was, the situation would be quite different. Under such circumstances his effort would have been not to destroy what he believed to be false but to destroy what he knew to be true. I think a lawyer, even in his zeal to extricate his client from a serious position, may not ethically go so far. This, however, was not the case. At the hearing of the instant proceeding Metzger testified that having had considerable experience in chirography he believed that the writing on the card was not by the same person as the writing on the envelope and in the letter. There is no apparent reason for disbelieving him. His purpose therefore was not the evil one of misleading the jury as to a fact which he knew existed but the laudable one of exposing what he believed to be an erroneous opinion. This was in the interest of justice and not against it. Metzger also testified that he had been unable after a long cross-examination of Bailey to discredit his opinion and that there was no other handwriting expert available whom he could consult or to whose opinion he could submit the writings. His only alternative therefore was in some way to lead Bailey to disclose his own fallibility.... I do not think that his treatment of the witness was unfair. A cross-examiner is certainly under no professional obligation to warn an expert witness, whose opinion he wishes to test, of the pit which has been dug for him and into

which he will fall unless he has sufficient technical learning to discover and avoid it.... It is a principle peculiar to the cross-examination of expert witnesses that in order to evaluate their opinions things may be assumed as facts which are not facts. This is all that Metzger really did. He in effect assumed, in the presence of the witness, the court and the jury, that the fabricated card was the real exhibit about which the witness had already testified and proceeded to ascertain by cross-examination whether he was capable of discovering that the assumption was false. In doing this he was entirely fair to the witness. According to his testimony he required Bailey to subject the fabricated card to the same tests to which he had subjected the real exhibit and to compare it with the writing on the envelope and the letter just as he had compared the real exhibit. It was an acid test of the value of Bailey's opinion, but no more severe than that to which a handwriting expert may properly be put.

Another variation of this kind of fraudulent cross-examination involves impeachment by learned treatises. Some trial lawyers suggest that if you are cross-examining a known charlatan, you can expose him or her as a faker if you are willing to create a little false evidence. They recommend that you ask the witness if he or she is familiar with the leading treatises, naming several well-known books but including in the list some fictitious authors.[40] If the witness is stupid enough to testify that he or she has studied a fictitious book, the impeachment obviously will be successful. However, to the extent that this tactic requires that you create false evidence, the practice is hard to justify as ethical. Your motives may be good, and you may take steps to insure that the jury understands (after the fact) that the evidence was false, but there is nothing in the Model Rules that permits the temporary use of false evidence even for good reasons.

D. DIRECT EXAMINATION

In almost every case you will have to decide whether you need to call any expert witnesses. If you decide to use expert testimony, you will have to locate and select appropriate witnesses, prepare them to testify, and plan and conduct effective direct examinations. The same is true, of course, for nonexpert witnesses. The techniques for preparing and conducting direct examinations in general are discussed in Chapter 6 and will not be repeated here. However, expert witnesses present some unique issues that deserve special attention.

1. WHETHER TO USE EXPERT TESTIMONY

Is it a good idea to call expert witnesses if the opportunity arises? Most lawyers think so; the majority of cases litigated today involve some sort of expert testimony.[41] Research by social psychologists backs this up. Experts can be quite persuasive and therefore are generally an asset to any case,[42] at

---

[40] *E.g.*, FRED LANE, LANE'S GOLDSTEIN TRIAL TECHNIQUES § 17.43 (3d ed. 1984).

[41] Gross, *supra* note 1, at 1119 (experts called in 86% of California civil cases).

[42] *See, e.g.*, Allan Raitz, Edith Greene, Jane Goodman, & Elizabeth F. Loftus, *The Influence of Expert Testimony on Jurors' Decision Making*, 14 LAW & HUM. BEHAV. 385, 390 (1990).

least as long as the expert's opinion verifies the jurors' intuition. Scientific and expert testimony that runs contrary to the personal anecdotal experiences of the jurors will tend to have little impact.[43]

In a few situations, the decision whether to use expert testimony may be taken out of your hands. In some kinds of cases, e.g., medical malpractice and insanity defense, state law may require you to present expert testimony or face a directed verdict. Other cases may involve a technical or scientific matter that simply cannot be proved without an expert, e.g., products liability, medical damages, possession of narcotics.

In many cases, however, expert testimony is not strictly necessary. For example, the state could try an accused based entirely on eyewitness testimony, but if experts can connect fingerprints, clothing fibers, and bullets found at the scene to the defendant, the case will be that much stronger. In these cases, you must engage in a benefit-cost analysis. Will an expert be of substantial assistance by providing unique evidence on an important issue, or of less help by offering redundant evidence or testifying on an unimportant issue? The potential benefits must be weighed against the costs. Not only are experts expensive, but also every time you use multiple experts on the same or closely related points you increase the risk that they might contradict each other.

One other reason for involving an expert should not be overlooked. An expert can assist you in the pretrial stages of a case involving technological issues. Even if you do not intend to call an expert yourself, you must be prepared to cross-examine experts called by the other side. An expert, even one who essentially agrees with the conclusions reached by opposing experts, can render valuable assistance by helping you understand the issues, decide whether to settle the case, and prepare for cross-examination by reviewing the procedures followed by the experts on the other side.

2. SELECTION OF EXPERT WITNESSES

If you decide to use experts, the next step is to select whom to use as a witness. Some experts have personal knowledge of relevant facts, and must be called, e.g., the emergency room physician who treated the plaintiff, or the police chemist who tested the cocaine. Beyond that, however, you probably have choices. The decision process involves two steps: preparing a list of names, and then selecting the best available candidate.

Numerous sources are can be consulted in order to compile a list of names. The following suggestions will get you started:

- The chair of a relevant academic department at a nearby university may be able to furnish the names of qualified alumni or faculty.
- Other attorneys who have handled similar cases may have already compiled such a list. Attorneys also may be able to tell you how the expert performed on the witness stand.

---

[43] *See* ROBERT NISBETT & LEE ROSS, HUMAN INFERENCE: STRATEGIES AND SHORTCOMINGS OF SOCIAL JUDGMENT 55-56 (1980); Neil J. Vidmar & Regina Schuller, *Juries and Expert Evidence: Social Framework Testimony*, 52 LAW & CONTEMP. PROBS. 133, 166-71 (1989).

- Professional directories, such as the American Chemical Society's Directory of Graduate Research, or the Directory of Medical Specialists put out by Who's Who.
- Classified advertisements in legal publications.
- The yellow pages.
- A computer-assisted search for recent similar cases in your vicinity will probably provide the names of experts that testified on unusual topics. If you wonder whether any experts have testified recently on cases of bubonic plague, try searching for it on LEXIS or WESTLAW.
- The indexes to scientific publications may yield names of experts who have written recent articles on the subject of interest to you. For example, a search through recent issues of Law and Human Behavior will provide names of experts who can testify about eyewitness unreliability.

The second step is to choose one of the experts from your list. The most important factor is the expert's inherent credibility. By this term we mean to distinguish between those factors affecting credibility that emerge during direct and cross-examination and factors affecting the way jurors will perceive the expert regardless of the content of testimony. The latter category can be called inherent credibility, and it is made up of three primary components: the personal reputation of the witness, the reputation of institutions with which the expert is associated, and the method used by the expert in arriving at an opinion.

- *The expert's personal reputation.* An expert witness who practices in your community may be well known to some of the jurors. For example, in selecting a medical expert, what better person could you choose than a local physician with a reputation as a good doctor, a doctor on whom many of the jurors routinely rely for advice? If jurors know in advance that this person is credible, they will be inclined to accept his or her opinions. Bear in mind, however, that reliance on local experts is a double-edged sword. Some jurors may have had bad experiences with that person. Particularly in small communities, a doctor may be accepted as the best in town and still not be perceived as especially skilled. This same kind of personal credibility can be a factor in selecting a local plumber or house builder as an expert.
- *The reputation of the institutions with which the expert is associated.* The credibility of experts will be affected by the quality of the institutions with which the expert is affiliated, such as the university attended or the place where the witness now works. In selecting an expert, you should look for people with connections to institutions that are perceived as particularly credible *to the jurors.* For two reasons, this is not always a question of the objective ranking of the institution: 1) Although The Johns Hopkins may be one of the best medical schools in the country, the jurors may never have heard of it and may give more credibility to graduates of the state medical school; and 2) There is some evidence that

jurors find most credible persons of slightly higher status, rather than much higher status.[44]

- *The method used to arrive at an opinion.* Did the expert conduct firsthand investigations, personally examining and testing the persons and objects involved, or did he or she simply review a file? Jurors probably find medical opinions more credible if they come from an expert who actually examined and treated the patient than if they come from experts who only reviewed the medical records.[45]

In addition, you might consider the following factors:

- Is the expert attractive? Research shows that physically attractive witnesses are perceived as more credible and more intelligent than unattractive witnesses.[46]
- Does the expert speak plain English? The expert needs to be able to explain things to the jury (and to you) in comprehensible terms.
- Is the expert's attitude and appearance professional without being aloof and patronizing?
- Can the expert be impeached with his or her own published words? Has the expert ever written books or articles espousing a viewpoint contrary to the stance the expert will take for you, or taking the position that no firm conclusions can be drawn in this area?
- Is the expert up-to-date? Has the person written recent articles or books, recently taught classes in the area, or recently attended continuing education seminars in the field? Developments in scientific and technical fields can happen very rapidly, and you need an expert who is familiar with the cutting edge of his or her field.
- Has the expert testified before? Previous courtroom experience will have helped the expert learn how to testify understandably and withstand cross-examination. A veteran expert may be able to offer good advice on how to present his or her evidence most persuasively, and may even have exhibits or scale models that have been used successfully in prior cases.
- Has the expert previously testified for both sides? An expert who testifies exclusively for one side or in defense of one industry (e.g., "whiplash doctors") are vulnerable to cross-examination. They have lost their aura of scientific impartiality.
- Is the person willing to testify? Rarely may you use the subpoena power to compel an expert to testify; nor would it be a good idea. You probably should consider this alternative only when absolutely necessary, when you cannot prove your case by any other means. Experts forced to testify may not be as helpful as you would like them to be — they may be resentful of the imposition and look for ways to teach you a lesson.

---

[44] Ellen Berscheid, *Opinion Change and Communicator-Communicatee Similarity and Dissimilarity*, 4 J. PERSONALITY & SOC. PSYCHOL. 670 (1966).

[45] *See* RITA J. SIMON, THE JURY: ITS ROLE IN AMERICAN SOCIETY 60 (1980).

[46] *See* Daniel Linz and Steven Penrod, *Increasing Attorney Persuasiveness in the Courtroom*, 8 LAW & PSYCHOL. REV. 1, 35-38 (1984).

3. PREPARATION

The first step in preparing for direct examination of an expert is to become an expert yourself. Before you can even effectively discuss specialized issues with an expert, you must acquire an in-depth knowledge of the subject matter. You should be able to speak the expert's language and understand the basic concepts of his or her field of specialty. You can acquire this knowledge by reading scientific texts and journals, or, in the more common fields of specialty, treatises written especially for lawyers.[47]

After you have acquired a general knowledge of the subject, you must turn your attention to the preparation of the direct examination of your expert. This process can be broken down into four separate tasks.

- Discuss the merits of the case with the expert.
- Prepare an outline of the direct examination.
- Work with the witness to make the direct examination clear and effective.
- Prepare the expert for the ordeal of courtroom testimony.

a. Initial Consultation

The first step in preparing expert testimony is the initial consultation. The scope of your interview with an expert is broader than that of an ordinary witness. You need to find out:

- The extent of the expert's personal knowledge of the events, just as you would interview any occurrence witness.
- The opinions the expert has reached and the reasons for them.
- The degree of certainty underlying the opinion, and if the expert is uncertain, what the next most likely conclusion is.

In addition to interviewing the expert, you need to use him or her as a consultant. You can:

- Go over any records, reports, or information gathered by or prepared by the expert.
- Involve the expert in planning the rest of your case. Would it help to gather additional data or conduct further tests? Does the expert know the opponent's experts? Where are the strengths and weaknesses in the case? Should you litigate or settle? An expert, especially one who has testified before, can be of great value early in the preparation process by acting as your consultant on a matter beyond your personal expertise.

b. Planning the Direct Examination

Planning the content and the organization of your direct examination should be carried out in cooperation with the expert. While the ultimate

---

[47] Examples of the kinds of texts written for lawyers include: ROBERT GORDON, FORENSIC PSYCHOLOGY (1977); ATTORNEYS' TEXTBOOK OF MEDICINE (1989); FREDERICK A. JAFFEE, A GUIDE TO PATHOLOGICAL EVIDENCE FOR LAWYERS AND POLICE (2d ed. 1983); ANDRE MOENSSENS ET AL., SCIENTIFIC EVIDENCE IN CRIMINAL CASES (3d ed. 1985).

responsibility for preparing the direct testimony is yours, the expert can assist you in deciding what to include or omit. The expert will be especially helpful in planning testimony about his or her qualifications and in drafting hypothetical questions.

(1) Introduction

What do you do first? In every other stage of the trial, our general strategy has been to start strong, emphasizing some important aspect of the case. There is no reason to abandon that strategy now. The introduction should inform the jury who the witness is and what the witness' role in the case is, and should emphasize an important point — usually, the witness' ultimate opinion. For example:

Q: What is your name?
A: Dr. Lauren Jones.
Q: Are you the psychiatrist who examined the defendant?
A: Yes.
Q: What was your diagnosis?
A: In my opinion, he knew what he was doing when he shot his wife. He was not clinically insane.

(2) Qualifications

You generally must begin direct examination by eliciting testimony about the expert's qualifications to establish his or her competence. If the witness is a doctor or other traditional expert, the subjects you will need to cover are fairly straightforward:

- Present occupation, title and rank.
- Experience and employment history.
- Formal education, including college and advanced degrees.
- Formal post-degree training, including apprenticeships, medical residencies, fellowships, continuing professional education seminars, or other specialized training.
- Teaching experience or affiliations with universities, especially any courses taught that relate to the opinion the expert will give.
- Publications in general, with special emphasis on any that relate to issues in the case.
- Membership in relevant professional societies, especially those in which membership is an honor.
- Membership on national committees or commissions.
- Honors and prizes received.
- Relevant inventions or scientific breakthroughs made by the expert, and any patents he or she holds.
- State licenses to practice that have been granted.
- Previous litigation experience.

If the expert is self-taught, or is an expert in a nontraditional field of specialty, you may have to modify these questions to emphasize the length of his or her experience and the frequency with which the witness is consulted by courts or businesses.

To what extent should you elicit testimony about qualifications? You must balance the necessity of convincing the jurors that the expert's testimony will be credible against the risk that jurors will become bored, or worse, view the process as needless and tasteless self-praise.

> The question of the extent to which you should prove those qualifications is primarily a matter of giving to the proof the amount of time and attention that will result in the most favorable impression on the jury. Laboring over insignificant details will bore the jury and perhaps lead them to the impression that you are trying to build up the witness beyond what the facts justify. There is also a possible advantage in omitting some of the details so the witness may have something further to offer in the event your adversary chooses to cross-examine regarding his qualifications. On the other hand, proof [only] of the bare essentials necessary to make the testimony admissible fails entirely to serve the second aim of persuading the jury that the witness is competent and his testimony accurate. In most cases in which you have an expert witness, your adversary will have one also and the jury must decide which one is right. Although the content of their testimony and their methods of expression will have more influence on the jury's choice between them, their respective qualifications are also likely to have weight. Accordingly, you should not be content with proving only the bare essentials.[48]

(3) Tender Witness as an Expert

Although it is not legally necessary to make a formal tender of the witness as an expert in a particular field, it is tactically advantageous. It gives you the opportunity to specify a particular field of expertise related to the case, to make it appear that your witness is a specialist. For example, if your medical expert is a general practitioner who will disagree with the other side's internal medicine specialist about the extent of internal injuries, you can close the expertise gap as follows:

Q: What do you do as a general practitioner?
A: Patients come to me first, with all sorts of symptoms and complaints. My job is to diagnose their ailments, and either treat them myself or refer them to a specialist.
Q: How many diagnoses do you do a day?
A: Twenty or thirty.
Q: That would be about 100 diagnoses a week, or 5,000 each year?
A: That's about right.
Attorney: Your Honor, we offer Dr. Jones as an expert witness in the diagnosis of medical problems.

The formal tender results in the judge accepting your witness as an expert in front of the jury. It also resolves the issue of whether your witness is properly

---

[48] ROBERT KEETON, TRIAL TACTICS AND METHODS 57-58 (2d ed. 1973).

qualified early in the examination, and prevents your opponent from disrupting the heart of your direct examination with an objection to qualifications.

(4) Facts and Opinions

Trial practitioners disagree about how to structure the remaining elements of an expert's testimony — facts and opinions. Rarely will an expert's testimony be amenable to the kind of orderly chronological presentation recommended for lay witnesses. There is general agreement that experts should be asked not only their opinions, but also the reasons for them and how they arrived at their conclusions. Without this information, the jurors will have difficulty deciding which expert is more credible. Beyond this, there are probably as many suggestions on organization as there are practicing attorneys.

If the expert has personal knowledge of the facts underlying an opinion, as in the case of a treating physician, a semblance of chronological order may be possible. You can start with the patient's first visit and have the doctor testify to the steps he or she took in reaching a diagnosis: medical history, observations, consultations with other doctors, examinations and laboratory tests. You then can elicit a diagnostic opinion of the patient's problem and an opinion as to the cause of that problem. If the doctor continued to treat the patient, you next can elicit testimony about that treatment and the results of subsequent examinations. Finally, you can end with a prognosis: the permanency of the injury, the likelihood of continuing pain, and the need for and cost of future medical care. Alternatively, you can ask the expert for his or her opinion about causation at the end, using it as the climax of direct examination.

If you are examining a consulting expert, you may still use a modified chronological order. You can begin with how the expert became involved in the case, including the expert's fees. Next, you can have the expert testify about the course of his or her investigation. This approach follows the chronological order of the investigation, not the original event. The consultant may have looked first at a patient's present condition, then at tests run a month before that, and lastly at the nature of the patient's early symptoms. This order generally follows a methodology that looks at aspects of the case history in order of importance. The expert can then explain any assumptions he or she has made that are important to the opinion. Finally, the expert states his or her opinion.

At times, chronological order will not be the best way to present expert testimony and another logical order must be found. This is especially likely for expert consultants. One technique is to ask the expert what investigative steps should be taken and then to elicit testimony about those steps in their order of importance. Professor James McElhaney uses as an example a physician who examined the plaintiff in the emergency room on a busy night.[49] Using chronological order may present a picture of chaos. The taking of the plaintiff's medical history may have been interrupted while the doctor treated a knife wound on another patient. The doctor may have returned to the plaintiff and begun an examination, only to be called away to tend to a head injury

---

[49]James McElhaney, *An Introduction to Direct Examination*, LITIGATION, Winter 1976, at 38.

victim from an automobile accident. The doctor may have returned to the plaintiff, decided that internal injuries were possible, and ordered X-rays and a hematology report. While awaiting the results, the doctor may have seen other patients. While eating a sandwich, the doctor may have examined two sets of X-rays at once, deciding that the plaintiff could go home but that another accident victim should be admitted. Before the doctor can complete the entry in the plaintiff's chart, she may have been called to emergency surgery, delivered a baby, and consulted with police officers about a shooting victim. Presenting these details in chronological order would give the jurors the impression of confusion, disorganization, and lack of attention. However, if the doctor is asked to list the tests that should be conducted to rule out internal injuries, and then testifies that she performed each test and made a diagnosis based on the results, the apparent state of confusion is minimized.

The easiest method of all, available in jurisdictions following the Federal Rules of Evidence, may be simply to elicit the expert's opinion and then ask how he or she drew that conclusion. This can be used both for experts with and experts without personal knowledge. For example:

Q: Were you asked to review and evaluate the plaintiff's medical files to determine the permanency of his paralysis?
A: Yes.
Q: Did you do so?
A: Yes.
Q: What is your conclusion?
A: Mr. Smith's paralysis is irreversible and permanent. There is no hope of a medical recovery.
Q: What is the basis for your opinion?

If the expert had personally treated the plaintiff, a similar format could be used:

Q: Are you the plaintiff's treating physician?
A: Yes.
Q: Did you examine and treat him for paralysis?
A: Yes, I did.
Q: Have you formed an opinion on the permanency of this condition?
A: Yes.
Q: What is your conclusion?
A: Mr. Smith's paralysis is irreversible and permanent. There is no hope of a medical recovery.
Q: Will you tell us how you arrived at that opinion?

If your expert lacks sufficient firsthand knowledge of the facts, you may decide to ask a hypothetical question, although they generally are not legally required. Hypothetical questions have been criticized as boring, confusing, too complex, repetitive of testimony, biased, and time consuming.[50] However,

---

[50] See MARSHALL HOUTS, DEATH, vol. 3 of COURTROOM MEDICINE, § 8.05 (1981): "In a recent case ... a typewritten hypothetical question which required 22 minutes to read was propounded with great seriousness to four consecutive medical witnesses.... By noon the attorney had lost his

well-phrased hypothetical questions may be tactically advantageous in some situations. Their use permits you to summarize the favorable evidence and to pinpoint the important facts on which the opinion is based. Unless the case is either so simple that no summary of the evidence is necessary or so complex that no brief and concise hypothetical question can be formulated, many trial practitioners continue to favor them.

If you decide to use hypothetical questions, they should be prepared in advance with the assistance of the expert. You are courting disaster if you either omit facts the expert thinks important or fail to show the question to your expert until trial. This advance preparation is necessary because your question must strike a delicate balance between being simple enough for the jury to follow and being detailed enough for an expert to use as the basis for a reliable opinion. On the one hand, you are striving for a concise question written in ordinary language that contains only the minimal facts necessary so that it will be listened to and understood by the jurors. On the other hand, the question should contain all important facts in precise detail; otherwise, it is subject to attack as misleading and may even be excluded by the judge.

c. Preparing the Content of the Expert's Testimony

The most important preparation task for most experts is to help the witness translate complicated medical or scientific concepts and jargon into lay terms. This is crucial, because expert testimony must be understood to be valuable. For the jurors to understand and accept an expert's opinions, they must understand not only the terminology, but also the technical concepts and principles used to arrive at a conclusion.

Many experts do not speak naturally in lay terms. They may be reluctant to do so, because ordinary language is too imprecise to express technical distinctions. They simply may have forgotten how to do so, having become used to speaking in the language of their profession. In either event, you must work with your expert on translating jargon into plain English and explaining scientific phenomena by analogy to events of everyday experience.

For example, if a medical expert tells a juror that she diagnosed a complete transection of the left sciatic nerve eight inches above the popliteal fossa, and performed surgery to re-proximate the nerve channels so that the nerve could regenerate, the jurors might understand some of it. However, if the expert uses plain language and analogies, all jurors will be able to understand what is going on:

> Mr. Jones' left leg was paralyzed and when we stuck pins in his leg he could not feel any pain from the knee down. Therefore it was obvious that the sciatic nerve — that's the main nerve for the whole leg — had been cut a few inches above the knee. A team of neurosurgeons operated on him to try to repair the nerve. This sciatic nerve is like a telephone cable, containing thousands of little wires or nerve fibers that follow the main channel until they branch off to a tiny piece of skin or muscle. Now, when

---

voice, the judge was reading a brief in another case, and the jury was mentally scattered between Yankee Stadium ... and Malibu."

the sciatic nerve is cut, all the fibers beyond that cut die. However, they can grow back, or regenerate — it's like pruning a plant. The problem is to make them grow back in the right direction. To do this, you have to reconnect the dead nerve fibers to the sciatic nerve. We actually sew them together. In this way, the new growing nerve fibers can use the old ones as pathways.

It is also important to anticipate potential weaknesses and misunderstandings inherent in expert testimony. Experts may use different standards in evaluating information than judges and juries. For example, an expert may believe that nothing can be proven with certainty; yet the jurors expect an unequivocal opinion. Alternatively, the expert may be comfortable basing a conclusion on a generally accepted theory that cannot be objectively verified while the jurors expect tangible proof. You must eliminate these areas of potential misunderstanding with your witness, either by convincing the expert to change his or her standards or by working out an explanation that will educate the jurors about the expert's standards.

Scott Baldwin provides some helpful illustrations about how this process might work in preparing a medical expert to testify. He suggests that you should explain to the expert the legal meanings of terms such as proximate cause and reasonable degree of medical certainty. If you are going to ask the expert for a prognosis, emphasize to him or her that the law does not require the expert to be absolutely certain — the plaintiff cannot wait for death to verify that his or her injury was permanent. Explain that the law recognizes that expert opinions can be given only in terms of probable results based on the limits of our medical knowledge and therefore a court will accept such opinions. If the expert understands this, he or she will be better able to give testimony without hedging.[51]

Baldwin also emphasizes that you must explain to the expert that the jury may be suspicious of theories and conclusions not objectively provable.[52] Rational scientific assumptions should not be taken for granted, but should be explained to the jury. For instance, if a diagnosis is based in large part on subjective complaints, you should prepare your medical expert to testify about the importance of a medical history in diagnosis, the fact that all doctors rely on them, and how hard it would be for a patient to know how to fake all the symptoms. If inconclusive tests were conducted, such as negative X-rays, the expert should be told that the jurors may not understand that this does not negate the presence of an injury. While all doctors may know that the kind of injuries suffered by the plaintiff do not often show up on X-rays, the jury must be given this basic medical education to interpret the facts correctly.

d. Preparing the Expert for the Courtroom

There is strong evidence that jurors initially have positive feelings about experts, hold them in high regard, and give considerable credit to their testi-

---

[51] SCOTT BALDWIN, ART OF ADVOCACY — DIRECT EXAMINATION § 22.01[11]-[15] (1981).

[52] For example, many people are suspicious of the theory of evolution in part because scientists cannot show them an actual example of a four-million-year-old primate. Simply calling something a "theory" may cause a lay juror to think it is only speculation.

mony.[53] However, experienced trial lawyers believe that this initial favorable feeling can turn into dislike or distrust by certain attitudes an expert may display at trial — condescending experts who talk to jurors as if they were simpletons, haughty experts who get angry if anyone questions their opinions, supercilious experts who give the impression they are wasting their valuable time testifying, and any expert who shows impatience, flippancy, disdain, or tends to try to prove his or her superiority over lawyers. If any of these traits appear in your expert, you should discuss them with your witness, and work on eliminating them. Lawyers suggest that you advise all your expert witnesses against volunteering information and going off on tangents, lecturing the jury, or expressing contempt for other experts, lawyers, or the judge. An expert's appearance may also be strengthened if he or she is told to be open about fees, to answer honestly without evasion, to avoid saying "I think so" if he or she means "yes," and to maintain academic neutrality. Above all, your expert must be made to understand that he or she is now in a legal context, and that you are in charge of directing the examination. In addition, if the expert is used to testifying in another jurisdiction, or has not testified before, you should explain any legal and procedural rules that restrict expert testimony or require that it be couched in certain terms. All of these suggestions will help the expert give more persuasive testimony.

The best way to assure effective courtroom testimony is probably to conduct a mock direct examination. If the witness has bad testifying habits, these can be pointed out and corrected. This practice examination will be especially helpful if the expert is going to use charts, diagrams, or models to illustrate his or her testimony. However, not all lawyers agree that a full practice examination is necessary. If the expert has considerable experience testifying, a complete practice session may be optional, as long as you go over carefully all important parts of the testimony.

Preparing an expert witness for cross-examination involves the same considerations as preparing any important witness. See Chapter 6, part G. In addition, you should discuss with your experts ways of dealing with special kinds of cross-examination to which only experts are susceptible: learned treatises and large fees.

You must explain that a learned treatise may be used to contradict the expert. Anything in a treatise that contradicts your expert's testimony is admissible, if your opponent can prove the book is authoritative, even if the book is outdated or every expert knows the author got that one passage wrong. For that reason, the expert should be cautioned against admitting that a treatise is authoritative unless he or she actually has read the relevant portions recently and knows they agree with his or her testimony. At the same time, the witness cannot very well refuse to recognize every treatise lest he or she appear uncooperative (or worse, lacking in expertise). The best solution is to make sure your expert rereads the relevant portions of the major texts and articles before trial and knows for sure which agree and which disagree with his or her conclusion. Be sure you remind the expert that you will pay for this time devoted to background reading.

---

[53] *See* Linz & Penrod, *supra* note 46, at 31-35.

Your expert also should be prepared to handle questions about his or her fee, and explain it by equating the fee charged to other income lost as a result of taking time off to testify. The witness should be able to make it clear that he or she is being compensated only for the time spent in preparation, consultation, and testimony. The expert can even be prepared to remind the cross-examining attorney that attorneys are paid far more than experts.[54]

4. CONDUCTING DIRECT EXAMINATION

Conducting the direct examination of an expert witness presents no issues substantially different from those arising during the direct examination of any witness. You should review Chapter 6, part F.

NOTES

1. *Including disputed facts in hypothetical questions.* Should you include in your hypothetical question a request that your expert assume facts that are disputed or that were objected to? Keeton cautions against inclusion unless the disputed facts are essential to a favorable answer. If evidence admitted over objection is found to be inadmissible on appeal, it probably will be harmless error if you can show that it was not essential to your case. However, if you based a hypothetical question in part on the inadmissible evidence, reversal is more likely. If you include sharply disputed facts in your question, you make the expert's opinion vulnerable to the argument that it is based on a false or unproved assumption and is therefore worthless. ROBERT KEETON, TRIAL TACTICS AND METHODS 53 (2d ed. 1973). *Cf.* SCOTT BALDWIN, ART OF ADVOCACY — DIRECT EXAMINATION § 22.04[3] (1981) (you may include disputed facts if solidly based on evidence).

2. *Simplified testimony under the Federal Rules of Evidence.* The Federal Rules of Evidence eliminated most of the common-law formalities governing expert testimony. They permit very short, summary testimony by experts. Without suggesting that it would be the most persuasive format, James McElhaney, *Expert Witnesses and the Federal Rules of Evidence*, 28 MERCER L. REV. 463, 478, 483-84 (1977), offers the following example of permissible abbreviated testimony:

Q: Dr. Willis — I take it you are a medical doctor, is that correct?
A: Yes, I am. I specialize in the field of neurology, which is treatment of disorders of the brain and nervous system.
Q: Are you familiar with the medical condition of Mr. Jon Price?
A: Yes, I am.
Q: Would you tell us about it, please?
A: Certainly. Jon Price hit his head on the side post of an automobile in which he was riding on January 5, 1976. That blow to the head caused a tear in the tissue of his brain, which formed a small scar as it healed. Because of that scar on his brain, he has a form of epilepsy. At times which cannot be predicted, his left hand and arm twitch and jerk

---

[54] *See* the cross-examination of the consulting expert in the movie *The Verdict*, starring Paul Newman.

uncontrollably. Unfortunately, there is no way to operate on his injury, and in his case, medication has been ineffective.

Q: Can you tell us, Doctor, how long this condition will last?

A: I am afraid it will be with him the rest of his life.

Q: In forming your opinion, Doctor Willis, did you rely on anything other than your examination of Mr. Price?

A: Yes, I did. I studied his complete medical file.

Q: What did this include?

A: Let's see — the notes of his family physician, Dr. Griffin, the medical file compiled by the late Dr. Young, which included his own findings, the electroencephalogram report, the cranial X-rays, Dr. Schuler's psychiatric report and the results of all the laboratory tests.

Q: Can you tell us, Doctor Willis, whether it is customary and reasonable for experts in the field of neurology to rely on such information in making professional judgments?

A: Certainly. We have to depend on each other. It would be literally impossible to do everything yourself. For example, I do not have the slightest idea how to do the biochemical tests in a simple urinalysis. Relying on other experts is actually more dependable than doing it yourself.

Q: Thank you, Doctor.

3. *Stipulating to qualifications.* As you start to prove the qualifications of your expert witness, your adversary may suddenly rise and offer to stipulate that your witness is an expert. Should you accept this stipulation? Trial practitioners unanimously agree that you should not, except in three situations: (1) if your witness is obviously less qualified than your opponent's; (2) if you have some doubt whether your witness will be accepted as an expert by the judge; or (3) if you are effectively forced to under pressure from the judge. *See* James H. Seckinger, *Presenting Expert Testimony*, 15 AM. J. TRIAL ADVOC. 215, 219-20 (1992). *Cf.* ANTHONY AMSTERDAM, TRIAL MANUAL 5 FOR THE DEFENSE OF CRIMINAL CASES § 398 (1988) (defense can accept a mutual stipulation if experts called by both prosecution and defense are equally qualified).

How can you gracefully refuse an offer to stipulate without appearing uncooperative? Three tactics may be considered. One is to explain to the judge and jury why you are refusing — because the jurors have to evaluate the professional credibility of the experts and you want them to know how qualified your expert is. The second is to offer a substitute stipulation that includes the expert's basic qualifications, e.g.:

> I would be willing to stipulate to Dr. Prandah's expertise if the stipulation includes his basic credentials — Dr. Prandah is a medical expert who graduated with honors from Harvard Medical School, is board certified in anesthesiology, is chief of anesthesiology at St. Vincent's Hospital, and has 25 years' experience in anesthesiology.

The third tactic, from the sarcastic school of trial practice, is to say you will accept the stipulation only if your opponent admits that your expert is one of the leading specialists in the country. *See* FRED LANE, LANE'S GOLDSTEIN

TRIAL TECHNIQUES §§ 14.47-14.48 (3d ed. 1984). This final tactic seems unwise unless your expert really is one of the country's leading specialists.

E. CROSS-EXAMINATION

Most of what you read in Chapter 7 on cross-examination of lay witnesses, applies to the cross-examination of expert witnesses. The basic concepts are the same: to be successful, the cross-examination should be planned carefully and organized to accomplish your purposes, and should be conducted in a way that allows you to maintain control over it. However, some aspects of the cross-examination of experts deserve special attention.

1. WHETHER TO CROSS-EXAMINE

The decision whether to cross-examine most witnesses is fairly straightforward. If a witness knows facts that can help you prove your case, or if you have the ammunition to successfully impeach a witness who has given damaging testimony, then you probably should conduct a cross-examination, whether that person is a lay or expert witness. If an expert such as a treating physician has any personal knowledge of the facts, some facts might be consistent with your own theory of the case and be worth eliciting. In some situations, an expert who gives damaging testimony can be impeached for interest or bias, or because he or she has made a significant prior inconsistent statement. In cases like these, the decision to cross-examine will be easy.

Often, however, an expert called by your opponent will not have any personal knowledge of the events and will appear reasonably credible. Thus, some trial practitioners recommend that cross-examination rarely should be attempted. Unless the expert is obviously dishonest or incompetent, a cross-examination is not likely to harm the expert's credibility, and may have the effect of strengthening his or her testimony by making it appear unassailable. Others argue that failing to cross-examine will be viewed by the jurors as a concession that the expert's opinion is authoritative, so that you always should attempt at least a token cross-examination.

As with most differences of opinion, the truth probably lies somewhere in between. Since your opponent has a choice of whom to call as an expert, it is likely that the expert witnesses who testify will give effective testimony against you. The more damaging the testimony, the greater the need for cross-examination. On the other hand, expert witnesses are likely to know more about their subjects than you do, increasing the risk that they will "get the better of you" in cross-examination. This risk suggests that you must be well prepared before you begin and should proceed cautiously, but not that you should forgo cross-examination altogether.

If you have the ammunition to attack an opposing expert's qualifications, you have an alternative to traditional cross-examination. You can object to the witness being qualified as an expert and assert your right to conduct a preliminary voir dire examination as to the witness' competence. This is a risky tactic, and some trial practitioners advise against it unless you are certain of success. If the judge overrules your objection and finds the witness qualified, the jurors may misinterpret the judge's ruling as settling the issue and will be less likely to consider weaknesses in the expert's qualifications. Others take the position that you should voir dire the witness if you know of any serious weakness in the proposed expert's qualifications. This view is supported by psychological evidence that jurors are likely to be less receptive to testimony if they know it is coming from a witness with credibility problems.[55]

2. PURPOSES OF CROSS-EXAMINATION

a. Eliciting Favorable Testimony

Favorable testimony can be elicited from expert witnesses in two different ways.

- If the expert has personal knowledge of the facts, he or she can be asked about aspects of the case that help prove or corroborate your theory.
- A consulting expert may be able to provide helpful testimony by answering hypothetical questions. This tactic will not work if the disputed issue concerns the proper conclusion to be drawn from undisputed facts, such as a criminal case in which experts give differing opinions on sanity based on essentially the same facts. However, if the controversy centers on disputed facts, the opposing expert may agree with your conclusion if asked to assume your version of the facts instead of your opponent's. For example, if a defense medical expert discounts plaintiff's self-report of symptoms and concludes that plaintiff has not been permanently injured, you could ask the expert to assume the truth of the plaintiff's statements. The expert then will probably have to agree with the conclusions reached by your own experts.[56]

b. Impeachment

Five avenues of impeachment are open to you in cross-examining expert witnesses. As with any witness, you can attack an expert's personal veracity and attempt to prove that the witness is deliberately lying or exaggerating, you can attack the credibility of the expert's testimony by showing that he or she has made honest mistakes, and you can attack the credibility of your opponent's case as a whole by emphasizing contradictions between opposing experts. In addition, you can attack an expert's degree of expertise and emphasize factors that make your opponent's witnesses less qualified than your own. Finally, you may be able to weaken expert testimony in inexact sciences by eliciting an admission from the witness that it is not possible to be absolutely certain.

(1) Attacking Personal Credibility

An expert may be cross-examined on the issue of bias like an ordinary witness. If you have the ammunition to attack the neutrality of an expert

---

[55] See Brian Sternthal et al., *The Persuasive Effect of Source Credibility*, 42 PUB. OPINION Q. 285 (1978).

[56] R. KEETON, *supra* note 48, at 162-65.

witness, this is a relatively easy kind of impeachment. You do not have to confront the witness in his or her own area of expertise. The concepts involved are the same as those for lay witness cross-examination. Some common areas of questioning are:

- *Employed by a party.* An expert who also is employed by one of the parties obviously has a built-in bias for that side and a personal interest in holding onto the job. The witness also may have a personal interest if he or she has been involved in the design, manufacture or marketing of a product now claimed to be defective or that was involved in the accident in some way.

- *Frequent witness for a party or industry.* Experts who are not permanent employees may still have a financial interest in testifying for one side or the other if they earn significant amounts of money as professional expert witnesses. If an expert frequently is retained by one party, or frequently testifies on behalf of one side of a controversy (e.g., "whiplash" doctors or American Tobacco Institute cancer experts), you can bring out the number of times the expert has worked for a party and the amount of income received over the years.

- *Accepts research funds from organization related to a party.* Especially if an expert comes from a university or medical school, the expert or a close colleague may be a recipient of research grants given by one of the parties, a related company within the same industry, or a trade association.

- *The hired gun.* If an expert no longer actually practices in his or her field, but has become a hired gun who spends all that person's time consulting and testifying, the jury may view him or her as less credible than an expert who actively practices. The hired-gun theme can be used in closing argument to suggest that a hired gun has to satisfy the client or nobody will hire that person again. This kind of argument is risky, because it impeaches the credibility of the lawyer (an obvious hired gun) at the same time as the witness. It obviously only works when your own expert is still engaged in practice. You can bolster this line of cross-examination if you can find advertisements in which the expert offers his or her services.

- *Amount of compensation.* Expert witnesses often are paid large sums of money. In some cases, they may be paid more per hour for consulting than they get at their regular jobs, especially if they teach at universities or work for the government. This kind of impeachment is common — so common, in fact that most attorneys prepare their experts on how to handle the questions. Experts will usually disclose their fees on direct examination, justify them, and affirm that they would never testify falsely just to earn a fee. For this reason, some attorneys suggest that cross-examining concerning fees is nitpicking and not worth it unless the fee is exceptionally large. However, if the fee is substantial, you probably should raise the issue whether or not it was defused during direct examination. A simple, "Did I hear you right? How much are you being paid for your testimony?" will usually make the point.

(2) Attacking the Credibility of the Testimony

Without insinuating that an expert witness is dishonest, it may be possible to impeach the credibility of the expert's testimony by demonstrating that it is unreliable. You can bring out that the expert had only limited exposure to firsthand information, is basing his or her opinion on unreliable or disputed facts, has failed to conduct a complete investigation, or has reached a conclusion different from most experts.

Probably the most fruitful line of attack is to bring out that the expert witness has had to rely on other people for the information on which his or her testimony is based. Often, an expert will have no personal knowledge of the facts at all, and will base an opinion solely on a review of records prepared by others. In personal injury cases, medical witnesses called on both sides may have examined the plaintiff only once or not at all. If your expert has personal knowledge of the case but the other side's does not, then it may be to your advantage to emphasize on cross-examination the limited opportunity the other expert had to observe and gather direct information.

This kind of cross-examination can be especially effective if the underlying facts are unverifiable. A good example is a medical expert who bases an opinion about the nature of the plaintiff's condition on the subjective complaints of the plaintiff. You may be able to show that the expert has to assume the truth of unverifiable statements by the plaintiff to arrive at a diagnosis; if the plaintiff is lying or exaggerating, then the diagnosis would be different. The expert's opinion then becomes only as credible as the plaintiff's complaints.

A closely related kind of impeachment is to demonstrate that the expert failed to properly conduct a complete investigation. This kind of impeachment is probably overused in criminal cases to attack "shoddy police work." The problem is that jurors are inclined to believe that experts know what they are doing. If you say an expert did not do a thorough investigation, but the expert says the investigation was adequate, why should the jury believe *you*? To be effective, this kind of cross-examination must be combined with positive testimony from your own experts that additional tests or investigations were needed. Three possible lines of inquiry are:

- Revealing that the expert did not perform certain tests commonly used in similar circumstances.
- Exposing the fact that the expert was poorly informed on the background data. For example, an economist testifying for the plaintiff that the defendant's anti-competitive actions probably caused the business damages for which compensation is sought can be undercut by exposing the fact that the expert was unaware of earlier unrelated events that could have produced the same damage.
- Discrediting underlying tests or experiments the expert relied on but that were conducted improperly. You may be able to expose methodological flaws or show dissimilarities between the conditions at the time of the incident and the conditions under which an experiment was conducted. However, challenging an expert on whether an experiment was properly

conducted is dangerous business and should not be attempted without assistance from experts qualified to critique experimental design.

One other approach for impeaching the reliability of an expert's opinion is to demonstrate that it is inconsistent with what has been published in that field of specialty. This impeachment through learned treatises will work only if the texts you use are genuinely authoritative (or written by the witness) and if no new developments in the field have made them obsolete. You will need expert guidance on these questions; you cannot just grab a book from the Medical School Library. Although modern evidence rules permit you to use treatises established as authoritative by your own witnesses, this kind of impeachment probably will be effective only if you can get the expert you are cross-examining to agree that the treatise is a leading one in the field.

To increase the likelihood of successful impeachment by learned treatises, trial practitioners routinely use two tactics: (1) interviewing or deposing an opposing expert in the expert's office and noting the treatises on the bookshelf; and (2) during the deposition, asking the expert about the books he or she consults.

> When you are using medical literature in cross-examination, one of the most effective methods is to get the witness committed to the authoritative standing of the particular book or of the writings of the particular author before you produce the writing itself for the expert to read and consider carefully. Sometimes you can do this by asking the witness to name the outstanding authorities in the field; it achieves much greater effect if he names your book in response to that question than if you ask only whether it is not true that your book is recognized as an authority in the field. Having established the authority of the book, you may then read selected passages contradicting his opinions, or you may hand him the book and ask that he read the marked passages. In that exceptional situation, on the other hand, in which the writings are those of the witness, it will often be more effective to ask him whether he agrees with certain extracted statements before advising him that the statements are extracted from his own works; occasionally such a witness is caught in the embarrassing situation of disagreeing with a passage from his own writings. As to the use of particular passages from a book, whether written by the witness or another, the advance advice of your own expert is essential unless you are certain that you have a full grasp of the subject; otherwise, with limited knowledge of the field you may misconstrue the writing and get out on a limb that the witness expertly saws off by pointing out the correct construction and other passages in the book that support it.[57]

(3) Emphasizing Contradictions Between Opposing Experts

On rare occasions, experts called by your opponent may contradict each other. They may disagree on proper procedures, or there may be discrepancies in their conclusions. If this happens, you should consider whether the differences of opinion are significant enough to cast doubt upon the ultimate conclu-

---

[57] R. KEETON, *supra* note 48, at 158-59.

sions they reached. For example, if you can elicit from two experts that each thinks that the other's methods were unreliable, you may be able to impeach both. The risks inherent in this tactic are enormous because it avoids the fact that both experts ultimately have reached the same conclusion, and it gives both witnesses a chance to reemphasize that their own methods were reliable.

(4) Attacking the Expert's Qualifications

In most cases, if one side calls an expert, the other side also will call one with a different opinion. The jurors then will be faced with deciding which expert to believe. One basis upon which this decision can be made is the respective qualifications of the competing experts. If jurors believe an expert to be unqualified, or less qualified than an opposing expert, they may be less likely to accept that person's opinions. Therefore, if you know about weaknesses in an expert's qualifications, and if these weaknesses are significant enough to cause a reasonable juror to question the validity of the expert's conclusions, this may be a fruitful area of inquiry.

The incompetence of an expert may be suggested in two ways: lack of training and lack of experience. Lack of training and knowledge may be shown through weaknesses in educational background, lack of advanced degrees, graduation from an inferior school, absence of professional certification, absence of writing or teaching in the particular subject, or nonmembership in relevant professional societies. Lack of practical experience can be demonstrated if the expert is new to the field, is a theorist with no hands-on experience, or does not regularly teach or do research in the field. The same caveat applies here, however. This kind of impeachment works best if it is done in conjunction with affirmative proof about the outstanding qualifications of your own expert.

(5) Attacking the Expert's Degree of Certainty

By far the most dangerous type of impeachment is to attack the expert's degree of certainty. This technique works best with academic experts and witnesses not used to testifying. Science is always a question of probability, and there are always qualifications and margins of error. These can sometimes be exploited to create the impression that the expert is really not very certain of his or her own conclusion.

> The fact that important aspects of the witness' testimony are opinions makes it worthwhile ... to look for and develop uncertainties and qualifications in these opinions. An expert will usually admit that some questions put to him are not subject to positive answers and that under these circumstances persons qualified in the field recognize that there is always a possibility that their opinions are wrong. In developing this idea, however, you should proceed with great caution. Expert witnesses who have stated qualified opinions on direct examination have a way of stating their opinions with more conviction, rather than less, when they are annoyed by the feeling that the cross-examiner is trying to make it appear that the opinions are arbitrary guesses.... With respect to develop-

ing particular uncertainties and qualifications, you should exercise even greater caution. Unless you have acquired a thorough knowledge of the subject from experience in trial of similar cases, you should not attempt this without advice from your own experts; otherwise you may fall into the trap of merely giving the witness an opportunity to explain more fully than he did on direct examination why, in reaching his final opinion, he excluded the other possibilities you have identified.[58]

3. PREPARATION

The same principles expressed in Chapter 7, part E, concerning cross-examination of lay witnesses apply to experts. It is critically important that you carefully prepare how you will phrase your questions.

- You probably should write out most of your questions, unless you can remember the Latin names for the bones.
- Ask only one fact per question.
- Always ask leading questions.
- Keep your questions simple.
- Do not repeat damaging direct examination.
- Use the witness' own words, from depositions, medical records, or publications, whenever possible.
- Don't ask the witness to agree to your conclusions; the witness is being paid a lot of money to hold opposite opinions.
- Don't ask the witness to explain an answer.

4. CONDUCTING THE CROSS-EXAMINATION

The same principles expressed in Chapter 7, section F, concerning cross-examination of lay witnesses apply to experts. To conduct the cross-examination of an expert, it is even more important (and even more difficult) that you be in control. Where you might have elected to allow a lay witness to be somewhat evasive rather than appear to be picking on a smaller opponent, this consideration does not apply to experts. You should more aggressively try to limit an expert's answers to "Yes" and "No," using all three techniques:

- Ask the witness to limit his or her answers to "Yes" or "No," both at the beginning and throughout the examination as needed.
- Move to strike any volunteered portions of the testimony as unresponsive and beyond the scope of your question.
- Ask the judge to instruct the witness to limit his or her answers to "Yes" or "No" if the witness persists in being evasive.

In addition, you should pay particular attention to:

- Knowing when to abandon a line of questions because you have gotten all you are going to get, or the testimony is taking an ugly turn.
- Choreography.

---

[58] R. KEETON, *supra* note 48, at 156-57.

- Maintaining a professional attitude of fairness to the witness. Trick questions in particular are not likely to work with an expert.

In one respect, conducting the cross-examination of an expert is different from an ordinary cross-examination. You probably cannot do it alone. You need your own expert consultant sitting beside you who can explain the importance of specific answers, suggest fruitful lines of new inquiry, and let you know when you have inadvertently phrased a question in a way that makes it ambiguous to the expert. Because of the rule permitting the separation of witnesses,[59] you may have to file a special motion to ask for permission for your expert to be in the courtroom and advise you during cross-examination.

NOTE

Apparent cross-examination of experts. When a witness has given damaging testimony but you have no effective means of cross-examining, some practitioners favor an apparent cross-examination that remains on the fringes of the witness' testimony. Three methods of apparent cross-examination have been suggested for experts:

- Asking the witness to agree to a sequence of general scientific principles that either will be used by your own experts in reaching their conclusions, or would lead to a different result if facts existed to support them. *See* Ted Warshafsky, *Cross-Examination of Technical Experts*, TRIAL DIPLOMACY J. at 20 (Spring 1978).
- Asking questions about the details of complicated principles in the field of specialty if you have any reason to believe the witness might not know the answers off the top of his or her head. *See* WAYNE STICHTER, A PRACTITIONER'S GUIDE TO THE USE OF EXHIBITS AND EXPERT TESTIMONY, IN ADVOCACY AND THE KING'S ENGLISH 121 (G. Rossman ed. 1960) (citing example of doctor who became confused over the Latin names for bones).
- In rare cases, demonstrating that the witness has claimed to be an expert in too many diverse fields to be taken seriously in any one. *See* ROBERT HABUSH, ART OF ADVOCACY — CROSS-EXAMINATION OF NON-MEDICAL EXPERTS § 4.05 (1981) (citing a case involving a design engineer who had previously testified about printing presses, snowmobiles, hoses, forklifts, fire trucks, ladders, car steering mechanisms, refrigeration and a dozen more areas).

F. BIBLIOGRAPHY

1. COMPREHENSIVE

JAMES W. JEANS, LITIGATION, chs. 11 and 16 (2d ed. 1992).
FRED LANE, LANE'S GOLDSTEIN TRIAL TECHNIQUE, chs. 15-17 (3d ed. 1984).
RALPH MCCULLOUGH & JAMES UNDERWOOD, CIVIL TRIAL MANUAL 391-410 (2d ed. 1980).
FAUST R. ROSSI, EXPERT WITNESSES (1991).

---

[59]*E.g.*, FED. R. EVID. 615.

2. LAW

Paul Giannelli, *The Admissibility of Novel Scientific Evidence: Frye v. United States a Half a Century Later*, 80 CALIF. L. REV. 1197 (1980).

Samuel R. Gross, *Expert Evidence*, 1991 WISC. L. REV. 1113.

James McElhaney, *Expert Witnesses and the Federal Rules of Evidence*, 28 MERCER L. REV. 463 (1977).

J. Alexander Tanford, David Pisoni & Keith Johnson, *Novel Scientific Evidence of Intoxication: Acoustic Analysis of Voice Recordings from the Exxon Valdez*, 82 J. CRIM. L. & CRIMINOLOGY 579 (1991).

3. DIRECT EXAMINATION

SCOTT BALDWIN, ART OF ADVOCACY — DIRECT EXAMINATION, ch. 22 (1981).

John Castles, *Selecting and Preparing the Expert Witness*, LITIGATION at 28 (Winter 1977).

James H. Seckinger, *Presenting Expert Testimony*, 15 AM. J. TRIAL ADVOC. 215 (1992).

4. CROSS-EXAMINATION

ROBERT HABUSH, ART OF ADVOCACY — CROSS-EXAMINATION OF NON-MEDICAL EXPERTS (1981).

Ted Warshafsky, *Cross-Examination of Technical Experts*, TRIAL DIPL. J. at 20 (Spring 1978).

CLOSING ARGUMENT

A. INTRODUCTION

Closing argument comes at the end of the trial. It is your final opportunity to address the jury. What should you try to accomplish? Many of you probably view closing argument as an opportunity to sway the jury and win your case with your powers of eloquence and persuasion. Much of the literature reinforces the view that closing argument is directed at those jurors who are thinking of voting against you: if you can only reveal to them the errors of their ways, you will convince them to change their minds and vote for you.

When you think about it, however, this scenario is improbable. After hearing the evidence, most jurors will already be inclined toward one side or the other; truly undecided jurors are rare. If a majority of jurors are inclined to vote against you based on the evidence, you are unlikely to persuade them otherwise, and you will probably lose the case. This should not come as any great shock to you — if your evidence is weak, you *ought* to lose the case. It is unrealistic to think that any amount of clever argument can turn a loser into a winner. On the other hand, if a majority of jurors are inclined to vote in your favor, based on the evidence, then you ought to win the case. Your closing argument can solidify and organize your supporters, arm them with the strongest arguments in your arsenal, help them find your opponent's weaknesses, and energize them to do battle in the jury room. This is the modern view of the role of closing argument:

> A lawsuit, like a chain, is only as strong as its weakest link. Contrary to popular myth, lawsuits are not won, although on rare occasions they may be lost, as a result of a summation. In fact, lawsuits are not usually won or lost during any one phase of the trial. They are generally won or lost on the evidence coupled with the effectiveness of the presentation by the lawyer from the moment he [or she] walks into the courthouse until the moment the verdict is returned.[1]

Viewed in this way, closing argument is not for the purpose of recruiting new troops, but for arming those already on your side. The big battle will take place in the jury room. Trial lawyers generally agree that you should try to accomplish six goals:

- Reiterate your theory of the case and make sure the jurors understand it. The importance of having a single, clear, simple theory cannot be overstated. It provides direction to your jurors. Alternative theories merely divide your forces into two groups that may start fighting with each other.

---

[1] Lawrence J. Smith, The Art of Advocacy — Summation § 1.11 (1978).

- Emphasize favorable evidence, but don't waste time with a detailed re-hashing of every detail as if the jurors were too stupid to remember anything.
- Rebut your opponent's allegations.
- Suggest specific reasons for the jury to resolve conflicts in your favor — both affirmative reasons why your position is right, and negative reasons why your opponent's position is wrong.
- Explain the law and show how the evidence satisfies all legal require-ments for a verdict in your favor.
- Most importantly, reduce your case to a good story, including plot, mo-tives, adventure, battles between good and evil, human weaknesses, temptation, drama, and a moral at the end.

NOTES

1. *The importance of closing argument.* Trial lawyers disagree about the importance of closing argument. Some believe that a good closing argu-ment is crucial to your case. *See* FRANCIS X. BUSCH, LAW AND TACTICS IN JURY TRIALS, vol. 5:411 (1963) (value of argument as instrument of persuasion cannot be overestimated); ROBERT MCCULLOUGH & JAMES UNDERWOOD, CIVIL TRIAL MANUAL 647 (2d ed. 1980) (importance cannot be overstated); LLOYD PAUL STRYKER, THE ART OF ADVOCACY 111 (1954) (high point in art of advo-cacy; opportunity to rescue lost cause). Others downplay the importance of argument, asserting that trials are won or lost based on the evidence and the attorney's entire presentation. JOHN APPLEMAN, PREPARATION AND TRIAL 189 (1967) (many jurors make up their minds early in the case); Michael F. Colley, *The Opening Statement*, TRIAL, Nov. 1982, at 53, 54 (interviews with jurors in Harris County, Texas, revealed that all had made up their minds on liability before closing arguments); Jacob Stein, *The Rhetorical Question and Other Forensic Speculations*, LITIGATION, Summer 1972, at 22, 23 (evidence deter-mines verdict).

2. *Can you convince jurors to change sides?* Social scientists who study persuasion and human behavior think not. An argument against a juror's tentative decision may only strengthen that juror's belief as he or she thinks up counter-arguments. HERBERT W. SIMONS, PERSUASION 48 (1976). If jurors feel they are being manipulated or pressured to change their views, they will tend to react to this threat by rejecting the message. This is a form of "reac-tance theory." RICHARD E. PETTY & JOHN T. CACIOPPO, COMMUNICATION AND PERSUASION 126-30 (1986). *See also* SHARON S. BREHM & JACK W. BREHM, PSYCHOLOGICAL REACTANCE: A THEORY OF FREEDOM AND CONTROL (1981) (de-tailed explanation of reactance theory). Anyone who has ever tried to per-suade a four-year-old child to change his or her mind will understand the problem.

B. EXAMPLE OF A CLOSING ARGUMENT

The following example should give you a feeling for the scope and structure of a closing argument. It is based loosely on an argument given by James E. Hullverson of the Missouri and Illinois bars, reprinted in LAWRENCE SMITH,

ART OF ADVOCACY — SUMMATION §§ 9.01 to 9.71 (1978). It illustrates most of the points raised in later sections.

May it please the court; members of the jury.

I have asked my client to leave the courtroom, as I had asked him not to be here during the medical testimony. We listened to the doctors explaining what a dismal future he has. He is going to be in a wheelchair, unable to walk more than a few steps because of his paralysis, a boy with no arms, only grotesque mechanical claws, for the rest of his life. That is a fact, and we have to accept it and base our decisions on it. John is only fourteen years old, and still has the hope — the dream of doctors inventing bionic arms that look natural, the dream of being able to run again. I did not want to be responsible for shattering that dream by making him sit here and listen to the brutal facts: He has been sentenced to life imprisonment in a wheelchair for a crime he didn't commit.

There has been a lot of medical and other testimony, and we want to thank you for being attentive. The burden on you is a grave one — to arrive at a fair and just verdict under all the circumstances. I will take a few minutes now to review the case as we see it.

There are three main points to this lawsuit. First, we are not dealing with an ordinary product, we're dealing with electrical power lines. They carry electricity — silent and invisible, but it can blow your arms off or kill you in a split second. Electricity is a dangerous, ultrahazardous force, and the defendant Electric Company should have taken precautions to prevent deadly currents from causing harm. They did not, so you should hold them responsible. Second, we are not dealing with an adult who was injured, but with a boy. John was twelve years old when he was crippled. Without any warning sign, he did not have the experience to know the small black wire was dangerous, so he is not contributorily negligent for doing what all young boys do: playing in a field near his home. And the third factor. John was crippled — given a life sentence — for which you should award him enough money to last him that lifetime.

How do these factors fit together? As we look at the overall lawsuit, what are the issues? Basically, we're talking about two things: Is the defendant Electric Company liable for John's injuries, and if so, what amount of money can compensate John for all he has suffered and continues to suffer?

First, let's talk about whether the Electric Company is liable. This boils down to two questions: Was this tragedy foreseeable, and was it preventable? The judge will read you an instruction on the law that says:

> Your verdict must be in favor of the plaintiff, John Wilson, if you find three things: First, that there was an uninsulated high voltage electric wire on the utility pole, and no warning sign of any kind. Second, that the Electric Company knew or should have known that young children were likely to climb the utility pole. Third, that the dangerous condition could have been eliminated without placing an undue burden on the Electric Company.

There is no question about the first element. You saw these photographs of the utility pole [attorney places two photographs on easels]. Witnesses pointed out the uninsulated high voltage line [attorney points to photograph], and the guy wire [attorney points to photograph], and you can clearly see for yourselves that there is no insulator on the guy wire and no warning sign of any kind. The parties are not in dispute about whether a dangerous condition existed.

The dispute centers on the second and third elements. Should the Electric Company have known that children were likely to climb the pole, and could the danger have been eliminated easily? In other words, if it was foreseeable that twelve-year-old boys like John would be tempted to climb the utility pole, then the law requires the Electric Company to try to prevent it and protect them from harm.

How do we know it was foreseeable that children will climb utility poles? You can look to the common experiences of all of us when we were young. We were all probably tempted to climb poles at one time or another. You can look to the testimony of Mr. Gilbert, the regional supervisor for the Electric Company. He admitted on cross-examination that even he had climbed poles as a child.

But what is the best evidence whether the Electric Company should have foreseen that children would climb poles? It is the National Electric Safety Code which was introduced into evidence. You heard the experts testify that this safety code was prepared by the power companies themselves, and that it sets out the minimum safety standards for the industry. And look at this [attorney holds out a copy of the code]: an entire section in this safety code is entitled, in boldface print, "Guarding Poles: Protection Against Climbing." Do they realize somebody might climb their poles? Yes, they realize it. They spell it out in a book. Not only is it reasonably foreseeable that children will climb utility poles, it is inevitable. Children do not know climbing is dangerous. How many times have they seen westerns on television in which the outlaws climb poles and cut the wires to the telegraph office? They never get electrocuted. It looks safe. And the pole John climbed looked just like the ones they climb in the movies. It was foreseeable.

Could this tragedy have been prevented? We are not talking about expensive fences or anything that would place an enormous burden on the defendant. The law only requires the Electric Company to take those safety measures that are easy and inexpensive. But you heard the testimony — it would have cost them two dollars to put an insulator on the guy wire. It would have cost them even less to put up a sign that said "Danger High Voltage," or something like that. I mean, someone could have written it on a piece of cardboard with a magic marker and tacked it on the pole for a few pennies. A few cents could have saved John from this terrible accident. The insulator would have made the shock impossible — every expert agreed to that. And a simple sign would have prevented it, because John told you he never would have gone up that pole if he had known there was electricity, if there had been a warning. Not only would it have been inexpensive and simple to prevent this tragedy, but also the safety code says that this is the kind of protection that is needed. In that code, in the section on protection against climbing, it says, "On poles carrying supply conductors exceeding three hundred volts" —

and remember, these lines carried seven thousand volts — "either guards or warning signs shall be used."

So it was foreseeable that a boy like John would climb the pole. It would have been simple and cost only a few cents to prevent it, but the Electric Company ignored the problem. They ignored the requirements of their own safety code and the requirements of common sense, and now the law says they are responsible.

Now, in some cases there is a defense to liability called contributory negligence. The judge will instruct you that if John was guilty of contributory negligence — that is, if he knew or should have known that there was a danger of high voltage, but ignored that danger — then he shares some of the responsibility for his own injuries. In this case, this is not a real defense because there is no evidence to support it. In the first place, how could John have known there was a danger of high voltage? There was no warning sign. The expert, the engineer, testified that you can't tell a high voltage wire from a telephone wire just by appearance. Did John disregard a known danger? Remember the first time he woke up in the hospital — what did he say? The nurse overheard it, and wrote it down in the hospital record [Attorney picks up hospital record and thumbs through it]. Here it is. He said, "What happened? I was climbing a telephone pole." John assumed this was like the poles in the movies, that it carried telephone wires, not high voltage lines. Remember that he was only twelve years old, and didn't have the experience of an adult. He was not told there were high voltage lines. He thought it was a telephone pole, and high voltage lines look just like telephone lines. Given what he knew, and what we expect twelve-year-olds to know, he bears no responsibility for his own injuries. If he had just fallen off the pole, that would be his own fault. He could see that danger. But he could not see and could not have known about the seven thousand volts of silent, deadly electricity.

The second issue for you to decide is damages. This is the important thing, in terms of John's future. The judge will instruct you that, "If you find for the plaintiff, John Wilson, it will be your duty to decide what sum will fairly and justly compensate him for the damages and injuries he has sustained and will sustain in the future." There is no simple yardstick by which to measure how much a near-fatal electric shock, how much a ten-foot fall, how much a month in the hospital, how much the loss of both arms, or how much life imprisonment in a wheelchair is worth. I will tell you this. If an Air Force pilot were in a fifteen-million-dollar Phantom jet that developed engine trouble, and the choice were between saving the life of the pilot or trying to save the plane, you can bet that the plane would be ditched — fifteen million dollars thrown into the ocean — so the pilot could parachute to safety. We can replace an airplane, but we cannot replace a destroyed, maimed human being. The value of human life far exceeds any sum of money.

So how can you arrive at a fair verdict? We have suggested that $7,736,000 would be fair. However, you the jury have the responsibility and the wisdom to decide what a ruined life is worth. Let me explain why we think seven and three-quarter million dollars is appropriate, and you can adjust the amount up or down to reflect your own experiences and knowledge of the cost of living.

The law says that John is entitled to be compensated for his injuries, and for the effects they will have on his life. The judge will instruct you that you may take into account the nature, extent, and permanency of the injuries; the reasonable expenses for past and future medical care; the value of any loss of ability to earn in the future; and any pain, suffering, and mental anguish experienced in the past or reasonably certain to be experienced in the future.

There's no question in this case about the nature, extent, and permanency of John's injuries. He lost both arms. The doctors testified that his other medical problems — the partial paralysis, phlebitis, and hernia — will be with him forever. This isn't like a broken arm that heals as good as new. It is uncontested that he will need a wheelchair and mechanical arms for the remaining sixty years of his life.

What are John's reasonable expenses for past and future medical care? It has been stipulated that his medical expenses, including hospitalization, therapy, and the cost of the mechanical arms, have been $100,000 through today. [Writes $100,000 on blackboard.] What about the future? Remember the testimony of Nancy Rhodes, the hospital therapist. Based on her experience, she testified that mechanical arms last only about eight to ten years each. The doctors testified that it costs about thirty thousand dollars to purchase and attach new mechanical arms. This chart, prepared by the government, shows that John has a life expectancy of sixty years from now. That means he probably will need six more pairs of arms during his lifetime — at thirty thousand dollars per pair, that's one hundred eighty thousand dollars. [Writes $180,000 on blackboard.] Plus, — and I won't review all the details here, I'm sure you recall them as well as I do — approximately forty thousand dollars for incidental medical expenses such as wheelchair repair, the additional hernia operation, and the other medical problems likely to arise that the doctors mentioned. [Writes $40,000 on board and adds.] So we submit that $320,000 is needed for past and future medical care.

The next thing you may consider is the value of any lost ability to earn a living. The right to work, to support yourself and your family, the right to join a union, the right to a paycheck on Friday, and to building up a pension for retirement, these are all important parts of our lives. John's injuries have taken that right away from him, and he should be compensated. We suggest the evidence demonstrates that $2,160,000 is the right figure. Remember the witness we called from the state unemployment office. She was a job counselor. We asked her if there were jobs he could do. He can't walk, carry a package, drive a car, or do physical labor. She said — let me find it, I wrote it down — she said, "No, it would be extremely difficult if not impossible to find a job for a person with John's handicaps." I know that we've all seen the ads on television showing a person in a wheelchair with a job. We asked about that, too, and the witness testified that she has never known of a person with handicaps as serious as John's who could get and keep a job. No witnesses came forward and said they had jobs for John.

If a normal person started work at twenty-two, after college, and retired at seventy, he would work for forty-eight years. Our economics experts said the average income for college-educated people is $40,000 in salary and another $5,000 a year in retirement benefits — and remember that both John's parents were college-educated, so it's reasonable to believe that John would also have gone to college. [Multiplies $45,000 × 48 on blackboard.] That comes out to $2,160,000 of work income that John cannot earn because the Electric Company decided not to put up a fifty-cent warning sign.

How much should he be compensated for the pain, suffering, and mental anguish? He is going to go through adolescence and not be able to hold a girl's hand, or go dancing, or play sports. He must sit on the sidelines and watch — longing to participate in normal life, and living every minute with the pain and frustration of being unable to do so. What are his realistic marital prospects? Zero. Most of us think of going through life married. John has been sentenced to a lonely and unfulfilled life.

What else does he have to look forward to? You heard the doctors testify that he has hernia problems and phlebitis, which cause daily pain. He has what they called phantom pains, where he thinks his arms hurt — only, of course, he has no arms. He will go through periods when he thinks full movement is returning to his leg, only to suffer the depressing reality of permanent paralysis. He will be reminded in his dreams of what it was like to be able to walk, run, eat and clothe himself, only to awaken to the truth. The mental suffering he will go through is immeasurable. He cannot even take care of his own bathroom needs or zip his pants. He needs help to eat. He needs help to attach his arms. He will go through life with these burdens weighing heavily on him.

It is humiliating for him not to be able to hold hands or ask a girl out? Is it embarrassing for this boy not to go to a party because he can't hold a Coke or smoke a cigarette? Is it painful each day to lie in bed helplessly until someone comes to reattach his mechanical arms? This is mental anguish and he will have it every day for the rest of his life. He is expected to live for sixty years, imprisoned in the hopelessness and despair of pain and suffering. Would anyone take his place for $10 an hour? Of course not; yet he must live with it 24 hours a day, 365 days a year for 60 years. The law says you must find some reasonable way to give him compensation for his pain and suffering. Even if all you award him is ten dollars an hour, that adds up to [attorney writes $10 × 24 × 365 × 60 on board] $5,256,000.

[Attorney adds up all numbers]. We are suggesting a total amount, then, of $7,736,000 for medical care, lost earnings, and pain and suffering. Considering that he will live with the results of this tragedy for sixty years, it really does not seem that much.

For a few cents, the defendant Electric Company could have prevented it. For a few hundred dollars, they could have put up signs on all the poles in the city. They chose not to. They gambled — gambled with the lives of children — gambled and lost. Now they must pay the gambling debt.

This is John's only day in court. This isn't like alimony or child support, where we can come back in a few years because the money's run out and ask for more. John cannot work, he cannot get married, he cannot live off his parents forever. He must live on whatever you award him. In the year 2035, he will be 65 years old, on his own, with no job, no retirement benefits. Will he still have enough left from today to support himself for the remaining fifteen years of his life?

I know budget planning for the future is difficult. But we all do it, day to day, and month to month, making sure there's enough money. You are being asked to budget sixty years into the future for John. We are confident that you will do so fairly and reasonably. John thanks you and I thank you.

NOTE

Other examples. Other examples of closing arguments can be found in LAWRENCE SMITH, THE ART OF ADVOCACY — SUMMATION (1978); FRANCIS X. BUSCH, LAW AND TACTICS OF JURY TRIALS, vol. 5: 556-600 (1963); JAMES W. JEANS, LITIGATION §§ 18.48-18.49 (2d ed. 1992); and THOMAS A. MAUET, FUNDAMENTALS OF TRIAL TECHNIQUES 301-32 (3d ed. 1992).

C. LEGAL FRAMEWORK

1. THE RIGHT TO MAKE AN ARGUMENT

Every party in a civil or criminal jury trial has a right to give a closing argument.[2] The following statute is typical:

> *Scope of argument.* At the close of the evidence, the respective parties, or their counsel, shall be entitled to sum up the facts to the jury. In their addresses to the jury they shall be allowed ample scope and latitude for argument upon, and illustration of any and all facts involved in the cause, and the evidence tending either to prove or disprove the same. They shall not be forbidden to argue the law of the case to the jury, but shall not assume to instruct the jury upon the law in such a manner as to encroach upon the function of the court to so instruct the jury.[3]

2. CLOSING ARGUMENT PROCEDURE

Closing arguments take place after all the evidence has been presented. The most common practice in ordinary two-party lawsuits is to have three arguments:[4]

- The plaintiff/prosecutor gives the first argument, which must be a full and fair statement of plaintiff's case.
- The defendant gives the second argument.
- The plaintiff gives the final argument. Final argument is not confined to "rebuttal," but may be a full argument covering all aspects of the case.

In multi-party lawsuits, the court may assign the order of argument. If the parties have diverse interests, they all have individual rights to give closing arguments, and the court has the discretion to set the order. If multiple parties have similar interests, the court has discretion to limit the number of arguments.[5] If a single party is represented by multiple attorneys, the court

---

[2] *See, e.g., Herring v. New York,* 422 U.S. 853 (1975) (criminal defendant has Sixth Amendment right to give closing argument); *Lyman v. Fidelity & Cas. Co.,* 65 App. Div. 27, 72 N.Y.S. 498 (1901) (civil litigant has right to argue).

[3] HAW. REV. STAT. § 635-52.

[4] *See, e.g.,* FED. R. CRIM. P. 29.1; MICH. CT. R. 2.507.

[5] *See, e.g., Sequoia Mfg. Co. v. Halex Constr. Co.,* 570 P.2d 782 (Ariz. App. 1977).

similarly has discretion to set the number who can participate in closing argument.[6]

Trial judges have broad discretion to set reasonable time limits on closing argument. For example, VERMONT RULE OF CIVIL PROCEDURE 51(a) provides:

> More than one hour on a side will not be allowed for argument to the jury, without leave granted before argument; and the court may limit argument to less time.

Restricting parties to as few as fifteen minutes has been approved in simple cases.[7] The court need not allow equal time to all parties if the interests of fairness indicate otherwise. For example, when multiple parties are arrayed on one side, and a single party on the other, it is common to allocate more time to the single party.[8] Otherwise, the single party's argument could be overwhelmed by adverse arguments lasting two to four times as long.

3. THE CONTENT OF CLOSING ARGUMENT

It generally is proper to include three things in closing argument: discussions of facts, statements of law and arguments about its applicability in this case, and comments on the justness of the case. Over 100 years ago, one court wrote:

> The largest and most liberal freedom of speech is allowed, and the law protects [counsel] in it. The right of discussing the merits of the cause, both as to the law and facts, is unabridged. The range of discussion is wide. [Counsel] may be heard in argument upon every question of law. In his addresses to the jury, it is his privilege to descant upon the facts proved or admitted in the pleadings; to arraign the conduct of parties; impugn, excuse, justify or condemn motives, so far as they are developed in evidence; assail the credibility of witnesses, when it is impeached by direct evidence, or by the inconsistency or incoherence of their testimony, their manner of testifying, their appearance on the stand, or by circumstances. His illustrations may be as various as the resources of his genius; his argumentation as full and profound as his learning can make it; and he may, if he will, give play to his wit, or wings to his imagination.[9]

a. Fact Arguments

Proper argument must be confined to facts introduced in evidence, facts of common knowledge, and logical inferences based on the evidence. If you stray beyond these somewhat vague boundaries, you may commit error.

---

[6]*See, e.g., Williams v. Greenfield Equip. Co.*, 361 S.E.2d 199 (Ga. App. 1987).

[7]*See, e.g., Brooks v. State*, 187 Tenn. 67, 213 S.W.2d 7 (1948). *Cf. Maleh v. Florida East Coast Props.*, 491 So. 2d 290 (Fla. App. 1986) (fifteen-minute limit was error in two-and-a-half-day trial with sixteen witnesses in which both liability and damages were hotly contested).

[8]*E.g., Aultman v. Dallas Ry. & Term. Co.*, 152 Tex. 509, 260 S.W.2d 596 (1953) (fifty minutes for plaintiff, thirty minutes each for two defendants).

[9]*Tucker v. Henniker*, 41 N.H. 317, 323 (1860).

It is improper to argue or allude to facts not in the record, to misstate a witness' testimony, or to attribute to a witness testimony that was not given.[10] However, courts usually make reasonable allowances for honest mistakes of memory and ignore misstatements of unimportant facts.[11] If the attorneys disagree on what the testimony was, the court usually will not resolve the dispute, but will instruct the jurors that they must decide what the facts are, based on their recollection (not the attorneys') of the testimony.

You also are permitted to allude to facts that are matters of common knowledge, whether or not those facts were introduced into evidence, and to ask a jury to use that information to arrive at a verdict. For example, an attorney may wish to remind the jury of inflation when arguing what the proper measure of future damages should be. Such an argument usually is allowed, as long as the attorney does not suggest a particular rate of inflation. In criminal cases, prosecutors like to remind the jury about "the problem of gangs and gang violence,"[12] the fact that crime is on the rise,[13] or that the jury is the voice and conscience of the community.[14] These arguments, too, are permitted as long as the prosecutor does not get too specific. Whether a fact is a matter of common knowledge is left to the discretion of the trial judge.[15]

You also may make reasonable inferences from the facts. For example, if the facts show that when a defendant was arrested for passing counterfeit bills, he had the counterfeit bills in one pocket and real money in the other pocket, the prosecutor may argue that the defendant had deliberately segregated real from counterfeit bills, which showed his knowledge that the bills were counterfeit.[16] An inference is reasonable if it is based on some remotely plausible interpretation of the evidence; it does not have to be logical or even likely. You may draw any inference you like, however absurd, as long as the facts on which it is based are in evidence.[17]

It is generally improper to insinuate the existence of unproved facts or to invite the jury to speculate about missing evidence.[18] However, in a few situations the law allows you to draw the jurors' attention to missing evidence. In all civil cases, you may point out that a party did not testify or failed to deny conduct or statements attributed to the party.[19] You also may comment on your adversary's failure to produce relevant evidence or call material wit-

---

[10]E.g., United States v. Santana-Camacho, 833 F.2d 371 (1st Cir. 1987) (prosecutor told jury that the defendant was an illegal alien; the evidence was contrary).

[11]See, e.g., Wilson v. State, 126 Ark. 354, 190 S.W. 441 (1916) (attributing testimony to wrong witness not error).

[12]Commonwealth v. Gwaltney, 442 A.2d 236 (Pa. 1982).

[13]State v. Williams, 485 P.2d 832 (Ariz. 1971) (but not that it went up exactly 116% last year).

[14]Brown v. State, 508 S.W.2d 91 (Tex. Crim. App. 1974).

[15]See Ronald Carlson, Argument to the Jury: Passion, Persuasion and Legal Controls, 33 ST. LOUIS U. L.J. 787, 805 (1989).

[16]United States v. Tucker, 820 F.2d 234 (7th Cir. 1987).

[17]Ladson v. State, 285 S.E.2d 508 (Ga. 1981).

[18]See, e.g., State v. Mork, 286 N.C. 509, 212 S.E.2d 125 (1975) (prosecutor implied that the defendant had a criminal record); People v. Terry, 57 Cal. 2d 538, 370 P.2d 985, 21 Cal. Rptr. 185 (1962) (prosecutor implied that a threat originated with defendant despite evidence that a third person had been responsible); Murray v. New York, N.H. & H.R. Co., 255 F.2d 42 (2d Cir. 1952) (defendant suggested that personal injury plaintiff would be able to retire at full pension).

[19]See City of Bessemer v. Clowdus, 261 Ala. 388, 74 So. 2d 259 (1954).

nesses that are in the possession of or under the control of the adverse party.[20] In both situations, you may argue that it is reasonable to infer that your adversary did not produce the evidence because it would have damaged his or her case. You also may read portions of the opponent's pleadings and comment upon the lack of evidence to support specific allegations.[21]

In criminal cases, the defendant usually is permitted to comment on missing evidence the prosecutor does not introduce. However, the courts are split on whether it is proper for the prosecution to comment on a criminal defendant's failure to produce witnesses or evidence within the defendant's exclusive control. The majority of courts follow the rule in civil cases allowing comment;[22] others hold that because a defendant has no obligation to present a defense, comment is improper.[23] Because of an accused's Fifth Amendment privilege, however, the state is never allowed to comment in any way upon the defendant's personal failure to testify.[24] Also, if evidence has been suppressed or ruled inadmissible, it is error for either side to comment on or refer to it.[25]

b. Arguments Concerning Damages

One common inferential argument that attorneys make is that, based on the evidence, a certain amount of damages should be awarded. Many kinds of damages are not susceptible to direct proof and are difficult to quantify in dollars. Especially difficult to articulate are emotional injuries, punitive damages, pain and suffering, and future business or financial losses. Since there is likely to be little direct evidence in the record concerning the value of such intangible harms, attempts by the attorneys to quantify how much the jury should award are rife with possibilities for straying beyond the "reasonable inference" limitation. The basic rule is that the attorneys may suggest specific damage amounts, even for intangible injuries, as long as they derive those amounts from the evidence. They may not base their requests on what their client *wants*, on what similar lawsuits have been worth, nor on their personal opinions.[26]

The most litigated of these issues is the so-called "per diem" argument, in which an attorney attempts to make a concrete estimate of intangible damages such as pain and suffering by breaking down a long period of time into small units — usually days — and asking the jury to assess a dollar amount to that unit, e.g., that it is reasonable to give a plaintiff fifty dollars for every day the plaintiff will have to spend in a wheelchair. The low figure probably will seem reasonable. Then, the attorney shows how many days (based on medical testimony and life expectancy tables) the plaintiff will be confined to

---

[20] See, e.g., Auto Owners Ins. Co. v. Bass, 684 F.2d 764, 769 (11th Cir. 1982).

[21] See, e.g., Stevenson v. Abbott, 251 Iowa 110, 99 N.W.2d 429 (1959).

[22] See, e.g., Lundy v. Campbell, 888 F.2d 467 (6th Cir. 1989).

[23] See United States v. Lombardozzi, 335 F.2d 414 (2d Cir. 1962); State v. Purvis, 525 S.W.2d 590 (Mo. App. 1975).

[24] Griffin v. California, 380 U.S. 609 (1965). Cf. Lockett v. Ohio, 438 U.S. 586 (1978) (dictum stating that prosecutor's repeated reference in closing argument to the state's evidence as unrefuted was not an impermissible comment on defendant's failure to testify).

[25] See, e.g., People v. Baker, 54 A.D. 2d 547, 387 N.Y.S.2d 129 (1976); United States v. Hickman, 468 F.2d 610 (5th Cir. 1972).

[26] See Carchidi v. Rodenhiser, 551 A.2d 1249 (Conn. 1989).

the wheelchair and computes total damages on the blackboard. For example, if a plaintiff had permanent injuries and a life expectancy of thirty years, she would be in a wheelchair for 10,950 days, which, when multiplied by the seemingly small amount of fifty dollars per day, comes to $547,500 in future damages. The courts are divided on whether this is proper argument. While the majority of jurisdictions permit it,[27] others have expressly held it to be improper.[28] Per diem arguments usually are accompanied by an instruction from the court that the monetary amount suggested by counsel is not binding in any way.[29]

In most jurisdictions you may suggest specific amounts as the proper measure of damages even for intangible injuries such as pain, provided that your suggested figures are based fairly on the evidence.[30] However, since the claim for damages in the pleadings (the "ad damnum" clause) almost always is inflated, many courts hold that it is improper to mention how much actually was sued for.[31] It usually is improper to suggest a figure for intangible damages by telling jurors how much other juries awarded in similar cases.[32]

One other common (but prohibited) damages argument is the "Golden Rule" argument, in which the plaintiff's lawyer invites the jury to do unto the plaintiff what they would do for themselves. It asks the jury to base an award on what they would *want* if they were similarly injured, rather than on the evidence. For example, in *Leathers v. General Motors Corp*,[33] the plaintiff argued:

> Mr. Leathers is going to live 26.9 years disabled. I don't know how to put a value on that. It's the loss of your legs, sports, hobbies, and enjoyment of life. 26.9 years are close to 9,000 days. How much would it be worth to you? What would you want? $20 a day? $30?

The argument was reversible error. Jurors are supposed to remain neutral between the parties and award damages based on evidence.

c. Arguments Concerning the Law

The rule concerning the propriety of arguments about the law is simple: you may review and discuss the law and suggest to the jury how it applies to the facts, but you must be accurate. Any misstatement of the law — by omitting part, by including an unnecessary element, or by an explanation that distorts the law — is error.[34] Any "jury nullification" argument suggesting that the jury disregard the law or circumvent an unfair law is similarly objection-

---

[27] *See, e.g., Rodrigue v. Hausman,* 33 Colo. App. 305, 519 P.2d 1216 (1974); *Christy v. Saliterman,* 288 Minn. 144, 179 N.W.2d 288 (1970).

[28] *See, e.g., Cox v. Valley Fair Corp.,* 83 N.J. 381, 416 A.2d 809 (1980); *Botta v. Brunner,* 26 N.J. 82, 138 A.2d 713, 60 A.L.R.2d 1331 (1958).

[29] *See Baron Tube Co. v. Transport Ins. Co.,* 365 F.2d 858 (5th Cir. 1966).

[30] *See, e.g., Carchidi v. Rodenhiser,* 551 A.2d 1249 (Ct. 1989).

[31] *E.g., Botta v. Brunner,* 26 N.J. 82, 138 A.2d 713 (1958); *Clark v. Essex Wire Corp.,* 361 Pa. 60, 63 A.2d 35 (1949).

[32] *See* Annot., 15 A.L.R.3d 1144.

[33] 546 F.2d 1083 (4th Cir. 1976).

[34] *See, e.g., United States v. Vargas,* 583 F.2d 380 (7th Cir. 1978); *State v. Tims,* 693 P.2d 333 (Ariz. 1985).

able.[35] This includes so-called "Ten Commandments" arguments that the Bible says, "Thou shalt not kill." The defendant is to be tried (in this world, at least) by state law, not God's law.[36]

In general, you must take the law from the jury instructions. You probably may read from statutes as well, at least if your cause of action is based on a statute. However, you may not read from legal treatises, law reviews, or appellate opinions, nor argue the policy behind the law.[37] You are addressing a jury, not the court of appeals.

d. Making Emotional Appeals

You certainly are permitted to *display* emotion in closing argument. Indeed, one court commented on an attorney weeping during closing argument by saying that "[t]ears have always been considered legitimate argument before the jury. If counsel has tears at his command, it may be ... his professional duty to shed them whenever the proper occasion arises."[38] However, you are not permitted to appeal to the emotions and prejudices of the jurors. This fundamental rule was stated in *Brown v. Swineford*:[39]

> It is the duty and right of counsel to indulge in all fair argument in favor of the right of his client; but he is outside of his duty and his right when he appeals to prejudice irrelevant to the case.

Therefore, it is improper to make the following kinds of arguments:

- Appeals to sympathy, e.g., referring to the tears of the victim's parents[40] or the client's recent heart attack.[41]
- Attempts to arouse racial prejudice.[42]
- Appeals to religious prejudice, e.g., anti-Semitic remarks.[43]
- Xenophobic arguments against foreigners.[44]
- Appeals to prejudice against corporations as large, wealthy or unfeeling.[45]
- Raising the relative financial conditions of the parties, discussing the existence of insurance (unless already in evidence), or otherwise arguing that the verdict should depend on ability to pay.[46]

---

[35] *See, e.g., People v. Babbitt*, 755 P.2d 253 (Cal. 1988); *State v. Thomas*, 239 N.W.2d 455 (Minn. 1976).

[36] *E.g., People v. Eckles*, 404 N.E.2d 358 (Ill. 1980).

[37] *E.g., State v. Austin*, 357 S.E.2d 641 (N.C. 1987); *Hawes v. State*, 240 S.E.2d 833 (Ga. 1977).

[38] *Ferguson v. Moore*, 98 Tenn. 342, 351-52 (1897). *But see People v. Dukes*, 12 Ill. 2d 334, 146 N.E.2d 14 (1957) (weeping during closing argument was reversible error).

[39] 44 Wis. 282, 293 (1878).

[40] *Williams v. State*, 544 So. 2d 1114 (Fla. App. 1989).

[41] *Cole v. Bertsch Vending Co.*, 766 F.2d 327 (7th Cir. 1985).

[42] *E.g., Seaboard Coastline R.R. v. Towns*, 274 S.E.2d 74 (1980).

[43] *E.g., McWilliams v. Sentinel Pub. Co.*, 339 Ill. App. 83, 89 N.W.2d 266 (1949).

[44] *Schotis v. North Coast Stevedoring Co.*, 1 P.2d 221 (Wash. 1931).

[45] *E.g., Bednar v. Commonwealth Edison*, 509 N.E.2d 687 (Ill. App. 1987); *Louisville & Nashville R.R. v. Mattingly*, 339 S.W.2d 155 (Ky. 1960).

[46] *E.g., Ashbee v. Brock*, 510 So. 2d 214 (Ala. 1984) (wealth and size of defendant); *Klein v. Herring*, 347 So. 2d 681 (Fla. App. 1977) (on plaintiff's side, you have a poor family). *But see Rodgers v. Fisher Body Div., Gen. Motors Corp.*, 739 F.2d 1102, 1105 (6th Cir. 1984) (wealth of defendant is a legitimate issue if case involves punitive damages).

- Asking jurors for vengeance, especially arguments that they should listen to the demands of the community and use this opportunity to get even for all the wrongs done to society, e.g., by linking a defendant with the problem of crime and drugs that is out of control, and suggesting that the community wants something done about the drug problem.[47]
- Asking jurors to make an example of the defendant or send a message to the community that they will not tolerate violence.[48]
- Appealing to jurors' fears for their own personal safety or suggesting that they will personally suffer (through higher taxes or insurance premiums) if they return a particular verdict.[49]

However, a distinction must be drawn between improper emotionalism and the emotions that are an inherent aspect of the case. You do not need to "sanitize" your case. If a child has been killed by a drunk driver, strong emotions are going to be an inherent part of the case, and it is not error to raise emotional issues in that context. For example, in *State v. Carter*, the prosecutor argued that the African-American defendants had murdered the victim just because he was white, in retaliation for the fact that a white man had killed a friend of theirs. He made references to a race war and suggested that these defendants had vowed to kill a white man every time a white man killed a black man. The court held that the possible racial motive in the killing made racial prejudice a central aspect of the case, and therefore a proper subject for argument.[50]

One way lawyers in criminal cases often try to play on the emotions of the jurors is by arguing about the consequences of a conviction. This is improper, regardless of which side is making the argument. The defendant may not tell the jury about mandatory terms of imprisonment or extreme potential sentences, because it may cause jurors to acquit a defendant they like (despite probative evidence) if they think the potential sentence too harsh. Similarly, the prosecutor is not supposed to tell the jurors about the possibility of early parole or pardon, or that a defendant can have the verdict reviewed on appeal, since such statements could result in conviction for an unproved serious crime if the jurors do not want a defendant released early. Such statements also encourage jurors to abdicate responsibility and convict more readily, believing (wrongly) that an appeals court will turn the defendant loose if the defendant should have been acquitted.[51] These rules seem to be honored more in the breach than in adherence to them.[52]

---

[47] *See e.g., Commonwealth v. Long*, 258 Pa. Super. 312, 392 A.2d 810 (1978); *United States v. Doe*, 860 F.2d 488 (1st Cir. 1988); *Prado v. State*, 626 S.W.2d 775 (Tex. 1982). However, if a suit involves punitive damages, the plaintiff has a limited ability to ask the jurors to make an example of the defendant.

[48] *E.g., Hines v. State*, 425 So. 2d 589 (Fla. App. 1983).

[49] *E.g., Byrns v. St. Louis Co.*, 295 N.W.2d 517 (Minn. 1988) (local taxes); *Rahmings v. State*, 425 So. 2d 1217 (Fla. App. 1983) (defendant would kill again in the community).

[50] 449 A.2d 1280 (1980).

[51] *E.g., Caldwell v. Mississippi*, 105 S. Ct. 2633 (1985).

[52] *See, e.g., State v. Monroe*, 397 So. 2d 1258 (La. 1981) (informing jury that defendant had automatic appeal of death sentence not error); *Moore v. State*, 240 Ga. 807, 243 S.E.2d 1 (1978) (jury told of right to appeal but instructed to disregard remark, no error); *Brothers v. State*, 236 Ala. 448, 183 So. 433 (Ala. 1938) (argument that appeals court would correct a mistake was improper but harmless error).

e. Personal Attacks and Comments

The rules of closing argument require that the attorneys remain detached from the cases they argue. You may not personally attack the honesty or impugn the motives of the opposing attorney, such as accusing your opponent of fabricating evidence or suborning perjury.[53] Similarly, you may not make personal references to yourself. For example, you may not state your personal belief as to the proper outcome of the case,[54] relate personal experiences that bear on the case,[55] use your personal knowledge of the credibility of witnesses to resolve conflicts in testimony,[56] or claim that you are impartial.[57]

Name-calling and other forms of personal attacks on the parties themselves are also technically improper unless connected to specific impeachment evidence. This error probably is committed most often by prosecutors, who seem unable to resist making derogatory remarks about defendants. For example, in the trial of Oliver North, the Independent Counsel analogized him to Adolf Hitler.[58] In other cases, it has been held to be error for a prosecutor to sarcastically refer to defendants as "four innocent bastards,"[59] or call a defendant a "liar" 40 times when he had not testified.[60] The rule is not strictly enforced, however, and courts have found that calling the defendants "scum"[61] or "drug lords"[62] was not error. In civil cases, counsel appear to act with greater decorum, and name calling is less common. However, in one case a lawyer referred to the adverse party as "a cheapskate, a scheming low-down pup, cheating and swindling, stealing and waiting like a snake in the grass." The error was found harmless.[63]

f. Use of Exhibits

Closing argument is not limited to words. You are permitted to use all kinds of visual aids to help communicate your theory. You are not limited to the exhibits introduced during trial. New exhibits — usually charts or blackboard drawings — may be used if they are based on the evidence. They may be used to clarify a dispute, emphasize certain facts, or calculate damages. The range of permissible uses of such charts is broad: you can list damages and calculate the total loss;[64] you can compute the number of weeks a plaintiff will suffer from permanent injury based on admitted evidence of life expectancy;[65] you can use a diagram of an accident scene to recreate the movements and relative positions of the parties;[66] you can outline the elements of a cause of action or

---

[53] See, e.g., People v. Smylie, 431 N.E.2d 1130 (Ill. 1982).

[54] E.g., State v. Jones, 604 S.W.2d 665 (Mo. Ct. App. 1980).

[55] E.g., Missouri Pac. R. Co. v. Foreman, 194 Ark. 490, 107 S.W.2d 546 (1937).

[56] United States v. Berry, 627 F.2d 193 (9th Cir. 1980).

[57] See, e.g., United States v. Morris, 568 F.2d 396 (5th Cir. 1978).

[58] United States v. North, 910 F.2d 843 (D.C. Cir. 1990).

[59] United States v. Doe, 860 F.2d 488 (1st Cir. 1988).

[60] Floyd v. Meachum, 907 F.2d 347 (2d Cir. 1990).

[61] Lindsey v. Smith, 820 F.2d 1137 (11th Cir. 1987).

[62] United States v. Castro, 908 F.2d 85 (6th Cir. 1990).

[63] Dudar v. Lewis, 282 S.E.2d 194 (Ga. 1981).

[64] E.g., Goldstein v. Gontarz, 364 Mass. 800, 309 N.E.2d 196 (1974); Crum v. Ward, 146 W. Va. 421, 122 S.E.2d 18 (1961).

[65] E.g., Timmerman v. Schroeder, 454 P.2d 522 (Kan. 1969).

[66] E.g., Boese v. Love, 300 S.W.2d 453 (Mo. 1957).

the questions in a special verdict and list what you believe to be the decisive evidence or the necessary result;[67] and you may be allowed to use new (unauthenticated) models or other illustrative exhibits to demonstrate your points.[68]

4. PROCEDURE FOR OBJECTING

Improper argument or conduct by your opponent always is subject to an objection. While the court may stop such an argument sua sponte,[69] the primary burden for objecting falls to the attorneys. An objection, accompanied by a motion to strike the offending argument, usually is the preferred procedure. As a general rule, all objections should be timely and must state clearly the grounds on which they are based. Failure to make a prompt, specific objection can amount to a waiver of that issue should you try to raise it on appeal.[70]

If your opponent's argument both is improper and impairs your client's ability to receive a fair trial, you can move for a mistrial. A mistrial is usually difficult to obtain for two reasons. First, most errors are deemed cured when the judge sustains your objection and instructs the jury to disregard the improper argument.[71] Second, if the improper argument is withdrawn by your opponent, any error usually will be cured.[72]

NOTES

1. *Unusual procedures.* A few jurisdictions limit the parties to one argument each, in which case the defendant usually goes first and the plaintiff or prosecution last. *E.g.,* N.Y. CIV. PRAC. LAW 4016 (McKinney 1992). In some jurisdictions, the defendant can earn the right to open and close argument in civil cases by admitting all the facts of the plaintiff's prima facie case and proceeding solely on an affirmative defense, *e.g., Phoenix Mut. Life Ins. Co. v. Bernfield*, 101 S.W.2d 1025 (Tex. Civ. App. 1937). In some jurisdictions, the defendant may have to concede the plaintiff's prima facie case and demand the right to go first before any evidence is introduced. *See Sirgany v. Equitable Life Ass'n*, 173 S.C. 120, 175 S.E. 209 (1934). In a few states, a criminal defendant may earn the right to argue last by presenting absolutely no evidence. *See Yeomans v. State*, 229 Ga. 488, 192 S.E.2d 362 (1972). If the defendant gives an opening statement or introduces an exhibit, the defendant may be deemed to have introduced evidence and may lose the right to open and close argument. *See Grimsley v. State*, 304 So. 2d 493 (Fla. App. 1974). In either case, the defendant must assert a claim to reverse the normal order of argument before closing argument begins.

---

[67] *E.g., Texas Employers' Ins. Ass'n v. Cruz*, 280 S.W.2d 388 (Tex. Civ. App. 1955).

[68] *Compare Peoples v. Commonwealth*, 147 Va. 692, 137 S.E. 603 (1927) (borrowing a police officer's revolver that had not been introduced was permitted to demonstrate impossibility of suicide) *with State v. Mayfield*, 506 S.W.2d 363 (Mo. 1974) (improper to brandish shotgun that had not been introduced during trial).

[69] *See, e.g., Aetna Life Ins. Co. v. Kelly*, 70 F.2d 589 (8th Cir. 1934).

[70] *See State v. Rollie*, 585 S.W.2d 78 (Mo. App. 1979). *Cf.* MINN. DIST. CT. R. 27(e) (objection still timely if made at the end of an argument).

[71] *See, e.g., Chavez v. Watts*, 515 N.E.2d 146 (Ill. App. 1987).

[72] *See, e.g., Parker v. Kangerga*, 482 S.W.2d 43 (Tex. Civ. App. 1972); *Hilton v. Thompson*, 360 Mo. 177, 227 S.W.2d 675 (1950); *Yellow Cab Co. v. Bradin*, 172 Md. 388, 191 A. 717 (1937).

2. Scope of final argument. The final argument generally is limited in scope, but it is more than just a two-minute rebuttal of the defendant's argument. The boundaries of final argument are determined by the issues raised in *both* preceding arguments, and the trial judge ultimately has the discretion to expand them even further. You are not supposed to introduce new issues in final argument that could have been raised (but were not) in your first argument, and also were not raised by the defense in their argument. *See, e.g., Heddendorf v. Joyce,* 178 So. 2d 126 (Fla. App. 1965); *Forguer v. Pinal Co.,* 22 Ariz. App. 266, 526 P.2d 1064 (1974). If the court does allow the plaintiff to raise new issues during final argument, fairness requires that the defendant be given a chance to reply. *See Thompson v. Bi-State Transit Sys.,* 458 S.W.2d 903 (Mo. App. 1970). Courts tend to be liberal in their findings of what constitutes proper scope of final argument. As long as no completely new issues are raised, you may bring up new lines of argument, new illustrations and exhibits, and additional details. *See Indianapolis Ry. v. Boyd,* 222 Ind. 481, 53 N.E.2d 762 (1944).

3. Reading from unofficial transcript of testimony. If the official transcript of testimony is not available for closing argument, can you quote from your own notes or from a private shorthand transcript? A majority of courts hold that it is within the judge's discretion to permit it. *See, e.g., Floen v. Sund,* 255 Minn. 211, 96 N.W.2d 563 (1959); *McLean v. San Francisco,* 151 Cal. App. 2d 133, 311 P.2d 158 (1957). However, some courts have held that, since there is no evidence that your personal transcript is correct, it is objectionable to hold it out as such to the jury. *See Chicago, I. & L. Ry. v. Gorman,* 58 Ind. App. 381, 106 N.E. 897 (1914); *Western Tube Co. v. Polobinski,* 192 Ill. 113, 61 N.E. 451 (1901).

4. Making up fictitious evidence. Attorneys often make up fictitious conversations that could have happened but about which there is no testimony. As long as this is clearly being done for purposes of argument and is not a distortion of the actual evidence, a court has the discretion to permit it. Consider the following argument, in which plaintiff's attorney put a Pepsi-Cola box in the witness chair during closing argument and said:

> Please testify, Mr. Pepsi-Cola Box. What is this box going to say? I don't know how old I am. I was born somewhere between 1936 and 1954. I was put together by Traub Box Company. I had metal bands and nails. I was loaded on a truck, pulled off other boxes, put on other boxes, put on rollers, [and] put on lines. One day, while I was working for Pepsi-Cola, carrying around 50 or 60 pounds, I lost one of my nails. I was all right. I was kept in service. At Christmastime, do you know what happened to me? I was hit, then I lost another nail. Although I lost another nail, I was still used. In 1959, I lost another nail. Sometimes I had to sit out in the rain, sometimes I had to sit out in the snow. [W]hile I was sitting there, my bottom was rotting out. Then I was delivered to a little grocery store in Murray Hill. A couple of days later a man tried to lift me up and finally the accumulation of all these years took its toll.

Would you permit it? The court in *Cusumano v. Pepsi-Cola Bottling Co.*, 9 Ohio App. 2d 105, 223 N.E.2d 477 (1967), did not. It held that it was error to allow the plaintiff to make the argument.

5. *Arguments concerning matters outside the record that affect plaintiff's compensation.* A number of factors indirectly affect how much compensation a plaintiff will actually receive. For example, since damages received as a result of personal injuries or in wrongful death cases are not subject to income taxes, 26 U.S.C. § 104(a)(2), a defense attorney may wish to point this out to the jury in an effort to reduce the final award. In most jurisdictions, however, it is not proper to do so. *See Cunningham v. Rederiet Vindeggen A/S*, 333 F.2d 308 (2d Cir. 1964); *Polster v. Griff's of Am., Inc.*, 32 Colo. App. 264, 514 P.2d 80 (1973); Annot., 63 A.L.R.2d 1393. The plaintiff may wish to ask the jury to take into account the effect of inflation when computing damages for future loss, in hopes of increasing the size of the verdict. Many courts also prohibit this argument, although there is a growing trend toward allowing it. *Compare Busch v. Busch Constr. Co.*, 262 N.W.2d 377 (Wis. 1977) (argument not permitted) *with Culver v. Slater Boat Co.*, 688 F.2d 280 (5th Cir. 1982) (argument permitted if based on expert testimony about wage trends). The plaintiff's attorney may not ask the jury to award his or her own fees and court costs in addition to the damage award, no matter how much these costs will otherwise reduce the client's actual recovery; *see Decks, Inc. v. Nunez*, 299 So. 2d 165 (Fla. App. 1974); *McElroy v. Swenson Constr. Co.*, 213 Mo. App. 160, 247 S.W. 209 (1923); nor may the defense attorney comment on the large fees the plaintiff's attorney is charging. *See Caplan v. Reynolds*, 191 Iowa 453, 182 N.W. 641 (1921). Finally, the "collateral source rule" prohibits a defense attorney from pointing out that someone else has already paid for the damages. It is common for some of the plaintiff's losses to have been paid by an insurance company, or for a plaintiff to have been taken care of by relatives. The defendant cannot argue that such payments should reduce the overall amount of damages. *E.g., Kniceley v. Migala*, 603 N.E.2d 843 (Ill. App. 1992).

D. ETHICAL CONSIDERATIONS

The MODEL RULES OF PROFESSIONAL CONDUCT contains two general provisions relevant to closing argument. Rule 3.3 prohibits a lawyer from "mak[ing] a false statement of material fact or law to a tribunal," and Rule 3.4 prohibits a lawyer from "stat[ing] a personal opinion as to the justness of a cause, the credibility of a witness, the culpability of a civil litigant, or the guilt or innocence of an accused."[73]

MODEL RULES OF PROFESSIONAL CONDUCT Rule 3.4(c) states that a lawyer shall not "knowingly disobey an obligation under the rules of a tribunal." It is therefore unethical to intentionally make an improper argument, and then withdraw it if your opponent objects. That may satisfy the legal requirement

---

[73] *See also State v. Locklear*, 294 N.C. 210, 241 S.E.2d 65 (1978) (unprofessional to assert opinion that a witness is lying); *State v. Vickroy*, 205 N.W.2d 748 (Iowa 1973) (unethical to state personal knowledge of defendant's guilt).

by removing improper matter from the jury's consideration, but it is still unethical. Under this general rule, it is unethical to:

- Allude to facts beyond the record.
- Distort or embellish the testimony.
- Invite speculation about unproved facts.
- Mention insurance or argue that someone else has already paid plaintiff's hospital bills.
- Distort or misstate the law.
- Make a jury nullification argument encouraging the jury to ignore an unpopular law (including the parole laws).
- Appeal to emotion, passion or prejudice that is not an inherent part of the case.
- Ask the jury to put themselves in your client's position.
- Suggest that the jurors will be personally affected by the verdict, e.g., through higher taxes or insurance premiums.
- Suggest that the court of appeals will correct any mistakes the jury makes.

The ABA STANDARDS FOR CRIMINAL JUSTICE address the ethics of closing argument in more detail:

Standard 3-5.8 Argument to the jury
   (a) The prosecutor may argue all reasonable inferences from evidence in the record. It is unprofessional conduct for the prosecutor intentionally to misstate the evidence or mislead the jury as to the inferences it may draw.
   (b) It is unprofessional conduct for the prosecutor to express his or her personal belief or opinion as to the truth or falsity of any testimony or evidence or the guilt of the defendant.
   (c) The prosecutor should not use arguments calculated to inflame the passions or prejudices of the jury.
   (d) The prosecutor should refrain from argument which would divert the jury from its duty to decide the case on the evidence, by injecting issues broader than the guilt or innocence of the accused under the controlling law, or by making predictions of the consequences of the jury's verdict.
   (e) It is the responsibility of the court to ensure that final argument to the jury is kept within proper, accepted bounds.

Standard 3-5.9. Facts outside the record
   It is unprofessional conduct for the prosecutor intentionally to refer to or argue on the basis of facts outside the record whether at trial or on appeal, unless such facts are matters of common public knowledge based on ordinary human experience or matters of which the court may take judicial notice.

The commentary to these standards points out that the prosecutor's argument is likely to have significant persuasive force with the jury, who will be inclined from the beginning to believe the prosecutor is less partisan than the defense attorney. Therefore, there is a special obligation on the prosecutor's part to act fairly. As the Supreme Court has remarked, although the prosecutor may "strike hard blows, he is not at liberty to strike foul ones."[74] The prosecutor may not misrepresent facts, insinuate that the state has additional information it could not present, appeal to prejudice, or play on the jurors' fear of crime.

NOTES

1. *Defense argument.* The ABA STANDARDS FOR CRIMINAL JUSTICE concerning defense argument are similar. Standard 4-7.8 contains one further restriction: It is unprofessional conduct for a lawyer "to attribute the crime to another person unless such an inference is warranted by the evidence."

2. *Referring to jurors by name.* It generally is held to be unethical to single out a particular juror during argument or call jurors by their names. *See* ABA Committee on Professional Ethics, Informal Opinion 739 (1963).

E. PREPARING CLOSING ARGUMENT

1. PLANNING STAGES

A closing argument is not a spontaneous outpouring of emotion and off-the-cuff eloquence. Although a few trial practitioners might disagree, most attorneys know that to give a good argument requires careful and thorough planning. Since some of the argument you will give will depend on the course of events at trial — the strength of your opponent's evidence, testimony unexpectedly excluded, or the success of trial motions — you cannot prepare your entire argument in advance. Nevertheless, you can prepare most of it before trial. Perhaps it will help to break down preparation into two stages.

a. First Stage — Outlining Your Argument

Your closing argument is simply an oral presentation of your theory of the case which you developed long before trial. It may, therefore, be valuable to review the section on developing a case theory in Chapter 2. In general, a good case theory has the following characteristics:

- It clearly tells the jury what verdict you want and why.
- It is logically based on the evidence.
- It is consistent with common sense.
- It accounts for all of the important evidence.
- It concentrates on the most important items of evidence.
- It avoids legal technicalities as much as possible.
- It explains both why you are right and why your opponent is wrong.
- It uses specific evidence and specific legal principles, not generalizations.
- It suggests reasonable ways to resolve disputes.
- It appeals to the jury's sense of fairness and justice.
- It is entertaining and incorporates visual aids.

---

[74]*Berger v. United States*, 295 U.S. 78, 88 (1935).

Despite the fact that you know your theory well, most lawyers recommend preparing either a detailed outline or a full version of your argument in advance. That forces you to think through exactly how you are going to present each argument, and to place them in some kind of logical order. A few practice rounds in front of friends, colleagues or a video camera will help improve your ability to deliver it. When you are satisfied with your argument, you might want to reduce it to a simple outline form to make sure you will not end up reading your argument to the jury.

This initial outline is not the final version of the argument you actually will deliver. Some changes inevitably will be necessary based on the testimony at trial and the statements made by your adversary. It is therefore a good idea to leave some working space on your outline to be filled in during the second stage of preparation.

b. Second Stage — Preparation During Trial

Most of your closing argument can (and should) be prepared in advance. However, there always will be a few unanticipated events that occur during trial. If you have a good working outline, it can be supplemented by a few notes as the trial progresses.

- During voir dire, the jurors may make statements or express concerns that provide ideas about how to phrase an argument, whether a particular point needs to be emphasized, or what kinds of analogies to draw. For example, if several jurors have young children and express concern about danger in the city schools, you may want to make a slight modification in your argument to work in a reference to your own client as a "a parent who has to worry about her children's safety every day," or to change your "safe streets" argument[75] to one that reminds the jury that the problems of crime are so great they are even threatening the schools.
- During opening statement, you can note any overstatements or exaggerations made by your opponent. These can be used later to argue that the other side has failed to prove its case. The standard argument goes something like this: "The prosecutor promised at the start of the trial that he would produce an eyewitness who could positively identify the defendant. He did not produce any such witness — only old Mr. Thornapple, who admitted he couldn't see very well. By his own admission, the prosecutor's case hinged on this testimony, and it did not measure up. He has failed to prove the most important part of his case beyond a reasonable doubt."
- During the examination of witnesses, you can note the exact words used by a witness at a critical time, so that they can be quoted accurately. If any evidence is unexpectedly excluded, that too should be noted so that you do not inadvertently refer to evidence outside the record.
- If either side is granted a partial directed verdict, or concedes an issue, whole sections can be eliminated from your argument.

---

[75] A "safe streets" argument is the standard rhetoric by prosecutors reminding the jury that crime is running rampant and they need to do their part to help make the streets safer by removing this particular miscreant from society.

Often there will be (or you can request) a recess between the conclusion of the evidence and closing arguments. This will give you time to make sure that you have all materials ready — notes, exhibits, charts, and so forth — and to make necessary rearrangements and modifications in your argument.

2. PRINCIPLES OF EFFECTIVE ARGUMENT

Good argument is not just oratory; nor is oratory necessarily good argument. Your goal is not to win an academy award for your dramatic performance, but to present your theory of the case to the jury so that they understand it and remember it. Whether you will give an effective closing argument is largely determined in advance as you decide how to organize and phrase your presentation. As you undertake this task, you might consider the following principles of effective argument:

- *Keep it simple.* Simple does not mean simplistic; it means uncomplicated. Concentrate on the real disputes, resist the temptation to offer several alternative theories, and avoid becoming bogged down in reviewing uncontested or trivial matters. Experiments by social psychologists indicate that about seven points are all you can argue persuasively. After that, arguments become confusing.[76]
- *Be specific.* Facts are more important than generalizations or rhetoric. Be specific about the important factual points, and the details that corroborate them. Don't just say you have proven that the goods were delivered, remind them which witnesses testified to the delivery and show them the warehouse receipt.
- *Be explicit.* Psychologists have demonstrated that an argument is more persuasive if the desired conclusions are explicitly suggested (but not demanded) than if you leave it up to the jury to draw its own conclusions.[77] Although in theory jurors might hold more strongly to a conclusion they reach on their own, if you do not suggest a conclusion, the jurors may reach a conclusion you do not like.
- *Be organized.*
- *Keep to your theory of the case.* If a fact, law or argument is not necessary to your theory of the case, do not mention it.
- *Use visual aids.* Presumably, you introduced exhibits during trial for a reason. Use them! But do not limit yourself to exhibits already introduced. Charts can be prepared specifically for closing argument, and arguments can be illustrated on the blackboard. The uses of descriptive exhibits are as varied as your creativity. You can list the elements of a cause of action, summarize evidence, calculate damages, draw a sketch of an intersection, and so on. The only requirement is that your exhibit be supported by the evidence. Some attorneys prefer the apparent spontane-

---

[76] *See* Daniel Linz & Steven Penrod, *Increasing Attorney Persuasiveness in the Courtroom,* 8 LAW & PSYCHOL. REV. 1, 28-29 (1984).

[77] Carl Hovland & Wallace Mandell, *An Experimental Comparison of Conclusion-Drawing by the Communicators and the Audience,* 47 J. ABNORMAL & SOC. PSYCHOL. 581 (1952); Bernard Fine, *Conclusion-Drawing, Communicator's Credibility, and Anxiety as Factors in Opinion Change,* 54 J. ABNORMAL & SOC. PSYCHOL. 369 (1957).

ity of blackboards; others prefer charts prepared in advance because they cannot be erased by the opponent and the likelihood of inadvertent errors is minimized.

- *Support your positions with jury instructions.* Rather than just summarize all the law at one time, weave instructions into the fabric of your argument. If you are arguing that a witness is not credible because the witness made a prior inconsistent statement and is the plaintiff's friend, that would be a good time to read a jury instruction that prior statements and bias may be taken into account in determining credibility.
- *Use the theme from your opening statement.*
- *Personalize your client and depersonalize the adverse witnesses.* You should make conscious efforts to personalize your client by referring to him or her by name and telling the jury personal things about your client's life. Similarly, you should depersonalize the other side's witnesses, by referring to the adverse party generically (e.g., the defendant, the corporation, the deceased) or with negative labels (e.g., the toxic-waste company).
- *Use analogies to common experiences.* If you think a jury may have difficulty understanding a legal concept, try to analogize it to some common experience. The classic example is the explanation of circumstantial evidence: suppose you got up one morning and saw a foot of snow on the ground that was not there when you went to bed. You can be certain it snowed during the night, even though no eyewitness saw it.
- *Be positive.* Spend your time arguing your own case, not your opponent's. Emphasize your strengths and concentrate on your main points. Discuss your opponent's case only to the extent necessary to refute it briefly.
- *Admit your weaknesses.* Every case has weaknesses. You should confront those inherent in your theory, admit them, and deal with them as best you can. The jury is probably already aware of them from the evidence, and your opponent is sure to bring them up, so you cannot make them go away. Therefore, you might as well at least earn points for candor and honesty. However, the dividing line between a candid discussion of your weaknesses and a defensive argument that focuses on your opponent's evidence is a fine one. It is not necessary to confront every piece of contradictory evidence. Rather, you should discuss and explain away the major weaknesses in your own theory.

3. LENGTH

Hugh Head, a Georgia trial attorney, has written that the one mistake that leads to the most lost lawsuits is talking too long:

> Mark Twain has a funny story about the preacher who was so spellbinding that he resolved to contribute all his money to the cause. The minister kept on, and he thought he would give him all his folding money. A few minutes later, he was down to all the loose change. The good pastor then kept on so long that finally Mark Twain vows he stole a quarter from the

plate when it was finally passed around. Few souls are saved, in church or court, after twenty minutes.[78]

Lengthy closing arguments can result in a number of undesirable consequences: your major point may become lost in a mass of trivial issues, the jury may become bored and stop listening, arguments may become disorganized, or you may even raise doubts about your own case.

What is the correct amount of time to spend on closing argument? The answer obviously will vary with the complexity of the issues you must discuss. Some writers have suggested absolute time limits for all arguments, ranging from twenty minutes to an hour. Such suggestions are important only because they demonstrate a near uniformity of opinion that relatively brief arguments are better than lengthy ones. While you should not be afraid to discuss the important issues fully, you should also be unafraid to sit down when you are finished. Taking unnecessary time simply to repeat arguments or to argue trivial or uncontested matters can only weaken your presentation.

4. STRUCTURING CLOSING ARGUMENT

There are probably as many ways to structure arguments as there are attorneys who give them. No one method of organization is categorically better than the others. In the next few pages, one method is suggested that emphasizes simplicity and clarity of organization. It is a good starting point for beginners, especially those who doubt their natural eloquence. Another organizational scheme is included in the notes following this section for comparison.

a. Introduction

Every argument starts with introductory remarks of some kind. The standard advice is that you should begin by thanking the jury for their patience and explaining the purpose of a closing argument. Many trial practitioners use these somewhat insincere, canned openings as crutches to ease themselves over those first tense moments. The usual opening remarks often sound like this:

> If Your Honor please, distinguished defense counsel, ladies and gentlemen of the jury. It is now my privilege to present what is known as a closing argument. This is my opportunity to discuss with you the evidence in this case and the law which will be given to you by the court. But first, Jane Porter and I want to thank you for your services as jurors. You have been taken away from your own personal affairs to do your civic duty, and I know it has been an inconvenience to sit patiently through days of tedious testimony. Without your conscientious service, trials like this would not be possible in our democracy. The burden on you will now become even greater. You must judge what is right and wrong, and decide

---

[78] Hugh Head, *Arguing Damages to the Jury*, TRIAL, Feb. 1980, at 28, 30.

whether Jane will recover any monetary damages from the defendants to compensate her for her crippling injuries.[79]

This kind of introduction is safe and inoffensive, but is also boring, insincere and misleading. Endless repetition of platitudes is boring. Even if you think thanking the jury is important, to do it first is so obviously currying favor that it cannot help but sound insincere. The introduction is misleading because it does not seem to acknowledge that there is a great battle raging between the two sides over millions of dollars.

It may make more sense to use your introductory remarks to further your case! Our strategy was to take advantage of the principle of primacy whenever we had the chance. You can set the mood, state your theme, summarize your theory and emphasize an important piece of information all in your first sentence or two while you have the jurors' attention. For example:

> During the four days of testimony concerning the injuries to Jane Porter, there have been a few times when certain events provoked a laugh — we all laughed. There was nothing wrong with that. For the law deals with love and laughter, and the events that affect lives. Laughter is one part of life. And perhaps, in a case like this, laughter was necessary for the momentary relief it provided from the catastrophe that has occupied our minds for four days. But now the time for laughter has passed, and we are confronted with a more difficult aspect of life — the suffering of Jane Porter, who because of the paralysis caused in the accident, will never love or laugh again.[80]

b. Brief Summary of Case

After the introduction, you should tell the jury *briefly* your theory of the case: who did what to whom and why. This should not take more than a few lines. This is not the time to go into detail, discuss specific witnesses, or resolve conflicting evidence. You simply should tell the jury, painting as vivid a picture as possible, your basic theory. For example:

> Jane Porter is now a cripple, and will remain so for the rest of her life. Her prospects of ever leading a normal life were shattered when a drunk college student ran a red light and smashed into Ms. Porter's car.

c. Identifying the Issues

The next step is to identify the issues and focus the jurors' attention on the important ones. It is not enough just to tell the jury what the issues are. They might not believe you — after all, your opponent may focus on other issues, and the court's instructions will not tell them which issues are truly important. Your conclusion about what the issues are must be credible. One method

---

[79] *See* L. SMITH, *supra* note 1, at §§ 3.01 to 3.03 (reprinting an actual argument given by Jack Werchick, a California attorney and adjunct trial practice instructor at Hastings College of Law that runs for three full paragraphs of platitudes).

[80] Suggested by JAMES JEANS, TRIAL ADVOCACY § 16.9 (1975). *See also* L. SMITH, *supra* note 1, at § 1.21 ("In the Bible it is stated that there is a time for joy and a time for sorrow").

of accomplishing this goal is to summarize the issues based on the instructions or verdict form they will receive. For example:

> The judge will instruct you that you should return a verdict for Jane Porter if you believe four things: first, that the defendant either drove at an excessive speed or was intoxicated; second, that his conduct was negligent; third, that Jane Porter sustained injuries as a result of such negligence; and fourth, that the truck driver was operating the Ajax Company truck within the scope of his employment by Ajax. These are the issues you must decide.

It often helps if you translate legalese into plain English. To the previous paragraph, you might add:

> In other words, we must prove four things: 1) the truck driver was either speeding or drunk; 2) the truck driver was negligent; 3) Jane was hurt; and 4) the truck driver was working for Ajax.

Some attorneys would put these simplified legal concepts on a chart, displayed in front of the jury.

The next step is to focus the attention of the jurors on the contested issues. This is done by eliminating the issues that are uncontested or only tokenly contested. For example:

> We don't have to worry about two of these issues — the fact that the truck driver was driving the truck as part of his job with Ajax is not contested. You heard the manager of Ajax testify that she personally told Jones to make this delivery. We also introduced the truck driver's employment contract (holding it up) signed by the president of Ajax. Therefore, it is clear from the evidence that he worked for Ajax and was making a routine delivery when the wreck occurred. The second issue also is not contested — if the truck driver were speeding or drunk while driving through city streets crowded with cars and pedestrians, his conduct was unreasonable and therefore negligent. That leaves two issues for your consideration.

Next, you should refine your definition of the issues by being detailed and specific. Does the dispute over intoxication concern whether the truck driver had been drinking at all, how much he had been drinking, or whether he was under the influence? Does the dispute over damages concern an allegation of a preexisting condition, a disagreement about the permanency of the injuries, or a question of how to value pain and suffering? Again, by a process of eliminating the uncontested facts, you can help the jurors (and your own argument) focus on the heart of the lawsuit. For example:

> The first issue is whether we have proved to you that the Ajax truck driver was drunk when he crashed into Jane Porter's car. There is no argument about the fact that the truck driver had been drinking in a bar only one hour before he smashed into Ms. Porter's car. The truck driver admitted on the stand that he stopped at Nick's Grill to drink beer at

about 2:30 p.m. The issue before you is how much he had to drink, and how that alcohol affected his ability to drive.

d. Order of Issues

If there is only a single issue, you can proceed directly to a discussion of it. If there are multiple issues, you should make clear to the jury the order in which you will discuss them. In general, it is better for a plaintiff to discuss liability first and damages last. A defendant in a civil case often reverses the order, discussing damages first and concluding with arguments against liability. It would be difficult to do it the other way. If, after you conclude that there is no basis for liability, you say: "But, in case you find liability, damages are very small," it weakens your argument against liability.

In criminal cases (and civil cases presenting only liability or only damage issues), it is usually advisable to discuss the issues in the order in which the jury will hear them in the instructions. However, you always must be careful to avoid an order that weakens a dispositive argument. If your primary argument is followed by a more technical argument, such as that your opponent has failed to prove some other element, it may appear that your main argument is not strong enough to entitle you to a verdict. For example, consider which of the following is the more effective:

(a) The evidence clearly establishes that the defendant was not even in Chicago when the alleged crime occurred. But even if you do not accept his alibi, the state failed to prove armed robbery. They did not show that a weapon was involved. They never produced it.

(b) The defendant is charged with armed robbery. You might ask why, since no weapon was introduced, and the state never proved that one was involved. But you do not have to worry about it, because the defendant was not even in Chicago when the incident occurred.

e. Resolving the Issues

The main body of your argument should be allocated to a resolution of these issues, one by one. This is the time to review the evidence — but only that portion that concerns the contested issue under discussion. There is rarely any need for a lengthy, boring recitation of the testimony of witnesses. If you have tried your case properly, the jury knows the basic story by now. You need only briefly summarizing the evidence on both sides of each contested issue to make the conflict clear, and then resolve the dispute in your favor.

If the issue is a factual one involving conflicting evidence, there are a number of ways to resolve it. Some are more effective than others, and you often will be able to combine two or more. You can argue that a conflict should be resolved in your favor because your version of the facts is:

- Consistent with physical evidence.
- Supported by the greater quantity of evidence.
- Consistent with common sense.
- Supported by the more credible witnesses.

The most effective way of resolving disputes in testimony is to show that your version is consistent with, and your adversary's is impossible to square with, uncontroverted physical evidence. For example, if there are 250 feet of skid marks, a car had to be going fast before the brakes were applied. If witnesses disagree about how long it took a person to walk thirty feet, you can demonstrate that it would take that person almost seven seconds to travel that distance at a normal walking pace.

Probably the second most effective way to resolve a dispute is to show that your version is corroborated by many witnesses and exhibits, while the other side's case rests only on one or two witnesses. The more witnesses there are, the less likely that any one could be mistaken. It is especially helpful if you can show that even witnesses called by your opponent corroborate important parts of your own case.

This argument often can be combined with a discussion of the burden of proof. The defendant can argue that its version of the case is supported by more evidence, and that the law of burden of proof says that the plaintiff's failure to produce the greater weight of evidence means the jury must decide against her. Plaintiff can argue that she has produced more evidence, and that is all the law requires. She need not negate all of the defendant's evidence entirely.

In the absence of physical evidence or corroborating witnesses, the argument most consistent with common sense and everyday experience is likely to prevail. Your version of the event should be both possible and probable. For example, the prosecution could negate a self-defense claim by pointing out that the defendant had taken a gun with him when he went to see the victim — something he was not likely to do unless he intended to use it.

The least effective method of resolving a factual dispute is to attack the credibility of your adversary's witnesses. Jurors do not readily believe that a witness would lie under oath unless that witness had a strong motive to do so. A good friend called as an alibi witness might lie for the defendant; a roll-over witnesses who is avoiding a long jail term by testifying might lie for the state. But you need a strong motive consistent with common sense to succeed in such an attack. Prior convictions (except for perjury), prior inconsistent statements, or biases and prejudices standing alone are not likely to be enough to convince a jury that the witness has lied. If you need to attack credibility, it is probably better to develop an argument that a witness was mistaken because of an inadequate opportunity to observe the events than to suggest that the witness is a liar.

These methods often can be combined into an effective argument, as in the following example:

> The second issue I mentioned was whether the Ajax truck driver was speeding when he crashed into Ms. Porter's car. You will recall that when the truck driver testified, he said he was going twenty to thirty miles per hour. The only other eyewitness was Ms. Frankel, the lady walking her dog. She estimated that the Ajax truck was going about fifty. How do we decide whom to believe? Let's look at the evidence. Remember the testimony of Jason Smith of the highway patrol. He measured over eighty feet

of skid marks. He testified to you that a truck going only thirty miles an hour would come to a complete stop within sixty feet. Did the Ajax truck come to a complete stop? No. It skidded another twenty feet and then (holding up a photograph of the truck) was still going fast enough to smash up the front end. Also, do not forget Ms. Porter's testimony. Although she did not see the Ajax truck bearing down on her, she felt the force of the impact. She said that she was thrown clear across the seat and hit the door handle on the other side of the car. Remember, too, that the truck driver's own boss testified that the delivery was supposed to be made by 3:00. The wreck occurred at 3:05, so the truck driver was already late. Which testimony makes more sense: that the driver would be driving five to fifteen miles per hour *below* the speed limit when he was late, or that he would be going faster than usual? The only evidence that he was driving slowly comes from the truck driver himself. Not only does he have a motive to claim he was going slowly, but his ability to estimate his speed accurately probably had been impaired by his drinking.

Many cases also will present issues of how to apply the facts to the law; for example, whether the defendant's conduct was unreasonable enough to amount to negligence. Making this kind of decision is the ultimate function of the jury. In one sense, there is little you can say beyond an argument such as:

We submit that it is not reasonable to drive fifty-five miles per hour on a narrow road in the pouring rain, even if that is within the speed limit.

However, you can employ a number of techniques that will make this kind of argument more effective. The most important is to translate the legal concepts into easily understood words. Then, through a series of analogies, you should demonstrate that the facts fit within that definition. For example:

The judge will instruct you that the defendant is negligent if he failed to use that degree of care that an ordinarily careful and prudent person would use under the same circumstances. That means you must measure the truck driver's conduct not against the way you drive, but against the way you expect your sons and daughters to be taught in drivers' education. His conduct must be measured against what a reasonable and careful driver, such as a parent taking his or her children to school, would do. Such a careful person might drive more slowly on narrow roads than on interstate highways. Such a careful person would certainly slow down in dense fog regardless of the speed limit, because it is not safe to drive fast when you cannot see. The careful driver would slow down if the roads were covered with ice. Similarly, if some other condition made it difficult to see and made the roads slippery, a careful driver would slow down. A hard rain presents just such a situation — obscured visibility and a slippery road. The truck driver's failure to slow down to a reasonably safe speed was therefore negligent.

Arguments about the value of intangible damages, such as pain and suffering, are difficult to formulate for similar reasons. This is also one of the ultimate functions of the jury. Trying to articulate the monetary value of pain

may seem almost impossible, so many lawyers mistakenly do not even attempt it. They choose instead to review the facts, make the pain as vivid as
possible, suggest a number, and trust the jury. The challenge is to make your
number reasonable. The same two techniques can help: translating the instruction into ordinary terms, and then using analogies and comparisons. For
example:

> The judge will instruct you that Jane Porter is entitled to reasonable
> compensation for her pain and suffering. How do you decide what is rea-
> sonable? Look around you at ordinary life, at the conduct of everyday
> affairs. What is the effect of pain? One effect is that it prevents Ms. Porter
> from getting a good night's sleep. She testified that she cannot sleep
> because of the pain. Her husband, Frank, testified that she tosses and
> turns, and often cries out at night. He told you about seeing the tears of
> frustration in his wife's eyes as another sleepless night goes by. Ms. Por-
> ter testified it was like trying to sleep in your car — you cannot get
> comfortable, your muscles cramp. What do reasonable people do when
> traveling? Instead of trying to sleep in their cars, they check into a motel.
> They recognize that a good night's sleep is worth something. It has a
> value — about sixty dollars for a night at the Holiday Inn. So I suggest
> that sixty dollars is a reasonable amount to award Ms. Porter for each
> night when the pain prevents her from sleeping. Since the evidence
> showed that she has not been able to get a single good night's sleep since
> the accident — that is two years and fifty-six days, or 786 days — she
> should be awarded $47,160 (doing calculations on the blackboard).

In arguing damages, it is particularly important to request a specific
amount, and to base that amount on reason and common sense. You are not
doing your job if all you can tell the jury is that they must decide on an
amount. If you, an experienced lawyer, cannot think up an amount, how do
you expect the jury to do so? Your adversary will probably step into this void
and suggest an amount quite different than what you wanted, which will be
the only estimate the jurors have in front of them. It is also helpful after
establishing the various components of damages, to compute them on the
blackboard so the jury can clearly see the total request.

f. Conclusion

The final part of your argument should be a strong statement of your position. Who did what to whom, why did they do it, why is it legal (or illegal), and
why does it entitle you to a verdict in your favor. Keep your summary *brief*
and stick to your own case. Don't rehash both sides of the argument or end on
a defensive note, because that gives too much credit to your adversary's position. Make clear to the jury exactly what verdict you expect them to return. If
they made any promises to you in voir dire, remind them of that. If the case
involves damages, repeat the specific amount you expect. Then, conclude with
a dramatic finish that sums up the central theme of your argument and the

justice of it. Thank the jury on behalf of your client, and sit down. For example:

> Two years ago, Jane Porter was wheeled into my office, laboring under the burden of having been crippled in an accident. For these past months, I have helped her carry some of that burden, but my task is now completed. The burden is being passed to you, the jury. Nothing you can do will totally lift the weight from Ms. Porter's shoulders. You cannot give her back the use of her legs. No matter what we do, she cannot walk out of this courtroom and down the stairs, cannot get into her car, press the gas pedal and drive home, as you and I will do. She has already been sentenced to life imprisonment in a wheelchair by the stupid, careless act of a drunken truck driver. But you do have the power to help her. How many of us have read of the heroic acts of ordinary people who help strangers who are in trouble, and wondered whether we would have had the courage to do the same? This is your opportunity. Ms. Porter will have to live the rest of her life with the result of your decision. We are confident that you will return a verdict for the plaintiff, Jane Porter. We have shown that $640,000 will reasonably compensate her. On behalf of Ms. Porter and myself, we thank you for your patience and attentiveness, and for your willingness to undertake the awesome responsibility placed upon you. We are confident that you will not shortchange a cripple.

5. SPECIAL PROBLEMS FOR PLAINTIFF

Plaintiffs (and prosecutors) usually have the opportunity to argue first and last. If you represent a plaintiff, how should you allocate your time? Most attorneys recommend that you allocate two-thirds to three-fourths of your time to your first argument. If you waive or give an abbreviated first argument, you sacrifice the psychological advantage of getting the first word. You also cede control over defining the issues to your opponent. If the defendant raises only a single issue, you may be precluded from raising new issues in final argument. This does not mean that you should shortchange your final argument. If you do, you have sacrificed the psychological advantage that comes from getting in the last word.[81] Final argument should be more than a spontaneous rebuttal of points made by your opponent. If you have thought through the case properly, you can anticipate the arguments your adversary will make and can prepare in advance the arguments that will refute them. Your final argument can then be structured in the same way as your first argument, with an introduction, a resolution of disputes, and a dramatic conclusion.

The second problem facing the person who argues first is whether to anticipate the defense argument. Trial practitioners agree that you cannot ignore conflicting evidence, but they disagree on the extent to which you should directly anticipate the defense's arguments. It is probably best to steer a middle ground, dealing with the large, obvious facts that seem to contradict

---

[81] *See, e.g.*, Chester Inkso, E. Allan Lind & Stephen LaTour, *Persuasion, Recall and Thoughts*, 7 REPRESENTATIVE RESEARCH IN SOCIAL PSYCHOLOGY 66 (1976).

your theory, but not trying to anticipate all the details of your opponent's argument. Experiments by psychologists have shown that if you forewarn jurors that the defendant is going to try to persuade them, and then refute a weakened version of the defense argument, you can to some extent inoculate them against your opponent's position.[82]

6. SPECIAL PROBLEMS FOR DEFENDANT

If you represent a defendant you will have only one argument, so your concerns will be slightly different than the plaintiff's. However, you still have to allocate time. How much time do you spend refuting the plaintiff, and how much in stating your own case? Experienced trial practitioners recommend that you stick to your own case — stay on the offensive. This strategy assumes that you have a plausible case, of course, and are not so desperate that your only argument is that the plaintiff or prosecutor has failed to meet the burden of proof.

You must accomplish two things in your one argument: refuting the plaintiff's case and offering your own theory. The usual order of an argument is to offer your own positive case first; this was the order suggested above. Beware of the temptation to attack the absurd arguments of your opponent first thing. It is especially important to avoid disrupting the natural organization of your argument by responding to individual silly remarks, lies and exaggerations made by the plaintiff during the opening argument. If they are relevant to your theory, you will get to them in due course, and can better refute them at that time.

How many issues should you raise? Some trial practitioners advise defendants to place as many issues as possible before the jury. The more arguments you have that there are disputes and unresolved problems, the more likely it is that you can convince a jury that the plaintiff has failed to carry its burden of proof. The problem with this approach is that the underlying argument — plaintiff failed to prove its case — is your weakest possible theory of the case. Do you not have *anything* positive to say about your own case? Is your client so obviously guilty that he or she could not even manage to take the stand and deny responsibility? In most cases, you will have something stronger to say — a particular reason why you are entitled to a verdict. As soon as we posit this scenario, the justification for a "shotgun" defense disappears. You would not want to risk burying your one good issue in a mass of unimportant ones.

Since you do not get another chance to speak, it is important that you anticipate plaintiff's final argument. If you know the case well, you know the points at which your opponent is likely to attack. You can warn the jurors of the coming assault, point out why it is not valid, and ask them to remember your argument since you cannot speak again. Psychologists have found that this process of inoculation is usually helpful.

---

[82]*See* Linz & Penrod, *supra* note 75, at 17-27; Steven Penrod et al., *The Implications of Social Psychological Research for Trial Practice Attorneys, in* PSYCHOLOGY AND LAW 448-49 (D. Muller et al., eds., 1984).

NOTES

1. *Other organizational schemes.* The suggested organizational model is not the only one available, although it is a good place to start. An alternative model is suggested by RALPH McCULLOUGH & JAMES UNDERWOOD, CIVIL TRIAL MANUAL 654-60 (2d ed. 1980):

- Brief opening remarks designed to get jurors' attention.
- Discussion of the burden of proof, especially by a plaintiff who needs to overcome the jurors' belief that civil cases must be proved beyond a reasonable doubt.
- Definition of the issues, narrowing them down as much as possible, and giving the jurors a logical and easy-to-understand analysis of each.
- Brief summary of the sequence of events from your perspective, told in narrative fashion like a story.
- A recap of the important testimony from important witnesses, being careful not to rehash everything said by every witness.
- Discussion of why your witnesses are credible, being candid about their weaknesses.
- Brief summary and refutation of the evidence introduced by your opponent, including any necessary attacks on the credibility of your adversary's witnesses.
- Discussion of the law as it applies to the case, paraphrasing any difficult passages.
- Discussion of damages.
- Conclusion that ends with a strong point, a summary of your main argument, and an emotional appeal.

2. *Should you ask rhetorical questions*? Mauet argues that it can be an effective technique to use rhetorical questions. THOMAS A. MAUET, FUNDAMENTALS OF TRIAL TECHNIQUES 282 (3d ed. 1992). He recommends using them to ask yourself the "tough" questions you imagine the jury is wondering about, and then answering them. There probably is nothing wrong with this technique, as in the following example from a plaintiff's attorney:

> "You're probably asking yourselves, 'Why should we award Ms. Johnson over $3,000,000? That's a lot of money.' You're right, of course. That is a lot of money. But in this case, Ms. Johnson's injuries were devastating and permanent. Recall the evidence ...."

However, Mauet goes on to recommend that you use rhetorical questions to challenge your opponent with questions you believe are unanswerable. For example, Mauet suggests the following question in a criminal case:

> "In this case, the evidence showed that the defendant *just happened* to be one block from where the robbery occurred moments earlier, *just happened* to have a nickel-plated revolver on him, *just happened* to have $47.00 in his pocket, and *just happened* to be wearing a red velour shirt. If he's so innocent, I'm sure his lawyer will have a great explanation for how all these things *just happened* at the same time when he argues to you."

This is a far more risky tactic. The question probably is either irrelevant to your opponent's theory, or your opponent, in fact, has an answer! For example, the defense attorney might respond to Mauet's argument as follows:

> "As I understood the prosecutor's argument, he said that if we could explain the coincidence of four pieces of incriminating evidence, it will prove Sammy's innocence. Why is it, the prosecutor asked in incredulous tones, that Sammy just happened to be one block from the robbery with a nickel-plated revolver on him, with $47.00 in his pocket, wearing a red velour shirt? Clever questions are not evidence, however. The evidence explains each of these items. Sammy is retarded, as everyone in the neighborhood knows. When Jack Ripple went to rob the grocery store, he took Sammy along. Sammy was happy to have anyone befriend him. Ripple told Sammy to wait for him, and then went to rob the store. Things went bad, and Jack needed to get away. He ran back and asked Sammy to hold some things for him — a gun, some money, and a red sweater. Sammy was happy to do this for his new "friend." Ripple then ran off down Fifth Street (where, you will remember, the ski mask was found) and disappeared. He left Sammy holding the bag.

F. CONDUCTING CLOSING ARGUMENT

1. MANNER AND STYLE

We have said throughout this book that style is largely a matter of individual personality. Nowhere is this more true than closing argument. You will be most effective if you are yourself, whether that means quiet reasoning, a sense of humor, or lofty rhetoric. If you try to adopt some artificial style that you saw on television, you will probably appear insincere and uncomfortable. The jurors may interpret this as discomfort with the *merits* of the case you must present.

Nevertheless, within the boundaries imposed by your own natural style of speaking, there are some suggestions you should consider:

- Informality is usually better than formality.
- Maintaining a courteous, professional demeanor is usually better than sarcasm, anger, or any other childish outburst. Try not to be rude, abrasive, or obnoxious.
- Histrionics should be used sparingly. You are likely to be more effective if you adopt a friendly, conversational manner than if you attempt to mimic the dramatic techniques of the actors who portray lawyers on television. However, this does not mean you should never use dramatic techniques, only that you should save them for the most important points in your argument.
- When the facts are emotional, you should display an emotional reaction yourself. If you represent a client who was crippled in an automobile accident, or are prosecuting a rape case, don't talk about the victim's plight in dry, matter-of-fact terms. Let your voice express your sympathy and your outrage.

- Be careful about using exaggeration and hyperbole. Remember that your personal credibility is on the line, and if you say outrageous things that are not true, the jury will believe you less.
- Notes should be used as minimally as possible so that your overall presentation is extemporaneous and conversational. Above all, do not read your closing argument.
- Maintain eye contact with the jury. Look from juror to juror during your argument, not at your notes or the floor. If looking directly at jurors makes you uncomfortable, look between two jurors.
- Avoid standing behind a lectern. If you need the security of a lectern, try standing beside it rather than hiding behind it.

Philip Corboy, former president of the ABA Section of Litigation, summarizes these suggestions as the five C's — five distinctive characteristics you must display in closing argument: courtesy, competence, credibility, charisma, and caring.[83]

2. SPEAKING RATE

How quickly or slowly should you speak when presenting a closing argument? The traditional advice given by trial practitioners (and their mothers) is to speak slowly and distinctly. You don't want to sound like a fast-talking used-car dealer trying to put something over on the audience. Lawyers also recommend that you vary your pace to alleviate monotony and boredom — speaking more quickly when covering relatively unimportant matters, and slowing down for emphasis when you make crucial points or refer to pivotal exhibits.

Surprisingly, there is some evidence that the traditional view may be wrong. Psychological experiments have shown that listeners rated fast talkers as more intelligent, more objective, and more persuasive than either normal or slow talkers, and that listener comprehension was not adversely affected.[84] There are two probable explanations for this. First, jurors can think faster than you can talk. The slower you talk, the more "spare" time jurors have to think of other things. Reactance theory suggests that one topic they will tend to think about when you are trying to sell them something, is the counterargument. The less time you give them to think about alternative explanations, the better. Second, if you talk faster, jurors have to work harder to keep up with you. This cognitive activity tends to implant your argument in their minds. To put this in perspective, think about which professors are more boring — the lively fast talkers, or the ones who speak slowly!

3. CHOREOGRAPHY

Unless you are in a courtroom where you are required to argue from a fixed position, you can make some choices about where to stand, when to move, and whether to use a lectern. In the typical courtroom, there is a great deal of

[83] Philip H. Corboy, *Final Argument: Earning the Jury's Trust*, TRIAL, Feb. 1992, at 61.

[84] Linz & Penrod, *supra* note 75, at 43-45 (1984); Stephan Peskin, *Non-verbal Communication in the Courtroom*, TRIAL DIPL. J., Fall 1980, at 4-5.

flexibility, and no two lawyers will choreograph their closing arguments in exactly the same way. In the last analysis, your argument probably will be most effective if you are comfortable, regardless of the general suggestions below.

Psychologists have experimented on the persuasive effect of arguments delivered from different distances. The results of one experiment indicated that distances between the speaker and listener of more than twelve feet were the most effective for formal one-way persuasion.[85] Other experiments have found that the most comfortable distances for less formal conversations are between four and eight feet — anything closer than four feet may cause the listener anxiety.[86] Where you choose to stand may therefore depend on your style. The more conversational and informal your argument, the closer you can be; the more formal or theatrical, the farther away you should be. It is also a good idea to stand out in front of the jurors, rather than at a sharp angle. You want to see the jurors' reactions, and you want them to be able to see you comfortably.

A second consideration in choreographing your closing argument is how much movement is appropriate. Some trial practitioners recommend that you stand still; others suggest that you change positions when you change topics. Some occasional movement is probably preferable, as it will help prevent monotony. All trial lawyers agree that random, nervous pacing is distracting to the jurors and should be avoided. Interestingly, there is some experimental evidence indicating that distraction is not necessarily bad. A moderate level of distraction may actually increase the persuasive impact of an argument because it tends to inhibit the natural tendency of listeners to think up counterarguments. This is an extension of the principle underlying the suggestion that you talk faster rather than slower. Of course, the level of distraction must not be so great as to prevent the jury from understanding your argument.

Your decision on whether to use a lectern should be made against this background. Some writers have simplistically formulated general rules about the use of lecterns. Professor James Jeans says that a lectern presents a physical obstacle to communication and should never be used.[87] He is partly right. Lecterns are obstacles, so there should be a *presumption* that you should not use them. However, the presumption is rebuttable. There are reasons for deciding to use one. If you are nervous, tend to pace rapidly, or cannot stand still, a lectern may help anchor you. If it gives you a feeling of security and an unobtrusive place to put your notes, making you more confident, then the benefits might outweigh the costs. If you do use a lectern, do not forget the importance of occasional movement. If you can get out from behind it periodically, your argument will appear more spontaneous and less like a lecture.

---

[85] Stuart Albert and James Dabbs, *Physical Distance and Persuasion*, 15 J. PERSONALITY & SOC. PSYCHOL. 265 (1970). *Cf.* EDWARD HALL, THE HIDDEN DIMENSION (1966) (ten to sixteen feet).

[86] *See* Carol Lassen, *Effect of Proximity on Anxiety and Communication in the Initial Psychiatric Interview*, 81 J. ABNORMAL PSYCHOLOGY 226 (1973).

[87] J. JEANS, *supra* note 79, at 384.

4. COPING WITH SURPRISES

Your opponent's closing argument inevitably will contain surprises. The two most common are the making of improper or unexpected arguments, and the way in which charts are used. Coping with the unexpected can be difficult. It often involves split-second decisions on whether to alter your own planned presentation. Bearing in mind that an unplanned argument is more dangerous than the one you carefully prepared in advance, you probably should be conservative in making impromptu changes. The tactical considerations for coping with some common surprises are discussed in the following sections.

a. Improper Arguments

If your opponent makes an improper argument, you have four possible responses:

- Do nothing.
- Object.
- Respond to it in a later argument.
- Retaliate in kind.

If you are going to object, you must do so immediately. The window of opportunity in which to make a timely objection is a narrow one. Despite the fact that some lawyers consider it a matter of courtesy bordering on obligation not to interrupt, if you try to save objections until the close of your opponent's argument, you will probably have waived them. Only a few jurisdictions permit you to reserve your objections and still preserve a claim of error.

Reasons to do nothing

- The improper argument is trivial.
- The argument is unimportant to your theory of the case.
- You have already made several objections and you sense that the jurors are growing impatient.
- Your opponent is exaggerating or misstating the evidence and you have no further opportunity to respond. It is unlikely that the judge will remember precisely what the witnesses said, and he or she will probably overrule you, instructing the jury that their recollection of the testimony controls.

Reasons to object

- You have already given your last argument and will not have the opportunity to retaliate or respond.
- The improper argument concerns a misstatement of law.
- Your adversary is committing serious error that will prejudice your client: asking the jury to speculate, quoting damage verdicts from other cases, making a direct appeal to emotion or prejudice, or commenting on suppressed evidence or the defendant's silence.

If you do object, you may choose to make a "speaking objection" in which you not only state the legal grounds, but also point out (for the jurors' benefit) the unfairness of your opponent's tactics. This may be a good tactic if your opponent misstates facts. For example, if the plaintiff tries to get a large verdict by referring incorrectly to your small business client as a "million-dollar corporation," a simple objection would only highlight the remark and might leave the jurors with the impression that you are trying to hide the wealth of your client from them. In such a situation, Professor Jeans suggests that you object as follows: "I object, Your Honor. Acme Industry is a small family-owned business with limited assets. The statement made by counsel is false and prejudicial, and a deliberate attempt to make the jury think my client has enough money to pay a large verdict."[88]

Reasons to wait and respond in later argument

- You have the opportunity to make further argument.[89]
- Your opponent misstated evidence (other kinds of errors deserve prompt attention).
- The misstatement was clear and obvious, so that it will look like your opponent was deliberately distorting the facts.

One common method of responding is to repeat your opponent's words, contrast them with the actual testimony, and point out how the other lawyer was trying to exaggerate the testimony in his or her own favor, impliedly admitting that the real testimony was too damaging. Such a response might sound like this:

> My opponent said something very interesting. I wrote down the exact words so that I would not misquote him. Mr. Scanlon said, "the evidence shows that Henry had one or two drinks." Was that the evidence? If you recall, Ms. Johnson testified under oath that the defendant had four drinks — not one or two, but four. She served them herself. Why is the defendant so interested in bringing down the number of drinks? It's because he knows, and we all know that the defendant should not have been driving after consuming four drinks.[90]

Reasons to retaliate in kind

- None.

One final tactical response to improper argument advocated by some trial practitioners is to retaliate in kind during your own argument. If your opponent makes an improper emotional appeal, you retaliate with an emotional appeal of your own. For example, Professor Jeans discusses the options available to a corporate defendant after the plaintiff improperly refers to the large assets of the corporation. The legal rule, of course, is that neither side may

---

[88]J. Jeans, *supra* note 79, at 382.

[89]Even if you have no formal opportunity, you may always ask the judge for a few minutes' surrebuttal to correct an erroneous statement by your adversary.

[90]Adapted from Alan Morrill, Trial Diplomacy 97-98 (2d ed. 1972).

appeal to the emotions of the jury. Nevertheless, Jeans suggests that you could retaliate as follows:

> If the corporation suffers a large financial loss, it's not some anonymous entity that pays it — the money comes out of profits; profits that would otherwise be distributed to the stockholders — widows, retired folks, maybe your own pension funds. Many stockholders depend on these dividends for their income.[91]

However, most trial lawyers reject retaliation as not only an unethical practice, but also an unwise tactic. They suggest that the more unfair your opponent becomes, the more fair and dignified you should be — pointing out the improper tactics, but not stooping to using them yourself.

b. Rhetorical Questions and Challenges

One fairly common tactic, usually used at the end of an argument, is to pose rhetorical questions or challenge the opponent to confront some particular issue. If this is done to you, how should you respond? In most cases, the challenge should be ignored. Give your prepared argument. It would obviously not be a wise idea to throw out your prepared argument and try to improvise an argument based on issues suggested by your adversary.

However, sometimes you may feel that you must respond to such a challenge. One compromise is suggested by Irving Goldstein:

> Members of the jury, I don't know whether counsel is deliberately trying to divert me from discussing our case and our evidence or not. He wants me to answer a whole series of questions which he knows would take up much of my allotted time. If I had the time I could answer each and every question as I am sure you can from the testimony that you have heard. For instance, he asked me to answer this question. (Repeat the question and then answer it using the evidence favorable to your side....) I could take each and every one of these questions and answer them in the same way to your satisfaction. However, first I am going to deal with the real issues and important evidence in this case. And I know you will find the answers to just about all of his questions in my comments.[92]

The other option is to write down the questions, plug them into your outline, and answer them as they come up naturally in your argument. If your closing argument is well prepared to cover all the relevant issues, then you can incorporate responses to challenges in the order that you have chosen, placing them in the context of your broader theory of the case. This method also helps you to decide which questions to answer. If you did not think the topic was important enough to be included in your argument, then there is little reason to waste time responding to it.

---

[91] J. JEANS, *supra* note 79, at § 16.27.
[92] FRED LANE, LANE'S GOLDSTEIN TRIAL TECHNIQUES § 23.106 (3d ed. 1984).

c. Plaintiff Waives or Gives a Short First Argument

The defense is put in a difficult tactical position if the plaintiff or prosecutor does not give a complete first argument. One response is for the defense to proceed as if a full first argument had been made, presenting the defense theory and rebutting the obvious issues plaintiff would have raised. This tactic is appropriate when the defense has a strong affirmative case.

Two other responses have been suggested by Professor Anthony Amsterdam.[93] If there are weaknesses in the prosecution's case, or if the evidence is confusing, you may waive your own closing argument (with the remark that the prosecution's weak case and absence of argument does not merit a reply). This leaves the prosecutor without the ability to argue, since there is no argument to rebut. A modified version of this tactic would be to limit your argument to a single favorable issue, thereby cutting the prosecutor off from arguing his or her strong issues. Remember that final argument is supposed to be limited to those issues raised in the previous arguments. The third alternative — probably the most common — is to object to the plaintiff's tactics (in open court if possible, so the jury understands the unfairness) and request leave to argue briefly in surrebuttal on any issues the plaintiff raises for the first time in final argument.

d. Charts

Two kinds of exhibits may be used by your opponent during closing argument: exhibits introduced during trial, and new demonstrative aids used to clarify the argument itself. Exhibits of this second type — charts of the elements of a cause of action, damage computations, lists of witnesses and corroborating evidence, and so on — are unpredictable. Your adversary may use none or many; they may be carefully prepared posters or hastily drawn sketches on the blackboard. Frequently, such visual aids present no special problems, because they are incorporated into your opponent's argument and removed when he or she has finished.

There will be times, however, when your opponent will try to gain a tactical advantage by leaving a chart in the jurors' sight after he or she finishes argument. As you rise to give your argument, a visual reminder of the opposing argument may still be on an easel or blackboard. It is probably safe to say that you should not allow it to remain. One option is simply to remove it. If your opponent has left a list of damages on the blackboard, you can erase it; if he or she has left a chart on an easel, you can take it down and give it back. However, unless you replace it with a chart of your own, such an action may look defensive (as indeed it is) to the jurors. You may appear to be afraid to let them measure your own argument against your adversary's.

Another possibility, especially if your opponent uses a blackboard, is to incorporate such a chart into your own argument by showing where it is in error and making graphic corrections. Melvin Belli provides a good example of this tactic. He recounts a personal injury case in which the plaintiff left a chart itemizing special damages on the blackboard. The defense counsel went

---

[93] ANTHONY AMSTERDAM, TRIAL MANUAL 5 FOR THE DEFENSE OF CRIMINAL CASES § 444 (1988).

to the same blackboard and made his argument. Whenever he reached a point where he had planned to challenge individual damage requests, he crossed out that item. When he was finished, he recomputed those damages that remained.[94]

NOTES

1. *Should you use notes?* Most experienced trial lawyers (to which group you do not yet belong) minimize their use of written notes, believing that jurors react negatively to closing arguments that appear to be read. The advice may be less valuable to a beginner. In your first few trials, you probably will be more confident if you speak from notes despite their marginal interference with eye contact and spontaneity. However, try not to read your notes verbatim, especially during the introduction and conclusion. Jurors remember best what they hear and see first and last, and the impression you convey during those times will be a lasting one. Consider JAMES JEANS, TRIAL ADVOCACY § 16.31 (1975):

> An ideal summation could be characterized as structured spontaneity. However it is quite a trick to develop your forensic ability to that degree which accommodates both features. Usually a choice must be made — shall I sacrifice some organization in order to enhance the spontaneity of my argument or shall I sacrifice some spontaneity in order to enhance the organization? Whether you use notes will depend on the choice which you make. If you find that notes are necessary then use them judiciously. Confine them to topic sentences or simply stated points you wish to cover. And don't feel confined to a legal size pad. Paper pads come in all sizes and you might find you function best with a six-by-four pad or three-by-five cards. As a rule of thumb, the less apparent the notes, the better.

2. *Ridicule and sarcasm.* Is there a place in closing argument for ridicule or sarcasm? Some trial practitioners say flatly to avoid it. *E.g.*, Hugh Head, *Arguing Damages to the Jury*, TRIAL, Feb. 1980, at 28, 29. Others encourage the use of scorn, ridicule, and vehemence, especially in final argument. *See* Craig Spangenberg, *Basic Values and the Techniques of Persuasion*, LITIGATION, Summer 1977, at 13, 16; Vogel, *Final Argument, in* CIVIL LITIGATION AND TRIAL TECHNIQUES 678 (H. Bodin ed. 1976) (ridicule of the contentions of an adversary or the unreasonable testimony given by witnesses may be effective as long as it does not become vituperative or inflammatory).

G. BIBLIOGRAPHY

1. GENERAL

FRANCIS X. BUSCH, LAW AND TACTICS OF JURY TRIALS, vol. 5: 408-600 (1963).
FRED LANE, LANE'S GOLDSTEIN TRIAL TECHNIQUE, ch. 23 (3d ed. 1984).
ABRAHAM ORDOVER, CRIMINAL LAW ADVOCACY — ARGUMENT TO THE JURY (1992).

---

[94]MELVIN BELLI, MODERN TRIALS, vol. 1: 882-83 (1954).

LAWRENCE SMITH, ART OF ADVOCACY — SUMMATION (1978).
JACOB STEIN, CLOSING ARGUMENTS (1991).

2. LAW

Ronald Carlson, *Argument to the Jury: Passion, Persuasion and Legal Controls*, 33 ST. LOUIS U. L.J. 787 (1989).

J. Alexander Tanford, *Closing Argument Procedure*, 10 AM. J. TRIAL ADVOC. 47 (1986).

J. Alexander Tanford, *An Introduction to Trial Law*, 51 Mo. L. REV. 623, 681-93 (1986).

3. TACTICS

William H. Ginsburg, *Final Argument: the Closing Effort, in* WINNING STRATEGIES AND TECHNIQUES FOR CIVIL LITIGATORS (J. E. Lyons ed., 1992).

Hugh Head, *Arguing Damages to the Jury*, TRIAL, Feb. 1980, at 28.

JAMES W. JEANS, TRIAL ADVOCACY, ch. 16 (1975).

JAMES W. JEANS, LITIGATION, ch. 18 (2d ed. 1992).

James McElhaney, *Analogies in Final Argument*, LITIGATION, Winter 1980, at 37.

James McElhaney, *Solving Problems with Final Argument*, LITIGATION, Winter 1983, at 43.

Stanley Preiser, *The Criminal Case: Tips on Summation*, TRIAL, Oct. 1979, at 49.

Craig Spangenberg, *Basic Values and the Techniques of Persuasion*, LITIGATION, Summer 1977, at 13.

Leslie Vogel, *Final Argument, in* CIVIL LITIGATION AND TRIAL TECHNIQUES (H. Bodin ed. 1976).

Chapter 10

NEGOTIATION

A. INTRODUCTION

It is no secret that the overwhelming majority of legal disputes are settled without trial.[1] Many reasons have been suggested for this apparent preference for negotiation over litigation. Attorneys in public practice, such as prosecutors, public defenders, and legal services lawyers, often have caseloads of such magnitude that taking every case to trial would be impossible. In civil cases, court backlogs can delay a case for several *years* before it reaches trial. This delay can place a devastating economic burden on a client who cannot afford to wait. Other external pressures to settle a case may be generated because of witnesses who are reluctant to testify, hostile judges, or unfavorable political climates. However, the single greatest factor in the preference for settlement may be fear: lawyers are afraid that jurors will return extreme verdicts against them.

Successful negotiation requires compromise from both sides. Both parties must gain something, and *both parties must lose something.* You must be prepared to give something up to which you are entitled. You cannot expect to defeat your opponent or "win" a negotiation by either the power of your negotiating skills or the compelling force of your logic. This is not to say that good negotiating ability is irrelevant. In most cases, a range of possible outcomes exists. A skilled negotiator often can achieve a settlement near the top of the range.

This chapter is primarily about negotiation as advocacy. It concentrates on the role of the attorney in persuading the other side to reach a reasonable settlement. It is not intended to teach the art of negotiation techniques; nor could the massive literature on bargaining be summarized adequately in one chapter. Instead, it focuses on issues common to trial advocacy generally: preparation, case analysis, anticipating your opponent, formulating persuasive factual and legal arguments, organization, and the ethical questions raised by various tactical maneuvers. It also includes enough of an introduction to the process of bargaining to enable you to conduct a negotiation.

NOTES

1. *Literature on negotiation.* To get some idea about how extensive the literature on bargaining is, *see* JEFFREY RUBIN & BERT BROWN, THE SOCIAL PSYCHOLOGY OF BARGAINING AND NEGOTIATION 301-41 (1975) (bibliography

---

[1]*See, e.g.,* ADMINISTRATIVE OFFICE OF THE U.S. COURTS, ANNUAL REPORT, Table C1, at 179, and C8, at 229 (1988) (only 5.3% of civil cases reached trial); U.S. DEPT. OF JUSTICE, BUREAU OF JUSTICE STATISTICS, SPECIAL REPORT: THE PREVALENCE OF GUILTY PLEAS 2 (1984) (approximately 8% of criminal cases go to trial). *See* Kevin C. McMunigal, *The Costs of Settlement: The Impact of Scarcity of Adjudication on Litigating Lawyers,* 37 UCLA L. REV. 833, 838-40 (1990).

containing 1000 references from the social sciences); Albert Matheny, *A Bibliography on Plea Bargaining*, 13 LAW & SOC. REV. 661 (1979) (430 references on plea bargaining). There also are journals devoted in whole or part to negotiation, *e.g.*, INDUSTRIAL AND LABOR RELATIONS REVIEW and JOURNAL OF CONFLICT RESOLUTION.

2. *Other approaches to negotiation.* Negotiation is treated in this chapter as part of litigation. Almost every case that goes to trial will have been preceded by settlement discussions. How you negotiate is, in turn, affected by the knowledge that the case will go to trial unless it has been settled. Negotiation, therefore, is an integral part of the life of a trial lawyer. However, this is a limited view of negotiation. In other contexts, notably professional sports, labor-management relationships, and diplomacy, negotiation is an alternative method of handling disputes because litigation is not available. One approaches negotiation quite differently if it is the primary method of dispute resolution than if it is merely an adjunct to trial practice. Probably the major book describing non-litigation negotiation is ROGER FISHER & WILLIAM URY, GETTING TO YES (2d ed. 1991).

B. LEGAL FRAMEWORK

1. SETTLEMENT PROCEDURE IN CIVIL CASES

Negotiation is primarily an extralegal process; it takes place outside of the formalized system of dispute resolution. Except for labor negotiation,[2] bargaining procedures are mostly unregulated by rules of law. As a general principle, you are free to engage in or decline to engage in negotiation and to follow whatever settlement procedures you choose. However, there are a few constraining legal rules.

One of the most common procedural devices to facilitate settlement is a rule of civil procedure requiring attorneys to meet before trial and explore the possibility of settlement.[3] While such rules may facilitate the opportunity for compromise, they do not compel negotiation because there is no sanction for failure to make a good faith effort to settle. FED. R. CIV. P. 68 goes farther. If a defendant makes a written settlement offer, and the plaintiff refuses it, plaintiff becomes liable for all the litigation costs if plaintiff does not do better at trial. However, Rule 68 operates only against plaintiffs. The Massachusetts Consumer Protection Act[4] is more evenly balanced. It penalizes both a plaintiff who refuses to accept a reasonable offer, and also a defendant who fails to make a reasonable offer. Either party can become liable for fees and costs of litigation for being unreasonable in negotiation.

The extent of judicial participation in settlement efforts varies. Generally, the judge is permitted to participate in negotiation as long as he or she acts as

---

[2]*See* Archibald Cox, *The Duty to Bargain in Good Faith*, 71 HARV. L. REV. 1401 (1958). Labor relations and collective bargaining are beyond the scope of this chapter.

[3]*See, e.g.*, IND. TRIAL R. 16(C)(5) (at least ten days before trial, attorneys must hold a pretrial meeting at which "the possibility of compromise settlement shall be fully discussed and explored"); MICH. CT. R. 2.301 (in every contested civil case, the court shall direct the parties to "discuss the possibility of settlement").

[4]MASS. GEN. L. ch. 93A, § 9(3), (4).

a catalyst, encouraging settlement but not taking sides.[5] The prevailing view is that settlement should come about as a natural by-product of preparation for trial, and should not be coerced by the court.[6] If the judge becomes too actively involved, he or she may become biased against a party who is reluctant to settle, disqualifying the judge from presiding further.[7]

In most cases in which a settlement is reached, court proceedings can be terminated without obtaining judicial approval. Under FED. R. CIV. P. 41, an action may be dismissed without order of the court by filing a stipulation of dismissal signed by all parties who have appeared in the action. In a few special cases, however, court approval of settlements must be obtained. Federal rules require court approval of settlements in class actions[8] and in cases in which a receiver has been appointed.[9] State laws generally require court approval of settlements of claims by minors or that involve payments to minors.[10]

2. PLEA BARGAINING IN CRIMINAL CASES

In criminal proceedings, negotiation usually is permitted but not required.[11] FED. R. CRIM. P. 11(e) is typical:

> The attorney for the government and the attorney for the defendant ... may engage in discussions with a view toward reaching an agreement that, upon the entering of a plea of guilty or nolo contendere to a charged offense or to a lesser or related offense, the attorney for the government will do any of the following:
>
> (A) move for dismissal of other charges; or
>
> (B) make a recommendation, or agree not to oppose the defendant's request, for a particular sentence, with the understanding that such recommendation or request shall not be binding upon the court; or
>
> (C) agree that a specific sentence is the appropriate disposition of the case.
>
> The court shall not participate in any such discussions.

---

[5]*Compare* U.S. DIST. CT., M.D.N.C., LOCAL RULE 22(k) (court will aid in settlement negotiations only if requested by the parties) with Edwin Naythons, *The Civil Settlement Conference*, 9 FORUM 75 (1973) (judge describes how he "nudges, encourages, and assists" counsel in negotiation).

[6]*See Wolff v. Laverne, Inc.*, 17 App. Div. 2d 213, 233 N.Y.S.2d 555 (1962) (abuse of discretion to impose sanction — in this case, an early trial date — against party who refused to settle at amount suggested by court).

[7]*Compare Rosenfield v. Vosper*, 45 Cal. App. 2d 365, 114 P.2d 29 (1941) (judge disqualified) with *Gardner v. Mobil Oil Co.*, 217 Cal. App. 2d 220, 31 Cal. Rptr. 731 (1963) (judge not disqualified). *Cf. Southern Bldrs., Inc. v. Carla Charcoal, Inc.*, 357 So. 2d 638 (La. App. 1978) (suggesting an appropriate settlement figure does not disqualify judge unless it reflects partiality toward one party).

[8]FED. R. CIV. P. 23(e).

[9]FED. R. CIV. P. 66.

[10]*See, e.g., State ex rel. Byrnes v. Goldman*, 59 Misc. 2d 570, 302 N.Y.S.2d 926 (1969). *See* Dan Dobbs, *Conclusiveness of Personal Injury Settlements: Basic Problems*, 41 N.C. L. REV. 665, 675-77 (1963).

[11]*E.g.*, MINN. R. CRIM. P. 15.04(1). *But see In re Rook*, 556 P.2d 1351 (Or. 1976) (district attorney sanctioned for refusing to bargain fifteen cases because of a feud with certain defense attorneys).

Plea bargaining has been upheld as necessary and proper by the United States Supreme Court[12] and by most state courts.[13] In only a few jurisdictions is plea bargaining unavailable, and then only because the prosecutor refuses to bargain, not because the law forbids it.[14]

Plea bargaining is subject to greater regulation than civil negotiations because it results in the accused's entering a guilty plea to a criminal charge. A guilty plea is valid only if "made voluntarily after proper advice and with full understanding of the consequences."[15] Guilty pleas generally are considered voluntary when they result from bargaining, even if a defendant who claims to be innocent cuts a deal only to avoid a disproportionately severe penalty that might follow if the defendant went to trial.[16] The defendant must be given proper advice, which usually means that he or she must be represented by counsel who must confer with the accused, investigate the case, understand the law, and advise the defendant accurately about his or her options.[17] To assure that the accused fully understands the consequences of the plea, most courts follow procedures requiring that the plea agreement be put on the record and that the judge question the defendant about his or her understanding of the potential consequences.[18]

The approval of the court usually is required before a criminal case may be disposed of by a plea bargain.[19] Even an outright dismissal of charges may require court approval.[20] Other forms of judicial participation generally are improper, although practices vary. Several jurisdictions prohibit any judicial involvement outright;[21] others permit only limited involvement — approving in advance the length of sentence, or participating only when specifically requested.[22]

In the last few years, a number of states have passed laws requiring that the victim of a crime participate in or approve a plea bargain in criminal cases. For example, Indiana Code § 35-35-3-2 requires the prosecutor to dis-

---

[12] *Santobello v. New York*, 404 U.S. 257 (1971).

[13] *E.g., People v. West*, 3 Cal. 3d 595, 477 P.2d 409 (1970); *Commonwealth ex. rel. Kerekes v. Maroney*, 423 Pa. 337, 223 A.2d 699 (1966). *But cf. State v. Buckalew*, 561 P.2d 289 (Alaska 1977) (judges forbidden to engage in bargaining).

[14] *See* JAMES E. BOND, PLEA BARGAINING AND GUILTY PLEAS § 1.9 (2d ed. 1983) (state of Alaska and one county in Arizona banned plea bargaining; mixed results).

[15] *Kercheval v. United States*, 274 U.S. 220, 223 (1927).

[16] *See Corbitt v. New Jersey*, 439 U.S. 212 (1978) (statutory scheme providing lesser sentence for guilty plea); *Bordenkircher v. Hayes*, 434 U.S. 357 (1978) (dictum) (threat to bring habitual offender charge); *North Carolina v. Alford*, 400 U.S. 25 (1970) (facing capital offense).

[17] *See* J. BOND, *supra* note 14, at §§ 4.8-4.9. Of course, the defendant can waive his or her right to counsel. *See* Note, *Accepting the Indigent Defendant's Waiver of Counsel and Plea of Guilty*, 22 U. FLA. L. REV. 453 (1970). Several states will not permit a defendant to plead guilty without first consulting an attorney. VA. RULES OF COURT 3A:11.

[18] *See, e.g.,* FED. R. CRIM. P. 11. Technical violations of Rule 11 do not necessarily render a guilty plea invalid. *United States v. Timmreck*, 441 U.S. 780 (1979) (court failed to inform accused of a mandatory special parole rule; no allegation that proper advice would have affected decision to plead guilty).

[19] *E.g.,* FED. R. CRIM. P. 11 (e).

[20] *See* FED. R. CRIM. P. 48 (a). If the trial has begun, charges cannot be dismissed without the consent of the defendant because of the double jeopardy prohibition.

[21] *E.g., State v. Buckalew*, 561 P.2d 289 (Alaska 1977).

[22] *See* J. BOND, *supra* note 14, at § 6.17.

cuss plea bargain proposals with the crime victim,[23] although it falls short of giving the victim a veto:

> *35-35-3-2. Notice of recommendation to victim.* — (a) In making a recommendation on a felony charge, a prosecuting attorney must:
>
> (1) Inform the victim that he has entered into discussions with defense counsel or the court concerning a recommendation;
>
> (2) Inform the victim of the contents of the recommendation before it is filed; and
>
> (3) Notify the victim so that he [or she] might be present when the court considers the recommendation.
>
> (b) A court may consider a recommendation on a felony charge only if the prosecuting attorney has complied with this section.

In the absence of such a statute, the broad concept of prosecutorial discretion encompasses the right of a prosecutor to reduce charges or otherwise engage in plea bargaining as he or she sees fit. The prosecutor's "client" has traditionally been defined as *all* the people of the state, so that the prosecutor owes no special obligation to the victim.

3. NEGOTIATED AGREEMENT AS CONTRACT

Once negotiation of a civil case has resulted in an agreement, whether written or oral, the parties have entered into a contract. From that point, their rights and duties are controlled by the law of contracts; there is no special law of settlements.[24] Generally, the agreement need not be in writing to create a valid contract unless it involves real property, is within the statute of frauds, or a writing is required by local rule.[25] A settlement agreement is fully binding on the parties in most cases.

Like any contract, however, a settlement can be overridden. If agreement is procured through fraud or duress, is based on a mutual mistake, or lacks consideration, it may be void.[26] Therefore, if you lie about the facts, misrepresent the law, or otherwise deliberately deceive your opponent in order to gain a bargaining advantage, the agreement you reach is voidable.

If a negotiated settlement is breached by one party, contract law applies in determining the remedies available to the aggrieved party — specific performance, compensatory damages, or treating the agreement as rescinded. If the settlement required and received court approval, the breaching party also may be in contempt of court, although the courts favor the enforcement of settlements through ordinary breach of contract actions.[27]

---

[23] *See also* ABA STANDARDS FOR CRIMINAL JUSTICE 3-3.2(g)-(h) (3d ed. 1992) (prosecutor should notify victims concerning plea bargaining, and provide them with opportunities for input into the decision).

[24] *See Plymouth Mut. Life Ins. Co. v. Illinois Mid-Continent Life Ins. Co.*, 378 F.2d 389 (3d Cir. 1967); *Putnam v. Otsego Mut. Fire Ins. Co.*, 45 App. Div. 2d 556, 360 N.Y.S.2d 331 (1974).

[25] *See, e.g.*, FED. R. CIV. P. 41 (a) (agreement to dismiss suit must be in writing); LA. CIV. CODE ANN. art. 3071 (all agreements must be reduced to writing or recited in open court).

[26] *See* Dan Dobbs, *Conclusiveness of Personal Injury Settlements: Basic Problems*, 41 N.C. L. REV. 665, 681-730 (1963).

[27] *See Mr. Steak, Inc. v. Sandquist Steaks, Inc.*, 309 Minn. 408, 245 N.W.2d 837 (1976).

In criminal cases, the most likely remedy for a broken plea bargain is to allow the defendant to withdraw his or her guilty plea and proceed to trial.[28] The other possible remedy is specific performance. This is uncommon, but may be appropriate if withdrawal and trial are unfair — for example, if the defendant exchanged testimony for a reduced sentence and already had completed his or her part of the bargain.[29] Some courts permit the defendant to elect his or her remedy;[30] others leave the choice of remedy to the trial judge's discretion.[31]

4. OTHER LEGAL RULES AFFECTING NEGOTIATION

a. Admissibility of Statements Made During Negotiation

Attorneys act and speak as authorized agents of their clients during negotiation. The statements they make are therefore potential admissions of their clients which could be used against a client in subsequent court proceedings.[32] Although final agreements and actual offers to compromise are not admissible,[33] jurisdictions follow a variety of practices with respect to the subsequent admissibility of statements that were made during negotiations but are not strictly settlement offers. The Federal Rules of Evidence declare all conduct and statements made during negotiations to be inadmissible on the main issues of liability and amount of damages:

> *Rule 408. Compromise and Offers to Compromise.*
>
> Evidence of (1) furnishing or offering or promising to furnish, or (2) accepting or offering or promising to accept, a valuable consideration in compromising or attempting to compromise a claim which was disputed as to either validity or amount, is not admissible to prove liability for or invalidity of the claim or its amount. Evidence of conduct or statements made in compromise negotiations is likewise not admissible. This rule does not require the exclusion of any evidence otherwise discoverable merely because it is presented in the course of compromise negotiations. This rule also does not require exclusion when the evidence is offered for another purpose, such as proving bias or prejudice of a witness, negativing a contention of undue delay, or proving an effort to obstruct a criminal investigation or prosecution.[34]

---

[28] *See* J. BOND, *supra* note 14, at §§ 7.2-7.3.

[29] *See Commonwealth v. Todd*, 186 Pa. Super. 272, 142 A.2d 174 (1958). *Compare Cooper v. United States*, 594 F.2d 12 (4th Cir. 1979) (specific performance usually available) with *Virgin Islands v. Scotland*, 614 F.2d 360 (3d Cir. 1980) (specific performance rarely available).

[30] *E.g., Miller v. State*, 322 A.2d 527 (Md. 1974); *In re Villa Fierro*, 18 Cal. App. 3d 612, 96 Cal. Rptr. 251 (1971).

[31] *See Santobello v. New York*, 404 U.S. 257 (1971).

[32] *See* FED. R. EVID. 801(d)(2) (a statement is admissible against a party if made either by an agent authorized to make statements or by an agent concerning a matter within the scope of employment).

[33] FED. R. EVID. 408 (offers to compromise civil suit not admissible); FED. R. EVID. 410 (offers to plead guilty in criminal cases). *Cf. Allen v. Kidd*, 197 Mass. 256, 84 N.E. 122 (1908) (judge informing jury that plaintiff refused a compromise proposal held to be reversible error).

[34] Statements made during plea bargaining are admissible only in subsequent perjury trials or if the defendant opens the door by introducing a related statement. FED. R. EVID. 410.

However, the common law generally drew a distinction between the actual offer and the statements of fact surrounding it, holding the statements admissible at a later trial if negotiations break down. In some jurisdictions, fact statements can be shielded if the attorney specifically denies that he or she is making a statement of fact. For example, if an attorney says, "I admit the brakes were bad, so we'll offer you $10,000," the statement that the brakes were bad is an unqualified admission of fact. On the other hand, if the attorney says, "I admit you could probably convince a jury the brakes were bad, so we'll offer you $10,000 even though we don't concede the point," the statement would not be admissible in a later trial. The more common rule employs a different test, holding that any statement that directly relates to a specific offer or counteroffer and is made to further the negotiation process is protected, and only collateral, unnecessary factual admissions are admissible.[35] Some attorneys, in an effort to avoid inadvertently admitting facts, will preface their entire negotiation with an agreement that all statements are made "without prejudice," which is effective in some states.[36]

b. Unintended Effects on Other Causes of Action

At common law, the release of one joint tortfeasor released all; a settlement with one was deemed a complete satisfaction of the tort. A partial settlement with one defendant for a share of damages could therefore result in the release of all other defendants, even though plaintiff had not yet been fully compensated. Even carefully worded agreements that explicitly said they were not releasing other joint tortfeasors were ineffective. This harsh result has been abrogated by statute in most jurisdictions.[37] States now generally follow one of three rules: (1) all settlements are to be interpreted according to the expressed intent of the parties, presuming neither release nor nonrelease; (2) the release of one joint tortfeasor presumptively releases all others unless a specific reservation of the right to sue is included; and (3) a release does not release other joint tortfeasors unless it contains a clear statement to the contrary.[38] Careful drafting of the terms of the release is essential.

Another hidden danger in a negotiated agreement arises when a plaintiff has multiple causes of action against a defendant and settles only one of them. If the plaintiff gives the defendant a general release, it could be interpreted as covering all causes of action between the parties, even though the plaintiff intended to keep the others alive. For example, if the parties reach a settlement for a single breach of an ongoing contract, if the release is not worded carefully, the agreement could be construed to include release from all pending claims, whether known or unknown. If the plaintiff then discovers a second breach of the contract, the right to sue may be lost.

---

[35] Jon Waltz & J. Patrick Huston, *The Rules of Evidence in Settlement*, LITIGATION, Fall 1978, at 12-13.

[36] *See Eagle Ins. Co. v. Albright*, 3 Wash. App. 256, 474 P.2d 920 (1970).

[37] *See* Robert S. Lindsey, *Documentation of Settlements*, 27 ARK. L. REV. 27, 31-34 (1973).

[38] Annot., 73 A.L.R.2d 431 (1960). *See* UNIFORM CONTRIBUTION AMONG TORTFEASORS ACT (adopted in nineteen states., *e.g.*, ARK. STAT. § 34-1004). *See also* CAL. CIV. P. CODE § 877.

NOTE

Defamation of character during negotiation. Settlement discussions invariably involve arguments about the credibility and motives of parties, witnesses, and even the attorneys themselves. For example, the defense attorney may accuse the plaintiff of malingering, a witness may be attacked as biased and untruthful, or one lawyer may suggest that the other is being stubborn, unreasonable, or unethical. As a general rule, no defamation action can be brought for any such remarks made by the attorneys during negotiation, provided that the statements are reasonably related to settlement. *Theiss v. Scherer*, 396 F.2d 646 (6th Cir. 1968); *Romero v. Prince*, 85 N.M. 474, 573 P.2d 717 (Ct. App. 1973). However, if a defamatory communication is completely unnecessary to negotiation, or if it is communicated to persons who are not involved in the negotiation, it is no longer privileged. *See Savage v. Stover*, 86 N.J. 478, 92 A. 284 (1914) (letter rejecting an offer contained spurious attack on adverse party as a cold-blooded man who treated his laborers like dogs); *Sussman v. Damian*, 355 So. 2d 809 (Fla. App. 1977) (heated negotiations continued in public elevator where attorney accused opponent of improprieties).

C. ETHICAL CONSIDERATIONS

1. HONESTY VS. GAMESMANSHIP

Several ethical questions arise constantly in negotiation.

- Must negotiations be conducted in good faith, without deception or trickery?
- May a lawyer resort to cleverness and benign deception in order to reach a fair and just result?
- May a lawyer take advantage of weaknesses and mistakes by his or her opponent and accept an unjust settlement?
- May a lawyer "bluff" during the negotiation game?

The answers to these basic ethical questions are far from clear. Some people argue that negotiations must be conducted with truthfulness and candor, and that a lawyer ethically may seek only just resolutions. The kind of all-out partisan advocacy appropriate in a courtroom may not be proper in negotiation.

In the American Bar Association's 1908 Canons of Professional Ethics, Canon 15 reflected this feeling that a lawyer had a moral obligation to be fair. It stated that "nothing operates more certainly to ... foster popular prejudice against lawyers ... than does the false claim ... that is it is the duty of the lawyer to do whatever may enable him to [win] his client's cause." Instead, the lawyer is exhorted to "obey his own conscience and not that of the client." Canon 22 required "candor and fairness" when dealing with other lawyers. The MODEL CODE OF PROFESSIONAL RESPONSIBILITY EC 9-2 (1969) forsook this ideal, eliminating the requirement of candor and replacing the lawyer's obligation to obey his or her conscience with: "A lawyer should determine his conduct by acting in a manner that promotes public confidence in the integrity ... of the legal system and the legal profession."

The latest revision, the MODEL RULES OF PROFESSIONAL CONDUCT, returns to the basic idea that you owe an ethical obligation of candor to your opponent. Rule 4.1 states that in "the course of representing a client a lawyer shall not knowingly make a false statement of material fact or law to a third person," a term that includes the opposing party in a negotiation. It is therefore improper to actively deceive your opponent. For example, it is unethical to suggest a settlement of $100,000 because that is the maximum under your client's insurance policy, when you know she has $250,000 coverage.[39]

But what are the parameters of this general prohibition? Consider Alvin Rubin, *A Causerie on Lawyers' Ethics in Negotiation*, 35 LA. L. REV. 577, 578-81, 584-86, 588-92 (1975):

> Is the lawyer-negotiator entitled, like Metternich, to depend on "cunning, precise calculation, and a willingness to employ whatever means justify the end of policy?" Few are so bold as to say so. Yet some whose personal integrity and reputation are scrupulous have [recommended] negotiating tactics that appear tacitly to countenance that kind of conduct.
>
> None would apparently deny that honesty and good faith in the sale of a house or a security implies telling the truth and not withholding information. But [neither the Code nor the Model Rules] exact that sort of integrity from lawyers who engage in negotiating the compromise of a lawsuit. [The ethical rule] forbids the lawyer to "knowingly make" a false statement of law or fact. Most lawyers say it would be improper to prepare a false document to deceive an adversary or to make a factual statement known to be untrue with the intention of deceiving him. But almost every lawyer can recount repeated instances where an adversary of reasonable repute dealt with facts in such an imaginative or hyperbolic way as to make them appear to be different from what he knew they were.
>
> Interesting answers are obtained if lawyers are asked whether it is proper to make false statements that concern negotiating strategy rather than the facts in litigation. Counsel for a plaintiff appears quite comfortable in stating, when representing a plaintiff, "My client won't take a penny less than $25,000," when in fact he knows that the client will happily settle for less; counsel for the defendant appears to have no qualms in representing that he has no authority to settle, or that a given figure exceeds his authority, when these are untrue statements. Many say that, as a matter of strategy, when they attend a pretrial conference with a judge known to press settlements, they disclaim any settlement authority both to the judge and adversary although in fact they do have settlement instructions; estimable members of the bar support the thesis that a lawyer may not misrepresent a fact in controversy but may misrepresent matters that pertain to his authority or negotiating strategy because this is expected by the adversary.

---

[39] *See In re McGrath*, 96 A.D. 2d 267, 468 N.Y.S.2d 349 (1983).

To most practitioners it appears that anything sanctioned by the rules of the game is appropriate. From this point of view, negotiations are merely, as the social scientists have viewed it, a form of game; observance of the expected rules, not professional ethics, is the guiding precept. But gamesmanship is not ethics.

The profession seldom confronts the necessity Vern Countryman and Ted Finman say the attorney-at-law must consider: "the need, if conflicting interests are to be protected, for the lawyer to serve as a source of restraint on his client, and, indeed, on himself." The lawyer is a professional because his role is not merely to represent his client as a mercenary in the client's war; he is also "a guardian of society's interests."

If he is a professional and not merely a hired, albeit skilled hand, the lawyer is not free to do anything his client might do in the same circumstances. The corollary of that proposition does set a minimum standard: the lawyer must be at least as candid and honest as his client would be required to be. The agent of the client, that is, his attorney-at-law, must not perpetrate the kind of fraud or deception that would vitiate a bargain if practiced by his principal. Beyond that, the profession should embrace an affirmative ethical standard for attorneys' professional relationships with courts, other lawyers and the public: The lawyer must act honestly and in good faith. Another lawyer, or a layman, who deals with a lawyer should not need to exercise the same degree of caution that he would if trading for reputedly antique copper jugs in an oriental bazaar. It is inherent in the concept of an ethic, as a principle of good conduct, that it is morally binding on the conscience of the professional, and not merely a rule of the game adopted because other players observe (or fail to adopt) the same rule.

Since bona fides and truthfulness do not inevitably lead to fairness in negotiations, an entirely truthful lawyer might be able to make an unconscionable deal when negotiating with a government agency, or a layman or another attorney who is representing his own client. Few lawyers would presently deny themselves and their clients the privilege of driving a hard bargain against any of these adversaries though the opponent's ability to negotiate effectively in his own interest may not be equal to that of the lawyer in question. The American Bar Association Committee on Ethics does not consider it improper for a lawyer to gain an unjust result in a tax controversy.

While it might strain present concepts of the role of the lawyer in an adversary system, surely the professional standards must ultimately impose upon him a duty not to accept an unconscionable deal. While some difficulty in line-drawing is inevitable when such a distinction is sought to be made, there must be a point at which the lawyer cannot ethically accept an arrangement that is completely unfair to the other side, be that opponent a patsy or a tax collector. So I posit a second precept: The lawyer may not accept a result that is unconscionably unfair to the other party.

The civil law has long had a principle that a sale of land would be set aside if made for less than half its value, regardless of circumstance. This doctrine, called lesion beyond moiety, looks purely to result. If the professional ethic is caveat negotiator, then we could not tolerate such a burden. But there certainly comes a time when a deal is too good to be true, where what has been accomplished passes the line of simply-a-good-deal and becomes a cheat.

The lawyer should not be free to negotiate an unconscionable result, however pleasing to his client, merely because it is possible, any more than he is free to do other reprobated acts. He is not to commit perjury or pay a bribe or give advice about how to commit embezzlement. Whether a mode of conduct available to the lawyer is illegal or merely unconscionably unfair, the attorney must refuse to participate. This duty of fairness is one owed to the profession and to society; it must supersede any duty owed to the client.

2. CONCEALMENT AND PASSIVE DECEPTION

The ethical prohibitions against making deliberate misrepresentations during negotiation are clear. MODEL RULES OF PROFESSIONAL CONDUCT Rule 4.1 prohibits you from knowingly making a false statement of law or fact at any time during your representation of a client. The rule provides no exception permitting false statements during negotiation. It covers not only false statements about the facts of the case but also false and misleading statements made to facilitate reaching a favorable agreement.[40] Nevertheless, this is probably the most frequently violated ethical rule.

The prohibition against active misrepresentation does not appear to require that you correct your opponent's misunderstanding of the facts or law, as long as you do nothing to encourage it. The Committee on Professional Ethics has stated that while a lawyer is under a duty not to mislead the opponent by misstatement or silence, he or she is under no duty to disclose the weaknesses of the client's case or correct his or her opponent's misconception of the law, even if a wrong or unjust result is reached.[41] Rule 4.1 continues to make it acceptable to take advantage of an opponent's misunderstanding. Proposed language in the 1981 Final Draft of the Model Rules that would have prohibited failure to disclose facts when such a failure would be the equivalent of making a material misrepresentation was not enacted.

Nevertheless, in extreme cases even passive deception may be unethical. If you conceal facts that you know would cause your opponent to break off negotiations completely, and permit a settlement to be based on material false assumptions, you may have acted unethically. For example, it is certainly unethical for a plaintiff's attorney to proceed with negotiations in a civil case if the client has died.[42]

---

[40] See Monroe v. State Bar, 55 Cal. 2d 145, 358 P.2d 529, 10 Cal. Rptr. 257 (1961) (falsely stating a cash escrow fund had been established to protect other side in case of breach of settlement); ABA Comm. on Ethics and Professional Responsibility, Informal Op. 1283 (1973) (falsely stating that class action would be filed if settlement not reached).

[41] ABA Comm. on Professional Ethics, Formal Op. 314 (1965).

[42] See RICHARD UNDERWOOD & WILLIAM FORTUNE, TRIAL ETHICS 515-16 (1988).

3. PROTECTING THE INTERESTS OF YOUR CLIENT

During negotiation, lawyers often forget that they are there to represent the interests of a client, not to engage in a battle of wits with another attorney. This gives rise to two common ethical violations: revealing confidential information without permission, and failing to adequately communicate with the client.

MODEL RULES OF PROFESSIONAL CONDUCT Rule 1.6 prohibits a lawyer from revealing a client confidence unless the client has given informed consent to its disclosure. Yet, lawyers routinely inform the opposing party about facts learned from their clients in order to bolster the strength of their cases,[43] or reveal some damaging piece of information about their clients in order to show that they are bargaining in good faith. Lawyers also tend to denigrate their clients' positions on some issues or distance themselves from a client's unreasonable demands, as if the lawyer were negotiating on his or her own behalf. All of these are unethical.

MODEL RULES OF PROFESSIONAL CONDUCT Rule 1.4 requires the lawyer to maintain prompt and reasonable communication with the client:

> *Rule 1.4 Communication*
> (a) A lawyer shall keep a client reasonably informed about the status of a matter and promptly comply with reasonable requests for information.
> (b) A lawyer shall explain a matter to the extent reasonably necessary to permit the client to make informed decisions regarding the representation.

The comments to the rule emphasize that:

> [A] lawyer negotiating on behalf of a client should provide the client with facts relevant to the matter, inform the client of communications from another party and take other reasonable steps that permit the client to make a decision regarding a serious offer from another party. A lawyer who receives from opposing counsel an offer of settlement in a civil controversy or a proffered plea bargain in a criminal case should promptly inform the client of its substance unless prior discussions with the client have left it clear that the proposal will be unacceptable. Even when a client delegates authority to the lawyer, the client should be kept advised of the status of the matter.

Despite this clear mandate that the client be kept informed so that the *client* can decide whether to accept or reject an offer of settlement,[44] lawyers routinely reject settlement offers within their authorized bargaining range without even communicating them to their clients because they believe they can "do better." If the tactic is successful, of course, the client is unlikely to complain. However, if you reject an offer without talking to the client and then *fail* to settle, you have breached your ethical duty to your client.[45]

---

[43] *See* Harold Baer & Aaron Broder, *How to Prepare and Negotiate Cases for Settlement — Pointers for Plaintiff*, 1968 TRIAL LAW. GUIDE 302, 305-06.

[44] MODEL RULES OF PROFESSIONAL CONDUCT Rule 1.2 requires that "[a] lawyer shall abide by a client's decision whether to accept an offer of settlement."

[45] *See* ABA Comm. on Professional Ethics, Formal Op. 325 (1970); Virginia Ethics Op. 143, *reprinted in* 28 VA. S.B. REP. 32 (1966).

4. CASELOAD PRESSURE

Many attorneys have such heavy caseloads that they cannot possibly take every case to trial, and must settle most by negotiation. This has always been a problem for lawyers in the public sector, such as public defenders and legal services attorneys. Recently it has also become a problem for many lawyers in the private sector who feel they need to maintain a high caseload in order to make money. Engaging in bargaining in order to alleviate caseload pressure, however necessary it may be, presents three potential ethical violations: conflict of interest, accepting cases on which you cannot give competent representation, and settling without being fully prepared.

The MODEL RULES OF PROFESSIONAL CONDUCT require that you refuse to accept or withdraw from employment if the exercise of judgment on behalf of a client is likely to be adversely affected by your other clients; that is, if you have a conflict of interest. Rule 1.7 provides the general rule that:

> (b) A lawyer shall not represent a client if the representation of that client may be materially limited by the lawyer's responsibilities to another client or to a third person, or by the lawyer's own interests.[46]

This stricture is given further definition by the comment that "a lawyer's need for income should not lead the lawyer to undertake matters that cannot be handled competently and at a reasonable fee." Clients have the right to expect the complete loyalty and undivided attention of their attorneys.[47] If caseload pressures dilute the services you can provide and force you to settle some cases quickly, you have violated your professional duty.

The Model Rules also prohibit accepting a case if you know you are not competent to handle it:

> *Rule 1.1 Competence*
> A Lawyer shall provide competent representation to a client. Competent representation requires the legal knowledge, skill, thoroughness and preparation reasonably necessary for the representation.

Taking on a large number of clients is prohibited if the resulting caseload pressures make competent representation of your clients impossible. If you do not adequately prepare for negotiation, you are not providing competent representation, whether it results from culpable neglect or from having too many clients. The ethical rules do not permit quality to be traded for quantity.[48]

5. BARGAINING DIRECTLY WITH OTHER PARTY

If the opposing party is represented by an attorney, ethical rules proscribe bypassing the attorney and attempting to settle directly with the client. MODEL RULES OF PROFESSIONAL CONDUCT Rule 4.2 states that during the

---

[46] An attorney may represent conflicting interests only if each client consents and it is reasonable to believe that all can be adequately represented. MODEL RULES OF PROFESSIONAL CONDUCT Rule 1.7.

[47] *See Grievance Comm. v. Rattner*, 152 Conn. 59, 65, 203 A.2d 82, 84 (1964).

[48] *See* Jeanne Kettleson, *Caseload Control*, 34 NLADA BRIEFCASE 111, 111-12 (1977). *See also* ABA STANDARDS FOR CRIMINAL JUSTICE 4-6.1 (2d ed. 1980) (defense lawyer may not recommend that a defendant accept a plea unless a full investigation of the law and facts has been completed).

course of representing your client, you shall not "communicate about the subject of the representation with a party" you know to have an attorney, unless you have the prior consent of that lawyer.[49] This prohibition extends to prosecutors who may wish to try to cut a deal with one of several codefendants in order to build a case against the others.[50]

A more difficult question is the propriety of negotiating directly with a person who does not have an attorney. Insurance companies frequently are accused of quickly offering unconscionably small settlements to people injured in accidents before they have the chance to contact attorneys or contemplate large damage claims. The Model Rules are ambiguous. Rule 4.1 forbids you from lying. Rule 4.3 forbids you from pretending to be disinterested, and the comment to that rule forbids "giv[ing] advice to an unrepresented person." No rule says anything about making settlement offers. Therefore, you presumably could make a settlement offer to an unrepresented person, but you could not advise that person to accept it.[51] The Model Rules do not, however, impose a special duty of fairness when dealing directly with a lay person unfamiliar with the negotiation process, nor do they make it unethical to take advantage of an unrepresented person's ignorance.

NOTES

1. *Questionable tactics.* In light of the foregoing materials, consider the following tactics that have been suggested: (1) Raise false demands and insert issues in which you have no interest to give yourself something to concede, and convince the other side they are real demands. HARRY T. EDWARDS & JAMES J. WHITE, THE LAWYER AS A NEGOTIATOR 116 (1977). (2) Make false demands, bluffs, and threats. HARROP FREEMAN & HENRY WEIHOFEN, CLINI-CAL LAW TRAINING 122 (1972). (3) Raise demands, reopen settled issues, claim you do not have authority to settle when you really do, have your client reject an agreement and raise his or her demand after settlement has been reached. MICHAEL MELTSNER & PHILIP SCHRAG, PUBLIC INTEREST ADVOCACY 237-38 (1974). (4) Incorporate your own terms and meanings into a drafted settlement agreement because the opponent probably will concede to a term rather than reargue it. Roger Thomasch, *Objectives and Techniques in Negotiating a Settlement, in* SETTLEMENT AND PLEA BARGAINING 105 (M. Edwards ed. 1981).

2. *Nuisance settlements.* Some attorneys may take a case that has no merit or may continue to press a case after it becomes clear it has no merit, hoping to settle it for its "nuisance value." *See* Philip Hermann, *Fair Dealing in Personal Injury Cases*, 10 CLEV. MAR. L. REV. 449, 455-56 (1961). This is a well-known practice of the "bottom third" of the plaintiff's personal injury bar. It is less well known, but perhaps more common among prosecuting attorneys, who may attempt to get a plea to a reduced offense after even it becomes clear that they cannot prove the crime charged (for example, if the

---

[49] *See* ABA Comm. on Ethics and Professional Responsibility, Informal Op. 1348 (1975); *id.*, Informal Op. 1190 (1971).

[50] *See* ABA STANDARDS FOR CRIMINAL JUSTICE 3-4.1(b) (2d ed. 1980) (prosecutor is not to plea bargain directly with accused without permission of counsel).

[51] See ABA Comm. on Professional Ethics and Grievances, Formal Op. 102 (1933) (permissible to submit formal settlement offer to unrepresented party).

victim refuses to testify). Is this ethical? While the matter is not directly addressed by the MODEL RULES OF PROFESSIONAL CONDUCT, it is probably unethical under the general provision of Rule 3.1 prohibiting a lawyer from pressing an issue "unless there is a basis for doing so that is not frivolous."

3. *Threatening criminal prosecution and similar coercive activity.* Under the 1969 ABA Model Code of Professional Conduct, it was unethical for "a lawyer [to] present, participate in presenting, or threaten to present criminal charges solely to obtain an advantage in a civil matter." *Cf.* Illinois State Bar Ass'n, Op. 539, *in* 64 ILL. B.J. 705 (1976) (prosecutor who agrees not to prosecute if defendant pays victim restitution is violating this provision). This provision was dropped when the ABA enacted the MODEL RULES OF PROFESSIONAL CONDUCT. There now seems to be no provision against trying to force a settlement by threatening criminal prosecution, disclosing the opponent's status as an illegal alien, filing an ethical complaint against a physician, etc. Despite the absence of a provision in the Model Rules, this tactic is probably unethical. *See* GARY BELLOW & BEA MOULTON, THE LAWYERING PROCESS 596 (1978). At the least, it is deceit and misrepresentation if you do not intend to go through with it. *But see* ABA Comm. on Ethics and Professional Responsibility, Informal Op. 1283 (1973) (permissible to threaten a class action suit if settlement not reached if that is really your intention). Whether or not it is unethical, it may be *criminal. See State v. Harrington*, 128 Vt. 242, 260 A.2d 692 (1969) (lawyer found guilty of attempted extortion for threatening to disclose adultery and turn other information over to the IRS unless defendant agreed to settlement).

4. *Unprepared bargaining.* The ABA STANDARDS FOR CRIMINAL JUSTICE 4-6.1(b) (2d ed. 1980) state that under no circumstances should a defense lawyer plea bargain "unless a full investigation and study of the case has been completed, including an analysis of the controlling law and the evidence likely to be introduced at trial." The reality is less than ideal. One survey of Arizona lawyers revealed that almost fifty percent engaged in felony plea bargaining before they had interviewed any witnesses. In misdemeanors, almost seventy percent bargained before talking to witnesses. Note, *Investigation of Facts in Preparation for Plea Bargaining*, 1981 ARIZ. ST. L.J. 557, 576. *See* Peter Perlman, *Fixing the Price: An Art or an Auction, in* SETTLEMENT AND PLEA BARGAINING 18 (M. Edwards ed. 1981). *Cf.* WELCOME D. PIERSON, THE DEFENSE ATTORNEY AND BASIC DEFENSE TACTICS 229 (1956) (never settle a case "involving a substantial amount" unless it has been fully investigated).

5. *Our ethical federal government?* In September, 1989, Attorney General Richard Thornburgh issued an internal memorandum exempting all Department of Justice lawyers from compliance with the ethical rule against direct contact with an opposing party known to be represented by counsel. Thornburgh asserted that federal prosecutors were above the law and could not be subjected to disciplinary action by the states that licensed them. *See* Roger Cramton & Lisa K. Urdell, *State Ethics Rules and Federal Prosecutors: The Controversies Over the Anti-Contact and Subpoena Rules*, 53 U. PITT. L. REV. 291, 319-22 (1992). A year later, Deputy Attorney General (later Attorney General) William Barr stated that it was the view of the federal government that the prosecuting attorneys working for the Department of Justice were not bound by the ethical standards of the states in which they were licensed. John M. Burkoff, *Prosecutorial Ethics: The Duty Not "To Strike Foul Blows,"* 53 U. PITT. L. REV. 271, 271-72 (1992). Implicit in this suggestion is the view that prosecutors may act unethically in trying to obtain convictions. Many people find this level of arrogance astonishing. *See* Bennett L. Greshman, *The New Prosecutors*, 53 U. PITT. L. REV. 393 (1992).

D. PREPARATION

1. UNDERSTANDING YOUR CASE

It is axiomatic that you cannot negotiate a case successfully unless you understand it. You must be fully familiar with the facts, the controlling law, and the persons who are involved in it. You should have completed your interviews, discovery, and research into the applicable substantive, procedural, and evidentiary law, so that you can analyze the strengths and weaknesses of your case and your opponent's. You must know the arguments you will make about why you are entitled to a verdict and exactly what damages are reasonably recoverable. In other words, you must be ready for trial.

Analyzing and understanding your case involves something other than creating arguments that might be possible if you can stretch the law or the facts. It cannot be done from an emotional perspective from which you attempt only to create plausible arguments favoring your client. You first must analyze the whole case objectively, as a juror would see it. You must be able to recognize where your case is strong, where it is weak, and what kind of verdict you are *realistically* likely to get from a jury. Otherwise, how can you decide what to demand, what to concede, and when to stop negotiating and take your chances at trial?

The kinds of factors that affect the strength of your case include more than just whether the admissible evidence is legally sufficient to entitle you to a verdict on a particular issue. The list of factors that go into evaluating your case is long. Some of them are listed below:

- Does the complaint state one or more legal causes of action that will survive a motion to dismiss?
- Can the plaintiff offer enough evidence on any of its causes of action to survive a directed verdict motion? Are you sure the victim or major eyewitnesses will testify?
- Can the defendant offer enough evidence on any of its defenses to survive a direct verdict motion?
- In what posture will the case go to a jury? What causes of action and defenses will probably remain in the case at that time?
- What are the chances that the jury will find in your favor on the question of liability?
- If the case involves comparative fault, how will the jury allocate fault between the two sides? Even in cases where the comparative fault doctrine does not apply, will the jury make a practical application of it during their deliberations and reduce plaintiff's damages?

- If the jury finds for plaintiff on liability, what is the most likely range of possible damage awards? In criminal cases, what sentence will a judge really give?
- Is there an emotional factor that will cause the jury to increase or decrease plaintiff's damage award, or a judge to raise or lower a sentence? For example, if the jury likes the plaintiff, they may award higher damages. Are any young children involved?
- Will the defendant be seen as having a "deep pocket" and the plaintiff as being in dire need of money?
- Does the case involve any controversial issues, such as drunk driving, abortion, allegations of sexual harassment, and so forth, likely to provoke extremely emotional reactions by some jurors?
- Who are the lawyers on each side? How good are they?
- Will the jury find out about the previous history and character of a plaintiff, victim or defendant? Will the plaintiff be able to introduce evidence of insurance?
- How much extra would it cost to go to trial?

2. SETTING YOUR BARGAINING RANGE IN CIVIL CASES

The first step in negotiation planning is to determine the "settlement value" of your case. A settlement value is based on three things:

- Your chances of winning on liability.
- An estimate of the amount of damages a jury would award. It is important that you be realistic. Ask what a jury will *probably* do, not what an irrational jury might do.
- Transaction costs.

In its simplest form, the calculation works as follows: Suppose that a plaintiff lost a hand in a table saw accident. The evidence will show that despite a clear warning not to operate the saw without a protective cover in place, plaintiff had removed the cover. Plaintiff alleges defective design because the cover was cheap plastic easily removed or broken. Because of contributory fault, plaintiff estimates that he has only a 50% chance of a favorable verdict on liability. If he wins, he figures the jury will award about $250,000 damages. However, it will cost an extra $15,000 to go to trial. This calculates out to a settlement value of $110,000 (50% × $250,000 − $15,000).

However, it is unlikely that you will be able to supply a precise number for any of these categories. Probably, each will consist of a range of likely results. If you represent the plaintiff in the table saw accident case, you might estimate your chances of winning on liability as 40-65%, the likely damage award as $100,000-$500,000, and your additional transaction costs for going to trial as $15,000-$25,000. That would give you a *bargaining range,* rather than a single settlement value. Your best case scenario is a 65% chance of winning $500,000 if you expend $15,000 in additional litigation costs, or $310,000. Your worst case scenario is a 40% chance of winning $100,000 after expending $25,000 in litigation costs, or $25,000. Your bargaining range is therefore $25,000-$310,000.

How do you predict the amount of damages a reasonable jury would award if it found the defendant liable, the likelihood it will find liability, and the additional costs of going to trial? Many attorneys simply rely on averages — either from their own experience or from sources that report typical jury awards.[52] The problem with using averages is that they are accurate only if you have an average case. For all the reasons discussed in the preceding section, your case may have many peculiar strengths or weaknesses that simply make it illogical to treat it as average. Every case should be evaluated on its own merits. That is, after all, the way the jury will treat it.

An estimate of the probable damage award consists of four components. First, uncontested provable damages should be included in your estimate at their full value. This category includes documented special damages — medical costs, property repair or replacement, lost wages and other out-of-pocket expenses — about which amount there is no dispute. Second, disputed and undocumented special damages must be evaluated. You must decide how likely the jury is to award such damages. Most attorneys would include only a portion of a disputed amount, a percentage that corresponds to the likelihood of proving it. Third, intangible damages, such as pain and suffering, must be estimated. This is a difficult and imprecise calculation based primarily on the factors that affect whether jurors will want to provide the plaintiff with a substantial award — the type of injury or disfigurement, the type of plaintiff, the obviousness of suffering, objective indications of pain such as heavy medication, length of hospital stay, and the permanency of the injury. Most attorneys rely on their experience or use a "multiplier" formula based on special damages; for example, that the pain and suffering award will be three times the special damages. Fourth, you must determine whether the law entitles the plaintiff to additional damages such as punitive damages, treble damages, or statutory attorney's fees.

3. VALUING NONMONETARY ISSUES

The negotiation of disputes may require resolving nonmonetary issues. A plaintiff may want a nuisance removed, a letter of apology from the defendant, delivery of goods in partial performance of a breached contract, child visitation rights in a divorce, public withdrawal of a defamatory statement, a particular method of payment, and so on. Although such demands cannot easily be translated into dollars, there is an old saying that "everything has its price." In a typical civil negotiation, a value must be put on them. For example, if the defendant is prepared to offer a maximum of $10,000 in settlement of a libel case, but the plaintiff demands a public retraction in addition to a monetary settlement, it is unreasonable to expect the defendant to give

---

[52] *See, e.g.,* JURY VERDICT RESEARCH, PERSONAL INJURY VALUATION HANDBOOKS, a multivolume set that reports average jury verdicts according to the kind of injury, and gives the likelihood of a verdict for plaintiff by type of accident and type of plaintiff and defendant. It also provides information necessary to adjust the expected verdicts based on overall verdict trends in different localities, and on secondary influences such as the age of the plaintiff and the percentage of permanent disability. Other sources that report actual verdict awards in areas other than personal injury include the Commerce Clearinghouse, Products Liability Reporter, and many state trial lawyers' association newsletters.

such a retraction in addition to the full $10,000. Both compensate the plaintiff; therefore, the defendant can expect the plaintiff to give up some economic compensation in return for the noneconomic compensation. Both parties must place a value on the retraction. Is it so embarrassing to the defendant to apologize that he or she is willing to pay an extra $5,000 to avoid doing so? Is the retraction so important to the plaintiff that he or she is willing to give up all or part of the monetary damages? Only the client can answer these questions.

4. SETTING YOUR BARGAINING RANGE IN CRIMINAL CASES

Bargaining limits in criminal cases may seem difficult to set because there are so many different things that can be bargained for. In a simple case of driving while intoxicated, there are at least the following variables:[53]

- Plea to the top charge, reduced charge, or multiple charges
- Nolo contendere vs. guilty plea
- Length of jail time
- Amount of fine
- Conditions of probation or suspended sentence
- Dismissal or reduction of companion charges
- Amount of time to pay out fines and costs
- Eligibility for delayed adjudication program
- Suspension of driver's license
- Alcohol or drug abuse programs
- Psychological evaluation or temporary commitment
- Type of community service

More complicated cases may present issues of civil forfeiture of property used in the crime, questions of whether prison time will be served in federal, state or county institutions, and restitution to victims.

To set a bargaining range, all possible results must be evaluated and placed in some kind of order based on a common denominator. In civil cases, that is usually money. For the criminal defendant, the measuring factor probably will be relative hardship. For the prosecution, the common measure will depend on why it wants the defendant prosecuted. If a prosecutor wants the defendant to be punished, he or she also will use a hardship scale in ordering bargaining options. However, if the state's goals are different — rehabilitation, deterrence of others, satisfaction of the victim, or the furthering of political or moral goals — then the valuing of bargaining options is likely to be different.

How a defendant orders these options will be a personal decision, and will vary according to the value the accused places on each option. Those defendants who already have criminal records may be concerned only about the length of time they will have to serve. For first offenders, the collateral consequences of a felony conviction may cause more hardship than going to jail,[54] so

---

[53] See Jim Lovett, *DWI Plea Bargaining, in* SETTLEMENT AND PLEA BARGAINING 303 (M. Edwards ed. 1981).

[54] *E.g.*, forfeiture of major assets, loss of voting privileges, deportation, loss of employment opportunities, or loss of special licenses (liquor, firearm). Mark Kadish, *Plea Bargaining in State*

that they would rather serve a sentence for pleading to a misdemeanor than
go free after pleading to a felony. To a wealthy defendant, a fine presents little
hardship, but an unemployed defendant may prefer to spend time in jail
rather than struggle to pay even a small fine. Unlike situations in which you
bargain for dollars, you cannot assume that all defendants will value hardship
the same way. Setting the bargaining limits — the points at which the defendant would rather go to trial than serve a long sentence, pay a high fine, plead
to a serious offense, or agree to a stringent a set of probation conditions — can
only be done in cooperation with your client. As in civil negotiations, how
high the limit is set depends upon both the odds of being convicted and the
probable sentence that will be imposed if your client is found guilty.

5. PLANNING THE NEGOTIATION

The actual negotiation can be understood as a recalculation of the settlement value limit set by the parties working together. If the parties can agree
on the value of damages, the likelihood of a finding of liability, and the transaction costs, then calculating a fair settlement is simply a matter of mathe-
matics. However, because of the large number of estimates and approxima-
tions involved, only rarely will the parties agree on the numbers. Places
where the parties disagree create disputes that must be resolved if you are to
reach agreement. This dispute resolution forms the heart of the negotiation.

Your planning must identify areas of probable dispute and how you will
compromise on them. This is a radically different approach from a trial plan.
For trial, you prepare arguments and stratagems for how you will *win* a
disputed issue by convincing a jury that you are *right* and your opponent is
wrong. For negotiation, you must abandon these winner-take-all attitudes.
You do not win on disputed issues, you concede that both sides have legitimate points, and you *compromise*.

When planning a negotiation, you must assume that you and your opponent's bargaining ranges overlap. Otherwise, settlement is impossible. If both
sides have done realistic jobs of estimating settlement value, there should be
plenty of room for agreement. However, bear in mind that it is always possible
that the two sides will have quite different bargaining ranges. First, the sides
may have access to different information that affects the probable outcome of
an issue. For example, a defendant sued for negligence may discover a new
eyewitness who confirms the defendant's denial of negligence, a discovery that
reduces the defense's evaluation of the likelihood of a plaintiff's verdict on
liability from 50% to 25%. Second, the two attorneys simply may have evaluated the available information differently, one calculating the likelihood of a
verdict at fifty percent, the other at sixty percent.

The following sections discuss some common suggestions about how pre-
negotiation planning can help achieve as favorable a settlement as possible
within the range of potential agreement.

---

and Federal Criminal Cases, in SETTLEMENT AND PLEA BARGAINING 295 (M. Edwards ed. 1981).
The collateral consequences of corporate crime include civil damages and forfeiture of assets. *See*
Paul Friedman and William Taylor, *Plea Negotiations in White Collar Crime Cases: Making the
Best of a Bad Deal, in* SETTLEMENT AND PLEA BARGAINING 335-37 (M. Edwards ed. 1981).

a. Agenda

Settlement is rarely a discussion of one issue. In most cases, the parties will have to compromise on many issues, each with its own range of possible resolutions. Negotiation, therefore, does not usually consist of exchanging lump sum offers and counteroffers, but is broken down into a series of mini-negotiations over the individual disputes. It is impossible to even conduct rational negotiation, then, unless the parties understand this concept and agree on an agenda that defines the disputes to be resolved and places them in some kind of order.

Many negotiators believe that this agenda plays a crucial role in the bargaining process. You should plan in advance the issues you want to raise, and the order in which you would like to talk about them. You probably should do this in writing and bring your proposal to the bargaining table. Of course, your opponent might bring a different agenda, requiring that you negotiate about the negotiation itself — which issues will be discussed, their order, and the procedure for structuring the process.

Defining the issues themselves should not prove difficult if you have a theory of the case. Your theory should already tell you which claims you will pursue, which you will drop, and which of your opponent's claims you think are groundless. It will tell you also what the components of damages are: what kinds of injuries can plaintiff be compensated for, and are they provable?

Some negotiators suggest that the best order is to raise major issues first. But what constitutes a "major" issue? Some negotiators place first those issues that are objectively important — where the most money is at stake. If agreement can be reached on the big-money issues, it will facilitate later bargaining over smaller amounts. If agreement is not reached, the parties can move to less important issues to try to start some momentum toward settlement. This approach assumes that if you start on the simple issues and a compromise cannot be reached, the parties may give up.

Other negotiators suggest putting issues that are *subjectively* important first. They suggest that the items on which you must reach an agreement of a certain kind should be first, whether or not they involve the most money. Negotiators who use this approach offer two justifications. It may enable you to obtain concessions on the most important issues during the initial "honeymoon" period when the other side wants to show its good faith. If not, then you can break off negotiations without wasting further time. You know immediately if an acceptable compromise is not possible.

This may be the best approach if your client has any nonnegotiable demands. It may be that there are issues on which your client is unwilling to negotiate. For example, a defendant faced with a criminal antitrust charge may refuse to enter a guilty plea because of the likelihood of treble damages in a pending civil suit, but may be willing to plead *nolo contendere*. A party to a divorce action may demand custody of children and be unwilling to settle without such an agreement. If the issue is genuinely nonnegotiable, it should be placed first on the bargaining agenda as a precondition. Why take up everyone's time on other issues if your opponent cannot agree to your precondition?

Most negotiators, however, prefer to raise at least some of the minor issues or the issues favoring their opponents first. They want to begin the bargaining session by making concessions, appearing reasonable, and establishing a pattern of cooperation. They want to dispel their opponent's fears that they will be "tough negotiators." The expectation is that by building a favorable atmosphere and some momentum, they will get concessions in return as the issues become more important.

b. First Offer Strategy

Skilled negotiators are in general agreement that the plaintiff's first offer should be high but reasonable, and the defendant's low but reasonable. Your offer should indicate your good faith while leaving you sufficient room to bargain and still settle above your limit. There are two reasons for this: 1) the other attorney probably will not accept your first offer because he or she assumes you have left yourself bargaining room, and 2) you want to allow a margin of error in case there is a more favorable settlement range than you expected. On the other hand, an extreme demand that far exceeds the reasonable settlement value of the case is counterproductive — it tells the other side either that you have not come to negotiate in good faith or that you have valued the case too optimistically for your own side. In either case, your opponent is likely to terminate negotiation. A good first offer is your best case scenario, as calculated when you set your bargaining range.

Your first offer not only should be reasonable, it should appear reasonable to your opponent. A lump sum offer, encompassing many small issues, unsupported by an explanation of its component parts, does not appear reasonable; it appears arbitrary. If you explain how you arrived at it — the damages you included, the demands you have dropped, and whether you have compensated for the possibility of an adverse verdict on liability — your offer will appear reasonable. Furthermore, your explanation will help focus on the contested issues that must be negotiated. The reasons you will put forward should be planned along with your offer.

Negotiators also agree about who should make the first offer, although unanimity in this instance is not the same as being right. Almost without exception, they advise you to force the other side to make the first offer. The reasons given for this include: 1) whoever makes the first offer gives an impression of weakness (that he or she really wants to settle); 2) the other side may have so misvalued the case that they offer far more than you would have asked for; or 3) you may have misvalued the case so that your opening offer would have been disastrous. Such fears seem misplaced. In the first place, both sides probably want to settle or they would not be wasting time negotiating; you give away no secrets by making an offer. In the second place, if both sides have prepared the case thoroughly, it is extremely unlikely that first offers will be unexpectedly favorable or disastrous.

The most obvious problem with this bizarre advice is that it makes negotiation impossible. If neither attorney is willing to make the first offer, what do they do — sit there and stare at each other? It also is inconsistent with the advice that you should try to control the agenda. How can you control the

agenda if you are unwilling to make the first move? The advantages of controlling first impressions far outweigh the imaginary fear that you will display weakness. It enables you to focus the negotiations on your own agenda
and may cause your opponent to move toward your offer or to reevaluate his or
her estimate of the settlement value in your favor. Besides, what do you care
if your opponent thinks you are weak? No consequence flows from it, as long
as you are not *actually* weak.

c. Concession Patterns

Bargaining is not finished after the exchange of first offers; it has only
begun. The negotiation will consist of a series of offers and counteroffers,
arguments and posturing, as both parties cautiously make concessions that
correspond to their uncertainties about potential weaknesses in their cases.
Each uncertainty or weakness in your case presents an apparent risk; the
amount of the concession depends upon the size of the apparent risk. You
should determine in advance how much you will concede on each issue and
how much concession you will demand. Bear in mind, however, that your
prearranged concession plan cannot be inflexible. You will learn new information during the negotiation. If it becomes apparent that your opponent has
identified a weakness that you had not considered, you may have to concede
more than you had planned. Similarly, if your opponent fails to recognize one
of your weaknesses, you may not have to concede as much.

Formulating a concession pattern requires that you make decisions about
the size of the concessions you will make and the reasons for which you will
compromise. JEFFREY RUBIN & BERT BROWN, THE SOCIAL PSYCHOLOGY OF BAR-
GAINING AND NEGOTIATION 269-72, 276-78 (1975) point out:

> Considered as a whole, the research suggests that the concession-mak-
> ing process has two important consequences for the bargaining relation-
> ship. First, concessions convey vital information about a bargainer's sub-
> jective utilities. They allow each party to gauge the other's preferences
> and intentions and, in turn, permit each party to present or misrepresent
> information about his own. For example, a bargainer who makes frequent
> concessions will probably be viewed as willing to settle for less than one
> who makes concessions only occasionally. Similarly, a bargainer who
> makes concessions up to a certain point and then refuses to move beyond
> this point will probably be seen as being close to some "cutoff point" on his
> utility scale below which he will leave the relationship rather than settle.
> On the other hand, a bargainer who makes negative concessions may be
> seen as threatening to toughen his position unless a particular offer is
> accepted. Thus, concessions may be shaped in a variety of ways, each of
> which has important consequences for the way in which one's preferences
> and intentions are viewed by the other.
>
> Second, concessions convey important information about a bargainer's
> perceptions of his adversary. They allow each party to find out how he
> looks in the other's eyes. And to the extent that a bargainer believes he is
> seen as capable and effective, we may expect him to behave in increas-
> ingly cooperative fashion. Consider the findings of the numerous studies

which have shown that a bargainer who makes positive concessions is more likely to elicit reciprocated concessions from the other than one who makes either negative concessions or none at all. The reason these findings hold, we would argue, has to do with the implications of concession making for a bargainer's self-concept. An adversary who follows a stance of initial toughness with a softening of demands may be seen as communicating a perception of the bargainer as a worthy opponent — an opponent who is effective, persuasive, and to whom one must gradually yield. Thus a bargainer may come to see the other's positive concessions as a reflection of his own bargaining effectiveness. To the extent that he views himself in this fashion, we may expect the bargainer's concern with how he looks in the other's eyes to be sharply reduced and to be followed by an increasing willingness to reciprocate. Conversely, the other's making of negative concessions or none at all may be seen by the bargainer as a reflection of his own incompetence — since he seems to be incapable of influencing the other to make offers that are increasingly attractive. Given this belief, we may expect the bargainer to become increasingly concerned with the apparent loss of face he has incurred in the other's eyes and to become increasingly competitive and vindictive as a result.

The fact that subjects tend to behave more cooperatively in the presence of another whose behavior is contingent upon, rather than independent of, their own behavior constitutes powerful evidence in support of our general argument. A bargainer wants to believe he is capable of shaping the other's behavior, of causing the other to choose as he (the other) does. In the presence of an adversary whose behavior appears to vary favorably in response to the bargainer's own moves and counter-moves, the bargainer may come to view himself as competent and may be expected to behave in increasingly cooperative fashion. On the other hand, in the presence of an opponent whose offers appear to be unrelated to the bargainer's behavior — even if these offers are consistently cooperative — the bargainer may see himself as fundamentally incompetent at the task of persuading the other and may come to behave in increasingly defensive or exploitative fashion. Thus, by making positive concessions, bargainers may communicate their perception of the other as a strong, worthy, and tough opponent and in so doing may increase the likelihood of inducing positive concessions in return.

Litigators stress the importance of advance planning about the precise concession points you will use. Remember that your agenda represents negotiations within negotiations. For example, if you are negotiating a personal injury case, you will have to resolve issues of liability, comparative fault, medical damages, property damages, lost income, and pain and suffering. Within medical damages may be hospital bills, doctor fees, and the cost of physical rehabilitation. Plaintiff's agenda might therefore look like this:

1. Concede contributory negligence
2. Defendant's liability
3. Comparative fault
4. Property damages

  5. Medical damages
     a. Hospital bills
     b. Doctor fees
     c. Rehabilitation
  6. Lost income
  7. Pain and suffering

An initial offer to settle for $325,000 is really just a total of all the numbers that will eventually be plugged into this list.

Your concession points should be tied specifically to particular agenda items. For example, you may make a first offer on comparative fault at 80% (best case) and be prepared to go to 50% (worst case). Do you jump right from 80% to 50% if the defense vehemently refuses to consider 80%? Or do you plan several stops in between? If you plan several stops, exactly what numbers will you offer and why? Suppose your own client had dropped a beer in his lap while driving, which caused him to suddenly hit the brakes, and that only one brake light was working at the time he was rear-ended by a speeding Greyhound bus. You might plan to concede twenty percentage points on the drinking issue, and five points on each of the other safety issues, based on your estimate of how seriously they would affect a jury.

The process works the same way for dollar-amount concessions. Your client may have been out of work for fifteen weeks, and averaged forty regular hours and five overtime hours a week, so you ask for 600 hours of lost income at $20 an hour plus seventy-five hours of overtime at $30 an hour, for an opening offer of $14,250. You are prepared to concede $2250 because the overtime is speculative, and another $800 because there were one-week layoffs during the summer.

In planning these concession points, experienced negotiators give the following general advice:

• Avoid large concessions because they weaken your credibility by communicating that your initial offer was not a serious one.
• Small concessions communicate that you have little room left to bargain, so they should be avoided unless you are in fact running out of negotiating room. If your adversary erroneously believes you have no room left, he or she may terminate the negotiating session prematurely.
• Plan concession points on each issue in an order that permits you to move in ever decreasing amounts. This avoids the problem of making premature small concessions.
• Try to have many, rather than few, concession points (without appearing ridiculous). That may enable you to move in smaller increments than your opponent, and it will be easier for you to make small concessions to keep the negotiations rolling.
• Since you cannot change the facts and law, and since you will not be credible if you offer only a small concession on a major issue on which your position is weak, your planning must concentrate on how the issues will be defined. For example, if all medical expenses are defined as one issue, the concessions will be large; if treated as separate issues of emer-

gency room expenses, room costs, surgeon fees, medication, and operating room charges, each concession will be smaller.

d. Strengthening Your Bargaining Positions

Part of your job as a negotiator is to sell your compromise proposals to your opponent. But bear in mind an important distinction: your job is not to "win" the negotiation by persuading your opponent to agree to your most optimistic position or give you everything you ask for in your opening offer. You must genuinely give something up (not just pretend to give up something you didn't really want anyway) if you expect to settle the case. But it is important that, when you make a concession and offer a reason for it, that you convince the other side of its soundness.

You can best accomplish this with facts. If plaintiff expects the defendant to accept $20 an hour as the basis for determining lost income, plaintiff must prove it — produce a paycheck stub. If defendant expects plaintiff to concede a week's income because of layoffs, defendant must prove it — produce the newspaper article announcing it. If either side expects to make a legal argument that attorney fees can be assessed to the losing side, bring the statute or case with you that says so. Do not expect your adversary to rely on your own assurances that a fact is true. Why should your opponent believe you? You are biased and would say anything to get a larger settlement.

Melvin Belli recommends that you go so far as to prepare a brochure to sell your commodity, in which the facts supporting your claims and positions are spelled out:[55]

> [The brochure] should have copies of police reports, the pleadings, the complaint, and if there is an answer filed, the answer, together with any pleas in abatement, some instructions, parts of the trial brief, pictures demonstrating liability and damage, enumeration of all items of special damage with supporting bills, statements of all of the witnesses, statements of all of the doctors, all of the hospital reports, both the emergency and ultimate treatment, life expectancy tables, a computation of all of the damages, both special and general, depositions if any are had, and the offer of settlement. Counsel for plaintiff says, "Look, here's our case, here are all the facts, here's our special damages, and we have every one itemized and proved and receipted, here's our future damages, here's our doctors' reports, here's our demand in this case, and you can make notes from this brochure and tell your home office what we've got, or you may take this brochure with you!"[56]

The problem with going this far is that it focuses too much on selling your opening offer, and not enough on documenting your compromises. For that reason, the popularity of the so-called "brochure method" has fallen in the last twenty years.

The point it makes is still valid, however. The more documentation you can produce in support of a compromise, the more likely it is to be accepted. If you

[55] For an example of a settlement brochure, *see* JAMES JEANS, TRIAL ADVOCACY 444-62 (1975).
[56] Melvin Belli, Modern Trials, vol. 1: 712-13 (1954).

and your opponent are arguing about what the impact of the plaintiff's drinking will have on comparative fault — you say 20%, the defendant says 30% — if you cannot document your position, you will eventually have to either "split the difference" and accept 25%, or break off negotiations. But, if you can produce a page from a law journal article reporting a statistical study of traffic accident cases in which the authors conclude that drinking affected verdicts by 20%, then your opponent will probably have to concede that your figure is the more accurate one.

NOTES

1. *Client sets bargaining limit.* Ultimately, it must be your client who sets the bargaining limit, deciding on the bottom line of your negotiating range. You have the responsibility to advise your client and assist him or her in evaluating where a realistic bargaining limit should be set. This is not always an easy task if the client is unwilling to accept the possibility that he or she might lose. *See* JAMES JEANS, TRIAL ADVOCACY 430-35 (1975). If the client demands an unreasonable settlement or refuses to authorize settlement negotiations at all, you must either withdraw from the case or carry out your client's wishes. Many attorneys forget that it is the client's claim and that they are playing with the client's money.

2. *The Sindell formula.* One method for predicting the settlement value of a case is by using the controversial Sindell formula. This formula evaluates seven areas that affect both the likelihood of verdict and the probable amount of verdict: (1) liability; (2) type of injuries; (3) age of plaintiff; (4) type of plaintiff; (5) type of defendant; (6) out-of-pocket expenses; and (7) probable jury verdict in perfect case. Each factor has been assigned a maximum number of potential points, reflecting the Sindells' estimate of the relative effect it has on the verdict:

50 — Liability
10 — Injuries
10 — Age of plaintiff
10 — Type of plaintiff
10 — Type of defendant
10 — Out-of-pocket expenses (one point per $100 of expenses, maximum ten points)

Each item is weighed independently and assigned its own value depending on your evaluation of how close the facts are to being ideally suited to recovery. For example, assume the case of a forty-year-old plaintiff whose leg was crushed when he was crossing a street and was hit by an oil company truck, who ran up $5,000 in medical expenses and lost $6,000 in wages. A lawyer might value the case as follows:

35 — Liability: There is conflicting testimony about whether the plaintiff was in or out of the crosswalk.
6 — Injury: Bruises would be worth 1, amputation 10. In this case, although the injuries were severe, the leg healed.

5 — Age of Plaintiff: Points are assigned as follows: 0-7 years, 10 pts.,
      8-15 years, 9 pts., 16-23 years, 8 pts., 24-31 years, 7 pts., 32-39 years,
      6 pts., 40-47 years, 5 pts., 48-55 years, 4 pts., 56-60 years, 3 pts.,
      61-65 years, 2 pts., over 66 years, 1 pt.
3 — Type of plaintiff: This plaintiff is unmarried and has a minor crimi-
      nal record.
9 — Type of defendant: This is a perfect defendant, a big oil company.
      Only nine points given because the actual truck driver is a likeable
      person.
10 — Out-of-pocket expenses: Ten points assigned because the special dam-
      ages exceed $1,000 [this number is now out-of-date]. The damages in
      excess of $1,000 (in this case, $10,000) will be added in later.
68 — Total points: Since there were 100 possible points, this is the same as
      sixty-eight percent.

The lawyer then estimates the average verdict for a serious leg injury; based
on experience or the Personal Injury Valuation Handbooks; multiplies it by
the total points, and adds excess expenses over $1,000:

Perfect jury verdict: $50,000
Multiply by total points (68%): $50,000 × .68 = $34,000
Add expenses over $1,000: $34,000 + $10,000
Full settlement value: $44,000

See David Sindell & Joseph Sindell, *Formulae to Evaluate Injury Cases*, in
SETTLEMENT AND PLEA BARGAINING 65-75 (M. Edwards ed. 1981). *See also*
MELVIN BELLI, MODERN TRIALS, vol. 1: 756-64 (1954). The use of this formula
has been criticized in Samuel Lindebaum, *Infant's Lost Earning Capacity:
Damages*, 1960 TRIAL LAW. GUIDE 139, and Joseph Kelner, *Settlement Techniques Part One*, TRIAL at 39, 40 (Feb. 1980), on the grounds that it contains
too many variables and estimates and actually may interfere with realistic
evaluation of the bargaining limit.

3. *Calculating a reasonable first offer.* Although negotiators suggest
that your first offer be reasonable, they do not tell you what "reasonable"
means, nor how you are supposed to arrive at it. Whether an offer appears
reasonable will depend on the facts and law of the case. A defense offer that
fails to include compensation for lost earnings when plaintiff was in a body
cast for six weeks is not reasonable. Similarly, a demand by the plaintiff in a
wrongful death case for damages for future lost earnings is not reasonable if
state law precludes recovery of such damages. We have suggested that your
first offer be the amount at the most optimistic end of your bargaining range.

One plaintiff's attorney suggests that, at least in cases in which a liability
verdict is fairly certain, you set your offer at the amount you would request
from a jury in final argument. Stuart Speiser, *The Psychology and Art of
Settlement, in* SETTLEMENT AND PLEA BARGAINING 54 (M. Edwards ed. 1981).
In other words, give yourself the full benefit of the doubt on all damages that
are contested or have to be estimated, and on all issues in which the legality of
recovery is questionable, conceding only those issues on which you know you

will lose, but that you start by assuming a 100% chance of a favorable verdict on liability.

4. *Using a multiplier.* The text mentions that many attorneys use a multiplier to arrive at a figure for pain and suffering damages. A multiplier is supposed to reflect local experience with real juries, and represents an average ratio between some known amount (usually "special damages" — medical expenses, lost income, and property damage) and pain and suffering awards. These generic multipliers generally range from 2 to 5. If you have $10,000 in hospital bills, you can expect a jury to award $20,000-$50,000 for pain and suffering. Like other averaging devices, the use of a multiplier is imprecise and does not reflect the realities of what a jury is likely to do in your particular case. Nevertheless, many attorneys blindly use the same multiplier in all cases. *See* KENNY HEGLAND, TRIAL AND PRACTICE SKILLS 282-83 (1978) (suggesting that a multiplier of three to four is usually appropriate, but that property damages are not included in the base figure). Multipliers obviously are arbitrary. An unemployed person can sustain the same degree of pain and suffering as a substantial wage earner; the same hold true for a person driving an old Subaru and one driving a new Mercedes, or a person living in a rural area where medical costs are low and New York City where they are high. In all cases, however, the special damages would be different. *See* MELVIN BELLI, MODERN TRIALS, vol. 1: 742 (1954).

E. CONDUCTING NEGOTIATIONS

1. BASIC PRINCIPLES: COOPERATION AND FLEXIBILITY

The evidence is overwhelming that cooperation is the surest road to successful settlement. Hostility, distrust, stubbornness, self-righteousness, conflict intensification, unjust demands, and attempts to gain unjustified advantages beget noncooperation rather than concessions, and tend to cause a breakdown in the communication necessary to reach a settlement. The key ingredient in cooperation, however, is mutuality — you cannot be unilaterally cooperative. If you are making concessions while your opponent is not, you are engaging in appeasement, not cooperative negotiation. Successful bargaining occurs when you are prepared both to be cooperative and to demand cooperation from your opponent.[57]

> The general conclusion implied by research is that cooperation begets cooperation; and, conversely, noncooperation begets noncooperation. But why should this be so? Bargainers ... are often concerned with intangible issues having to do with how they look in the eyes of others. In the presence of an adversary who behaves in consistently competitive fashion, the need to maintain or not lose face emerges as a central theme in the relationship and drives the bargainer to defend himself through competitive behavior. On the other hand, to the extent that one's adversary chooses to cooperate, a bargainer's need to maintain face (to look tough) is

---

[57] *See, e.g.*, Donald Harnett et al., *Personality, Bargaining Style and Payoff*, 36 SOCIOMETRY 325 (1973).

dramatically reduced, and he can and does risk the reciprocation of cooperation.[58]

Genuine cooperation requires flexibility, not just the appearance of flexibility. There is a real possibility that your pre-negotiation evaluation may have
been too optimistic, evidence exists of which you are unaware, or you failed to
consider an issue. If during bargaining you realize you have over or underval-
ued your case, you must be prepared to modify your original expectations.
Many lawyers know how to appear flexible, through pre-negotiation planning
of concessions, but stubbornly cling to their initial evaluation even after new
information becomes available during bargaining that changes the facts under which that evaluation was made.

For example, suppose plaintiff's attorney in a breach of contract case estimates that damages are fixed at $100,000, her chances of a favorable verdict
on liability are 50-65%, and it will cost $5000 to go to trial. Her initial settle-
ment range was therefore $45,000 to 60,000. However, during bargaining, the
defendant convinces her that only $80,000 of the damages are recoverable
because of a statute of limitations problem on the other $20,000. Many attor-
neys are not flexible enough to realize that the bottom line in their bargaining
range must be reduced because they had misvalued the case. It should have
been $35,000 to $47,000. Instead, it is common for bargainers to try to "make
up the difference," e.g., by irrationally raising their estimate to the chances of
a favorable verdict to 60-75%.

2. PRELIMINARY NEGOTIATIONS: AGENDA, AUTHORITY, AND GROUND RULES

Social psychologists have found that bargaining effectiveness is usually
increased if the channels of communication are structured in advance and
agreed upon by both parties. Uncertainty about the ground rules of a negotiating session leads to competitive rather than cooperative behavior. Mutual
discussion of the issues to be bargained produces better outcomes than unilat-
eral planning. If the parties do not structure the negotiation, they take longer
to reach agreement, remain farther apart on the issues, and are less yielding.[59]

Despite this evidence, it is apparent that most lawyers do not negotiate over
the agenda, preferring to keep their agendas hidden. This leads inevitably to
competitive behavior in which both sides strive for psychological control over
the negotiations, which in turn leads to antagonism and the breakdown of
cooperation. Even those attorneys who recognize that this happens see little
advantage in overt agenda negotiation, preferring the tacit agreement that
arises from the process of exchanging offers. They argue that agenda negotia-

---

[58]JEFFREY RUBIN & BERT BROWN, THE SOCIAL PSYCHOLOGY OF BARGAINING AND NEGOTIATION
270-72 (1975). The authors cite twenty-two studies that support this conclusion, but also cite
eight studies that have found no systematic relationship between one party's cooperativeness and
the behavior of the other party, and two studies finding that noncooperative behavior by one
party induced greater cooperation by the other party.

[59]*See* J. RUBIN & B. BROWN, *supra* note 58, at 104-15; Daniel Druckman, *Dogmatism,
Prenegotiation Experience, and Simulated Group Representation as Determinants of Dyadic Behavior in a Bargaining Situation*, 6 J. PERSONALITY & SOC. PSYCHOL. 279 (1967).

tions add more disputes to already contentious situations, and that attorneys never stick to any agreed-upon plan anyway.

One good way of beginning a discussion of agenda and ground rules is for you to prepare a written offer in advance and send it to the other attorney. In your letter, you can express concerns you have, suggest a timetable for discussion, provide a proposed agenda, and include your first offer. When the actual negotiation starts, you can suggest that you follow the outline of your proposal, unless your opponent has any objections. This forces even a reluctant attorney to discuss these preliminary issues.

Even though they might not see it as agenda negotiation, lawyers consistently recommend that there be at least one prenegotiation discussion — the extent of the bargainers' authority to settle. Two aspects of authority affect whether a final settlement can be reached: whether the attorney has authority to bind his or her client, and, in situations involving multiple negotiators, which attorney has the ultimate authority. The simplest way to find out your opponent's authority in this regard is to ask.

Two other matters often are agreed upon in advance: the length of the session, and whether to use item-by-item or lump-sum negotiation. Time limits are important because they increase the likelihood of agreement and tend to result in reductions in demands and the elimination of bluffing as the "eleventh hour" approaches. Open-ended negotiation sessions tend to be just that — sessions without end, in which the parties avoid final settlement and renege on tentative agreements. Negotiations also are affected by whether binding commitments are made item-by-item or only on lump sums. Of course, individual issues undoubtedly will be discussed one at a time and tentative agreements reached. However, some trial lawyers oppose making these settlements binding because a party who has gained an advantage may become harder to deal with as the pressure to settle diminishes, and one who has suffered a setback may be reluctant to continue. They argue that only if all agreements are contingent upon a final lump-sum settlement figure is there still as much pressure to settle at the end as there was at the start.

3. BARGAINING TACTICS

Experienced negotiators have suggested tactics ranging from such relatively innocuous ones as offering to split the difference when deadlocked over a trivial amount, to outright lying and fraud. One federal judge has criticized even informing law students about the kinds of tactics used by lawyers who think the ends justify any cunning means.[60] Obviously, tactics involving bluffing, lying, and fraud are unethical. They also are strategically unwise, because they will probably be found out, and may make your opponent unwilling to negotiate with you. Their use even may constitute grounds for invalidating the settlement. You also should not forget that, on the whole, cooperation begets cooperation and aggressive tactics beget aggressive counter tactics.

---

[60] Alvin B. Rubin, *A Causerie on Lawyers' Ethics in Negotiation*, 35 LA. L. REV. 577, 580-81 (1975).

In his book FUNDAMENTALS OF NEGOTIATING, Gerard Nierenberg discusses at length many of the commonly used negotiating tactics.[61] They can be grouped into four categories: 1) procedural tactics, 2) tactics relating to the presentation of substantive issues, 3) deadlock avoidance tactics, and 4) psychological ploys.

The first group of tactics contains general procedural maneuvers for controlling or changing the agenda.

- *Blanketing* is presenting many issues together. It can be used for a number of purposes. Many weak issues can be grouped together in hopes of achieving a concession on one or two of them. A single weak issue can be buried among strong ones. You may be able to discover how strong your opponent thinks he or she is on individual issues from the order in which he or she responds. Blanketing also can be used to gain agenda control. If you raise only a single issue, your opponent may take control of the next issue, but if you present a group of issues simultaneously, you may keep control during the entire discussion.
- *Pairing* is introducing two issues together so that you can make concessions on one and gain concessions on the other. This tactic often is used to present two of your weaker issues. If you discuss them separately, you might have to make concessions on both, but if taken together, you can demand one concession from your opponent, arguing that it is unfair for him or her to expect you to be making all the concessions.
- *Retroactive pairing* is reopening a settled issue and pairing it with a current issue to counter an unreasonable demand from your opponent. You can then demand that the issues be treated together or that the current issue be dropped. Nierenberg uses the example of a labor negotiation in which the union demands a shorter workweek, and the employer replies that it can be considered only if the union is prepared to give up some of the holidays already agreed upon.
- *Slicing the salami* consists of seeking concessions in small increments — like gaining possession of a salami one thin slice at a time. If you overtly try to take something big away from your adversary, particularly on a major issue, he or she is likely to put up a strenuous defense. However, if a big issue can be divided into smaller issues on which the stakes are low, cooperation and compromise may be easier to obtain.
- *Limited authority* is a tactic in which the scope of the negotiator's agency is temporarily limited by the client, or by turning part of the negotiation over to an associate with limited authority. It may occasionally be easier to obtain agreement on a couple of sub-issues first, and return to bargain more difficult issues on another day when a person with full authority will be present. This tactic has a potential drawback — the other side may refuse to negotiate if the agent's authority is too narrow.
- *Limits* is a related tactic. You may set artificial limitations, especially time limits. Setting time limits can create an atmosphere conducive to compromise as long as both sides take the time limit seriously. This

---

[61] GERARD NIERENBERG, FUNDAMENTALS OF NEGOTIATING 149-75 (1973). In the following pages, Nierenberg's suggestions are mixed with those from other authors listed in the bibliography.

rarely happens because limits usually are arbitrary and bind no one. Some negotiators try to schedule bargaining sessions at times when natural time limits operate — on Friday afternoons, a few days before Christmas or Thanksgiving, and so on.

- *Boulwareism*, named after a labor negotiator named Lemuel R. Boulware, is presenting a take-it-or-leave-it proposition. You make a fair offer at or near your bottom line and stick to it. This tactic is not recommended. Almost no one uses it, so you probably will not be taken seriously. Your opponent will misperceive your offer as a first offer, and will refuse it. This tactic invites the opponent to call your bluff and break off negotiations if the offer is unacceptable; therefore, it should be reserved for situations in which you are prepared to go to trial if the offer is refused.

The second group of tactics are those relating to the manner in which you present and negotiate your individual issues.

- *Association* is a tactic in which you link an issue to a factor outside of the case likely to influence your opponent. For example, you can link your client's desire for a quick settlement to the opponent's patriotism if you represent a soldier about to be sent into combat. Most frequently, this tactic is used in criminal plea bargaining to link settlement to the opposing lawyer's self-interest in reducing a heavy caseload.
- *Authority* is a tactic familiar to all of you — cite a case, statute, or document to support your position.
- *Misdirection* involves making an apparent move in one direction to divert attention from your real goal. The classic example of this is the story of Br'er Rabbit. The line between misdirection and outright fraud and lying is a fine one, however.
- *Reversal* involves acting contrary to normal expectations or normal procedures. For example, a union could propose that wages be cut if company profits go down. If management accepts this principle, it will be easier to negotiate that wages also should go up if profits go up.
- *Mutt and Jeff* is the familiar good cop/bad cop routine. Two lawyers for the same side feign an internal dispute concerning their position; one takes the hard line, offering almost no compromise, while the other appears to desire to make small concessions, and occasionally the "good lawyer" prevails. Lawyers opposing such a team may accept the marginal concessions because they seem substantial in relation to the position of the hard-liner.
- *Trollope ploy* is one in which a rejected demand is followed not by a concession, but by a stronger demand, encouraging the opponent to accept the milder of the two. It is often used in criminal cases, in which a defendant's refusal to bargain results in additional charges being filed, to "apply pressure." In a normal case, this ploy cannot hope to succeed, because the opponent will simply break off negotiations if you use this tactic. It can be used, however, by the more powerful side in a case where one side has a strong advantage.

- *Cooling-off periods* are an important tactic. Negotiation takes patience. Giving yourself time to think, to calculate, or to caucus with your associates can prevent you from being stampeded into an unwise agreement. Cooling-off periods can restore a level of decorum and rationality to emotionally charged bargaining.
- *Silence* is similar to a cooling-off period. Simply waiting the other side out may elicit a new concession or new proposal. Knowing when to stop talking and to let the other side respond is also crucial to effective negotiation.

A number of tactics have been suggested to help prevent impasses or deadlocks.

- *Go to mediation* by enlisting the help of a neutral person who can encourage settlement and suggest compromises. The judge is often willing to act in this role, or you can hire a mediation service.
- *Use subcommittees* — assign one person from each negotiating team to try to resolve difficulties away from the negotiating table.
- *Substitution* is the assigning of new negotiators to take over when the original ones seem to have reached an impasse.
- *Splitting the difference.* This is probably the oldest negotiation tactic, used to reach final settlement when the parties are near agreement. Logically, this tactic makes little sense, because it is unrelated to any aspect of the case. It is unwise to use it unless the amounts in dispute are small.

4. COUNTERTACTICS

a. Making Counteroffers

If you are negotiating in good faith and wish to facilitate settlement through cooperation, it would seem logical for you to respond to an offer with a counteroffer. This exchange of offers, accompanied by discussions of the reasons underlying them, helps isolate differences of opinion and helps structure the negotiation. Indeed, the wisdom of this approach is borne out by a number of experimental studies. Maximum cooperation is achieved when the parties alternate concessions. You may imagine that it is a good tactic to try to get your opponent to make several concessions in a row, and feel you are gaining an advantage in so doing. The problem is that if you fail to respond to a legitimate compromise with a compromise offer of your own, the party making the first move may feel betrayed. The result may well be a breakdown in negotiation.[62]

Some attorneys who employ a more competitive negotiating technique try to delay the making of counteroffers as long as possible. They expect that their opponents will continue to submit lower and lower offers (make all the concessions) while they do nothing, only submitting a counteroffer when they believe the opponent is near his or her bargaining limit. This tactic, however,

---

[62] *See* J. RUBIN & B. BROWN, *supra* note 58, at 274-76 (summarizing experiments by social psychologists).

is likely to work only if the opponent is desperate to settle. Otherwise, he or she is unlikely to make a second offer or to continue negotiations at all unless you submit a counteroffer.

b. Dealing With Hard or Unreasonable Tactics

So far the discussion has assumed that both parties genuinely are interested in trying to reach a mutually beneficial settlement and understand that cooperation is the best way to achieve this. However, you never can be certain that your opponent is negotiating in good faith unless he or she proves it by honest bargaining. How should you respond to hard tactics — threats, ultimatums, unreasonable offers, stalling, and so forth — that threaten to deadlock the negotiation and make settlement impossible? In most cases, you probably should accept the inevitable and terminate the discussion. Negotiation will not be successful unless both sides wish it to be.

(1) Unreasonable First Offers

Your opponent may make an unreasonable first offer for one of three reasons: he or she is not bargaining in good faith, has reached a very different estimate of the value of the case than you have, or is trying it only as an exploratory tactic to test your reaction. In the first two situations, the probability of eventually reaching a settlement is extremely small. In the third situation, if you indicate a willingness to consider the outrageous offer, your opponent may interpret your reaction as an indication that you are desperate to settle at any amount and may raise his or her bargaining limit. This also makes eventual settlement unlikely. Therefore, your reaction to an unreasonable first offer should be the same regardless of the reason it was made. You should be honest and tell your opponent that the offer is way out of line and indicates that agreement is probably impossible. You can either ask for justification or for a more rational offer, or you can make your own offer. It is then up to your opponent to decide whether he or she wishes to negotiate. You should not be afraid to break off negotiations that cannot result in agreement.

Some attorneys play the I-can-be-more-childish-than-you game, and counter an unreasonable first offer with a similarly unreasonable offer of your own. Obviously, this is a silly tactic if your goal is to reach a settlement.

(2) Failure to Make an Offer (Not Bargaining in Good Faith)

Your opponent may refuse to make an offer or counteroffer. He or she may try to force you into changing your own offer (making concessions) without making any counterproposal. You may be asked to change your first offer because it is too high or low, or your opponent may tender a few offers and then stop making concessions. Effective negotiation requires that both sides cooperate. If your opponent stops, it is pointless for you to continue. You should never bid against yourself.

(3) Deadlocks

If your opponent refuses to make further concessions before you have arrived at an agreement, you have reached a deadlock. Deadlocks are more likely to occur when negotiating a component issue than in the exchange of lump-sum offers. A number of tactics are available when you are deadlocked. If the parties are far apart, if the issue is important enough, or if you have no bargaining room left, you may have to break off negotiations. It may be that your opponent genuinely cannot settle within your limits.

In many deadlocked situations the parties will be close to agreement, the issue unimportant in relation to the whole controversy, or your opponent's last offer will be within your bargaining range, so that breaking off negotiations and going to trial is a disproportionate response. Available alternatives include:

- Offering to split the difference, if the two side are close.
- Offering to trade concessions, one party conceding on this issue and the other conceding on another deadlocked issue.
- Combining the deadlocked issue with several related issues (this may require reopening an earlier agreement) and trying to negotiate the package.
- Making a final compromise offer at your bargaining limit, making it clear that it is a take-it-or-leave-it proposition.

(4) Attempts to Reopen Settled Issues

Your opponent may attempt to reopen an issue on which agreement had been reached or may try to change a negotiated agenda by adding a new issue. Obviously, this kind of tactic amounts to "unnegotiating." If unjustified, it demonstrates bad faith, and it should not be tolerated. If the negotiations are allowed to start to unravel, progress has stopped and begun to move backwards. Probably the best response is to demand that the negotiations continue, and suggest to your opponent that he or she wait until a final agreement is worked out, at which time he or she can accept or reject the package. Another tactic that can make this problem less likely to occur is to write down the points of agreement as they are reached — it may be harder for your opponent to try to reopen an agreement that has been reduced to writing.

On some occasions, a brinkmanship response — which, in effect, threatens to break off negotiation unless the other side drops its demand to reopen or add an issue — may be disproportionate to the controversy. Your opponent may have a valid reason for wishing to reopen an agreement. He or she may have made a mathematical error in arriving at an amount, may have discovered new facts that alter the premises on which an issue was negotiated, or may be trying to work out a way around an impasse. Before you take precipitous action, you should consider carefully whether your opponent's request is justified. Also, if the settled issue resulted in an agreement disproportionately in your favor, and you still had bargaining room left, it is probably better to reopen than risk an eventual rejection of the final settlement proposal.

(5) Walkouts

Your opponent may terminate the negotiations at any time. You have no control over whether he or she chooses to bargain or decides to go to trial. A walkout may be a genuine expression of your opponent's inability or unwillingness to negotiate further, or may be just a tactic to scare you into a major concession. In either case, you have a choice: offer a concession to encourage the other side to return, or do nothing and hope your opponent makes overtures to reconvene. If you have bargaining room, you probably should offer a concession. On the other hand, if you are already at or near your bargaining limit, or have already made several concessions in a row, you should wait for the other side to be reasonable. Do not let a walkout panic you into going below your bargaining limit.

NOTES

1. *Negotiation as discovery.* One collateral benefit to bargaining is that, even if it breaks down, you have learned more about your opponent's case. If you are willing to listen to your adversary, you may discover additional facts, you may be referred to other legal sources, you may discern how he or she intends to present the case, and (perhaps most importantly) you may discover weaknesses in your case you had not noticed before. The information you gain will be useful in the negotiation itself and also in preparing for trial if no agreement is reached.

> When the negotiations are in the stage in which you and your opponent are exchanging views, positions, facts and arguments, it is best to put the burden of talking on your opponent. Ask him position questions, such as:
>   1. How do you size up this case?
>   2. What is your best judgment of the value of the case?
>   3. How did you get to that figure?
>   4. What is your client looking for?
>   5. How do you feel about ... (specify some aspect of the case)?
> The worst situation which can occur during a settlement negotiation is to have both negotiators talking at once. Neither is convincing the other, and each is losing a chance to hear the position of the other.

Roger Thomasch, *Objectives and Techniques in Negotiating a Settlement, in* SETTLEMENT AND PLEA BARGAINING 102 (M. Edwards ed. 1981).

2. *Face-to-face, telephone, or written negotiation.* Negotiations can be conducted in three ways: in a face-to-face meeting between attorneys, over the telephone, or by an exchange of written offers. Is there any reason to prefer one of these methods over the others? Negotiators seem to prefer face-to-face bargaining, because it allows you to judge your opponent not only by what he or she says, but also by how the negotiator appears. Face-to-face negotiation also allows you to present visual or other sensory evidence to support your position. For example, bringing a jar of effluent to a negotiating session may help convince negotiators representing a chemical plant that you easily can prove to a jury that the smell is a nuisance. *See* JOHN ILICH, THE ART AND SKILL OF SUCCESSFUL NEGOTIATION 45-48 (1973). Experiments have shown

that greater cooperation is achieved if both parties can see and hear each other than if they are isolated. *See* JEFFREY RUBIN & BERT BROWN, THE SOCIAL PSYCHOLOGY OF BARGAINING AND NEGOTIATION 96-99 (1975) (communication, both verbal and nonverbal, is essential to effective bargaining).

3. *Presence of client at negotiation.* In almost every episode of the television series "L.A. Law," the lawyers bring their clients with them to a negotiation session. There are some possible reasons for doing this — it will show the client you are working on the case, it will make final agreement easier, and, if the client is a good witness or has suffered sympathetic injuries, it may convince your opponent that you can present a good case to the jury. Harold Baer & Aaron Broder, *How to Prepare and Negotiate Cases for Settlement — Pointers for Plaintiff*, 1968 TRIAL LAW. GUIDE 302, 303-04. However, the dangers usually far outweigh these small advantages:

- The client may make damaging admissions or be goaded into making threats, unaware of the consequences of the statements.
- Because of unfamiliarity with bargaining tactics, the client may be influenced by your opponent's tactics into agreeing to an unfavorable settlement.
- The presence of the client prevents you from using the tactic of limited authority.
- The client's actions, such as showing surprise at your tactics or eagerness to accept an opponent's offer, may limit your bargaining ability.
- The client's presence may distract your attention from the negotiation.

See JOHN ILICH, THE ART AND SKILL OF SUCCESSFUL NEGOTIATIONS 25-29 (1973). Social psychologists agree that the client's presence interferes with successful negotiation because the attorney will become concerned with his or her appearance to the client, and will try to be a tough negotiator. Steven Penrod et al., *The Implications of Social Psychological Research for Trial Practice Attorneys, in* PSYCHOLOGY AND LAW (D. Muller ed., 1984). For these reasons, clients rarely are present during civil negotiations. Although the same reasons militate against having a client present during plea bargaining, in practice it is somewhat more common for a criminal defendant to be present during bargaining, especially if the defendant has something to trade, such as testimony against confederates.

4. *Final agreement.* Should the final agreement be written and formalized, and if so, who should draft it? The answer to the first question would seem to be that it must be written and signed by both parties if it is to have any binding effect. The answer to the second question is that you should not abdicate your responsibility for the drafting of the agreement. Most negotiators recommend that you should volunteer to write up the agreement yourself, so that you can be sure that your client is completely protected. *See* Roger Thomasch, *Objectives and Techniques in Negotiating a Settlement, in* SETTLEMENT AND PLEA BARGAINING 105 (M. Edwards ed. 1981). In reality, however, the agreement itself usually will have to be negotiated — from an outline through various drafts, until both sides agree on its wording — so that it makes little difference who prepares the final draft. *See* Palmer Madden,

Drafting Settlement Agreements in Commercial Litigation, LITIGATION, Fall 1978, at 40.

F. BIBLIOGRAPHY

1. GENERAL

HARRY T. EDWARDS & JAMES J. WHITE, THE LAWYER AS A NEGOTIATOR (1977).
Albert Matheny, *A Bibliography on Plea Bargaining*, 13 LAW & SOC. REV. 661 (1979).
HENRY G. MILLER, THE ART OF ADVOCACY — SETTLEMENT (1983).
GERARD NIERENBERG, FUNDAMENTALS OF NEGOTIATING (1973).

2. LAW

JAMES BOND, PLEA BARGAINING AND GUILTY PLEAS (2d ed. 1983).
Dan Dobbs, *Conclusiveness of Personal Injury Settlements: Basic Problems*, 41 N.C. L. REV. 665 (1963).
Robert S. Lindsey, *Documentation of Settlements*, 27 ARK. L. REV. 27 (1973).

3. ETHICS

Alvin B. Rubin, *A Causerie on Lawyers' Ethics in Negotiation*, 35 LA. LAW REV. 577 (1975).
Thomas Shaffer, *Negotiation Ethics: A Report to Cartaphila*, LITIGATION, Winter 1981, at 37.

4. PSYCHOLOGY

Donald Harnett et al., *Personality, Bargaining Style and Payoff*, 36 SOCIOMETRY 325 (1973).
JEFFREY RUBIN & BERT BROWN, THE SOCIAL PSYCHOLOGY OF BARGAINING AND NEGOTIATION (1975).

5. TACTICS

ANTHONY AMSTERDAM, TRIAL MANUAL 5 FOR THE DEFENSE OF CRIMINAL CASES, ch. 13 (1988).
Harold Baer and Aaron Broder, *How to Prepare and Negotiate Cases for Settlement — Pointers for Plaintiff*, 1968 TRIAL LAW. GUIDE 302.
Philip Bourne, *Ruminations on the Psychology and Methodology of Settlement Negotiations*, in SETTLEMENT AND PLEA BARGAINING 1 (M. Edwards ed. 1981).
ROGER FISHER & WILLIAM URY, GETTING TO YES (2d ed. 1991).
JOHN ILICH, THE ART AND SKILL OF SUCCESSFUL NEGOTIATION (1973).
Joseph Kelner, *Settlement Techniques Part One*, TRIAL, Feb. 1980, at 39.
FRED LANE, LANE'S GOLDSTEIN TRIAL TECHNIQUE, ch. 7A (3d ed. 1984).
David Sindell & Joseph Sindell, *Formulae to Evaluate Injury Cases*, in SETTLEMENT AND PLEA BARGAINING 65-75 (M. Edwards ed. 1981).
Stuart Speiser, *The Psychology and Art of Settlement*, in SETTLEMENT AND PLEA BARGAINING 55 (M. Edwards ed. 1981).

Roger Thomasch, *Objectives and Techniques in Negotiating a Settlement, in*
SETTLEMENT AND PLEA BARGAINING 105 (M. Edwards ed. 1981).
Gary Weiss, *Settlement Techniques: The Need Theory, in* SETTLEMENT AND
PLEA BARGAINING 80 (M. Edwards ed. 1981).

Table of Cases

References are to pages. Principal cases and the pages
where they appear are in italics.

Index

A

B

C

D

E

O

V